CONTENTS

MW00980105

v

2

TABLES AND FORMS: DESIGN, PROPERTIES, VIEWS, AND WIZARDS 49

3

INFORMATION FROM THE DATABASE: REPORTS AND QUERIES 101

PROFICIENCY: RELATIONAL DATABASES, EXTERNAL DATA, CHARTS, AND THE SWITCHBOARD   161

ONE-TO-MANY RELATIONSHIPS: SUBFORMS AND MULTIPLE TABLE QUERIES   205

6

MANY-TO-MANY RELATIONSHIPS: A MORE COMPLEX SYSTEM   259

7

BUILDING APPLICATIONS: THE SWITCHBOARD, MACROS, AND PROTOTYPING   317

CREATING MORE POWERFUL APPLICATIONS: INTRODUCTION TO VBA   367

PREREQUISITES: ESSENTIALS OF WINDOWS 95/98

INDEX

PREFACE

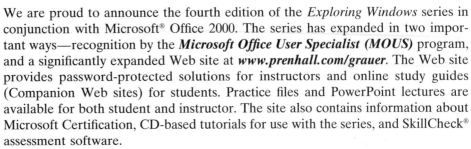

We are proud to announce the fourth edition of the *Exploring Windows* series in conjunction with Microsoft® Office 2000. The series has expanded in two important ways—recognition by the ***Microsoft Office User Specialist (MOUS)*** program, and a significantly expanded Web site at ***www.prenhall.com/grauer***. The Web site provides password-protected solutions for instructors and online study guides (Companion Web sites) for students. Practice files and PowerPoint lectures are available for both student and instructor. The site also contains information about Microsoft Certification, CD-based tutorials for use with the series, and SkillCheck® assessment software.

The organization of the series is essentially unchanged. There are separate titles for each application—*Word 2000, Excel 2000, Access 2000,* and *PowerPoint 2000,* a book on *Windows® 98,* and eventually, *Windows® 2000.* There are also four combined texts—*Exploring Microsoft Office Professional, Volumes I* and *II, Exploring Microsoft Office Proficient Certification Edition,* and *Brief Office. Volume I* is a unique combination of applications and concepts for the introductory computer course. It covers all four Office applications and includes supporting material on Windows 95/98, Internet Explorer, and Essential Computing Concepts. The modules for Word and Excel satisfy the requirements for proficient certification. The *Proficient Certification Edition* extends the coverage of Access and PowerPoint from *Volume I* to meet the certification requirements, but (because of length) deletes the units on Internet Explorer and Essential Computing Concepts that are found in *Volume I. Volume II* includes the advanced features in all four applications and extends certification to the expert level. *Brief Office* is intended to get the reader "up and running," without concern for certification requirements.

The Internet and World Wide Web are integrated throughout the series. Students learn Office applications as before, and in addition are sent to the Web as appropriate for supplementary exercises. The sections on Object Linking and Embedding, for example, not only draw on resources within Microsoft Office, but on the Web as well. Students are directed to search the Web for information, and then download resources for inclusion in Office documents. The icon at the left of this paragraph appears throughout the text whenever there is a Web reference.

The *Exploring Windows* series is part of the Prentice Hall custom-binding (*Right PHit*) program, enabling instructors to create their own texts by selecting modules from *Volume I, Volume II,* the *Proficient Certification Edition,* and/or *Brief Office* to suit the needs of a specific course. An instructor could, for example, create a custom text consisting of the proficient modules in Word and Excel, coupled with the brief modules for Access and PowerPoint. Instructors can also take advantage of our *ValuePack program* to shrink-wrap multiple books together at a substantial saving for the student. A ValuePack is ideal in courses that require complete coverage of multiple applications.

Instructors will want to obtain the *Instructor's Resource CD* from their Prentice Hall representative. The CD contains the student data disks, solutions to all exercises in machine-readable format, PowerPoint lectures, and the Instructor Manuals themselves in Word format. The CD also has a Windows-based test generator. Please visit us on the Web at ***www.prenhall.com/grauer*** for additional information.

FEATURES AND BENEFITS

Exploring Microsoft® Access 2000 is written for the novice and assumes no previous knowledge of the operating system. A 64-page appendix covers the essentials of Windows 95/98/NT and emphasizes the file operations the reader will need.

Database design is stressed throughout the text, beginning in Chapter 1, where the reader is shown the power of a relational database. Full-color illustrations help clarify the relationships between tables and provide an intuitive understanding of select queries. Appendix B presents additional material on database design.

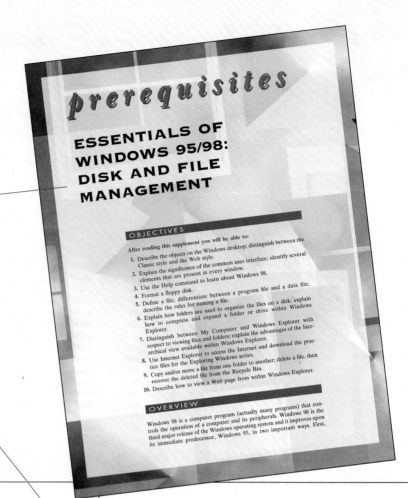

prerequisites

ESSENTIALS OF WINDOWS 95/98: DISK AND FILE MANAGEMENT

OBJECTIVES

After reading this supplement you will be able to:

1. Describe the objects on the Windows desktop; distinguish between the Classic style and the Web style.
2. Explain the significance of the common user interface; identify several elements that are present in every window.
3. Use the Help command to learn about Windows 98.
4. Format a floppy disk.
5. Define a file; differentiate between a program file and a data file; describe the rules for naming a file.
6. Explain how folders are used to organize the files on a disk; explain how to compress and expand a folder or drive within Windows Explorer.
7. Distinguish between My Computer and Windows Explorer with respect to viewing files and folders; explain the advantages of the hierarchical view available within Windows Explorer.
8. Use Internet Explorer to access the Internet and download the practice files for the Exploring Windows series.
9. Copy and/or move a file from one folder to another; delete a file, then recover the deleted file from the Recycle Bin.
10. Describe how to view a Web page from within Windows Explorer.

OVERVIEW

Windows 98 is a computer program (actually many programs) that controls the operation of a computer and its peripherals. Windows 98 is the third major release of the Windows operating system and it improves upon its immediate predecessor, Windows 95, in two important ways. First,

---

LOOKING AHEAD: A RELATIONAL DATABASE

The Bookstore and Employee databases are both examples of simple databases in that they each contained only a single table. The real power of Access, however, is derived from multiple tables and the relationships between those tables. This type of database is known as a *relational database* and is illustrated in Figure 1.9. This figure expands the original Employee database by adding two tables, for locations and titles, respectively.

The Employees table in Figure 1.9a is the same table we used at the beginning of the previous exercise, except for the substitution of a LocationID and TitleID for the location and title, respectively. The Locations table in turn has all

SSN	LastName	FirstName	LocationID	TitleID	Salary	Gender	Performance
000-01-0000	Milgrom	Pamela	L02	T02	$57,500	F	Average
000-02-2222	Adams	Jennifer	L01	T03	$19,500	F	Average
111-12-1111	Johnson	James	L03	T01	$47,500	M	Good
123-45-6789	Coulter	Tracey	L01	T02	$100,000	F	Good
222-23-2222	Marlin	Billy	L04	T02	$125,000	M	Good
222-52-5555	Smith	Mary	L03	T01	$42,500	F	Average
333-34-3333	Manin	Ann	L02	T01	$49,500	F	Average
333-43-4444	Smith	Frank	L01	T01	$65,000	M	Good
333-66-1234	Brown	Marietta	L01	T03	$18,500	F	Poor
444-45-4444	Frank	Vernon	L04	T01	$75,000	M	Good
555-22-3333	Rubin	Patricia	L02	T01	$45,000	F	Average
555-56-5555	Charles	Kenneth	L02	T01	$40,000	M	Poor
776-67-6666	Adamson	David	L03	T02	$52,000	M	Poor
777-78-7777	Marder	Kelly	L03	T01	$38,500	F	Average

(a) The Employees Table

LocationID	Location	Address	State	Zipcode	OfficePhone
L01	Atlanta	450 Peachtree Road	GA	30316	(404) 333-5555
L02	Boston	3 Commons Blvd	MA	02190	(617) 123-4444
L03	Chicago	500 Loop Highway	IL	60620	(312) 444-6666
L04	Miami	210 Biscayne Blvd	FL	33103	(305) 787-9999

(b) The Locations Table

TitleID	Title	Description	EducationRequired	MinimumSalary	MaximumSalary
T01	Account Rep	A marketing ...	Four year degree	$25,000	$75,000
T02	Manager	A supervisory ...	Four year degree	$50,000	$150,000
T03	Trainee	An entry-level ...	Two year degree	$18,000	$25,000

(c) The Titles Table

FIGURE 1.9 A Relational Database

of the fields that pertain to each location: LocationID, Location, Address, State, Zipcode, and Office Phone. One field, the LocationID, appears in both Employees and Locations tables and links the two tables to one another. In similar fashion, the Titles table has the information for each title: the TitleID, Title, Description, Education Required, and Minimum and Maximum Salary. The TitleID appears in both the Employees and Titles tables to link those tables to one another.

It sounds complicated, but it is really quite simple and very elegant. More importantly, it enables you to obtain detailed information about any employee, location, or title. To show how it works, we will ask a series of questions that require you to look in one or more tables for the answer. Consider:

Query: At which location does Pamela Milgrom work? What is the phone number of her office?
Answer: Pamela works in the Boston office, at 3 Commons Blvd., Boston, MA, 02190. The phone number is (617) 123-4444.

Did you answer the question correctly? You had to search the Employees table for Pamela Milgrom to obtain the LocationID (L02 in this example) corresponding to her office. You then searched the Locations table for this LocationID to obtain the address and phone number for that location. The process required you to use both the Locations and Employees tables, which are linked to one another through a *one-to-many relationship*. One location can have many employees, but a specific employee can work at only one location. Let's try another question:

Query: Which employees are managers?
Answer: There are four managers: Pamela Milgrom, Tracey Coulter, Billy Marlin, and David Adamson.

The answer to this question is based on the one-to-many relationship that exists between titles and employees. One title can have many employees, but a given employee has only one title. To answer the query, you search the Titles table for "manager" to determine its TitleID (T02). You then go to the Employees table and select those records that have this value in the TitleID field.

The design of a relational database enables us to extract information from multiple tables in a single query. Equally important, it simplifies the way data is changed in that modifications are made in only one place. Consider:

Query: Which employees work in the Boston office? What is their phone number? How many changes would be necessary if the Boston office were to get a new phone number?
Answer: There are four employees in Boston: Pamela Milgrom, Ann Manin, Patricia Rubin, and Kenneth Charles, each with the same number (617 123-4444). Only one change (in the Locations table) would be necessary if the phone number changed.

Once again, we draw on the one-to-many relationship between locations and employees. Thus, we begin in the Locations table where we search for "Boston" to determine its LocationID (L02) and phone number (617 123-4444). Then we go to the Employees table to select those records with this value in the LocationID field. Realize, however, that the phone number is stored in the Locations table. Thus, the new phone number is entered in the Boston record, where it is reflected automatically for each employee with a LocationID of L02 (corresponding to the Boston office).

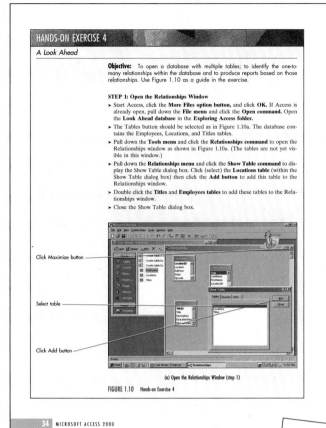

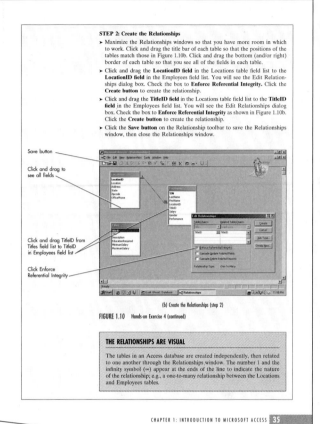

A total of 30 in-depth tutorials provide hands-on instruction at the computer and guide the reader every step of the way. Each tutorial is illustrated with annotated screen captures and expanded through appropriate tips that further explain the task at hand.

All discussions are accompanied by multiple illustrations that explain the underlying conceptual material. This example describes the different types of reports that can be created from a database. The reader learns concepts as well as keystrokes, which in turn increases his or her proficiency in Access.

United States
by Region

Prepared by Gregg Kuehnel

Region	Name	Capital	Population	Area	Population Density
Middle Atlantic					
	Delaware	Dover	666,168	2,057	323.85
	Maryland	Annapolis	4,781,468	10,577	452.06
	New Jersey	Trenton	7,730,188	7,836	986.50
	New York	Albany	17,990,455	49,576	362.89
	Pennsylvania	Harrisburg	11,881,643	45,333	262.10
	Total for Region		**43,049,922**	**115,379**	
	Average for Region		**8,609,984**	**23,076**	**477.48**
Mountain					
	Arizona	Phoenix	3,665,228	113,909	32.18
	Colorado	Denver	3,294,394	104,247	31.60
	Idaho	Boise	1,006,749	83,557	12.05
	Montana	Helena	799,065	147,138	5.43
	Nevada	Carson City	1,201,833	110,540	10.87
	New Mexico	Santa Fe	1,515,069	121,666	12.45
	Utah	Salt Lake City	1,722,850	84,916	20.29
	Wyoming	Cheyenne	453,588	97,914	4.63
	Total for Region		**13,658,776**	**863,887**	
	Average for Region		**1,707,347**	**107,986**	**16.19**
New England					
	Connecticut	Hartford	3,287,116	5,009	656.24
	Maine	Augusta	1,227,928	33,215	36.97
	Massachusetts	Boston	6,016,425	8,257	728.65
	New	Concord	1,109,252	9,304	119.22
	Rhode Island	Providence	1,003,464	1,214	826.58
	Vermont	Montpelier	562,758	9,609	58.57
	Total for Region		**13,206,943**	**66,608**	
	Average for Region		**2,201,157**	**11,101**	**404.37**
North Central					
	Illinois	Springfield	11,430,602	56,400	202.67
	Indiana	Indianapolis	5,544,159	36,291	152.77
	Iowa	Des Moines	2,776,755	56,290	49.33
	Kansas	Topeka	2,477,574	82,264	30.12

Friday, February 19, 1999   Page 1 of 3

FIGURE 3.13   The United States Database (Exercise 3)

University of Miami
Book Store

Prepared by Gregg Kuehnel

Publisher	ISBN	Author	Title	ListPrice
Macmillan Publishing				
	1-56686-127-6	Rosch	The Hardware Bible	$35.00
			Number of Books:	1
			Average List Price:	$35.00
McGraw Hill				
	0-07-029387-2	Hofstetter	Internet Literacy	$45.00
	0-07-041127-1	Martinez	Getting Ahead by Getting	$39.95
	0-07-054048-9	Rothstein	Ace the Technical Interview	$24.95
	0-07-070318-3	Willard	The Cybernetics Reader	$15.75
			Number of Books:	4
			Average List Price:	$31.41
Prentice Hall				
	013-011100-7	Grauer/Barber	Exploring Microsoft Office 2000	$45.00
	0-13-011108-2	Grauer/Barber	Exploring Excel 2000	$28.95
	0-13-011190-0	Grauer/Barber	Exploring Microsoft Office 2000	$45.00
	0-13-011816-8	Grauer/Barber	Exploring PowerPoint 2000	$28.95
	0-13-020476-5	Grauer/Barber	Exploring Access 2000	$28.95
	0-13-020489-7	Grauer/Barber	Exploring Word 2000	$28.95
	0-13-065541-4	Grauer/Barber	Exploring Windows 3.1	$24.95
	0-13-504077-9	Grauer/Barber	Exploring Windows 95	$28.95
	0-13-754193-7	Grauer/Barber	Exploring Windows 98	$28.95
	0-13-754201-1	Grauer/Barber	Exploring Word 97	$30.95
	0-13-754219-1	Grauer/Barber	Exploring Excel 97	$30.95
	0-13-754227-5	Grauer/Barber	Exploring Access 97	$30.95
	0-13-754235-6	Grauer/Barber	Exploring PowerPoint 97	$30.95
	0-13-790817-2	Grauer/ Villar	COBOL: From Micro to Mainframe	$52.95
			Number of Books:	14
			Average List Price:	$33.24

Friday, February 19, 1999   Page 1 of 2

FIGURE 3.14   The Bookstore Database (Exercise 4)

Every chapter ends with multiple practice exercises to reinforce the material and avoid repetition from one semester to the next. There are objective multiple-choice questions, guided computer exercises, and less structured case studies.

The case studies challenge the reader by extending the material in the chapter. The Web icon appears whenever the reader is directed to the World Wide Web as a source of additional material. Object Linking and Embedding (OLE) is also highlighted.

CASE STUDIES

The United States of America

What is the total population of the United States? What is its area? Can you name the 13 original states or the last five states admitted to the Union? Do you know the 10 states with the highest population or the five largest states in terms of area? Which states have the highest population density (people per square mile)?

The answers to these and other questions can be obtained from the United States database that is available on the data disk. The key to the assignment is to use the Top Values property within a query that limits the number of records returned in the dynaset. Use the database to create several reports that you think will be of interest to the class.

The Super Bowl

How many times has the NFC won the Super Bowl? When was the last time the AFC won? What was the largest margin of victory? What was the closest game? What is the most points scored by two teams in one game? How many times have the Miami Dolphins appeared? How many times did they win? Use the data in the Super Bowl database to create a trivia sheet on the Super Bowl, then incorporate your analysis into a letter addressed to NBC Sports. Convince them you are a super fan and that you merit two tickets to next year's game. Go to the home page of the National Football League (www.nfl.com) to obtain score(s) from the most recent game(s) to update our table if necessary.

Mail Merge

A mail merge takes the tedium out of sending form letters, as it creates the same letter many times, changing the name, address, and other information as appropriate from letter to letter. The form letter is created in a word processor (e.g., Microsoft Word), but the data file may be taken from an Access table or query. Use the Our Students database as the basis for two different form letters sent to two different groups of students. The first letter is to congratulate students on the Dean's list (GPA of 3.50 or higher). The second letter is a warning to students on academic probation (GPA of less than 2.00).

Compacting versus Compressing

An Access database becomes fragmented, and thus unnecessarily large, as objects (e.g., reports and forms) are modified or deleted. It is important, therefore, to periodically compact a database to reduce its size (enabling you to back it up on a floppy disk). Choose a database with multiple objects; e.g., the Our Students database used in this chapter. Use the Windows Explorer to record the file size of the database as it presently exists. Start Access, open the database, pull down the Tools menu and select Database Utilities to compact the database, then record the size of the database after compacting. You can also compress a compacted database (using a standard Windows utility such as WinZip) to further reduce the requirement for disk storage. Summarize your findings in a short report to your instructor. Try compacting and compressing at least two different databases to better appreciate these techniques.

Exploring Microsoft® Access 2000 goes beyond the Expert level in the MOUS (Microsoft Office User Specialist) program to include a capstone chapter on VBA. This material enables the reader to take Access to the next level as he or she learns how to put VBA code behind Access objects.

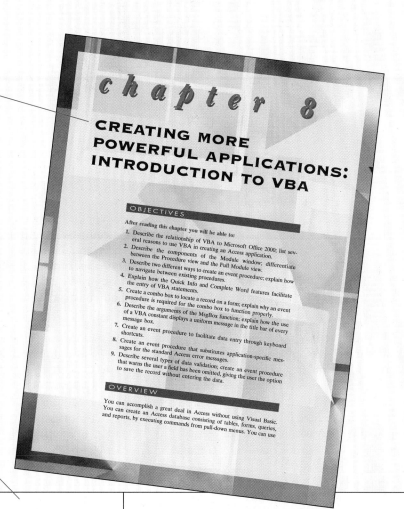

Students are exposed to a wide variety of practical applications with which they can identify. The case study on a sports league appears in Chapter 7 and includes material on multilevel switchboards and macros.

database into two files—one containing the tables and the other containing the remaining objects (the forms, reports, queries, and macros). The tables are then linked to the other objects through the Link Tables command. It sounds complicated but this approach has several advantages, as you will see.

The chapter also covers macros and prototyping, two techniques that are used by developers in creating applications. A macro automates common command sequences and further simplifies the system for the end user. Prototyping is used in conjunction with developing the various switchboards to demonstrate the "look and feel" of an application, even before the application is complete. Three hands-on exercises are included in the chapter to progressively build the application as you develop your skills in Access.

CASE STUDY: A RECREATIONAL SPORTS LEAGUE

You have probably played in a sports league at one time or another, whether in Little League as a child or in an intramural league at school or work. Whatever the league, it had teams, players, and coaches. The typical league registers the players and coaches individually then holds a draft among the coaches to divide the players into teams according to ability. The league may have been organized informally, with manual procedures for registering the participants and creating the teams. Now we automate the process.

Let's think for a moment about the tables and associated relationships that will be necessary to create the database. There are three tables, one each for players, coaches, and teams. There is a one-to-many relationship between teams and players (one team has many players, but a player is assigned to only one team). There is also a one-to-many relationship between teams and coaches (one team has many coaches, but a coach is assigned to only one team).

In addition to the tables, the database will contain multiple forms, queries, and reports based on these tables. A Players form is necessary in order to add a new player, or edit or delete the record of an existing player. A similar form should exist for Coaches. There might also be a sophisticated main and subform combination for the Teams table that displays the players and coaches on each team, and through which data for any table (Team, Player, or Coach) can be added, edited, or deleted. And, of course, there will be a variety of reports and queries.

Let's assume that this database has been created. It would not be difficult for a person knowledgeable in Access to open the database and select the various objects as the need arose. He or she would know how to display the Database window and how to select the various buttons in order to open the appropriate object. But what if the system is to be used by someone who does not know Access, which is typically the case? You can see that the user interface becomes the most important part of the system, at least from the viewpoint of the end user. An interface that is intuitive and easy to use will be successful. Conversely, a system that is difficult to use or visually unappealing is sure to fail.

Figure 7.1a displays the switchboard that will be created for this application. We have added a soccer ball as a logo, but the application applies to any type of recreational sports league. The interface is intuitive and easy to use. Click the About Sports button, the first button on our menu, and the system displays the informational screen we like to include in all of our applications. Click any other button, and you display the indicated form. Click the Teams button, for example, and you see the form in Figure 7.1b where you can add a new team, view, edit, or print the data for any existing team, then click the Close Form button to return to the main menu.

The switchboard in Figure 7.1a exists as a form within the database. Look closely, however, and you will see it is subtly different from the forms you have developed in previous chapters. The record selector and navigation buttons, for example, have been suppressed because they are not needed. In other words, this

Click About Sports button to display informational message

Hyperlink

Click Teams button to display Team form

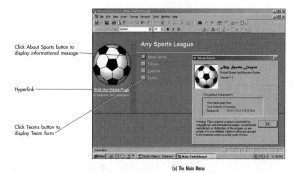

(a) The Main Menu

Add, edit, delete a team

Add, edit, delete a coach

Add, edit, delete a player

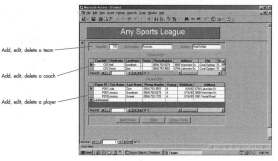

(b) The Teams Form

FIGURE 7.1   Building a User Interface

Acknowledgments

We want to thank the many individuals who have helped to bring this project to fruition. We are especially grateful to Nancy Evans and PJ Boardman, who continue to offer inspiration and guidance. Alex von Rosenberg, executive editor at Prentice Hall, has provided new leadership in extending the series to Office 2000. Nancy Welcher did an absolutely incredible job on our Web site. Susan Rifkin coordinated the myriad details of production and the certification process. Greg Christofferson was instrumental in the acquisition of supporting software. Lynne Breitfeller was the project manager. Paul Smolenski was senior manufacturing supervisor. Greg Hubit has been masterful as the external production editor for every book in the series. Cecil Yarbrough did an outstanding job in checking the manuscript for technical accuracy. Jennifer Surich was the editorial assistant. Leanne Nieglos was the supplements editor. Cindy Stevens, Karen Vignare, and Michael Olmstead wrote the Instructor Manuals. Patricia Smythe developed the innovative and attractive design. We also want to acknowledge our reviewers who, through their comments and constructive criticism, greatly improved the series.

Lynne Band, Middlesex Community College
Don Belle, Central Piedmont Community College
Stuart P. Brian, Holy Family College
Carl M. Briggs, Indiana University School of Business
Kimberly Chambers, Scottsdale Community College
Alok Charturvedi, Purdue University
Jerry Chin, Southwest Missouri State University
Dean Combellick, Scottsdale Community College
Cody Copeland, Johnson County Community College
Larry S. Corman, Fort Lewis College
Janis Cox, Tri-County Technical College
Martin Crossland, Southwest Missouri State University
Paul E. Daurelle, Western Piedmont Community College
David Douglas, University of Arkansas
Carlotta Eaton, Radford University
Judith M. Fitspatrick, Gulf Coast Community College
Raymond Frost, Central Connecticut State University
Midge Gerber, Southwestern Oklahoma State University
James Gips, Boston College
Vernon Griffin, Austin Community College
Michael Hassett, Fort Hays State University
Wanda D. Heller, Seminole Community College
Bonnie Homan, San Francisco State University
Ernie Ivey, Polk Community College
Mike Kelly, Community College of Rhode Island
Jane King, Everett Community College
Rose M. Laird, Northern Virginia Community College

John Lesson, University of Central Florida
David B. Meinert, Southwest Missouri State University
Alan Moltz, Naugatuck Valley Technical Community College
Kim Montney, Kellogg Community College
Bill Morse, DeVry Institute of Technology
Kevin Pauli, University of Nebraska
Mary McKenry Percival, University of Miami
Delores Pusins, Hillsborough Community College
Gale E. Rand, College Misericordia
Judith Rice, Santa Fe Community College
David Rinehard, Lansing Community College
Marilyn Salas, Scottsdale Community College
John Shepherd, Duquesne University
Barbara Sherman, Buffalo State College
Robert Spear, Prince George's Community College
Michael Stewardson, San Jacinto College—North
Helen Stoloff, Hudson Valley Community College
Margaret Thomas, Ohio University
Mike Thomas, Indiana University School of Business
Suzanne Tomlinson, Iowa State University
Karen Tracey, Central Connecticut State University
Sally Visci, Lorain County Community College
David Weiner, University of San Francisco
Connie Wells, Georgia State University
Wallace John Whistance-Smith, Ryerson Polytechnic University
Jack Zeller, Kirkwood Community College

A final word of thanks to the unnamed students at the University of Miami, who make it all worthwhile. Most of all, thanks to you, our readers, for choosing this book. Please feel free to contact us with any comments and suggestions.

Robert T. Grauer
rgrauer@sba.miami.edu
www.bus.miami.edu/~rgrauer
www.prenhall.com/grauer

Maryann Barber
mbarber@sba.miami.edu
www.bus.miami.edu/~mbarber

chapter 1

INTRODUCTION TO MICROSOFT ACCESS: WHAT IS A DATABASE?

OBJECTIVES

After reading this chapter you will be able to:

1. Define the terms field, record, table, and database.
2. Start Microsoft Access; describe the Database window and the objects in an Access database.
3. Add, edit, and delete records within a table; use the Find command to locate a specific record.
4. Describe the record selector; explain when changes are saved to a table.
5. Explain the importance of data validation in table maintenance.
6. Apply a filter (by form or by selection) to a table; sort a table on one or more fields.
7. Describe a relational database; identify the one-to-many relationships that exist within a database.

OVERVIEW

All businesses and organizations maintain data of one kind or another. Companies store data about their employees. Schools and universities store data about their students and faculties. Magazines and newspapers store data about their subscribers. The list goes on and on, and while each of these examples refers to different types of data, they all operate under the same basic principles of database management.

The chapter introduces you to Microsoft Access, the application in the Microsoft Office suite that performs database management. We describe the objects in an Access database and show you how to add, edit, and delete records to a table. We explain how to obtain information from the database by running reports and queries that have been previously created. We discuss how to display selected records through a filter and how to display those records in different sequences. And finally, we provide a look ahead, by showing how the real power of Access is derived from a relational database that contains multiple tables.

The hands-on exercises in the chapter enable you to apply all of the material at the computer, and are indispensable to the learn-by-doing philosophy we follow throughout the text. As you do the exercises, you may recognize many commands from other Windows applications, all of which share a common user interface and consistent command structure.

CASE STUDY: THE COLLEGE BOOKSTORE

Imagine, if you will, that you are the manager of a college bookstore and that you maintain data for every book in the store. Accordingly, you have recorded the specifics of each book (the title, author, publisher, price, and so on) in a manila folder, and have stored the folders in one drawer of a file cabinet.

One of your major responsibilities is to order books at the beginning of each semester, which in turn requires you to contact the various publishers. You have found it convenient, therefore, to create a second set of folders with data about each publisher such as the publisher's phone number, address, discount policy, and so on. You also found it necessary to create a third set of folders with data about each order such as when the order was placed, the status of the order, which books were ordered, how many copies, and so on.

Normal business operations will require you to make repeated trips to the filing cabinet to maintain the accuracy of the data and keep it up to date. You will have to create a new folder whenever a new book is received, whenever you contract with a new publisher, or whenever you place a new order. Each of these folders must be placed in the proper drawer in the filing cabinet. In similar fashion, you will have to modify the data in an existing folder to reflect changes that occur, such as an increase in the price of a book, a change in a publisher's address, or an update in the status of an order. And, lastly, you will need to remove the folder of any book that is no longer carried by the bookstore, or of any publisher with whom you no longer have contact, or of any order that was canceled.

The preceding discussion describes the bookstore of 40 years ago—before the advent of computers and computerized databases. The bookstore manager of today needs the same information as his or her predecessor. Today's manager, however, has the information readily available, at the touch of a key or the click of a mouse, through the miracle of modern technology. The concepts are identical in both the manual and computerized systems.

Information systems have their own vocabulary. A *field* is a basic fact (or data element) such as the name of a book or the telephone number of a publisher. A *record* is a set of fields. A *table* is a set of records. Every record in a table contains the same fields in the same order. A *database* consists of one or more tables. In our example, each record in the Books table will contain the identical six fields—ISBN (a unique identifying number for the book), title, author, year of publication, price, and publisher. In similar fashion, every record in the Publishers table will have the same fields for each publisher just as every record in the Orders table has the same fields for each order. This terminology (field, record, file, and database) is extremely important and will be used throughout the text.

You can think of the file cabinet in the manual system as a database. Each set of folders in the file cabinet corresponds to a table within the database. Thus the bookstore database consists of three separate tables—for books, publishers, and orders. Each table, in turn, consists of multiple *records,* corresponding to the folders in the file cabinet. The Books table, for example, contains a record for every book title in the store. The Publishers table has a record for each publisher, just as the Orders table has a record for each order.

Microsoft Access, the fourth major application in the Microsoft Office, is used to create and manage a database such as the one for the college bookstore. Consider now Figure 1.1, which shows how Microsoft Access appears on the desktop. Our discussion assumes a basic familiarity with the Windows operating system and the user interface that is common to all Windows applications. You should recognize, therefore, that the desktop in Figure 1.1 has two open windows—an application window for Microsoft Access and a document (database) window for the database that is currently open.

Each window has its own title bar and Minimize, Maximize (or Restore), and Close buttons. The title bar in the application window contains the name of the application (Microsoft Access). The title bar in the document (database) window contains the name of the database that is currently open (Bookstore). The application window for Access has been maximized to take up the entire desktop, and hence the Restore button is visible. The database window has not been maximized.

A menu bar appears immediately below the application title bar. A toolbar (similar to those in other Office applications) appears below the menu bar and offers alternative ways to execute common commands. The Windows taskbar appears at the bottom of the screen and shows the open applications.

The Database Window

The *Database window* displays the various objects in an Access database. There are seven types of objects—tables, queries, forms, reports, pages, macros, and modules. Every database must contain at least one table, and it may contain any

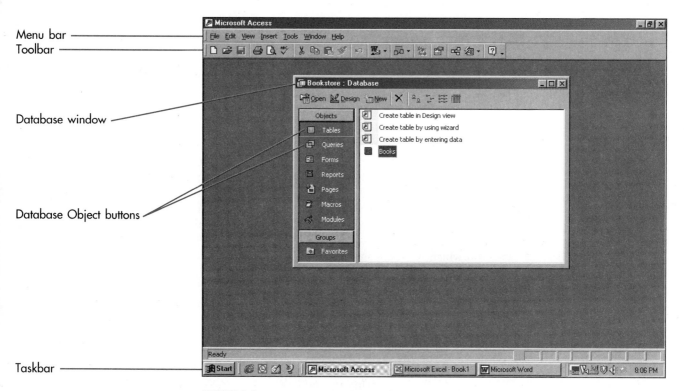

FIGURE 1.1   The Database Window

or all (or none) of the other objects. Each object type is accessed through the appropriate button within the Database window. In this chapter we concentrate on tables, but we briefly describe the other types of objects as a preview of what you will learn as you read our book.

- A *table* stores data about an entity (a person, place, or thing) and is the basic element in any database. A table is made up of records, which in turn are made up of fields. It is columnar in appearance, with each record in a separate row of the table and each field in a separate column.
- A *form* provides a more convenient and attractive way to enter, display, and/or print the data in a table.
- A *query* answers a question about the database. The most common type of query specifies a set of criteria, then searches the database to retrieve the records that satisfy the criteria.
- A *report* presents the data in a table or query in attractive fashion on the printed page.
- A *page* is an HTML document that can be posted to a Web server or Local Area Network, and which can be viewed by a Web browser.
- A *macro* is analogous to a computer program and consists of commands that are executed automatically one after the other. Macros are used to automate the performance of any repetitive task.
- A *module* provides a greater degree of automation through programming in Visual Basic for Applications (VBA).

ONE FILE HOLDS ALL

All of the objects in an Access database (tables, forms, queries, reports, pages, macros, and modules) are stored in a single file on disk. The database itself is opened through the Open command in the File menu or by clicking the Open button on the Database toolbar. The individual objects within a database are opened through the database window.

Tables

A table (or set of tables) is the heart of any database, as it contains the actual data. In Access a table is displayed in one of two views—the Design view or the Datasheet view. The *Design view* is used to define the table initially and to specify the fields it will contain. It is also used to modify the table definition if changes are subsequently necessary. The Design view is discussed in detail in Chapter 2. The *Datasheet view*—the view you use to add, edit, or delete records—is the view on which we focus in this chapter.

Figure 1.2 shows the Datasheet view for the Books table in our bookstore. The first row in the table contains the *field names.* Each additional row contains a record (the data for a specific book). Each column represents a field (one fact about a book). Every record in the table contains the same fields in the same order: ISBN Number, Title, Author, Year, List Price, and Publisher.

The status bar at the bottom of Figure 1.2a indicates that there are five records in the table and that you are positioned on the first record. This is the record you are working on and is known as the *current record.* (You can work on only one record at a time.) There is a *record selector symbol* (a triangle, asterisk, or pencil) next to the current record to indicate its status.

Field names

Triangle indicates data
has been saved to disk

Current record

Total number of records

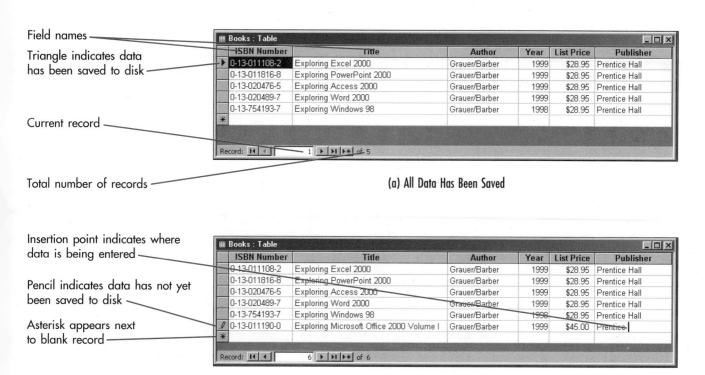

(a) All Data Has Been Saved

Insertion point indicates where
data is being entered

Pencil indicates data has not yet
been saved to disk

Asterisk appears next
to blank record

(b) During Data Entry

FIGURE 1.2   Tables

A *triangle* indicates that the record has been saved to disk. A *pencil* indicates that you are working on the record and that the changes have not yet been saved. As soon as you move to the next record, however, the pencil changes to a triangle to indicate that the record on which you were working has been saved. (Access, unlike other Office applications, automatically saves changes made to a record without your having to execute the Save command.) An *asterisk* appears next to the blank record at the end of every table.

Figure 1.2a shows the table as it would appear immediately after you opened it. The first field in the first record is selected (highlighted), and anything you type at this point will replace the selected data. (This is the same convention as in any other Windows application.) The triangle next to the current record (record 1) indicates that changes have not yet been made. An asterisk appears as the record selector symbol next to the blank record at the end of the table. The blank record is used to add a record to the table and is not counted in determining the number of records in the table.

Figure 1.2b shows the table as you are in the process of entering data for a new record at the end of the table. The current record is now record 6. The *insertion point* (a flashing vertical bar) appears at the point where text is being entered. The record selector for the current record is a pencil, indicating that the record has not yet been saved. The asterisk has moved to the blank record at the end of the table, which now contains one more record than the table in Figure 1.2a.

Note, too, that each table in a database must have a field (or combination of fields) known as the *primary key,* which is unique for every record in the table. The ISBN (International Standard Book Number) is the primary key in our example, and it ensures that each record in the Books table is different from every other record. (Other fields may also have a unique value for every record, but only one field is designated as the primary key.)

Introduction to Microsoft Access

Objective: To open an existing database; to add a record to a table within the database. Use Figure 1.3 as a guide in the exercise.

STEP 1: Welcome to Windows

➤ Turn on the computer and all of its peripherals. The floppy drive should be empty prior to starting your machine. This ensures that the system starts by reading from the hard disk, which contains the Windows files, as opposed to a floppy disk, which does not.

➤ Your system will take a minute or so to get started, after which you should see the desktop in Figure 1.3a. Do not be concerned if the appearance of your desktop is different from ours. If necessary, click the **Close button** to close the Welcome window.

Start button

(a) Welcome to Windows (step 1)

FIGURE 1.3   Hands-on Exercise 1

TAKE THE WINDOWS TOUR

Windows 98 greets you with a Welcome window that describes the high-lights in the operating system. Click Discover Windows 98 to take a guided tour or select one of the topics at the left of the window. If you do not see the Welcome window when you start your computer, click the Start button, click Run, type C:\Windows\Welcome in the text box, and press the enter key. Relax and enjoy the show.

STEP 2: Obtain the Practice Files:

➤ We have created a series of practice files for you to use throughout the text. Your instructor will make these files available to you in a variety of ways:

- You can download the files from our Web site if you have access to the Internet and World Wide Web (see boxed tip).

- The files may be on a network drive, in which case you use the Windows Explorer to copy the files from the network to a floppy disk.

- There may be an actual "data disk" that you are to check out from the lab in order to use the Copy Disk command to duplicate the disk.

➤ Check with your instructor for additional information.

DOWNLOAD THE PRACTICE FILES

Download the practice files for any book in the *Exploring Windows* series from the Exploring Windows home page. Go to www.prenhall.com/grauer, click the Office 2000 text, click the link to student resources, then click the link to download the student data disk. Our Web site has many other features such as the Companion Web Sites (online study guides) to enhance your learning experience. See problem 6 at the end of the chapter.

STEP 3: Start Microsoft Access

➤ Click the **Start button** to display the Start menu. Click (or point to) the **Programs menu,** then click **Microsoft Access** to start the program. Click and drag the Office Assistant out of the way if it appears. (The Office Assistant is described in the next hands-on exercise.)

➤ You should see the Microsoft Access dialog box with the option button to **Open an existing file** already selected. Click **More Files,** then click **OK** to display the Open dialog box in Figure 1.3b.

➤ Click the **down arrow** on the Views button, then click **Details** to change to the Details view. Click and drag the vertical border between columns to increase (or decrease) the size of a column.

➤ Click the **drop-down arrow** on the Look In list box. Click the appropriate drive (drive C is recommended rather than drive A), depending on the location of your data. Double click the **Exploring Access folder.**

➤ Click the **down scroll arrow** until you can click the **Bookstore database.** Click the **Open command button** to open the database.

WORK ON DRIVE C

Even in a lab setting it is preferable to work on the local hard drive, as opposed to a floppy disk. The hard drive is much faster, which becomes especially important when working with the large file sizes associated with Access. Use the Windows Explorer to copy the database from the network drive to the local hard drive prior to the exercise, then work on drive C throughout the exercise. Once you have completed the exercise, use the Explorer a second time to copy the modified database to a floppy disk that you can take with you.

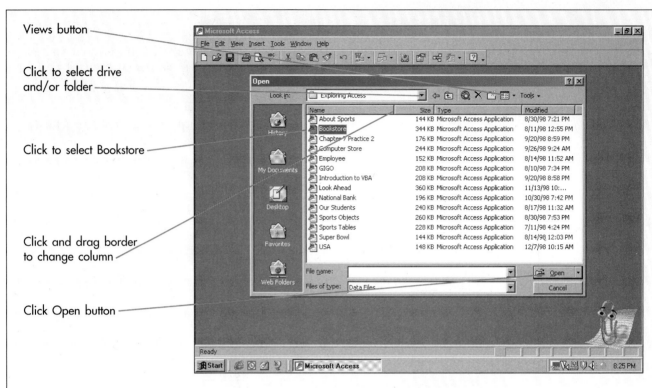

Views button

Click to select drive and/or folder

Click to select Bookstore

Click and drag border to change column

Click Open button

(b) Open an Existing Database (step 3)

FIGURE 1.3   Hands-on Exercise (continued)

STEP 4: Open the Books Table

➤ If necessary, click the **Maximize button** in the application window so that Access takes the entire desktop.

➤ You should see the Database window for the Bookstore database with the **Tables button** already selected. Double click the **Books table** to open the table as shown in Figure 1.3c.

➤ Click the **Maximize button** so that the Books table fills the Access window and reduces the clutter on the screen.

A SIMPLER DATABASE

The real power of Access is derived from a database with multiple tables that are related to one another. For the time being, however, we focus on a database with only one table so that you can learn the basics of Access. After you are comfortable working with a single table, we will show you how to work with multiple tables and how to relate them to one another.

STEP 5: Moving within a Table

➤ Click in any field in the first record. The status bar at the bottom of the Books Table indicates record 1 of 22.

➤ The triangle symbol in the record selector indicates that the record has not changed since it was last saved.

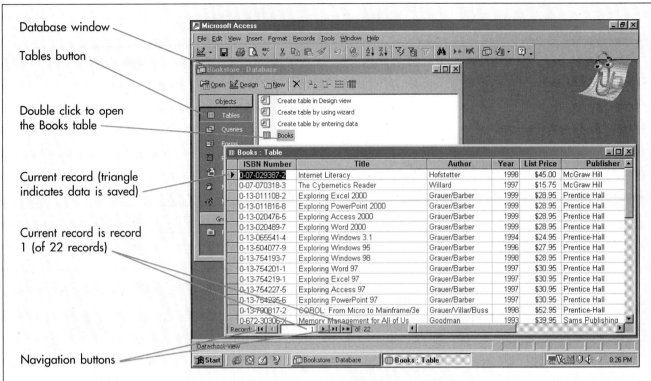

Database window

Tables button

Double click to open
the Books table

Current record (triangle
indicates data is saved)

Current record is record
1 (of 22 records)

Navigation buttons

(c) Open the Books Table (step 4)

FIGURE 1.3   Hands-on Exercise 1 (continued)

➤ You can move from record to record (or field to field) using either the mouse or the arrow keys:

- Click in any field in the second record. The status bar indicates record 2 of 22.

- Press the **down arrow key** to move to the third record. The status bar indicates record 3 of 22.

- Press the **left and right arrow keys** to move from field to field within the third record.

➤ You can also use the navigation buttons above the status bar to move from one record to the next:

- Click |◄ to move to the first record in the table.

- Click ► to move forward in the table to the next record.

- Click ◄ to move back in the table to the previous record.

MOVING FROM FIELD TO FIELD

Press the Tab key, the right arrow key, or the enter key to move to the next field in the current record (or the first field in the next record if you are already in the last field of the current record). Press Shift+Tab or the left arrow key to return to the previous field in the current record (or the last field in the previous record if you are already in the first field of the current record).

- Click ►| to move to the last record in the table.
- Click ►* to move beyond the last record in order to insert a new record.

➤ Click |◄ to return to the first record in the table.

STEP 6: Add a New Record

➤ Pull down the **Insert menu** and click **New Record** (or click the **New Record button** on the Table Datasheet toolbar). The record selector moves to the last record (now record 23). The insertion point is positioned in the first field (ISBN Number).

➤ Enter data for the new record as shown in Figure 1.3d. The record selector changes to a pencil as soon as you enter the first character in the new record.

➤ Press the **enter key** when you have entered the last field for the record. The new record is saved, and the record selector changes to a triangle and moves automatically to the next record.

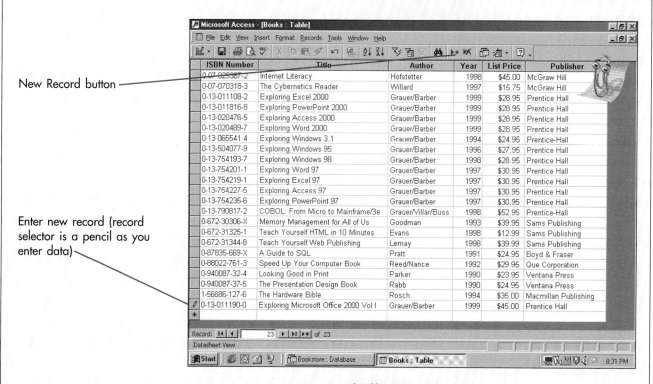

New Record button

Enter new record (record selector is a pencil as you enter data)

(d) Add a New Record (step 6)

FIGURE 1.3   Hands-on Exercise 1 (continued)

WHEN IS DATA SAVED?

There is one critical difference between Access and other Office applications such as Word for Windows or Microsoft Excel. *Access automatically saves any changes in the current record as soon as you move to the next record or when you close the table.* In other words, you do *not* have to execute the Save command explicitly to save the data in the table.

STEP 7: Add a Second Record

➤ The record selector is at the end of the table where you can add another record. Enter **0-07-054048-9** as the ISBN number for this record. Press the **Tab, enter,** or **right arrow key** to move to the Title field.

➤ Enter the title of this book as **Ace teh Technical Interview** (deliberately misspelling the word "the"). Try to look at the monitor as you type to see the AutoCorrect feature (common to all Office applications) in action. Access will correct the misspelling and change *teh* to *the*.

➤ If you did not see the correction being made, press the **backspace key** several times to erase the last several characters in the title, then re-enter the title.

➤ Complete the entry for this book. Enter **Rothstein** for the author. Enter **1998** for the year of publication. Enter **24.95** for the list price. Enter **McGraw Hill** for the publisher, then press **enter.**

CREATE YOUR OWN SHORTHAND

Use the AutoCorrect feature that is common to all Office applications to expand abbreviations such as "PH" for Prentice Hall. Pull down the Tools menu, click AutoCorrect, type the abbreviation in the Replace text box and the expanded entry in the With text box. Click the Add command button, then click OK to exit the dialog box and return to the document. The next time you type PH (in uppercase) as you enter a record, it will automatically be expanded to Prentice Hall.

STEP 8: Print the Table

➤ Pull down the **File menu.** Click **Page Setup** to display the Page Setup dialog box in Figure 1.3e.

➤ Click the **Page tab.** Click the **Landscape option button.** Click **OK** to accept the settings and close the dialog box.

➤ Click the **Print button** on the toolbar to print the table. Alternatively, you can pull down the **File menu,** click **Print** to display the Print dialog box, click the **All option button,** then click **OK.**

ABOUT MICROSOFT ACCESS

Pull down the Help menu and click About Microsoft Access to display the specific release number as well as other licensing information, including the Product ID. This help screen also contains two very useful command buttons, System Info and Tech Support. The first button displays information about the hardware installed on your system, including the amount of memory and available space on the hard drive. The Tech Support button provides telephone numbers for technical assistance.

Print button ———

Page tab ———

Landscape option ———

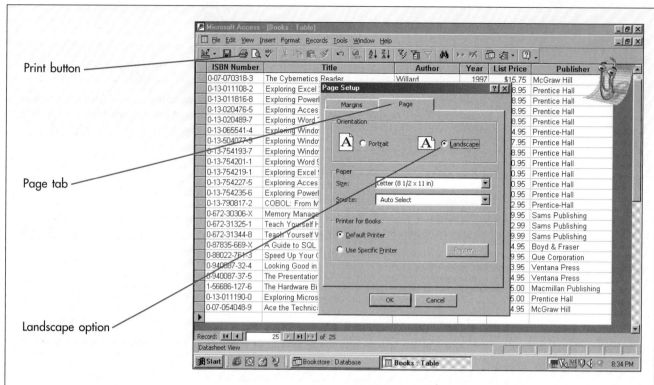

(e) Print the Table (step 8)

FIGURE 1.3   Hands-on Exercise 1 (continued)

STEP 9: Exit Access

➤ You need to close both the Books table and the Bookstore database:

• Pull down the **File menu** and click **Close** (or click the **Close button**) to close the Books table. Answer **Yes** if asked to save changes to the layout of the table.

• Pull down the **File menu** and click **Close** (or click the **Close button**) to close the Bookstore database.

➤ Pull down the **File menu** and click **Exit** to close Access if you do not want to continue with the next exercise at this time.

OUR FAVORITE BOOKSTORE

This exercise has taken you through our hypothetical bookstore database. It's more fun, however, to go to a real bookstore. Amazon Books (www.amazon.com), with a virtual inventory of more than three million titles, is one of our favorite sites on the Web. You can search by author, subject, or title, read reviews written by other Amazon visitors, or contribute your own review. It's not as cozy as your neighborhood bookstore, but you can order any title for mail-order delivery. And you never have to leave home.

The exercise just completed showed you how to open an existing table and add records to that table. You will also need to edit and/or delete existing records in order to maintain the data as changes occur. These operations require you to find the specific record and then make the change. You can search the table manually, or more easily through the Find and Replace commands.

Find and Replace Commands

The Find and Replace commands are similar in function to the corresponding commands in all other Office applications. (The commands are executed from within the same dialog box by selecting the appropriate tab.) The ***Find command*** enables you to locate a specific record(s) by searching a table for a particular value. You could, for example, search the Books table for the title of a book, then move to the appropriate field to change its price. The ***Replace command*** incorporates the Find command and allows you to locate and optionally replace (one or more occurrences of) one value with another. The Replace command in Figure 1.4 searches for *PH* in order to substitute *Prentice Hall.*

Searches can be made more efficient by making use of the various options. A case-sensitive search, for example, matches not only the specific characters, but also the use of upper- and lowercase letters. Thus, *PH* is different from *ph,* and a case-sensitive search on one will not identify the other. A case-insensitive search (where Match Case is *not* selected) will find both *PH* and *ph.* Any search may specify a match on whole fields to identify *Davis,* but not *Davison.* And finally, a search can also be made more efficient by restricting it to the current field.

The replacement can be either selective or automatic. Selective replacement lets you examine each successful match in context and decide whether to replace it. Automatic replacement makes the substitution without asking for confirmation (and is generally not recommended). Selective replacement is implemented by clicking the Find Next command button, then clicking (or not clicking) the Replace button to make (or not make) the substitution. Automatic replacement (through the entire table) is implemented by clicking the Replace All button.

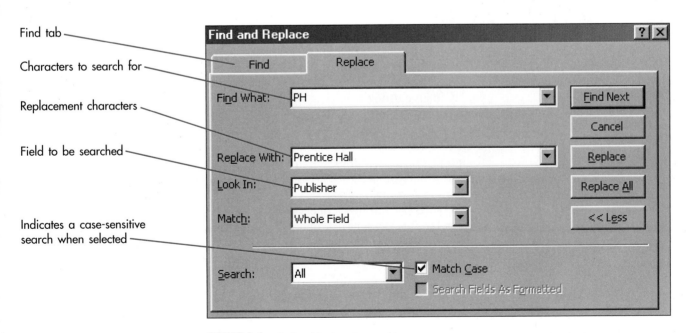

FIGURE 1.4   Find and Replace Commands

Data Validation

It is unwise to simply add (edit or delete) a record without adequate checks on the validity of the data. Ask yourself, for example, whether a search for all books by Prentice Hall (without a hyphen) will also return all books by *Prentice-Hall* (with a hyphen). The answer is *no* because the publisher's name is spelled differently and a search for one will not locate the other. *You* know the publisher is the same in both instances, but the computer does not.

Data validation is a crucial part of any system. Good systems are built to anticipate errors you might make and reject those errors prior to accepting data. Access automatically implements certain types of data validation. It will not, for example, let you enter letters where a numeric value is expected (such as the Year and List Price fields in our example). More sophisticated types of validation are implemented by the user when the table is created. You may decide, for example, to reject any record that omits the title or author. Data validation is described more completely in Chapter 2.

GARBAGE IN, GARBAGE OUT (GIGO)

A computer does exactly what you tell it to do, which is not necessarily what you want it to do. It is absolutely critical, therefore, that you validate the data that goes into a system, or else the associated information may not be correct. No system, no matter how sophisticated, can produce valid output from invalid input. In other words: garbage in, garbage out.

FORMS, QUERIES, AND REPORTS

As previously indicated, an Access database can contain as many as seven different types of objects. Thus far we have concentrated on tables. Now we extend the discussion to include other objects such as forms, queries, and reports as illustrated in Figure 1.5.

Figure 1.5a contains the Books table as it exists after the first hands-on exercise. There are 24 records in the table and six fields for each record. The status bar indicates that you are currently positioned in the first record. You can enter new records in the table as was done in the previous exercise. You can also edit or delete an existing record, as will be illustrated in the next exercise.

Figure 1.5b displays a form that is based on the table of Figure 1.5a. A form provides a friendlier interface than does a table and is easier to understand and use. Note, for example, the command buttons in the form to add a new record, or to find and/or delete an existing record. The status bar at the bottom of the form indicates that you are on the first of 24 records, and is identical to the status bar for the table in Figure 1.5a.

Figure 1.5c displays a query to list the books for a particular publisher (Prentice Hall in this example). A query consists of a question (e.g., enter the publisher name) and an answer (the records that satisfy the query). The results of the query are similar in appearance to that of a table, except that the query results contain selected records and/or selected fields for those records. The query may also list the records in a different sequence from that of the table.

Current record

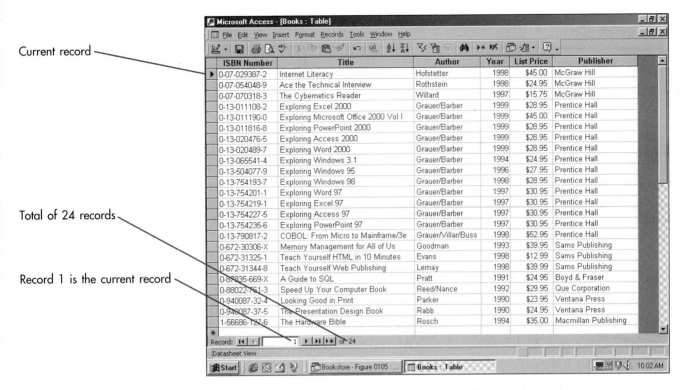

Total of 24 records

Record 1 is the current record

(a) The Books Table

Command buttons

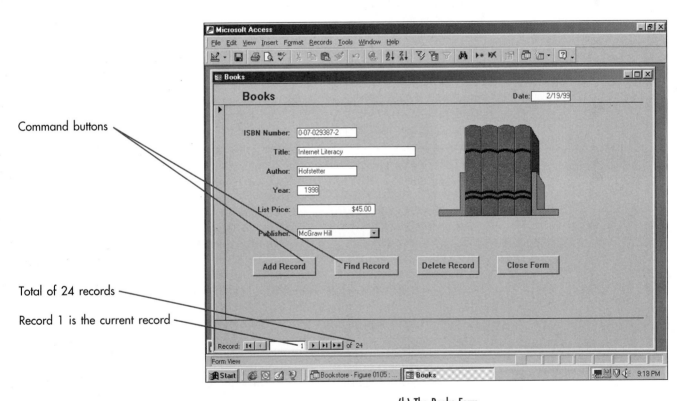

Total of 24 records

Record 1 is the current record

(b) The Books Form

FIGURE 1.5   The Objects in a Database

Records are sequenced
by title within author

Query has total of 13 records

Publisher	Author	Title	ISBN Number	Year	List Price
Prentice Hall	Grauer/Barber	Exploring Access 2000	0-13-020476-5	1999	$28.95
Prentice Hall	Grauer/Barber	Exploring Access 97	0-13-754227-5	1997	$30.95
Prentice Hall	Grauer/Barber	Exploring Excel 2000	0-13-011108-2	1999	$28.95
Prentice Hall	Grauer/Barber	Exploring Excel 97	0-13-754219-1	1997	$30.95
Prentice Hall	Grauer/Barber	Exploring Microsoft Office 2000 Vol I	0-13-011190-0	1999	$45.00
Prentice Hall	Grauer/Barber	Exploring PowerPoint 2000	0-13-011816-8	1999	$28.95
Prentice Hall	Grauer/Barber	Exploring PowerPoint 97	0-13-754235-6	1997	$30.95
Prentice Hall	Grauer/Barber	Exploring Windows 3.1	0-13-065541-4	1994	$24.95
Prentice Hall	Grauer/Barber	Exploring Windows 95	0-13-504077-9	1996	$27.95
Prentice Hall	Grauer/Barber	Exploring Windows 98	0-13-754193-7	1998	$28.95
Prentice Hall	Grauer/Barber	Exploring Word 2000	0-13-020489-7	1999	$28.95
Prentice Hall	Grauer/Barber	Exploring Word 97	0-13-754201-1	1997	$30.95
Prentice Hall	Grauer/Villar/Buss	COBOL: From Micro to Mainframe/3e	0-13-790817-2	1998	$52.95

Record: 1 of 13

(c) The Publisher Query

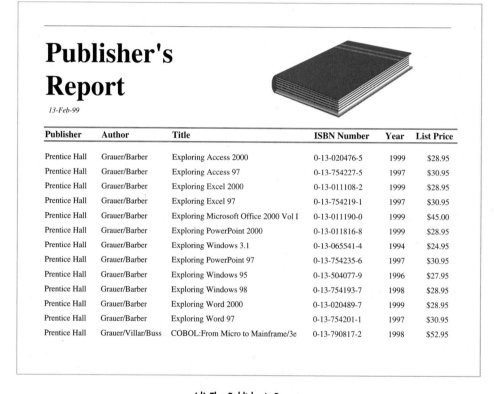

Publisher's Report

13-Feb-99

Publisher	Author	Title	ISBN Number	Year	List Price
Prentice Hall	Grauer/Barber	Exploring Access 2000	0-13-020476-5	1999	$28.95
Prentice Hall	Grauer/Barber	Exploring Access 97	0-13-754227-5	1997	$30.95
Prentice Hall	Grauer/Barber	Exploring Excel 2000	0-13-011108-2	1999	$28.95
Prentice Hall	Grauer/Barber	Exploring Excel 97	0-13-754219-1	1997	$30.95
Prentice Hall	Grauer/Barber	Exploring Microsoft Office 2000 Vol I	0-13-011190-0	1999	$45.00
Prentice Hall	Grauer/Barber	Exploring PowerPoint 2000	0-13-011816-8	1999	$28.95
Prentice Hall	Grauer/Barber	Exploring Windows 3.1	0-13-065541-4	1994	$24.95
Prentice Hall	Grauer/Barber	Exploring PowerPoint 97	0-13-754235-6	1997	$30.95
Prentice Hall	Grauer/Barber	Exploring Windows 95	0-13-504077-9	1996	$27.95
Prentice Hall	Grauer/Barber	Exploring Windows 98	0-13-754193-7	1998	$28.95
Prentice Hall	Grauer/Barber	Exploring Word 2000	0-13-020489-7	1999	$28.95
Prentice Hall	Grauer/Barber	Exploring Word 97	0-13-754201-1	1997	$30.95
Prentice Hall	Grauer/Villar/Buss	COBOL:From Micro to Mainframe/3e	0-13-790817-2	1998	$52.95

(d) The Publisher's Report

FIGURE 1.5   The Objects in a Database (continued)

Figure 1.5d illustrates a report that includes only the books from Prentice Hall. A report provides presentation-quality output and is preferable to printing the datasheet view of a table or query. Note, too, that a report may be based on either a table or a query. You could, for example, base the report in Figure 1.5d on the Books table, in which case it would list every book in the table. Alternatively, the report could be based on a query, as in Figure 1.5d, and list only the books that satisfy the criteria within the query.

Later chapters discuss forms, queries, and reports in depth. The exercise that follows is intended only as a brief introduction to what can be accomplished in Access.

Maintaining the Database

Objective: To add, edit, and delete a record; to demonstrate data validation; to introduce forms, queries, and reports. Use Figure 1.6 as a guide.

STEP 1: Open the Bookstore Database

➤ Start Access. The Bookstore database should appear within the list of recently opened databases as shown in Figure 1.6a.

➤ Select the **Bookstore database** (its drive and folder may be different from that in Figure 1.6a). Click **OK** to open the database.

➤ Right click the Office Assistant if it appears and click the **Hide** command.

Right click the Office Assistant for shortcut menu

Click Bookstore to select it

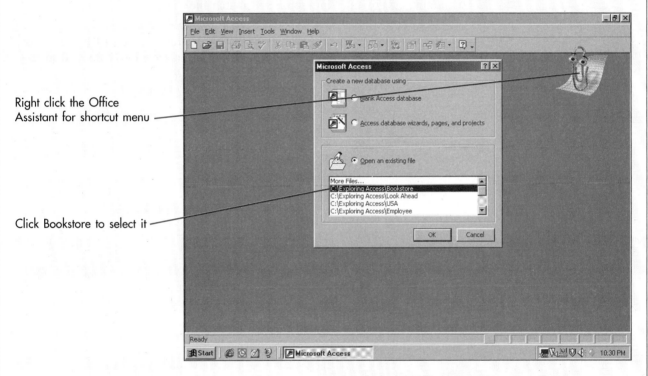

(a) Open the Bookstore Database (step 1)

FIGURE 1.6 Hands-on Exercise 2

ABOUT THE ASSISTANT

The Assistant is very powerful and hence you want to experiment with various ways to use it. To ask a question, click the Assistant's icon to toggle its balloon on or off. If you find the Assistant distracting, click and drag the character out of the way or hide it altogether by pulling down the Help menu and clicking the Hide the Office Assistant command. Pull down the Help menu and click the Show the Office Assistant command to return the Assistant to the desktop.

STEP 2: The Find Command

➤ If necessary, click the **Tables button** in the Database window. Double click the icon for the **Books table** to open the table from the previous exercise.

➤ You should see the Books table in Figure 1.6b. (The Find dialog box is not yet displayed).

➤ If necessary, click the **Maximize button** to maximize the Books table within the Access window.

➤ *Exploring Microsoft Office 2000 Vol 1* and *Ace the Technical Interview,* the books you added in the previous exercise, appear in sequence according to the ISBN number because this field is the primary key for the Books table.

➤ Click in the **Title field** for the first record. Pull down the **Edit menu** and click **Find** (or click the **Find button** on the toolbar) to display the dialog box in Figure 1.6b. (You are still positioned in the first record.)

➤ Enter **Exploring Windows 95** in the Find What text box. Check that the other parameters for the Find command match the dialog box in Figure 1.6b. Be sure that the **Title field** is selected in the Look in list.

➤ Click the **Find Next command button.** Access moves to record 10, the record containing the designated character string, and selects the Title field for that record. Click **Cancel** to close the Find dialog box.

➤ Press the **tab key** three times to move from the Title field to the List Price field. The current price ($27.95) is already selected. Type **28.95,** then press the **enter key** to change the price to $28.95.

Find button

Click in Title field
for first record

New books are in order by
ISBN number (primary key)

Title is found

Title should be selected
in Look In list box

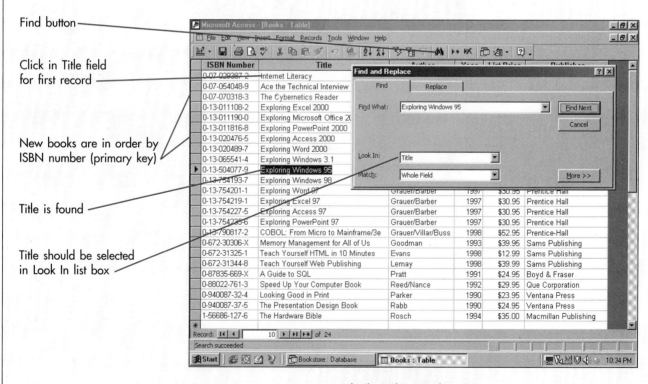

(b) The Find Command (step 2)

FIGURE 1.6   Hands-on Exercise 2 (continued)

EDITING A RECORD

The fastest way to replace the value in an existing field is to select the field, then type the new value. Access automatically selects the field for you when you use the keyboard (Tab, enter, or arrow keys) to move from one field to the next. Click the mouse within the field (to deselect the field) if you are replacing only one or two characters rather than the entire field.

STEP 3: The Undo Command

➤ Pull down the **Edit menu** and click **Undo Current Field/Record** (or click the **Undo button** on the toolbar). The price for Exploring Windows 95 returns to its previous value.

➤ Pull down the **Edit menu** a second time. The Undo command is dim (as is the Undo button on the toolbar), indicating that you can no longer undo any changes. Press **Esc.**

➤ Correct the List Price field a second time and move to the next record to save your change.

THE UNDO COMMAND

The Undo command is common to all Office applications, but is implemented differently from one application to the next. Microsoft Word, for example, enables you to undo multiple operations. Access, however, because it saves changes automatically as soon as you move to the next record, enables you to undo only the most recent command.

STEP 4: The Delete Command

➤ Click any field in the record for **A Guide to SQL.** (You can also use the **Find command** to search for the title and move directly to its record.)

➤ Pull down the **Edit menu.** Click **Select Record** to highlight the entire record.

➤ Press the **Del key** to delete the record. You will see a dialog box as shown in Figure 1.6c, indicating that you are about to delete a record and asking you to confirm the deletion. Click **Yes.**

➤ Pull down the **Edit menu.** The Undo command is dim, indicating that you cannot undelete a record. Press **Esc** to continue working.

THE RECORD SELECTOR

Click the record selector (the box immediately to the left of the first field in a record) to select the record without having to use a pull-down menu. Click and drag the mouse over the record selector for multiple rows to select several sequential records at the same time.

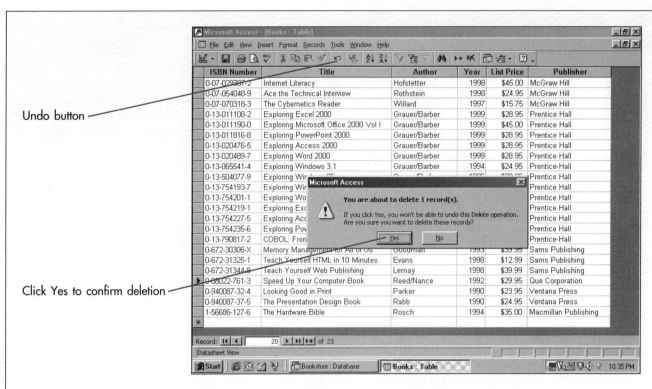

Undo button

Click Yes to confirm deletion

(c) The Delete Command (step 4)

FIGURE 1.6   Hands-on Exercise 2 (continued)

STEP 5: Data Validation

➤ Click the **New Record button** on the toolbar. The record selector moves to the last record (record 24).

➤ Add data as shown in Figure 1.6d, being sure to enter an invalid price **(XXX)** in the List Price field. Press the **Tab key** to move to the next field.

➤ Access displays the dialog box in Figure 1.6d, indicating that the value you entered (XXX) is inappropriate for the List Price field; in other words, you cannot enter letters when Access is expecting a numeric entry.

➤ Click the **OK command button** to close the dialog box and return to the table. Drag the mouse to select XXX, then enter the correct price of **$39.95.**

➤ Press the **Tab key** to move to the Publisher field. Type **McGraw Hill.** Press the **Tab key, right arrow key,** or **enter key** to complete the record.

➤ Click the **Close button** to close the Books table.

STEP 6: Open the Books Form

➤ Click the **Forms button** in the Database window. Double click the **Books form** to open the form as shown in Figure 1.6e, then (if necessary) maximize the form so that it takes the entire window.

➤ Click the **Add Record command button** to move to a new record. The status bar shows record 25 of 25.

➤ Click in the text box for **ISBN number,** then use the **Tab key** to move from field to field as you enter data for the book as shown in Figure 1.6e.

➤ Click the **drop-down arrow** on the Publisher's list box to display the available publishers and to select the appropriate one. The use of a list box ensures that you cannot misspell a publisher's name.

New Record button

Enter invalid price

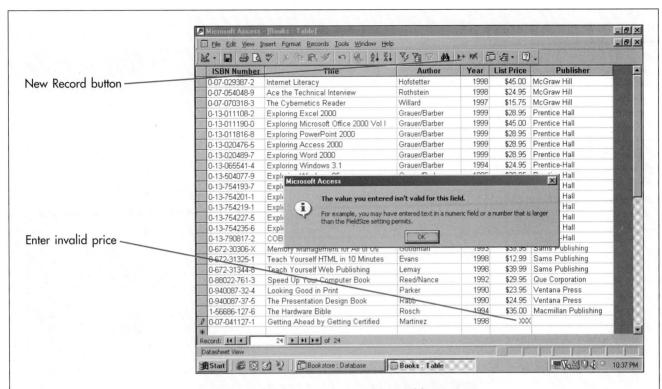

(d) Data Validation (step 5)

Click and enter data

Click to display list of publishers

Add Record button

Current record is record 25

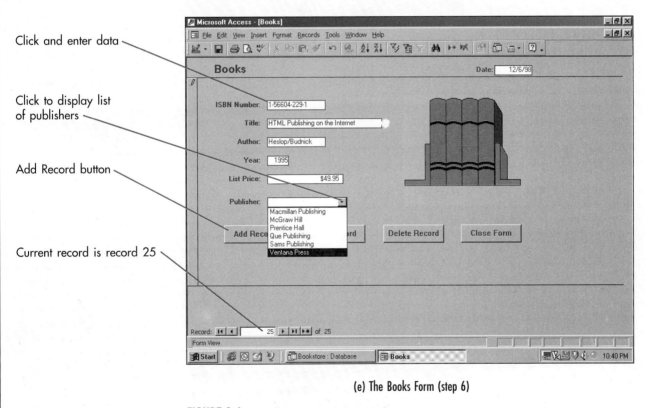

(e) The Books Form (step 6)

FIGURE 1.6   Hands-on Exercise 2 (continued)

STEP 7: The Replace Command

➤ Pull down the **View menu.** Click **Datasheet View** to switch from the Form view to the Datasheet view and display the table on which the form is based.

➤ Press **Ctrl+Home** to move to the first record in the Books table, then click in the **Publisher field** for that record. Pull down the **Edit menu.** Click **Replace.**

➤ Enter the parameters as they appear in Figure 1.6f, then click the **Find Next button** to move to the first occurrence of Prentice-Hall.

➤ Click **Replace** to make the substitution in this record and move to the next occurrence.

➤ Click **Replace** to make the second (and last) substitution, then close the dialog box when Access no longer finds the search string. Close the table.

Click in Publisher field for first record

Enter Prentice-Hall

Enter Prentice Hall (without hyphen)

Search Publisher field

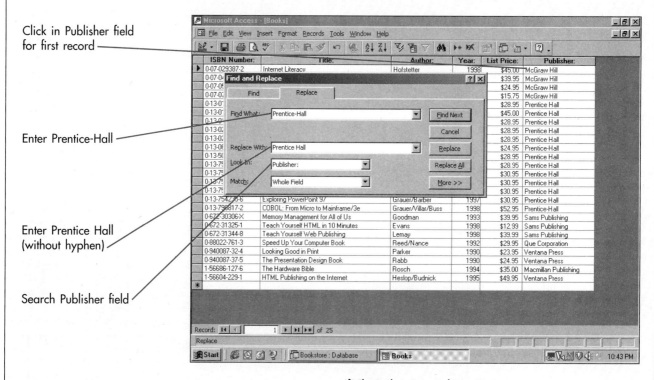

(f) The Replace Command (step 7)

FIGURE 1.6   Hands-on Exercise 2 (continued)

THE MENUS CHANGE

All applications in Office 2000 display a series of short menus that contain only basic commands. There is, however, a double arrow at the bottom of each menu that you can click to display the additional commands. In addition, each time you execute a command it is added to the menu, and conversely, commands are removed from a menu if they are not used after a period of time. You can, however, display the full menus through the Customize command in the Tools menu by clearing the check boxes in the Personalized Menus and Toolbars section.

STEP 8: Print a Report

➤ Click the **Reports button** in the Database window to display the available reports. Double click the icon for the **Publisher report.**

➤ Type **Prentice Hall** (or the name of any other publisher) in the Parameter dialog box. Press **enter** to create the report.

➤ If necessary, click the **Maximize button** in the Report Window so that the report takes the entire screen as shown in Figure 1.6g.

➤ Click the **drop-down arrow** on the Zoom box, then click **Fit** to display the whole page. Note that all of the books in the report are published by Prentice Hall, which is consistent with the parameter you entered earlier.

➤ Click the **Print button** on the Report toolbar to print the report.

➤ Click the **Close button** on the Print Review toolbar to close the Report window.

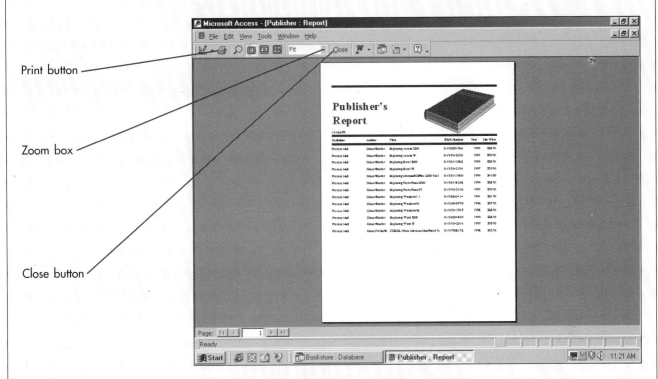

(g) Run a Report (step 8)

FIGURE 1.6 Hands-on Exercise 2 (continued)

TIP OF THE DAY

You can set the Office Assistant to greet you with a "tip of the day" each time you start Access. Click the Microsoft Access Help button (or press the F1 key) to display the Assistant, then click the Options button to display the Office Assistant dialog box. Click the Options tab, then check the Show the Tip of the Day at Startup box and click OK. The next time you start Access, you will be greeted by the Assistant, who will offer you the tip of the day.

STEP 9: The Office Assistant

➤ If necessary, pull down the **Help menu** and click the command to **Show the Office Assistant.** (You may see a different character.) Click the Assistant, then enter the question, **How do I get Help** in the balloon.

➤ Click the **Search button** in the Assistant's balloon to look for the answer. The size of the Assistant's balloon expands as the Assistant suggests several topics that may be appropriate.

➤ Select any topic (we selected **Ways to get assistance while you work**), which in turn displays a Help window with multiple links as shown in Figure 1.6h. Click any of the links in the Help window to read the information.

➤ Click the **Show button** in the Help window to display the Contents, Answer Wizard, and Index tabs. Click the **Contents tab,** then click the **plus sign** that appears next to the various book icons to expand the various help topics. Click the **icon** next to any topic to display the associated information.

➤ Continue to experiment, then close the Help window when you are finished.

➤ Exit Access if you do not want to continue with the next exercise at this time.

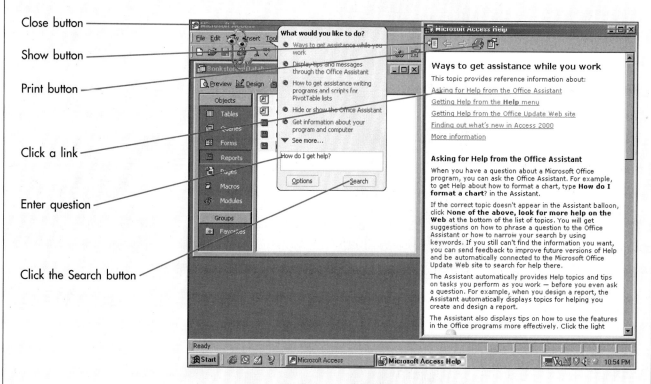

(h) The Office Assistant (step 9)

FIGURE 1.6   Hands-on Exercise 2 (continued)

CHOOSE YOUR OWN ASSISTANT

Choose your own personal assistant from one of several available candidates. Press the F1 key to display the Assistant, click the Assistant to display the balloon, click the Options button to display the Office Assistant dialog box, then click the Gallery tab where you choose your character. (The Office 2000 CD is required to select some characters.)

The exercise just completed described how to use an existing report to obtain information from the database. But what if you are in a hurry and don't have the time to create the report? There is a faster way. You can open the table in the Datasheet view, then apply a filter and/or a sort to the table to display selected records in any order. A *filter* displays a subset of records from the table according to specified criteria. A *sort* lists those records in a specific sequence such as alphabetically by last name or by social security number. We illustrate these concepts in conjunction with Figure 1.7.

Figure 1.7a displays an employee table with 14 records. Each record has 8 fields. The records in the table are displayed in sequence according to the social security number, which is also the primary key (the field or combination of fields that uniquely identifies a record). The status bar indicates that there are 14 records in the table.

Figure 1.7b displays a filtered view of the same table in which we see only the Account Reps. The status bar shows that this is a filtered list, and that there are 8 records that satisfy the criteria. (The employee table still contains the original 14 records, but only 8 records are visible with the filter in effect.) Note, too, that the selected employees are displayed in alphabetical order as opposed to social security order.

Two operations are necessary to go from Figure 1.7a to Figure 1.7b—filtering and sorting. The easiest way to implement a filter is to click in any cell that contains the value of the desired criterion (such as any cell that contains "Account Rep" in the Title field) then click the **Filter by Selection button** on the Database toolbar. To sort the table, click in the field on which you want to sequence the records (the LastName field in this example) then click the **Sort Ascending button** on the Database toolbar. The **Sort Descending button** is appropriate for numeric fields such as salary, if you want to display the records with the highest value listed first.

The operations can be done in any order; that is, you can filter a table to show only selected records, then you can sort the filtered table to display the records in a different order. Conversely, you can sort a table and then apply a filter. It does not matter which operation is performed first, and indeed, you can go back and forth between the two. You can also filter the table further, by applying a second (or third) criterion; e.g., click in a cell containing "Good," then click the Filter by Selection button a second time to display the Account Reps with good performance. You can also click the **Remove Filter button** at any time to display the complete table.

Figure 1.7c illustrates an alternate and more powerful way to apply a filter known as **Filter by Form,** in which you can select the criteria from a drop-down list, and/or apply multiple criteria simultaneously. However, the real advantage of the Filter by Form command extends beyond these conveniences to two additional capabilities. First, you can specify relationships within a criterion; for example, you can select employees with a salary greater than (or less than) $40,000. Filter by Selection, on the other hand, requires you to specify criteria equal to an existing value. Figure 1.7d displays the filtered table of Chicago employees earning more than $40,000.

A second advantage of the Filter by Form command is that you can specify alternative criterion (such as employees in Chicago *or* employees who are account reps) by clicking the Or tab. (The latter capability is not implemented in Figure 1.7.) Suffice it to say, however, that the availability of the various filter and sort commands enable you to obtain information from a database quickly and easily. And as you may have guessed, it's time for another hands-on exercise.

Records are in sequence by SSN (primary key) —

Total of 14 records in table —

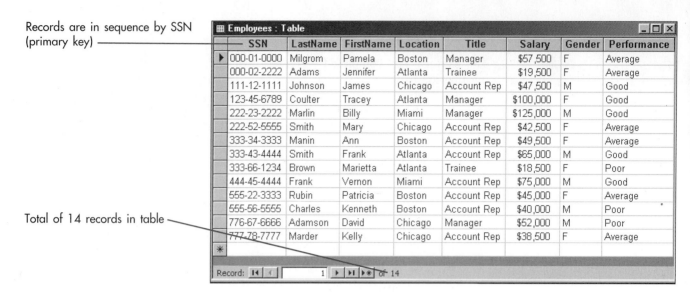

(a) The Employee Table (by Social Security Number)

Records are in alphabetical order by last name —

Total of 8 records in filtered list —

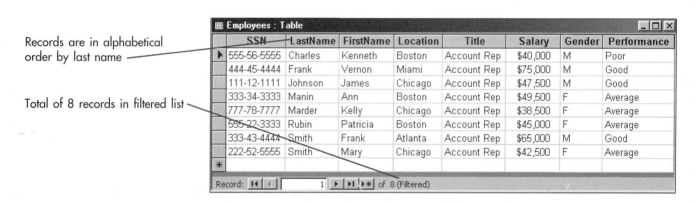

(b) A Filtered List (Account Reps by last name)

Select from a drop-down list to establish criteria —

Or tab —

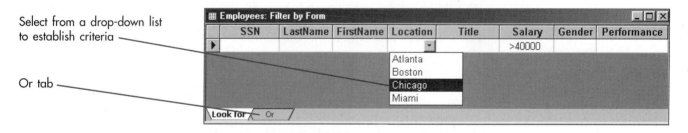

(c) Filter by Form

(d) Filtered List

FIGURE 1.7   Filters and Sorting

Filters and Sorting

Objective: To display selected records within a table by applying the Filter by Selection and Filter by Form criteria; to sort the records in a table. Use Figure 1.8 as a guide in the exercise.

STEP 1: Open the Employees Table

➤ Start Access as you did in the previous exercises, but this time you will open a different database. Click **More Files,** and click **OK** (if you see the Microsoft Access dialog box) or pull down the **File menu** and click the **Open command.** Either way, open the **Employees database** in the **Exploring Access folder.**

➤ If necessary, click the **Tables button** in the database window, then double click the **Employees table,** as shown in Figure 1.8a. Click the **maximize button** so that the Employees table fills the Access window. If necessary, click the **maximize button** in the application window so that Access takes the entire desktop.

➤ Pull down the **Insert menu** and click **New Record** (or click the **New Record button** on either the toolbar or the status bar). The record selector moves to the last record (now record 15).

➤ Add data for yourself, using your own social security number, and your first and last name. Assign yourself to **the Miami office** as an **Account Rep** with a salary of **$32,000** and a **Good performance.**

➤ Press **enter** after you have completed the last field.

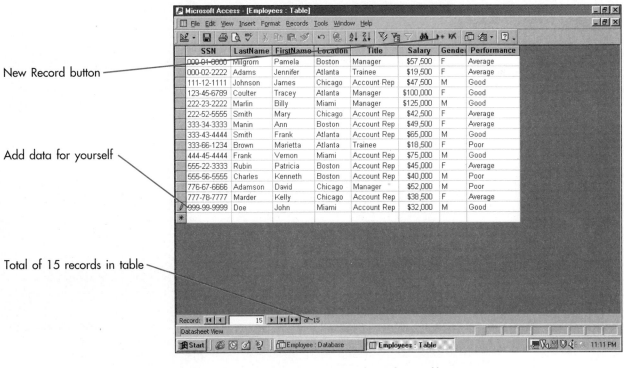

New Record button

Add data for yourself

Total of 15 records in table

(a) Open the Employees Table (step 1)

FIGURE 1.8 Hands-on Exercise 3

STEP 2: Filter By Selection

➤ The Employees table should contain 15 records, including the record you added for yourself. Click in the Title field of any record that contains the title **Account Rep,** then click the **Filter by Selection button.**

➤ You should see 9 employees, all of whom are Account Reps, as shown in Figure 1.8b. The status bar indicates that there are 9 records (as opposed to 15) and that there is a filter condition in effect.

➤ Click in the performance field of any employee with a good performance (we clicked in the performance field of the first record, which should be yours), then click the **Filter by Selection button** a second time.

➤ This time you see 4 employees, each of whom is an Account Rep with a performance evaluation of good. The status bar indicates that 4 records satisfy this filter condition.

➤ Click the **Print button** to print the filtered table.

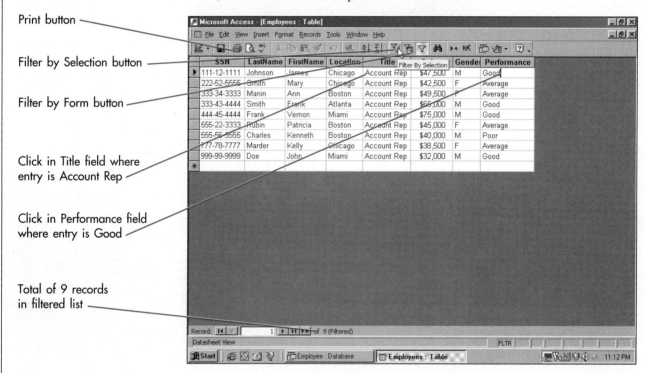

(b) Filter by Selection (step 2)

FIGURE 1.8 Hands-on Exercise 3 (continued)

FILTER EXCLUDING SELECTION

The Filter by Selection button on the Database toolbar selects all records that meet the designated criterion. The Filter Excluding Selection command does just the opposite and displays all records that do not satisfy the criterion. First, click the Remove Filter button to remove any filters that are in effect, then click in the appropriate field of any record that contains the value you want to exclude. Pull down the Records menu, click (or point to) the Filter command, then click the Filter Excluding Selection command to display the records that do not meet the criterion.

STEP 3: Filter by Form

➤ Click the **Filter by Form button** to display the form in Figure 1.8c where you can enter or remove criteria in any sequence. Each time you click in a field, a drop-down list appears that displays all of the values for the field that occur within the table.

➤ Click in the columns for Title and Performance to remove the criteria that were entered in the previous step. Select the existing entries and press the **Del key.**

➤ Click in the cell underneath the Salary field and type **>30000** (as opposed to selecting a specific value). Click in the cell underneath the Location Field and select **Chicago.**

➤ Click the **Apply Filter button** to display the records that satisfy these criteria. (You should see 4 records.) Click the **Print button.**

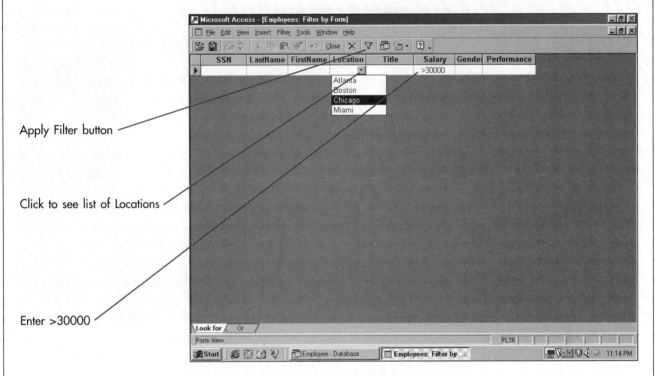

Apply Filter button

Click to see list of Locations

Enter >30000

(c) Filter by Form (step 3)

FIGURE 1.8   Hands-on Exercise 3 (continued)

FILTER BY FORM VERSUS FILTER BY SELECTION

The Filter by Form command has all of the capabilities of the Filter by Selection command, and provides two additional capabilities. First, you can use relational operators such as >, >=, <, or <=, as opposed to searching for an exact value. Second, you can search for records that meet one of several conditions (the equivalent of an "Or" operation). Enter the first criteria as you normally would, then click the Or tab at the bottom of the window to display a second form in which you enter the alternate criteria. (To delete an alternate criterion, click the associated tab, then click the Delete button on the toolbar.)

STEP 4: Sort the Table

➤ Click the **Remove Filter button** to display the complete table of 15 employees. Click in the LastName field of any record, then click the **Sort Ascending button.** The records are displayed in alphabetical (ascending) order by last name.

➤ Click in the Salary field of any record, then click the **Sort Descending button.** The records are in descending order of salary; that is, the employee with the highest salary is listed first.

➤ Click in the Location field of any record, then click the **Sort Ascending button** to display the records by location, although the employees within a location are not in any specific order. You can sort on two fields at the same time provided the fields are next to each other, as described in the next step.

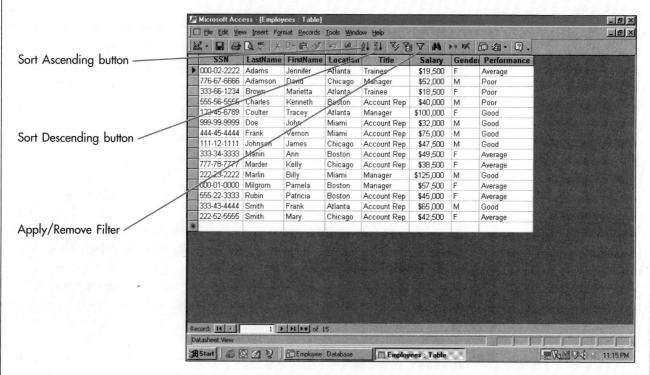

(d) Sort the Table (step 4)

FIGURE 1.8   Hands-on Exercise 3 (continued)

THE SORT OR FILTER—WHICH IS FIRST?

It doesn't matter whether you sort a table and then apply a filter, or filter first and then sort. The operations are cumulative. Thus, once a table has been sorted, any subsequent display of filtered records for that table will be in the specified sequence. Alternatively, you can apply a filter, then sort the filtered table by clicking in the desired field and clicking the appropriate sort button. Remember, too, that all filter commands are cumulative, and hence you must remove the filter to see the original table.

STEP 5: Sort on Two Fields

➤ Click the header for the Location field to select the entire column. Click and drag the Location header so that the Location field is moved to the left of the LastName field as shown in Figure 1.8e.

➤ Click anywhere to deselect the column, then click on the Location header and click and drag to select both the Location header and the LastName Header. Click the **Sort Ascending button.** The records are sorted by location and alphabetically within location.

➤ Click the **Print button** to print the table to prove to your instructor that you completed the exercise. Click the **close button** to close the Employees table.

➤ Click **Yes** when asked whether to save the changes to the Employees table. Saving the table automatically saves the filter and the associated sort.

➤ Exit Access if you do not want to continue with the next exercise at this time.

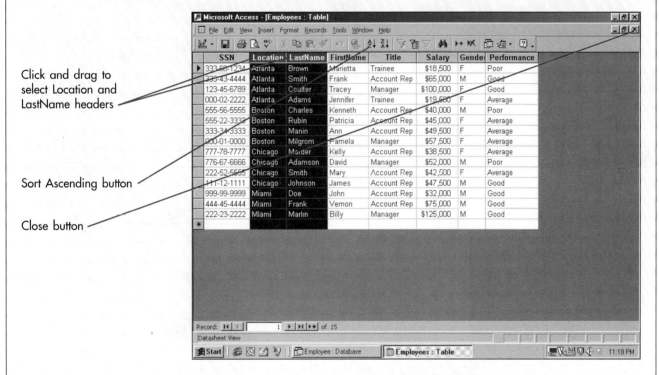

Click and drag to select Location and LastName headers

Sort Ascending button

Close button

(e) Sort on Two Fields (step 5)

FIGURE 1.8   Hands-on Exercise 3 (continued)

REMOVING VERSUS DELETING A FILTER

Removing a filter displays all of the records in a table, but it does not delete the filter because the filter is stored permanently with the table. To delete the filter entirely is more complicated than simply removing it. Pull down the Record menu, click Filter, then click the Advanced Filter/Sort command to display a grid containing the criteria for the filter. Clear the Sort and Criteria rows by clicking in any cell containing an entry and deleting that entry, then click the Apply Filter button when all cells are clear to return to the Datasheet view. The Apply Filter button should be dim, indicating that the table does not contain a filter.

LOOKING AHEAD:
A RELATIONAL DATABASE

The Bookstore and Employee databases are both examples of simple databases in that they each contained only a single table. The real power of Access, however, is derived from multiple tables and the relationships between those tables. This type of database is known as a *relational database* and is illustrated in Figure 1.9. This figure expands the original Employee database by adding two tables, for locations and titles, respectively.

The Employees table in Figure 1.9a is the same table we used at the beginning of the previous exercise, except for the substitution of a LocationID and TitleID for the location and title, respectively. The Locations table in turn has all

SSN	LastName	FirstName	LocationID	TitleID	Salary	Gender	Performance
000-01-0000	Milgrom	Pamela	L02	T02	$57,500	F	Average
000-02-2222	Adams	Jennifer	L01	T03	$19,500	F	Average
111-12-1111	Johnson	James	L03	T01	$47,500	M	Good
123-45-6789	Coulter	Tracey	L01	T02	$100,000	F	Good
222-23-2222	Marlin	Billy	L04	T02	$125,000	M	Good
222-52-5555	Smith	Mary	L03	T01	$42,500	F	Average
333-34-3333	Manin	Ann	L02	T01	$49,500	F	Average
333-43-4444	Smith	Frank	L01	T01	$65,000	M	Good
333-66-1234	Brown	Marietta	L01	T03	$18,500	F	Poor
444-45-4444	Frank	Vernon	L04	T01	$75,000	M	Good
555-22-3333	Rubin	Patricia	L02	T01	$45,000	F	Average
555-56-5555	Charles	Kenneth	L02	T01	$40,000	M	Poor
776-67-6666	Adamson	David	L03	T02	$52,000	M	Poor
777-78-7777	Marder	Kelly	L03	T01	$38,500	F	Average

(a) The Employees Table

LocationID	Location	Address	State	Zipcode	OfficePhone
L01	Atlanta	450 Peachtree Road	GA	30316	(404) 333-5555
L02	Boston	3 Commons Blvd	MA	02190	(617) 123-4444
L03	Chicago	500 Loop Highway	IL	60620	(312) 444-6666
L04	Miami	210 Biscayne Blvd	FL	33103	(305) 787-9999

(b) The Locations Table

TitleID	Title	Description	EducationRequired	MinimumSalary	MaximumSalary
T01	Account Rep	A marketing ...	Four year degree	$25,000	$75,000
T02	Manager	A supervisory ...	Four year degree	$50,000	$150,000
T03	Trainee	An entry-level ...	Two year degree	$18,000	$25,000

(c) The Titles Table

FIGURE 1.9   A Relational Database

of the fields that pertain to each location: LocationID, Location, Address, State, Zipcode, and Office Phone. One field, the LocationID, appears in both Employees and Locations tables and links the two tables to one another. In similar fashion, the Titles table has the information for each title: the TitleID, Title, Description, Education Required, and Minimum and Maximum Salary. The TitleID appears in both the Employees and Titles tables to link those tables to one another.

It sounds complicated, but it is really quite simple and very elegant. More importantly, it enables you to obtain detailed information about any employee, location, or title. To show how it works, we will ask a series of questions that require you to look in one or more tables for the answer. Consider:

Query: At which location does Pamela Milgrom work? What is the phone number of her office?

Answer: Pamela works in the Boston office, at 3 Commons Blvd., Boston, MA, 02190. The phone number is (617) 123-4444.

Did you answer the question correctly? You had to search the Employees table for Pamela Milgrom to obtain the LocationID (L02 in this example) corresponding to her office. You then searched the Locations table for this LocationID to obtain the address and phone number for that location. The process required you to use both the Locations and Employees tables, which are linked to one another through a *one-to-many relationship.* One location can have many employees, but a specific employee can work at only one location. Let's try another question:

Query: Which employees are managers?

Answer: There are four managers: Pamela Milgrom, Tracey Coulter, Billy Marlin, and David Adamson

The answer to this question is based on the one-to-many relationship that exists between titles and employees. One title can have many employees, but a given employee has only one title. To answer the query, you search the Titles table for "manager" to determine its TitleID (T02). You then go to the Employees table and select those records that have this value in the TitleID field.

The design of a relational database enables us to extract information from multiple tables in a single query. Equally important, it simplifies the way data is changed in that modifications are made in only one place. Consider:

Query: Which employees work in the Boston office? What is their phone number? How many changes would be necessary if the Boston office were to get a new phone number?

Answer: There are four employees in Boston: Pamela Milgrom, Ann Manin, Patricia Rubin, and Kenneth Charles, each with the same number (617 123-4444). Only one change (in the Locations table) would be necessary if the phone number changed.

Once again, we draw on the one-to-many relationship between locations and employees. Thus, we begin in the Locations table where we search for "Boston" to determine its LocationID (L02) and phone number (617 123-4444). Then we go to the Employees table to select those records with this value in the LocationID field. Realize, however, that the phone number is stored in the Locations table. Thus, the new phone number is entered in the Boston record, where it is reflected automatically for each employee with a LocationID of L02 (corresponding to the Boston office).

Objective: To open a database with multiple tables; to identify the one-to-many relationships within the database and to produce reports based on those relationships. Use Figure 1.10 as a guide in the exercise.

STEP 1: Open the Relationships Window

➤ Start Access, click the **More Files option button,** and click **OK.** If Access is already open, pull down the **File menu** and click the **Open command.** Open the **Look Ahead database** in the **Exploring Access folder.**

➤ The Tables button should be selected as in Figure 1.10a. The database contains the Employees, Locations, and Titles tables.

➤ Pull down the **Tools menu** and click the **Relationships command** to open the Relationships window as shown in Figure 1.10a. (The tables are not yet visible in this window.)

➤ Pull down the **Relationships menu** and click the **Show Table command** to display the Show Table dialog box. Click (select) the **Locations table** (within the Show Table dialog box) then click the **Add button** to add this table to the Relationships window.

➤ Double click the **Titles** and **Employees tables** to add these tables to the Relationships window.

➤ Close the Show Table dialog box.

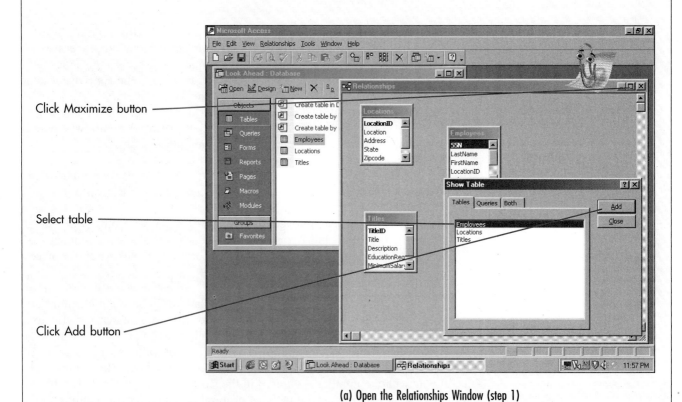

Click Maximize button

Select table

Click Add button

(a) Open the Relationships Window (step 1)

FIGURE 1.10   Hands-on Exercise 4

STEP 2: Create the Relationships

➤ Maximize the Relationships windows so that you have more room in which to work. Click and drag the title bar of each table so that the positions of the tables match those in Figure 1.10b. Click and drag the bottom (and/or right) border of each table so that you see all of the fields in each table.

➤ Click and drag the **LocationID field** in the Locations table field list to the **LocationID field** in the Employees field list. You will see the Edit Relationships dialog box. Check the box to **Enforce Referential Integrity.** Click the **Create button** to create the relationship.

➤ Click and drag the **TitleID field** in the Locations table field list to the **TitleID field** in the Employees field list. You will see the Edit Relationships dialog box. Check the box to **Enforce Referential Integrity** as shown in Figure 1.10b. Click the **Create button** to create the relationship.

➤ Click the **Save button** on the Relationship toolbar to save the Relationships window, then close the Relationships window.

Save button

Click and drag to see all fields

Click and drag TitleID from Titles field list to TitleID in Employees field list

Click Enforce Referential Integrity

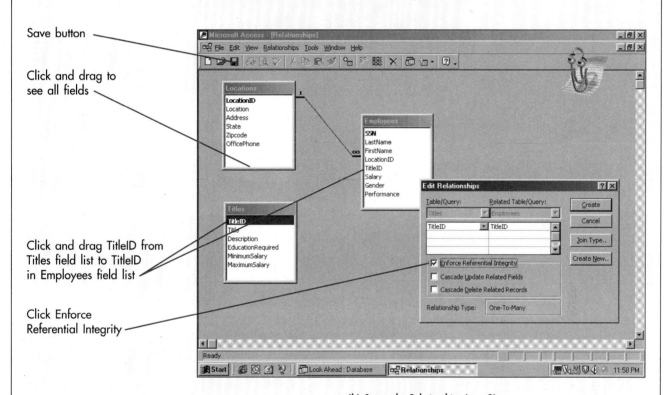

(b) Create the Relationships (step 2)

FIGURE 1.10   Hands-on Exercise 4 (continued)

THE RELATIONSHIPS ARE VISUAL

The tables in an Access database are created independently, then related to one another through the Relationships window. The number 1 and the infinity symbol (∞) appear at the ends of the line to indicate the nature of the relationship; e.g., a one-to-many relationship between the Locations and Employees tables.

STEP 3: Enter Your Own Record

➤ Double click the **Employees table** to open the table. Maximize the window. Pull down the **Insert** menu and click the **New Record** command (or click the **New Record button**) on the Table Datasheet toolbar.

➤ Enter data for yourself, using your own social security number, and your first and last name as shown in Figure 1.10c. Enter an invalid LocationID (e.g., **L44**) then complete the record as shown in the figure.

➤ Press the **enter key** when you have completed the data entry, then click **OK** when you see the error message. Access prevents you from entering a location that does not exist.

➤ Click in the **LocationID field** and enter **L04**, the LocationID for Miami. Press the **down arrow key** to move to the next record, which automatically saves the current record. Close the Employees table.

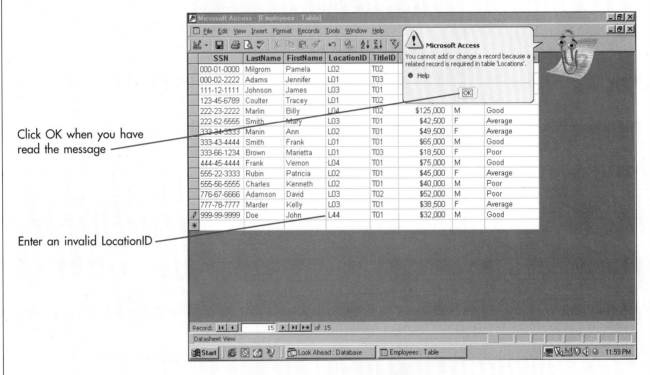

Click OK when you have read the message

Enter an invalid LocationID

(c) Referential Integrity (step 3)

FIGURE 1.10   Hands-on Exercise 4 (continued)

REFERENTIAL INTEGRITY

The tables in a database must be consistent with one another, a concept known as referential integrity. Thus, Access automatically implements certain types of data validation to prevent such errors from occurring. You cannot, for example, enter a record in the Employees table that contains an invalid value for either the LocationID or the TitleID. Nor can you delete a record in the Locations or Titles table if it has related records in the Employees table.

STEP 4: Simplified Data Entry

➤ Click the **Forms button** in the Database window, then double click the **Employees Form** to open this form as shown in Figure 1.10d. Click the **Add Record button** then click in the text box for the Social Security Number.

➤ Enter the data for **Bob Grauer** one field at a time, pressing the **Tab key** to move from one field to the next. Click the **down arrow** when you come to the location field to display the available locations, then select (click) **Miami.**

➤ Press the **Tab key** to move to the Title field and choose **Account Rep.** Complete the data for Bob's record by entering **$150,000, M,** and **Excellent** in the Salary, Gender, and Performance fields, respectively.

➤ Click the **Close Form button** when you have finished entering the data.

Enter data for Bob Grauer

Click to drop down list of cities

Add Record button

Click to drop down list of titles

Close Form

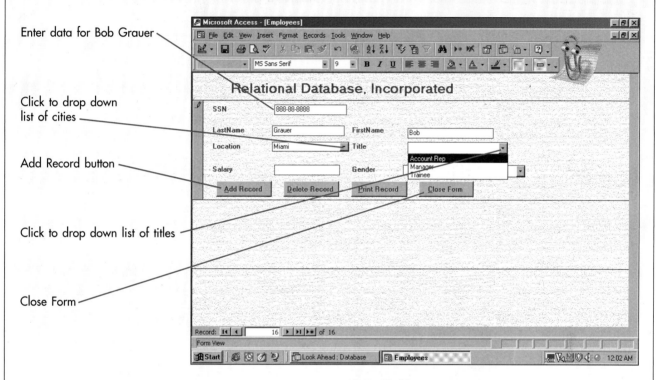

(d) Simplified Data Entry (step 4)

FIGURE 1.10   Hands-on Exercise 4 (continued)

SIMPLIFIED DATA ENTRY

The success of any system depends on the accuracy of its data as well as its ease of use. Both objectives are met through a well-designed form that guides the user through the process of data entry and simultaneously rejects invalid responses. The drop-down list boxes for the Location, Title, and Performance fields ensure that the user can enter only valid values in these fields. Data entry is also simplified in these fields in that you can enter just the first letter of a field, then press the Tab key to move to the next field.

STEP 5: View the Employee Master List

➤ Click the **Reports button** in the Database window. Double click the **Employee Master List** report to open the report as shown in figure 1.10e.

➤ This report lists selected fields for all employees in the database. Note that the two new employees, you and Bob Grauer, appear in alphabetical order. Both employees are in the Miami Office.

➤ Close the Report window.

Close button

The two new employees are listed in alphabetical order

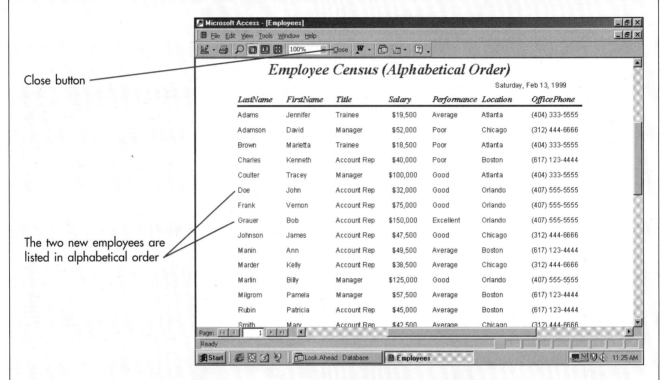

(e) View the Employee Master List (step 5)

FIGURE 1.10   Hands-on Exercise 4 (continued)

ADVICE FROM THE ASSISTANT

The Office Assistant monitors your work and displays a lightbulb when it has a suggestion to help you work more efficiently. Click the lightbulb to display the tip, then click OK or press the Esc key after you have read the information. The Assistant will not, however, repeat a tip from an earlier session unless it is reset at the start of a session. This is especially important in a laboratory situation where you are sharing a computer with many students. To reset the tips, click the Assistant to display its balloon, click the Options button in the balloon, then click the Options tab, then click the button to Reset My Tips.

STEP 6: Change the Locations Table

➤ Click the **Tables button** in the Database window, then double click the **Locations table** to open this table as shown in figure 1.10f. Maximize the window.

➤ Click the **plus sign** next to location L04 (Miami) to view the employees in this office. The plus sign changes to a minus sign as the employee records for this location are shown. Your name appears in this list as does Bob Grauer's. Click the **minus sign** and the list of related records disappears.

➤ Click and drag to select **Miami** (the current value in the Location field). Type **Orlando** and press the **Tab key.** Enter the corresponding values for the other field: **1000 Kirkman Road, FL, 32801** and **(407) 555-5555** for the address, state, zip code, and office phone, respectively.

➤ Close the **Locations table.** You have moved the Miami Office to Orlando.

Change address and phone number

Change Miami to Orlando

Click + sign to display employees at Location LO4 (+ changes to a −)

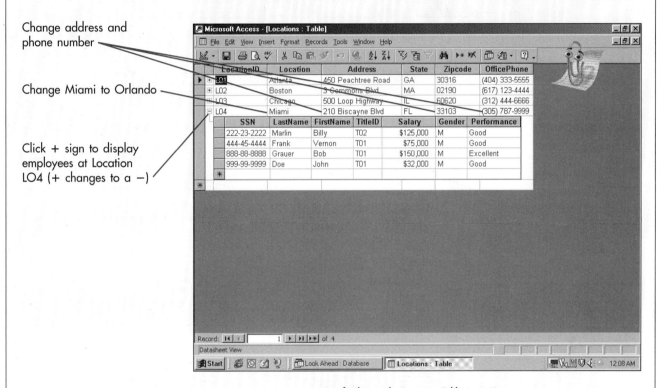

(f) Change the Locations Table (step 6)

FIGURE 1.10   Hands-on Exercise 4 (continued)

ADD AND DELETE RELATED RECORDS

Take advantage of the one-to-many relationship between locations and employees (or titles and employees) to add and/or delete records in the Employees table. Open the Locations table, then click the plus sign next to the location where you want to add or delete an employee record. To add a new employee, click the New Record navigation button within the Employees table for that location, then add the new data. To delete a record, click the record, then click the Delete Record button on the Table Datasheet toolbar. Click the minus sign to close the employee list.

STEP 7: View the Employees by Title Report

➤ Click the **Reports button** in the Database window, then double click the **Employees by Title** report to open the report shown in Figure 1.10g.

➤ This report lists employees by title, rather than alphabetically. Note that you and Bob Grauer are both listed as Account Reps in the Orlando office; i.e., the location of the office was changed in the Locations table and that change is automatically reflected for all employees assigned to that office.

➤ Close the Report window. Close the Database window. Exit Access. Welcome to the world of relational databases.

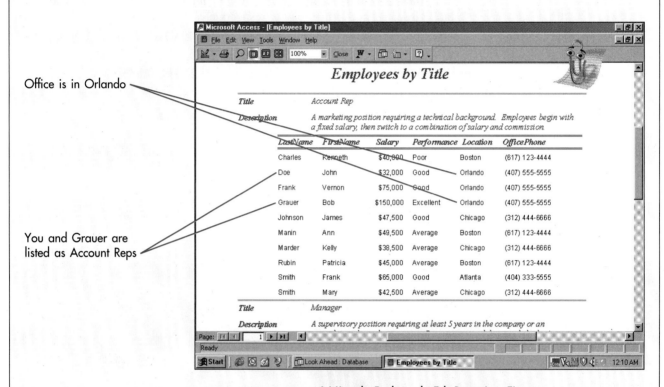

Office is in Orlando

You and Grauer are listed as Account Reps

(g) View the Employees by Title Report (step 7)

FIGURE 1.10   Hands-on Exercise 4 (continued)

THE WHAT'S THIS COMMAND

Use the What's This command to obtain a detailed explanation for any toolbar button. Pull down the Help menu and click the What's This command (or press the Shift+F1 key) to change the mouse pointer to an arrow with a question mark. Now click any toolbar button for an explanation of that button. Press the Esc key to return the mouse pointer to normal and continue working.

An Access database has seven types of objects—tables, forms, queries, reports, pages, macros, and modules. The database window displays these objects and enables you to open an existing object or create a new object.

Each table in the database is composed of records, and each record is in turn composed of fields. Every record in a given table has the same fields in the same order.

A table is displayed in one of two views—the Design view or the Datasheet view. The Design view is used to define the table initially and to specify the fields it will contain. The Datasheet view is the view you use to add, edit, or delete records.

A record selector symbol is displayed next to the current record and signifies the status of that record. A triangle indicates that the record has been saved. A pencil indicates that the record has not been saved and that you are in the process of entering (or changing) the data. An asterisk appears next to the blank record present at the end of every table, where you add a new record to the table.

Access automatically saves any changes in the current record as soon as you move to the next record or when you close the table. The Undo Current Record command cancels (undoes) the changes to the previously saved record.

No system, no matter how sophisticated, can produce valid output from invalid input. Data validation is thus a critical part of any system. Access automatically imposes certain types of data validation during data entry. Additional checks can be implemented by the user.

A filter is a set of criteria that is applied to a table in order to display a subset of the records in that table. Microsoft Access lets you filter by selection or filter by form. The application of a filter does not remove the records from the table, but simply suppresses them from view. The records in a table can be displayed in ascending or descending sequence by clicking the appropriate button on the Database toolbar.

A relational database contains multiple tables and enables you to extract information from those tables in a single query. The tables must be consistent with one another, a concept known as referential integrity. Thus, Access automatically implements certain types of data validation to prevent such errors from occurring.

KEY WORDS AND CONCEPTS

Asterisk (record selector) symbol
AutoCorrect
Current record
Data validation
Database
Database window
Datasheet view
Design view
Field
Field name
Filter
Filter by Form
Filter by Selection
Filter Excluding Selection

Find command
Form
GIGO (garbage in, garbage out)
Insertion point
Macro
Microsoft Access
Module
One-to-many relationship
Page
Pencil (record selector) symbol
Primary key
Query
Record

Record selector symbol
Referential Integrity
Relational database
Remove filter
Replace command
Report
Sort
Sort Ascending
Sort Descending
Table
Triangle (record selector) symbol
Undo command

1. Which sequence represents the hierarchy of terms, from smallest to largest?
   (a) Database, table, record, field
   (b) Field, record, table, database
   (c) Record, field, table, database
   (d) Field, record, database, table

2. Which of the following is true regarding movement within a record (assuming you are not in the first or last field of that record)?
   (a) Press Tab or the right arrow key to move to the next field
   (b) Press Shift+Tab or the left arrow key to return to the previous field
   (c) Both (a) and (b)
   (d) Neither (a) nor (b)

3. You're performing routine maintenance on a table within an Access database. When should you execute the Save command?
   (a) Immediately after you add, edit, or delete a record
   (b) Periodically during a session—for example, after every fifth change
   (c) Once at the end of a session
   (d) None of the above since Access automatically saves the changes as they are made

4. Which of the following objects are contained within an Access database?
   (a) Tables and forms
   (b) Queries and reports
   (c) Macros and modules
   (d) All of the above

5. Which of the following is true about the objects in an Access database?
   (a) Every database must contain at least one object of every type
   (b) A database may contain at most one object of each type
   (c) Both (a) and (b)
   (d) Neither (a) nor (b)

6. Which of the following is true of an Access database?
   (a) Every record in a table has the same fields as every other record in that table
   (b) Every table contains the same number of records as every other table
   (c) Both (a) and (b)
   (d) Neither (a) nor (b)

7. Which of the following is a *false* statement about the Open Database command?
   (a) It can be executed from the File menu
   (b) It can be executed by clicking the Open button on the Database toolbar
   (c) It loads a database from disk into memory
   (d) It opens the selected table from the Database window

8. Which of the following is true regarding the record selector symbol?
   (a) A pencil indicates that the current record has already been saved
   (b) A triangle indicates that the current record has not changed
   (c) An asterisk indicates the first record in the table
   (d) All of the above

9. Which view is used to add, edit, and delete records in a table?
   (a) The Design view
   (b) The Datasheet view
   (c) Either (a) or (b)
   (d) Neither (a) nor (b)

10. Which of the following is true with respect to a table within an Access database?
    (a) Ctrl+End moves to the last field in the last record of a table
    (b) Ctrl+Home moves to the first field in the first record of a table
    (c) Both (a) and (b)
    (d) Neither (a) nor (b)

11. What does GIGO stand for?
    (a) Gee, I Goofed, OK
    (b) Grand Illusions, Go On
    (c) Global Indexing, Global Order
    (d) Garbage In, Garbage Out

12. The find and replace values in a Replace command must be:
    (a) The same length
    (b) The same case
    (c) Both (a) and (b)
    (d) Neither (a) nor (b)

13. An Access table containing 10 records, and 10 fields per record, requires two pages for printing. What, if anything, can be done to print the table on one page?
    (a) Print in Landscape rather than Portrait mode
    (b) Decrease the left and right margins
    (c) Both (a) and (b)
    (d) Neither (a) nor (b)

14. Which of the following capabilities is available through Filter by Selection?
    (a) The imposition of a relational condition
    (b) The imposition of an alternate (OR) condition
    (c) Both (a) and (b)
    (d) Neither (a) nor (b)

15. Which of the following best describes the relationship between locations and employees as implemented in the Look Ahead database within the chapter?
    (a) One to one
    (b) One to many
    (c) Many to many
    (d) Impossible to determine

Answers

1. b	**6.** a	**11.** d
2. c	**7.** d	**12.** d
3. d	**8.** b	**13.** c
4. d	**9.** b	**14.** d
5. d	**10.** c	**15.** b

PRACTICE WITH ACCESS 2000

1. The Employee Database: Review and/or complete the third hands-on exercise that introduced the Employee database. Be sure to remove any filters that are in effect at the end of the exercise, then implement the following transactions:

   a. Delete the record for Kelly Marder.

   b. Change Pamela Milgrom's salary to $59,500.

   c. Use the Replace command to change all occurrences of "Manager" to "Supervisor."

   d. Print the Employee Census Report as shown in Figure 1.11 after making the changes in parts (a) through (c).

   e. Create a cover page (in Microsoft Word) and submit the assignment to your instructor.

FIGURE 1.11   The Employee Database (Exercise 1)

2. Do the two hands-on exercises in the chapter, then modify the Bookstore database to accommodate the following:
   a. Add the book, *Exploring Microsoft Office 2000 Vol II* (ISBN: 013-011100-7) by Grauer/Barber, published in 1999 by Prentice Hall, selling for $45.00.
   b. Change the price of *Memory Management for All of Us* to $29.95.
   c. Delete *The Presentation Design Book*.
   d. Print the *All Books Report* after these changes have been made.

3. The United States: Figure 1.12 displays a table from the United States (USA) database that is one of our practice files. The database contains statistical data about all 50 states and enables you to produce various reports such as the 10 largest states in terms of population.
   a. Open the USA database, then open the USstates table. Click anywhere in the Population field, then click the Sort Descending button to list the states in descending order. Click and drag to select the first ten records so that you have selected the ten most populous states.
   b. Pull down the File menu, click the Print command, then click the option button to print the selected records. Be sure to print in Landscape mode so that all of the data fits on one page. (Use the Page Setup command in the File menu prior to printing.)
   c. Repeat the procedure in steps a and b, but this time print the ten states with the largest area.
   d. Repeat the procedure once again to print the first thirteen states admitted to the Union. (You have to sort in ascending rather than descending sequence.)
   e. Submit all three pages together with a title page (created in Microsoft Word) to your instructor.

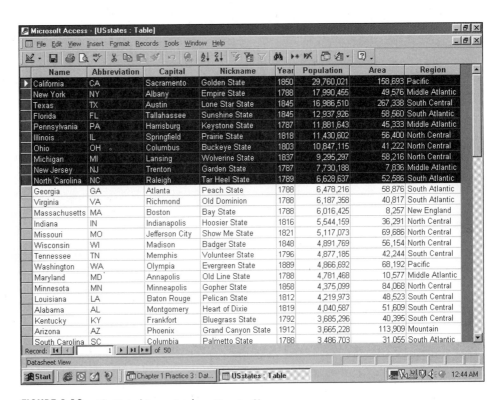

FIGURE 1.12   The United States Database (Exercise 3)

4. The Super Bowl: Open the Super Bowl database on the data disk and display the table in Figure 1.13. Our data stops with the 1999 Super Bowl and it may no longer be current. Thus, the first thing you will need to do is update our table.

a. Pull down the View menu, click Toolbars, then toggle the Web toolbar on. Enter the address of the NFL home page (www.nfl.com) in the Address bar, then click the link to the Super Bowl. Follow the links that will allow you to determine the teams and score of any game(s) not included in our table.

b. Click the New Record button and enter the additional data in the table. The additional data will be entered at the end of the table, and hence you need to sort the data after it is entered. Click anywhere in the Year field, then click the Descending Sort button to display the most recent Super Bowl first as shown in Figure 1.13c.

c. Select the winner in any year that the AFC won. Click the Filter by Selection button to display only those records (i.e., the years in which the AFC won the game). Print these records.

d. Click the Remove Filter button. Select any year in which the NFC won, then click the Filter by Selection button to display the years in which the NFC won. Print these records. Remove the filter.

e. Create one additional filter (e.g., the years in which your team won the big game). Print these records as well.

f. Create a cover sheet, then submit all three reports to your instructor.

FIGURE 1.13 The Super Bowl (Exercise 4)

5. A Look Ahead: Review and/or complete the fourth hands-on exercise that pertained to the Look Ahead database. Enter the following additional transactions, then print the Employees by Location report shown in Figure 1.14.

   a. Add a new location to the Locations table. Use L05, New York, 1000 Broadway, NY, 10020, and (212) 666-6666 for the LocationID, Location, Address, State, ZipCode, and OfficePhone fields, respectively.

   b. Change the assigned location for Bob Grauer, Frank Smith, and yourself to the New York Office. Bob will be the manager of the New York office.

   c. Delete the record for Kenneth Charles.

   d. Change the title, "Account Rep" to "Account Exec."

   e. Print the Employees by Location report and submit it to your instructor as proof you did this exercise.

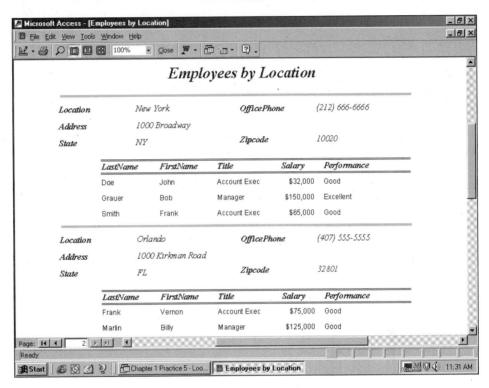

FIGURE 1.14   A Look Ahead (Exercise 5)

6. A Companion Web site (or online study guide) accompanies each book in the *Exploring Microsoft Office 2000* series. Go to the Exploring Windows home page at www.prenhall.com/grauer, click the book to Office 2000, and click the Companion Web site tab at the top of the screen. Choose the appropriate text (Exploring Access 2000) and the chapter within the text (e.g., Chapter 1).

   Each chapter contains a series of short-answer exercises (multiple-choice, true/false, and matching) to review the material in the chapter. You can take practice quizzes by yourself and/or e-mail the results to your instructor. You can try the essay questions for additional practice and engage in online chat sessions. We hope you will find the online guide to be a valuable resource.

Planning for Disaster

This case has nothing to do with databases per se, but it is perhaps the most important case of all, as it deals with the question of backup. Do you have a backup strategy? Do you even know what a backup strategy is? Now is a good time to learn because sooner or later you will wish you had one. There will come a time when you will accidentally erase a file, be unable to read from a floppy disk, or worse yet, suffer a hardware failure in which you are unable to access the hard drive. The problem always seems to occur the night before an assignment is due. The ultimate disaster is the disappearance of your computer, by theft or natural disaster (e.g., Hurricane Andrew, the floods in the Midwest, or the Los Angeles earthquake). Describe in 250 or fewer words the backup strategy you plan to implement in conjunction with your work in this class.

The Common User Interface

One of the most significant benefits of the Windows environment is the common user interface, which provides a sense of familiarity when you go from one application to another—for example, when you go from Excel to Access. How many similarities can you find between these two applications? Which menus are common to both? Which keyboard shortcuts? Which formatting conventions? Which toolbar icons? Which shortcut menus?

Garbage In, Garbage Out

Your excellent work in this class has earned you an internship in the registrar's office. Your predecessor has created a student database that appears to work well, but in reality has several problems in that many of its reports do not produce the expected information. One problem came to light in conjunction with a report listing business majors: the report contained far fewer majors than were expected. Open the GIGO database on the data disk and see if you can find and correct the problem.

Changing Menus and Toolbars

Office 2000 implements one very significant change over previous versions of Office in that it displays a series of short menus that contain only basic commands. The additional commands are made visible by clicking the double arrow that appears at the bottom of the menu. New commands are added to the menu as they are used, and conversely, other commands are removed if they are not used. A similar strategy is followed for the Standard and Formatting toolbars which are displayed on a single row, and thus do not show all of the buttons at one time. The intent is to simplify Office 2000 for the new user by limiting the number of commands that are visible. The consequence, however, is that the individual is not exposed to new commands, and hence may not use Office to its full potential. Which set of menus do you prefer? How do you switch from one set to the other?

chapter 2

TABLES AND FORMS: DESIGN, PROPERTIES, VIEWS, AND WIZARDS

OBJECTIVES

After reading this chapter you will be able to:

1. Describe in general terms how to design a table; discuss three guidelines you can use in the design process.
2. Describe the data types and properties available within Access and the purpose of each; set the primary key for a table.
3. Use the Table Wizard to create a table; add and delete fields in an existing table.
4. Discuss the importance of data validation and how it is implemented in Access.
5. Use the Form Wizard to create one of several predefined forms.
6. Distinguish between a bound control, an unbound control, and a calculated control; explain how each type of control is entered on a form.
7. Modify an existing form to include a combo box, command buttons, and color.
8. Switch between the Form view, Design view, and Datasheet view; use a form to add, edit, and delete records in a table.

OVERVIEW

This chapter introduces a new case study, that of a student database, which we use to present the basic principles of table and form design. Tables and forms are used to input data into a system from which information can be produced. The value of that information depends entirely on the quality of the underlying data, which must be both complete and accurate. We begin, therefore, with a conceptual discussion emphasizing the importance of proper design and develop essential guidelines that are used throughout the book.

After the design has been developed, we turn our attention to implementing that design in Access. We show you how to create a table using the Table Wizard, then show you how to refine its design by changing the properties of various fields within the table. We also stress the importance of data validation during data entry.

The second half of the chapter introduces forms as a more convenient way to enter and display data. We introduce the Form Wizard to create a basic form, then show you how to modify that form to include command buttons, a list box, a check box, and an option group.

As always, the hands-on exercises in the chapter enable you to apply the conceptual material at the computer. This chapter contains three exercises, after which you will be well on your way toward creating a useful database in Access.

CASE STUDY: A STUDENT DATABASE

As a student you are well aware that your school maintains all types of data about you. They have your social security number. They have your name and address and phone number. They know whether or not you are receiving financial aid. They know your major and the number of credits you have completed.

Think for a moment about the information your school requires, then write down all of the data needed to produce that information. This is the key to the design process. You must visualize the output the end user will require to determine the input to produce that output. Think of the specific fields you will need. Try to characterize each field according to the type of data it contains (such as text, numbers, or dates) as well as its size (length).

Our solution is shown in Figure 2.1, which may or may not correspond to what you have written down. The order of the fields within the table is not significant. Neither are the specific field names. What is important is that the table contain all necessary fields so that the system can perform as intended.

Field Name	Type
SSN	Text
FirstName	Text
LastName	Text
Address	Text
City	Text
State	Text
PostalCode	Text
PhoneNumber	Text
Major	Text
BirthDate	Date/Time
FinancialAid	Yes/No
Gender	Text
Credits	Number
QualityPoints	Number

FIGURE 2.1   The Students Table

Figure 2.1 may seem obvious upon presentation, but it does reflect the results of a careful design process based on three essential guidelines:

1. Include all of the necessary data
2. Store data in its smallest parts
3. Do not use calculated fields

Each guideline is discussed in turn. As you proceed through the text, you will be exposed to many applications that help you develop the experience necessary to design your own systems.

Include the Necessary Data

How do you determine the necessary data? The best way is to create a rough draft of the reports you will need, then design the table so that it contains the fields necessary to create those reports. In other words, ask yourself what information will be expected from the system, then determine the data required to produce that information. Consider, for example, the type of information that can and cannot be produced from the table in Figure 2.1:

- You can contact a student by mail or by telephone. You cannot, however, contact the student's parents if the student lives on campus or has an address different from his or her parents.
- You can calculate a student's grade point average (GPA) by dividing the quality points by the number of credits. You cannot produce a transcript listing the courses a student has taken.
- You can calculate a student's age from his or her date of birth. You cannot determine how long the student has been at the university because the date of admission is not in the table.

Whether or not these omissions are important depends on the objectives of the system. Suffice it to say that you must design a table carefully, so that you are not disappointed when it is implemented. *You must be absolutely certain that the data entered into a system is sufficient to provide all necessary information;* otherwise the system is almost guaranteed to fail.

DESIGN FOR THE NEXT 100 YEARS

Your system will not last 100 years, but it is prudent to design as though it will. It is a fundamental law of information technology that systems evolve continually and that information requirements will change. Try to anticipate the future needs of the system, then build in the flexibility to satisfy those demands. Include the necessary data at the outset and be sure that the field sizes are large enough to accommodate future expansion.

Store Data in Its Smallest Parts

Figure 2.1 divides a student's name into two fields (first name and last name) to reference each field individually. You might think it easier to use a single field consisting of both the first and last name, but that approach is inadequate. Consider, for example, the following list in which the student's name is stored as a single field:

Allison Foster
Brit Reback
Carrie Graber
Danielle Ferrarro

The first problem in this approach is one of flexibility, in that you cannot separate a student's first name from her last name. You could not, for example, create a salutation of the form "Dear Allison" or "Dear Ms. Foster" because the first and last name are not accessible individually.

A second difficulty is that the list of students cannot be put into alphabetical order because the last name begins in the middle of the field. Indeed, whether you realize it or not, the names in the list are already in alphabetical order (according to the design criteria of a single field) because sorting always begins with the leftmost position in a field. Thus the "A" in Allison comes before the "B" in Brit, and so on. The proper way to sort the data is on the last name, which can be done only if the last name is stored as a separate field.

CITY, STATE, AND ZIP CODE: ONE FIELD OR THREE?

The city, state, and zip code should always be stored as separate fields. Any type of mass mailing requires you to sort on zip code to take advantage of bulk mail. Other applications may require you to select records from a particular state or zip code, which can be done only if the data is stored as separate fields. The guideline is simple—store data in its smallest parts.

Avoid Calculated Fields

A *calculated field* is a field whose value is derived from a formula or function that references an existing field or combination of fields. Calculated fields should not be stored in a table because they are subject to change, waste space, and are otherwise redundant.

The Grade Point Average (GPA) is an example of a calculated field as it is computed by dividing the number of quality points by the number of credits. It is both unnecessary and undesirable to store GPA in the Students table, because the table contains the fields on which the GPA is based. In other words, Access is able to calculate the GPA from these fields whenever it is needed, which is much more efficient than doing it manually. Imagine, for example, having to manually recalculate the GPA for 10,000 students each semester.

BIRTH DATE VERSUS AGE

A person's age and date of birth provide equivalent information, as one is calculated from the other. It might seem easier, therefore, to store the age rather than the birth date, and thus avoid the calculation. That would be a mistake because age changes continually (and would need to be updated continually), whereas the date of birth remains constant. Similar reasoning applies to an employee's length of service versus date of hire.

There are two ways to create a table. The easier way is to use the **Table Wizard,** an interactive coach that lets you choose from many predefined tables. The Table Wizard asks you questions about the fields you want to include in your table, then creates the table for you. Alternatively, you can create a table yourself by defining every field in the table. Regardless of how a table is created, you can modify it to include a new field or to delete an existing field.

Every field has a **field name** to identify the data that is entered into the field. The field name should be descriptive of the data and can be up to 64 characters in length, including letters, numbers, and spaces. We do not, however, use spaces in our field names, but use uppercase letters to distinguish the first letter of a new word. This is consistent with the default names provided by Access in its predefined tables.

Every field also has a **data type** that determines the type of data that can be entered and the operations that can be performed on that data. Access recognizes nine data types: Number, Text, Memo, Date/Time, Currency, Yes/No, OLE Object, AutoNumber, and Hyperlink.

- A **Number field** contains a value that can be used in a calculation such as the number of quality points or credits a student has earned. The contents of a number field are restricted to numbers, a decimal point, and a plus or minus sign.
- A **Text field** stores alphanumeric data such as a student's name or address. It can contain alphabetic characters, numbers, and/or special characters (e.g., an apostrophe in O'Malley). Fields that contain only numbers but are not used in a calculation (e.g., social security number, telephone number, or zip code) should be designated as text fields for efficiency purposes. A text field can hold up to 255 characters.
- A **Memo field** can be up to 64,000 characters long. Memo fields are used to hold lengthy, descriptive data (several sentences or paragraphs).
- A **Date/Time field** holds formatted dates or times (e.g., mm/dd/yy) and allows the values to be used in date or time arithmetic.
- A **Currency field** can be used in a calculation and is used for fields that contain monetary values.
- A **Yes/No field** (also known as a Boolean or Logical field) assumes one of two values such as Yes or No, or True or False, or On or Off.
- An **OLE Object field** contains an object created by another application. OLE objects include pictures, sounds, or graphics.
- An **AutoNumber field** is a special data type that causes Access to assign the next consecutive number each time you add a record. The value of an AutoNumber field is unique for each record in the file, and thus AutoNumber fields are frequently used as the primary key.
- A **Hyperlink field** stores a Web address (URL). All Office 97 documents are Web-enabled so that you can click a hyperlink within an Access database and display the associated Web page, provided that you have access to the Internet.

Primary Key

The **primary key** is a field (or combination of fields) that uniquely identifies a record. There can be only one primary key per table and, by definition, every record in the table must have a different value for the primary key.

A person's name is not used as the primary key because names are not unique. A social security number, on the other hand, is unique and is a frequent choice for the primary key, as in the Students table in this chapter. The primary key emerges naturally in many applications, such as a part number in an inventory system, or the ISBN in the Books table of Chapter 1. If there is no apparent primary key, a new field can be created with the AutoNumber field type.

Views

A table has two views—the Datasheet view and the Design view. The Datasheet view is the view you used in Chapter 1 to add, edit, and delete records. The Design view is the view you will use in this chapter to create (and modify) a table.

Figure 2.2a shows the Datasheet view corresponding to the table in Figure 2.1. (Not all of the fields are visible.) The ***Datasheet view*** displays the record selector symbol for the current record (a pencil or a triangle). It also displays an asterisk in the record selector column next to the blank record at the end of the table.

Figure 2.2b shows the Design view of the same table. The ***Design view*** displays the field names in the table, the data type of each field, and the properties of the selected field. The Design view also displays a key indicator next to the field (or combination of fields) designated as the primary key.

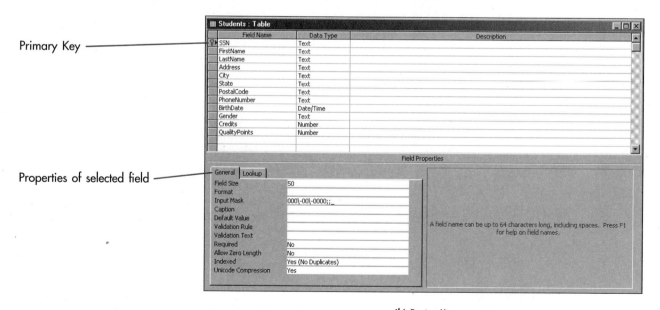

FIGURE 2.2   The Views of a Table

Properties

A *property* is a characteristic or attribute of an object that determines how the object looks and behaves. Every Access object (tables, forms, queries, and reports) has a set of properties that determine the behavior of that object. The properties for an object are displayed and/or changed in a *property sheet,* which is described in more detail later in the chapter.

Each field has its own set of properties that determine how the data in the field are stored and displayed. The properties are set to default values according to the data type, but can be modified as necessary. The properties are displayed in the Design view and described briefly below:

- The *Field Size property* adjusts the size of a text field or limits the allowable value in a number field. Microsoft Access uses only the amount of space it needs even if the field size allows a greater number.
- The *Format property* changes the way a field is displayed or printed, but does not affect the stored value.
- The *Input Mask property* facilitates data entry by displaying literal characters, such as hyphens in a social security number or slashes in a date. It also imposes data validation by ensuring that the data entered by the user fits within the mask.
- The *Caption property* specifies a label other than the field name for forms and reports.
- The *Default Value property* automatically enters a designated (default) value for the field in each record that is added to the table.
- The *Validation Rule property* rejects any record where the data entered does not conform to the specified rules for data entry.
- The *Validation Text property* specifies the error message that is displayed when the validation rule is violated.
- The *Required property* rejects any record that does not have a value entered for this field.
- The *Allow Zero Length property* allows text or memo strings of zero length.
- The *Indexed property* increases the efficiency of a search on the designated field. (The primary key in a table is always indexed.)

The following exercise has you create a table using the Table Wizard and then modify the table by including additional fields. It also has you change the properties for various fields within the table.

CHANGE THE DEFAULT FOLDER

The default folder is the folder Access uses to retrieve (and save) a database unless it is otherwise instructed. To change the default folder, pull down the Tools menu, click Options, then click the General tab in the Options dialog box. Enter the name of the default database folder (e.g., C:\Exploring Access), then click OK to accept the settings and close the Options dialog box. The next time you access the File menu the default folder will reflect the change.

Creating a Table

Objective: To use the Table Wizard to create a table; to add and delete fields in an existing table; to change the primary key of an existing table; to establish an input mask and validation rule for fields within a table; to switch between the Design and Datasheet views of a table. Use Figure 2.3 as a guide.

STEP 1: Create a New Database

➤ Click the **Start button** to display the Start menu. Click (or point to) the **Programs menu,** then click **Microsoft Access** to start the program.

➤ You should see the Microsoft Access dialog box. Click the option button to create a new database using a **Blank Access Database.** Click **OK.** You should see the File New Database dialog box shown in Figure 2.3a.

➤ Click the **drop-down arrow** on the Save In list box. Click the appropriate drive (e.g., drive C), depending on the location of your data. Double click the **Exploring Access folder** to make it the active folder.

➤ Click in the **File Name text box** and drag to select **db1.** Type **My First Database** as the name of the database you will create. Click the **Create button.**

Click to select drive and/or folder

Create Button

Enter file name

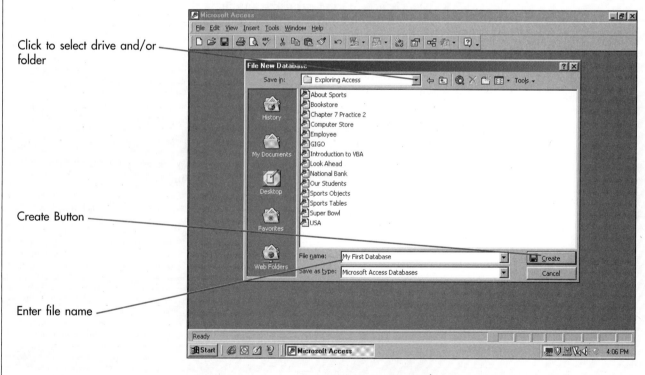

(a) Create a New Database (step 1)

FIGURE 2.3   Hands-on Exercise 1

STEP 2: Create the Table

➤ The Database window for My First Database should appear on your monitor. The **Tables button** is selected by default.

➤ Click and drag an edge or border of the Database window to change its size to match that in Figure 2.3b. Click and drag the title bar of the Database window to change its position on the desktop.

➤ Click the **New button** to display the New Table dialog box shown in Figure 2.3b. Click (select) **Table Wizard** in the New Table dialog box, then click **OK** to start the Table Wizard.

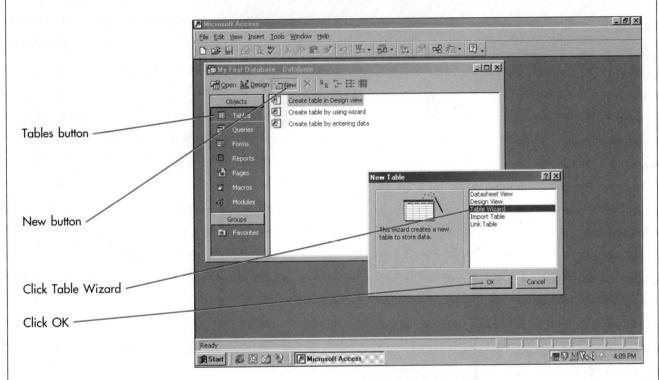

Tables button

New button

Click Table Wizard

Click OK

(b) The Table Wizard (step 2)

FIGURE 2.3 Hands-on Exercise 1 (continued)

STEP 3: The Table Wizard

➤ If necessary, click the **Business option button.** Click the **down arrow** on the **Sample Tables list box** to scroll through the available business tables. Click (select) **Students** within the list of sample tables. The tables are *not* in alphabetical order, and the Students table is found near the very bottom of the list.

➤ The **StudentID field** is already selected in the Sample Fields list box. Click the > **button** to enter this field in the list of fields for the new table as shown in Figure 2.3c.

➤ Enter the additional fields for the new table by selecting the field and clicking the > **button** (or by double clicking the field). The fields to enter are: **FirstName, LastName, Address, City,** and **StateOrProvince** as shown in the figure.

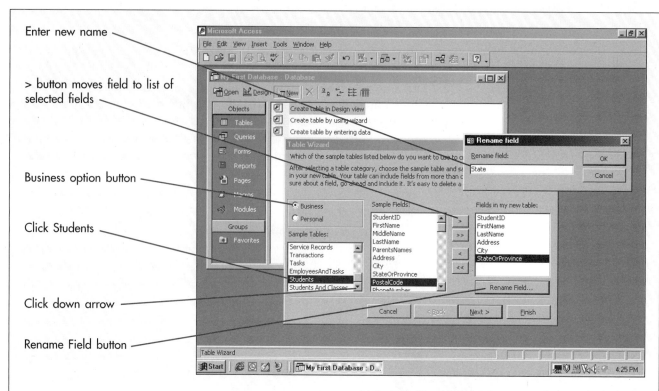

Enter new name

> button moves field to list of selected fields

Business option button

Click Students

Click down arrow

Rename Field button

(c) The Table Wizard (step 3)

FIGURE 2.3   Hands-on Exercise 1 (continued)

➤ Click the **Rename Field command button** after adding the StateOrProvince field to display the Rename Field dialog box. Enter **State** to shorten the name of this field. Click **OK.**

➤ Add **PostalCode** and **PhoneNumber** as the last two fields in the table. Click the **Next command button** when you have entered all the fields.

WIZARDS AND BUTTONS

Many Wizards present you with two open list boxes and expect you to copy some or all fields from the list box on the left to the list box on the right. The > and >> buttons work from left to right. The < and << buttons work in the opposite direction. The > button copies the selected field from the list box on the left to the box on the right. The >> button copies all of the fields. The < button removes the selected field from the list box on the right. The << removes all of the fields.

STEP 4: The Table Wizard (continued)

➤ The next screen in the Table Wizard asks you to name the table and determine the primary key.

• Accept the Wizard's suggestion of **Students** as the name of the table.

• Make sure that the option button **Yes, set a primary key for me** is selected.

• Click the **Next command button** to accept both of these options.

➤ The final screen in the Table Wizard asks what you want to do next.
- Click the option button to **Modify the table design.**
- Click the **Finish command button.** The Students table should appear on your monitor.

➤ Pull down the **File menu** and click **Save** (or click the **Save button** on the Table Design toolbar) to save the table.

STEP 5: Add the Additional Fields

➤ Click the **Maximize button** to give yourself more room to work. Click the cell immediately below the last field in the table (PhoneNumber). Type **Birth-Date** as shown in Figure 2.3d.

➤ Press the **Tab key** to move to the Data Type column. Click the **down arrow** on the drop-down list box. Click **Date/Time.**

➤ Add the remaining fields to the Students table. Add **Gender** as a Text field. Add **Credits** as a Number field. Add **QualityPoints** as a Number field. (There is no space in the field name.)

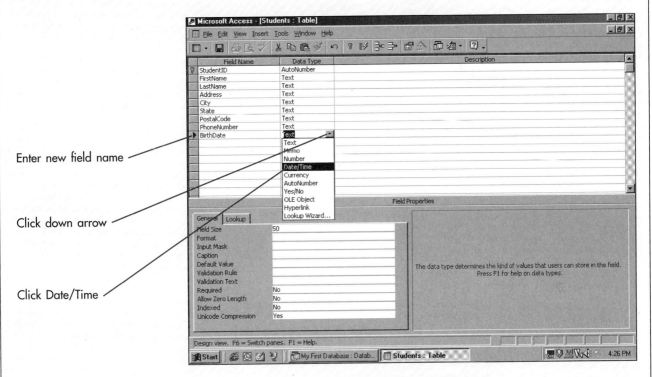

Enter new field name

Click down arrow

Click Date/Time

(d) Add the Additional Fields (step 5)

FIGURE 2.3   Hands-on Exercise 1 (continued)

CHOOSING A DATA TYPE

The fastest way to specify the data type is to type the first letter—T for Text, D for Date/Time, N for Number, and Y for Yes/No. Text is the default data type and is entered automatically.

STEP 6: Change the Primary Key

➤ Point to the first field in the table and click the **right mouse button** to display the shortcut menu in Figure 2.3e. Click **Insert Rows.**

➤ Click the **Field Name column** in the newly inserted row. Type **SSN** (for social security number) as the name of the new field. Press **enter.** The data type will be set to Text by default.

➤ Click the **Required box** in the Properties area. Click the drop-down arrow and select **Yes.**

➤ Click in the Field Name column for **SSN,** then click the **Primary Key button** on the Table Design toolbar to change the primary key to social security number. The primary key symbol has moved to SSN.

➤ Point to the **StudentID field** in the second row. Click the **right mouse button** to display the shortcut menu. Click **Delete Rows** to remove this field from the table definition. Save the table.

Point to first row and click right mouse button to display shortcut menu

Click Insert Rows

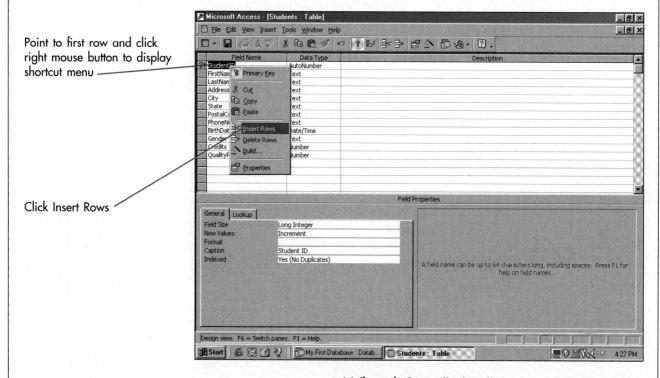

(e) Change the Primary Key (step 6)

FIGURE 2.3 Hands-on Exercise 1 (continued)

INSERTING OR DELETING FIELDS

To insert or delete a field, point to an existing field, then click the right mouse button to display a shortcut menu. Click Insert Rows or Delete Rows to add or remove a field as appropriate. To insert (or delete) multiple fields, point to the field selector to the left of the field name, click and drag the mouse over multiple rows to extend the selection, then click the right mouse button to display a shortcut menu.

STEP 7: Add an Input Mask

➤ Click the field selector column for **SSN.** Click the **Input Mask box** in the Properties area. (The box is currently empty.)

➤ Click the **Build button** to display the Input Mask Wizard. Click **Social Security Number** in the Input Mask Wizard dialog box as shown in Figure 2.3f.

➤ Click the **Try It** text box and enter a social security number to see how the mask works. If necessary, press the **left arrow key** until you are at the beginning of the text box, then enter a social security number (digits only). Click the **Finish command button** to accept the input mask.

➤ Click the field selector column for **BirthDate,** then follow the steps detailed above to add an input mask. (Choose the **Short Date** format.) Click **Yes** if asked whether to save the table.

➤ Save the table.

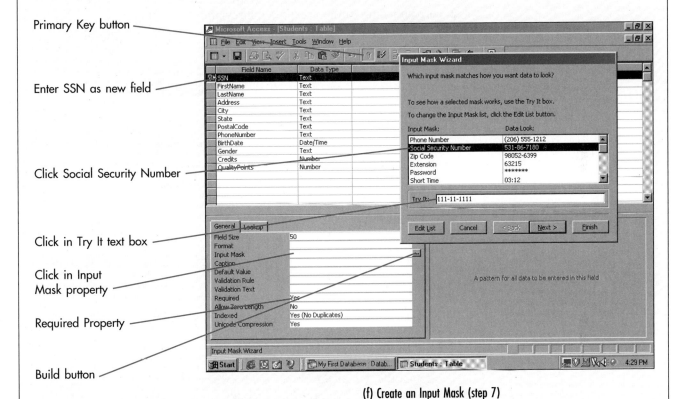

Primary Key button

Enter SSN as new field

Click Social Security Number

Click in Try It text box

Click in Input Mask property

Required Property

Build button

(f) Create an Input Mask (step 7)

FIGURE 2.3 Hands-on Exercise 1 (continued)

SHOW THE KEYBOARD SHORTCUT IN A SCREENTIP

You can expand the ScreenTip associated with any toolbar button to include the equivalent keyboard shortcut. Pull down the View menu, click Toolbars, then click Customize to display the Customize dialog box. Click the Options tab and check the box to show the shortcut keys in the Screen-Tips. Close the dialog box, then point to any toolbar button and you should see the name of the button as well as the equivalent keyboard shortcut.

STEP 8: Change the Field Properties

➤ Click the field selector column for the **FirstName** field:
  • Click the **Field Size box** in the Properties area and change the field size to **25.** (You can press the F6 key to toggle between the field name and the Properties area.)
  • Click the **Required box** in the Properties area. Click the **drop-down arrow** and select **Yes.**

➤ Click the field selector column for the **LastName** field:
  • Click the **Field Size box** in the Properties area. Change the field size to **25.**
  • Click the **Required box** in the Properties area. Click the **drop-down arrow** and select **Yes.**

➤ Click the field selector column for the **State** field.
  • Click the **Field Size box** in the Properties area and change the field size to **2,** corresponding to the accepted abbreviation for a state.
  • Click the **Format box** in the Properties area. Type a **> sign** to display the data in uppercase.

➤ Click the field selector column for the **Credits** field:
  • Click the **Field Size box** in the Properties area, click the **drop-down arrow** to display the available field sizes, then click **Integer.**
  • Click the **Default Value box** in the Properties area. Delete the **0.**

➤ Click the field selector column for the **QualityPoints** field:
  • Click the **Field Size box** in the Properties area, click the **drop-down arrow** to display the available field sizes, then click **Integer.**
  • Click the **Default Value box** in the Properties area. Delete the **0.**

➤ Save the table.

THE FIELD SIZE PROPERTY

The field size property for a Text or Number field determines the maximum number of characters that can be stored in that field. The property should be set to the smallest possible setting because smaller data sizes are processed more efficiently. A text field can hold from 0 to 255 characters (50 is the default). Number fields (which do not contain a decimal value) can be set to Byte, Integer, or Long Integer field sizes, which hold values up to 255, or 32,767, or 2,147,483,647, respectively. The Single or Double sizes are required if the field is to contain a decimal value, as they specify the precision with which a value will be stored. (See online Help for details.)

STEP 9: Add a Validation Rule

➤ Click the field selector column for the **Gender** field. Click the **Field Size box** and change the field size to **1** as shown in Figure 2.3g.

➤ Click the **Format box** in the Properties area. Type a **> sign** to display the data entered in uppercase.

➤ Click the **Validation Rule box.** Type **"M" or "F"** to accept only these values on data entry.

➤ Click the **Validation Text box.** Type **You must specify M or F.**

➤ Save the table.

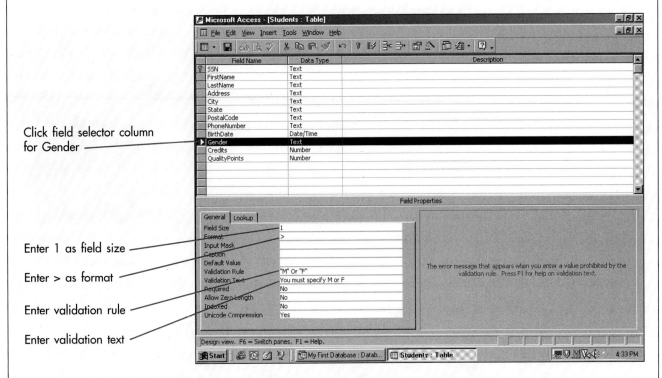

Click field selector column for Gender ⎯

Enter 1 as field size ⎯

Enter > as format ⎯

Enter validation rule ⎯

Enter validation text ⎯

(g) Add a Validation Rule (step 9)

FIGURE 2.3   Hands-on Exercise 1 (continued)

STEP 10: The Datasheet View

➤ Pull down the **View menu** and click **Datasheet View** (or click the **View button** on the toolbar) to change to the Datasheet view as shown in Figure 2.3h.

➤ The insertion point (a flashing vertical line indicating the position where data will be entered) is automatically set to the first field of the first record.

➤ Type **111111111** to enter the social security number for the first record. (The input mask will appear as soon as you enter the first digit.)

➤ Press the **Tab key,** the **right arrow key,** or the **enter key** to move to the First-Name field. Enter the data for Ronnie Adili as shown in Figure 2.3h. Make up data for the fields you cannot see.

➤ Scrolling takes place automatically as you move within the record.

CHANGE THE FIELD WIDTH

Drag the border between field names to change the displayed width of a field. Double click the right boundary of a field name to change the width to accommodate the widest entry in that field.

View button

Enter data

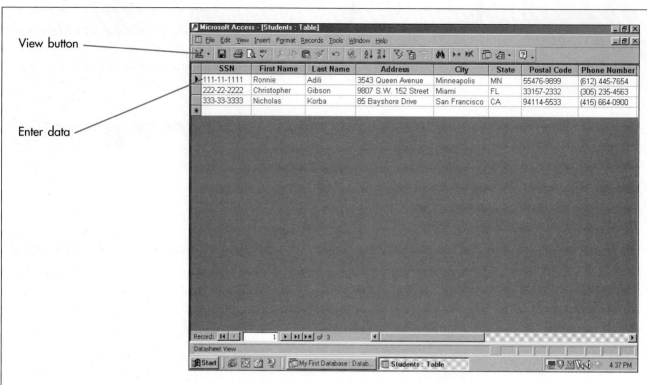

(h) Datasheet View (steps 10 & 11)

FIGURE 2.3   Hands-on Exercise 1 (continued)

STEP 11: Enter Additional Data

➤ Enter data for the two additional students shown in the figure, but enter deliberately invalid data to experiment with the validation capabilities built into Access. Here are some of the errors you may encounter:

- The message, *The value you entered isn't valid for this field,* implies that the data type is wrong—for example, alphabetic characters in a numeric field such as Credits.

- The message, *You must specify M or F,* means you entered a letter other than "M" or "F" in the Gender field (or you didn't enter a value at all).

- The message, *The changes you requested to the table were not successful because they would create duplicate values in the index, primary key, or relationship,* indicates that the value of the primary key is not unique.

- The message, *The field 'Students.LastName' can't contain a Null value,* implies that you left a required field blank.

- If you encounter a data validation error, press **Esc** (or click **OK**), then reenter the data.

STEP 12: Print the Students Table

➤ Pull down the **File menu** and click **Print** (or click the **Print button**). Click the **All option button** to print the entire table. Click **OK.** Do not be concerned if the table prints on multiple pages. (You can, however, use the Page Setup command to change the way the data are printed.)

➤ Pull down the **File menu** and click **Close** to close the Students table. Click **Yes** if asked to save the changes to the layout of the table.

> Pull down the **File menu** and click the **Close** command to close the database and remain in Access.

> Pull down the **File menu** a second time and click **Exit** if you do not want to continue with the next exercise at this time.

THE PAGE SETUP COMMAND

The Page Setup command controls the margins and orientation of the printed page and may enable you to keep all fields for a single record on the same page. Pull down the File menu, click Page Setup, click the Margins tab, then decrease the left and right margins (to .5 inch each) to increase the amount of data that is printed on one line. Be sure to check the box to Print Headings so that the field names appear with the table. Click the Page tab, then click the Landscape option button to change the orientation, which further increases the amount of data printed on one line. Click OK to exit the Page Setup dialog box.

FORMS

A **form** provides an easy way to enter and display the data stored in a table. You type data into a form, such as the one in Figure 2.4, and Access stores the data in the corresponding (underlying) table in the database. One advantage of using a form (as opposed to entering records in the Datasheet view) is that you can see all of the fields in a single record without scrolling. A second advantage is that a form can be designed to resemble a paper form, and thus provide a sense of familiarity for the individuals who actually enter the data.

A form has different views, as does a table. The **Form view** in Figure 2.4a displays the completed form and is used to enter or modify the data in the underlying table. The **Design view** in Figure 2.4b is used to create or modify the form.

Controls

All forms consist of **controls** (objects) that accept and display data, perform a specific action, decorate the form, or add descriptive information. There are three types of controls—bound, unbound, and calculated. A **bound control** (such as the text boxes in Figure 2.4a) has a data source (a field in the underlying table) and is used to enter or modify the data in that table. An **unbound control** has no data source. Unbound controls are used to display titles, labels, lines, graphics, or pictures. Note, too, that every bound control (**text box**) in Figure 2.4a is associated with an unbound control (**label**). The bound control for social security number, for example, is preceded by a label (immediately to the left of the control) that indicates to the user the value that is to be entered.

A **calculated control** has as its data source an expression rather than a field. An **expression** is a combination of operators (e.g., +, −, *, and /), field names, constants, and/or functions. A student's Grade Point Average (GPA in Figure 2.4a) is an example of a calculated control, since it is computed by dividing the number of quality points by the number of credits.

Unbound control

Bound control

Calculated control

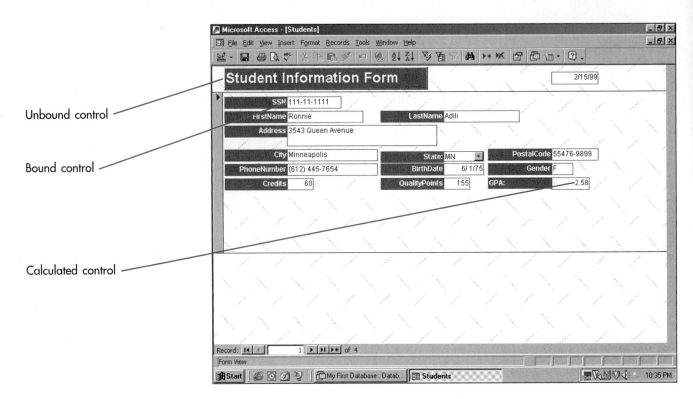

(a) Form View

Unbound control

Bound control

Calculated control

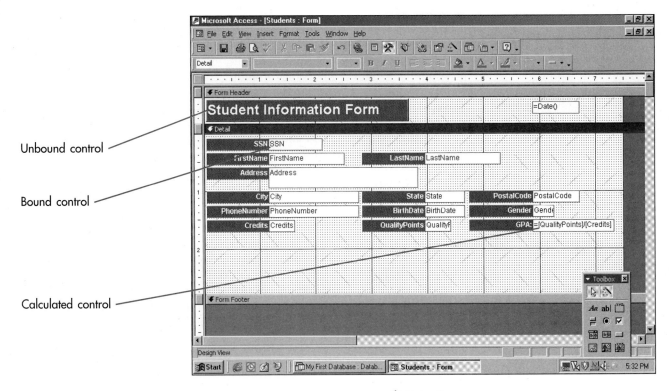

(b) Design View

FIGURE 2.4   Forms

Properties

As previously stated, a ***property*** is a characteristic or attribute of an object that determines how the object looks and behaves. Each control in a form has its own set of properties, just as every field in a table has its own set of properties. The properties for a control are displayed in a ***property sheet,*** as shown in Figure 2.5.

Figure 2.5a displays the property sheet for the Form Header Label. There are many different properties (note the vertical scroll bar) that control every aspect of the label's appearance. The properties are determined automatically as the object is created; that is, as you move and size the label on the form, the properties related to its size and position (Left, Top, Width, and Height in Figure 2.5a) are established for you.

Other actions, such as various formatting commands, set the properties that determine the font name and size (MS Sans Serif and 14 point in Figure 2.5a). You can change the appearance of an object in two ways—by executing a command to change the object on the form, which in turn changes the property sheet, *or* by changing the property within the property sheet, which in turn changes the object's appearance on the form.

Figure 2.5b displays the property sheet for the bound SSN control. The name of the control is SSN. The source for the control is the SSN field in the Students table. Thus, various properties of the SSN control, such as the input mask, are inherited from the SSN field in the underlying table. Note, too, that the list of properties in Figure 2.5b, which reflects a bound control, is different from the list of properties in Figure 2.5a for an unbound control. Some properties, however (such as left, top, width, and height, which determine the size and position of an object), are present for every control and determine its location on the form.

The Form Wizard

The easiest way to create a form is with the ***Form Wizard.*** The Form Wizard asks a series of questions, then builds a form according to your answers. You can use the form as is, or you can customize it to better suit your needs.

Figure 2.6 displays the Database Window from which you call the Form Wizard. The Form Wizard, in turn, requires that you specify the table or query on which the form will be based. (Queries are discussed in Chapter 3.) The form in this example will be based on the Students table created in the previous exercise. Once you specify the underlying table, you select one or more fields from that table as shown in Figure 2.6b. Each field that is selected is entered automatically on the form as a bound control. The Form Wizard asks you to select a layout (e.g., Columnar in Figure 2.6c) and a style (e.g., Blends in Figure 2.6d). The Form Wizard then has all of the information it needs, and creates the form for you. You can enter data immediately, or you can modify the form in the Form Design view.

ANATOMY OF A FORM

A form is divided into one or more sections. Virtually every form has a detail section to display or enter the records in the underlying table. You can, however, increase the effectiveness or visual appeal of a form by adding a header and/or footer. Either section may contain descriptive information about the form such as a title, instructions for using the form, or a graphic or logo.

Properties for Form Header Label

Properties related to size

Font name

Font size

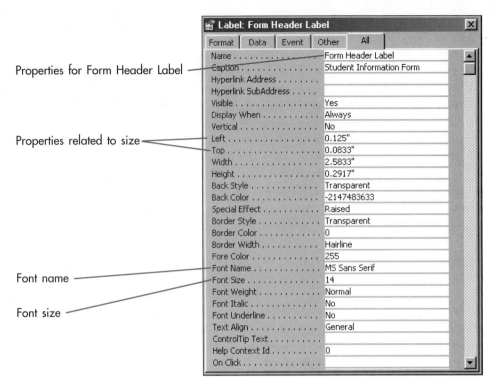

(a) Form Header Label (unbound control)

Properties for SSN

SSN is data source
for this control

Input mask was inherited from
table design for underlying table

Properties related to size

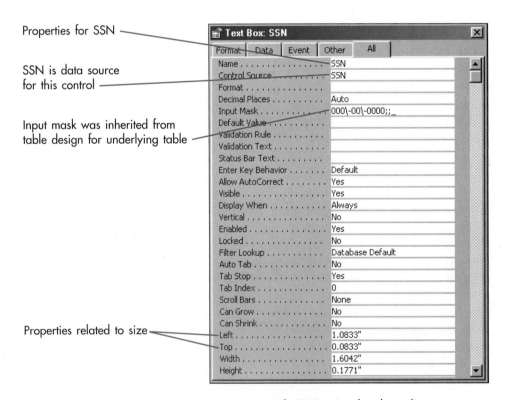

(b) SSN Text Box (bound control)

FIGURE 2.5   Property Sheets

Table on which form will be based

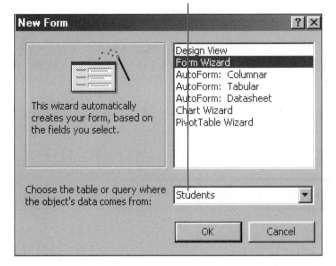

Underlying table   Available fields   Selected fields

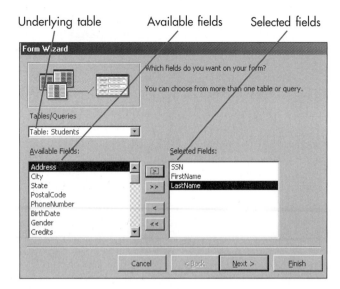

(a) Specify the Underlying Table

(b) Select the Fields

Selected layout

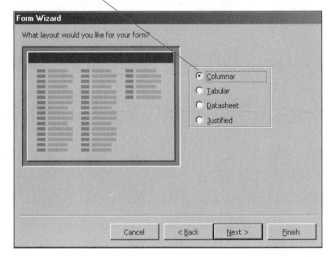

Selected style

(c) Choose the Layout

(d) Choose the Style

FIGURE 2.6   The Form Wizard

Modifying a Form

The Form Wizard provides an excellent starting point, but you typically need to customize the form by adding other controls (e.g., the calculated control for GPA) and/or by modifying the controls that were created by the Wizard. Each control is treated as an object, and moved or sized like any other Windows object. In essence, you select the control, then click and drag to resize the control or position it elsewhere on the form. You can also change the properties of the control through buttons on the various toolbars or by displaying the property sheet for the control and changing the appropriate property. Consider:

■ *To select a bound control and its associated label (an unbound control),* click either the control or the label. If you click the control, the control has sizing handles and a move handle, but the label has only a move handle. If you click the label, the opposite occurs; that is, the label will have both sizing handles and a move handle, but the control will have only a move handle.

- *To size a control,* click the control to select the control and display the sizing handles, then drag the sizing handles in the appropriate direction. Drag the handles on the top or bottom to size the box vertically. Drag the handles on the left or right side to size the box horizontally. Drag the handles in the corner to size both horizontally and vertically.

- *To move a control and its label,* click and drag the border of either object. To move either the control or its label, click and drag the move handle (a tiny square in the upper left corner) of the appropriate object.

- *To change the properties of a control,* point to the control, click the right mouse button to display a shortcut menu, then click Properties to display the property sheet. Click the text box for the desired property, make the necessary change, then close the property sheet.

- *To select multiple controls,* press and hold the Shift key as you click each successive control. The advantage of selecting multiple controls is that you can modify the selected controls at the same time rather than working with them individually.

HANDS-ON EXERCISE 2

Creating a Form

Objective: To use the Form Wizard to create a form; to move and size controls within a form; to use the completed form to enter data into the associated table. Use Figure 2.7 as a guide in the exercise.

STEP 1: Open the Existing Database

➤ Start Access as you did in the previous exercise. Select (click) **My First Database** from the list of recently opened databases, then click **OK.** (Click **More Files** if you do not see My First Database.)

➤ Click the **Forms button** in the Database window. Click the **New command button** to display the New Form dialog box as shown in Figure 2.7a.

➤ Click **Form Wizard** in the list box. Click the **drop-down arrow** to display the available tables and queries in the database on which the form can be based.

➤ Click **Students** to select the Students table from the previous exercise. Click **OK** to start the Form Wizard.

THE MOST RECENTLY OPENED FILE LIST

The easiest way to open a recently used database is to select it from the Microsoft Access dialog box that appears when Access is first started. Check to see if your database appears on the list of the four most recently opened databases, and if so, simply double click the database to open it. The list of the most recently opened databases can also be found at the bottom of the File menu.

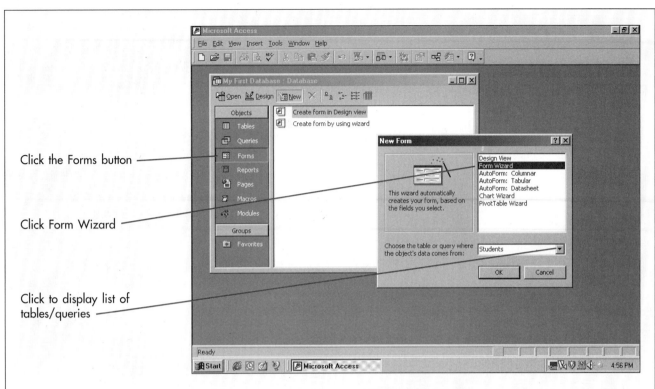

Click the Forms button

Click Form Wizard

Click to display list of tables/queries

(a) Create a Form (step 1)

FIGURE 2.7   Hands-on Exercise 2

STEP 2: The Form Wizard

➤ You should see the dialog box in Figure 2.7b, which displays all of the fields in the Students table. Click the **>> button** to enter all of the fields in the table on the form. Click the **Next command button.**

➤ The **Columnar layout** is already selected. Click the **Next command button.**

➤ Click **Industrial** as the style for your form. Click the **Next command button.**

➤ The Form Wizard asks you for the title of the form and what you want to do next.

 • The Form Wizard suggests **Students** as the title of the form. Keep this entry.

 • Click the option button to **Modify the form's design.**

➤ Click the **Finish command button** to display the form in Design view.

FLOATING TOOLBARS

A toolbar is typically docked (fixed) along the edge of the application window, but it can be displayed as a floating toolbar within the application window. To move a docked toolbar, drag the toolbar background (or the toolbar's move handle). To move a floating toolbar, drag its title bar. To size a floating toolbar, drag any border in the direction you want to go. Double click the background of any toolbar to toggle between a floating toolbar and a docked (fixed) toolbar.

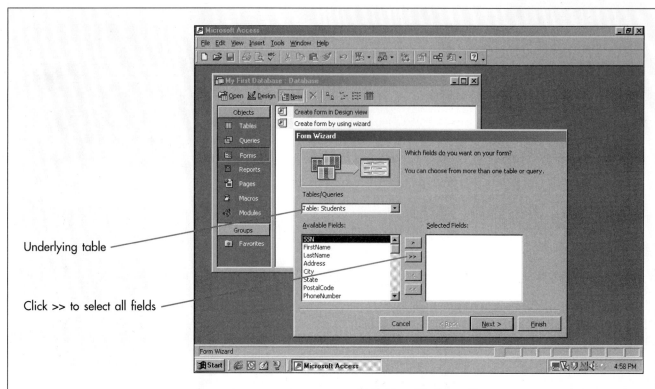

Underlying table

Click >> to select all fields

(b) The Form Wizard (step 2)

FIGURE 2.7   Hands-on Exercise 2 (continued)

STEP 3: Move the Controls

➤ If necessary, click the **Maximize button** so that the form takes the entire screen as shown in Figure 2.7c. The Form Wizard has arranged the controls in columnar format, but you need to rearrange the controls.

➤ Click the **LastName control** to select the control and display the sizing handles. (Be sure to select the text box and *not* the attached label.) Click and drag the **border** of the control (the pointer changes to a hand) so that the LastName control is on the same line as the FirstName control. Use the grid to space and align the controls.

➤ Click and drag the **Address control** under the FirstName control (to take the space previously occupied by the last name).

➤ Click and drag the **border** of the form to **7 inches** so that the City, State, and PostalCode controls will fit on the same line. (Click and drag the title bar of the Toolbox toolbar to move the toolbar out of the way.)

➤ Click and drag the **State control** so that it is next to the City control, then click and drag the **PostalCode control** so that it is on the same line as the other two. Press and hold the **Shift key** as you click the **City, State,** and **PostalCode controls** to select all three, then click and drag the selected controls under the Address control.

➤ Place the controls for **PhoneNumber, BirthDate,** and **Gender** on the same line. Move the controls under City, State, PostalCode.

➤ Place the controls for **Credits** and **QualityPoints** on the same line. Move the controls under PhoneNumber.

➤ Pull down the **File menu** and click **Save** (or click the **Save button**) to save the form.

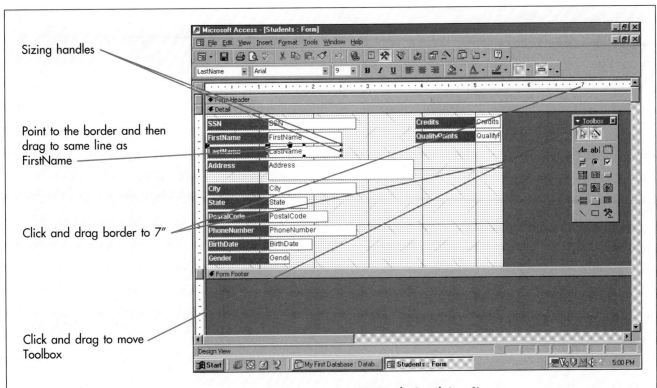

Sizing handles

Point to the border and then drag to same line as FirstName

Click and drag border to 7"

Click and drag to move Toolbox

(c) Move the Controls (step 3)

FIGURE 2.7 Hands-on Exercise 2 (continued)

THE UNDO COMMAND

The Undo command is invaluable at any time, and is especially useful when moving and sizing controls. Pull down the Edit menu and click Undo (or click the Undo button on the toolbar) immediately to reverse the effects of the last command.

STEP 4: Add a Calculated Control (GPA)

➤ Click the **Text Box tool** in the toolbox as shown in Figure 2.7d. The mouse pointer changes to a tiny crosshair with a text box attached.

➤ Click and drag in the form where you want the text box (the GPA control) to go. Release the mouse. You will see an Unbound control and an attached label containing a field number (e.g., Text25) as shown in Figure 2.7d.

➤ Click in the **text box** of the control. The word Unbound will disappear, and you can enter an expression:

• Enter **=[QualityPoints]/[Credits]** to calculate a student's GPA. Do not be concerned if you cannot see the entire entry as scrolling will take place as necessary.

• You must enter the field names *exactly* as they were defined in the table; that is, do *not* include a space between Quality and Points.

➤ Select the attached label (Text25), then click and drag to select the text in the attached label. Type **GPA** as the label for this control and press enter.

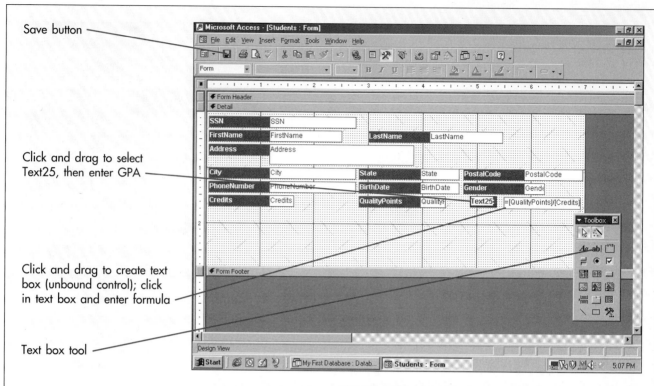

Save button

Click and drag to select
Text25, then enter GPA

Click and drag to create text
box (unbound control); click
in text box and enter formula

Text box tool

(d) Add a Calculated Control (step 4)

FIGURE 2.7   Hands-on Exercise 2 (continued)

➤ Size the text box appropriately for GPA. Size the bound control as well. Move either control as necessary.

➤ Click the **Save button.**

SIZING OR MOVING A CONTROL AND ITS LABEL

A bound control is created with an attached label. Select (click) the control, and the control has sizing handles and a move handle, but the label has only a move handle. Select the label (instead of the control), and the opposite occurs; the control has only a move handle, but the label will have both sizing handles and a move handle. To move a control and its label, click and drag the border of either object. To move either the control or its label, click and drag the move handle (a tiny square in the upper left corner) of the appropriate object.

STEP 5: Modify the Property Sheet

➤ Point to the GPA control and click the **right mouse button** to display a shortcut menu. Click **Properties** to display the Properties dialog box.

➤ If necessary, click the **All tab** as shown in Figure 2.7e. The Control Source text box contains the entry =[QualityPoints]/[Credits] from the preceding step.

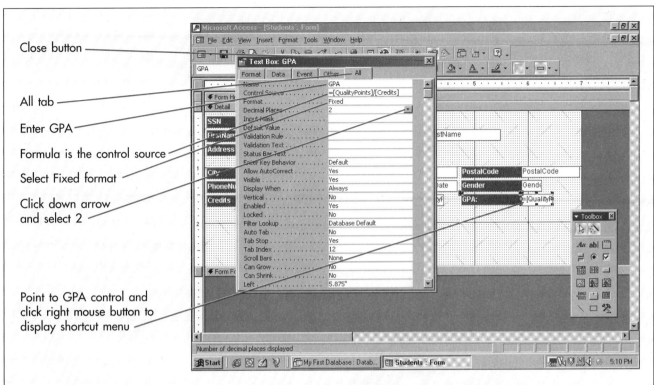

Close button

All tab

Enter GPA

Formula is the control source

Select Fixed format

Click down arrow
and select 2

Point to GPA control and
click right mouse button to
display shortcut menu

(e) Modify the Property Sheet (step 5)

FIGURE 2.7   Hands-on Exercise 2 (continued)

> Click the **Name text box.** Replace the original name (e.g., Text24) with **GPA.**
> Click the **Format box.** Click the **drop-down arrow,** then scroll until you can select **Fixed.**
> Click the box for the **Decimal places.** Click the **drop-down arrow** and select **2** as the number of decimal places.
> Close the Properties dialog box to accept these settings and return to the form.

USE THE PROPERTY SHEET

You can change the appearance or behavior of a control in two ways—by changing the actual control on the form itself or by changing the underlying property sheet. Anything you do to the control automatically changes the associated property, and conversely, any change to the property sheet is reflected in the appearance or behavior of the control. In general, you can obtain greater precision through the property sheet, but we find ourselves continually switching back and forth between the two techniques.

STEP 6: Align the Controls

➤ Click the label for SSN, then press and hold the **Shift key** as you click the label for the other controls on the form. This enables you to select multiple controls at the same time in order to apply uniform formatting to the selected controls.

➤ All labels should be selected as shown in Figure 2.7f. Click the **Align Right button** on the Formatting toolbar to move the labels to the right so that each label is closer to its associated control.

➤ Click anywhere on the form to deselect the controls, then fine-tune the form as necessary to make it more attractive. We moved LastName to align it with State. We also made the SSN and PostalCode controls smaller.

➤ Save the form.

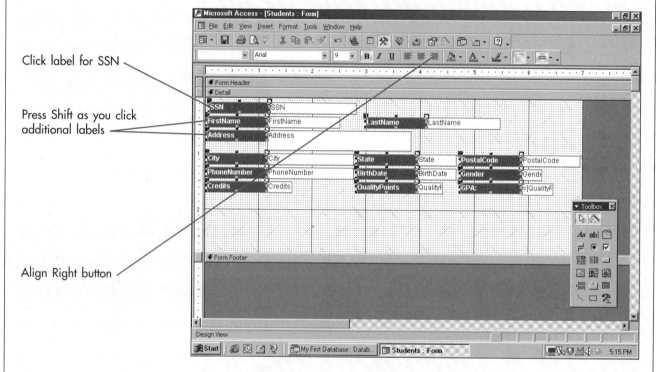

Click label for SSN

Press Shift as you click additional labels

Align Right button

(f) Align the Controls (step 6)

FIGURE 2.7   Hands-on Exercise 2 (continued)

ALIGN THE CONTROLS

To align controls in a straight line (horizontally or vertically), press and hold the Shift key and click the labels of the controls to be aligned. Pull down the Format menu, click Align, then select the edge to align (Left, Right, Top, and Bottom). Click the Undo command if you are not satisfied with the result.

STEP 7: Create the Form Header

➤ Click and drag the line separating the border of the Form Header and Detail to provide space for a header as shown in Figure 2.7g.

➤ Click the **Label tool** on the Toolbox toolbar (the mouse pointer changes to a cross hair combined with the letter A). Click and drag the mouse pointer to create a label within the header. The insertion point (a flashing vertical line) is automatically positioned within the label.

➤ Type **Student Information Form.** Do not be concerned about the size or alignment of the text at this time. Click outside the label when you have completed the entry, then click the control to select it.

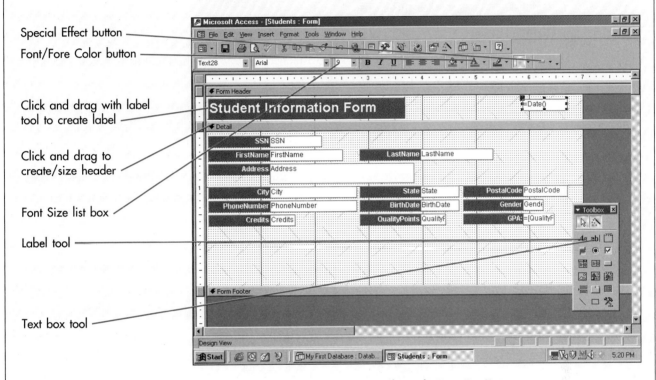

Special Effect button

Font/Fore Color button

Click and drag with label tool to create label

Click and drag to create/size header

Font Size list box

Label tool

Text box tool

(g) Create the Header (steps 7 & 8)

FIGURE 2.7   Hands-on Exercise 2 (continued)

THE FORMATTING TOOLBAR

The Formatting toolbar contains many of the same buttons that are found on the Formatting toolbars of the other Office applications. These include buttons for boldface, italics, and underlining, as well as left, center, and right alignment. You will find drop-down list boxes to change the font or point size. The Formatting toolbar also contains drop-down palettes to change the foreground or background color, the border color and width, and the special effect.

➤ Click the **drop-down arrow** on the **Font Size list box** on the Formatting toolbar. Click **18.** The size of the text changes to the larger point size.

➤ Click the **drop-down arrow** next to the **Special Effect button** on the Formatting toolbar to display the available effects. Click the **Raised button** to highlight the label.

➤ Click outside the label to deselect it. Click the **Save button** to save the form.

STEP 8: Add the Date

➤ Click the **Textbox tool** on the Toolbox toolbar. The mouse pointer changes to a tiny crosshair with a text box attached.

➤ Click and drag in the form where you want the text box for the date, then release the mouse.

➤ You will see an Unbound control and an attached label containing a number (e.g., Text28). Click in the text box, and the word Unbound will disappear. Type =**Date().** Click the attached label. Press the **Del key** to delete the label.

STEP 9: The Form View

➤ Click the **View button** to switch to the Form view. You will see the first record in the table that was created in the previous exercise.

➤ Click the **New Record button** to move to the end of the table to enter a new record as shown in Figure 2.7h. Enter data for yourself:

- The record selector symbol changes to a pencil as you begin to enter data.
- Press the **Tab key** to move from one field to the next within the form. All properties (masks and data validation) have been inherited from the Students table created in the first exercise.

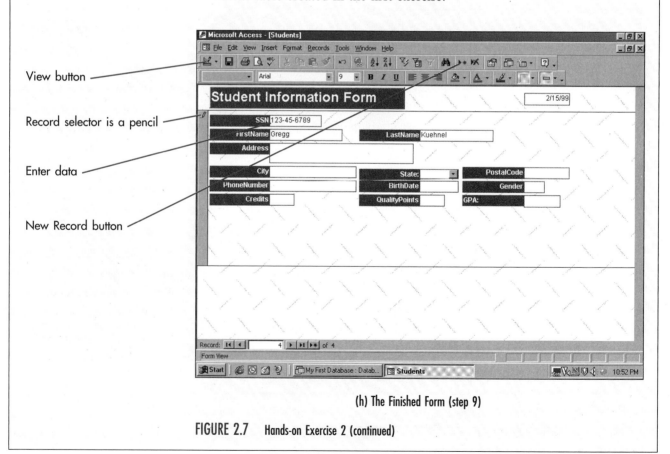

(h) The Finished Form (step 9)

FIGURE 2.7   Hands-on Exercise 2 (continued)

➤ Pull down the **File menu** and click **Close** to close the form. Click **Yes** if asked to save the changes to the form.

➤ Pull down the **File menu** and click **Close** to close the database and remain in Access. Pull down the **File menu** a second time and click **Exit** if you do not want to continue with the next exercise at this time.

ERROR MESSAGES—#NAME? OR #ERROR?

The most common reason for either message is that the control source references a field that no longer exists, or a field whose name is misspelled. Go to the Design view, right click the control, click the Properties command, then click the All tab within the Properties dialog box. Look at the Control Source property and check the spelling of every field. Be sure there are brackets around each field in a calculated control; for example =[QualityPoints]/[Credits].

A MORE SOPHISTICATED FORM

The Form Wizard provides an excellent starting point but stops short of creating the form you really want. The exercise just completed showed you how to add controls to a form that were not in the underlying table, such as the calculated control for the GPA. The exercise also showed how to move and size existing controls to create a more attractive and functional form.

Consider now Figure 2.8, which further improves on the form from the previous exercise. Three additional controls have been added—for major, financial

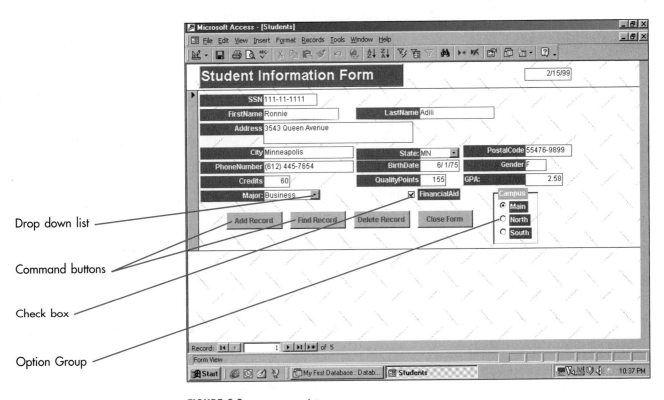

FIGURE 2.8   An Improved Form

aid, and campus—to illustrate other ways to enter data than through a text box. The student's major is selected from a **drop-down list box.** The indication of financial aid (a Yes/No field) is entered through a **check box.** The student's campus is selected from an **option group,** in which you choose one of three mutually exclusive options.

    Command buttons have also been added to the bottom of the form to facilitate the way in which the user carries out certain procedures. To add a record, for example, the user simply clicks the Add Record command button, as opposed to having to click the New Record button on the Database toolbar or having to pull down the Insert menu. The next exercise has you retrieve the form you created in Hands-on Exercise 2 in order to add these enhancements.

HANDS-ON EXERCISE 3

A More Sophisticated Form

Objective: To add fields to an existing table; to use the Lookup Wizard to create a combo box; to add controls to an existing form to demonstrate inheritance; to add command buttons to a form. Use Figure 2.9 as a guide in the exercise.

STEP 1: Modify the Table

➤ Open **My First Database** that we have been using throughout the chapter. If necessary, click the **Tables button** in the Database window. The **Students table** is already selected since that is the only table in the database.

➤ Click the **Design command button** to open the table in Design view as shown in Figure 2.9a. (The FinancialAid, Campus, and Major fields have not yet been added.) Maximize the window.

➤ Click the **Field Name box** under QualityPoints. Enter **FinancialAid** as the name of the new field. Press the **enter (Tab,** or **right arrow) key** to move to the Data Type column. Type **Y** (the first letter in a Yes/No field) to specify the data type.

➤ Click the **Field Name box** on the next row. Type **Campus.** (There is no need to specify the Data Type since Text is the default.)

➤ Press the **down arrow key** to move to the Field Name box on the next row. Enter **Major.** Press the **enter (Tab,** or **right arrow) key** to move to the Data Type column. Click the **drop-down arrow** to display the list of data types as shown in Figure 2.9a. Click **Lookup Wizard.**

STEP 2: The Lookup Wizard

➤ The first screen in the Lookup Wizard asks how you want to look up the data. Click the option button that indicates **I will type in the values that I want.** Click **Next.**

➤ You should see the dialog box in Figure 2.9b. The number of columns is already entered as one. Click the **text box** to enter the first major. Type **Business.** Press **Tab** or the **down arrow key** (do *not* press the enter key) to enter the next major.

➤ Complete the entries shown in Figure 2.9b. Click **Next.** The Wizard asks for a label to identify the column. (Major is already entered.) Click **Finish** to exit the Wizard and return to the Design View.

➤ Click the **Save button** to save the table. Close the table.

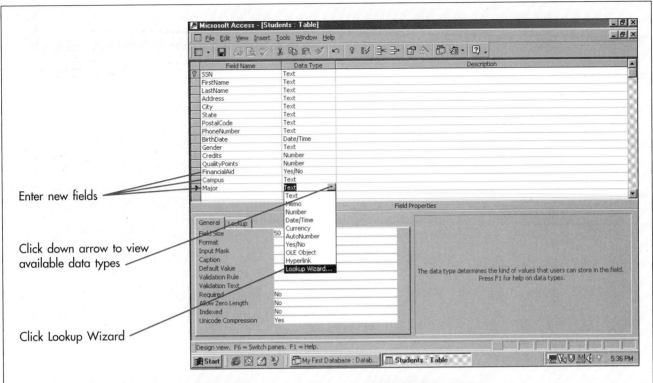

Enter new fields

Click down arrow to view available data types

Click Lookup Wizard

(a) Modify the Table (step 1)

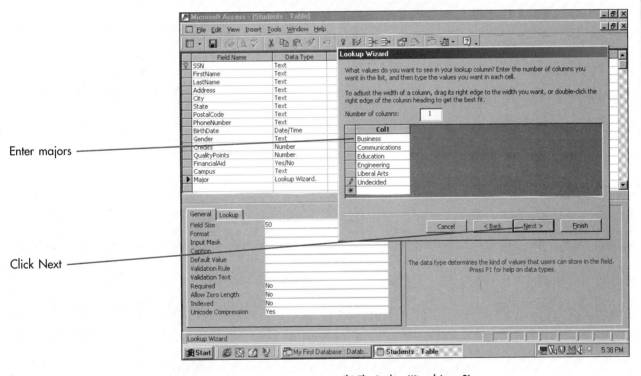

Enter majors

Click Next

(b) The Lookup Wizard (step 2)

FIGURE 2.9 Hands-on Exercise 3

STEP 3: Add the New Controls

➤ Click the **Forms button** in the Database window. If necessary, click the Students form to select it.

➤ Click the **Design command button** to open the form from the previous exercise. If necessary, click the **Maximize button** so that the form takes the entire window.

➤ Pull down the **View menu.** Click **Field List** to display the field list for the table on which the form is based. You can move and size the field list just like any other Windows object.

- Click and drag the **title bar** of the field list to the position in Figure 2.9c.
- Click and drag a **corner** or **border** of the field list so that you can see all of the fields at the same time.

➤ Fields can be added to the form from the field list in any order. Click and drag the **Major field** from the field list to the form. The Major control is created as a combo box because of the lookup list in the underlying table.

➤ Click and drag the **FinancialAid field** from the list to the form. The FinancialAid control is created as a check box because FinancialAid is a Yes/No field in the underlying table.

➤ Save the form.

INHERITANCE

A bound control inherits its properties from the associated field in the underlying table. A check box, for example, appears automatically next to any bound control that was defined as a Yes/No field. In similar fashion, a drop-down list will appear next to any bound control that was defined through the Lookup Wizard. Changing the property setting of a field *after* the form has been created will *not* change the property of the associated control. And finally, changing the property setting of a control does *not* change the property setting of the field because the control inherits the properties of the field rather than the other way around.

STEP 4: Create an Option Group

➤ Click the **Option Group button** on the Toolbox toolbar. The mouse pointer changes to a tiny crosshair attached to an option group icon when you point anywhere in the form. Click and drag in the form where you want the option group to go, then release the mouse.

➤ You should see the Option Group Wizard as shown in Figure 2.9d. Enter **Main** as the label for the first option, then press the **Tab key** to move to the next line. Type **North** and press **Tab** to move to the next line. Enter **South** as the third and last option. Click **Next.**

➤ The option button to select Main (the first label that was entered) as the default is selected. Click **Next.**

➤ Main, North, and South will be assigned the values 1, 2, and 3, respectively. (Numeric entries are required for an option group.) Click **Next.**

➤ Click the **drop-down arrow** to select the field in which to store the value selected through the option group, then scroll until you can select **Campus.** Click **Next.**

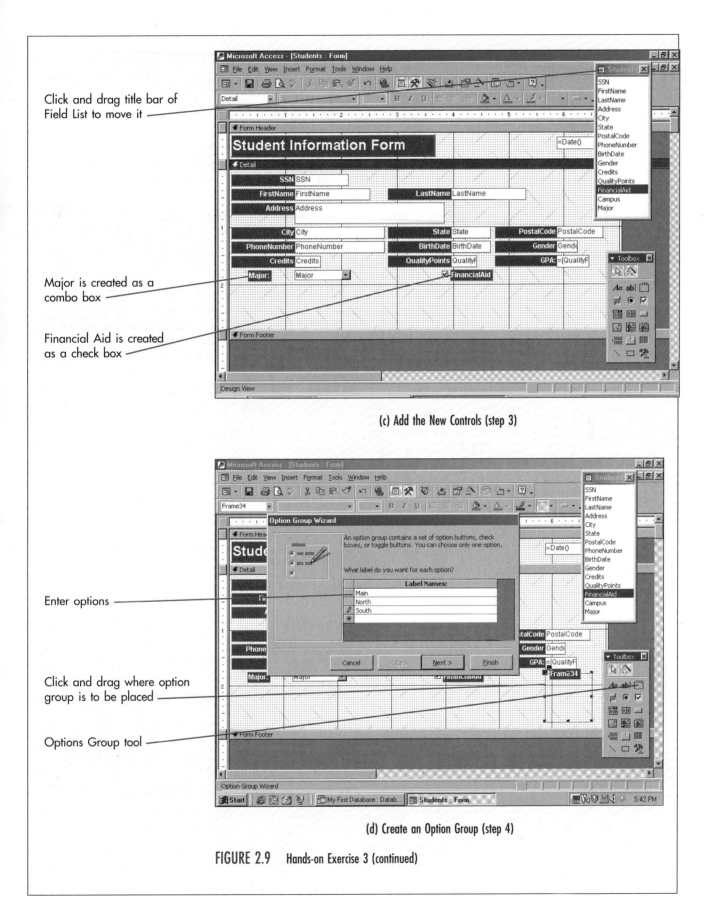

Click and drag title bar of Field List to move it

Major is created as a combo box

Financial Aid is created as a check box

(c) Add the New Controls (step 3)

Enter options

Click and drag where option group is to be placed

Options Group tool

(d) Create an Option Group (step 4)

FIGURE 2.9   Hands-on Exercise 3 (continued)

➤ Make sure the Option button is selected as the type of control.

➤ Click the option button for the **Sunken style** to match the other controls on the form. Click **Next.**

➤ Enter **Campus** as the caption for the group. Click the **Finish command button** to create the option group on the form. Click and drag the option group to position it on the form under the GPA control.

➤ Point to the border of the option group on the form, click the **right mouse button** to display a shortcut menu, and click **Properties.** Click the **All tab.** Change the name to **Campus.**

➤ Close the dialog box. Close the field list. Save the form.

MISSING TOOLBARS

The Form Design, Formatting, and Toolbox toolbars appear by default in the Form Design view, but any (or all) of these toolbars may be hidden at the discretion of the user. Point to any visible toolbar, click the right mouse button to display a shortcut menu, then check the name of any toolbar you want to display. You can also click the Toolbox button on the Form Design toolbar to display (hide) the Toolbox toolbar.

STEP 5: Add a Command Button

➤ Click the **Command Button tool.** The mouse pointer changes to a tiny crosshair attached to a command button when you point anywhere in the form.

➤ Click and drag in the form where you want the button to go, then release the mouse. This draws a button and simultaneously opens the Command Button Wizard as shown in Figure 2.9e. (The number in your button may be different from ours.)

➤ Click **Record Operations** in the Categories list box. Choose **Add New Record** as the operation. Click **Next.**

➤ Click the **Text option button** in the next screen. Click **Next.**

➤ Type **Add Record** as the name of the button, then click the **Finish command button.** The completed command button should appear on your form. Save the form.

STEP 6: Create the Additional Command Buttons

➤ Click the **Command Button tool.** Click and drag on the form where you want the second button to go.

➤ Click **Record Navigation** in the Categories list box. Choose **Find Record** as the operation. Click the **Next command button.**

➤ Click the **Text option button.** Click the **Next command button.**

➤ Type **Find Record** as the name of the button, then click the **Finish command button.** The completed command button should appear on the form.

➤ Repeat these steps to add the command buttons to delete a record (Record Operations) and close the form (Form Operations).

➤ Save the form.

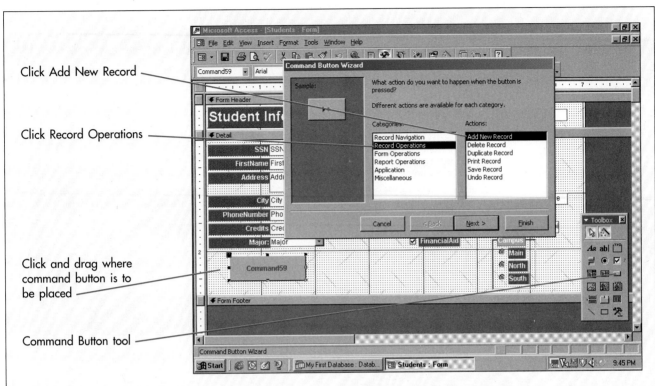

Click Add New Record

Click Record Operations

Click and drag where command button is to be placed

Command Button tool

(e) Add a Command Button (step 5)

FIGURE 2.9   Hands-on Exercise 3 (continued)

STEP 7: Align the Command Buttons

➤ Select the four command buttons by pressing and holding the **Shift key** as you click each button. Release the Shift key when all buttons are selected.

➤ Pull down the **Format menu.** Click **Size** to display the cascade menu shown in Figure 2.9f. (Click the double arrow at the bottom of the menu if you don't see the Size command.) Click **to Widest** to set a uniform width.

➤ Pull down the **Format menu** a second time, click **Size,** then click **to Tallest** to set a uniform height.

➤ Pull down the **Format menu** again, click **Horizontal Spacing,** then click **Make Equal** so that each button is equidistant from the other buttons.

➤ Pull down the **Format menu** a final time, click **Align,** then click **Bottom** to complete the alignment. Drag the buttons to the center of the form.

MULTIPLE CONTROLS AND PROPERTIES

Press and hold the Shift key as you click one control after another to select multiple controls. To view or change the properties for the selected controls, click the right mouse button to display a shortcut menu, then click Properties to display a property sheet. If the value of a property is the same for all selected controls, that value will appear in the property sheet; otherwise the box for that property will be blank. Changing a property when multiple controls are selected changes the property for all selected controls.

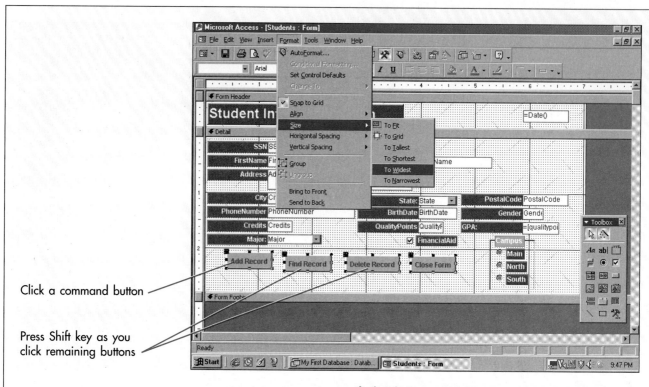

Click a command button

Press Shift key as you click remaining buttons

(f) Align the Buttons (step 7)

FIGURE 2.9 Hands-on Exercise 3 (continued)

STEP 8: Reset the Tab Order

➤ Click anywhere in the Detail section. Pull down the **View menu.** Click **Tab Order** to display the Tab Order dialog box in Figure 2.9g. (Click the double arrow at the bottom of the menu if you don't see the Tab Order command.)

➤ Click the **AutoOrder command button** so that the tab key will move to fields in left-to-right, top-to-bottom order as you enter data in the form. Click **OK** to close the Tab Order dialog box.

➤ Check the form one more time in order to make any last-minute changes.

➤ Save the form.

CHANGE THE TAB ORDER

The Tab key provides a shortcut in the finished form to move from one field to the next; that is, you press Tab to move forward to the next field and Shift+Tab to return to the previous field. The order in which fields are selected corresponds to the sequence in which the controls were entered onto the form, and need not correspond to the physical appearance of the actual form. To restore a left-to-right, top-to-bottom sequence, pull down the View menu, click Tab Order, then select AutoOrder. Alternatively, you can specify a custom sequence by clicking the selector for the various controls within the Tab Order dialog box, then moving the row up or down within the list.

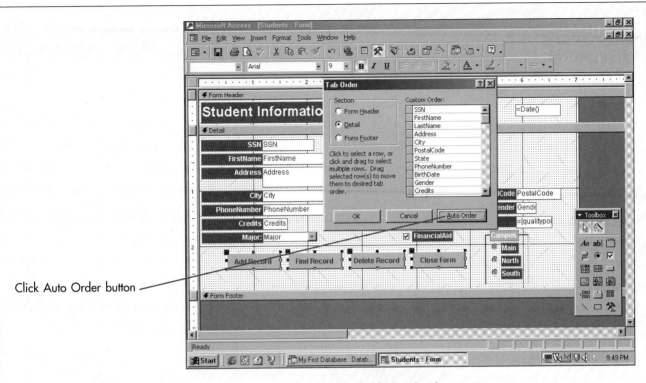

Click Auto Order button

(g) Modify the Tab Order (step 8)

FIGURE 2.9   Hands-on Exercise 3 (continued)

STEP 9: The Page Setup Command

➤ Point to any blank area in the Detail section of the form. Click the **right mouse button** to display a shortcut menu, then click **Properties** to display the Properties dialog box for the Detail section. Click the **All tab.**

➤ Click the text box for **Height.** Enter **3.5** to change the height of the Detail section to three and one-half inches. Close the Properties dialog box.

➤ If necessary, click and drag the **right border** of the form so that all controls are fully visible. Do *not* exceed a width of 7 inches for the entire form.

➤ Pull down the **File menu.** Click **Page Setup** to display the Page Setup dialog box. If necessary, click the **Margins tab.**

➤ Change the left and right margins to **.75** inch. Click **OK** to accept the settings and close the Page Setup dialog box.

CHECK YOUR NUMBERS

The width of the form, plus the left and right margins, cannot exceed the width of the printed page. Thus increasing the width of a form may require a corresponding decrease in the left and right margins or a change to landscape (rather than portrait) orientation. Pull down the File menu and choose the Page Setup command to modify the dimensions of the form prior to printing.

STEP 10: The Completed Form

➤ Click the **View button** to switch to the Form view and display the first record in the table.

➤ Complete the record by adding appropriate data (choose any values you like) for the Major, FinancialAid, and Campus fields that were added to the form in this exercise.

➤ Click the **Add Record command button** to create a new record. Click the text box for **Social Security Number.** Add the record shown in Figure 2.9h. The record selector changes to a pencil as soon as you begin to enter data to indicate the record has not been saved.

➤ Press the **Tab key** or the **enter key** to move from field to field within the record. Click the **arrow** on the drop-down list box to display the list of majors, then click the desired major.

➤ Complete all of the information in the form. Press **enter** to move to the next record.

➤ Click the **selection area** (the thin vertical column to the left of the form) to select only the current record. The record selector changes from a pencil to an arrow. The selection area is shaded to indicate that the record has been selected.

➤ Pull down the **File menu.** Click **Print** to display the Print dialog box. Click the option button to print **Selected Record**—that is, to print only the one record. Click **OK.**

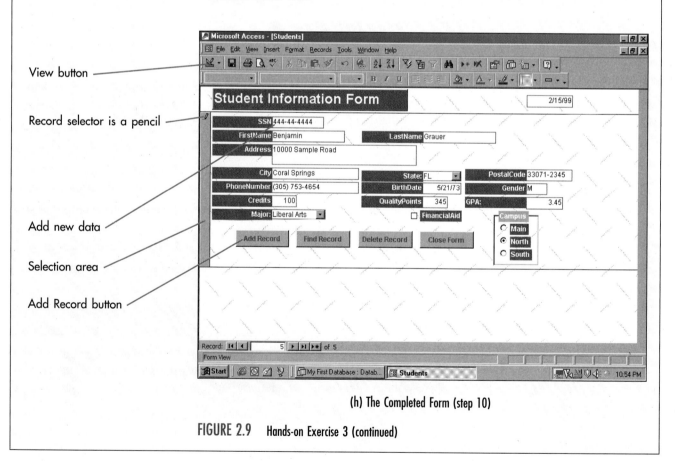

(h) The Completed Form (step 10)

FIGURE 2.9   Hands-on Exercise 3 (continued)

KEYBOARD SHORTCUTS

Press Tab to move from one field to the next in a finished form. Press Shift+Tab to return to the previous field. Type the first letter of an item's name to select the first item in a drop-down list beginning with that letter; for example, type "B" to select the first item in Major beginning with that letter. Type the first two letters quickly—for example, Bu—and you will go directly to Business. Press the space bar to toggle a check box on and off. Press the down arrow key to move from one option to the next within an option group.

STEP 11: Exit Access

➤ Examine your printed output to be sure that the form fits on a single page.

➤ It if doesn't, you need to adjust the margins of the form itself and/or change the margins using the Page Setup command in the File menu, then print the form a second time.

➤ Click the **Close Form command button** on the form after you have printed the record for your instructor.

➤ Click **Yes** if you see a message asking to save changes to the form design.

➤ Pull down the **File menu.** Click **Exit** to leave Access. Congratulations on a job well done.

SUMMARY

The information produced by a system depends entirely on the underlying data. The design of the database is of critical importance and must be done correctly. Three guidelines were suggested. These are to include the necessary data, to store data in its smallest parts, and to avoid the use of calculated fields in a table.

The Table Wizard is the easiest way to create a table. It lets you choose from a series of business or personal tables, asks you questions about the fields you want, then creates the table for you.

A table has two views—the Design view and the Datasheet view. The Design view is used to create the table and determine the fields within the table, as well as the data type and properties of each field. The Datasheet view is used after the table has been created to add, edit, and delete records.

A form provides a user-friendly way to enter and display data, in that it can be made to resemble a paper form. The Form Wizard is the easiest way to create a form. The Design view enables you to modify an existing form.

A form consists of objects called controls. A bound control has a data source such as a field in the underlying table. An unbound control has no data source. A calculated control contains an expression. Controls are selected, moved, and sized the same way as any other Windows object.

A property is a characteristic or attribute of an object that determines how the object looks and behaves. Every Access object (e.g., tables, fields, forms, and controls) has a set of properties that determine the behavior of that object. The properties for an object are displayed in a property sheet.

Allow Zero Length
  property
AutoNumber field
AutoOrder
Bound control
Calculated control
Calculated field
Caption property
Check box
Combo box
Command button
Control
Currency field
Data type
Datasheet view
Date/Time field
Default Value property
Design view

Drop-down list box
Expression
Field name
Field Size property
Form
Form view
Form Wizard
Format property
Hyperlink field
Indexed property
Inheritance
Input Mask property
Label
Lookup Wizard
Memo field
Number field
OLE Object field
Option group

Page Setup
Primary key
Print Preview
Property
Property sheet
Required property
Selection area
Tab Order
Table Wizard
Text box
Text field
Toolbox toolbar
Unbound control
Validation Rule
  property
Validation Text
  property
Yes/No field

MULTIPLE CHOICE

1. Which of the following is true?
  (a) The Table Wizard must be used to create a table
  (b) The Form Wizard must be used to create a form
  (c) Both (a) and (b)
  (d) Neither (a) nor (b)

2. Which of the following is implemented automatically by Access?
  (a) Rejection of a record with a duplicate value of the primary key
  (b) Rejection of numbers in a text field
  (c) Both (a) and (b)
  (d) Neither (a) nor (b)

3. Social security number, phone number, and zip code should be designated as:
  (a) Number fields
  (b) Text fields
  (c) Yes/No fields
  (d) Any of the above depending on the application

4. Which of the following is true of the primary key?
  (a) Its values must be unique
  (b) It must be defined as a text field
  (c) It must be the first field in a table
  (d) It can never be changed

5. Social security number rather than name is used as a primary key because:
   (a) The social security number is numeric, whereas the name is not
   (b) The social security number is unique, whereas the name is not
   (c) The social security number is a shorter field
   (d) All of the above

6. Which of the following is true regarding buttons within the Form Wizard?
   (a) The > button copies a selected field from a table onto a form
   (b) The < button removes a selected field from a form
   (c) Both (a) and (b)
   (d) Neither (a) nor (b)

7. Which of the following was *not* a suggested guideline for designing a table?
   (a) Include all necessary data
   (b) Store data in its smallest parts
   (c) Avoid calculated fields
   (d) Designate at least two primary keys

8. Which of the following are valid parameters for use with a form?
   (a) Portrait orientation, a width of 6 inches, left and right margins of 1¼ inch
   (b) Landscape orientation, a width of 9 inches, left and right margins of 1 inch
   (c) Both (a) and (b)
   (d) Neither (a) nor (b)

9. Which view is used to add, edit, or delete records in a table?
   (a) The Datasheet view
   (b) The Form view
   (c) Both (a) and (b)
   (d) Neither (a) nor (b)

10. Which of the following is true?
    (a) Any field added to a table after a form has been created is automatically added to the form as a bound control
    (b) Any calculated control that appears in a form is automatically inserted into the underlying table
    (c) Every bound and unbound control in a form has an underlying property sheet
    (d) All of the above

11. In which view will you see the record selector symbols of a pencil and a triangle?
    (a) Only the Datasheet view
    (b) Only the Form view
    (c) The Datasheet view and the Form view
    (d) The Form view, the Design view, and the Datasheet view

12. To move a control (in the Design view), you select the control, then:
    (a) Point to a border (the pointer changes to an arrow) and click and drag the border to the new position
    (b) Point to a border (the pointer changes to a hand) and click and drag the border to the new position

(c) Point to a sizing handle (the pointer changes to an arrow) and click and drag the sizing handle to the new position

(d) Point to a sizing handle (the pointer changes to a hand) and click and drag the sizing handle to the new position

13. Which fields are commonly defined with an input mask?
    (a) Social security number and phone number
    (b) First name, middle name, and last name
    (c) City, state, and zip code
    (d) All of the above

14. Which data type appears as a check box in a form?
    (a) Text field
    (b) Number field
    (c) Yes/No field
    (d) All of the above

15. Which properties would you use to limit a user's response to two characters, and automatically convert the response to uppercase?
    (a) Field Size and Format
    (b) Input Mask, Validation Rule, and Default Value
    (c) Input Mask and Required
    (d) Field Size, Validation Rule, Validation Text, and Required

Answers

1. d	**6.** c	**11.** c
2. a	**7.** d	**12.** b
3. b	**8.** c	**13.** a
4. a	**9.** c	**14.** c
5. b	**10.** c	**15.** a

PRACTICE WITH ACCESS 2000

1. A Modified Student Form: Modify the Student form created in the hands-on exercises to match the form in Figure 2.10. (The form contains three additional controls that must be added to the Students table.)

   a. Add the DateAdmitted and EmailAddress as a date and a text field, respectively, in the Students table. Add a Yes/No field to indicate whether or not the student is an International student.

   b. Add controls for the additional fields as shown in Figure 2.10.

   c. Modify the State field in the underlying Students table to use the Lookup Wizard, and set CA, FL, NJ, and NY as the values for the list box. (These are the most common states in the Student population.) The control in the form will not, however, inherit the list box because it was added to the table after the form was created. Hence you have to delete the existing control in the form, display the field list, then click and drag the State field from the field list to the form.

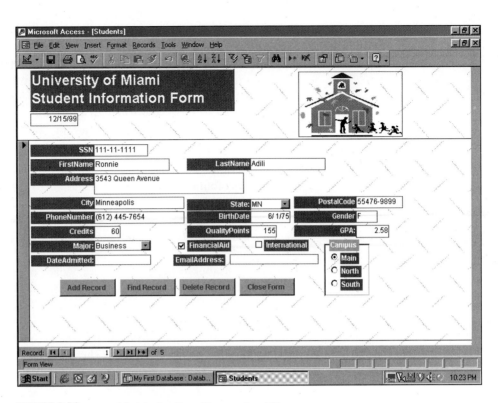

FIGURE 2.10 A Modified Student Form (Exercises 1 and 2)

d. Resize the control in the Form Header so that *University of Miami Student Information Form* takes two lines. Press Ctrl+Enter to force a line break within the control. Resize the Form Header.

e. Change the tab order to reflect the new fields in the form.

f. Add a graphic as described in problem 2.

2. Object Linking and Embedding: This exercise is a continuation of problem 1 and describes how to insert a graphic created by another application onto an Access form.

a. Open the Students form in My First Database in the Design view. Move the date in the header under the label.

b. Click the Unbound Object Frame tool on the toolbox. (If you are unsure as to which tool to click, just point to the tool to display the name of the tool.)

c. Click and drag in the Form Header to size the frame, then release the mouse to display an Insert Object dialog box.

d. Click the Create New option button. Select the Microsoft Clip Gallery as the object type. Click OK.

e. Click the Pictures tab in the Microsoft Clip Gallery dialog box. Choose the category and picture you want from within the Clip Gallery. Click the Insert Clip icon to insert the picture into the Access form and simultaneously close the Clip Gallery dialog box. Do *not* be concerned if only a portion of the picture appears on the form.

f. Right click the newly inserted object to display a shortcut menu, then click Properties to display the Properties dialog box. Select (click) the Size Mode property and select Stretch from the associated list. If necessary, change the Back Style property to Transparent, the Special Effect property to Flat, and the Border Style property to Transparent. Close the Properties dialog box.

g. You should see the entire clip art image, although it may be distorted because the size and shape of the frame you inserted in steps (b) and (c) do not match the image you selected. Click and drag the sizing handles on the frame to size the object so that its proportions are correct. Click anywhere in the middle of the frame (the mouse pointer changes to a hand) to move the frame elsewhere in the form.

h. If you want to display a different object, double click the clip art image to return to the Clip Gallery in order to select another object.

3. The Employee Database: Open the Employee database in the Exploring Access folder to create a form similar to the one in Figure 2.11. (This is the same database that was referenced in problem 1 in Chapter 1.)

a. The form was created using the Form Wizard and Standard style. The various controls were then moved and sized to match the arrangement in the figure.

b. The label in the Form Header, date of execution, and command buttons were added after the form was created, using the techniques in the third hands-on exercise.

c. To add lines to the form, click the Line tool in the toolbox, then click and drag on the form to draw the line. To draw a straight line, press and hold the Shift key as you draw the line.

d. You need not match our form exactly, and we encourage you to experiment with a different design.

e. Use the command buttons on the form to test the indicated operations. Add a record for yourself (if you have not already done so in Chapter 1), then print the form containing your data. Submit the printed form to your instructor as proof you did this exercise.

f. Click the close button on the form to close the form.

g. Exit Access.

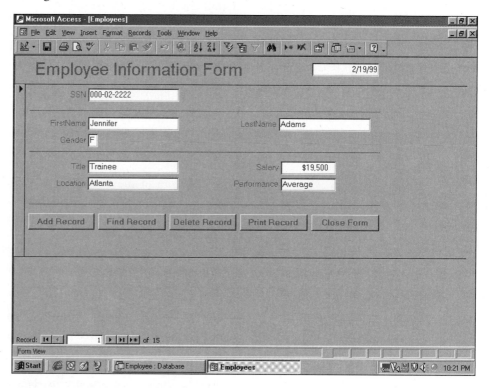

FIGURE 2.11   The Employee Database (Exercise 3)

4. The United States Database: Open the USA database found in the Exploring Access folder to create a form similar to the one in Figure 2.12.

   a. The form was created using the Form Wizard and Blends style. The controls were moved and sized to match the arrangement in the figure.

   b. Population density is a calculated control and is computed by dividing the population by the area. Format the density to two decimal places.

   c. You need not match our form exactly, and we encourage you to experiment with different designs.

   d. Add the graphic, following the steps in the second exercise.

   e. Print the form of your favorite state and submit it to your instructor. Be sure to choose the option to print only the selected record.

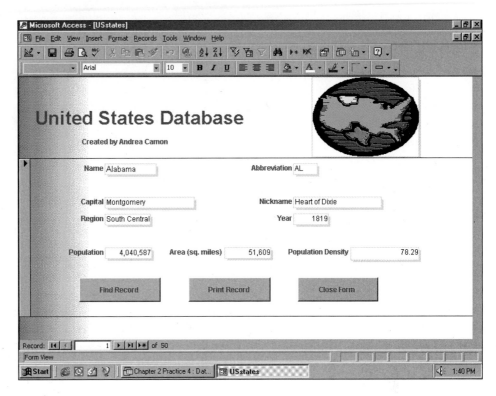

FIGURE 2.12   The United States Database (Exercise 4)

5. The Address Book: Figure 2.13 displays the Design view of a form to maintain an address book of friends and acquaintances. The picture requires you to obtain pictures of your friends in machine-readable form. Each picture is stored initially in its own file (in GIF or JPEG format). The form and underlying table build upon the information in the chapter.

   a. Create an Address Book database containing a table and associated form, using Figure 2.13 as a guide. You can add or delete fields as appropriate with the exception of the FriendID field, which is designated as the primary key. The FriendID should be defined as an AutoNumber field whose value is created automatically each time a record is added to the table.

   b. Include a logical field (e.g., SendCard) in the underlying table. This will enable you to create a report of those people who are to receive a birthday card (or season's greetings card) once the data have been entered.

   c. Include an OLE field in the table, regardless of whether or not you actually have a picture, and be sure to leave space in the form for the picture. Those records that have an associated picture will display the picture in the form. Those records without a picture will display a blank space.

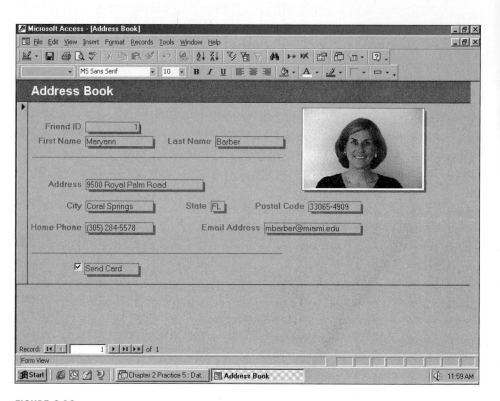

FIGURE 2.13   The Address Book (Exercise 5)

d. To insert a picture into the database, open the table, click in the OLE field, pull down the Insert menu, and click the Object command. Click the Create from File option button, click the Browse button in the associated dialog box, then select the appropriate file name and location.

e. Enter data for yourself in the completed form, then print the associated form to submit to your instructor as proof you did this exercise.

6. The NBA: The potential of Access is limited only by your imagination. Figure 2.14, for example, shows a (partially completed) table to hold statistics for players in the National Basketball Association. The decision on which fields to include is up to you; e.g., you can include statistics for the player's career and/or the current year. We suggest, however, the inclusion of a memo field to add descriptive notes (e.g., career highlights) about each player. You can also include an optional picture field provided you can obtain the player's picture. Design the table, create the associated form, then go the home page of the NBA to obtain statistics for your favorite player. Print the completed form for your player as proof you did this exercise.

7. Help for Your Users: Figure 2.15 shows the Design view of a form that we create for all of our databases. The form is designed to display information about the system such as a version number or product serial number, and hence is not based on a table or query. The default properties of the form have been changed and are set to suppress the scroll bars, record selector, and navigation buttons.

To change the properties of a form, go to the Design view and right click the Form Select button (the tiny square in the upper-left corner) to display a context-sensitive menu. Choose Properties to display the Property sheet for the form, and then look for the appropriate property. Note, too, that the dimensions of the form are also smaller than the typical form. Create the form in Figure 2.15, add your name as indicated, then print the completed form and submit it to your instructor.

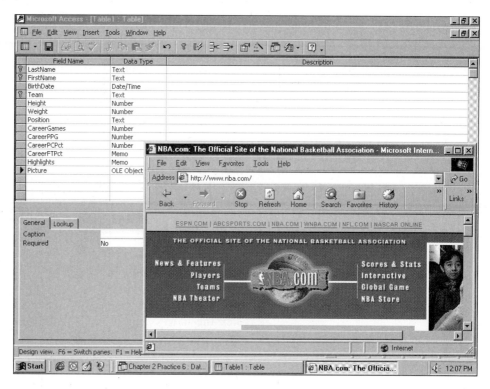

FIGURE 2.14　The NBA (Exercise 6)

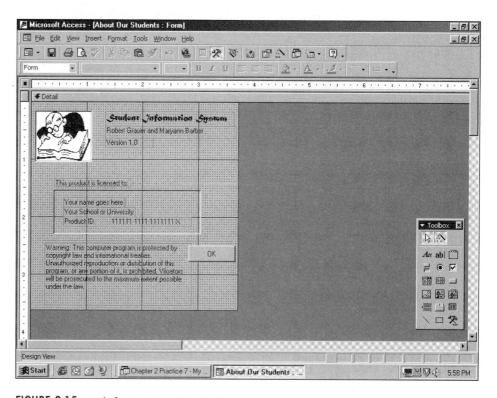

FIGURE 2.15　Help for Your Users (Exercise 7)

8. Add a Hyperlink: Figure 2.16 displays a modified version of the form that was created for the United States database in problem 4. We have added an additional field that is defined as a hyperlink. The new field enables you to click the hyperlink from within Access to start your Web browser and display the associated Web page provided you have an Internet connection. Do the following:

a. Open the United States database, select the USStates table, add a new field called WebPage, and specify hyperlink as the field type.

b. Open the existing form, pull down the View menu, and click Field List. Drag the newly added WebPage field onto the form. Size and align the controls as shown in Figure 2.16.

c. Pull down the View menu a second time. Click the Tab Order command and click the AutoOrder command button. Save the form.

d. Go to the Form view, select the state (e.g., California), and enter the address http://www.yahoo.com/Regional/U_S_States/California, substituting the appropriate name of the state. (This is the address returned by the Yahoo Search engine and it provides generalized information about all fifty states.)

e. Click the newly created link to start your browser and go to the appropriate site provided you have an Internet connection. Explore the site, then print one or two pages about your state using the Print command in the browser.

f. Click the Access button on the taskbar to return to the Access database. Choose a second state, then repeat steps (a) through (e) for that state. Can you appreciate the utility of including hyperlinks within a database? Do you see the advantages of multitasking within the Windows environment?

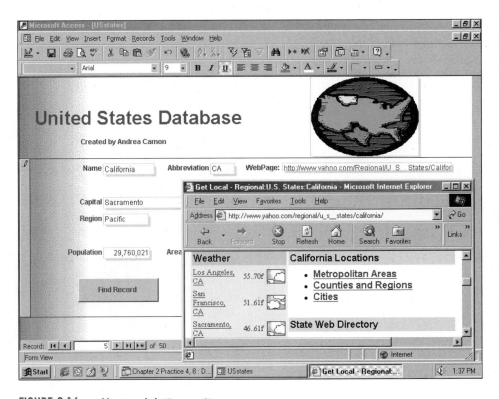

FIGURE 2.16   Add a Hyperlink (Exercise 8)

Personnel Management

You have been hired as the Personnel Director for a medium-sized firm (500 employees) and are expected to implement a system to track employee compensation. You want to be able to calculate the age of every employee as well as the length of service. You want to know each employee's most recent performance evaluation. You want to be able to calculate the amount of the most recent salary increase, both in dollars and as a percentage of the previous salary. You also want to know how long the employee had to wait for that increase—that is, how much time elapsed between the present and previous salary. Design a table capable of providing this information. Create a supporting form, then use that form to enter data for two employees.

The Stockbroker

A good friend has come to you for help. He is a new stockbroker whose firm provides computer support for existing clients, but does nothing in the way of data management for prospective clients. Your friend wants to use a PC to track the clients he is pursuing. He wants to know when he last contacted a person, how the contact was made (by phone or through the mail), and how interested the person was. He also wants to store the investment goals of each prospect, such as growth or income, and whether a person is interested in stocks, bonds, and/or a retirement account. And finally, he wants to record the amount of money the person has to invest. Design a table suitable for the information requirements. Create a supporting form, then use that form to enter data for two clients.

Metro Zoo

Your job as Director of Special Programs at the Metro Zoo has put you in charge of this year's fund-raising effort. You have decided to run an "Adopt an Animal" campaign and are looking for contributions on three levels: $25 for a reptile, $50 for a bird, and $100 for a mammal. Adopting "parents" will receive a personalized adoption certificate, a picture of their animal, and educational information about the zoo. You already have a great mailing list—the guest book that is maintained at the zoo entrance. Your main job is to computerize that information and to store additional information about contributions that are received. Design a table that will be suitable for this project.

Form Design

Collect several examples of such real forms as a magazine subscription, auto registration, or employment application. Choose the form you like best and implement the design in Access. Start by creating the underlying table (with some degree of validation), then use the Form Wizard to create the form. How closely does the form you create resemble the paper form with which you began? To what extent does the data validation ensure the accuracy of the data?

File Compression

Photographs add significantly to the value of a database, but they also add to its size. Accordingly, you might want to consider acquisition of a file compression program to facilitate copying large documents to a floppy disk in order to transport your documents to and from school, home, or work. You can download an evaluation copy of the popular WinZip program at www.winzip.com. Investigate the subject of file compression, then submit a summary of your findings to your instructor.

Copyright Infringement

It's fun to download images from the Web for inclusion into a database, but is it legal? Copyright protection (infringement) is one of the most pressing legal issues on the Web. Search the Web for sites that provide information on current copyright law. One excellent site is the copyright page at the Institute for Learning Technologies at www.ilt.columbia.edu/projects/copyright. Another excellent reference is the page at www.benedict.com. Research these and other sites, then summarize your findings in a short note to your instructor.

The Digital Camera

The art of photography is undergoing profound changes with the introduction of the digital camera. The images are stored on disk rather than traditional film and are available instantly. Search the Internet for the latest information on digital cameras and report back to the class with the results of your research. Perhaps one of your classmates has access to a digital camera, in which case you can take pictures of the class for inclusion in an Access database.

chapter 3

INFORMATION FROM THE DATABASE: REPORTS AND QUERIES

OBJECTIVES

After reading this chapter you will be able to:

1. Describe the various types of reports available through the Report Wizard.
2. Describe the various views in the Report Window and the purpose of each.
3. Describe the similarities between forms and reports with respect to bound, unbound, and calculated controls.
4. List the sections that may be present in a report and explain the purpose of each.
5. Differentiate between a query and a table; explain how the objects in an Access database (tables, forms, queries, and reports) interact with one another.
6. Use the design grid to create and modify a select query.
7. Explain the use of multiple criteria rows within the design grid to implement AND and OR conditions in a query.
8. Define an action query; list the different types of action queries that are available and explain how they are used to update a table.
9. Create a crosstab query.

OVERVIEW

Data and information are not synonymous. Data refers to a fact or facts about a specific record, such as a student's name, major, quality points, or number of completed credits. Information can be defined as data that has been rearranged into a more useful format. The individual fields within a student record are considered data. A list of students on the Dean's List, however, is information that has been produced from the data about the individual students.

Chapters 1 and 2 described how to enter and maintain data through the use of tables and forms. This chapter shows how to convert the data to information through queries and reports. Queries enable you to ask questions about the database. A special type of query, known as an action query, allows you to update a database by changing multiple records in a single operation. Reports provide presentation quality output and display detail as well as summary information about the records in a database.

As you read the chapter, you will see that the objects in an Access database (tables, forms, reports and queries) have many similar characteristics. We use these similarities to build on what you have learned in previous chapters. You already know, for example, that the controls in a form inherit their properties from the corresponding fields in a table. The same concept applies to the controls in a report. And since you know how to move and size controls within a form, you also know how to move and size the controls in a report. As you read the chapter, look for these similarities to apply your existing knowledge to new material.

REPORTS

A *report* is a printed document that displays information from a database. Figure 3.1 shows several sample reports, each of which will be created in this chapter. The reports were created with the Report Wizard and are based on the Students table that was presented in Chapter 2. (The table has been expanded to 24 records.) As you view each report, ask yourself how the data in the table was rearranged to produce the information in the report.

The *columnar (vertical) report* in Figure 3.1a is the simplest type of report. It lists every field for every record in a single column (one record per page) and typically runs for many pages. The records in this report are displayed in the same sequence (by social security number) as the records in the table on which the report is based.

The *tabular report* in Figure 3.1b displays fields in a row rather than in a column. Each record in the underlying table is printed in its own row. Unlike the previous report, only selected fields are displayed, so the tabular report is more concise than the columnar report of Figure 3.1a. Note, too, that the records in the report are listed in alphabetical order rather than by social security number.

The report in Figure 3.1c is also a tabular report, but it is very different from the report in Figure 3.1b. The report in Figure 3.1c lists only a selected set of students (those students with a GPA of 3.50 or higher), as opposed to the earlier reports, which listed every student. The students are listed in descending order according to their GPA.

The report in Figure 3.1d displays the students in groups, according to their major, then computes the average GPA for each group. The report also contains summary information (not visible in Figure 3.1d) for the report as a whole, which computes the average GPA for all students.

DATA VERSUS INFORMATION

Data and information are not synonymous although the terms are often interchanged. Data is the raw material and consists of the table (or tables) that compose a database. Information is the finished product. Data is converted to information by selecting records, performing calculations on those records, and/or changing the sequence in which the records are displayed. Decisions in an organization are made on the basis of information rather than raw data.

Student Roster

SSN	111-11-1111
FirstName	Jared
LastName	Berlin
Address	900 Main Highway
City	Charleston
State	SC
PostalCode	29410-0560
PhoneNumber	(803) 223-7868
BirthDate	1/15/72
Gender	M
Credits	100
QualityPoints	250
FinancialAid	Yes
Campus	1
Major	Engineering

Saturday, January 11, 1997 — Page 1 of 24

(a) Columnar Report

Student Master List

Last Name	First Name	Phone Number	Major
Adili	Ronnie	(612) 445-7654	Business
Berlin	Jared	(803) 223-7868	Engineering
Camejo	Oscar	(716) 433-3321	Liberal Arts
Coe	Bradley	(415) 235-6543	Undecided
Cornell	Ryan	(404) 755-4490	Undecided
DiGiacomo	Kevin	(305) 531-7652	Business
Faulkner	Eileen	(305) 489-8876	Communications
Frazier	Steven	(410) 995-8755	Undecided
Gibson	Christopher	(305) 235-4563	Business
Heltzer	Peter	(305) 753-4533	Engineering
Huerta	Carlos	(212) 344-5654	Undecided
Joseph	Cedric	(404) 667-8955	Communications
Korba	Nickolas	(415) 664-0900	Education
Ortiz	Frances	(303) 575-3211	Communications
Parulis	Christa	(410) 877-6565	Liberal Arts
Price	Lori	(310) 961-2323	Communications
Ramsay	Robert	(212) 223-9889	Business
Slater	Erica	(312) 545-6978	Communications
Solomon	Wendy	(305) 666-4532	Engineering
Watson	Ana	(305) 595-7877	Liberal Arts
Watson	Ana	(305) 561-2334	Business
Weissman	Kimberly	(904) 388-8605	Liberal Arts
Zacco	Michelle	(617) 884-3434	Undecided
Zimmerman	Kimberly	(713) 225-3434	Education

Saturday, January 11, 1997 — Page 1 of 1

(b) Tabular Report

Dean's List

First Name	Last Name	Major	Credits	Quality Points	GPA
Peter	Heltzer	Engineering	25	100	4.00
Cedric	Joseph	Communications	45	170	3.78
Erica	Slater	Communications	105	390	3.71
Kevin	DiGiacomo	Business	105	375	3.57
Wendy	Solomon	Engineering	50	175	3.50

Saturday, January 11, 1997 — Page 1 of 1

(c) Dean's List

GPA by Major

Major	Last Name	First Name	GPA
Business			
	Adili	Ronnie	2.58
	Cornell	Ryan	1.78
	DiGiacomo	Kevin	3.57
	Gibson	Christopher	1.71
	Ramsay	Robert	3.24
	Watson	Ana	2.50
	Average GPA for Major		2.56
Communications			
	Faulkner	Eileen	2.67
	Joseph	Cedric	3.78
	Ortiz	Frances	2.14
	Price	Lori	1.75
	Slater	Erica	3.71
	Average GPA for Major		2.81
Education			
	Korba	Nickolas	1.66
	Zimmerman	Kimberly	3.29
	Average GPA for Major		2.48
Engineering			
	Berlin	Jared	2.50
	Heltzer	Peter	4.00
	Solomon	Wendy	3.50
	Average GPA for Major		3.33
Liberal Arts			
	Camejo	Oscar	2.80
	Parulis	Christa	1.80
	Watson	Ana	2.79
	Weissman	Kimberly	2.63
	Average GPA for Major		2.51

Saturday, January 11, 1997 — Page 1 of 2

(d) Summary Report

FIGURE 3.1   Report Types

Anatomy of a Report

All reports are based on an underlying table or query within the database. (Queries are discussed later in the chapter, beginning on page 102.) A report, however, displays the data or information in a more attractive fashion because it contains various headings and/or other decorative items that are not present in either a table or a query.

The easiest way to learn about reports is to compare a printed report with its underlying design. Consider, for example, Figure 3.2a, which displays the tabular report, and Figure 3.2b, which shows the underlying design. The latter shows how a report is divided into sections, which appear at designated places when the report is printed. There are seven types of sections, but a report need not contain all seven.

The *report header* appears once, at the beginning of a report. It typically contains information describing the report, such as its title and the date the report was printed. (The report header appears above the page header on the first page of the report.) The *report footer* appears once at the end of the report, above the page footer on the last page of the report, and displays summary information for the report as a whole.

The *page header* appears at the top of every page in a report and can be used to display page numbers, column headings, and other descriptive information. The *page footer* appears at the bottom of every page and may contain page numbers (when they are not in the page header) or other descriptive information.

A *group header* appears at the beginning of a group of records to identify the group. A *group footer* appears after the last record in a group and contains summary information about the group. Group headers and footers are used only when the records in a report are sorted (grouped) according to a common value in a specific field. These sections do not appear in the report of Figure 3.2, but were shown earlier in the report of Figure 3.1d.

The *detail section* appears in the main body of a report and is printed once for every record in the underlying table (or query). It displays one or more fields for each record in columnar or tabular fashion, according to the design of the report.

The Report Wizard

The *Report Wizard* is the easiest way to create a report, just as the Form Wizard is the easiest way to create a form. The Report Wizard asks you questions about the report you want, then builds the report for you. You can accept the report as is, or you can customize it to better suit your needs.

Figure 3.3a displays the New Report dialog box, from which you can select the Report Wizard. The Report Wizard, in turn, requires you to specify the table or query on which the report will be based. The report in this example will be based on an expanded version of the Students table that was created in Chapter 2.

After you specify the underlying table, you select one or more fields from that table, as shown in Figure 3.3b. The Report Wizard then asks you to select a layout (e.g., Tabular in Figure 3.3c.) and a style (e.g., Soft Gray in Figure 3.3d). This is all the information the Report Wizard requires, and it proceeds to create the report for you. The controls on the report correspond to the fields you selected and are displayed in accordance with the specified layout.

Apply What You Know

The Report Wizard provides an excellent starting point, but typically does not create the report exactly as you would like it to be. Accordingly, you can modify a

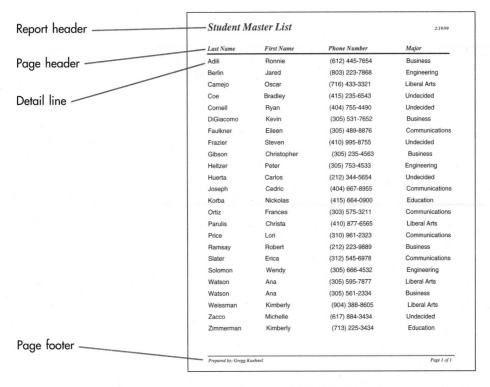

(a) The Printed Report

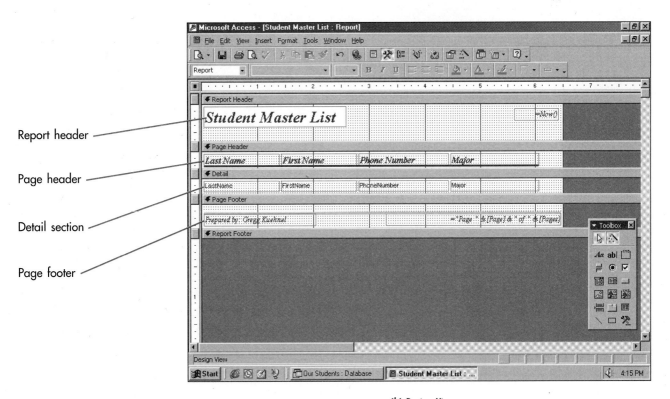

(b) Design View

FIGURE 3.2   Anatomy of a Report

Click to select table/query on which report will be based

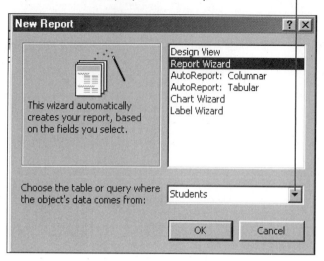

(a) Select the Underlying Table

Underlying table   Available fields   Selected fields

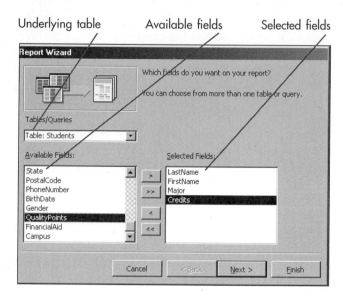

(b) Select the Fields

Selected layout

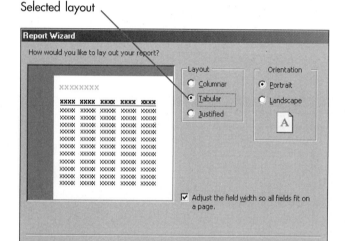

(c) Choose the Layout

Selected style

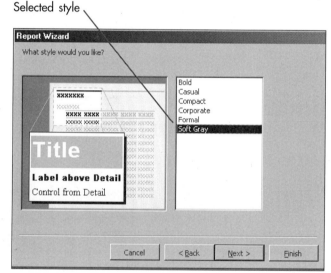

(d) Choose the Style

FIGURE 3.3   The Report Wizard

report created by the Report Wizard, just as you can modify a form created by the Form Wizard. The techniques are the same, and you should look for similarities between forms and reports so that you can apply what you already know. Knowledge of one is helpful in understanding the other.

Controls appear in a report just as they do in a form, and the same definitions apply. A **bound control** has as its data source a field in the underlying table. An **unbound control** has no data source and is used to display titles, labels, lines, rectangles, and graphics. A **calculated control** has as its data source an expression rather than a field. A student's Grade Point Average is an example of a calculated control since it is computed by dividing the number of quality points by the number of credits. The means for selecting, sizing, moving, aligning, and deleting controls are the same, regardless of whether you are working on a form or a report. Thus:

- To select a control, click anywhere on the control. To select multiple controls, press and hold the Shift key as you click each successive control.
- To size a control, click the control to select it, then drag the sizing handles. Drag the handles on the top or bottom to size the box vertically. Drag the handles on the left or right side to size the box horizontally. Drag the handles in the corner to size both horizontally and vertically.
- To move a control, point to any border, but not to a sizing handle (the mouse pointer changes to a hand), then click the mouse and drag the control to its new position.
- To change the properties of a control, point to the control, click the right mouse button to display a shortcut menu, then click Properties to display the property sheet. Click the text box for the desired property, make the necessary change, then close the property sheet.

INHERITANCE

A bound control inherits the same property settings as the associated field in the underlying table. Changing the property setting for a field after the report has been created does *not*, however, change the property of the corresponding control in the report. In similar fashion, changing the property setting of a control in a report does *not* change the property setting of the field in the underlying table.

HANDS-ON EXERCISE 1

The Report Wizard

Objective: To use the Report Wizard to create a new report; to modify an existing report by adding, deleting, and/or modifying its controls. Use Figure 3.4 as a guide in the exercise.

STEP 1: Open the Our Students Database
➤ Start Access. You should see the Microsoft Access dialog box with the option button to **Open an existing file** already selected.
➤ Double click the **More Files** selection to display the Open dialog box. Click the **drop-down arrow** on the Look In list box, click the drive containing the **Exploring Access folder,** then open that folder.

THE OUR STUDENTS DATABASE

The Our Students database has the identical design as the database you created in Chapter 2. We have, however, expanded the Students table so that it contains 24 records. The larger table enables you to create more meaningful reports and to obtain the same results as we do in the hands-on exercise.

➤ Click the **down scroll arrow,** if necessary, and select the **Our Students** database. Click the **Open command button** to open the database.

➤ Click the **Reports button** in the Database window, then click the **New command button** to display the New Report dialog box in Figure 3.4a. Select the **Report Wizard** as the means of creating the report.

➤ Click the **drop-down arrow** to display the tables and queries in the database in order to select the one on which the report will be based. Click **Students,** then click **OK** to start the Report Wizard.

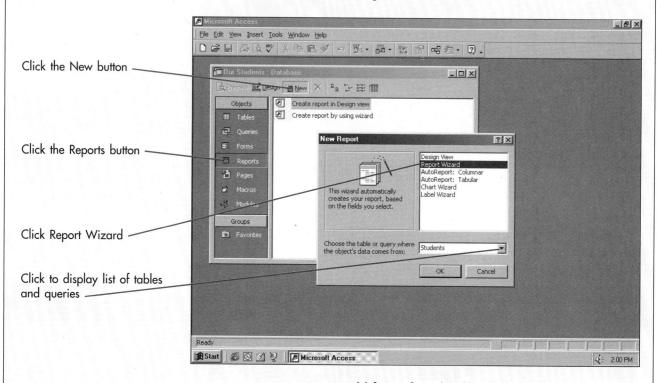

Click the New button

Click the Reports button

Click Report Wizard

Click to display list of tables and queries

(a) Create a Report (step 1)

FIGURE 3.4   Hands-on Exercise 1

STEP 2: The Report Wizard

➤ You should see the dialog box in Figure 3.4b, which displays all of the fields in the Students table. Click the **LastName field** in the Available Fields list box, then click the **> button** to enter this field in the Selected Fields list, as shown in Figure 3.4b.

➤ Enter the remaining fields (FirstName, PhoneNumber, and Major) one at a time, by selecting the field name, then clicking the **> button.** Click the **Next command button** when you have entered the four fields.

WHAT THE REPORT WIZARD DOESN'T TELL YOU

The fastest way to select a field is by double clicking; that is, double click a field in the Available Fields list box, and it is automatically moved to the Selected Fields list for inclusion in the report. The process also works in reverse; that is, you can double click a field in the Selected Fields list to remove it from the report.

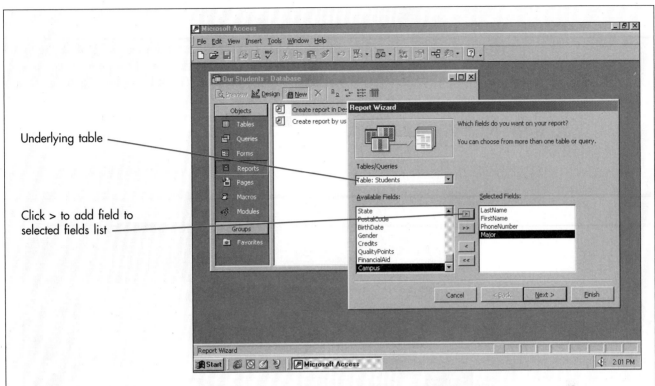

(b) The Report Wizard (step 2)

FIGURE 3.4   Hands-on Exercise 1 (continued)

STEP 3: The Report Wizard (continued)

➤ The Report Wizard displays several additional screens asking about the report you want to create. The first screen asks whether you want to choose any grouping levels. Click **Next** without specifying a grouping level.

➤ The next screen asks whether you want to sort the records. Click the **drop-down arrow** to display the available fields, then select **LastName.** Click **Next.**

➤ The **Tabular layout** is selected, as is **Portrait orientation.** Be sure the box is checked to **Adjust field width so all fields fit on a page.** Click **Next.**

➤ Choose **Corporate** as the style. Click **Next.**

➤ Enter **Student Master List** as the title for your report. The option button to **Preview the Report** is already selected. Click the **Finish command button** to exit the Report Wizard and view the report.

AUTOMATIC SAVING

The Report Wizard automatically saves a report under the name you supply for the title of the report. To verify that a report has been saved, change to the Database window by pulling down the Window menu or by clicking the Database Window button that appears on every toolbar. Once you are in the Database window, click the Reports tab to see the list of existing reports. Note, however, that any subsequent changes must be saved explicitly by clicking the Save button in the Report Design view, or by clicking Yes in response to the warning prompt should you attempt to close the report without saving the changes.

STEP 4: Preview the Report

➤ Click the **Maximize button** so the report takes the entire window as shown in Figure 3.4c. Note the report header at the beginning of the report, the page header (column headings) at the top of the page, and the page footer at the bottom of the page.

➤ Click the **drop-down arrow** on the Zoom Control box so that you can view the report at **75%.** Click the **scroll arrows** on the vertical scroll bar to view the names of additional students.

➤ Click the **Close button** to close the Print Preview window and change to the Report Design view.

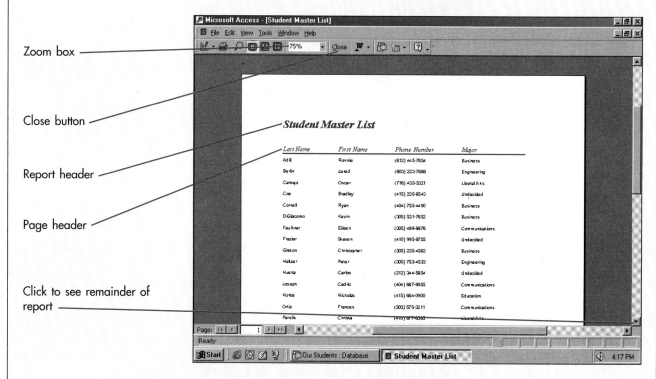

(c) The Initial Report (step 4)

FIGURE 3.4   Hands-on Exercise 1 (continued)

THE PRINT PREVIEW WINDOW

The Print Preview window enables you to preview a report in various ways. Click the One Page, Two Pages, or Multiple Pages buttons for different views of a report. Use the Zoom button to toggle between the full page and zoom (magnified) views, or use the Zoom Control box to choose a specific magnification. The Navigation buttons at the bottom of the Print Preview window enable you to preview a specific page, while the vertical scroll bar at the right side of the window lets you scroll within a page.

STEP 5: Modify an Existing Control

➤ Click and drag the border of control containing the **Now function** from the report footer to the report header as shown in Figure 3.4d.

➤ Size the control as necessary, then check that the control is still selected and click the **Align Right button** on the Formatting toolbar.

➤ Point to the control, then click the **right mouse button** to display a shortcut menu and click **Properties** to display the Properties sheet.

➤ Click the **Format tab** in the Properties sheet, click the **Format property,** then click the **drop-down arrow** to display the available formats. Click **Short Date,** then close the Properties sheet.

➤ Pull down the **File menu** and click **Save** (or click the **Save button**) to save the modified design.

Click and drag control to the Report header

Point to control and click right mouse button to display shortcut menu

Click and drag in Page Footer where label is to be placed

Label tool

Click in Font Size box

Click to display font sizes

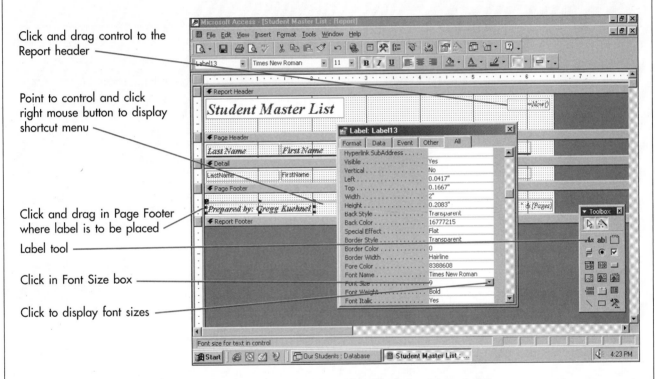

(d) Modify the Report (steps 5 & 6)

FIGURE 3.4   Hands-on Exercise 1 (continued)

ACCESS FUNCTIONS

Access contains many built-in functions, each of which returns a specific value or the result of a calculation. The Now function, for example, returns the current date and time. The Page and Pages functions return the specific page number and total number of pages, respectively. The Report Wizard automatically adds these functions at appropriate places in a report. You can also add these (or other) functions explicitly, by creating a text box, then replacing the default unbound control by an equal sign, followed by the function name (and associated arguments if any)—for example, =Now( ) to insert the current date and time.

STEP 6: Add an Unbound Control

➤ Click the **Label tool** on the Toolbox toolbar, then click and drag in the report footer where you want the label to go and release the mouse. You should see a flashing insertion point inside the label control. (If you see the word *Unbound* instead of the insertion point, it means you selected the Text box tool rather than the Label tool; delete the text box and begin again.)

➤ Type **Prepared by** followed by your name as shown in Figure 3.4d. Press **enter** to complete the entry and also select the control. Point to the control, click the **right mouse button** to display the shortcut menu, then click **Properties** to display the Properties dialog box.

➤ Click the **down arrow** on the scroll bar, then scroll until you see the Font Size property. Click in the **Font Size box,** click the **drop-down arrow,** then scroll until you can change the font size to **9.** Close the Property sheet.

MISSING TOOLBARS

The Report Design, Formatting, and Toolbox toolbars appear by default in the Report Design view, but any (or all) of these toolbars may be hidden at the discretion of the user. If any of these toolbars do not appear, point to any visible toolbar, click the right mouse button to display a shortcut menu, then click the name of the toolbar you want to display. You can also click the Toolbox button on the Report Design toolbar to display (hide) the Toolbox toolbar.

STEP 7: Change the Sort Order

➤ Pull down the **View menu.** Click **Sorting and Grouping** to display the Sorting and Grouping dialog box. The students are currently sorted by last name.

➤ Click the **drop-down arrow** in the Field Expression box. Click **Major.** (The ascending sequence is selected automatically.)

➤ Click on the next line in the Field Expression box, click the **drop-down arrow** to display the available fields, then click **LastName** to sort the students alphabetically within major as shown in Figure 3.4e.

➤ Close the Sorting and Grouping dialog box. Save the report.

STEP 8: View the Modified Report

➤ Click the **Print Preview button** to preview the finished report. If necessary, click the **Zoom button** on the Print Preview toolbar so that the display on your monitor matches Figure 3.4f. The report has changed so that:

- The date appears in the report header (as opposed to the report footer). The format of the date has changed to a numbered month, and the day of the week has been eliminated.

- The students are listed by major and, within each major, alphabetically according to last name.

- Your name appears in the Report Footer. Click the **down arrow** on the vertical scroll bar to move to the bottom of the page to see your name.

➤ Click the **Print button** to print the report and submit it to your instructor. Click the **Close button** to exit the Print Preview window.

➤ Click the **Close button** in the Report Design window. Click **Yes** if asked whether to save the changes to the Student Master List report.

Print Preview button

Close button

Select Major

Click on second line

Click to drop-down list
of field names

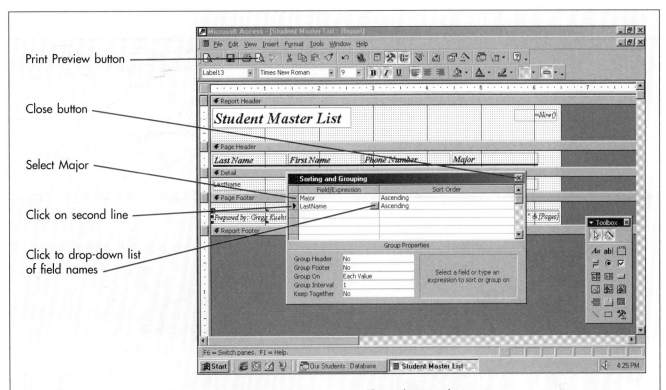

(e) Change the Sort Order (step 7)

Print button

Zoom button

Close button

Date is in Report header

Students are listed by last
name within major

Click to see bottom of report

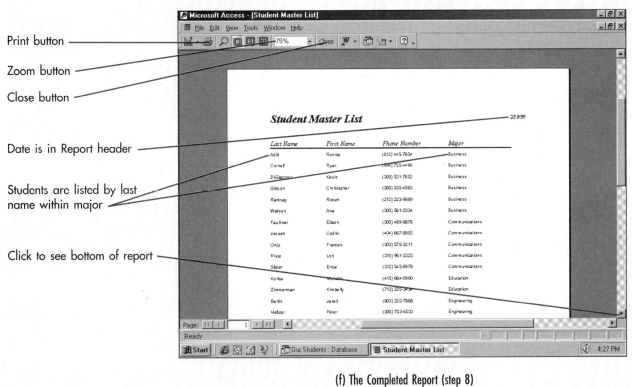

(f) The Completed Report (step 8)

FIGURE 3.4   Hands-on Exercise 1 (continued)

STEP 9: Report Properties

➤ The Database window for the Our Students database should be displayed on the screen as shown in Figure 3.4g. Click the **Restore button** to restore the window to its earlier size.

➤ The **Reports button** is already selected. Point to the **Student Master List**, click the **right mouse button** to display a shortcut menu, then click **Properties** to display the Properties dialog box as shown in Figure 3.4g.

➤ Click the **Description text box,** then enter the description shown in the figure. Click **OK** to close the Properties dialog box.

➤ Close the database. Exit Access if you do not wish to continue with the next exercise at this time.

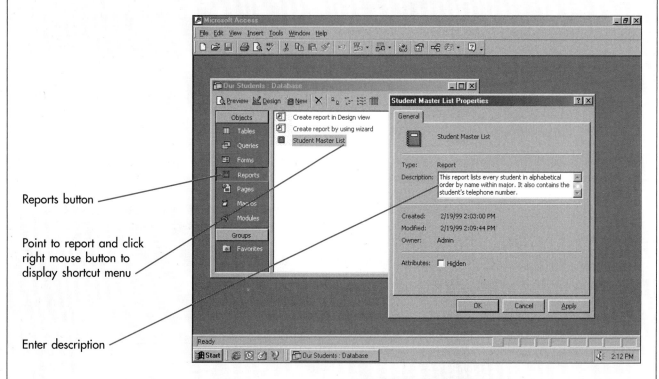

Reports button

Point to report and click right mouse button to display shortcut menu

Enter description

(g) Report Properties (step 9)

FIGURE 3.4   Hands-on Exercise 1 (continued)

DESCRIBE YOUR OBJECTS

A working database will contain many different objects of the same type, making it all too easy to forget the purpose of the individual objects. It is important, therefore, to use meaningful names for the objects themselves, and further to take advantage of the Description property to enter additional information about the object. Once a description has been created, you can right click any object in the Database window, then click the Properties command from the shortcut menu to display the Properties dialog box with the description of the object.

INTRODUCTION TO QUERIES

The report you just created displayed every student in the underlying table. What if, however, we wanted to see just the students who are majoring in Business? Or the students who are receiving financial aid? Or the students who are majoring in Business *and* receiving financial aid? The ability to ask questions such as these, and to see the answers to those questions, is provided through a query. Queries represent the real power of a database.

A *query* lets you see the data you want in the sequence that you want it. It lets you select specific records from a table (or from several tables) and show some or all of the fields for the selected records. It also lets you perform calculations to display data that is not explicitly stored in the underlying table(s), such as a student's GPA.

A query represents a question and an answer. The question is developed by using a graphical tool known as the *design grid.* The answer is displayed in a *dynaset,* which contains the records that satisfy the criteria specified in the query.

A dynaset looks and acts like a table, but it isn't a table; it is a *dyna*mic sub*set* of a table that selects and sorts records as specified in the query. A dynaset is similar to a table in appearance and, like a table, it enables you to enter a new record or modify or delete an existing record. Any changes made in the dynaset are automatically reflected in the underlying table.

Figure 3.5a displays the Students table we have been using throughout the chapter. (We omit some of the fields for ease of illustration.) Figure 3.5b contains the design grid used to select students whose major is "Undecided" and further, to list those students in alphabetical order. (The design grid is explained in the next section.) Figure 3.5c displays the answer to the query in the form of a dynaset.

The table in Figure 3.5a contains 24 records. The dynaset in Figure 3.5c has only five records, corresponding to the students who arc undecided about their major. The table in Figure 3.5a has 15 fields for each record (some of the fields are hidden). The dynaset in Figure 3.5c has only four fields. The records in the table are in social security number order (the primary key), whereas the records in the dynaset are in alphabetical order by last name.

The query in Figure 3.5 is an example of a *select query,* which is the most common type of query. A select query searches the underlying table (Figure 3.5a in the example) to retrieve the data that satisfies the query. The data is displayed in a dynaset (Figure 3.5c), which you can modify to update the data in the underlying table(s). The specifications for selecting records and determining which fields will be displayed for the selected records, as wcll as the sequence of the selected records, are established within the design grid of Figure 3.5b.

The design grid consists of columns and rows. Each field in the query has its own column and contains multiple rows. The *Field row* displays the field name. The *Sort row* enables you to sort in *ascending* or *descending sequence.* The *Show row* controls whether or not the field will be displayed in the dynaset. The *Criteria row(s)* determine the records that will be selected, such as students with an undecided major.

REPORTS, QUERIES, AND TABLES

Every report is based on either a table or a query. The design of the report may be the same with respect to the fields that are included, but the actual reports will be very different. A report based on a table contains every record in the table. A report based on a query contains only the records that satisfy the criteria in the query.

Records are in order by SSN (primary key)

Total of 24 records

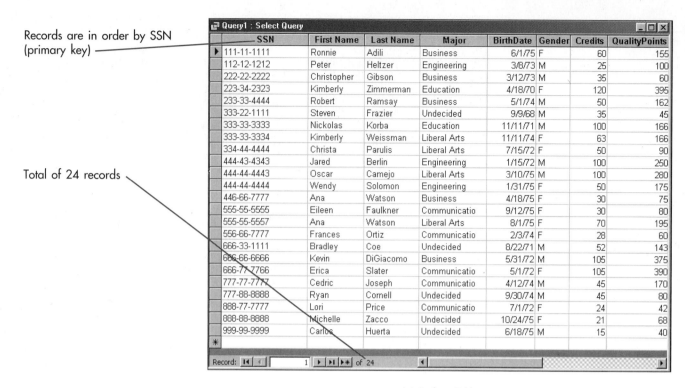

SSN	First Name	Last Name	Major	BirthDate	Gender	Credits	QualityPoints
111-11-1111	Ronnie	Adili	Business	6/1/75	F	60	155
112-12-1212	Peter	Heltzer	Engineering	3/8/73	M	25	100
222-22-2222	Christopher	Gibson	Business	3/12/73	M	35	60
223-34-2323	Kimberly	Zimmerman	Education	4/18/70	F	120	395
233-33-4444	Robert	Ramsay	Business	5/1/74	M	50	162
333-22-1111	Steven	Frazier	Undecided	9/9/68	M	35	45
333-33-3333	Nickolas	Korba	Education	11/11/71	M	100	166
333-33-3334	Kimberly	Weissman	Liberal Arts	11/11/74	F	63	166
334-44-4444	Christa	Parulis	Liberal Arts	7/15/72	F	50	90
444-43-4343	Jared	Berlin	Engineering	1/15/72	M	100	250
444-44-4443	Oscar	Camejo	Liberal Arts	3/10/75	M	100	280
444-44-4444	Wendy	Solomon	Engineering	1/31/75	F	50	175
446-66-7777	Ana	Watson	Business	4/18/75	F	30	75
555-55-5555	Eileen	Faulkner	Communicatio	9/12/75	F	30	80
555-55-5557	Ana	Watson	Liberal Arts	8/1/75	F	70	195
556-66-7777	Frances	Ortiz	Communicatio	2/3/74	F	28	60
666-33-1111	Bradley	Coe	Undecided	8/22/71	M	52	143
666-66-6666	Kevin	DiGiacomo	Business	5/31/72	M	105	375
666-77-7766	Erica	Slater	Communicatio	5/1/72	F	105	390
777-77-7777	Cedric	Joseph	Communicatio	4/12/74	M	45	170
777-88-8888	Ryan	Cornell	Undecided	9/30/74	M	45	80
888-77-7777	Lori	Price	Communicatio	7/1/72	F	24	42
888-88-8888	Michelle	Zacco	Undecided	10/24/75	F	21	68
999-99-9999	Carlos	Huerta	Undecided	6/18/75	M	15	40

Record: 1 of 24

(a) Students Table

Sort order

Criteria

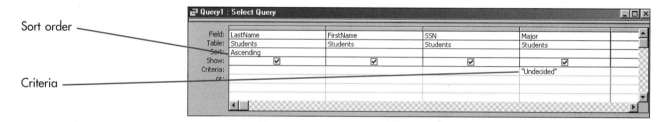

Field:	LastName	FirstName	SSN	Major	
Table:	Students	Students	Students	Students	
Sort:	Ascending				
Show:	☑	☑	☑	☑	
Criteria:				"Undecided"	
or:					

(b) Design Grid

Records are in alphabetical order by last name

Total of 5 records

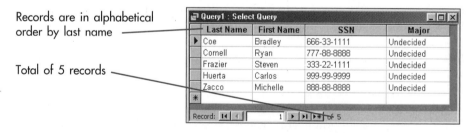

Last Name	First Name	SSN	Major
Coe	Bradley	666-33-1111	Undecided
Cornell	Ryan	777-88-8888	Undecided
Frazier	Steven	333-22-1111	Undecided
Huerta	Carlos	999-99-9999	Undecided
Zacco	Michelle	888-88-8888	Undecided

Record: 1 of 5

(c) Dynaset

FIGURE 3.5 Queries

Query Window

The **Query window** has three views. The **Design view** is displayed by default and is used to create (or modify) a select query. The **Datasheet view** displays the resulting dynaset. The **SQL view** enables you to use SQL (Structured Query Language) statements to modify the query and is beyond the scope of the present

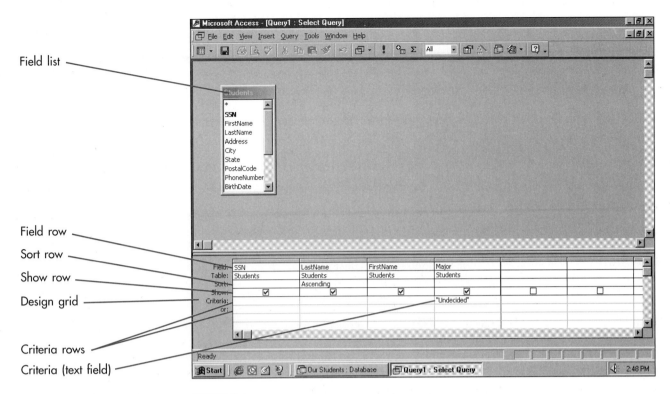

Field list

Field row

Sort row

Show row

Design grid

Criteria rows

Criteria (text field)

FIGURE 3.6   Query Design View

discussion. The View button on the Query Design toolbar lets you display all three views.

A select query is created in the Design view as shown in Figure 3.6a. The upper portion of the Design view window contains the field list for the table(s) on which the query is based (the Students table in this example). The lower portion of the window displays the design grid, which is where the specifications for the select query are entered. A field is added to the design grid by dragging it from the field list.

The data type of a field determines the way in which the criteria are specified for that field. The criterion for a text field is enclosed in quotation marks. The criteria for number, currency, and counter fields are shown as digits with or without a decimal point. (Commas and dollar signs are not allowed.) Dates are enclosed in pound signs and are entered in the mm/dd/yy format. The criterion for a Yes/No field is entered as Yes (or True) or No (or False).

CONVERSION TO STANDARD FORMAT

Access accepts values for text and date fields in the design grid in multiple formats. The value for a text field can be entered with or without quotation marks (Undecided or "Undecided"). A date can be entered with or without pound signs (1/1/97 or #1/1/97#). Access converts your entries to standard format as soon as you move to the next cell in the design grid. Thus, text entries are always shown in quotation marks, and dates are enclosed in pound signs.

Selection Criteria

To specify selection criteria in the design grid, enter a value or expression in the Criteria row of the appropriate column. Figure 3.7 contains several examples of simple criteria and provides a basic introduction to select queries.

The criterion in Figure 3.7a selects the students majoring in Business. The criteria for text fields are case-insensitive. Thus, *"Business"* is the same as *"business"* or *"BUSINESS"*.

Values entered in multiple columns of the same Criteria row implement an **AND condition** in which the selected records must meet *all* of the specified criteria. The criteria in Figure 3.7b select students who are majoring in Business *and* who are from the state of Florida. The criteria in Figure 3.7c select Communications majors who are receiving financial aid.

Values entered in different Criteria rows are connected by an **OR condition** in which the selected records may satisfy *any* of the indicated criteria. The criteria in Figure 3.7d select students who are majoring in Business *or* who are from Florida or both.

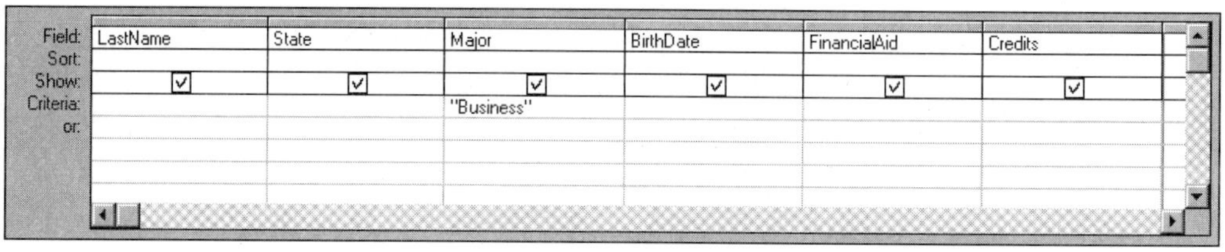

(a) Business Majors

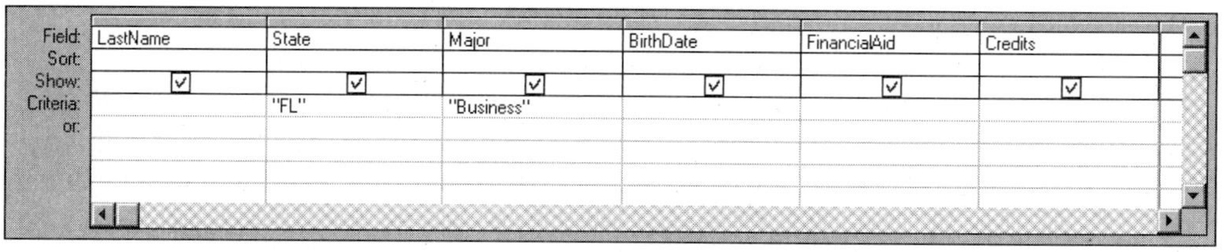

(b) Business Majors from Florida

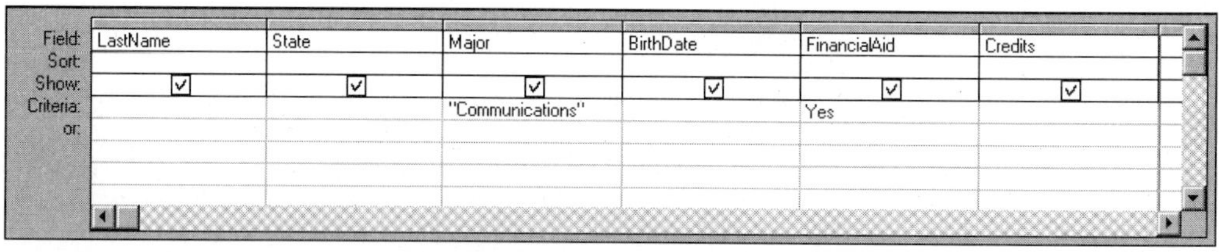

(c) Communications Majors Receiving Financial Aid

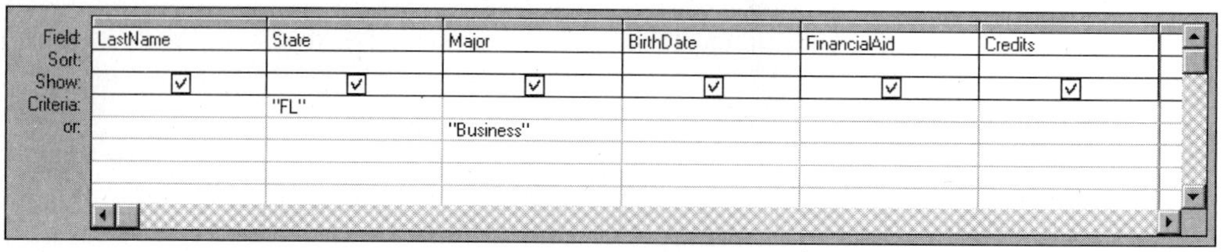

(d) Business Majors or Students from Florida

FIGURE 3.7   Criteria

Relational operators (>, <, >=, <=, =, and <>) are used with date or number fields to return records within a designated range. The criteria in Figure 3.7e select Engineering majors with fewer than 60 credits. The criteria in Figure 3.7f select Communications majors who were born on or after April 1, 1974.

Field:	LastName	State	Major	BirthDate	FinancialAid	Credits
Sort:						
Show:	✓	✓	✓	✓	✓	✓
Criteria:			"Engineering"			<60
or:						

(e) Engineering Majors with Fewer than 60 Credits

Field:	LastName	State	Major	BirthDate	FinancialAid	Credits
Sort:						
Show:	✓	✓	✓	✓	✓	✓
Criteria:			"Communications"	>=#4/1/74#		
or:						

(f) Communications Majors Born on or after April 1, 1974

Field:	LastName	State	Major	BirthDate	FinancialAid	Credits
Sort:						
Show:	✓	✓	✓	✓	✓	✓
Criteria:			"Engineering"			<60
or:			Communications	>=#4/1/74#		

(g) Engineering Majors with Fewer than 60 Credits or Communications Majors Born on or after April 1, 1974

Field:	LastName	State	Major	BirthDate	FinancialAid	Credits
Sort:						
Show:	✓	✓	✓	✓	✓	✓
Criteria:						Between 60 and 90
or:						

(h) Students with between 60 and 90 Credits

Field:	LastName	State	Major	BirthDate	FinancialAid	Credits
Sort:						
Show:	✓	✓	✓	✓	✓	✓
Criteria:			Not "Liberal Arts"			
or:						

(i) Students with Majors Other Than Liberal Arts

FIGURE 3.7   Criteria (continued)

Criteria can grow more complex by combining multiple AND and OR conditions. The criteria in Figure 3.7g select Engineering majors with fewer than 60 credits *or* Communications majors who were born on or after April 1, 1974.

Other functions enable you to impose still other criteria. The ***Between function*** selects records that fall within a range of values. The criterion in Figure 3.7h selects students who have between 60 and 90 credits. The ***NOT function*** selects records that do not contain the designated value. The criterion in Figure 3.7i selects students with majors other than Liberal Arts.

WILD CARDS

Select queries recognize the question mark and asterisk wild cards that enable you to search for a pattern within a text field. A question mark stands for a single character in the same position as the question mark; thus H?ll will return Hall, Hill, and Hull. An asterisk stands for any number of characters in the same position as the asterisk; for example, S*nd will return Sand, Stand, and Strand.

HANDS-ON EXERCISE 2

Creating a Select Query

Objective: To create a select query using the design grid; to show how changing values in a dynaset changes the values in the underlying table; to create a report based on a query. Use Figure 3.8 as a guide in the exercise.

STEP 1: Open the Existing Database

➤ Start Access as you did in the previous exercise. Our Students (the database you used in the previous exercise) should appear within the list of recently opened databases.

➤ Select (click) **Our Students,** then click **OK** (or simply double click the name of the database) to open the database and display the database window.

➤ Click the **Queries button** in the Database window. Click the **New command button** to display the New Query dialog box as shown in Figure 3.8a.

➤ **Design View** is already selected as the means of creating a query. Click **OK** to begin creating the query.

THE SIMPLE QUERY WIZARD

The Simple Query Wizard is exactly what its name implies—simple. It lets you select fields from an underlying table, but it does not let you enter values or a sort sequence. We prefer, therefore, to bypass the Wizard and to create the query entirely from the Query Design window.

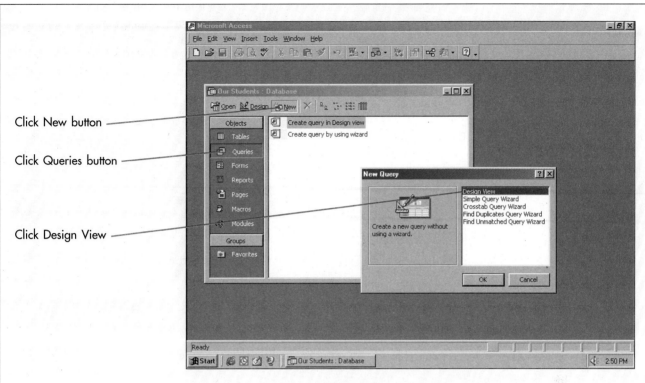

Click New button

Click Queries button

Click Design View

(a) Open the Students Database (step 1)

FIGURE 3.8 Hands-on Exercise 2

STEP 2: Add the Students Table

➤ The Show Table dialog box appears as shown in Figure 3.8b, with the **Tables tab** already selected.

➤ Select the **Students table,** then click the **Add button** to add the Students table to the query. (You can also double click the Students table.)

➤ The field list should appear within the Query Design window. Click **Close** to close the Show Table dialog box.

➤ Click the **Maximize button** so that the Query Design window takes up the entire screen.

➤ Drag the border between the upper and lower portions of the window to give yourself more room in the upper portion. Make the field list larger to display more fields at one time.

CUSTOMIZE THE QUERY WINDOW

The Query window displays the field list and design grid in its upper and lower halves, respectively. To increase (decrease) the size of either portion of the window, drag the line dividing the upper and lower sections. Drag the title bar to move a field list. You can also size a field list by dragging a border just as you would size any other window. Press the F6 key to toggle between the upper and lower halves of the Design window.

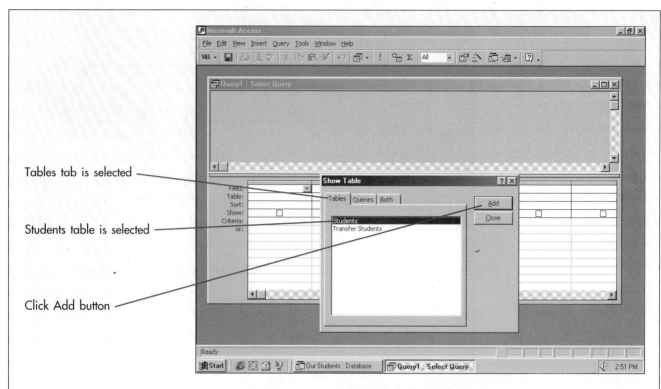

Tables tab is selected

Students table is selected

Click Add button

(b) Add the Students Table (step 2)

FIGURE 3.8   Hands-on Exercise 2 (continued)

STEP 3: Create the Query

➤ Click and drag the **LastName field** from the Students field list to the Field row in the first column of the QBE grid as shown in Figure 3.8c.

➤ Click and drag the **FirstName, PhoneNumber, Major,** and **Credits fields** (in that order) in similar fashion, dragging each field to the next available column in the Field row.

➤ A check appears in the Show row under each field name to indicate that the field will be displayed in the dynaset. (The show box functions as a toggle switch; thus, you can click the box to clear the check and hide the field in the dynaset. Click the box a second time to display the check and show the field.)

ADDING AND DELETING FIELDS

The fastest way to add a field to the design grid is to double click the field name in the field list. To add more than one field at a time, press and hold the Ctrl key as you click the fields within the field list, then drag the group to a cell in the Field row. To delete a field, click the column selector above the field name to select the column, then press the Del key.

STEP 4: Specify the Criteria

➤ Click the **Criteria row** for Major. Type **Undecided.**

➤ Click the **Sort row** under the LastName field, click the **drop-down arrow,** then select **Ascending** as the sort sequence.

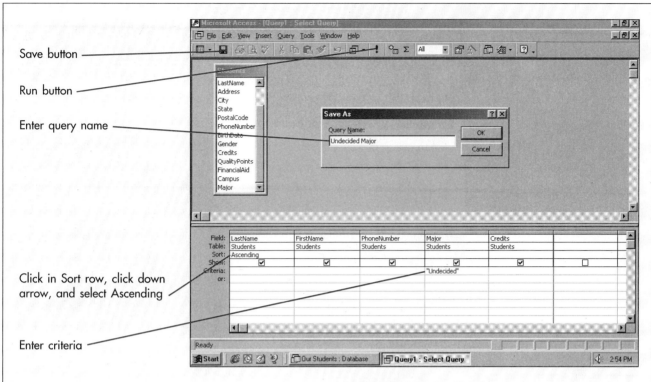

Save button

Run button

Enter query name

Click in Sort row, click down
arrow, and select Ascending

Enter criteria

(c) Create the Query (steps 3 & 4)

FIGURE 3.8   Hands-on Exercise 2 (continued)

➤ Pull down the **File menu** and click **Save** (or click the **Save button**) to display
the dialog box in Figure 3.8c.

➤ Type **Undecided Major** as the query name. Click **OK.**

FLEXIBLE CRITERIA

Access offers a great deal of flexibility in the way you enter the criteria
for a text field. Quotation marks and/or an equal sign are optional. Thus
"Undecided", Undecided, =Undecided, or ="Undecided" are all valid,
and you may choose any of these formats. Access will convert your entry
to standard format ("Undecided" in this example) after you have moved
to the next cell.

STEP 5: Run the Query

➤ Pull down the **Query menu** and click **Run** (or click the **Run button**) to run
the query and change to the Datasheet view.

➤ You should see the five records in the dynaset of Figure 3.8d. Change Ryan
Cornell's major to Business by clicking in the **Major field,** clicking the **drop-
down arrow,** then choosing **Business** from the drop-down list.

➤ Click the **View button** to change the query.

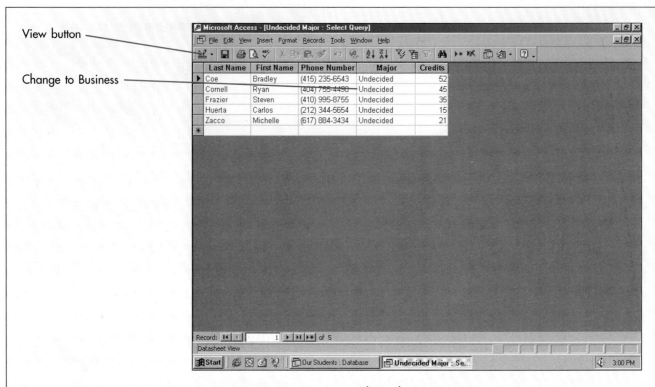

(d) Run the Query (step 5)

FIGURE 3.8   Hands-on Exercise 2 (continued)

STEP 6: Modify the Query

➤ Click the **Show check box** in the Major field to remove the check as shown in Figure 3.8e.

➤ Click the **Criteria row** under credits. Type **>30** to select only the Undecided majors with more than 30 credits.

➤ Click the **Save button** to save the revised query. Click the **Run button** to run the revised query. This time there are only two records (Bradley Coe and Steven Frazier) in the dynaset, and the major is no longer displayed.

  • Ryan Cornell does not appear because he has changed his major.

  • Carlos Huerta and Michelle Zacco do not appear because they do not have more than 30 credits.

STEP 7: Create a Report

➤ Pull down the **Window menu** and click **1 Our Students: Database** (or click the **Database window button** on the toolbar). You will see the Database window in Figure 3.8f.

➤ Double click the icon next to **Create report by using Wizard.**

➤ Click the **drop-down arrow** on the **Tables/Queries** list box and select **Query:Undecided Major.** All of the visible fields (major has been hidden) are displayed. Click the **>>button** to select all of the fields in the query for the report. Click **Next.**

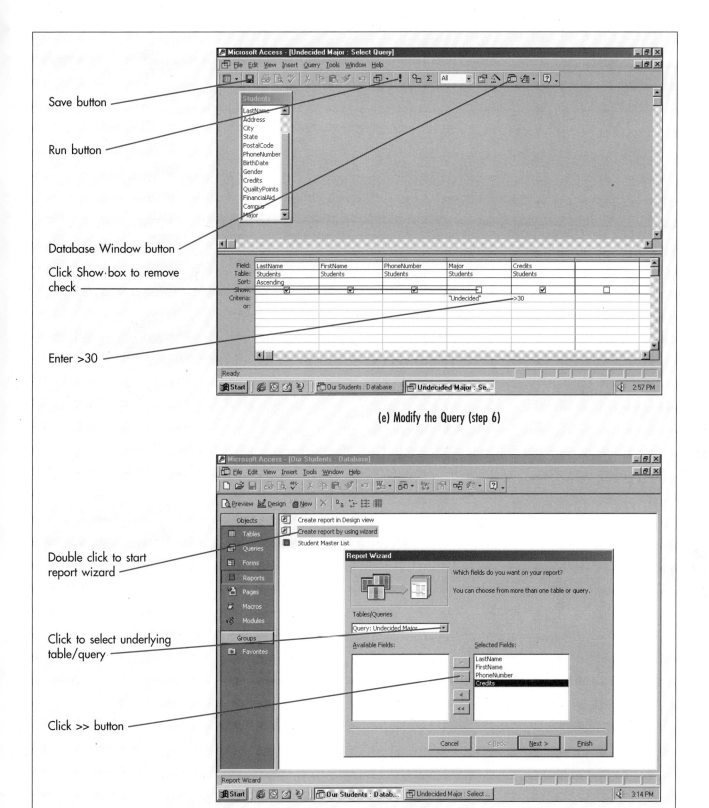

Save button

Run button

Database Window button

Click Show box to remove check

Enter >30

(e) Modify the Query (step 6)

Double click to start report wizard

Click to select underlying table/query

Click >> button

(f) Create a Report (step 7)

FIGURE 3.8   Hands-on Exercise 2 (continued)

➤ You do not want to choose additional grouping levels. Click **Next** to move to the next screen.

➤ There is no need to specify a sort sequence. Click **Next.**

➤ The **Tabular layout** is selected, as is **Portrait orientation.** Be sure the box is checked to **Adjust field width so all fields fit on a page.** Click **Next.**

➤ Choose **Soft Gray** as the style. Click **Next.**

➤ If necessary, enter **Undecided Major** as the title for your report. The option button to **Preview the Report** is already selected. Click the **Finish command button** to exit the Report Wizard and view the report.

THE BACK BUTTON

The Back button is present on every screen within the Report Wizard and enables you to recover from mistakes or simply to change your mind about how you want the report to look. Click the Back button at any time to return to the previous screen, then click it again if you want to return to the screen before that, and continue, if necessary, all the way back to the beginning.

STEP 8: View the Report

➤ If necessary, click the **Maximize button** to see the completed report as shown in Figure 3.8g. Click the **down arrow** on the **Zoom box** to see the full page.

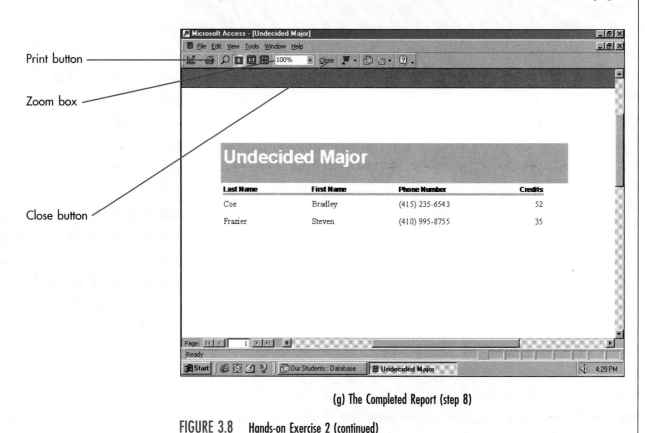

Print button

Zoom box

Close button

(g) The Completed Report (step 8)

FIGURE 3.8   Hands-on Exercise 2 (continued)

➤ Click the **Print button** to print the report and submit it to your instructor. Click the **Close button** to exit the Print Preview window.

➤ Switch to the Query window, then close the Query window.

➤ If necessary, click the **Database Window button** on the toolbar to return to the Database window. Click the **Maximize button**:

- Click the **Queries tab** to display the names of the queries in the Our Students database. You should see the *Undecided Major* query created in this exercise.

- Click the **Reports tab.** You should see two reports: *Student Master List* (created in the previous exercise) and *Undecided Major* (created in this exercise).

- Click the **Forms tab.** You should see the *Students* form corresponding to the form you created in Chapter 2.

- Click the **Tables tab.** You should see the *Students* table that is the basis of the report and query you just created. The *Transfer Students* table will be used later in the chapter.

➤ Close the **Our Students database** and exit Access if you do not wish to continue with the next exercise. Click **Yes** if asked to save changes to any of the objects in the database.

THE BORDER PROPERTY

The Border property enables you to display a border around any type of control. Point to the control (in the Design view), click the right mouse button to display a shortcut menu, then click Properties to display the Properties dialog box. Select the Format tab, click the Border Style property, then choose the type of border you want (e.g., solid to display a border or transparent to suppress a border). Use the Border Color and Border Width properties to change the appearance of the border.

GROUPING RECORDS

The records in a report are often grouped according to the value of a specific field. The report in Figure 3.9a, for example, groups students according to their major, sorts them alphabetically according to last name within each major, then calculates the average GPA for all students in each major. A group header appears before each group of students to identify the group and display the major. A group footer appears at the end of each group and displays the average GPA for students in that major

Figure 3.9b displays the Design view of the report in Figure 3.9a, which determines the appearance of the printed report. Look carefully at the design to relate each section to the corresponding portion of the printed report:

■ The report header contains the title of the report and appears once, at the beginning of the printed report.

■ The page header contains the column headings that appear at the top of each page. The column headings are labels (or unbound controls) and are formatted in bold.

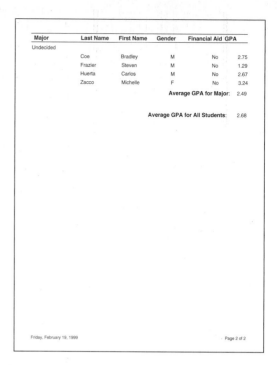

GPA by Major

Major	Last Name	First Name	Gender	Financial Aid	GPA
Business					
	Adili	Ronnie	F	No	2.58
	Cornell	Ryan	M	No	1.78
	DiGiacomo	Kevin	M	Yes	3.57
	Gibson	Christopher	M	Yes	1.71
	Ramsay	Robert	M	Yes	3.24
	Watson	Ana	F	No	2.50
				Average GPA for Major:	2.56
Communications					
	Faulkner	Eileen	F	No	2.67
	Joseph	Cedric	M	Yes	3.78
	Ortiz	Frances	F	Yes	2.14
	Price	Lori	F	Yes	1.75
	Slater	Erica	F	Yes	3.71
				Average GPA for Major:	2.81
Education					
	Korba	Nickolas	M	No	1.66
	Zimmerman	Kimberly	F	No	3.29
				Average GPA for Major:	2.48
Engineering					
	Berlin	Jared	M	Yes	2.50
	Heltzer	Peter	M	No	4.00
	Solomon	Wendy	F	No	3.50
				Average GPA for Major:	3.33
Liberal Arts					
	Camejo	Oscar	M	Yes	2.80
	Parulis	Christa	F	No	1.80
	Watson	Ana	F	Yes	2.79
	Weissman	Kimberly	F	Yes	2.63
				Average GPA for Major:	2.51

Friday, February 19, 1999   Page 1 of 2

Major	Last Name	First Name	Gender	Financial Aid	GPA
Undecided					
	Coe	Bradley	M	No	2.75
	Frazier	Steven	M	No	1.29
	Huerta	Carlos	M	No	2.67
	Zacco	Michelle	F	No	3.24
				Average GPA for Major:	2.49
				Average GPA for All Students:	2.68

Friday, February 19, 1999   Page 2 of 2

(a) The Printed Columnar Report

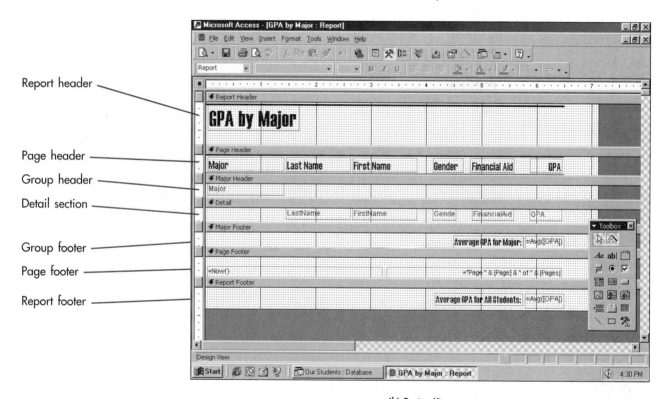

(b) Design View

FIGURE 3.9   Summary Reports

- The group header consists of a single bound control that displays the value of the major field prior to each group of detail records.
- The detail section consists of bound controls that appear directly under the corresponding heading in the page header. The detail section is printed once for each record in each group.

- The group footer appears after each group of detail records. It consists of an unbound control (Average GPA for Major:) followed by a calculated control that computes the average GPA for each group of students.
- The page footer appears at the bottom of each page and contains the date, page number, and total number of pages in the report.
- The report footer appears at the end of the report. It consists of an unbound control (Average GPA for All Students:) followed by a calculated control that computes the average GPA for all students.

Grouping records within a report enables you to perform calculations on each group, as was done in the group footer of Figure 3.9. The calculations in our example made use of the *Avg function,* but other types of calculations are possible:

- The *Sum function* computes the total for a specific field for all records in the group.
- The *Min function* determines the minimum value for all records in the group.
- The *Max function* determines the maximum value for all records in the group.
- The *Count function* counts the number of records in the group.

The following exercise has you create the report in Figure 3.9. The report is based on a query containing a calculated control, GPA, which is computed by dividing the QualityPoints field by the Credits field. The Report Wizard is used to design the basic report, but additional modifications are necessary to create the group header and group footer.

HANDS-ON EXERCISE 3

Grouping Records

Objective: To create a query containing a calculated control, then create a report based on that query; to use the Sorting and Grouping command to add a group header and group footer to a report. Use Figure 3.10 as a guide.

STEP 1: Create the Query

➤ Start Access and open the **Our Students database** from the previous exercise.

➤ Click the **Queries button** in the Database window. Double click **Create query in Design view** to display the Query Design window.

➤ The Show Table dialog box appears; the **Tables tab** is already selected, as is the **Students table.** Click the **Add button** to add the table to the query (the field list should appear within the Query window). Click **Close** to close the Show Table dialog box.

➤ Click the **Maximize button** so that the window takes up the entire screen as shown in Figure 3.10a. Drag the border between the upper and lower portions of the window to give yourself more room in the upper portion. Make the field list larger, to display more fields at one time.

➤ Scroll (if necessary) within the field list, then click and drag the **Major field** from the field list to the query. Click and drag the **LastName, FirstName, Gender, FinancialAid, QualityPoints,** and **Credits fields** (in that order) in similar fashion.

Click and drag to change
size of Field list

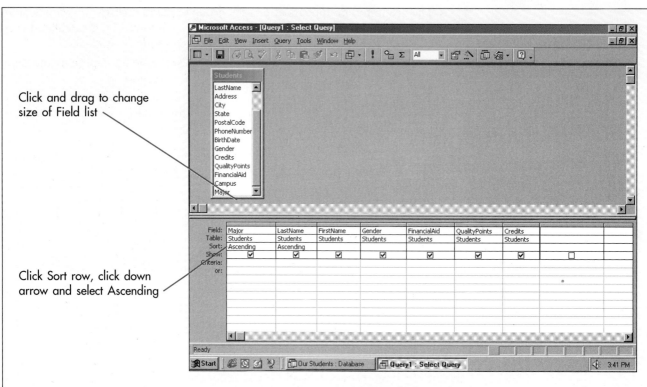

Click Sort row, click down
arrow and select Ascending

(a) Create the Query (step 1)

FIGURE 3.10   Hands-on Exercise 3

➤ Click the **Sort row** for the Major field. Click the **down arrow** to open the drop-down list box. Click **Ascending.**

➤ Click the **Sort row** for the LastName field. Click the **down arrow** to open the drop-down list box. Click **Ascending.**

SORTING ON MULTIPLE FIELDS

You can sort a query on more than one field, but you must be certain that the fields are in the proper order within the design grid. Access sorts from left to right (the leftmost field is the primary sort key), so the fields must be arranged in the desired sort sequence. To move a field within the design grid, click the column selector above the field name to select the column, then drag the column to its new position.

STEP 2: Add a Calculated Control

➤ Click in the first blank column in the Field row. Enter the expression **=[QualityPoints]/[Credits].** Do not be concerned if you cannot see the entire expression.

➤ Press **enter.** Access has substituted Expr1: for the equal sign you typed initially. Drag the **column selector boundary** so that the entire expression is visible as in Figure 3.10b. (You may have to make some of the columns narrower to see all of the fields in the design grid.)

➤ Pull down the **File menu** and click **Save** (or click the **Save button**) to display the dialog box in Figure 3.10b. Enter **GPA By Major** for the Query Name. Click **OK.**

USE DESCRIPTIVE NAMES

An Access database contains multiple objects—tables, forms, queries, and reports. It is important, therefore, that the name assigned to each object be descriptive of its function so that you can select the proper object from the Database window. The name of an object can contain up to 64 characters and can include any combination of letters, numbers, and spaces. (Names may not, however, include leading spaces, a period, an exclamation mark, or brackets ([ ]).

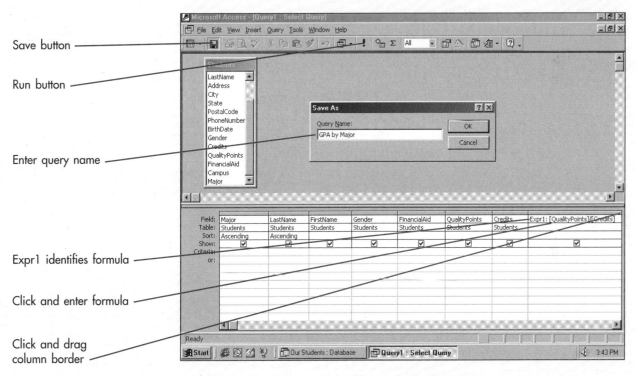

Save button

Run button

Enter query name

Expr1 identifies formula

Click and enter formula

Click and drag column border

(b) Add a Calculated Field (step 2)

FIGURE 3.10   Hands-on Exercise 3 (continued)

STEP 3: Run the Query

➤ Pull down the **Query menu** and click **Run** (or click the **Run button** on the Query Design toolbar). You will see the dynaset in Figure 3.10c:

• Students are listed by major and alphabetically by last name within major.

• The GPA is calculated to several places and appears in the Expr1 field.

➤ Click the **View button** in order to modify the query.

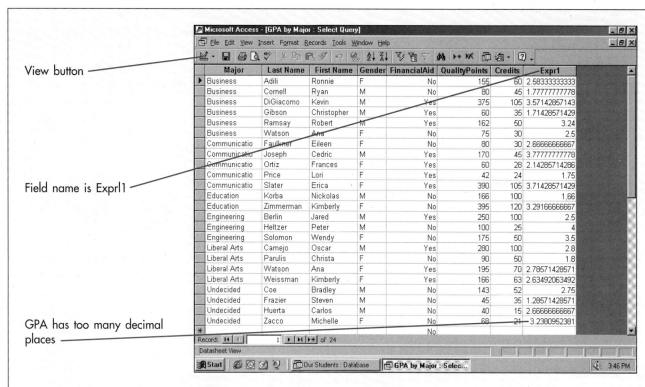

View button

Field name is Exprl1

GPA has too many decimal places

(c) Run the Query (step 3)

FIGURE 3.10   Hands-on Exercise 3 (continued)

ADJUST THE COLUMN WIDTH

Point to the right edge of the column you want to resize, then drag the mouse in the direction you want to go; drag to the right to make the column wider or to the left to make it narrower. Alternatively, you can double click the column selector line (right edge) to fit the longest entry in that column. Adjusting the column width in the Design view does not affect the column width in the Datasheet view, but you can use the same technique in both views.

STEP 4: Modify the Query

➤ Click and drag to select **Expr1** in the Field row for the calculated field. (Do not select the colon). Type **GPA** to substitute a more meaningful field name.

➤ Point to the column and click the **right mouse button** to display a shortcut menu. Click **Properties** to display the Field Properties dialog box in Figure 3.10d. Click the **General tab** if necessary:

- Click the **Description text box.** Enter **GPA** as shown in Figure 3.10d.
- Click the **Format text box.** Click the **drop-down arrow** to display the available formats. Click **Fixed.** Set Decimals to 2.
- Close the Field Properties dialog box.

➤ Click the **Save button** to save the modified query.

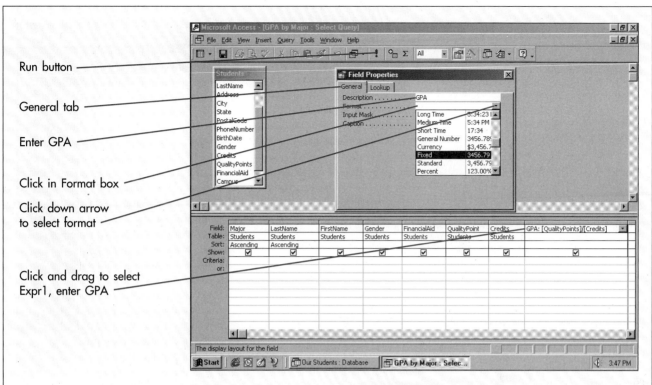

Run button

General tab

Enter GPA

Click in Format box

Click down arrow
to select format

Click and drag to select
Expr1, enter GPA

(d) Modify the Query (step 4)

FIGURE 3.10   Hands-on Exercise 3 (continued)

THE TOP VALUES PROPERTY

Can you create a query that lists only the five students with the highest or lowest GPA? It's easy, if you know about the Top Values property. First, sort the query according to the desired sequence—such as students in descending order by GPA to see the students with the highest GPA. (Remove all other sort keys within the query.) Point anywhere in the gray area in the upper portion of the Query window, click the right mouse button to display a shortcut menu, then click Properties to display the Query Properties sheet. Click the Top Values box and enter the desired number of students (e.g., 5 for five students, or 5% for the top five percent). When you run the query you will see only the top five students. (You can see the bottom five instead if you specify ascending rather than descending as the sort sequence.)

STEP 5: Rerun the Query

➤ Click the **Run button** to run the modified query. You will see a new dynaset corresponding to the modified query as shown in Figure 3.10e. Resize the column widths (as necessary) within the dynaset.

• Students are still listed by major and alphabetically within major.

• The GPA is calculated to two decimal places and appears under the GPA field.

Students are grouped by major and listed alphabetically within major

Field name is GPA

GPA has 2 decimal places

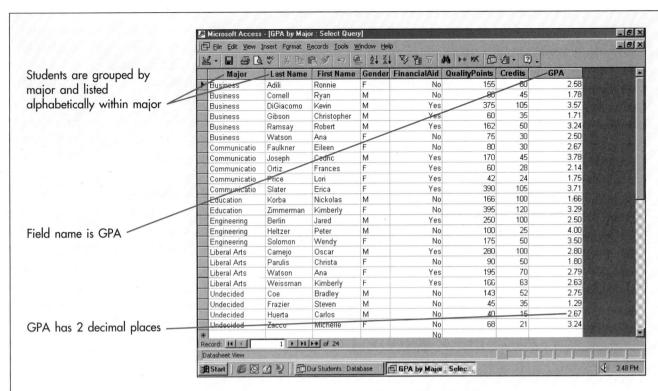

(e) Rerun the Query (step 5)

FIGURE 3.10   Hands-on Exercise 3 (continued)

> ➤ Click the **QualityPoints field** for Christopher Gibson. Replace 60 with **70.** Press **enter.** The GPA changes automatically to 2.
> ➤ Pull down the **Edit menu** and click **Undo Current Field/Record** (or click the **Undo button** on the Query toolbar). The GPA returns to its previous value.
> ➤ Tab to the **GPA field** for Christopher Gibson. Type **2.** Access will beep and prevent you from changing the GPA because it is a calculated field as indicated on the status bar.
> ➤ Click the **Close button** to close the query and return to the Database window. Click **Yes** if asked whether to save the changes.

THE DYNASET

A query represents a question and an answer. The question is developed by using the design grid in the Query Design view. The answer is displayed in a dynaset that contains the records that satisfy the criteria specified in the query. A dynaset looks and acts like a table but it isn't a table; it is a dynamic subset of a table that selects and sorts records as specified in the query. A dynaset is like a table in that you can enter a new record or modify or delete an existing record. It is dynamic because the changes made to the dynaset are automatically reflected in the underlying table.

STEP 6: The Report Wizard

➤ You should see the Database window. Click the **Reports button,** then double click **Create report by using Wizard** to start the Report Wizard.

➤ Select **GPA By Major** from the Tables/Queries drop-down list. The Available fields list displays all of the fields in the GPA by Major query.

  • Click the **Major field** in the Available fields list box. Click the **> button.**

  • Add the **LastName, FirstName, Gender, FinancialAid,** and **GPA fields** one at a time.

  • Do not include the QualityPoints or Credits fields. Click **Next.**

➤ You should see the screen asking whether you want to group the fields. Click (select) the **Major field,** then click the **> button** to display the screen in Figure 3.10f. The Major field appears above the other fields to indicate that the records will be grouped according to the value of the Major field. Click **Next.**

➤ The next screen asks you to specify the order for the detail records. Click the **drop-down arrow** on the list box for the first field. Click **LastName** to sort the records alphabetically by last name within each major. Click **Next.**

➤ The **Stepped Option button** is already selected for the report layout, as is **Portrait orientation.** Be sure the box is checked to **Adjust field width so all fields fit on a page.** Click **Next.**

➤ Choose **Compact** as the style. Click **Next.**

➤ **GPA By Major** (which corresponds to the name of the underlying query) is already entered as the name of the report. Click the Option button to **Modify the report's design.** Click **Finish** to exit the Report Wizard.

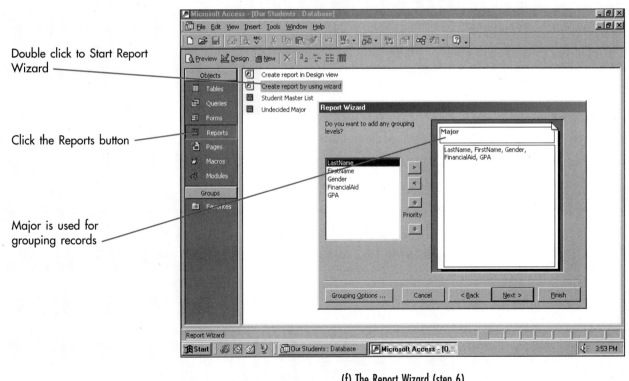

Double click to Start Report Wizard

Click the Reports button

Major is used for grouping records

(f) The Report Wizard (step 6)

FIGURE 3.10   Hands-on Exercise 3 (continued)

STEP 7: Sorting and Grouping

➤ You should see the Report Design view as shown in Figure 3.10g. (The Sorting and Grouping dialog box is not yet visible.)

➤ Maximize the Report window (if necessary) so that you have more room in which to work.

➤ Move, size, and align the column headings and bound controls as shown in Figure 3.10g. We made GPA (label and bound control) smaller. We also moved **Gender** and **FinancialAid** (label and bound control) to the right.

➤ Pull down the **View menu.** Click **Sorting and Grouping** to display the Sorting and Grouping dialog box.

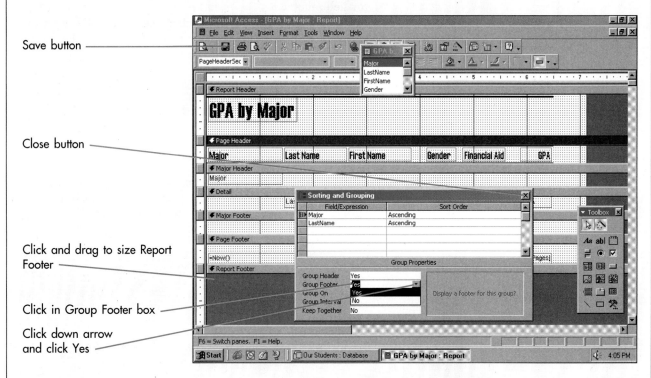

(g) Sorting and Grouping (step 7)

FIGURE 3.10   Hands-on Exercise 3 (continued)

SELECTING MULTIPLE CONTROLS

Select (click) a column heading in the page header, then press and hold the Shift key as you select the corresponding bound control in the Detail section. This selects both the column heading and the bound control and enables you to move and size the objects in conjunction with one another. Continue to work with both objects selected as you apply formatting through various buttons on the Formatting toolbar, or change properties through the property sheet. Click anywhere on the report to deselect the objects when you are finished.

> ➤ The **Major field** should already be selected. Click the **Group Footer** property, click the **drop-down arrow,** then click **Yes** to create a group footer for the Major field.

> ➤ Close the dialog box. The Major footer has been added to the report. Click the Save button to save the modified report.

STEP 8: Create the Group Footer

> ➤ Click the **Text Box button** on the Toolbox toolbar. The mouse pointer changes to a tiny crosshair with a text box attached.

> ➤ Click and drag in the group footer where you want the text box (which will contain the average GPA) to go. Release the mouse.

> ➤ You will see an Unbound control and an attached label containing a field number (e.g., Text 19).

> ➤ Click in the **text box** of the control (Unbound will disappear). Enter **=Avg(GPA)** to calculate the average of the GPA for all students in this group as shown in Figure 3.10h.

> ➤ Click in the attached unbound control, click and drag to select the text (Text19), then type **Average GPA for Major** as the label for this control. Size, move, and align the label as shown in the figure. (See the boxed tip on sizing or moving a control and its label.)

> ➤ Point to the **Average GPA control,** click the **right mouse button** to display a shortcut menu, then click **Properties** to display the Properties dialog box. If necessary, click the **All tab,** then scroll to the top of the list to view and/or modify the existing properties:

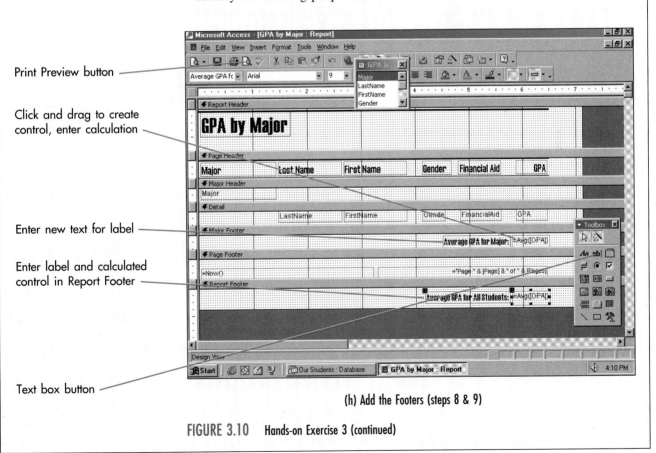

Print Preview button

Click and drag to create control, enter calculation

Enter new text for label

Enter label and calculated control in Report Footer

Text box button

(h) Add the Footers (steps 8 & 9)

FIGURE 3.10   Hands-on Exercise 3 (continued)

- The Control Source text box contains the entry =Avg([GPA]) from the preceding step.
- Click the **Name text box.** Replace the original name (e.g., Text19) with **Average GPA for Major.**
- Click the **Format box.** Click the **drop-down arrow** and select **Fixed.**
- Click the box for the **Decimal places.** Click the **drop-down arrow** and select (click) **2.**
- Close the Properties dialog box to accept these settings and return to the report.

➤ Click the **Save button** on the toolbar.

SIZING OR MOVING A BOUND CONTROL AND ITS LABEL

A bound control is created with an attached label. Select (click) the control, and the control has sizing handles and a move handle, but the label has only a move handle. Select the label (instead of the control), and the opposite occurs: the control has only a move handle, but the label will have both sizing handles and a move handle. To move a control and its label, click and drag the border of either object. To move either the control or its label (but not both), click and drag the move handle (a tiny square in the upper left corner) of the appropriate object. (Use the Undo command if the result is not what you expect; then try again.)

STEP 9: Create the Report Footer

➤ The report footer is created in similar fashion to the group footer. Click and drag the bottom of the report footer to extend the size of the footer as shown in Figure 3.10h.

➤ Click the **Text Box button** on the Toolbox toolbar, then click and drag in the report footer where you want the text box to go. Release the mouse. You will see an Unbound control and an attached label containing a field number (e.g., Text21).

➤ Click in the **text box** of the control (Unbound will disappear). Enter **=Avg(GPA)** to calculate the average of the grade point averages for all students in the report.

➤ Click in the attached label, click and drag to select the text (Text21), then type **Average GPA for All Students** as the label for this control. Move, size, and align the label appropriately.

➤ Size the text box, then format the control:
- Point to the control, click the **right mouse button** to display a shortcut menu, then click **Properties** to display the Properties dialog box. Change the properties to **Fixed Format** with **2 decimal places.** Change the name to **Average GPA for All Students.**
- Close the Properties dialog box to accept these settings and return to the report.

➤ Click the **Save button** on the toolbar.

SECTION PROPERTIES

Each section in a report has properties that control its appearance and behavior. Point to the section header, click the right mouse button to display a shortcut menu, then click Properties to display the property sheet and set the properties. You can hide the section by changing the Visible property to No. You can also change the Special Effect property to Raised or Sunken.

STEP 10: View the Report

➤ Click the **Print Preview button** to view the completed report as shown in Figure 3.10i. The status bar shows you are on page 1 of the report.

➤ Click the **Zoom button** to see the entire page. Click the **Zoom button** a second time to return to the higher magnification, which lets you read the report.

➤ Be sure that you are satisfied with the appearance of the report and that all controls align properly with their associated labels. If necessary, return to the Design view to modify the report.

➤ Pull down the **File menu** and click **Print** (or click the **Print button**) to display the Print dialog box. The **All option button** is already selected under Print Range. Click **OK** to print the report.

➤ Pull down the **File menu** and click **Close** to close the GPA by Major report. Click **Yes** if asked to save design changes to the report.

➤ Close the **Our Students database** and exit Access.

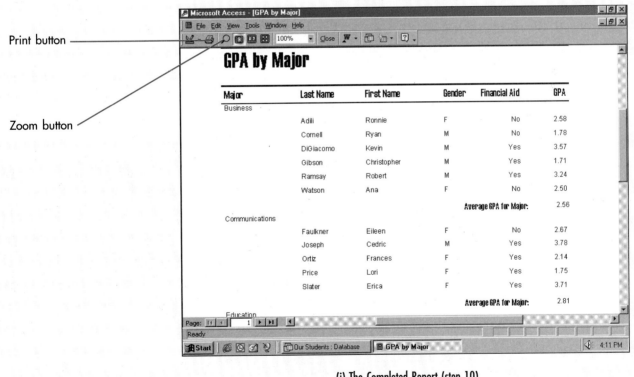

Print button

Zoom button

(i) The Completed Report (step 10)

FIGURE 3.10   Hands-on Exercise 3 (continued)

CROSSTAB QUERIES

We continue the earlier discussion on queries to include more powerful types of queries. A *crosstab query* consolidates data from an Access table and presents the information in a row and column format (similar to a pivot table in Excel). Figure 3.11 shows a crosstab query that displays the average GPA for all students by major and gender. A crosstab query aggregates (sums, counts, or averages) the values of one field (e.g., GPA), then groups the results according to the values of another field listed down the left side of the table (major), and a set of values listed across the top of the table (gender).

A crosstab query can be created in the Query Design view but it is easier to use the Crosstab Query Wizard, as you will see in the hands-on exercise. The Wizard allows you to choose the table (or query) on which the crosstab query is based, then prompts you for the fields to be used for the row and column values (major and gender in our example). You then select the field that will be summarized (GPA), and chose the desired calculation (average). It's easy and you get a chance to practice in the hands-on exercise that follows shortly.

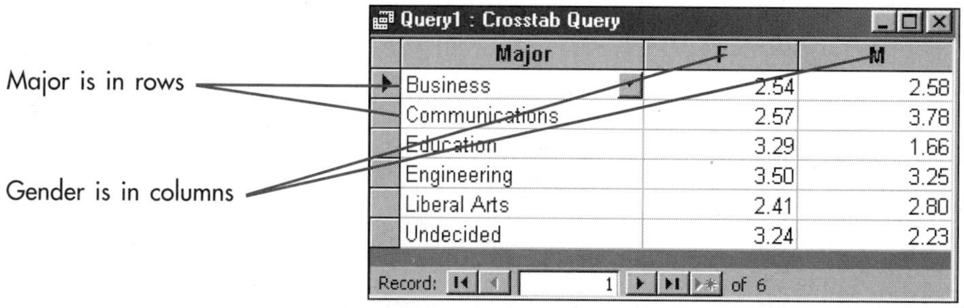

Major is in rows

Gender is in columns

Major	F	M
Business	2.54	2.58
Communications	2.57	3.78
Education	3.29	1.66
Engineering	3.50	3.25
Liberal Arts	2.41	2.80
Undecided	3.24	2.23

FIGURE 3.11   Crosstab Query

ACTION QUERIES

Queries are generally used to extract information from a database. A special type of query, however, known as an *action query,* enables you to update the database by changing multiple records in a single operation. There are four types of action queries: update, append, delete, and make-table.

An *update query* changes multiple records within a table. You could, for example, create an update query to raise the salary of every employee by 10 percent. You can also use criteria in the update query; for example, you can increase the salaries of only those employees with a specified performance rating.

An *append query* adds records from one table to the end of another table. It could be used in the context of the student database to add transfer students to the Students table, given that the transfer records were stored originally in a separate table. An append query can include criteria, so that it adds only selected records from the other table, such as those students with a designated GPA.

A *delete query* deletes one or more records from a table according to designated criteria. You could, for example, use a delete query to remove employees who are no longer working for a company, students who have graduated, or products that are no longer kept in inventory.

A *make-table query* creates a new table from records in an existing table. This type of query is especially useful prior to running a delete query in that you can back up (archive) the records you are about to delete. Thus, you could use a make-table query to create a table containing those students who are about to graduate (e.g., those with 120 credits or more), then run a delete query to remove the graduates from the Students table. You're ready for another hands-on exercise.

Crosstab and Action Queries

Objective: To use action queries to modify a database; to create a crosstab query to display summarized values from a table. Use Figure 3.12 as a guide.

STEP 1: Create the Make-Table Query

➤ Start Access and open the **Our Students database.** Click the **Queries button** in the Database window, then double click **Create query in Design view.**

➤ The Show Table dialog box appears automatically with the Tables tab already selected. If necessary, select the **Students table,** then click the **Add button** to add the table to the query as shown in Figure 3.12a. Close the Show Table dialog box. Maximize the query window.

➤ Click the **SSN** (the first field) in the Students table. Press and hold the **Shift key,** then scroll (if necessary) until you can click **Major** (the last field) in the table. Click and drag the selected fields (i.e., every field in the table) from the field list to the design grid in Figure 3.12a.

➤ Scroll in the design grid until you can see the Credits field. Click in the Criteria row for the Credits field and enter **>=120.**

➤ Click the **drop-down arrow** next to the **Query Type button** on the toolbar and select (click) the **make-table query** as shown in Figure 3.12a. Enter **Graduating Seniors** as the name of the table you will create.

➤ Verify that the option button for Current Database is selected then click **OK.**

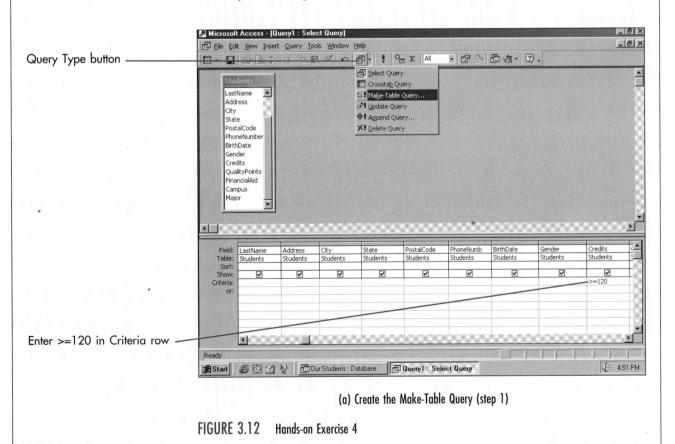

(a) Create the Make-Table Query (step 1)

FIGURE 3.12 Hands-on Exercise 4

STEP 2: Run the Make-Table Query

➤ Click the **Run button** to run the make-table query. Click **Yes** in response to the message in Figure 3.12b indicating that you are about to paste one record (for the graduating seniors) into a new table.

➤ Do not be concerned if you do not see the Graduating Seniors table at this time; i.e., unlike a select query, you remain in the Design view after executing the make-table query. Close the make-table query. Save the query as **Archive Graduating Seniors.**

➤ Click the **Tables button** in the Database window, then open the **Graduating Seniors** table you just created. The table should contain one record (for Kim Zimmerman) with 120 or more credits. Close the table.

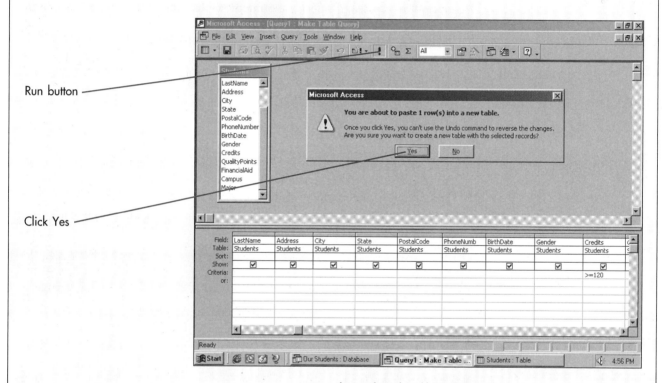

(b) Run the Make-Table Query (step 2)

FIGURE 3.12 Hands-on Exercise 4 (continued)

LOOK BEFORE YOU LEAP

The result of an action query is irreversible; that is, once you click Yes in the dialog box displayed by the query, you cannot undo the action. You can, however, preview the result before creating the query by clicking the View button at the left of the Query design toolbar. Click the button and you see the results of the query displayed in a dynaset, then click the View button a second time to return to the Design view. Click the Run Query button to execute the query, but now you can click Yes with confidence since you have seen the result.

STEP 3: Create the Delete Table Query

➤ Click the **Queries button** in the Database window, then click the **Archive Graduating Seniors** query to select the query. Pull down the **Edit menu.** Click **Copy** to copy the query to the clipboard.

➤ Pull down the **Edit menu** a second time, then click the **Paste command** to display the Paste As dialog box in Figure 3.12c. Type **Purge Graduating Seniors** as the name of the query, then click **OK.**

➤ The Database window contains the original query (Archive Graduating Seniors) as well as the copied version (Purge Graduating Seniors) you just created.

Click the Queries button

Click Archive Graduating Seniors

Enter name for new query

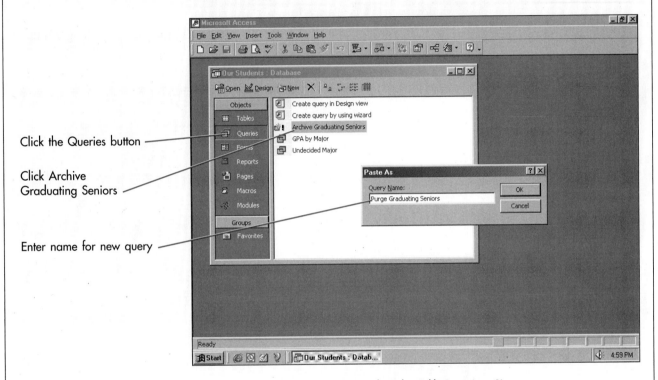

(c) Create the Delete Table Query (step 3)

FIGURE 3.12   Hands-on Exercise 4 (continued)

COPY, RENAME, OR DELETE AN ACCESS OBJECT

Use the Copy and Paste commands in the Database window to copy any object in an Access database. To copy an object, select the object, pull down the Edit menu and click Copy (or use the Ctrl+C keyboard shortcut). Pull down the Edit menu a second time and select the Paste command (or use the Ctrl+V shortcut), then enter a name for the copied object. To delete or rename an object, point to the object then click the right mouse button to display a shortcut menu and select the desired operation.

STEP 4: Complete and Run the Delete Table Query

➤ Open the newly created query in the Design view. Maximize the window. Click the **drop-down arrow** next to the **Query Type button** on the toolbar and select (click) the **Delete Query.**

➤ Click and drag the box on the horizontal scroll bar until you can see the Credits field as shown in Figure 3.12d. The criteria, >= 120, is already entered because the Delete query was copied originally from Make Table query and the criteria are identical.

➤ Click the **Run button** to execute the query. Click **Yes** when warned that you are about to delete one record from the specified table. Once again, you remain in the design view after the query has been executed. Close the query window. Click **Yes** if asked to save the changes.

➤ Open the **Students table.** The record for Kim Zimmerman is no longer there. Close the Students table.

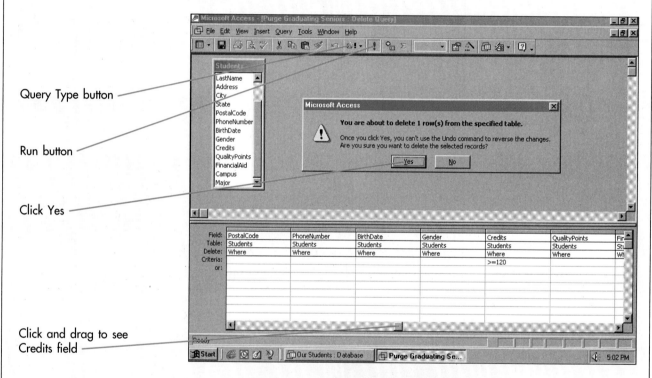

Query Type button

Run button

Click Yes

Click and drag to see Credits field

(d) Run the Delete Table Query (step 4)

FIGURE 3.12   Hands-on Exercise 4 (continued)

PLAN FOR THE UNEXPECTED

Deleting records is cause for concern in that once the records are removed from a table, they cannot be restored. This may not be a problem, but it is comforting to have some means of recovery. Accordingly, we always execute a Make Table query, with the identical criteria as in the delete query, prior to running the latter. The records in the newly created table can be restored through an append query should it be necessary.

STEP 5: Create the Append Table Query

➤ Click the **Queries button** then double click **Create query in Design view.** The Show Tables dialog box opens and contains the following tables:

• The Students table that you have used throughout the chapter.

• The Graduating Seniors table that you just created.

• The Transfer Students table that will be appended to the Students table.

➤ Select the **Transfer Students** table then click the **Add button** to add this table to the query. Close the Show Table dialog box. Maximize the window. Click and drag the **asterisk** from the field list to the query design grid.

➤ Click the **drop-down arrow** next to the **Query Type button** on the toolbar and select (click) **Append Query** to display the Append dialog box. Click the **drop-down arrow** on the Append to Table name list box and select the **Students table** as shown in Figure 3.12e. Click **OK.**

➤ Click the **Run button.** Click **Yes** when warned that you are about to add 4 rows (from the Transfer Students table to the Students table).

➤ Save the query as **Append Transfer Students.** Close the query window.

➤ Open the **Students table.** Four records have been added (Liquer, Thomas, Rudolph, Milgrom). Close the table.

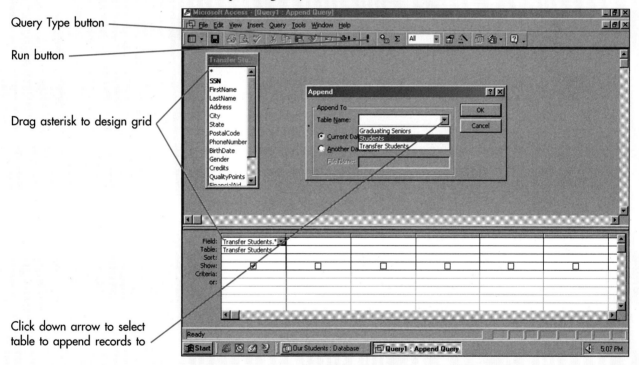

Query Type button

Run button

Drag asterisk to design grid

Click down arrow to select table to append records to

(e) Create the Append Table Query (step 5)

FIGURE 3.12 Hands-on Exercise 4 (continued)

THE ASTERISK VERSUS INDIVIDUAL FIELDS

Click and drag the asterisk in the field list to the design grid to add every field in the underlying table to the query. The advantage to this approach is that it is quicker than selecting the fields individually. The disadvantage is that you cannot sort or specify criteria for individual fields.

STEP 6: Create an Update Query

➤ Click the **Query button** in the Database window. Select (click) the **GPA by Major query,** press **Ctrl+C** to copy the query, then press **Ctrl+V** to display the Paste as dialog box. Enter **Update Financial Aid.** Click **OK.**

➤ Open the newly created query in the Design view as shown in Figure 3.12f. Click the **drop-down arrow** next to the **Query Type button** on the toolbar and select (click) **Update Query.** The query grid changes to include an Update To:row and the Sort row disappears.

➤ Click in the Criteria row for the **GPA field** and enter **>=3.** Click in the Update To row for the FinancialAid field and enter **Yes.** The combination of these entries will change the value of the Financial Aid field to "yes" for all students with a GPA of 3.00 or higher.

➤ Click the **Run button** to execute the query. Click **Yes** when warned that you are about to update nine records. Close the query window. Click **Yes** if asked whether to save the changes.

Query Type button

Run button

Click Yes

Enter Yes in Update to row

Enter >=3 in Criteria row

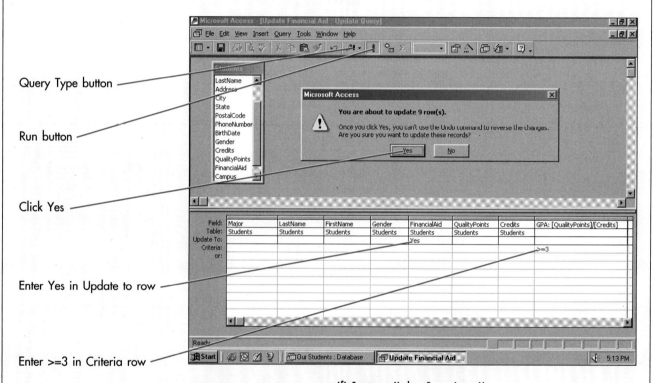

(f) Create an Update Query (step 6)

FIGURE 3.12   Hands-on Exercise 4 (continued)

VERIFY THE RESULTS OF THE UPDATE QUERY

You have run the Update Query, but are you sure it worked correctly? Press the F11 key to return to the Database window, click the Queries button, and rerun the GPA by Major query that was created earlier. Click in the GPA field for the first student, then click the Sort Descending button to display the students in descending order by GPA. Every student with a GPA of 3.00 or higher should be receiving financial aid.

STEP 7: Check Your Progress

➤ Click the **Tables button** in the Database window. Open (double click) the Students, Graduating Seniors, and Transfer Students tables one after another. You have to return to the Database window each time you open a table.

➤ Pull down the **Window menu** and click the **Tile Vertically command** to display the tables as shown in Figure 3.12g. The arrangement of your tables may be different from ours.

➤ Check your progress by comparing the tables to one another:

- Check the first record in the Transfer Students table, Lindsey Liquer, and note that it has been added to the Students table via the Append Transfer Students query.

- Check the record in the Graduating Senior table, Kim Zimmerman, and note that it has been removed from the Students table via the Purge Graduating Seniors query.

- The Students table reflects the current student database. The other two tables function as back up.

➤ Close the Students, Transfer Students, and Graduating Seniors tables.

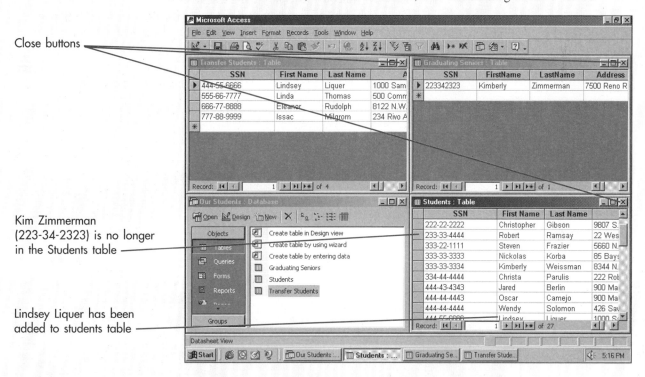

(g) Check Results of the Action Queries (step 7)

FIGURE 3.12   Hands-on Exercise 4 (continued)

DATABASE PROPERTIES

The buttons within the Database window display the objects within a database, but show only one type of object at a time. You can, for example, see all of the reports or all of the queries, but you cannot see the reports and queries at the same time. There is another way. Pull down the File menu, click Database Properties, then click the Contents tab to display the contents (objects) in the database.

STEP 8: Create a Crosstab Query

➤ Click the **Queries button** in the Database window, click **New,** click the **Crosstab Query Wizard** in the New Query dialog box and click **OK** to start the wizard.

➤ Click the **Queries option button** and select the **GPA by Major query.** Click **Next.**

• Click **Major** in the available field list, then click **>** to place it in the selected fields list. Click **Next.**

• Click **Gender** as the field for column headings. Click **Next.**

• Click **GPA** as the field to calculate and select the **Avg function** as shown in Figure 3.12h. Clear the check box to include row sums. Click **Next.**

• The name of the query is suggested for you, as is the option button to view the query. Click **Finish.**

➤ The results of the crosstab query are shown. The query lists the average GPA for each combination of major and gender. The display is awkward, however, in that the GPA is calculated to an unnecessary number of decimal places.

➤ Click the **View button** to display the Design view for this query. Right click in the **GPA column** to display a context-sensitive menu, click **Properties** to display the Field Properties dialog box, click in the **Format row,** and select **Fixed.** Set the number of decimals to **two.**

➤ Click the **Run button** to re-execute the query. This time the GPA is displayed to two decimal places. Save the query. Close the Query window.

➤ Close the Our Students database. Exit Access.

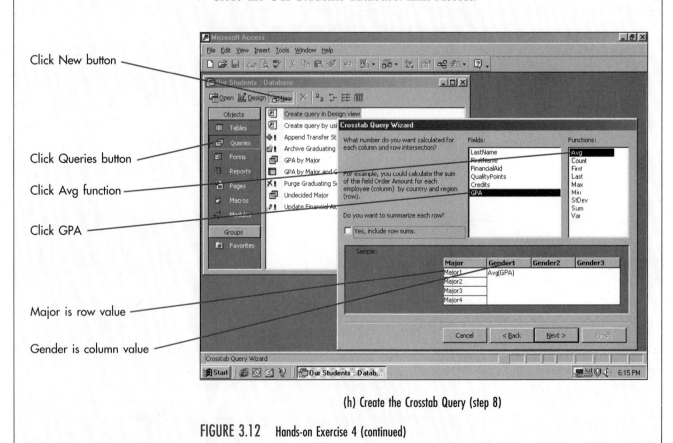

(h) Create the Crosstab Query (step 8)

FIGURE 3.12   Hands-on Exercise 4 (continued)

Data and information are not synonymous. Data refers to a fact or facts about a specific record. Information is data that has been rearranged into a more useful format. Data may be viewed as the raw material, whereas information is the finished product.

A report is a printed document that displays information from the database. Reports are created through the Report Wizard, then modified as necessary in the Design view. A report is divided into sections. The report header (footer) occurs at the beginning (end) of the report. The page header (footer) appears at the top (bottom) of each page. The detail section is found in the main body of the report and is printed once for each record in the report.

Each section is comprised of objects known as controls. A bound control has a data source such as a field in the underlying table. An unbound control has no data source. A calculated control contains an expression. Controls are selected, moved, and sized the same way as any other Windows object.

Every report is based on either a table or a query. A report based on a table contains every record in that table. A report based on a query contains only the records satisfying the criteria in the query.

A query enables you to select records from a table (or from several tables), display the selected records in any order, and perform calculations on fields within the query. A select query is the most common type of query and is created using the design grid. A select query displays its output in a dynaset that can be used to update the data in the underlying table(s).

The records in a report are often grouped according to the value of a specific field within the record. A group header appears before each group to identify the group. A group footer appears at the end of each group and can be used to display the summary information about the group.

An action query modifies one or more records in a single operation. There are four types of action queries: update, append, delete, and make-table. An update query changes multiple records within a table. An append query adds records from one table to the end of another table. A delete query deletes one or more records from a table according to designated criteria. A make-table query creates a new table from records in an existing table.

A crosstab query displays aggregated information as opposed to individual records. It can be created directly in the Query Design view, but is created more easily through the Crosstab Query Wizard.

KEY WORDS AND CONCEPTS

Action query	Crosstab query	Inheritance
AND condition	Database Properties	Label tool
Append query	Datasheet view	Make-table query
Ascending sequence	Delete query	Max function
Avg function	Descending sequence	Min function
Between function	Design grid	NOT function
Bound control	Design view	Now function
Calculated control	Detail section	OR condition
Columnar report	Dynaset	Page footer
Compacting	Field row	Page header
Count function	Group footer	Print Preview
Criteria row	Group header	Query

Query window	Select query	Text box tool
Relational operators	Show row	Top Values property
Report	Sort row	Unbound control
Report footer	Sorting and Grouping	Update query
Report header	Sum function	Wild card
Report Wizard	Tabular report	

MULTIPLE CHOICE

1. Which of the following is a reason for basing a report on a query rather than a table?
   (a) To limit the report to selected records
   (b) To include a calculated field in the report
   (c) Both (a) and (b)
   (d) Neither (a) nor (b)

2. An Access database may contain:
   (a) One or more tables
   (b) One or more queries
   (c) One or more reports
   (d) All of the above

3. Which of the following is true regarding the names of objects within an Access database?
   (a) A form or report may have the same name as the underlying table
   (b) A form or report may have the same name as the underlying query
   (c) Both (a) and (b)
   (d) Neither (a) nor (b)

4. The dynaset created by a query may contain:
   (a) A subset of records from the associated table but must contain all of the fields for the selected records
   (b) A subset of fields from the associated table but must contain all of the records
   (c) Both (a) and (b)
   (d) Neither (a) nor (b)

5. Which toolbar contains a button to display the properties of a selected object?
   (a) The Query Design toolbar
   (b) The Report Design toolbar
   (c) Both (a) and (b)
   (d) Neither (a) nor (b)

6. Which of the following does *not* have both a Design view and a Datasheet view?
   (a) Tables
   (b) Forms
   (c) Queries
   (d) Reports

7. Which of the following is true regarding the wild card character within Access?
   (a) A question mark stands for a single character in the same position as the question mark
   (b) An asterisk stands for any number of characters in the same position as the asterisk
   (c) Both (a) and (b)
   (d) Neither (a) nor (b)

8. Which of the following will print at the top of every page?
   (a) Report header
   (b) Group header
   (c) Both (a) and (b)
   (d) Neither (a) nor (b)

9. A query, based on the Our Students database within the chapter, contains two fields from the Student table (QualityPoints and Credits) as well as a calculated field (GPA). Which of the following is true?
   (a) Changing the value of Credits or QualityPoints in the query's dynaset automatically changes these values in the underlying table
   (b) Changing the value of GPA automatically changes its value in the underlying table
   (c) Both (a) and (b)
   (d) Neither (a) nor (b)

10. Which of the following must be present in every report?
    (a) A report header and a report footer
    (b) A page header and a page footer
    (c) Both (a) and (b)
    (d) Neither (a) nor (b)

11. Which of the following may be included in a report as well as in a form?
    (a) Bound control
    (b) Unbound control
    (c) Calculated control
    (d) All of the above

12. The navigation buttons ▶ and ◀ will:
    (a) Move to the next or previous record in a table
    (b) Move to the next or previous page in a report
    (c) Both (a) and (b)
    (d) Neither (a) nor (b)

13. Assume that you created a query based on an Employee table, and that the query contains fields for Location and Title. Assume further that there is a single criteria row and that New York and Manager have been entered under the Location and Title fields, respectively. The dynaset will contain:
    (a) All employees in New York
    (b) All managers
    (c) Only the managers in New York
    (d) All employees in New York and all managers

14. You have decided to modify the query from the previous question to include a second criteria row. The Location and Title fields are still in the query, but this time New York and Manager appear in *different* criteria rows. The dynaset will contain:
   (a) All employees in New York
   (b) All managers
   (c) Only the managers in New York
   (d) All employees in New York and all managers

15. Which of the following is true about a query that lists employees by city and alphabetically within city?
   (a) The design grid should specify a descending sort on both city and employee name
   (b) The City field should appear to the left of the employee name in the design grid
   (c) Both (a) and (b)
   (d) Neither (a) nor (b)

Answers

1. c	6. d	11. d
2. d	7. c	12. c
3. c	8. d	13. c
4. d	9. a	14. d
5. d	10. d	15. b

PRACTICE WITH MICROSOFT ACCESS 2000

1. The Our Students Database: Use the Our Students database as the basis for the following queries and reports:
   a. Create a select query for students on the Dean's List (GPA >= 3.50). Include the student's name, major, quality points, credits, and GPA. List the students alphabetically.
   b. Use the Report Wizard to prepare a tabular report based on the query in part a. Include your name in the report header as the academic advisor.
   c. Create a select query for students on academic probation (GPA < 2.00). Include the same fields as the query in part a. List the students in alphabetical order.
   d. Use the Report Wizard to prepare a tabular report similar to the report in part b.
   e. Print both reports and submit them to your instructor as proof that you did this exercise.

2. The Employee Database: Use the Employee database in the Exploring Access folder to create the reports listed in parts (a) and (b). (This is the same database that was used earlier in Chapters 1 and 2.)
   a. A report containing all employees in sequence by location and alphabetically within location. Show the employee's last name, first name, location, title, and salary. Include summary statistics to display the total salaries in each location as well as for the company as a whole.

   b. A report containing all employees in sequence by title and alphabetically within title. Show the employee's last name, first name, location, title, and salary. Include summary statistics to show the average salary for each title as well as the average salary in the company.

   c. Add your name to the report header in the report so that your instructor will know the reports came from you. Print both reports and submit them to your instructor.

3. The United States Database: Use the United States database in the Exploring Access folder to create the report shown in Figure 3.13 on page 154. (This is the same database that was used in Chapters 1 and 2.) The report lists states by geographic region, and alphabetically within region. It includes a calculated field, Population Density, which is computed by dividing a state's population by its area. Summary statistics are also required as shown in the report.

   Note that the report header contains a map of the United States that was taken from the Microsoft Clip Gallery. The instructions for inserting an object can be found on page 100 in conjunction with an earlier problem. Be sure to include your name in the report footer so that your instructor will know that the report comes from you.

4. The Bookstore Database: Use the Bookstore database in the Exploring Access folder to create the report shown in Figure 3.14 on page 155. (This is the same database that was used in the hands-on exercises in Chapter 1.)

   The report header in Figure 3.14 contains a graphic object that was taken from the Microsoft Clip Gallery. You are not required to use this specific image, but you are required to insert a graphic. The instructions for inserting an object can be found on page 100 in conjunction with an earlier problem. Be sure to include your name in the report header so that your instructor will know that the report comes from you.

5. Use the Super Bowl database in the Exploring Access folder to create the report in Figure 3.15 on page 156, which lists the participants and scores in every game played to date. It also displays the Super Bowl logo, which we downloaded from the home page of the NFL (www.nfl.com). Be sure to include your name in the report footer so that your instructor will know that the report comes from you. (See the Super Bowl case study for suggestions on additional reports or queries that you can create from this database.)

6. Database Properties: Do the four hands-on exercises in the chapter, then prove to your instructor that you have completed the exercises by capturing the screen in Figure 3.16 on page 157. Proceed as follows:

   a. Complete the exercises, then pull down the File menu and select Database Properties to display the Properties dialog box in Figure 3.16. Click the Contents tab to list all of the objects in the database.

   b. Press the Alt+PrintScreen key to copy the screen to the clipboard (an area of memory that is available to every Windows application).

   c. Click the Start button, click Programs, click Accessories, then click Paint to open the Paint accessory. If necessary, click the maximize button so that the Paint window takes the entire desktop.

   d. Pull down the Edit menu. Click Paste to copy the screen from the clipboard to the drawing. Click Yes if you are asked to enlarge the bitmap.

   e. Click the text tool (the capital A), then click and drag in the drawing area to create a dotted rectangle that will contain the message to your instructor. Type the text indicating that you did the exercises. (If necessary, pull down the View menu and check the command for the Text toolbar. This enables you to change the font and/or point size.) Click outside the text to deselect it.

United States by Region

Prepared by Gregg Kuehnel

Region	Name	Capital	Population	Area	Population Density
Middle Atlantic					
	Delaware	Dover	666,168	2,057	323.85
	Maryland	Annapolis	4,781,468	10,577	452.06
	New Jersey	Trenton	7,730,188	7,836	986.50
	New York	Albany	17,990,455	49,576	362.89
	Pennsylvania	Harrisburg	11,881,643	45,333	262.10
	Total for Region		**43,049,922**	**115,379**	
	Average for Region		**8,609,984**	**23,076**	**477.48**
Mountain					
	Arizona	Phoenix	3,665,228	113,909	32.18
	Colorado	Denver	3,294,394	104,247	31.60
	Idaho	Boise	1,006,749	83,557	12.05
	Montana	Helena	799,065	147,138	5.43
	Nevada	Carson City	1,201,833	110,540	10.87
	New Mexico	Santa Fe	1,515,069	121,666	12.45
	Utah	Salt Lake City	1,722,850	84,916	20.29
	Wyoming	Cheyenne	453,588	97,914	4.63
	Total for Region		**13,658,776**	**863,887**	
	Average for Region		**1,707,347**	**107,986**	**16.19**
New England					
	Connecticut	Hartford	3,287,116	5,009	656.24
	Maine	Augusta	1,227,928	33,215	36.97
	Massachusetts	Boston	6,016,425	8,257	728.65
	New	Concord	1,109,252	9,304	119.22
	Rhode Island	Providence	1,003,464	1,214	826.58
	Vermont	Montpelier	562,758	9,609	58.57
	Total for Region		**13,206,943**	**66,608**	
	Average for Region		**2,201,157**	**11,101**	**404.37**
North Central					
	Illinois	Springfield	11,430,602	56,400	202.67
	Indiana	Indianapolis	5,544,159	36,291	152.77
	Iowa	Des Moines	2,776,755	56,290	49.33
	Kansas	Topeka	2,477,574	82,264	30.12

FIGURE 3.13 The United States Database (Exercise 3)

University of Miami
Book Store

Prepared by Gregg Kuehnel

Publisher	ISBN	Author	Title	ListPrice
Macmillan Publishing				
	1-56686-127-6	Rosch	The Hardware Bible	$35.00
			Number of Books:	1
			Average List Price:	$35.00
McGraw Hill				
	0-07-029387-2	Hofstetter	Internet Literacy	$45.00
	0-07-041127-1	Martinez	Getting Ahead by Getting	$39.95
	0-07-054048-9	Rothstein	Ace the Technical Interview	$24.95
	0-07-070318-3	Willard	The Cybernetics Reader	$15.75
			Number of Books:	4
			Average List Price:	$31.41
Prentice Hall				
	013-011100-7	Grauer/Barber	Exploring Microsoft Office 2000	$45.00
	0-13-011108-2	Grauer/Barber	Exploring Excel 2000	$28.95
	0-13-011190-0	Grauer/Barber	Exploring Microsoft Office 2000	$45.00
	0-13-011816-8	Grauer/Barber	Exploring PowerPoint 2000	$28.95
	0-13-020476-5	Grauer/Barber	Exploring Access 2000	$28.95
	0-13-020489-7	Grauer/Barber	Exploring Word 2000	$28.95
	0-13-065541-4	Grauer/Barber	Exploring Windows 3.1	$24.95
	0-13-504077-9	Grauer/Barber	Exploring Windows 95	$28.95
	0-13-754193-7	Grauer/Barber	Exploring Windows 98	$28.95
	0-13-754201-1	Grauer/Barber	Exploring Word 97	$30.95
	0-13-754219-1	Grauer/Barber	Exploring Excel 97	$30.95
	0-13-754227-5	Grauer/Barber	Exploring Access 97	$30.95
	0-13-754235-6	Grauer/Barber	Exploring PowerPoint 97	$30.95
	0-13-790817-2	Grauer/ Villar	COBOL: From Micro to Mainframe	$52.95
			Number of Books:	14
			Average List Price:	$33.24

Friday, February 19, 1999   **Page 1 of 2**

FIGURE 3.14   *The Bookstore Database (Exercise 4)*

Super Bowl

Year	AFC Team	AFC Score	NFC Team	NFC Score
1999	Denver	34	Atlanta	19
1998	Denver	31	Green Bay	24
1997	New England	21	Green Bay	35
1996	Pittsburgh	17	Dallas	27
1995	San Diego	26	San Francisco	49
1994	Buffalo	13	Dallas	30
1993	Buffalo	17	Dallas	52
1992	Buffalo	24	Washington	37
1991	Buffalo	19	Giants	20
1990	Denver	10	San Francisco	55
1989	Cincinnati	16	San Francisco	20
1988	Denver	10	Washington	42
1987	Denver	20	Giants	39
1986	New England	10	Chicago	46
1985	Miami	16	San Francisco	38
1984	Los Angeles Raiders	38	Washington	9
1983	Miami	17	Washington	27
1982	Cincinnati	21	San Francisco	26
1981	Oakland	27	Philadelphia	10
1980	Pittsburgh	31	Los Angeles	19
1979	Pittsburgh	35	Dallas	31
1978	Denver	10	Dallas	27
1977	Oakland	32	Minnesota	14
1976	Pittsburgh	21	Dallas	17
1975	Pittsburgh	16	Minnesota	6
1974	Miami	24	Minnesota	7
1973	Miami	14	Washington	7
1972	Miami	3	Dallas	24
1971	Baltimore	16	Dallas	13
1970	Kansas City	23	Minnesota	7

Friday, February 19, 1999   Page 1 of 2

FIGURE 3.15   The Super Bowl Database (Exercise 5)

f. Pull down the File menu and click the Page Setup command to display the Page Setup dialog box. Click the Landscape option button. Change the margins to one inch all around. Click OK.

g. Pull down the File menu a second time. Click Print. Click OK.

h. Exit Paint. Submit the document to your instructor.

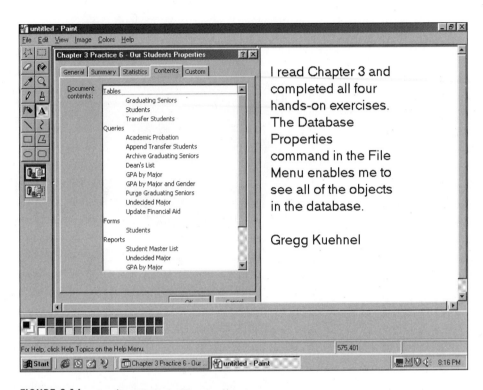

FIGURE 3.16   Database Properties (Exercise 6)

7. Action Queries: Open the Employees database that has been referenced throughout the text. The table in Figure 3.17 reflects the results of the earlier exercises in Chapters 1 and 2. If necessary, modify the data in your table so that it matches ours, then create and run the following action queries:

   a. A make-table query containing the complete records for all employees with poor performance.

   b. A Delete query to remove the employees with poor performance from the Employee table.

   c. An Update query to award a 10% increase to all employees with a good performance rating. (Use Salary*1.1 as the entry in the Update to column.) Be sure to run this query only once.

   d. Print the Employees table after all of the queries have been run.

8. The Switchboard Manager: The Switchboard Manager was not covered in the chapter, but it is worth exploring, especially if you want to develop a database that is easy to use. A switchboard is a user interface that enables a nontechnical person to access the various objects in an Access database by clicking the appropriate command button. The switchboard in Figure 3.18 enables the user to click any button to display the indicated form or report. Use the Help command to learn about the Switchboard Manager, then try your hand at creating your own switchboard. It's much easier than you might think. Note, too, you can modify the design of the Switchboard form (just as you can change the design of any form) to include your name and/or a graphic image as in Figure 3.18.

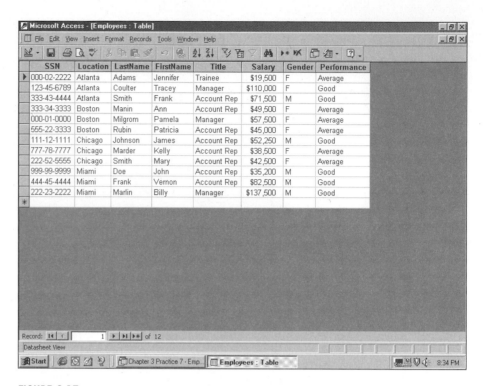

FIGURE 3.17   Action Queries (Exercise 7)

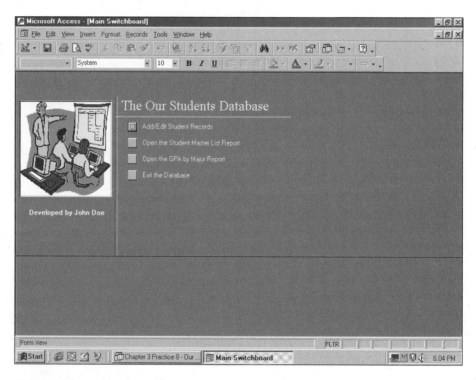

FIGURE 3.18   The Switchboard Manager (Exercise 8)

The United States of America

What is the total population of the United States? What is its area? Can you name the 13 original states or the last five states admitted to the Union? Do you know the 10 states with the highest population or the five largest states in terms of area? Which states have the highest population density (people per square mile)?

The answers to these and other questions can be obtained from the United States database that is available on the data disk. The key to the assignment is to use the Top Values property within a query that limits the number of records returned in the dynaset. Use the database to create several reports that you think will be of interest to the class.

The Super Bowl

How many times has the NFC won the Super Bowl? When was the last time the AFC won? What was the largest margin of victory? What was the closest game? What is the most points scored by two teams in one game? How many times have the Miami Dolphins appeared? How many times did they win? Use the data in the Super Bowl database to create a trivia sheet on the Super Bowl, then incorporate your analysis into a letter addressed to NBC Sports. Convince them you are a super fan and that you merit two tickets to next year's game. Go to the home page of the National Football League (www.nfl.com) to obtain score(s) from the most recent game(s) to update our table if necessary.

Mail Merge

A mail merge takes the tedium out of sending form letters, as it creates the same letter many times, changing the name, address, and other information as appropriate from letter to letter. The form letter is created in a word processor (e.g., Microsoft Word), but the data file may be taken from an Access table or query. Use the Our Students database as the basis for two different form letters sent to two different groups of students. The first letter is to congratulate students on the Dean's list (GPA of 3.50 or higher). The second letter is a warning to students on academic probation (GPA of less than 2.00).

Compacting versus Compressing

An Access database becomes fragmented, and thus unnecessarily large, as objects (e.g., reports and forms) are modified or deleted. It is important, therefore, to periodically compact a database to reduce its size (enabling you to back it up on a floppy disk). Choose a database with multiple objects; e.g., the Our Students database used in this chapter. Use the Windows Explorer to record the file size of the database as it presently exists. Start Access, open the database, pull down the Tools menu and select Database Utilities to compact the database, then record the size of the database after compacting. You can also compress a compacted database (using a standard Windows utility such as WinZip) to further reduce the requirement for disk storage. Summarize your findings in a short report to your instructor. Try compacting and compressing at least two different databases to better appreciate these techniques.

chapter 4

PROFICIENCY: RELATIONAL DATABASES, EXTERNAL DATA, CHARTS, AND THE SWITCHBOARD

OBJECTIVES

After reading this chapter you will be able to:

1. Describe the one-to-many relationships in an Access database; explain how these relationships facilitate the retrieval of information.

2. Use the Relationships window to create a one-to-many relationship; print the relationships in a database.

3. Use the Get External Data command to import and/or link data from an external source into an Access database; export database objects to an Excel workbook.

4. Create and modify a multiple-table select query.

5. Use aggregate functions to create a totals query.

6. Use Microsoft Graph to create a chart based on a table or query for inclusion in a form or report.

7. Use the Switchboard Manager to create and/or modify a switchboard.

8. Use Access utilities to compact and repair a database, and to convert a database to a previous version of Access.

OVERVIEW

Each application in Microsoft Office is independent of the others, but it is often necessary or advantageous to share data between the applications. Data may be collected in Excel, imported or linked to an Access database to take advantage of its relational capability, then exported back to Excel for data analysis, or to Microsoft Word for a mail merge. This chapter describes how to share data between applications in the context of a database for an investment firm.

Unlike the examples from Chapters 2 and 3, the investment database is a relational database with two tables, one for clients, and one for financial consultants. Data from both tables can be displayed in a single query that contains fields from each table, and therein lies the real power of Microsoft Access. The chapter also introduces the concept of a total query that aggregates results from groups of records to produce summary information. The results of a total query are then presented in graphical form through Microsoft Graph, an application that is contained in Microsoft Office.

The last portion of the chapter describes the creation of a user interface (or switchboard) that lets a nontechnical person move easily from one object to another by clicking a menu item. The switchboard is created through the Switchboard Manager, one of several utilities in Microsoft Access. Other utilities, to compact or repair a database and/or convert it to a previous version, are also discussed.

THE INVESTMENT DATABASE

The database in Figure 4.1 is designed for an investment firm that monitors its clients and their financial consultants. The firm requires the typical data for each client—name, birth date, telephone, assets under management, and so on. The firm also stores data about its employees who are the financial consultants that service the clients. Each entity (clients and consultants) requires its own table in the database in order to add, edit, and/or delete data for individual clients and consultants, independently of one another.

If, for example, you wanted to know (or change) the account type and assets for Bradley Adams, you would search the Clients table for Bradley's record, where you would find the account type (Retirement), and assets ($90,000). In similar fashion you could search the Consultants table for Andrea Carrion and learn that she was hired on September 1, 1995, and that she is a partner in the firm. You could also use the ConsultantID field in Bradley Adams' record to learn that Andrea Carrion is Bradley's financial consultant.

Bradley Adams' record —

The ConsultantID points to Andrea Carrion —

SSN	FirstName	LastName	ConsultantID	BirthDate	Gender	Account Type	Assets
100-00-0000	Eileen	Marder	2	9/12/35	F	Standard	$14,000
111-11-1111	Bradley	Adams	1	8/22/61	M	Retirement	$90,000
200-00-0000	Kevin	Stutz	3	5/31/72	M	Retirement	$150,000
222-22-2222	Nickolas	Gruber	2	11/11/61	M	Corporate	$90,000
300-00-0000	Cedric	Stewart	4	4/12/74	M	Retirement	$90,000
333-33-3333	Lori	Graber	3	7/1/72	F	Deluxe	$120,000
400-00-0000	Ryan	Yanez	1	9/30/74	M	Standard	$18,000
444-44-4444	Christopher	Milgrom	4	3/12/53	M	Corporate	$100,000
500-00-0000	Erica	Milgrom	2	5/1/72	F	Retirement	$150,000
555-55-5555	Peter	Carson	1	3/8/53	M	Standard	$12,000
600-00-0000	Michelle	Zacco	3	10/24/75	F	Deluxe	$90,000
666-66-6666	Kimberly	Coulter	2	11/11/74	F	Corporate	$180,000
700-00-0000	Steven	Frazier	4	9/9/68	M	Retirement	$150,000
777-77-7777	Ana	Johnson	3	4/18/48	F	Standard	$12,000
800-00-0000	Christa	Parulis	1	7/15/72	F	Corporate	$120,000
888-88-8888	David	James	4	8/1/45	M	Deluxe	$100,000
900-00-0000	Ronnie	Jones	2	6/1/49	F	Standard	$12,000
999-99-9999	Wendy	Simon	1	1/31/45	F	Retirement	$10,000

(a) The Clients Table

Andrea Carrion is Bradley Adams' consultant —

ConsultantID	FirstName	LastName	Phone	DateHired	Status
1	Andrea	Carrion	(954) 346-1980	9/1/95	Partner
2	Ken	Grauer	(954) 346-1955	9/1/95	Associate
3	Robert	Arnold	(954) 346-1958	10/18/97	Associate
4	Issac	Milgrom	(954) 346-1961	3/16/98	Partner

(b) The Consultants Table

FIGURE 4.1   The Investment Database

The investment firm imposes a ***one-to-many relationship*** between financial consultants and their clients. One consultant can have many clients, but a given client is assigned to one consultant. This relationship is implemented in the database by including a common field, ConsultantID, in both tables. The ConsultantID is the primary key (the field or combination of fields that ensures each record is unique) in the Consultants tables. It also appears as a ***foreign key*** (the primary key of another table) in the Clients table in order to relate the two tables to one another.

The data from both tables can be combined through this relationship to provide complete information about any client and the consultant who serves him/her, or about any consultant and the clients they service. For example, to determine the name, telephone number, and status of Bradley Adams' financial consultant, you would search the Clients table to determine the ConsultantID assigned to Bradley (consultant number 1). You would then search the Consultants table for that consultant number, Andrea Carrion, and retrieve the associated data.

Multiple-Table Queries

You have just seen how to manually relate data from the Clients and Consultants tables to one another. As you might expect, it can also be done automatically through the creation of a multiple-table query as shown in Figure 4.2. Figure 4.2a shows the Design view whereas Figure 4.2b displays the associated dynaset. Bradley Adams appears first in the dynaset since the query lists clients in alphabetical order by last name. Note, too, that Carrion appears as Bradley's financial consultant, which is the same conclusion we reached when we looked at the tables initially.

The one-to-many relationship between consultants and clients is shown graphically in the Query window. The tables are related through the ConsultantID

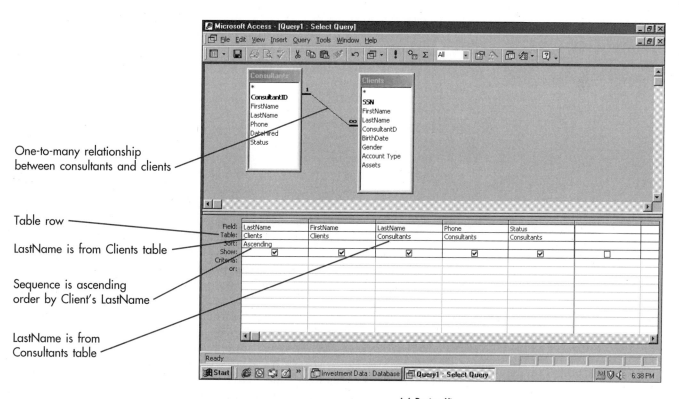

(a) Design View

FIGURE 4.2   Multiple-Table Query

Clients are listed in
alphabetical order

Carrion is the consultant
for Bradley Adams

Clients.LastName	FirstName	Consultants.LastName	Phone	Status
Adams	Bradley	Carrion	(954) 346-1980	Partner
Carson	Peter	Carrion	(954) 346-1980	Partner
Coulter	Kimberly	Grauer	(954) 346-1955	Associate
Frazier	Steven	Milgrom	(954) 346-1961	Partner
Graber	Lori	Arnold	(954) 346-1958	Associate
Gruber	Nickolas	Grauer	(954) 346-1955	Associate
James	David	Milgrom	(954) 346-1961	Partner
Johnson	Ana	Arnold	(954) 346-1958	Associate
Jones	Ronnie	Grauer	(954) 346-1955	Associate
Marder	Eileen	Grauer	(954) 346-1955	Associate
Milgrom	Erica	Grauer	(954) 346-1955	Associate
Milgrom	Christopher	Milgrom	(954) 346-1961	Partner
Parulis	Christa	Carrion	(954) 346-1980	Partner
Simon	Wendy	Carrion	(954) 346-1980	Partner
Stewart	Cedric	Milgrom	(954) 346-1961	Partner
Stutz	Kevin	Arnold	(954) 346-1958	Associate
Yanez	Ryan	Carrion	(954) 346-1980	Partner
Zacco	Michelle	Arnold	(954) 346-1958	Associate

(b) Dynaset

FIGURE 4.2   Multiple-Table Query (continued)

field that appears in both tables. ConsultantID is the primary key of the "one"
table (the Consultants table in this example), but it is also a field in the "many"
table (the Clients table). This in turn links the tables to one another, making it
possible to join data from the two tables in a single query.

The lower half of the Query window is similar to the queries you created
earlier in Chapter 3. The difference is that the Design grid contains a **Table row**
to indicate the table from where the field was taken. The client's last name and
first name are taken from the Clients table. The consultant's last name, phone,
and status are taken from the Consultants table. The records appear in alphabetical order (in ascending sequence) according to the value of the client's last name.

Maintaining the Database

You have seen how easy it is to obtain information from the investment database.
The design of the investment database, with separate tables for clients and consultants, makes it easy to add, edit, or delete information about a client or consultant. Thus, to add a new client or consultant, just go to the respective table and
add the record. In similar fashion, to change the data for an existing client or consultant, you again go to the appropriate table, locate the record, and make the
change. The advantage of the relational database, however, is that you only have
to change the consultant information in one place; for example, change the phone
number of a consultant and the change will be automatically reflected for every
client associated with that consultant.

Realize, too, that the tables in the database must be consistent with one
another, a concept known as **referential integrity**. For example, you can always
delete a record from the Clients table (the "many" table in this example). You
cannot, however, delete a record from the Consultants table (the "one" table)
when there are clients assigned to that consultant, because those clients would then
be assigned to a financial consultant who did not exist. Access monitors the relationships that are in effect and prevents you from making changes that do not
make sense.

THE IMPORT SPREADSHEET WIZARD

It is important to realize that data is data regardless of where it originates. You may prefer to work in Access, but others in the organization may use Excel or vice versa. In any event, there is a need to send data back and forth between applications. The ***Get External Data command*** imports or links data from an external source into Access. The data may come from an Excel workbook (as in our next hands-on exercise), or from a text file that was created by an application outside of Microsoft Office. The ***Export command*** does the reverse and copies an Access database object to an external destination.

The ***Import Spreadsheet Wizard*** is illustrated in Figure 4.3. The Wizard asks you a series of questions, then it imports the Excel worksheet into the Access table. You select the worksheet in Figure 4.3a, designate the Excel column headings and Access field names in Figure 4.3b, and specify the primary key in Figure 4.3c. You can then view and/or modify the resulting table as shown in Figure 4.3d.

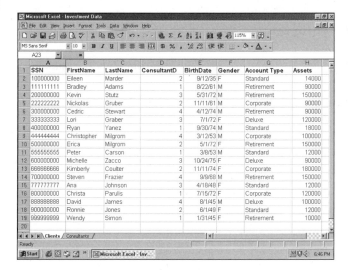

(a) The Excel Workbook

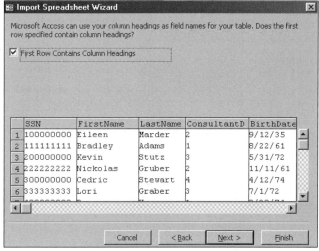

(b) Designate Column Headings (Field Names)

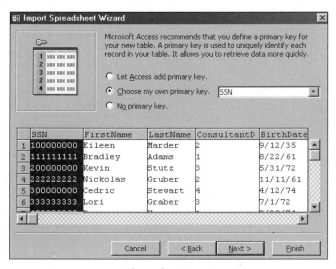

(c) Choose the Primary Key

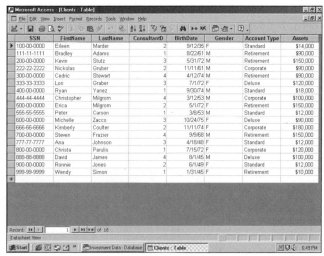

(d) The Clients Table

FIGURE 4.3   The Import Spreadsheet Wizard

Importing and Exporting Access Objects

Objective: To import an Access table from an Excel workbook; to create a one-to-many relationship between tables in a database; to create a multiple-table query. Use Figure 4.4 as a guide in the exercise.

STEP 1: Open the Investment Database

➤ Start Access, click the **Open an existing file option button**, click **More Files**, and click **OK**. If Access is already open, pull down the **File menu** and click the **Open command**.

➤ Open the **Investment database** in the **Exploring Access folder**. If necessary, click the **Tables button**.

➤ The database does not contain any tables as of yet, but it does contain other objects (click the Forms or Reports button to see these objects). The tables will be imported from Excel.

➤ Pull down the **File menu**, click (or point to) the **Get External Data command**, then click **Import** to display the Import dialog box in Figure 4.4a.

➤ Click the **down arrow** on the Look in list box and change to the **Exploring Access folder** (the same folder that contains the Access databases).

➤ Click the **down arrow** on the Files of type list box and select **Microsoft Excel**. Select the **Investment Data workbook**. Click the **Import button** to start the Import Spreadsheet Wizard.

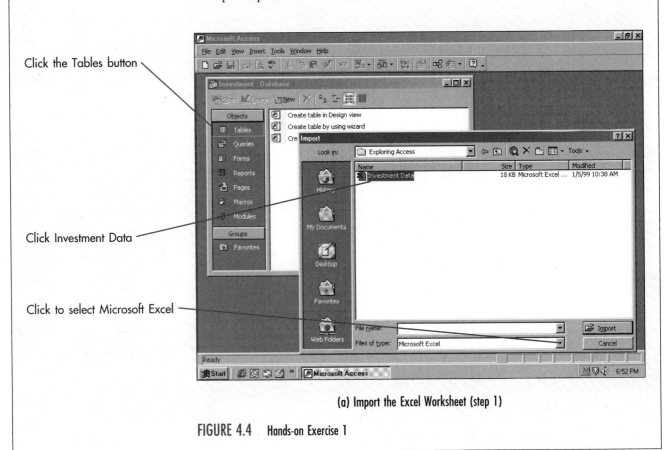

Click the Tables button

Click Investment Data

Click to select Microsoft Excel

(a) Import the Excel Worksheet (step 1)

FIGURE 4.4   Hands-on Exercise 1

STEP 2: The Import Spreadsheet Wizard

➤ You should see the first step in the Import Spreadsheet Wizard as shown in Figure 4.4b. The option button to **Show Worksheets** is selected. The Clients worksheet is also selected. Click **Next**.

➤ Access will use the column headings in the Excel workbook as field names in the Access table, provided you check the box indicating that the first row contains column headings. Click **Next**.

➤ Select the option button to store the data in a new table. Click **Next**.

➤ You do not need information about the individual fields. Click **Next**.

➤ Select the option to choose your own primary key. Click the **drop-down arrow** on the list box, and select the Social Security Number. Click **Next**.

➤ Click the **Finish button**, then click **OK** when the Wizard indicates it has finished importing the data. The Import Spreadsheet Wizard disappears from the screen and the Clients table appears within the Database window.

➤ Repeat the steps to import the Consultants table into the Investment database from the Investment Data workbook. Use the **ConsultantID field** as the primary key for this table.

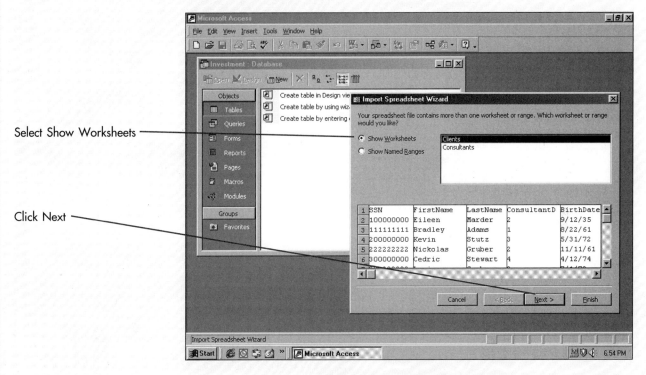

Select Show Worksheets

Click Next

(b) The Import Spreadsheet Wizard (step 2)

FIGURE 4.4   Hands-on Exercise 1 (continued)

THE IMPORT TEXT WIZARD

The most common format for data originating outside of Microsoft Office is a text (or ASCII) file that stores the data without formatting of any kind. Pull down the File menu, click the Get External Data command, and specify Text as the file format to start the Import Text Wizard.

STEP 3: Create the Relationship

➤ Pull down the **Tools menu** and click the **Relationships command** to open the Relationships window in Figure 4.4c. (The tables are not yet visible.)

➤ Pull down the **Relationships menu** and click the **Show Table command** to display the Show Table dialog box. Click (select) the **Clients table** (within the Show Table dialog box) then click the **Add button**.

➤ Double click the **Consultants table** to add this table to the Relationships window. Close the Show Table dialog box. Click and drag the title bar of each table so that the positions of the tables match those in Figure 4.4c.

➤ Click and drag the bottom (and/or right) border of each table so that you see all of the fields in each table.

➤ Click and drag the **ConsultantID field** in the Consultants table field list to the **ConsultantID field** in the Clients field list. You will see the Edit Relationships dialog box. Check the box to **Enforce Referential Integrity**. Click the **Create button** to create the relationship.

➤ Click the **Save button** to save the Relationships window.

Save button ————

Click and drag ConsultantID field from Consultants table to the ConsultantID field in the Clients table

Click Enforce Referential Integrity

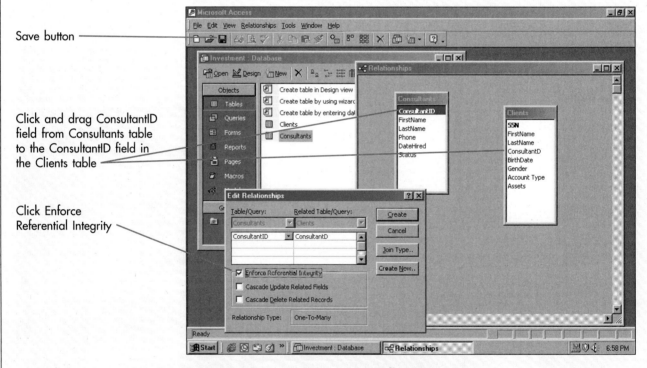

(c) Create the Relationship (step 3)

FIGURE 4.4   Hands-on Exercise 1 (continued)

REFERENTIAL INTEGRITY

The tables in a database must be consistent with one another, a concept known as referential integrity. Thus, Access automatically implements certain types of data validation to prevent such errors from occurring. You cannot, for example, enter a record in the Clients table that references a Consultant who does not exist. Nor can you delete a record in the Consultants table if it has related records in the Clients table.

STEP 4: Print the Relationship

➤ Pull down the **File menu** and click the **Print Relationships command**. You will see the Print Preview screen of a report. Maximize the window.

➤ Click the **View button** to change to the Design view as shown in Figure 4.4d. If necessary, click the **Toolbox button** to display the Toolbox toolbar.

➤ Click the **Label tool** on the Toolbox toolbar, then click and drag in the Report Header section of the report to create an unbound control.

➤ The insertion point is positioned automatically within the label you just created. Type **Prepared by:** followed by your name.

➤ Click the **Save button** to display the Save As dialog box. Change the name of the report to **Relationships Diagram**, then click **OK**.

➤ Click the **View button** to change to the **Print Preview** view of the report. Click the **Print button**. Close the Print Preview window.

➤ Close the Report window. Close the Relationships window.

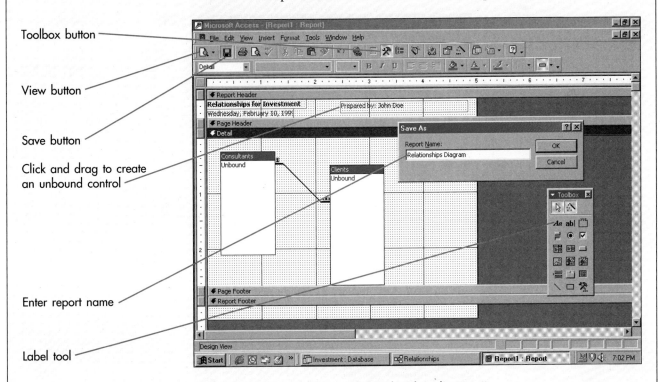

Toolbox button

View button

Save button

Click and drag to create
an unbound control

Enter report name

Label tool

(d) Print the Relationship (step 4)

FIGURE 4.4   Hands-on Exercise 1 (continued)

DISPLAY THE CURRENT DATE

A report typically displays one of two dates, the date it was created, or the current date (i.e., the date on which it is printed). We prefer the latter and it is obtained through the Now( ) function. Click in the Report header and delete the label containing today's (fixed) date. Click the Text box tool, click and drag where you want the date to appear, then release the mouse. Click in the text box and enter the function =Now( ). Save the report. The next time you open the report it will display the current date.

STEP 5: Add the New Data

➤ Click the **Forms button** in the Database window, then double click the **Consultants form** to open the form.

➤ Click the **Add Record button** and enter the data for your instructor. Enter **5** as the ConsultantID, enter your instructor's name, and use today's date as the date of hire. Your instructor is a partner. Close the form.

➤ Double click the **Clients form** in the Database window to open the form as shown in Figure 4.4e. Click the **Add Record button** then enter the appropriate data for yourself. Use the **Standard Account** and enter assets of **$25,000**.

➤ Click the **down arrow** on the Consultant's list box, then select your instructor as your financial consultant. Finish entering the data for your record, then click the **Print Record** button to print the form.

➤ Add a second client record for a classmate. Assign your instructor as your classmate's financial consultant. Click the **Close Form button**.

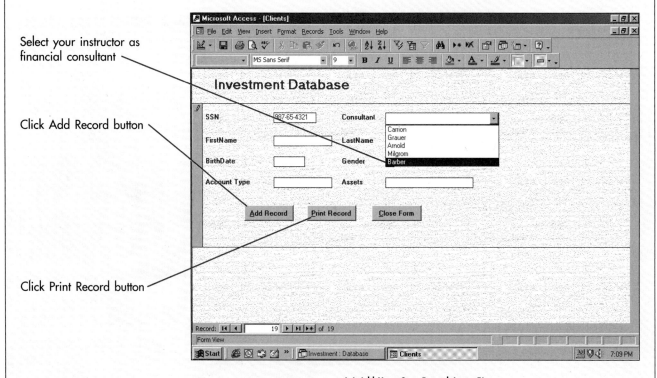

(e) Add Your Own Record (step 5)

FIGURE 4.4   Hands-on Exercise 1 (continued)

OPEN THE SUBDATASHEET

Take advantage of the one-to-many relationship that exists between consultants and clients to add and/or delete records in the Clients table while viewing the information for the associated consultant. Go to the Database window, open the Consultants table in Datasheet view, then click the plus sign next to the consultant. You now have access to all of the client records for that consultant and can add, edit, or delete a record as necessary. Click the minus sign to close the client list.

STEP 6: Create the Multiple-Table Query

➤ Click the **Queries button** in the Database window. Double click the icon to **Create query in design view** to open the Design window. The Show Table dialog box appears automatically.

➤ Press and hold the **Ctrl key** to select the Clients and Consultants tables, then click the **Add button** to add these tables to the query. Close the Show Table dialog box.

➤ Click the **maximize button** so that the Query Design window takes the entire desktop. Point to the line separating the field lists from the QBE grid (the mouse pointer changes to a cross), then click and drag in a downward direction. This gives you more space to display the field lists.

➤ Click and drag the title bars of each table to arrange the tables as shown in Figure 4.4f. Click and drag the bottom of each field list until you can see all of the fields in the table.

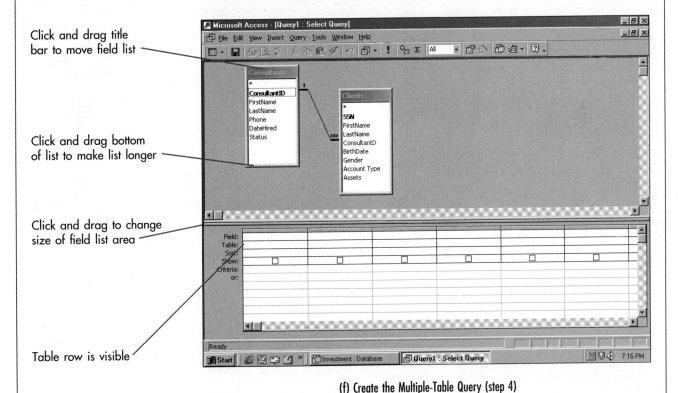

(f) Create the Multiple-Table Query (step 4)

FIGURE 4.4   Hands-on Exercise 1 (continued)

THE JOIN LINE

Access joins the tables in a query automatically if a relationship exists between the tables. Access will also join the tables (even if no relationship exists) if both tables have a field with the same name and data type, and if one of the fields is a primary key. And finally, you can create the join yourself by dragging a field from one table to the other, but this type of join applies only to the query in which it was created.

STEP 7: Complete the Multiple-Table Query

➤ The Table row should be visible within the QBE grid. If not, pull down the **View menu** and click **Table Names** to display the Table row in the QBE grid as shown in Figure 4.4g.

➤ Double click the **LastName** and **Status** fields from the Consultants table to add these fields to the QBE grid. Double click the LastName, Assets, and Account Type fields from the Clients table to add these fields as well.

➤ Click the **Sort row** under the **LastName** field from the **Consultants table**, then click the **down arrow** to open the drop-down list box. Click **Ascending**.

➤ Click the **Save button** on the Query Design toolbar. Save the query as **Assets Under Management**. Click **OK** to save the query. Click the **Run button** (the exclamation point) to run the query.

Run button

Double click field name to add it to the QBE grid

Click Sort row and select ascending

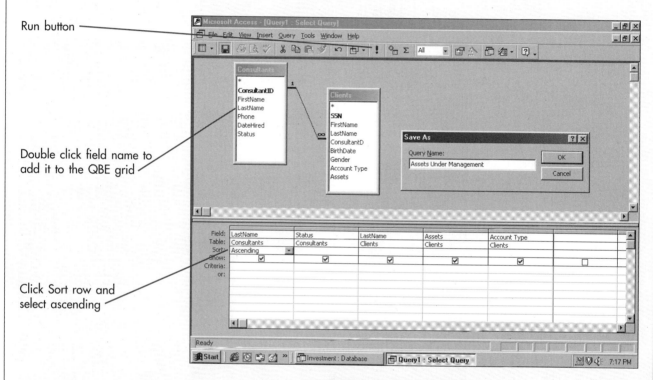

(g) Complete the Multiple-Table Query (step 7)

FIGURE 4.4   Hands-on Exercise 1 (continued)

SORT ON MULTIPLE FIELDS

A query can be sorted on multiple fields (e.g., by consultant, and by client's last name within consultant) provided the fields are in the proper order within the Design grid. Access sorts from left to right (the leftmost field is the more important field), so the consultant's last name must appear to the left of the client's last name. To move a field within the QBE grid, click the column selector above the field name to select the column, then drag the column to its new position. Click the Sort row for both fields and choose the ascending sequence.

STEP 8: Export the Query and Modified Tables

➤ You should see the dynaset created by the query as shown in Figure 4.4h. The query lists all of the client records according to the last name of the financial consultant. There should be two records for your instructor.

➤ Pull down the **File menu**, click (or point to) the **Export command** to display the Export Query dialog box. Click the **down arrow** in the Save as type list box to select **Microsoft Excel 97-2000**.

➤ Select the **Investment Data workbook** and click the **Save All button** to save the query as a worksheet in the Investment Data workbook. The Export Query dialog box closes automatically. Close the Query window.

➤ Click the **Tables button**. Select the **Clients table**, pull down the **File menu**, click the **Export command** and check that the file type is **Microsoft Excel 97-2000**. Select (click) the **Investment Data workbook**. Click **Save**.

➤ Export the Consultants table in similar fashion. Exit Access.

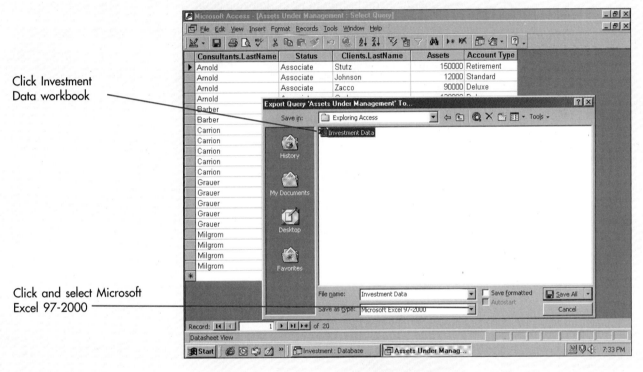

Click Investment Data workbook

Click and select Microsoft Excel 97-2000

(h) Export the Query (step 8)

FIGURE 4.4   Hands-on Exercise 1 (continued)

REPORT QUALITY OUTPUT

The authors have previously created the Assets Under Management report, based on the query you just created. Go to the Database window, click the Reports button, and open the Assets Under Management report in the Design view. Enter your name in the Report Header, save the report, then click the Print button to print the report. If you have any difficulty, it is because you misnamed the query on which the report is based. Go to the Database window, right click the query you created in step 7, click the Rename command, then be sure you enter the name correctly.

STEP 9: View the Excel Workbook

➤ Click the **Start button**, click (or point to) the **Programs command**, then select **Microsoft Excel** to start the program. Click the **Open button**, change to the Exploring Access folder, then open the **Investment Data workbook**.

➤ Click the **Assets_Under_Management tab** to see the worksheet in Figure 4.4i. Format the worksheet to improve its appearance.

➤ There are two client worksheets, Clients and Clients1, corresponding to the original and modified client data. Click the **Clients1 tab**.

➤ There are also two consultant worksheets, Consultants and Consultants1. Click the **Consultants1 tab** to view the data for your instructor.

➤ Press and hold the **Ctrl key** as you click the tab for each worksheet to select all five worksheets. Pull down the **File** menu, click the **Page Setup command** to display the Page Setup dialog box, then click the **Sheet tab**. Check the boxes to print **Gridlines** and **Row and Column headings**. Click **OK**.

➤ Click the **Print button** to print the workbook. Save the workbook. Exit Excel.

Sheet created with updated data from Consultants data

Sheet created with updated data from Clients table

Click Assets_Under_ Management tab

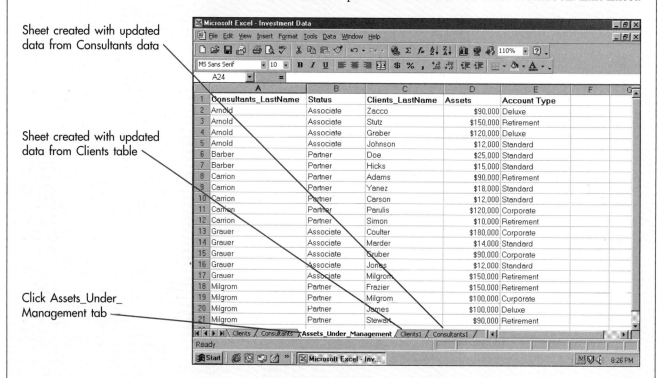

(i) View the Excel Workbook (step 9)

FIGURE 4.4   Hands-on Exercise 1 (continued)

IMPORTING VERSUS LINKING

The Get External Data command displays a cascaded menu to import or link tables. Importing a table brings a copy of the table into the database and does not maintain a tie to the original data. Linking, on the other hand, does not bring the table into the database but only a pointer to the data source. Any changes to the data are made in the original data source and are reflected automatically in any database that is linked to that source. See problem 5 at the end of the chapter.

A *total query* performs calculations on a group of records using one of several *summary (aggregate) functions* available within Access. These include the Sum, Count, Avg, Max, and Min functions to determine the total, number, average, maximum, and minimum values, respectively. Figure 4.5 shows a total query to compute the total assets under management for each financial consultant.

Figure 4.5a displays the results of a select query similar to the query created in the first exercise. The records are displayed in alphabetical order according to the last name of the financial consultant. The dynaset contains one record for each client in the Clients table and enables us to verify the results of the total query in Figure 4.5c. Arnold, the first consultant listed, has four clients (Johnson, Zacco, Graber, and Stutz). The total assets that Arnold has under management are $372,000, which is obtained by adding the Assets field in the four records.

Figure 4.5b shows the Design view of the total query to calculate the total assets managed by each consultant. The query contains three fields, the LastName (from the Consultants table), followed by the LastName and Assets fields from the Clients table. The QBE grid also displays a *Total row* in which each field in the query has either a Group By or aggregate entry. The *Group By* entry under the consultant's last name indicates that the records in the dynaset are to be grouped (aggregated) according to the like values of the consultant's last name; that is, there will be one record in the total query for each consultant. The *Count function* under the client's last name indicates that the query is to count the number of records for each consultant The *Sum function* under the Assets field specifies the values in this field are to be summed for each consultant.

The dynaset in Figure 4.5c displays the result of the total query and contains *aggregate* records as opposed to *individual* records. There are four records for Arnold in Figure 4.5a, but only one record in Figure 4.5c. This is because each record in a total query contains a calculated result for a group of records.

Microsoft Graph

Microsoft Office 2000 includes a supplementary application called *Microsoft Graph* that enables you to create a graph (or chart) within an Access form or report. The chart can be based on any table or query, such as the Assets Under Management query in Figure 4.5. The easiest way to create the chart is to open the report or form in Design view, pull down the Insert menu, click the Chart command, then let the *Chart Wizard* take over.

The Chart Wizard guides you every step of the way as can be seen in Figure 4.6. The Wizard asks you to choose the table or query (Figure 4.6a), the fields within the table or query (Figure 4.6b), and the type of chart (Figure 4.6c). You then have the chance to preview or modify the chart (Figure 4.6d) and add a title (Figure 4.6e). Figure 4.6f displays the completed chart.

EMPHASIZE YOUR MESSAGE

A graph is used to deliver a message, and you want that message to be as clear as possible. One way to help put your point across is to choose a title that leads the audience. A neutral title, such as "Assets Under Management," is nondescriptive and requires the audience to reach its own conclusion. A better title might be, "Grauer Leads All Consultants," if the objective is to emphasize an individual's performance.

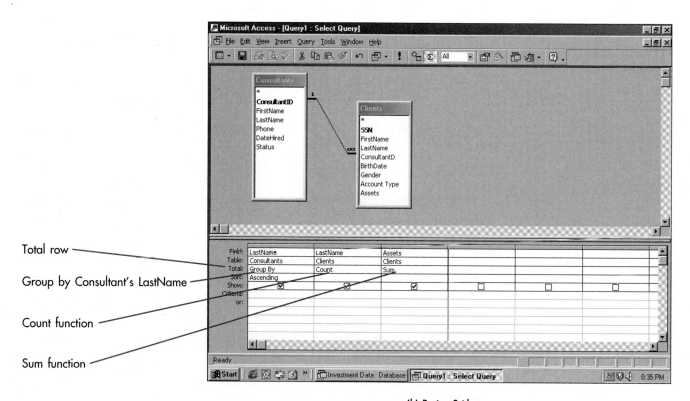

Consultants.LastName	Status	Clients.LastName	Assets	Account Type
Arnold	Associate	Stutz	$150,000	Retirement
Arnold	Associate	Johnson	$12,000	Standard
Arnold	Associate	Zacco	$90,000	Deluxe
Arnold	Associate	Graber	$120,000	Deluxe
Barber	Partner	Doe	$25,000	Standard
Barber	Partner	Hicks	$15,000	Standard
Carrion	Partner	Yanez	$18,000	Standard
Carrion	Partner	Carson	$12,000	Standard
Carrion	Partner	Parulis	$120,000	Corporate
Carrion	Partner	Simon	$10,000	Retirement
Carrion	Partner	Adams	$90,000	Retirement
Grauer	Associate	Marder	$14,000	Standard
Grauer	Associate	Gruber	$90,000	Corporate
Grauer	Associate	Milgrom	$150,000	Retirement
Grauer	Associate	Jones	$12,000	Standard
Grauer	Associate	Coulter	$180,000	Corpurate
Milgrom	Partner	Stewart	$90,000	Retirement
Milgrom	Partner	Milgrom	$100,000	Corporate
Milgrom	Partner	Frazier	$150,000	Retirement
Milgrom	Partner	James	$100,000	Deluxe

Arnold is the consultant for the first four clients

Arnold's total assets under management is $372,000

(a) Detail Records

Total row

Group by Consultant's LastName

Count function

Sum function

(b) Design Grid

LastName	CountOfLastName	SumOfAssets
Arnold	4	$372,000
Barber	2	$40,000
Carrion	5	$250,000
Grauer	5	$446,000
Milgrom	4	$440,000

There is one aggregate record for Arnold

(c) Summary Totals

FIGURE 4.5   A Total Query

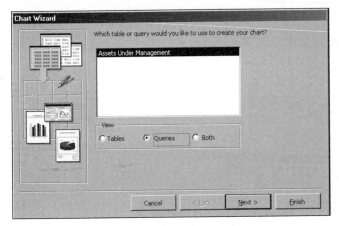

(a) Choose the Query

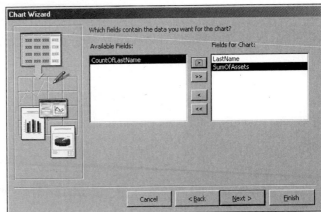

(b) Choose the Fields

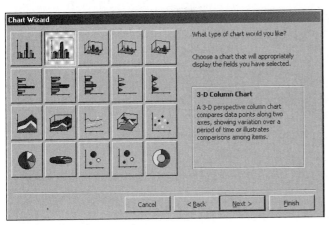

(c) Choose the Chart Type

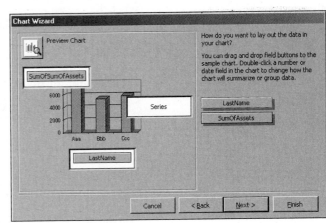

(d) Preview the Chart

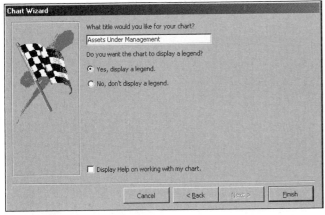

(e) Title the Chart

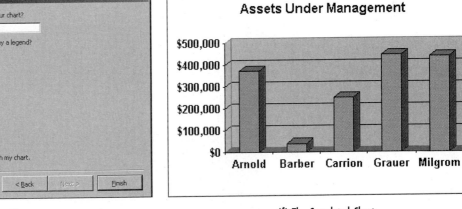

(f) The Completed Chart

FIGURE 4.6   The Chart Wizard

Total Queries and Charts

Objective: To create a total query; to use Microsoft Graph to present data from an Access object in graphical form. Use Figure 4.7 as a guide in the exercise.

STEP 1: Copy the Assets Under Management Query

➤ Open the **Investment database** from the previous exercise. Click the **Queries button** in the Database window and select the **Assets Under Management** query that was created in the previous exercise.

➤ Click the **Copy button** on the Database toolbar (or press **Ctrl+C**) to copy the query to the clipboard. Click the **Paste button** (or press **Ctrl+V**) to display the Paste As dialog box in Figure 4.7a.

➤ Enter **Assets Under Management Summary** as the name of the new query. Click **OK**.

➤ There are now two queries in the database window, the original query that was created in the previous exercise, as well as a copy of that query that you will modify in this exercise.

➤ Select (click) the **Assets Under Management Summary** query that was just created via the copy and paste commands.

➤ Click the **Design button** to open the query in Design view.

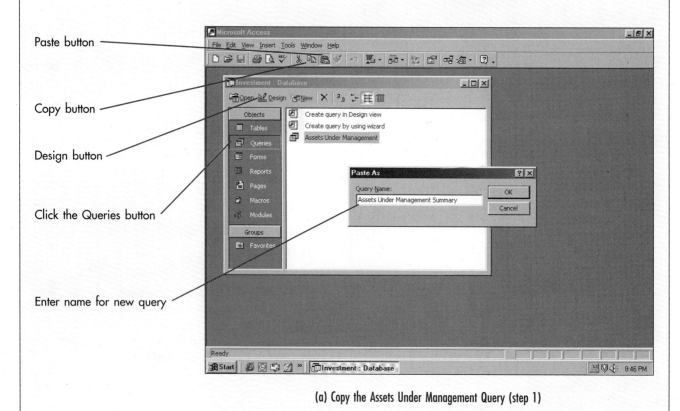

Paste button

Copy button

Design button

Click the Queries button

Enter name for new query

(a) Copy the Assets Under Management Query (step 1)

FIGURE 4.7   Hands-on Exercise 2

STEP 2: Create the Total Query

➤ You should see the Assets Under Management Summary in Design view as shown in Figure 4.7b. Maximize the window. Pull down the **View menu** and click **Totals** to display the Total row.

➤ Click the **Total row** under the **Client's LastName field**, click the **down arrow** to display the list of summary functions, then click the **Count function**.

➤ Click the **Total row** under the Assets field, click the **down arrow** to display the list of summary functions, then click the **Sum function**.

➤ Click the column selector for the Consultant's Status field to select the entire column, then press the **Del key** to remove the column from the query. Delete the column containing the Client's Account Type field in similar fashion. Your query should now contain three fields.

➤ Pull down the **Query menu** and click **Run** (or click the **Run button**) to run the query. You should see a dynaset with five records, one for each financial consultant. Save the query.

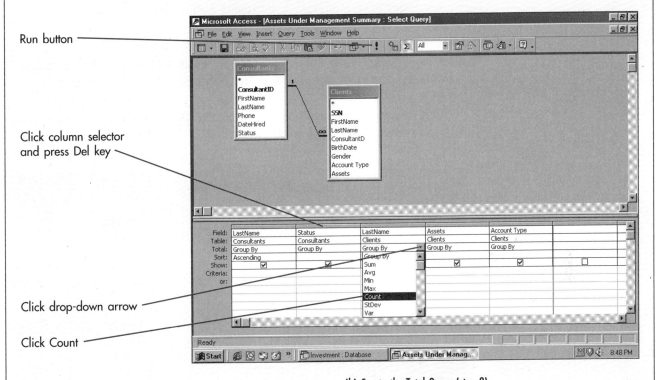

Run button

Click column selector and press Del key

Click drop-down arrow

Click Count

(b) Create the Total Query (step 2)

FIGURE 4.7   Hands-on Exercise 2 (continued)

CUSTOMIZE THE QUERY WINDOW

The query window displays the field list and design grid in its upper and lower halves, respectively. To increase (decrease) the size of either portion of the window, drag the line dividing the upper and lower sections. Drag the title bar to move a field list. You can also size a field list by dragging a border just as you can size any window. Press the F6 key to switch back and forth between the upper and lower halves of the window.

STEP 3: Check Your Progress

➤ Press the **F11 key** or click the **Investment button** on the Windows taskbar to return to the Database window. Maximize the window.

➤ Pull down the **File menu**, click **Database Properties**, then click the **Contents tab** to display the contents (objects) in the database as shown in Figure 4.7c:

- There are two tables, Clients and Consultants, that you imported earlier from an Excel workbook.

- There are two queries, Assets Under Management, and Assets Under Management Summary; the latter will be the basis of the chart we create in the next several steps.

- There are three forms, About Investments, Clients, and Consultants. The About Investments form is an informational form that will be referenced later in the chapter.

- There are two reports, Assets Under Management and Relationships Diagram. The first report was created for you and it will contain the chart you are about to create. The second report is the one that you created to print the Relationships diagram.

- Click **OK** to close the Investment Properties window.

➤ Click the **Reports button** in the Database window. Double click the **Assets Under Management report** to run the report. Maximize the window.

➤ The report contains the list of clients, grouped by consultant, with the consultants listed in alphabetical order. Click the **Design button** to switch to the Design view.

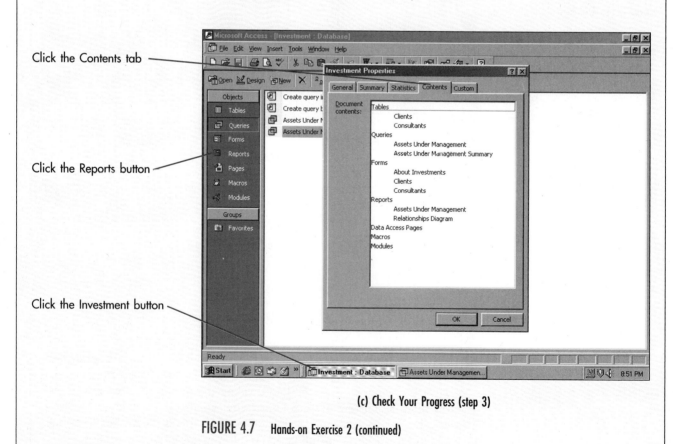

Click the Contents tab

Click the Reports button

Click the Investment button

(c) Check Your Progress (step 3)

FIGURE 4.7   Hands-on Exercise 2 (continued)

STEP 4: Start the Chart Wizard

➤ You should see the Assets Under Management Report in Design view as shown in Figure 4.7d. Click and drag the **Report Header** down in the report to increase the size of the report header.

➤ Click the control that is to contain the name of the person who prepared the report and enter your name.

➤ Pull down the **Insert menu** and click the **Chart command**. The mouse pointer changes to a tiny crosshair. Click and drag in the Report Header to draw the outline of the chart as shown in Figure 4.7d.

➤ The Chart Wizard starts automatically and asks for the table or query on which to base the chart. Click the **Queries button**, click the **Assets Under Management Summary query**, and click **Next**.

Click and drag to draw the chart area

Add your name to the report header

Click Assets Under Management Summary Query

Click and drag the bottom of the Report Header

Click the Queries button

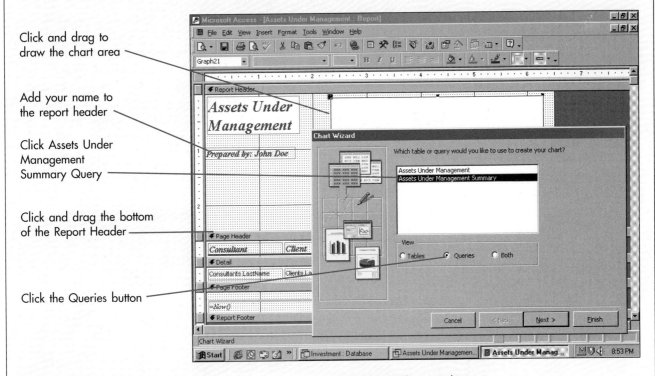

(d) Start the Chart Wizard (step 4)

FIGURE 4.7   Hands-on Exercise 2 (continued)

ANATOMY OF A REPORT

All reports are divided into sections that print at designated times. The report header and report footer are each printed once at the beginning and end of the report. The page header appears under the report header on the first page and at the top of every page thereafter. The page footer appears at the bottom of every page in the report, including the last page where it appears after the report footer. The detail section is printed once for each record in the underlying query or table.

STEP 5: Complete the Chart Wizard

➤ Answer the questions posed by the Chart Wizard in order to complete the chart:

- Double click the **LastName** and **SumOfAssets** fields to move these fields from the list of available fields to the list containing the fields for the chart. Click **Next**.

- Select the 3-D Column Chart as the chart type. Click **Next.**

- The Chart Wizard lays out the chart for you, with the SumOfAssets field on the Y-axis and the LastName field on the X-axis. Click **Next.**

- The chart should not change from record to record because we are plotting the total for each consultant. Thus, click the down arrow in both the Report Fields list and the Chart Fields list and select No Field. Click **Next**.

- Assets Under Management Summary is entered automatically as the title for the chart. Click the option button that indicates you do not want to display a legend. Click **Finish**.

➤ The completed chart appears in the report as shown in Figure 4.7e. Do not be concerned that the values along the Y-axis do not match the Asset totals or that the labels on the Y-axis do not correspond to the names of the financial consultants.

➤ Click the **Save button** to save the report. Click the **View button** to view the chart within the report. The appearance of the chart more closely resembles the finished product, but the chart still needs work.

➤ Click the **View button** to return to the Design view.

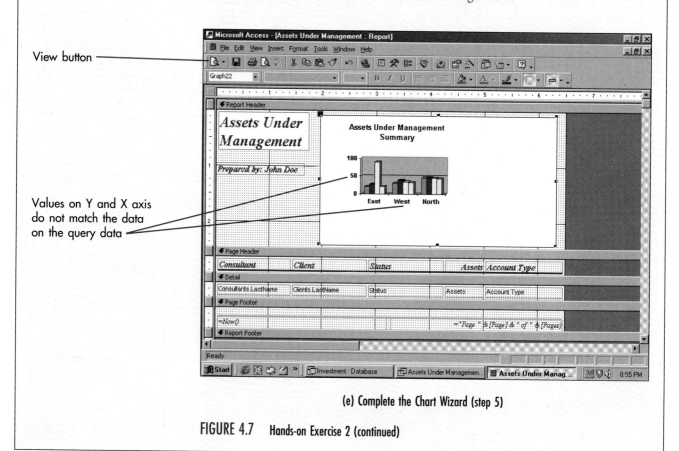

View button

Values on Y and X axis do not match the data on the query data

(e) Complete the Chart Wizard (step 5)

FIGURE 4.7   Hands-on Exercise 2 (continued)

STEP 6: Increase the Plot Area

➤ Click anywhere in the chart to display the sizing handles, then (if necessary) drag the sizing handle on the right border to increase the width of the chart.

➤ You might also want to drag the Report Header down (to increase the size of the header), then click and drag the bottom border of the chart to make it deeper. The chart area should be large enough so that you will be able to see the names of all the financial consultants along the X-axis.

➤ Click off the chart to deselect it, then double click within the chart to display the hashed border as shown in Figure 4.7f. Close the chart datasheet if it appears. Click (select) the title of the chart and press the **Del key**.

➤ Drag the right and bottom edges of the hashed border to fill the chart area. Right click the **Y-axis**, click **Format Axis**, click the **Number tab**, and set to **Currency format** with zero decimals. Click **OK**.

➤ Click off the chart to deselect the chart, then click the **View button**. Continue to move back and forth between the Design view and the finished report, until you can see the consultants' names along the X-axis.

➤ Close the report. Click **Yes** if asked whether to save the changes to the report.

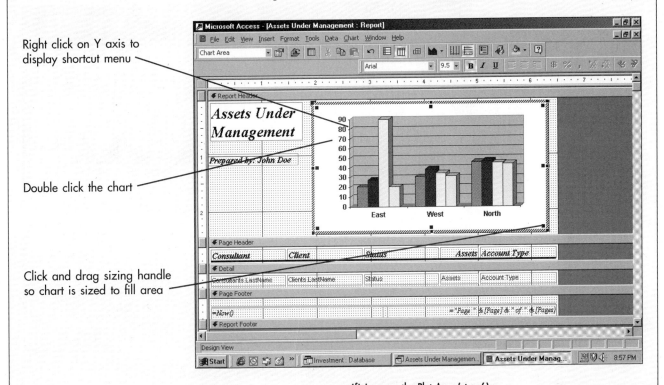

(f) Increase the Plot Area (step 6)

FIGURE 4.7 Hands-on Exercise 2 (continued)

TO CLICK OR NOT TO CLICK

Click anywhere on the chart to select the chart and display the sizing handles; this allows you to move and/or size the chart within the report. Click off the chart to deselect it, then double click the chart to start the Microsoft Graph in order to modify the chart itself.

STEP 7: Change the Data

➤ Click the **Investment Database** button on the taskbar to return to the Database window. Click the **Forms button**, open the **Clients form**, locate your record, and change your assets to **$1,000,000**. Click the ▶ **button** to record your changes and move to the next record. Close the Clients form.

➤ Click the **Queries button**, then double click the **Assets Under Management Summary query** to rerun the query. The increased value of your account should be reflected in the Assets Under Management of your instructor. Close the query.

➤ Click the **Reports button**, and double click the **Assets Under Management report** to open the report as shown in Figure 4.7g.

➤ The detailed information for your account (Doe in this example) appears within the detailed records in the body of the report. The value of your account ($1,000,000) is reflected in the total for your instructor.

➤ Click the **Print button** to print the report for your instructor. Exit Access if you do not want to continue with the next exercise at this time.

Value of Doe account is reflected in Barber's total

Detail record for Doe reflects assets of $1,000,000

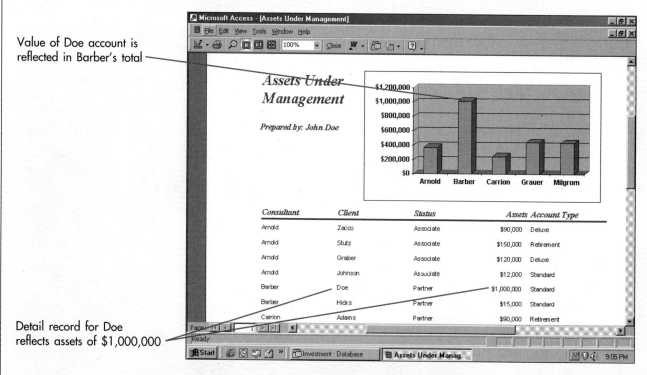

(g) The Completed Report (step 7)

FIGURE 4.7   Hands-on Exercise 2 (continued)

BACK UP YOUR DATA

We cannot overemphasize the importance of adequate backup. Our suggested strategy is very simple, namely that you back up whatever you cannot afford to lose and that you do so at the end of every session. You can always get another copy of Access 2000, but you are the only one who has a copy of the actual database. Develop an effective strategy and follow it!

THE USER INTERFACE

The investment database has grown in sophistication throughout the chapter. It contains two tables, for clients and consultants, and a form to enter data in each table. There are also queries and reports based on these tables. You are proficient in Access and are familiar with its Database window to the extent that you can select different objects to accomplish the work you have to do. But what if the system is to be used by a nontechnical user who might not know how to open the various forms and reports within the system?

It is important, therefore, to create a user interface that ties the objects together so that the database is easy to use. The interface displays a menu (or series of menus) that enable a nontechnical person to open the various objects within the database, and to move easily from one object to another. This type of interface is called a **_switchboard_** and it is illustrated in Figure 4.8. The switchboard itself is stored as a form within the database, but it is subtly different from the forms you have developed in previous chapters. Look closely and note that the record selector and navigation buttons have been suppressed because the switchboard is not used for data entry, but rather as a menu for the user.

The switchboard is intuitive and easy to use. Click About Investments, the first button on the switchboard in Figure 4.8a, and the system displays the informational screen we like to include in all of our applications. Click any other button, and you display the indicated form or report. Close the form or report and you will be returned to the switchboard, where you can select another item.

You should try to develop a switchboard that will appeal to your users. Speak in depth to the people who will use your application to determine what they expect from the system. Identify the tasks they consider critical and be sure you have an easily accessible menu option for those tasks.

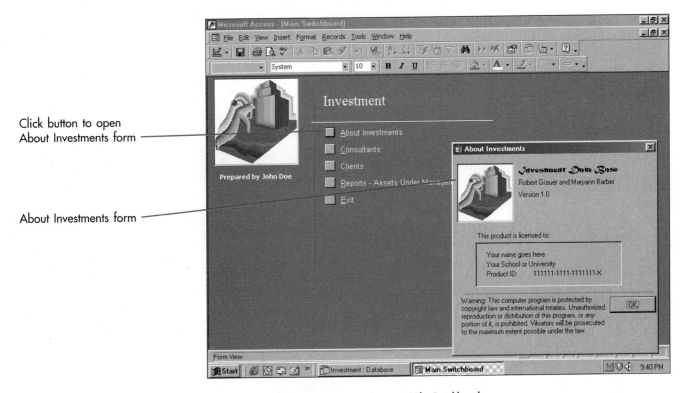

(a) The Switchboard

FIGURE 4.8   The Switchboard

Position of menu items

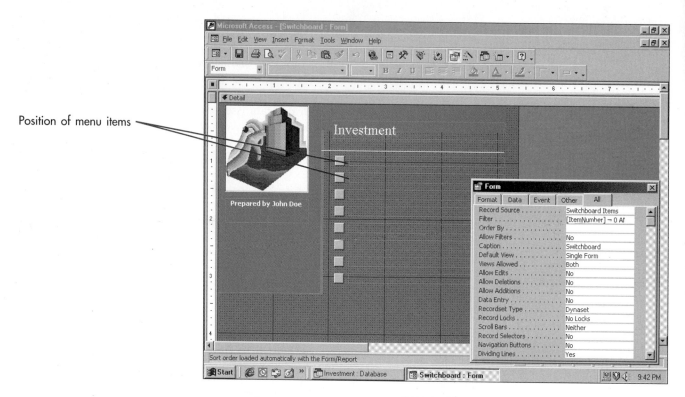

(b) Design View

Item Number reflects
position on menu

& reflects underlined letter

3 indicates an
Open Form command

Name of form to be opened

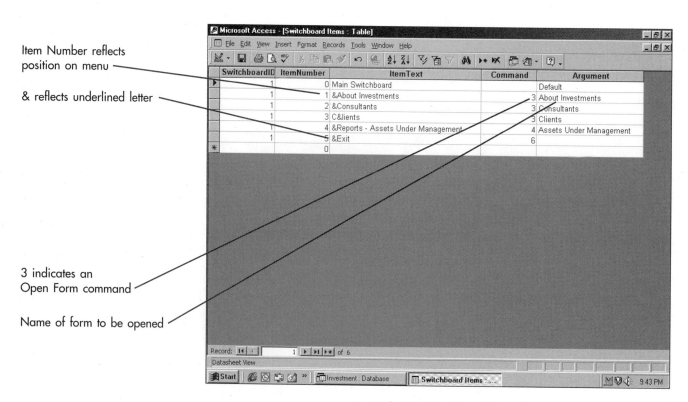

(c) The Switchboard Items Table

FIGURE 4.8   The Switchboard (continued)

The Switchboard Manager

The switchboard is quite powerful, but it is also very easy to create. All of the work is done by the **Switchboard Manager**, an Access utility that prompts you for information about each menu item that you want to add to the switchboard. You supply the text of the item, as it is to appear on the switchboard (e.g., Clients), together with the underlying command (e.g., Open Clients Form). Access does the rest. It creates the switchboard form and an associated **Switchboard Items table** that is the basis for the switchboard. Figure 4.8b displays the Design view of the switchboard in Figure 4.8a.

At first, the two views do not appear to correspond to one another, in that text appears next to each button in the Form view, but it is absent in the Design view. This, however, is the nature of a switchboard, because the text for each button is taken from the Switchboard Items table in Figure 4.8c, which is the record source for the form, as can be inferred from the Form property sheet shown in Figure 4.8b. In other words, each record in the Switchboard Items table has a corresponding menu item in the switchboard form.

The Switchboard Items table is created automatically and need never be modified explicitly. It helps, however, to have an appreciation for each field in the table. The SwitchboardID field identifies the number of the switchboard, which becomes important in applications with more than one switchboard. Access limits each switchboard to eight items, but you can create as many switchboards as you like, each with a different value for the SwitchboardID. Every database has a main switchboard by default, which can in turn display other switchboards as necessary.

The ItemNumber and ItemText fields identify the position and text of the item, respectively, as it appears on the switchboard form. (The & that appears within the ItemText field will appear as an underlined letter on the switchboard to enable a keyboard shortcut; e.g., &Consultants is displayed as Consultants and recognizes the Alt+C keyboard shortcut in lieu of clicking the button.) The Command and Argument fields determine the action that will be taken when the corresponding button is clicked. Command number 3, for example, opens a form.

Other Access Utilities

The Switchboard Manager is only one of several utility programs. Two other utilities, Convert Database, and Compact and Repair Database, are important and useful commands. Both commands are executed from the Tools menu.

The **Convert Database command** changes the file format of an Access 2000 database to the format used by earlier versions of the program. Think, for a moment, why such a command is necessary. Access 2000 is the current release of the program, and thus, it is able to read files that were created in all previous versions of Access. The converse is not true, however. Access 97, for example, cannot read an Access 2000 database because the latter uses a file format that was unknown when Access 97 was developed. The Convert Database command solves the problem by translating an Access 2000 database to the earlier format.

The **Compact and Repair Database command** serves two functions, as its name suggests. The compacting process eliminates the fragmentation and wasted disk space that occurs during development as you add, edit, and delete the various objects in a database. Compacting can be done when the database is open or closed. Compacting a database when it's open saves the database under the same name. Compacting a database when it is closed is safer, however, since the compacted database is stored as a new file (enabling you to return to the original file should anything go wrong). The Repair function takes place automatically if Access is unable to read a database when the database is opened initially. The **Encrypt/Decrypt command** compacts a database, and also makes it indecipherable by a utility program or word processor.

The Switchboard Manager

Objective: To create a switchboard and user interface; to compact a database. Use Figure 4.9 as a guide in the exercise.

STEP 1: Start the Switchboard Manager

➤ Open the Investment database. Minimize the Database window to give yourself more room in which to work. Pull down the **Tools menu**, click the **Database Utilities command**, and choose **Switchboard Manager**.

➤ Click **Yes** if you see a message indicating that there is no valid switchboard and asking if you want to create one. You should see the Switchboard Manager dialog box as shown in Figure 4.9a.

➤ Click the **Edit command button** to edit the Main Switchboard, which displays the Edit Switchboard Page dialog box. Click the **New command button** to add an item to this page, which in turn displays the Edit Switchboard item dialog box. Add the first switchboard item as follows.

  • Click in the Text list box and type **&About Investments**, which is the name of the command, as it will appear in the switchboard.

  • Click the **drop-down arrow** on the Command list box and choose the command to open the form in either the Add or Edit mode.

  • Click the **down arrow** in the Form list box and choose **About Investments**.

➤ Click **OK** to create the switchboard item. The Edit Switchboard Item dialog box closes and the item appears in the Main Switchboard Page.

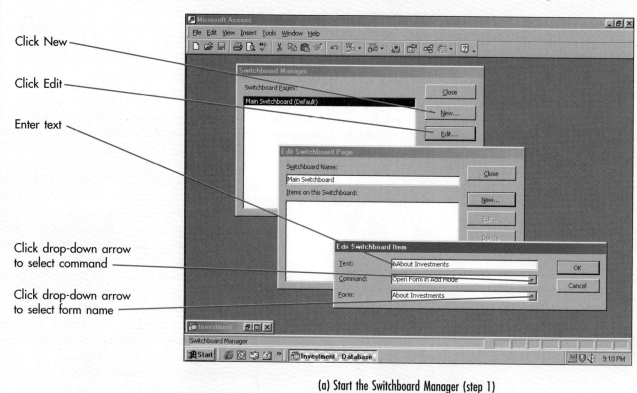

(a) Start the Switchboard Manager (step 1)

FIGURE 4.9   Hands-on Exercise 3

STEP 2: Complete the Switchboard

➤ Click the **New command button** in the Edit Switchboard Page dialog box to add a second item to the switchboard.

➤ Click in the Text list box and type **&Consultants**. Click the **drop-down arrow** on the Command list box and choose **Open Form in Edit Mode**. Click the **drop-down arrow** in the Form list box and choose **Consultants**. Click **OK**. The &Consultants command appears as an item on the switchboard.

➤ Add the remaining items to the switchboard as shown in Figure 4.9b. The menu items are as follows:

- **C&lients**—Opens the Clients form in Edit mode.
- **Assets Under &Management**—Opens the Assets report.
- **&Exit**—Exits the application (closes the database but remains in Access).

➤ Click the **Close button** to close the Edit Switchboard Page dialog box after you have added the last item. Close the Switchboard Manager dialog box.

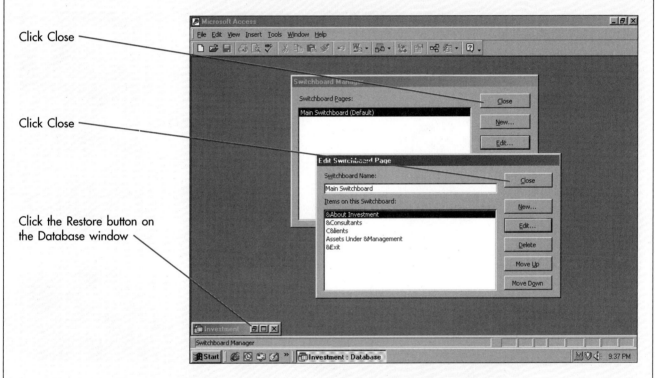

(b) Complete the Switchboard (step 2)

FIGURE 4.9   Hands-on Exercise 3 (continued)

CREATE A KEYBOARD SHORTCUT

The & has special significance when used within the name of an Access object because it creates a keyboard shortcut to that object. Enter "&About Investments", for example, and the letter A (the letter immediately after the ampersand) will be underlined and appear as "About Investments" on the switchboard. From there, you can execute the item by clicking its button, or you can use the Alt+A keyboard shortcut (where "A" is the underlined letter in the menu option).

STEP 3: Test the Switchboard

➤ Click the **Restore button** in the Database window to view the objects in the database, then click the **Forms button**. The Switchboard Manager has created the Switchboard form automatically.

➤ Double click the **Switchboard form** to open the Main Switchboard. Do not be concerned about the design of the switchboard at this time, as your immediate objective is to make sure that the buttons work.

➤ Click the **About Investments button** (or use the **Alt+A** shortcut) to display the About Investments form as shown in Figure 4.9c. Click the **OK button** to close the form.

➤ Click the **Consultants button** (or use the **Alt+C** shortcut) to open the Consultants form. Click the **Close button** on the form to close this form and return to the switchboard.

➤ Test the remaining items on the switchboard (except the Exit button).

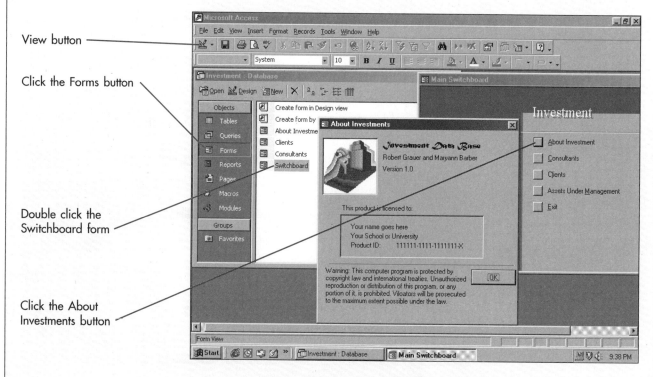

View button

Click the Forms button

Double click the Switchboard form

Click the About Investments button

(c) Test the Switchboard (step 3)

FIGURE 4.9   Hands-on Exercise 3 (continued)

THE SWITCHBOARD ITEMS TABLE

You can modify an existing switchboard in one of two ways—by using the Switchboard Manager or by making changes directly in the underlying table of switchboard items. Press the F11 key to display the Database window, click the Tables button, then open the Switchboard Items table where you can make changes to the various entries on the switchboard. We encourage you to experiment, but start by changing one entry at a time. The ItemText field is a good place to begin.

STEP 4: Insert the Clip Art

➤ Change to the Design View. Click in the left side of the form, where you want the clip art to go.

➤ Pull down the **Insert menu** and click **Object**, then choose **Microsoft Clip Gallery**. Click **OK**.

➤ Click the **Business category**, then select the appropriate image as shown in Figure 4.9d. Click the **Insert Clip button** to insert the picture.

➤ The clip art will be distorted; i.e., you will not see the entire image. Right click the clip art to display its property sheet, click the **All tab**, click the **Size Mode** property text box, and select **Stretch**.

➤ Move and size the picture as appropriate. Our object is a square, 1.5 inches × 1.5 inches. Close the property sheet.

➤ Right click to the right of the picture in the Detail (gray) area of the form. Click the **Fill/Back Color command** from the context-sensitive menu to display a color palette. Choose the same shade as appears on the rest of the form. (It is the fifth square from the left in the second row.)

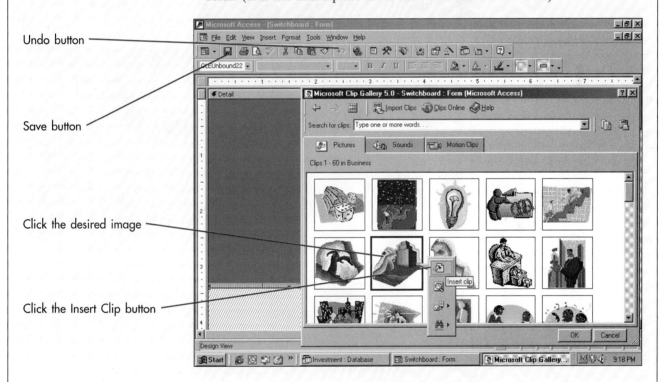

Undo button

Save button

Click the desired image

Click the Insert Clip button

(d) Insert the Clip Art (step 4)

FIGURE 4.9   Hands-on Exercise 3 (continued)

THE OBJECT BOX

The easiest way to familiarize yourself with the design of the switchboard is to click the down arrow on the object box on the Formatting toolbar, scrolling as necessary to see the various objects. Select (click) any object in the Object box and it is selected automatically in the form. Right click the selected object to display its property sheet where you can make design changes as appropriate.

STEP 5: Complete the Design

➤ If necessary, click the **Toolbox** tool to display the toolbox. Click the **Label tool**, then click and drag to create a text box under the picture. Enter your name in an appropriate font, point size, and color. Move and/or size the label containing your name as appropriate.

➤ Press and hold the **Shift button** as you click each text box in succession. Be sure that you select all eight, even if you do not have eight menu choices.

➤ Click the **drop-down arrow** on the Font/Fore color button and change the font to white as shown in Figure 4.9e. Change the font and point size to **Arial** and **10pt**, respectively.

➤ Click the **Save button** to save the changes, then switch to the Form view to see the modified switchboard. Return to the Design view as necessary to make the final adjustments to the switchboard. Save the form.

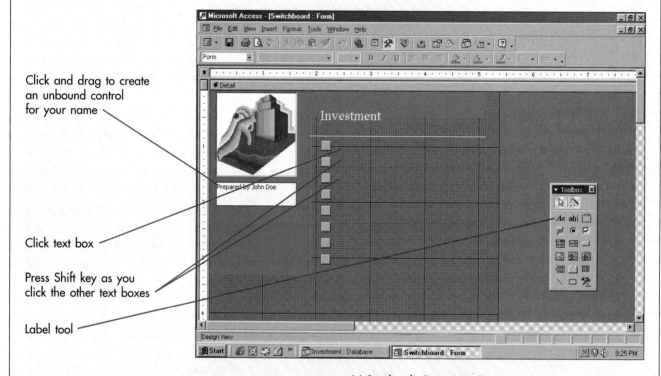

Click and drag to create an unbound control for your name

Click text box

Press Shift key as you click the other text boxes

Label tool

(e) Complete the Design (step 5)

FIGURE 4.9 Hands-on Exercise 3 (continued)

THE STARTUP PROPERTY

The ideal way to open a database is to present the user with the main switchboard, without the user having to take any special action. Pull down the Tools menu, click Startup to display the Startup dialog box, click the drop-down arrow in the Display Form list box, and select the Switchboard as the form to open. Add a personal touch to the database by clicking in the Application Title text box and entering your name. Click OK to accept the settings and close the Startup dialog box. The next time the database is opened, the switchboard will be displayed automatically.

STEP 6: The Completed Switchboard

➤ You should see the completed switchboard in Figure 4.9f. Click the **maximize button** so that the switchboard takes the entire screen. Repeat the testing process for the various menu items, but this time use the keyboard shortcuts.

➤ Press **Alt+L** (when the switchboard is active) to open the Clients form. Locate your record. Change the balance to $2,000,000 (wishful thinking).

➤ Look closely at the command buttons on the Clients form and note that those buttons also have keyboard shortcuts; e.g., press **Alt+C** to close the Clients form and return to the switchboard.

➤ Press **Alt+M** to open the Assets Under Management Report. The chart should reflect the increased value of your account. Close the report.

➤ Test the remaining items to be sure that the switchboard works as intended. Press **Alt+E** to exit the application. (Click **Yes** if asked whether to save the switchboard.) The Investment database is closed, but Access is still open.

Alt+L will open Clients form —

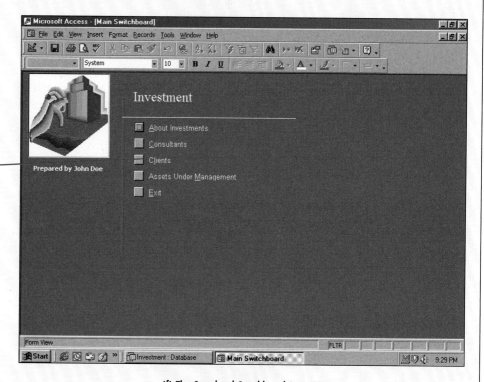

(f) The Completed Switchboard (step 6)

FIGURE 4.9   Hands-on Exercise 3 (continued)

ADD A HYPERLINK

You can enhance the appeal of your switchboard through inclusion of a hyperlink. Open the switchboard form in Design view, then click the Insert Hyperlink button to display the Insert Hyperlink dialog box. Enter the Web address and click OK to close the dialog box and return to the Design view. Right click the hyperlink to display a shortcut menu, click the Properties command to display the Properties dialog box, then change the caption, font, and/or point size as appropriate.

STEP 7: Compact the Database

➤ Pull down the **Tools menu**, click (or point to) **Database Utilities**, and click the **Compact and Repair Database command** to display the Database to Compact From dialog box in Figure 4.9g. Click the **Views button** and change to the **Details view**.

➤ Click the **drop-down arrow** in the Look in list box to change to the **Exploring Access folder** you have used throughout the text. Select (click) the **Investment** database and note the file size. Do not be concerned if your file is a different size than ours. Click the **Compact button**.

➤ Access then displays the Compact Into dialog box and supplies db1 as the default file name for the compacted database. Type **Investment Compacted** as the new name (to distinguish it from the database you have been working with). Click the **Save button**.

➤ Access will create the compacted database, then it will close the Compact Into dialog box. Access is still open, however, and you can use the File menu to see the effect of the compacting operation.

➤ Pull down the **File menu** and click the **Open command** to display the Open dialog box. Click the **Views button** and change to the **Details view**.

➤ Click the **drop-down arrow** in the Look in list box to change to the **Exploring Access folder**. You should see the Investment database as well as the Investment Compacted database that was just created. The latter should be significantly smaller.

➤ Click the **Cancel button** since we do not want to open either database at this time. Exit Access.

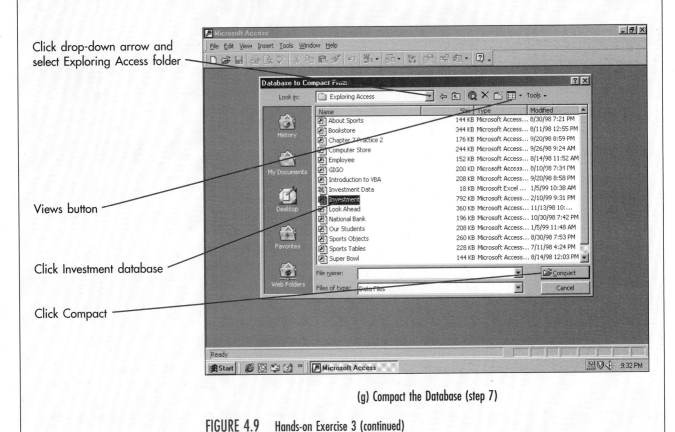

Click drop-down arrow and select Exploring Access folder

Views button

Click Investment database

Click Compact

(g) Compact the Database (step 7)

FIGURE 4.9   Hands-on Exercise 3 (continued)

A relational database contains multiple tables. Each table stores data about a specific entity in the physical system, such as clients and consultants in the investment database. The tables are related to one another through a one-to-many relationship; for example, one consultant can have many clients, as in the database from this chapter. The relationship is created in the Relationships window by dragging the join field from the one table to the related table. Referential integrity ensures that the data in the two tables are consistent.

A select query can contain fields from multiple tables. The relationship between those tables is shown graphically in the Query Design view. The Tables Row displays the name of the table that contains each field in the query.

The Get External Data command starts a Wizard that will import (or link) data from an external source such as an Excel workbook into an Access database. The Export command does the reverse and copies an Access object to an external destination.

A total query performs calculations on a group of records using one of several summary (aggregate) functions. Execution of the query displays a summary record for each group and individual records do not appear. The results of a total query can be input to Microsoft Graph to display the information graphically in a form or report.

A switchboard is a user interface that enables a nontechnical person to open the objects in an Access database by selecting commands from a menu. The switchboard is created through the Switchboard Manager, a tool that prompts you for the information about each menu item. The switchboard itself is stored as a form within the database that reads data from an underlying table of switchboard items.

The Convert Database command changes the file format of an Access 2000 database to the format used by earlier versions of the program. The Compact and Repair Database command serves two functions, as its name suggests. The compacting process eliminates the fragmentation and wasted disk space that occurs during development as you add, edit, and delete the various objects in a database. The Repair function takes place automatically if Access is unable to read a database when the database is opened initially.

KEY WORDS AND CONCEPTS

Aggregate functions

Chart Wizard

Compact and Repair
 command

Convert Database
 command

Export command

Get External Data
 command

Group By

Import Spreadsheet
 Wizard

Imported data

Insert Hyperlink
 command

Join field

Join line

Linked data

Microsoft Graph

One-to-many
 relationship

Primary key

Referential integrity

Relationships window

Startup property

Switchboard

Switchboard Items
 table

Switchboard Manager

Table row

Total query

Total row

1. A database has a one-to-many relationship between physicians and patients (one physician can have many patients). Which of the following is true?
   (a) The PhysicianID will appear in the Patients table
   (b) The PatientID will appear in the Physicians table
   (c) Both (a) and (b)
   (d) Neither (a) nor (b)

2. You are creating a database for an intramural league that has a one-to-many relationship between teams and players. Which of the following describes the correct database design?
   (a) Each record in the Teams table should contain the PlayerID field
   (b) Each record in the Players table should contain the TeamID field
   (c) Both (a) and (b)
   (d) Neither (a) nor (b)

3. Which of the following will create a problem of referential integrity in the Investments database that was developed in the chapter?
   (a) The deletion of a consultant record that has a corresponding client record
   (b) The deletion of a consultant record that does not have any client records
   (c) The deletion of a client record who is assigned to a consultant
   (d) All of the above

4. Which of the following is true about a select query?
   (a) It may reference fields from more than one table
   (b) It may have one or more criteria rows
   (c) It may sort on one or more fields
   (d) All of the above

5. Which of the following is a true statement about Access tables?
   (a) An Access query can be exported to an Excel workbook
   (b) An Excel worksheet can be imported as an Access table
   (c) Both (a) and (b)
   (d) Neither (a) nor (b)

6. The Get External Data command will:
   (a) Import a worksheet from an Excel workbook as a new Access table
   (b) Import a text file as a new Access table
   (c) Both (a) and (b)
   (d) Neither (a) nor (b)

7. An Excel worksheet has been imported into an Access database as a new table, after which the data in the table has been modified. Which of the following is *false*?
   (a) The Excel worksheet will be updated to reflect the modified table
   (b) A query that is run after the table has been modified will reflect the new data
   (c) A report that is run after the table has been modified will reflect the new data
   (d) All of the above

8. Which of the following is true about the rows in the Query Design grid?
   (a) The Total row can contain different aggregate functions for different fields
   (b) The Table row can reflect different tables
   (c) The Sort row can include entries for multiple fields
   (d) All of the above

9. Which of the following is available as an aggregate function within a query?
   (a) Sum and Avg
   (b) Min and Max
   (c) Both (a) and (b)
   (d) Neither (a) nor (b)

10. Which of the following is true about clicking and double clicking a chart within a report?
   (a) Clicking the chart selects the chart, enabling you to change the size of the chart, click and drag it to a new position, or delete it altogether
   (b) Double clicking the chart opens the underlying application (Microsoft Graph), enabling you to change the appearance of the chart
   (c) Both (a) and (b)
   (d) Neither (a) nor (b)

11. Which of the following is created by the Switchboard Manager?
   (a) A switchboard form
   (b) A switchboard items table
   (c) Both (a) and (b)
   (d) Neither (a) nor (b)

12. How do you insert clip art into a switchboard?
   (a) Start the Switchboard Manager, then use the Insert Clip Art command
   (b) Open the switchboard form in Design view, then add the clip art using the same techniques as for any other form
   (c) Both (a) and (b)
   (d) Neither (a) nor (b)

13. Which of the following is true about compacting a database?
   (a) Compacting a database when the database is open saves the compacted database under the original file name
   (b) Compacting a closed database saves the compacted database under a different file name
   (c) Both (a) and (b)
   (d Neither (a) nor (b)

14. Which of the following was suggested as essential to a backup strategy?
   (a) Backing up data files at the end of every session
   (b) Storing the backup file(s) at another location
   (c) Both (a) and (b)
   (d) Neither (a) nor (b)

15. Which of the following is a *false* statement?
   (a) A database created in Access 97 can always be read by Access 2000
   (b) A database created in Access 2000 can always be read by Access 97
   (c) A database created in Access 2000 can be converted to a format that can be read by earlier versions of Access
   (d) All of the above

ANSWERS

1. a	**6.** c	**11.** c
2. b	**7.** a	**12.** b
3. a	**8.** d	**13.** c
4. d	**9.** c	**14.** c
5. c	**10.** c	**15.** b

PRACTICE WITH ACCESS 2000

1. The Client Master List: The report in Figure 4.10 is based on a query that displays all clients in alphabetical order by last name. Use the Investment database to create the appropriate query, then create the report from your query. The query will contain fields from both the clients and consultants tables.

   You need not follow our design exactly, provided that your report contains all of the indicated fields. Include your name in the report header, then submit the completed report to your instructor. You can enhance your report by including the same clip art image that appeared on the switchboard.

   Expand the switchboard that you created in the third hands-on exercise to include an option to print this report. Print the switchboard form and table of switchboard items for your professor as proof that you did this exercise. Create a cover sheet for this assignment.

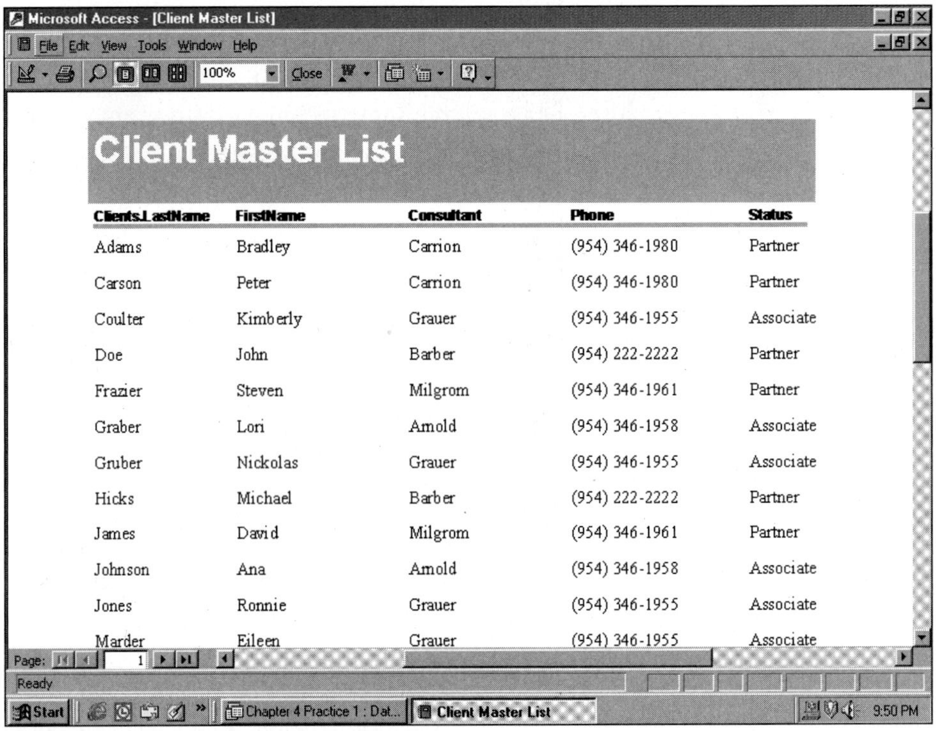

FIGURE 4.10 The Client Master List (Exercise 1)

2. The HMO Database: Figure 4.11 displays two worksheets, one for patients and one for physicians, that are contained in an Excel workbook intended as the basis for an Access database.

   a. Start Access and create a new database, *Chapter 4 Practice 2*. Use the Get External Data command to import the worksheets from the *Chapter 4 Practice 2* Excel workbook into the new Access database.

   b. Create a one-to-many relationship between the Physicians and Patients tables. Enforce referential integrity.

   c. Create a query that lists all patients in alphabetical order by last name. Your query should include the patient's first and last name, their birth date and gender. It should also include the last name of the patient's physician and the physician's phone number.

   d. Create a report based on the query from part (c). Print the report for your instructor.

   e. Create a second report to print the relationships that are in the database. Add your name to the report header.

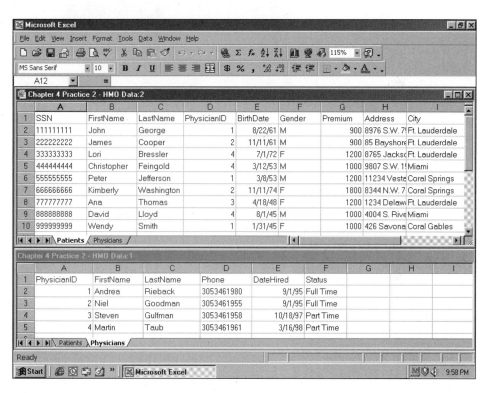

FIGURE 4.11   The HMO Database (Exercise 2)

3. Creating a Switchboard: Expand the previous exercise by creating a switchboard and an appropriate set of forms as shown in Figure 4.12. The forms do not have to be elaborate but they should enable you to modify data in both the patients and physicians table.

   You are also asked to create a simple Help form similar to the form that was presented in the chapter. (The easiest way to do this task is to use the Get External Data command to import the Help form from the Investment database, then modify it accordingly.) Print the switchboard for your instructor as proof that you did this exercise. In addition, print the first record in each table using the forms that you created.

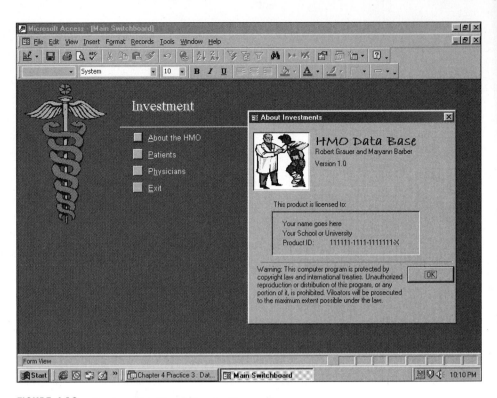

FIGURE 4.12   Creating a Switchboard (Exercise 3)

4. The Look Ahead Database: The Look Ahead database was presented at the end of Chapter 1 as an introduction to relational databases. It contained three tables—for employees, locations, and titles, respectively. There was a one-to-many relationship between locations and employees and a second one-to-many relationship between titles and employees. Open this database, and if necessary, complete the fourth hands-on exercise in Chapter 1. Create a switchboard and help form for the database similar to the one in Figure 4.13.

5. Linking Versus Importing: Look closely at the Database window in Figure 4.14 and note that it differs slightly from the window that appeared throughout the chapter. There is an arrow next to each table, indicating that the table is not contained in the database, but that the data for the table is linked to an underlying data source.

   a. Complete the three hands-on exercises in the chapter.

   b. Go to the Database window and click the Tables button. Select the Clients table and press the Del key to delete the table from the database. Delete the Consultants table in similar fashion.

   c. Pull down the File menu, click the Get External Data command, but this time select the command to link, rather than import a table. Follow the steps in the Link Spreadsheet Wizard to link the Clients table in the Investment database to the Clients tab in the Excel Workbook. Repeat the process to link the Consultants table to the Consultants tab.

   d. Click the Form button in the Database Window, open the Clients form, and increase your assets to $3,000,000. Open the Consultant's form and add Maryann Barber as a new financial consultant.

   e. Close the Access database. Open the Excel workbook, click the Clients tab, and view your record within Excel. You should have $3,000,000 in the Assets field. Click the Consultants tab and verify that Maryann Barber appears as the last consultant.

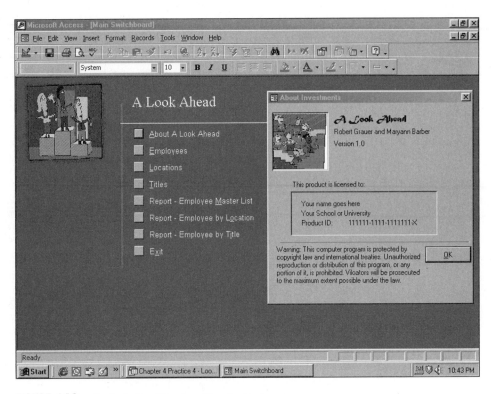

FIGURE 4.13   The Look Ahead Database (Exercise 4)

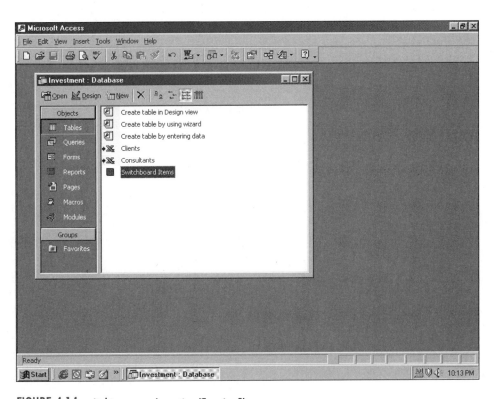

FIGURE 4.14   Linking versus Importing (Exercise 5)

6. **Pivot Tables:** A crosstab query consolidates data from an Access table or query in a row and column format. It is a powerful capability, but it pales in comparison to the pivot tables that are available in Microsoft Excel.

    a. Open the Investment database that was created in this chapter. Create a crosstab query based on the Assets Under Management query that was created in the first hands-on exercise. Use the Consultant's last name as the row field and the Client's Account type as the Column field.

    b. Open the Excel workbook you have used throughout the chapter. The workbook should contain an Assets_Under_Management worksheet that was exported from the Access database.

    c. Use the Help menu to learn how to create an Excel pivot table similar to the one in Figure 4.15. The pivot table parallels the Access crosstab query except that it contains a page field for the consultant's status.

    d. Click and drag the various field buttons (Status, Consultant, and Account Type) to create an entirely different pivot table. Compare the capabilities of the Excel pivot table to the Access crosstab query in a short note to your instructor.

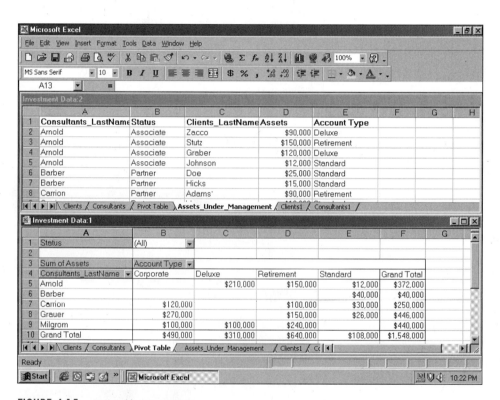

FIGURE 4.15   Pivot Tables (Exercise 6)

7. **Pivot Charts:** Access enables you to add a chart to a form or report, but that capability pales in comparison to what you can do with an Excel pivot chart. Create the Excel pivot table in problem 6, then use that table as the basis for the pivot chart in Figure 4.16. Click and drag the field buttons on the pivot chart to create an entirely different chart. Right click any of the field buttons to display a context-sensitive menu, then modify the chart using one of the commands in the menu. Compare the capabilities of an Excel pivot chart to an Access chart created through Microsoft Graph.

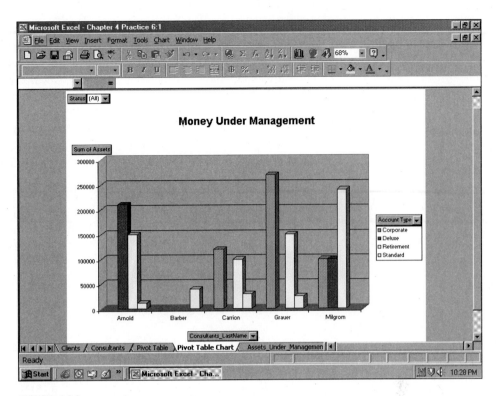

FIGURE 4.16   Pivot Charts (Exercise 7)

CASE STUDIES

Your First Consultant's Job

Go to a real installation such as a doctor or an attorney's office, the company where you work, or the computer lab at school. Determine the backup procedures that are in effect then write a one-page report indicating whether the policy is adequate and, if necessary, offering suggestions for improvement. Your report should be addressed to the individual in charge of the business and it should cover all aspects of the backup strategy. Be sure to indicate which files are backed up, the individual responsible, how often the files are backed up, and where the backup copies are stored.

Compacting versus Compressing

The importance of adequate backup has been stressed throughout the text. As a student, however, your backup may be limited to what you can fit on a single floppy disk, which, in turn, creates a problem if the size of your database grows beyond 1.4Mb. Two potential solutions involve compacting and/or compressing the database. Compacting is done from within Access whereas compressing requires additional software. Investigate both of these techniques with respect to the Sports league database created in the chapter. Be sure to indicate to your instructor the reduction in file size that you were able to achieve.

The Wellness Center

The Director of the Wellness Center has asked you to design a database that will track its members and personal trainers, as well as the predefined fitness programs that it offers to its members. In designing the database, keep in mind that each member is assigned to a personal trainer and is enrolled in a predefined fitness program. A personal trainer may work with many different members, but a member is assigned to one, and only one, personal trainer. In addition, each member is enrolled in one, and only one, of seven different predefined fitness programs (although the center is continually adding new programs and modifying the existing ones).

The center would like to be able to retrieve all data on a given member (name, address, phone, birth date, enrollment date), personal trainer (name, address, phone, certification date), and program (name, activities), as well as issue reports on all members assigned to a given personal trainer and all members enrolled in a given program.

The Database Wizard

The Database Wizard provides an easy way to create a database as it creates the database for you. The advantage of the Wizard is that it creates the tables, forms, and reports, together with a Main Menu (called a switchboard) in one operation. The disadvantage is that the Wizard is inflexible compared to creating the database yourself. Use the online Help facility to learn about the Database Wizard, then use the Wizard to create a simple database for your Music Collection. Is the Wizard a useful shortcut or is it easier to create the database yourself?

Two Different Clipboards

The Office clipboard is different from the Windows clipboard, but both clipboards share some functionality. Thus, whenever you copy an object to the Office clipboard, it is also copied to the Windows clipboard. However, each successive copy operation adds an object to the Office clipboard (up to a maximum of 12 objects), whereas it replaces the contents of the Windows clipboard. The Office clipboard also has its own toolbar. Experiment with the Office clipboard from different applications, then summarize your findings in a brief note to your instructor.

chapter 5

ONE-TO-MANY RELATIONSHIPS: SUBFORMS AND MULTIPLE TABLE QUERIES

OBJECTIVES

After reading this chapter you will be able to:

1. Explain how a one-to-many relationship is essential in the design of a database; differentiate between a primary key and a foreign key.

2. Use the Relationships window to implement a one-to-many relationship within an Access database.

3. Define referential integrity; explain how the enforcement of referential integrity maintains consistency within a database.

4. Distinguish between a main form and a subform; explain how a subform is used in conjunction with a one-to-many relationship.

5. Create a query based on multiple tables, then create a report based on that query.

6. Create a main form containing two subforms linked to one another

OVERVIEW

The real power of Access stems from its use as a relational database that contains multiple tables, and the objects associated with those tables. We introduced this concept at the end of Chapter 1, when we looked briefly at a database that had three tables. We revisited the concept in the previous chapter when we looked at a second relational database.

    This chapter presents an entirely new case study that focuses on a relational database. The case is that of a consumer loan system within a bank. The database contains two tables, one for customers and one for loans. There is a one-to-many relationship between the tables, in that one customer can have many loans, but a loan is tied to only one customer.

The case solution includes a discussion of database concepts. It reviews the definition of a primary key and explains how the primary key of one table exists as a foreign key in a related table. It also reviews the concept of referential integrity, which ensures that the tables within the database are consistent with one another. And most important, it shows how to implement these concepts in an Access database.

The chapter builds on what you already know by expanding the earlier material on forms, queries, and reports. It describes how to create a main form and a corresponding subform that contains data from a related table. It develops a query that contains data from multiple tables, then creates a report based on that query.

Suffice it to say that this is a critically important chapter because it is built around a relational database, as opposed to a single table. Thus, when you complete the chapter, you will have a much better appreciation of what can be accomplished within Access. As always, the hands-on exercises are essential to your understanding of the material.

CASE STUDY: CONSUMER LOANS

Let us assume that you are in the Information Systems department of a commercial bank and are assigned the task of implementing a system for consumer loans. The bank needs complete data about every loan (the amount, interest rate, term, and so on). It also needs data about the customers holding those loans (name, address, telephone, etc.).

The problem is how to structure the data so that the bank will be able to obtain all of the information it needs from its database. The system must be able to supply the name and address of the person associated with a loan. The system must also be able to retrieve all of the loans for a specific individual.

The solution calls for a database with two tables, one for loans and one for customers. To appreciate the elegance of this approach, consider first a single table containing a combination of loan and customer data as shown in Figure 5.1. At first glance this solution appears to be satisfactory. You can, for example, search for a specific loan (e.g., L022) and determine that Lori Sangastiano is the customer associated with that loan. You can also search for a particular customer (e.g., Michelle Zacco) and find all of her loans (L028, L030, and L060).

There is a problem, however, in that the table duplicates customer data throughout the database. Thus, when one customer has multiple loans, the customer's name, address, and other data are stored multiple times. Maintaining the data in this form is a time-consuming and error-prone procedure, because any change to the customer's data has to be made in many places.

A second problem arises when you enter data for a new customer that occurs before a loan has been approved. The bank receives the customer's application data prior to granting a loan, and it wants to retain the customer data even if a loan is turned down. Adding a customer to the database in Figure 5.1 is awkward, however, because it requires the creation of a "dummy" loan record to hold the customer data.

The deletion (payoff) of a loan creates a third type of problem. What happens, for example, when Ted Myerson pays off loan L020? The loan record would be deleted, but so too would Ted's data as he has no other outstanding loans. The bank might want to contact Mr. Myerson about another loan in the future, but it would lose his data with the deletion of the existing loan.

The database in Figure 5.2 represents a much better design because it eliminates all three problems. It uses two different tables, a Loans table and a Customers table. Each record in the Loans table has data about a specific loan (LoanID, Date, Amount, Interest Rate, Term, Type, and CustomerID). Each record in the Customers table has data about a specific customer (CustomerID, First Name, Last Name, Address, City, State, Zip Code, and Phone Number).

LoanID	Loan Data (Date, Amount, Interest Rate...)	Customer Data (First Name, Last Name, Address...)
L001	Loan Data for Loan L001	Customer Data for Wendy Solomon
L004	Loan Data for Loan L004	Customer Data for Wendy Solomon
L010	Loan Data for Loan L010	Customer Data for Alex Rey
L014	Loan Data for Loan L014	Customer Data for Wendy Solomon
L020	Loan Data for Loan L020	Customer Data for Matt Hirsch
L022	Loan Data for Loan L022	Customer Data for Lori Sangastiano
L026	Loan Data for Loan L026	Customer Data for Matt Hirsch
L028	Loan Data for Loan L028	Customer Data for Michelle Zacco
L030	Loan Data for Loan L030	Customer Data for Michelle Zacco
L031	Loan Data for Loan L031	Customer Data for Eileen Faulkner
L032	Loan Data for Loan L032	Customer Data for Scott Wit
L033	Loan Data for Loan L033	Customer Data for Alex Rey
L039	Loan Data for Loan L039	Customer Data for David Powell
L040	Loan Data for Loan L040	Customer Data for Matt Hirsch
L047	Loan Data for Loan L047	Customer Data for Benjamin Grauer
L049	Loan Data for Loan L049	Customer Data for Eileen Faulkner
L052	Loan Data for Loan L052	Customer Data for Eileen Faulkner
L053	Loan Data for Loan L053	Customer Data for Benjamin Grauer
L054	Loan Data for Loan L054	Customer Data for Scott Wit
L057	Loan Data for Loan L057	Customer Data for Benjamin Grauer
L060	Loan Data for Loan L060	Customer Data for Michelle Zacco
L062	Loan Data for Loan L062	Customer Data for Matt Hirsch
L100	Loan Data for Loan L100	Customer Data for Benjamin Grauer
L109	Loan Data for Loan L109	Customer Data for Wendy Solomon
L120	Loan Data for Loan L120	Customer Data for Lori Sangastiano

FIGURE 5.1   Single Table Solution

Each record in the Loans table is associated with a matching record in the Customers table through the CustomerID field common to both tables. This solution may seem complicated, but it is really quite simple and elegant.

Consider, for example, how easy it is to change a customer's address. If Michelle Zacco were to move, you would go into the Customers table, find her record (Customer C08), and make the necessary change. You would not have to change any of the records in the Loans table, because they do not contain customer data, but only a CustomerID that indicates who the customer is. In other words, you would change Michelle's address in only one place, and the change would be automatically reflected for every associated loan.

The addition of a new customer is done directly in the Customers table. This is much easier than the approach of Figure 5.1, which required an existing loan in order to add a new customer. And finally, the deletion of an existing loan is also easier than with the single table organization. A loan can be deleted from the Loans table without losing the corresponding customer data.

The database in Figure 5.2 is composed of two tables in which there is a *one-to-many relationship* between customers and loans. One customer (Michelle Zacco) can have many loans (Loan numbers L028, L030, and L060), but a specific loan (L028) is associated with only one customer (Michelle Zacco). The tables are related to one another by a common field (CustomerID) that is present in both the Customers and the Loans table.

Access enables you to create the one-to-many relationship between the tables, then uses that relationship to answer questions about the database. It can retrieve information about a specific loan, such as the name and address of the customer holding that loan. It can also find all loans for a particular customer.

LoanID	Date	Amount	Interest Rate	Term	Type	CustomerID
L001	1/15/99	$475,000	6.90%	15	M	C04
L004	1/23/99	$35,000	7.20%	5	C	C04
L010	1/25/99	$10,000	5.50%	3	C	C05
L014	1/31/99	$12,000	9.50%	10	O	C04
L020	2/8/99	$525,000	6.50%	30	M	C06
L022	2/12/99	$10,500	7.50%	5	O	C07
L026	2/15/99	$35,000	6.50%	5	O	C10
L028	2/20/99	$250,000	8.80%	30	M	C08
L030	2/21/99	$5,000	10.00%	3	O	C08
L031	2/28/99	$200,000	7.00%	15	M	C01
L032	3/1/99	$25,000	10.00%	3	C	C02
L033	3/1/99	$20,000	9.50%	5	O	C05
L039	3/3/99	$56,000	7.50%	5	C	C09
L040	3/10/99	$129,000	8.50%	15	M	C10
L047	3/11/99	$200,000	7.25%	15	M	C03
L049	3/21/99	$150,000	7.50%	15	M	C01
L052	3/22/99	$100,000	7.00%	30	M	C01
L053	3/31/99	$15,000	6.50%	3	O	C03
L054	4/1/99	$10,000	8.00%	5	C	C02
L057	4/15/99	$25,000	8.50%	4	C	C03
L060	4/18/99	$41,000	9.90%	4	C	C08
L062	4/22/99	$350,000	7.50%	15	M	C10
L100	5/1/99	$150,000	6.00%	15	M	C03
L109	5/3/99	$350,000	8.20%	30	M	C04
L120	5/8/99	$275,000	9.20%	15	M	C07

(a) Loans Table

CustomerID	First Name	Last Name	Address	City	State	Zip Code	Phone Number
C01	Eileen	Faulkner	7245 NW 8 Street	Minneapolis	MN	55346	(612) 894-1511
C02	Scott	Wit	5660 NW 175 Terrace	Baltimore	MD	21224	(410) 753-0345
C03	Benjamin	Grauer	10000 Sample Road	Coral Springs	FL	33073	(305) 444-5555
C04	Wendy	Solomon	7500 Reno Road	Houston	TX	77090	(713) 427-3104
C05	Alex	Rey	3456 Main Highway	Denver	CO	80228	(303) 555-6666
C06	Ted	Myerson	6545 Stone Street	Chapel Hill	NC	27515	(919) 942-7654
C07	Lori	Sangastiano	4533 Aero Drive	Santa Rosa	CA	95403	(707) 542-3411
C08	Michelle	Zacco	488 Gold Street	Gainesville	FL	32601	(904) 374-5660
C09	David	Powell	5070 Battle Road	Decatur	GA	30034	(301) 345-6556
C10	Matt	Hirsch	777 NW 67 Avenue	Fort Lee	NJ	07624	(201) 664-3211

(b) Customers Table

FIGURE 5.2   Multiple Table Solution

Query: What are the name, address, and phone number of the customer associated with loan number L010?

Answer: Alex Rey, at 3456 Main Highway is the customer associated with loan L010. His phone number is (303) 555-6666.

To determine the answer, Access searches the Loans table for loan L010 to obtain the CustomerID (C05 in this example). It then searches the Customers table for the customer with the matching CustomerID and retrieves the name, address, and phone number. Consider a second example:

Query: What loans are associated with Wendy Solomon?

Answer: Wendy Solomon has four loans: loan L001 for $475,000, loan L004 for $35,000, loan L014 for $12,000, and loan L109 for $350,000.

This time Access begins in the Customers table and searches for Wendy Solomon to determine the CustomerID (C04). It then searches the Loans table for all records with a matching CustomerID.

Referential Integrity

Microsoft Access automatically implements certain types of data validation during data entry to ensure that the database will produce accurate information. Access always lets you enter a record in the "one" table, the Customers table in this example, provided that all existing rules for data validation are met. You cannot, however, enter a record in the "many" table (the Loans table in this example) if that record contains an invalid (nonexistent) value for the CustomerID. This type of data validation is known as *referential integrity* and it guarantees that the tables within a database are consistent with one another. Consider:

Query: Can you add a loan to the Loans table (as it presently exists) for Customer C01? Can you add a loan for Customer C20?

Answer: Yes, you can add a loan for Customer C01 provided that the other rules for data validation are met. You cannot add a loan for Customer C20, because that customer is not in the Customers table.

Implementation in Access

Figure 5.3a displays the *Relationships window* that is used to create the one-to-many relationship between customers and loans. Each table stores data about a specific subject, such as customers or loans. Each table has a *primary key*, which is a field (or combination of fields) that uniquely identifies each record. CustomerID is the primary key in the Customers table. LoanID is the primary key in the Loans table.

The one-to-many relationship between the tables is based on the fact that the same field (CustomerID) appears in both tables. The CustomerID is the primary key in the Customers table where its values are unique, but it is a *foreign key* in the Loans table where its values are not unique. (A foreign key is simply the primary key of another table.) In other words, multiple records in the Loans table can have the same CustomerID to implement the one-to-many relationship between customers and loans.

To create a one-to-many relationship, you open the *Relationships window* in Figure 5.3a and add the necessary tables. You then drag the field on which the relationship is built from the field list of the "one" table (Customers) to the matching field in the related table (Loans). Once the relationship has been established, you will see a *relationship line* connecting the tables that indicates the one and many side of the relationship. The line extends from the primary key in the "one" table to the foreign key in the "many" table.

Figure 5.3b displays the Customers table after the one-to-many relationship has been created. A plus (or minus) sign appears to the left of the CustomerID to indicate that there are corresponding records in a related table. You can click the plus sign next to any customer record to display the related records (called a *subdatasheet*) for that customer. Conversely, you can click the minus sign (after the related records have been displayed) and the records are hidden. Look carefully at the related records for customer C04 (Wendy Solomon) and you will see the answer to one of our earlier queries.

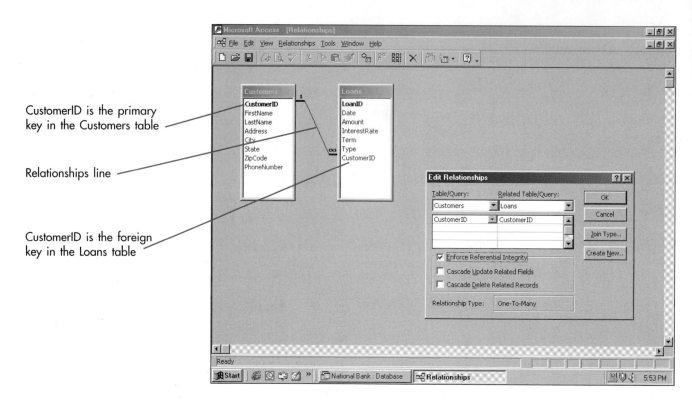

CustomerID is the primary key in the Customers table

Relationships line

CustomerID is the foreign key in the Loans table

(a) The Relationships Window

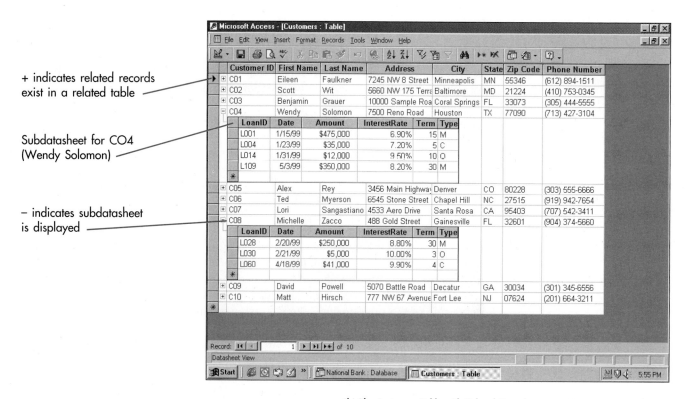

+ indicates related records exist in a related table

Subdatasheet for CO4 (Wendy Solomon)

– indicates subdatasheet is displayed

(b) The Customers Table with Related Records

FIGURE 5.3   One-to-Many Relationship

One-to-Many Relationships

Objective: To create a one-to-many relationship between existing tables in a database; to demonstrate referential integrity between the tables in a one-to-many relationship. Use Figure 5.4 as a guide in the exercise.

STEP 1: The Relationships Window

➤ Start Access. Open the **National Bank database** in the **Exploring Access folder**. The database contains three tables: for Customers, Loans, and Payments. (The Payments table will be used later in the chapter.)

➤ Pull down the **Tools menu** and click **Relationships** to open the Relationships window as shown in Figure 5.4a. (The Customers and Loans tables are not yet visible.) If you do not see the Show Table dialog box, pull down the **Relationships menu** and click the **Show Table command**.

➤ The **Tables tab** is selected within the Show Table dialog box. Click (select) the **Customers table**, then click the **Add Command button** to add the table to the Relationships window.

➤ Click the **Loans table**, then click the **Add Command button** (or simply double click the **Loans table**) to add this table to the Relationships window.

➤ Do *not* add the Payments table at this time. Click the **Close button** to close the Show Table dialog box.

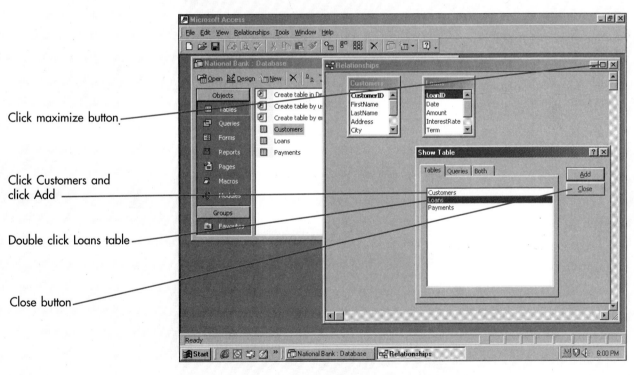

(a) The Relationships Window (step 1)

FIGURE 5.4   Hands-on Exercise 1

STEP 2: Create the Relationship

➤ Maximize the Relationships window. Point to the bottom border of the **Customers field list** (the mouse pointer changes to a double arrow), then click and drag the border until all of the fields are visible.

➤ Click and drag the bottom border of the **Loans field list** until all of the fields are visible. Click and drag the title bar of the **Loans field list** so that it is approximately one inch away from the Customers field list.

➤ Click and drag the **CustomerID field** in the Customers field list to the **CustomerID field** in the Loans field list. You will see the Relationships dialog box in Figure 5.4b.

➤ Check the **Enforce Referential Integrity** check box. (If necessary, clear the check boxes to Cascade Update Related Fields and Delete Related Records.)

➤ Click the **Create Command button** to establish the relationship and close the Relationships dialog box. You should see a line indicating a one-to-many relationship between the Customers and Loans tables.

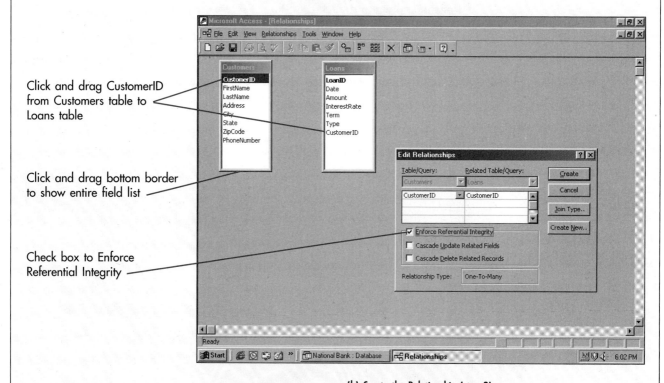

Click and drag CustomerID from Customers table to Loans table

Click and drag bottom border to show entire field list

Check box to Enforce Referential Integrity

(b) Create the Relationship (step 2)

FIGURE 5.4   Hands-on Exercise 1 (continued)

THE TABLE ANALYZER WIZARD

Duplicating data within a database results in wasted space, or worse, in erroneous information. Access, however, provides the Table Analyzer Wizard, which will examine the tables within a database to prevent such errors from occurring. The Wizard offers a brief explanation of the consequences of poor design, then it will examine your tables and make the appropriate suggestions. See problem 6 at the end of the chapter.

STEP 3: Delete a Relationship

➤ Access displays a relationship line between related tables, containing the number 1 and the infinity symbol (∞), to indicate a one-to-many relationship in which referential integrity is enforced.

➤ Point to the line indicating the relationship between the tables, then click the **right mouse button** to select the relationship and display a shortcut menu.

➤ Click the **Delete command**. You will see the dialog box in Figure 5.4c, asking whether you are sure you want to delete the relationship. Click **No** since you do *not* want to delete the relationship.

➤ Close the Relationships window. Click **Yes** if asked whether to save the layout changes.

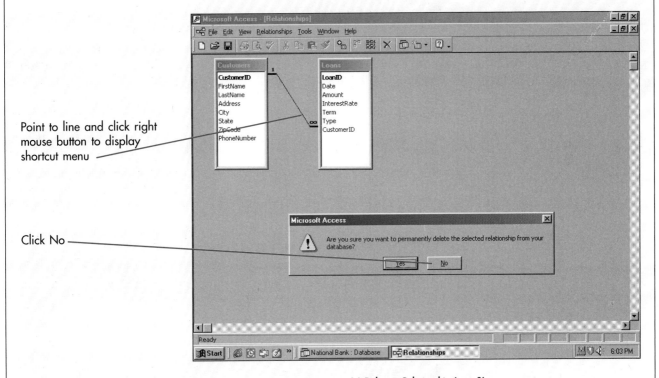

Point to line and click right mouse button to display shortcut menu

Click No

(c) Delete a Relationship (step 3)

FIGURE 5.4   Hands-on Exercise 1 (continued)

RELATED FIELDS AND DATA TYPES

The fields on both sides of a relationship must have the same data type; for example, both fields should be text fields or both fields should be number fields. In addition, Number fields must also have the same field size. The exception is an AutoNumber (counter) field in the primary table, which is matched against a Long Integer field in the related table. AutoNumber fields are discussed in Chapter 6.

STEP 4: Add a Customer Record

➤ The Database window is again visible with the Tables button selected. Open the **Customers table**. If necessary, click the **Maximize button** to give yourself additional room when adding a record. Widen the fields as necessary to see the data.

➤ Click the **New Record button** on the toolbar. The record selector moves to the last record (record 11).

➤ Enter **C11** as the CustomerID as shown in Figure 5.4d. The record selector changes to a pencil as soon as you enter the first character.

➤ Enter data for yourself as the new customer. Data validation has been built into the Customers table, so you must enter the data correctly, or it will not be accepted.

   • The message, *Customer ID must begin with the letter C followed by a two-digit number,* indicates that the CustomerID field is invalid.

   • The message, *The field 'Customers.LastName' can't contain a Null value because the Required property for this field is set to True,* indicates that you must enter a last name.

   • A beep in either the ZipCode or PhoneNumber field indicates that you are entering a nonnumeric character.

   • If you encounter a data validation error, press **Esc** (or Click **OK**), then reenter the data.

➤ Press **enter** when you have completed your record. Remember your CustomerID (C11) because you will need to enter it in the corresponding loan records.

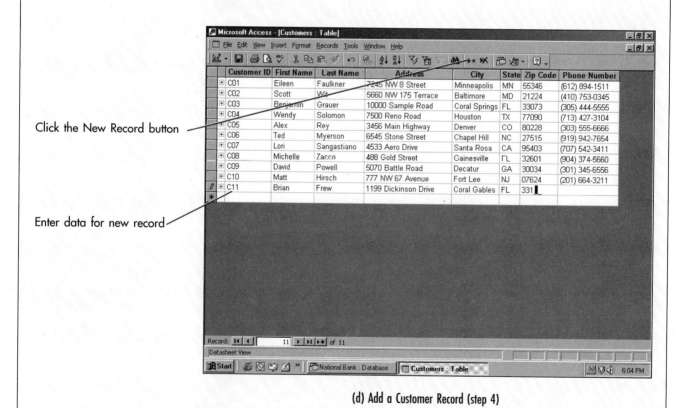

Click the New Record button

Enter data for new record

(d) Add a Customer Record (step 4)

FIGURE 5.4   Hands-on Exercise 1 (continued)

STEP 5: Add a Loan Record

➤ Click the **plus sign** next to the record selector for customer C03 (Benjamin Grauer). The plus sign changes to a minus sign and you see the related records as shown in Figure 5.4e. Click the **minus sign** and it changes back to a plus sign. The related records for this customer are no longer visible.

➤ Click the **plus sign** next to your customer record (record C11 in our figure). The plus sign changes to a minus sign but there are no loans as yet. Click in the LoanID field and enter data for a new loan record as shown in Figure 5.4e.

 • Use **L121** for the LoanID and enter the terms of the loan as you see fit.

 • Data validation has been built into the Loans table. The term of the loan, for example, cannot exceed 30 years. The interest rate must be entered as a decimal. The type of the loan must be C, M, or O for Car, Mortgage, or Other. Enter **C** for a car loan.

➤ Press **enter** when you have completed the loan record.

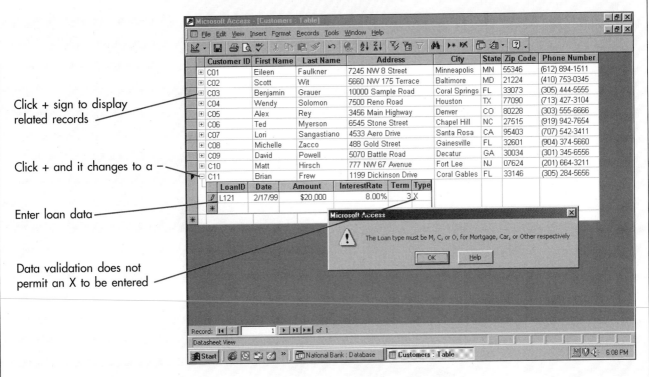

(e) Add a Loan Record (step 5)

FIGURE 5.4   Hands-on Exercise 1 (continued)

ADD AND DELETE RELATED RECORDS

Take advantage of the one-to-many relationship that exists between Customers and Loans to add or delete records in the Loans table from within the Customers table. Open the Customers table, then click the plus sign next to the Customer for whom you want to add or delete a loan record. To add a Loan, click in the blank row marked by the asterisk, then enter the new data. To delete a loan, select the Loan record, then click the Delete Record button on the Standard toolbar.

STEP 6: Referential Integrity

➤ Click the **plus sign** next to the record selector for Customer C09 (David Powell). Click in the CustomerID field for this customer, then click the Delete Record button to (attempt to) delete this customer.

➤ You will see the error message in Figure 5.4f indicating that you cannot delete the customer record because there are related loan records. Click **OK**.

➤ Click in the LoanID for L039 (the loan for this customer). Click the **Delete Record button**. Click **Yes** when warned that you will not be able to undo this operation. The loan disappears.

➤ Click in the CustomerID field, click the **Delete Record button**, then click **Yes** to delete the record. The deletion was permitted because there were no longer any related records in the Loans table.

➤ Close the Customers table. Close the National Bank database. Exit Access if you do not want to continue with the next exercise at this time.

Delete Record button

Click + to display related records

Click in CustomerID field

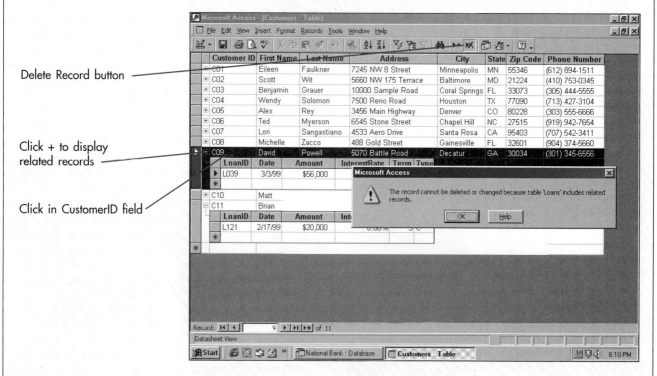

(f) Referential Integrity (step 6)

FIGURE 5.4   Hands-on Exercise 1 (continued)

CASCADE DELETED RECORDS

The enforcement of referential integrity will prevent the deletion of a record in the primary (Customers) table if there is a corresponding record in the related (Loans) table. (Thus, to delete a customer, you would first have to delete all loans for that customer.) This restriction is relaxed if you modify the relationship by checking the Cascade Delete Related Records option in the Relationships dialog box. The option is discussed further in the next chapter.

SUBFORMS

A *subform* is a form within a form. It appears inside a main form to display records from a related table. A main form and its associated subform, to display the loans for one customer, are shown in Figure 5.5. The **main form** (also known as the primary form) is based on the **primary table** (the Customers table). The subform is based on the related table (the Loans table).

The main form and the subform are linked to one another so that the subform displays only the records related to the record currently displayed in the main form. The main form shows the "one" side of the relationship (the customer). The subform shows the "many" side of the relationship (the loans). The main form displays the customer data for one record (Eileen Faulkner with CustomerID C01). The subform shows the loans for that customer. The main form is displayed in the **Form view**, whereas the subform is displayed in the **Datasheet view**. (A subform can also be displayed in the Form view, in which case it would show one loan at a time.)

Each form in Figure 5.5a has its own status bar and associated navigation buttons. The status bar for the main form indicates that the active record is record 1 of 10 records in the Customers table. The status bar for the subform indicates record 1 of 3 records. (The latter shows the number of loans for this customer rather than the number of loans in the Loans table.) Click the navigation button to move to the next customer record and you will automatically see the loans associated with that customer. If, for example, you were to move to the last customer record (C11, which contains the data you entered in the first hands-on exercise), you would see your customer and loan information.

The Loans form also contains a calculated control, the payment due, which is based on the loan parameters. Loan L031, for example (a $200,000 mortgage at 7% with a 15-year term), has a monthly payment of $1,797.66. The amount of the payment is calculated using a predefined function, as will be described in the next hands-on exercise.

Figure 5.5b displays the Design view of the Customers form in Figure 5.5a. The Loans subform control is an object on the Customers form and can be moved and sized (or deleted) just like any other object. It should also be noted that the Loans subform is a form in and of itself, and can be opened in either the Datasheet view or the Form view. It can also be opened in the Design view (to modify its appearance) as will be done in the next hands-on exercise.

Note, too, that reports can be linked to one another in exactly the same way that forms are linked to each other. Thus, you could create a main report/subreport combination to display the same information as the forms in Figure 5.5a. The choice between a form and a report depends on the information requirements of the system. Access, however, gives you the capability to create both. Everything that you learn about creating a subform also pertains to creating a subreport.

THE PMT FUNCTION

The PMT function is one of several predefined *functions* built into Access. It calculates the payment due on a loan based on the principal, interest rate, and term and is similar to the PMT function in Excel. The PMT function is reached most easily through the Expression Builder and can be entered onto any form, query, or report.

Payment Due is a calculated field —

Status bar for subform —

Status bar for main form —

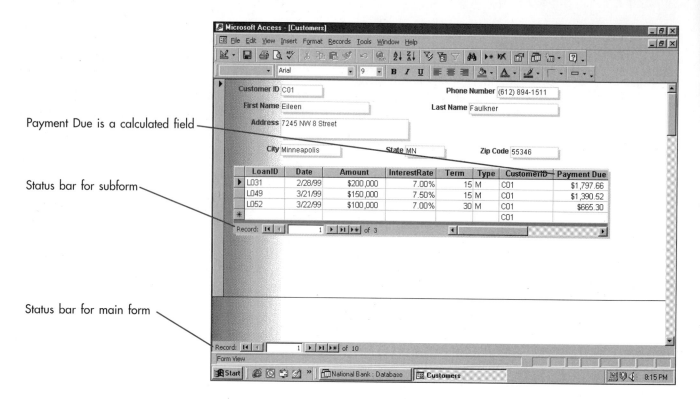

(a) Form View

Loans subform control —

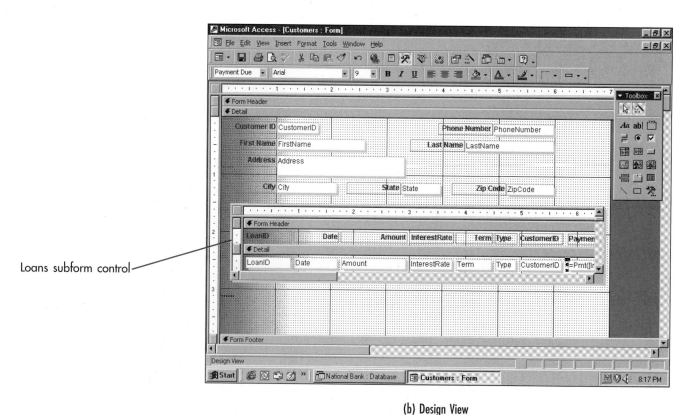

(b) Design View

FIGURE 5.5   A Main Form and a Subform

The Form Wizard

A subform is created in different ways depending on whether or not the main form already exists. The easiest way is to create the two forms at the same time by using the Form Wizard as depicted in Figure 5.6. The Wizard starts by asking you which fields you want to include in your form. You will need to select fields from the Customers table, as shown in Figure 5.6a, as well as from the Loans table as shown in Figure 5.6b, since these tables are the basis for the main form and subform, respectively.

The Wizard will do the rest. It gives you the opportunity to view the records by customer, as shown in Figure 5.6c. (Additional screens, not shown in Figure 5.6, let you choose the style of the forms.) Finally, you save each form as a separate object as shown in Figure 5.6d. You will find that the Wizard provides an excellent starting point, but you usually have to customize the forms after they have been created. This is done in the Form Design view using the identical techniques that were presented earlier to move and size controls and/or modify their properties.

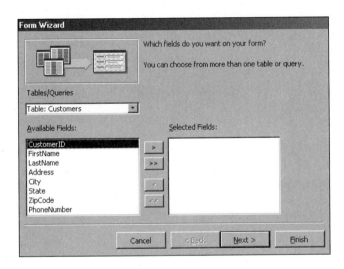

(a) The Customers Table

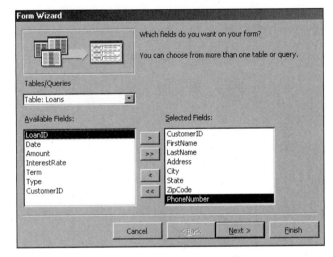

(b) The Loans Table

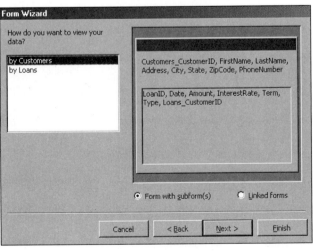

(c) View Data by Customers

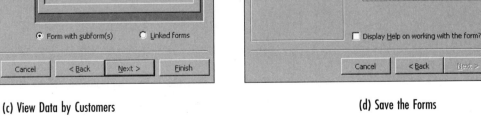

(d) Save the Forms

FIGURE 5.6   The Form Wizard

Creating a Subform

Objective: To create a subform that displays the many records in a one-to-many relationship; to move and size controls in an existing form; to enter data in a subform. Use Figure 5.7 as a guide in doing the exercise.

STEP 1: Start the Form Wizard

➤ Open the **National Bank** database from the previous exercise. Click the **Forms button** in the Database window, then double click the **Create form by using Wizard button** to start the Form Wizard.

➤ You should see the Form Wizard dialog box in Figure 5.7a, except that no fields have been selected.

➤ The Customers table is selected by default. Click the **>> button** to enter all of the fields in the Customers table on the form.

➤ Click the **drop-down arrow** in the Tables/Queries list box to display the tables and queries in the database.

➤ Click **Loans** to select the Loans table as shown in Figure 5.7a. Click the **>> button** to enter all of the fields in the Loans table on the form.

➤ Be sure that the Selected Fields area contains the fields from both the Loans form and the Customers form.

➤ Click **Next** to continue with the Form Wizard.

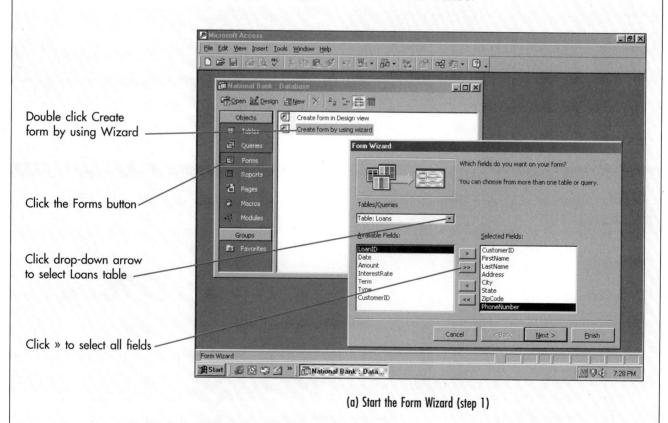

Double click Create form by using Wizard

Click the Forms button

Click drop-down arrow to select Loans table

Click » to select all fields

(a) Start the Form Wizard (step 1)

FIGURE 5.7 Hands-on Exercise 2

STEP 2: Complete the Forms

➤ The Wizard will prompt you for the additional information it needs to create the Customers form and the associated Loans subform:

• The next screen suggests that you view the data by customers and that you are going to create a form with subforms. Click **Next**.

• The Datasheet option button is selected as the default layout for the subform. Click **Next**.

• Click **Blends** as the style for your form. Click **Next**.

• You should see the screen in Figure 5.7b in which the Form Wizard suggests **Customers** as the title of the form and **Loans Subform** as the title for the subform. Click the option button to **Modify the form's design**, then click the **Finish command button** to create the form and exit the Form Wizard.

➤ You should be in the Design view of the Customer form you just created. Click the **Save button** to save the form and continue working.

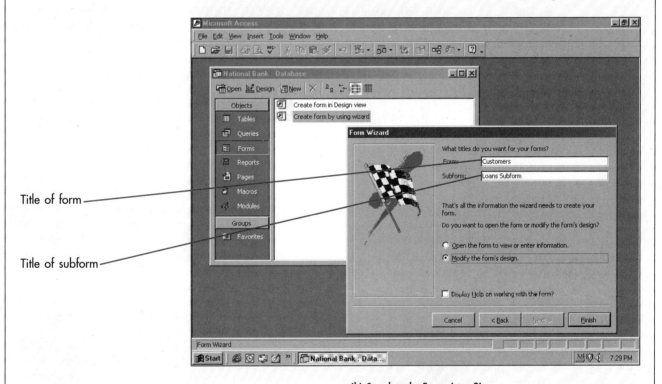

Title of form

Title of subform

(b) Complete the Forms (step 2)

FIGURE 5.7   Hands-on Exercise 2 (continued)

THE NAME'S THE SAME

The Form Wizard automatically assigns the name of the underlying table (or query) to each form (subform) it creates. The Report Wizard works in similar fashion. The intent of the similar naming convention is to help you select the proper object from the Database window when you want to subsequently open the object. This becomes increasingly important in databases that contain a large number of objects.

STEP 3: Modify the Customers Form

➤ You should see the Customers form in Figure 5.7c. The appearance of your form will be different from our figure, however, as you need to rearrange the position of the fields on the form. Maximize the form window.

➤ Click and drag the bottom of the Details section down to give yourself additional room in which to work.

➤ It takes time (and a little practice) to move and size the controls within a form. Try the indicated command, then click the **Undo button** if you are not satisfied with the result.

• Move the **City, State, ZipCode, and PhoneNumber** to the bottom of the detail section. (This is only temporary, but we need room to work.)

• Increase the width of the form to seven inches. Click the **LastName** control to select the control and display the sizing handles, then drag the Last-Name control and its attached label so that it is next to the FirstName control. Align the top of the LastName and FirstName controls.

• Move the **Address** control up. Place the controls for **City, State,** and **Zip-Code** on the same line, then move these controls under the Address control. You may need to size some of the other labels to fit everything on one line. Align the top of these controls as well.

• Click and drag the control for **PhoneNumber** to the right of the CustomerID field. Align the top of the controls.

• Right align all of the labels so that they appear close to the bound control they identify.

➤ Your form should now match Figure 5.7c. Click the label attached to the subform control and press the **Del key**. Be sure you delete only the label and not the control for the subform. Save the form.

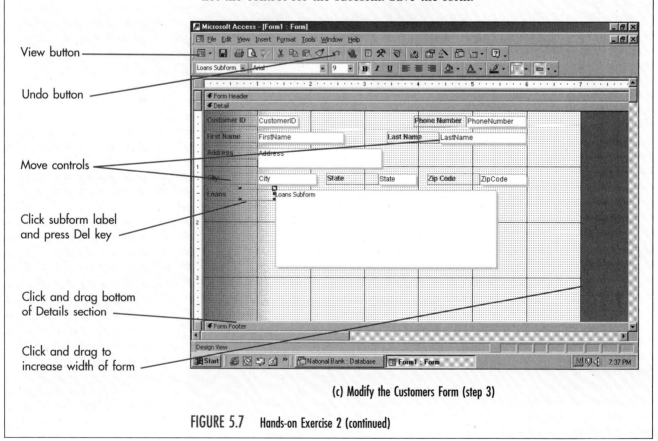

View button

Undo button

Move controls

Click subform label
and press Del key

Click and drag bottom
of Details section

Click and drag to
increase width of form

(c) Modify the Customers Form (step 3)

FIGURE 5.7   Hands-on Exercise 2 (continued)

STEP 4: Change the Column Widths

➤ Click the **View button** to change to the Form view. You should see the first customer in the database, together with the associated loan information. You may, however, have to adjust the width of the columns within the subform and/or the size and position of the subform within the main form.

➤ To change the width of the columns within the subform:

- Click the **drop-down arrow** on the **View button** to change to the **Datasheet view**. Click the **plus sign** next to the CustomerID column for the first customer to display the associated records in the Loans table as shown in Figure 5.7d.

- Click and drag the border between the column headings until you can read all of the information. Click the **Save button** to save the new layout, then **close** the form. You must close the main form, then reopen the form in order for the changes in the subform to be visible.

- You should be back in the Database window. Double click the **Customers form** to reopen the form and check the width of the columns in the subform. If necessary, click the **View button** to return to the Datasheet view to further adjust the columns.

➤ It may also be necessary to change the size or position of the subform control within the main form. Click the **View button** and change to **the Design view**.

- Click the **subform control** to select it, then click and drag a sizing handle to change the size of the subform control.

- Click and drag a border of the control to change its position.

➤ You will have to switch back and forth between the Form and Design view a few times to get the correct sizing. Save the completed form.

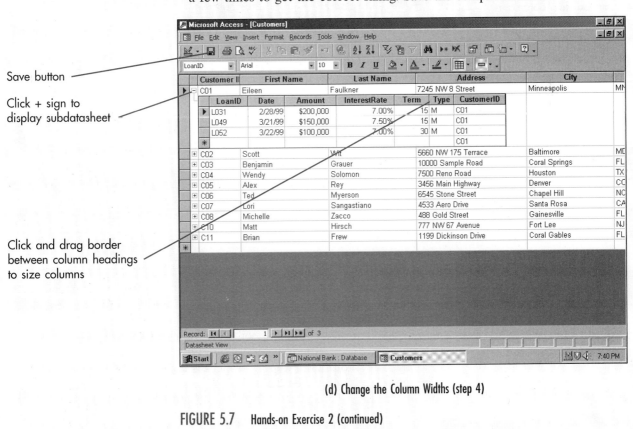

(d) Change the Column Widths (step 4)

FIGURE 5.7   Hands-on Exercise 2 (continued)

STEP 5: View the Customers Form

➤ You should see the Customer form in the **Form View** as in Figure 5.7e.

  • The customer information for the first customer (C01) is displayed in the main portion of the form. The loans for that customer are in the subform.

  • The status bar at the bottom of the window (corresponding to the main form) displays record 1 of 10 records (you are looking at the first record in the Customers table).

  • The status bar for the subform displays record 1 of 3 records (you are on the first of three loan records for this customer).

➤ Click the ▶ **button** on the status bar for the main form to move to the next customer record. The subform is updated automatically to display the two loans belonging to this customer.

➤ Close the Customers form. Click **Yes** if asked to save the changes.

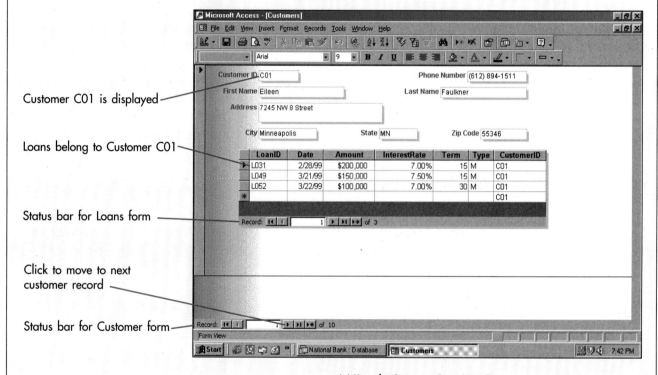

Customer C01 is displayed

Loans belong to Customer C01

Status bar for Loans form

Click to move to next customer record

Status bar for Customer form

(e) View the Customers Form (step 5)

FIGURE 5.7   Hands-on Exercise 2 (continued)

WHY IT WORKS

The main form (Customers) and subform (Loans) work in conjunction with one another so that you always see all of the loans for a given customer. To see how the link is actually implemented, change to the Design view of the Customers form and point anywhere inside the Loans subform. Click the right mouse button to display a shortcut menu, click Properties to display the Subform/Subreport properties dialog box, and, if necessary, click the All tab within the dialog box. You should see CustomerID next to two properties (Link Child Fields and Link Master Fields).

STEP 6: Add the Payment Amount

➤ Click the **Forms button** in the Database window. Open the **Loans subform** in Design view. Click and drag the right edge of the form to **7 inches**.

➤ Click the **Label button** on the Toolbox toolbar, then click and drag in the Form Header to create an unbound control. Enter **Payment Due** as the text for the label as shown in Figure 5.7f. Size and align the label.

➤ Click the **Text box button**, then click and drag in the Detail section to create an unbound control that will contain the amount of the monthly payment. Click the label for the control (e.g., Text 15), then press the **Del key**.

➤ Point to the unbound control, click the **right mouse button**, then click **Properties** to open the properties dialog box. Click the **All tab**.

➤ Click the **Name property**. Enter **Payment Due** in place of the existing label.

➤ Click the **Control Source property**, then click the **Build (...) button** to display the Expression Builder dialog box.

  • Double click **Functions** (if there is a plus sign in its icon), then click **Built-In Functions**. Click **Financial** in the second column, then double click **PMT**.

  • You need to replace each of the arguments in the Pmt function with the appropriate field names from the Loans table. Select the arguments one at a time and enter the replacement for that argument exactly as shown in Figure 5.7f. Click **OK** when finished.

➤ Click the **Format property**, click the **down arrow**, and specify **Currency**. Click the **Decimal Places property**, click the **down arrow**, and select **2**.

➤ Close the Properties dialog box. Change to the Datasheet view and check the column widths, making adjustments as necessary. Close the Loans subform. Click **Yes** to save the changes.

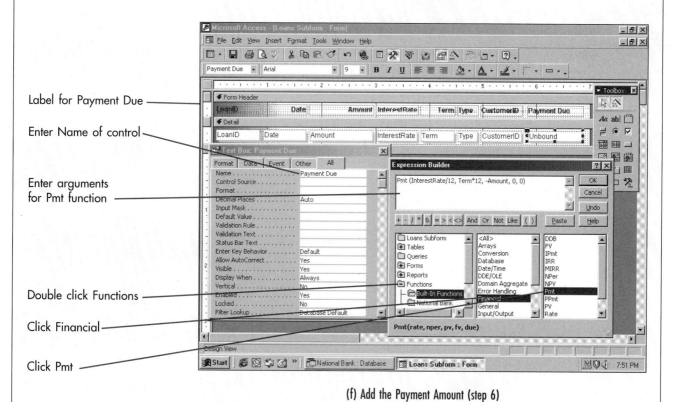

Label for Payment Due

Enter Name of control

Enter arguments for Pmt function

Double click Functions

Click Financial

Click Pmt

(f) Add the Payment Amount (step 6)

FIGURE 5.7   Hands-on Exercise 2 (continued)

STEP 7: Complete the Customers Form

➤ Select the **Customers form**, then click the **Design button** to reopen the form as shown in Figure 5.7g. Click and drag the right border of the subform control to make it larger. Pull down the **View menu**.

➤ Click the **Tab Order command** to display the Tab Order dialog box as shown in Figure 5.7g. Click the **Auto Order button**, then click **OK** to accept the new tab order and close the dialog box.

➤ Click the **Page Break** tool in the toolbox, then click below the subform control. This will print one customer form per page.

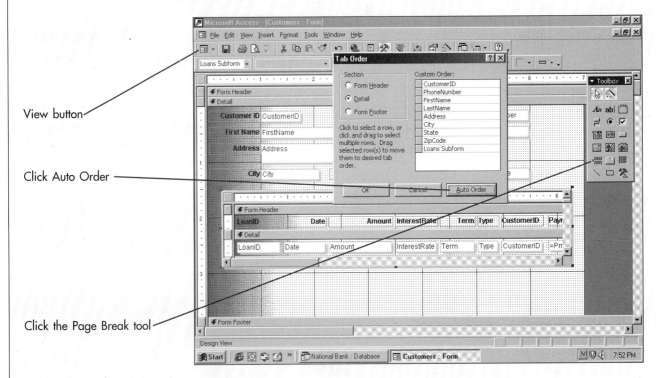

View button

Click Auto Order

Click the Page Break tool

(g) Complete the Customers Form (step 7)

FIGURE 5.7 Hands-on Exercise 2 (continued)

#ERROR AND HOW TO AVOID IT

A #Error message will be displayed in the Form view if the Pmt function is unable to compute a payment; for example, in a new record prior to entering the term of the loan. You can, however, suppress the display of the message by using the IIf (Immediate If) function to test for a null argument. In other words, if the term of the loan has not been entered, do not display anything; otherwise compute the payment in the usual way. Use the IIf function =IIf([Term] Is Null,"",Pmt([InterestRate]/12, [Term]*12,−[Amount],)) as the control source for the payment amount. See Help for additional information.

STEP 8: Enter a New Loan

➤ Click the **View button** to switch to the Form view as shown in Figure 5.7h. (You may have to return to the Design view of the Customers form to increase the space allotted for the Loans subform. You may also have to reopen the Loans subform to adjust the column widths.)

➤ Click the ►| on the status bar of the main form to move to the last record (customer C11) which is the record you entered in the previous exercise. (Click the **PgUp key** if you are on a blank record.)

➤ Click the **LoanID field** next to the asterisk in the subform. Enter data for the new loan as shown in Figure 5.7h:

• The record selector changes to a pencil as soon as you begin to enter data.

• The payment due will be computed automatically as soon as you complete the Term field.

• You do *not* have to enter the CustomerID since it appears automatically due to the relationship between the Customers and Loans tables.

➤ Press the **down arrow** when you have entered the last field (Type), which saves the data in the current record. (The record selector symbol changes from a pencil to a triangle.)

➤ Check that you are still on the record for customer 11 (the record containing your data), then click the **selection area** at the left of the form.

➤ Pull down the **File menu** and click **Print** (or click the Print button) to display the Print dialog box. Click the **Selected Record(s) option button**. Click **OK**.

➤ Close the Customers form. Click **Yes** if asked to save the changes to the form. Close the National Bank database. Exit Access if you do not want to continue with the next hands-on exercise at this time.

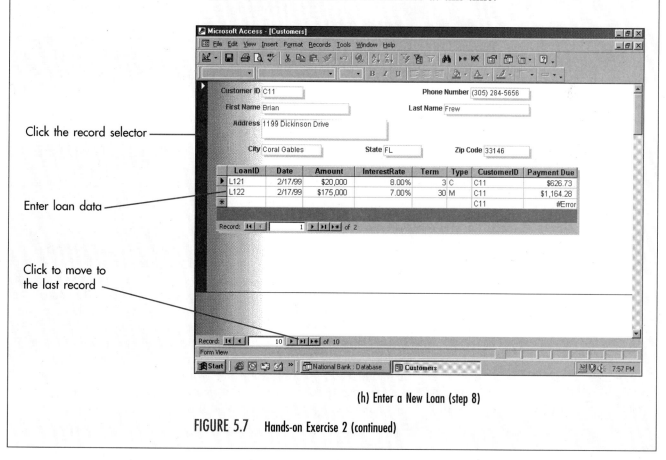

(h) Enter a New Loan (step 8)

FIGURE 5.7   Hands-on Exercise 2 (continued)

The chapter began with a conceptual view of the National Bank database, in which we described the need for separate tables to store data for customers and loans. We created a database with sample data, asked several questions about various customers and their loans, then intuitively drew on both tables to derive the answers. Access simply automates the process through creation of a **multiple-table query**. This type of query was introduced in the previous chapter, but it is reviewed in this section because of its importance.

Let's assume that you wanted to know the name of every customer who held a 15-year mortgage that was issued after April 1, 1999. To answer that question, you would need data from both the Customers table and the Loans table, as shown in Figure 5.8. You would create the query using the same grid as for a simple select query, but you would have to add fields from both tables to the query. The Design view of the query is shown in Figure 5.8a. The resulting dynaset is displayed in Figure 5.8b.

The Query window contains the Field, Sort, Show, and Criteria rows that appear in simple select queries. The **Table row** is necessary only in multiple-table queries and indicates the table where the field originates. The customer's last name and first name are taken from the Customers table. All of the other fields are from the Loans table. The one-to-many relationship between the Customers table and the Loans table is shown graphically within the Query window. The tables are related through the CustomerID field, which is the primary key in the Customers table and a foreign key in the Loans table. The line between the two field lists is called a **join line** and its properties determine how the tables will be accessed within the query.

Figure 5.8 extends the earlier discussion on multiple-table queries to include the **SQL** statement in Figure 5.8c and the Join Properties dialog box in Figure 5.8d. This information is intended primarily for the reader who is interested in the theoretical concepts of a relational database. **Structured Query Language** (SQL) is the universal way to access a relational database, meaning that the information provided by any database is obtained through SQL queries. Access simplifies the creation of an SQL query, however, by providing the Design grid, then converting the entries in the grid to the equivalent SQL statements. You can view the SQL statements from within Access as we did in Figure 5.8c, by changing to the SQL view, and in so doing you can gain a better appreciation for how a relational database works.

The concept of a "join" is also crucial to a relational database. In essence, Access, or any other relational database, combines (joins) all of the records in the Customers table with all of the records in the Loans table to create a temporary working table. The result is a very large table in which each record contains all of the fields from both the Customers table and the Loans table. The number of records in this table is equal to the product of the number of Customer records times the number of Loans records; for example, if there were 10 records in the Customers table, and 30 records in the Loans table, there would be 300 records in the combined table. However, Access displays only those records where the value of the joined field (CustomerID) is the same in both tables. It sounds complicated (it is), but Access does the work for you. And as we said earlier, you only need to master the Design grid in Figure 5.8a and let Access do the rest.

The power of a relational database is its ability to process multiple-table queries, such as the example in Figure 5.8. The forms and reports within a database also become more interesting when they contain information based on multiple table queries. Our next exercise has you create a query similar to the one in Figure 5.8, then create a report based on that query.

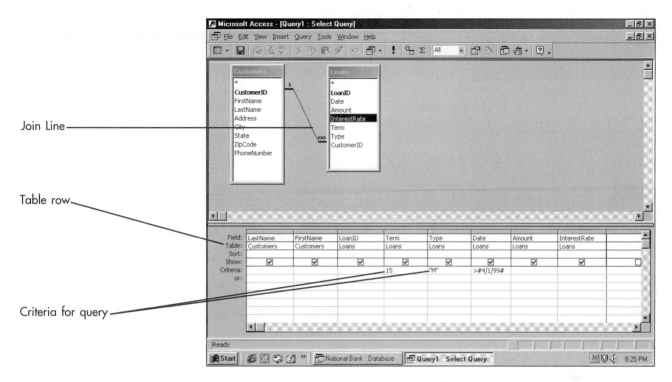

(a) Query Window

	Last Name	First Name	LoanID	Term	Type	Date	Amount	InterestRate
▶	Hirsch	Matt	L062	15	M	4/22/99	$350,000	7.50%
	Grauer	Benjamin	L100	15	M	5/1/99	$150,000	6.00%
	Sangastiano	Lori	L120	15	M	5/8/99	$275,000	9.20%
*								

(b) Dynaset

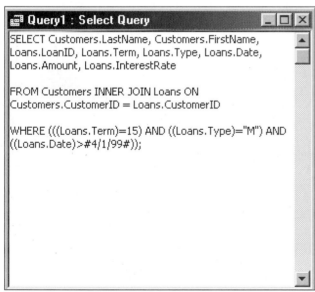

```
SELECT Customers.LastName, Customers.FirstName,
Loans.LoanID, Loans.Term, Loans.Type, Loans.Date,
Loans.Amount, Loans.InterestRate

FROM Customers INNER JOIN Loans ON
Customers.CustomerID = Loans.CustomerID

WHERE (((Loans.Term)=15) AND ((Loans.Type)="M") AND
((Loans.Date)>#4/1/99#));
```

(c) SQL View

Join Properties

Left Table Name: Customers
Right Table Name: Loans

Left Column Name: CustomerID
Right Column Name: CustomerID

⦿ 1: Only include rows where the joined fields from both tables are equal.

◯ 2: Include ALL records from 'Customers' and only those records from 'Loans' where the joined fields are equal.

◯ 3: Include ALL records from 'Loans' and only those records from 'Customers' where the joined fields are equal.

OK   Cancel   New

(d) Join Properties

FIGURE 5.8 A Multiple-Table Query

Objective: To create a query that relates two tables to one another, then create a report based on that query. Use Figure 5.9 as a guide in the exercise.

STEP 1: Create a Select Query

➤ Open the **National Bank database** from the previous exercise.

➤ Click the **Queries button** in the Database window. Double click **Create query in Design view**.

➤ The Show Table dialog box appears as shown in Figure 5.9a, with the Tables tab already selected. Click the **Customers table,** then click the **Add button** (or double click the **Customers table**) to add the Customers table to the query.

➤ Double click the **Loans table** to add the Loans table to the query.

➤ Click **Close** to close the Show Table dialog box.

Click maximize button

Double click Customers table

Double click Loans table

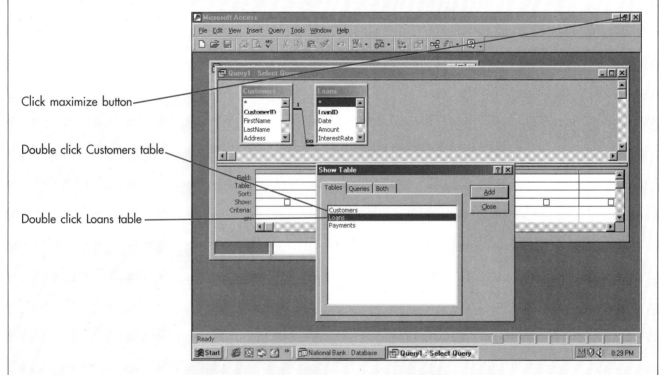

(a) Add the Tables

FIGURE 5.9   Hands-on Exercise 3

ADDING AND DELETING TABLES

To add a table to an existing query, pull down the Query menu, click Show Table, then double click the name of the table from the Table/Query list. To delete a table, click anywhere in its field list and press the Del key, or pull down the Query menu and click Remove Table.

STEP 2: Move and Size the Field Lists

➤ Click the **Maximize button** so that the Query Design window takes the entire desktop.

➤ Point to the line separating the field lists from the design grid (the mouse pointer changes to a cross), then click and drag in a downward direction. This gives you more space to display the field lists for the tables in the query as shown in Figure 5.9b.

➤ Click and drag the bottom of the **Customers table field list** until you can see all of the fields in the Customers table. Click and drag the bottom of the **Loans table field list** until you can see all of the fields in the Loans table.

➤ Click and drag the title bar of the **Loans table** to the right until you are satisfied with the appearance of the line connecting the tables.

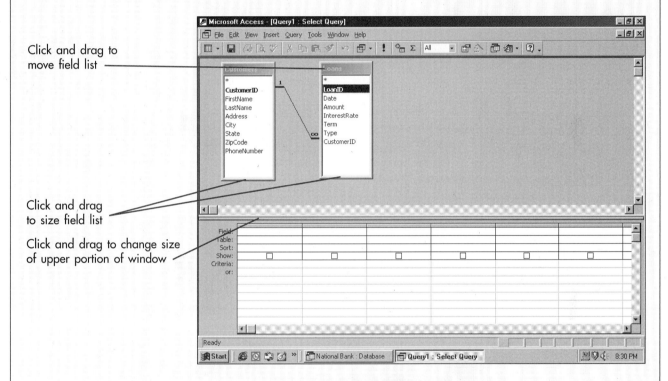

Click and drag to move field list

Click and drag to size field list

Click and drag to change size of upper portion of window

(b) Move and Size the Field Lists (step 2)

FIGURE 5.9 Hands-on Exercise 3 (continued)

CONVERSION TO STANDARD FORMAT

Access is flexible in accepting text and date expressions in the Criteria row of a select query. A text entry can be entered with or without quotation marks (e.g., M or "M"). A date entry can be entered with or without pound signs (you can enter 1/1/96 or #1/1/96#). Access does, however, convert your entries to standard format as soon you move to the next cell in the design grid. Thus, text entries are always displayed in quotation marks, and dates are always enclosed in pound signs.

STEP 3: Create the Query

➤ The Table row should be visible within the design grid. If not, pull down the **View menu** and click **Table Names** to display the Table row in the design grid as shown in Figure 5.9c.

➤ Double click the **LastName** and **FirstName fields**, in that order, from the Customers table to add these fields to the design grid. Double click the **title bar** of the Loans table to select all of the fields, then drag the selected group of fields to the design grid.

➤ Enter the selection criteria (scrolling if necessary) as follows:

  • Click the **Criteria row** under the **Date field**. Type **Between 1/1/99 and 3/31/99**. (You do not have to type the pound signs.)

  • Click the **Criteria row** for the **Amount field**. Type **>200000**.

  • Type **M** in the Criteria row for the **Type field**. (You do not have to type the quotation marks.)

➤ Select all of the columns in the design grid by clicking the column selector in the first column, then pressing and holding the **Shift key** as you scroll to the last column and click its column selector.

➤ Double click the right edge of any column selector to adjust the column width of all the columns simultaneously.

➤ Click the **Sort row** under the LastName field, then click the **down arrow** to open the drop-down list box. Click **Ascending**.

➤ Click the **Save button** on the Query Design toolbar. Save the query as **First Quarter 1999 Jumbo Loans**.

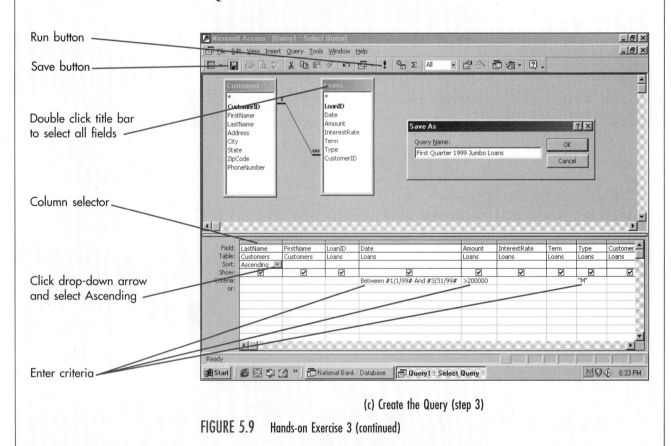

(c) Create the Query (step 3)

FIGURE 5.9   Hands-on Exercise 3 (continued)

STEP 4: Run the Query

➤ Click the **Run button** (the exclamation point) to run the query and create the dynaset in Figure 5.9d. Three jumbo loans are listed.

➤ Click the **Amount field** for loan L028. Enter **100000** as the corrected amount and press **enter**. (This will reduce the number of jumbo loans in subsequent reports to two.)

➤ Return to the Design view and rerun the query. Only two loans are listed, because loan L028 is no longer a jumbo loan. Changing a value in a dynaset automatically changes the underlying query.

➤ Click the **Close button** to close the query. Click **Yes** if asked whether to save the changes to the query.

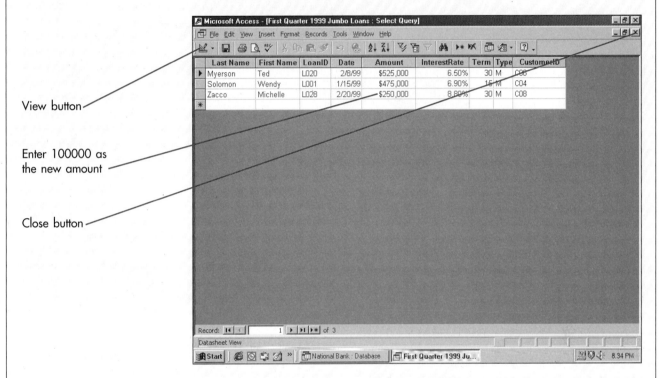

View button

Enter 100000 as the new amount

Close button

(d) The Dynaset (step 4)

FIGURE 5.9 Hands-on Exercise 3 (continued)

DATA TYPE MISMATCH

The data type determines the way in which criteria appear in the design grid. A text field is enclosed in quotation marks. Number, currency, and counter fields are shown as digits with or without a decimal point. Dates are enclosed in pound signs. A Yes/No field is entered as Yes or No without quotation marks. Entering criteria in the wrong format produces a Data Type Mismatch error when attempting to run the query.

STEP 5: Create a Report

➤ The National Bank database should still be open (although the size of your window may be different from the one in the figure).

➤ Click the **Reports button** in the Database window. Double click **Create report by using Wizard**.

➤ Click the **drop-down arrow** to display the tables and queries in the database in order to select the one on which the report will be based.

➤ Select **First Quarter 1999 Jumbo Loans** (the query you just created) as the basis of your report as shown in Figure 5.9e.

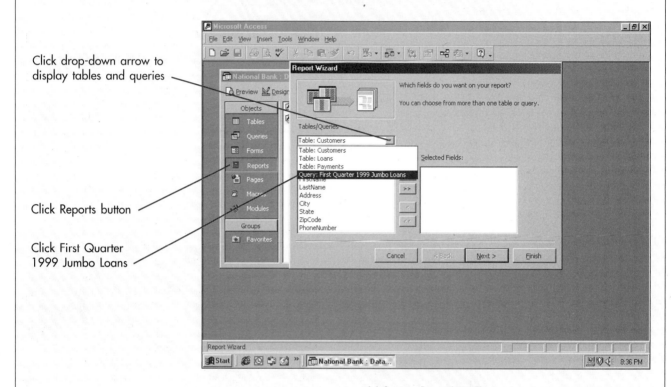

Click drop-down arrow to display tables and queries

Click Reports button

Click First Quarter 1999 Jumbo Loans

(e) Create a Report (step 5)

FIGURE 5.9   Hands-on Exercise 3 (continued)

CHANGE THE REPORT PROPERTIES

Do you want the page header or page footer appearing on every page of a report, or would you prefer to suppress the information on pages where there is a report header or footer? You can customize a report to accommodate this and other subtleties by changing the report properties. Open the report in Design view, right click the Report Selector button (the solid square in the upper left corner), then click the Properties command to display the property sheet for the report. Click the All tab, locate the Page Header or Page Footer property, and make the appropriate change.

STEP 6: The Report Wizard

➤ Double click **LoanID** from the Available Fields list box to add this field to the report. Add the **LastName**, **FirstName**, **Date**, and **Amount** fields as shown in Figure 5.9f. Click **Next**.

➤ There is no need to group the records. Click **Next**.

➤ There is no need to sort the records. Click **Next**.

➤ The **Tabular layout** is selected, as is **Portrait orientation**. Be sure the box is checked to **Adjust field width so all fields fit on a page**. Click **Next**.

➤ Choose **Soft Gray** as the style. Click **Next**.

➤ **First Quarter 1999 Jumbo Loans** is already entered as the title for your report. The option button to **Preview the Report** is already selected.

➤ Click the **Finish Command button** to exit the Report Wizard and preview the report.

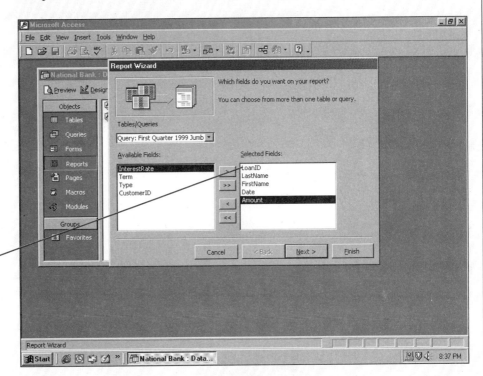

Select fields for report

(f) The Report Wizard (step 6)

FIGURE 5.9   Hands-on Exercise 3 (continued)

SYNCHRONIZING REPORTS

The easiest way to link two reports to one another is to create the reports simultaneously through the Report Wizard, by selecting fields from multiple tables. You can, however, add a subreport to an existing report at any time. Open the existing (main) report in Design view, click the Subform/Subreport tool on the Toolbox toolbar, then click and drag on the main report where you want the subreport to go. Supply the information requested by the Wizard and Access will do the rest. See problem 7 at the end of the chapter.

STEP 7: Print the Completed Report

➤ Click the **Maximize button**. If necessary, click the **Zoom button** in the Print Preview window so that you can see the whole report as in Figure 5.9g.

➤ The report is based on the query created earlier. Michelle Zacco is *not* in the report because the amount of her loan was updated in the query's dynaset in step 4.

➤ Click the **Print button** to print the report. Close the Preview window, then close the Report window. Click **Yes** if asked to save the changes.

➤ Close the National Bank database and exit Access if you do not want to continue with the next exercise at this time.

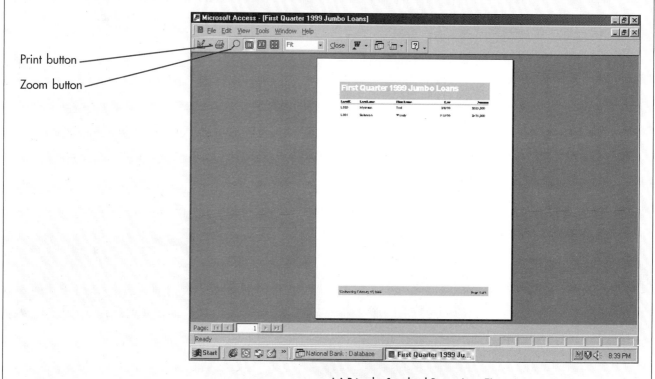

(g) Print the Completed Report (step 7)

FIGURE 5.9   Hands-on Exercise 3 (continued)

DATA ACCESS PAGES

The information produced by an Access database can be displayed in a query, form, or a printed report. It can also be saved as a data access page that exists as a separate object within an Access database and as an HTML document. The latter can be viewed in Internet Explorer, without having Microsoft Access installed on the client computer. The data within a data access page can be grouped (e.g., by customer), and sorted within a group (e.g., by loan number). See problem 8 at the end of the chapter.

One of the advantages of a relational database is that it can be easily expanded to include additional tables without disturbing the existing tables. The database used throughout the chapter consisted of two tables: a Customers table and a Loans table. Figure 5.10 extends the database to include a partial listing of the Payments table containing the payments received by the bank. Each record in the Payments table has four fields: LoanID, PaymentNumber, Date (the date the payment was received), and PaymentReceived (the amount sent in).

The original database had a one-to-many relationship between customers and loans. One customer may have many loans, but a given loan is associated with only one customer. The expanded database contains a second one-to-many relationship between loans and payments. One loan has many payments, but a specific payment is associated with only one loan. Thus, the primary key of the Loans table (LoanID) appears as a foreign key in the Payments table.

Look carefully at the Payments table and note that it contains multiple records with the same payment number (e.g., every loan has a payment number 1). In similar fashion, there are multiple records with the same LoanID. Loan L001, for example, has five payments. The combination of LoanID and Payment-Number is unique, however (there is only one payment 1 for loan L001), and thus the combination of the two fields serves as the primary key. Consider:

Query: How many payments have been received for loan L022? What was the date of the most recent payment?

Answer: Four payments have been received for loan L022. The most recent payment was received on 6/12/99.

The query can be answered with reference to just the Payments table by finding all payments for loan L022. To determine the most recent payment, you would retrieve the records in descending order by Date and retrieve the first record.

Query: How many payments have been received from Michelle Zacco since May 1, 1999?

Answer: Four payments have been received. Two of the payments were for loan L028 on May 20th and June 20th. Two were for loan L030 on May 21st and June 21st.

To answer this query, you would look in the Customers table to determine the CustomerID for Ms. Zacco, search the Loans table for all loans for this customer, then retrieve the corresponding payments from the Payments table. (Michelle is also associated with loan L060. The Payments table, however, is truncated in Figure 5.10, and hence the payments for this loan are not visible.)

A CONCATENATED PRIMARY KEY

The primary key is defined as the field, or combination of fields, that is unique for every record in a table. The Payments table contains multiple records with the same payment number (i.e., every loan has a payment number 1, 2, 3, and so on) as well as multiple payments for the same LoanID. The combination of LoanID and PaymentNumber is unique, however, and serves as the primary key for the Payments table.

CustomerID	First Name	Last Name	Address	City	State	Zip Code	Phone Number
C01	Eileen	Faulkner	7245 NW 8 Street	Minneapolis	MN	55346	(612) 894-1511
C02	Scott	Wit	5660 NW 175 Terrace	Baltimore	MD	21224	(410) 753-0345
C03	Benjamin	Grauer	10000 Sample Road	Coral Springs	FL	33073	(305) 444-5555
C04	Wendy	Solomon	7500 Reno Road	Houston	TX	77090	(713) 427-3104
C05	Alex	Rey	3456 Main Highway	Denver	CO	80228	(303) 555-6666
C06	Ted	Myerson	6545 Stone Street	Chapel Hill	NC	27515	(919) 942-7654
C07	Lori	Sangastiano	4533 Aero Drive	Santa Rosa	CA	95403	(707) 542-3411
C08	Michelle	Zacco	488 Gold Street	Gainesville	FL	32601	(904) 374-5660
C09	David	Powell	5070 Battle Road	Decatur	GA	30034	(301) 345-6556
C10	Matt	Hirsch	777 NW 67 Avenue	Fort Lee	NJ	07624	(201) 664-3211

(a) Customers Table

LoanID	Date	Amount	Interest Rate	Term	Type	CustomerID
L001	1/15/99	$475,000	6.90%	15	M	C04
L004	1/23/99	$35,000	7.20%	5	C	C04
L010	1/25/99	$10,000	5.50%	3	C	C05
L014	1/31/99	$12,000	9.50%	10	O	C04
L020	2/8/99	$525,000	6.50%	30	M	C06
L022	2/12/99	$10,500	7.50%	5	O	C07
L026	2/15/99	$35,000	6.50%	5	O	C10
L028	2/20/99	$250,000	8.80%	30	M	C08
L030	2/21/99	$5,000	10.00%	3	O	C08
L031	2/28/99	$200,000	7.00%	15	M	C01
L032	3/1/99	$25,000	10.00%	3	C	C02
L033	3/1/99	$20,000	9.50%	5	O	C05
L039	3/3/99	$56,000	7.50%	5	C	C09
L040	3/10/99	$129,000	8.50%	15	M	C10
L047	3/11/99	$200,000	7.25%	15	M	C03
L049	3/21/99	$150,000	7.50%	15	M	C01
L052	3/22/99	$100,000	7.00%	30	M	C01
L053	3/31/99	$15,000	6.50%	3	O	C03
L054	4/1/99	$10,000	8.00%	5	C	C02
L057	4/15/99	$25,000	8.50%	4	C	C03
L060	4/18/99	$41,000	9.90%	4	C	C08
L062	4/22/99	$350,000	7.50%	15	M	C10
L100	5/1/99	$150,000	6.00%	15	M	C03
L109	5/3/99	$350,000	8.20%	30	M	C04
L120	5/8/99	$275,000	9.20%	15	M	C07

(b) Loans Table

LoanID	Payment Number	Date	Payment Received
L001	1	2/15/99	$4,242.92
L001	2	3/15/99	$4,242.92
L001	3	4/15/99	$4,242.92
L001	4	5/15/99	$4,242.92
L001	5	6/15/99	$4,242.92
L004	1	2/23/99	$696.35
L004	2	3/23/99	$696.35
L004	3	4/23/99	$696.35
L004	4	5/23/99	$696.35
L004	5	6/23/99	$696.35
L010	1	2/25/99	$301.96
L010	2	3/25/99	$301.96

LoanID	Payment Number	Date	Payment Received
L010	3	4/25/99	$301.96
L010	4	5/25/99	$301.96
L010	5	6/25/99	$301.96
L014	1	2/28/99	$155.28
L014	2	3/31/99	$155.28
L014	3	4/30/99	$155.28
L014	4	5/30/99	$155.28
L014	5	6/30/99	$155.28
L020	1	3/8/99	$3,318.36
L020	2	4/8/99	$3,318.36
L020	3	5/8/99	$3,318.36
L020	4	6/8/99	$3,318.36
L022	1	3/12/99	$210.40
L022	2	4/12/99	$210.40

LoanID	Payment Number	Date	Payment Received
L022	3	5/12/99	$210.40
L022	4	6/12/99	$210.40
L026	1	3/15/99	$684.82
L026	2	4/15/99	$684.82
L026	3	5/15/99	$684.82
L026	4	6/15/99	$684.82
L028	1	3/20/99	$1,975.69
L028	2	4/20/99	$1,975.69
L028	3	5/20/99	$1,975.69
L028	4	6/20/99	$1,975.69
L030	1	3/21/99	$161.34
L030	2	4/21/99	$161.34
L030	3	5/21/99	$161.34
L030	4	6/21/99	$161.34

(c) Payments Table (partial list)

FIGURE 5.10   Expanding the Database

Multiple Subforms

Subforms were introduced earlier in the chapter as a means of displaying data from related tables. Figure 5.11 continues the discussion by showing a main form with two levels of subforms. The main (Customers) form has a one-to-many relationship with the first (Loans) subform. The Loans subform in turn has a one-to-many relationship with the second (Payments) subform. The Customers form and the Loans subform are the forms you created in the second hands-on exercise. (The Loans subform is displayed in the Form view as opposed to the Data sheet view.) The Payments subform is new and will be developed in our next exercise.

The records displayed in the three forms are linked to one another according to the relationships within the database. There is a one-to-many relationship between customers and loans so that the first subform displays all of the loans for one customer. There is also a one-to-many relationship between loans and payments so that the second subform (Payments) displays all of the payments for the selected loan. Click on a different loan (for the same customer), and the Payments subform is updated automatically to show all of the payments for that loan.

The status bar for the main form indicates record 5 of 10, meaning that you are viewing the fifth of 10 Customer records. The status bar for the Loans subform indicates record 2 of 2, corresponding to the second of two loan records for the fifth customer. The status bar for the Payments subform indicates record 1 of 3, corresponding to the first of three Payment records for this loan for this customer.

The three sets of navigation buttons enable you to advance to the next record(s) in any of the forms. The records move in conjunction with one another. Thus, if you advance to the next record in the Customers form you will automatically display a different set of records in the Loans subform, as well as a different set of Payment records in the Payments subform.

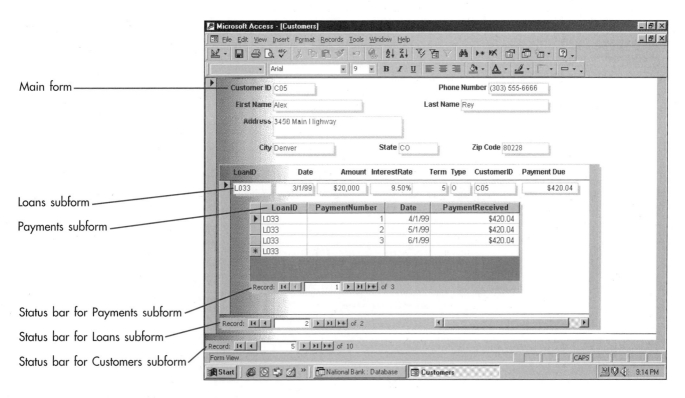

FIGURE 5.11 Multiple Subforms

Linked Subforms

Objective: To create a main form with two levels of subforms; to display a subform in Form view or Datasheet view. Use Figure 5.12 as a guide.

STEP 1: Add a Relationship

➤ Open the **National Bank database**. Pull down the **Tools menu**. Click **Relationships** to open the Relationships window as shown in Figure 5.12a.

➤ Maximize the Relationships window. Pull down the **Relationships menu**. Click **Show Table** to display the Show Table dialog box.

➤ The **Tables tab** is selected within the Show Table dialog box. Double click the **Payments table** to add the table to the Relationships window. Close the Show Table dialog box.

➤ Click and drag the title bar of the **Payments Field list** so that it is positioned approximately one inch from the Loans table.

➤ Click and drag the **LoanID field** in the Loans field list to the **LoanID field** in the Payments field list. You will see the Relationships dialog box.

➤ Check the **Enforce Referential Integrity** check box. (If necessary, clear the check boxes to Cascade Update Related Fields and Delete Related Records.)

➤ Click the **Create button** to establish the relationship. You should see a line indicating a one-to-many relationship between the Loans and Payments tables.

➤ Click the **Save button**, then close the Relationships window.

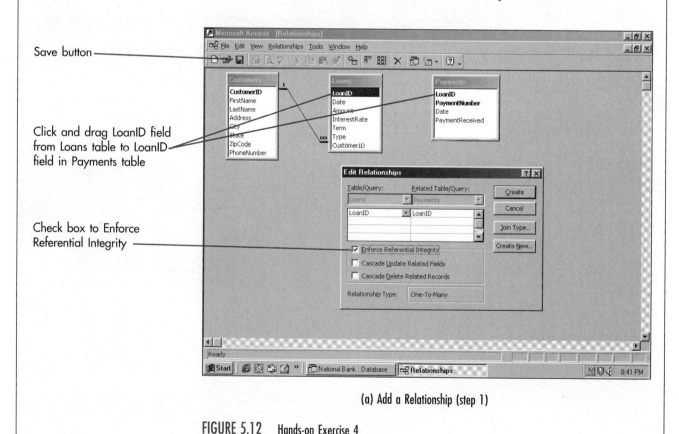

Save button

Click and drag LoanID field from Loans table to LoanID field in Payments table

Check box to Enforce Referential Integrity

(a) Add a Relationship (step 1)

FIGURE 5.12   Hands-on Exercise 4

STEP 2: Create the Payments Subform

➤ You should be back in the Database window. Click the **Forms button**, then open the **Loans subform** in Design view as shown in Figure 5.12b.

➤ Click and drag the top edge of the **Details section** so that you have approximately 2 to 2½ inches of blank space in the Detail section.

➤ Click the **Subform/Subreport button** on the Toolbox toolbar, then click and drag in the Loans form to create the Payments subform. Release the mouse.

➤ The **Use Existing Tables and Queries option button** is selected, indicating that we will build the subform from a table or query. Click **Next**. You should see the Subform/Subreport dialog box in Figure 5.12b.

➤ Click the **drop-down arrow** on the Tables and Queries list box to select the **Payments table**. Click the **>> button** to add all of the fields in the Payments table to the subform. Click **Next**.

➤ The Subform Wizard asks you to define the fields that link the main form to the subform. The option button to **Choose from a list** is selected, as is **Show Payments for each record in Loans using LoanID**. Click **Next**.

➤ **Payments subform** is entered as the name of the subform. Click **Finish**.

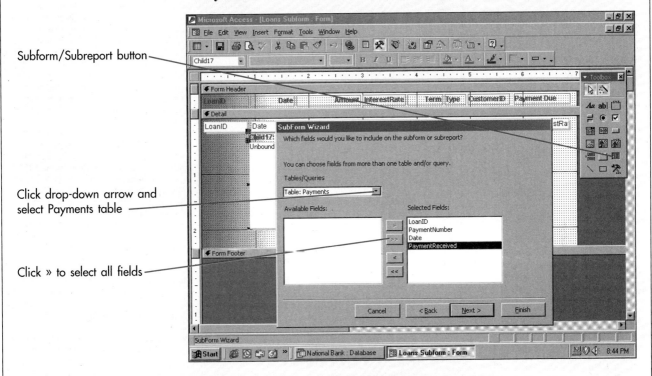

(b) Create the Payments Subform (step 2)

FIGURE 5.12   Hands-on Exercise 4 (continued)

LINKING FIELDS, FORMS, AND SUBFORMS

Linking fields do not have to appear in the main form and subform but must be included in the underlying table or query. The LoanID, for example, links the Loans form and the Payments form and need not appear in either form. We have, however, chosen to display the LoanID in both forms to emphasize the relationship between the corresponding tables.

STEP 3: Change the Default View

➤ Maximize the window. Point to the **Form Selector box** in the upper-left corner of the Design window, click the **right mouse button** to display a shortcut menu, and click **Properties** to display the Form Properties dialog box in Figure 5.12c.

➤ Click in the **Default View box,** click the **drop-down arrow** to display the views, then click **Single Form.** Close the Properties dialog box.

➤ Select the label for the Payments subform control, then press the **Del key** to delete the label.

➤ Save the form.

Click drop-down arrow on View button

Point to form selector box and click right mouse button

Delete label

Click in Default View box

Click drop-down arrow

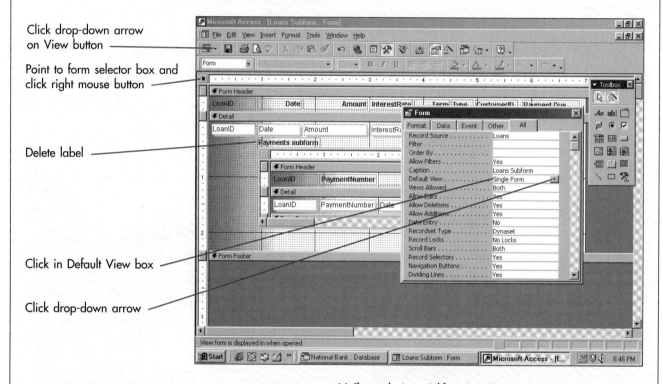

(c) Change the Loans Subform (step 3)

FIGURE 5.12   Hands-on Exercise 4 (continued)

THE DEFAULT VIEW PROPERTY

The Default View property determines how a form is dislayed initially and is especially important when working with multiple forms. In general, the highest level form(s) is (are) displayed in the Single Form view and the lowest level in the Datasheet view. In this example, the Customers and Loans forms are both set to the Single Form view, whereas the Payment form is set to the Datasheet view. To change the default view, right click the Form Selector box to display the property sheet, click the All tab, then change the entry in the Default View property.

STEP 4: The Loans Subform in Form View

➤ Click the **drop-down arrow** next to the **View button** to switch to the Form view for the Loans subform as shown in Figure 5.12d.

➤ Do not be concerned if the size and/or position of your form is different from ours as you can return to the Design view in order to make the necessary changes.

• The status bar of the Loans form indicates record 1 of 26, meaning that you are positioned on the first of 26 records in the Loans table.

• The status bar for the Payments subform indicates record 1 of 5, corresponding to the first of five payment records for this loan.

➤ Change to the **Design view** to size and/or move the Payments subform control within the Loans subform. Save, then close, the Loans subform.

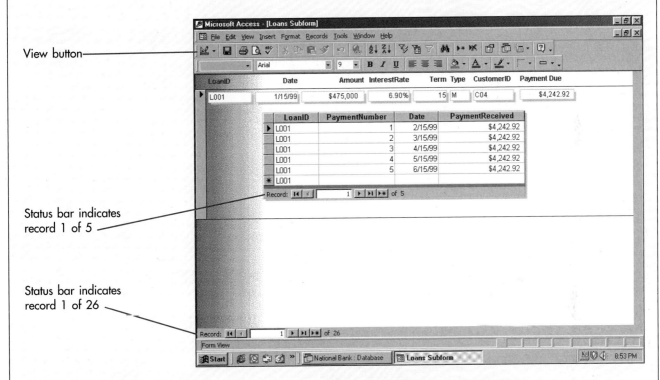

(d) The Loans Subform in Form View (step 4)

FIGURE 5.12   Hands-on Exercise 4 (continued)

USER FRIENDLY FORMS

The phrase "user friendly" appears so frequently that we tend to take it for granted. The intention is clear, however, and you should strive to make your forms as clear as possible so that the user is provided with all the information he or she may need. It may be obvious to the designer that one has to click the Navigation buttons to move to a new loan, but a novice unfamiliar with Access may not know that. Adding a descriptive label to the form goes a long way toward making a system successful.

STEP 5: The Customers Form

➤ You should be back in the Database window. Click the **Forms button** (if necessary), then open the **Customers form** as shown in Figure 5.12e.

➤ Do not be concerned if the size of the subforms are different from ours as you can return to the Design view to make the necessary changes.

- The status bar of the Customers form indicates record 1 of 10, meaning that you are positioned on the first of 10 records in the Customers table.

- The status bar for the Loans subform indicates record 1 of 3, corresponding to the first of three records for this customer.

- The status bar for the Payments subform indicates record 1 of 4, corresponding to the first of four payments for this loan.

➤ Change to the **Design view** to move and/or size the control for the Loans subform as described in step 6.

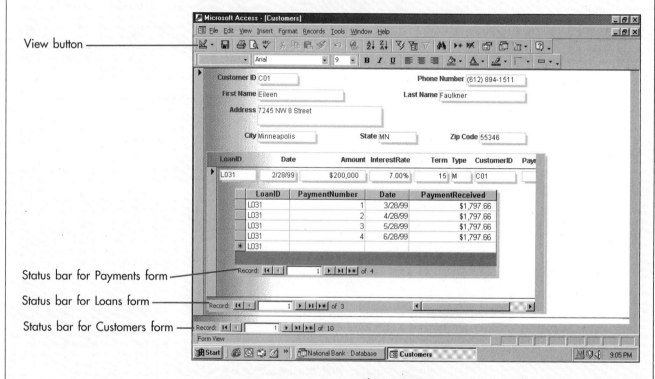

(e) The Customers Form (step 5)

FIGURE 5.12 Hands-on Exercise 4 (continued)

THE STARTUP PROPERTY

The Startup property determines how a database will appear when it is opened. One very common option is to open a form automatically so that the user is presented with the form without having to navigate through the Database window. Pull down the Tools menu, click Startup to display the Startup dialog box, then click the drop-down arrow in the Display Form list box. Select the desired form, such as the Customers form created in this exercise, then click OK. The next time you open the database the designated form will be opened automatically.

STEP 6: The Finishing Touches

➤ You may need to increase the size of the Loans subform control. Click and drag the bottom edge of the **Detail Section** in Figure 5.12f to make the section larger. You may also have to click and drag the Loans subform to the left, then click and drag its right border to make it wider.

➤ We also found it necessary to decrease the size of the Amount field within the Loans subform. Click the label for the **Amount field** in the Form header. Press and hold the **Shift key** as you select the bound control for the Amount field in the detail section, then click and drag the right border to make both controls narrower.

➤ Click the **Interest Rate label**. Press and hold the **Shift key** as you select the remaining controls to the left of the amount field, then click and drag these fields to the left. Save the changes.

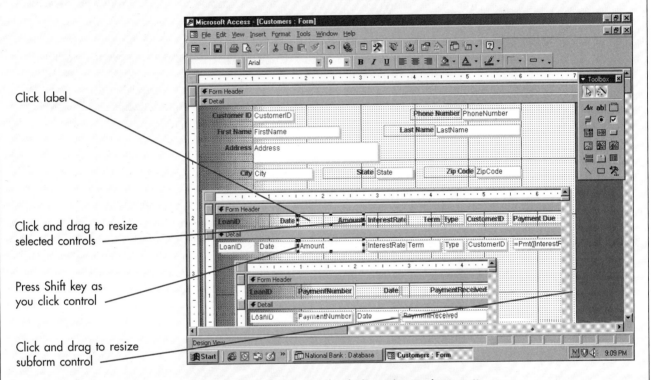

Click label

Click and drag to resize selected controls

Press Shift key as you click control

Click and drag to resize subform control

(f) The Finishing Touches (step 6)

FIGURE 5.12   Hands-on Exercise 4 (continued)

MULTIPLE CONTROLS AND PROPERTIES

Press and hold the Shift key as you click one control after another in order to select multiple controls. To view or change the properties for the selected controls, click the right mouse button to display a shortcut menu, then click Properties to display a property sheet. If the value of a property is the same for all selected controls, that value will appear in the property sheet; otherwise the box for that property will be blank. Changing a property when multiple controls are selected changes the property for all selected controls.

STEP 7: Make Your Payments

➤ Change to the **Form view.** Click the ▶❘ on the status bar for the Customers form to move to the last record as shown in Figure 5.12g. This should be Customer C11 (your record) that you entered in the earlier exercises in this chapter. You currently have two loans, L121 and L122, the first of which is displayed.

➤ Click in the **Payments subform.** Enter the payment number, press **Tab,** enter the date of your first payment, press **Tab,** then enter the amount paid. Press **enter** to move to the next payment record and enter this payment as well. Press **enter** and enter a third payment.

➤ Click the **selection area** at the left of the form to select this record. Pull down the **File menu** and click **Print** to display the Print dialog box. Click the **Selected Records Option button.** Click **OK** to print the selected form.

➤ Close the Customers form. Click **Yes** if asked to save the changes to the form.

➤ Close the National Bank database and exit Access.

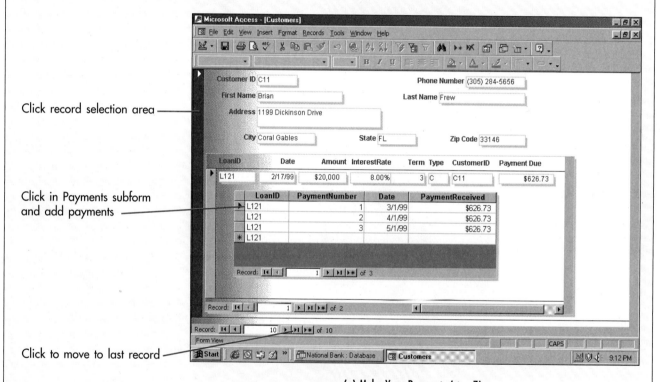

Click record selection area —

Click in Payments subform and add payments —

Click to move to last record —

(g) Make Your Payments (step 7)

FIGURE 5.12 Hands-on Exercise 4 (continued)

THREE SETS OF NAVIGATION BUTTONS

Each form or subform has its own set of navigation buttons. Thus, you are looking at record 10 of 10 in the Customers form, loan 1 of 2 in the Loans form for this customer, and payment 3 of 3 in the Payments form for this loan.

An Access database may contain multiple tables. Each table stores data about a specific subject. Each table has a primary key, which is a field (or combination of fields) that uniquely identifies each record.

A one-to-many relationship uses the primary key of the "one" table as a foreign key in the "many" table. (A foreign key is simply the primary key of the related table.) The Relationships window enables you to graphically create a one-to-many relationship by dragging the join field from one table to the other.

Referential integrity ensures that the tables in a database are consistent with one another. When referential integrity is enforced, Access prevents you from adding a record to the "many" table if that record contains an invalid foreign key. It also prevents you from deleting a record in the "one" table if there is a corresponding record in the related table. You can, however, always add a record to the "one" table, and you can always delete a record from the "many" table.

A subform is a form within a form and is used to display data from a related table. It is created most easily with the Form Wizard, then modified in the Form Design view just as any other form. A main form can have any number of subforms. Subforms can extend to two levels, enabling a subform to be created within a subform.

The power of a select query lies in its ability to include fields from several tables. The query shows the relationships that exist between the tables by drawing a join line that indicates how to relate the data. The Tables row displays the name of the table containing the corresponding field. Once created, a multiple table query can be the basis for a form or report.

Tables can be added to a relational database without disturbing the data in existing tables. A database can have several one-to-many relationships. All relationships are created in the Relationships window.

KEY WORDS AND CONCEPTS

Build button	Main form	Relationship line
Control Source property	One-to-many relationship	Relationships window
Datasheet view	Primary key	Subform
Foreign key	Primary table	Subform Wizard
Form view	Referential integrity	Table row
Function	Related table	

MULTIPLE CHOICE

1. Which of the following will cause a problem of referential integrity when there is a one-to-many relationship between customers and loans?

(a) The deletion of a customer record that has corresponding loan records

(b) The deletion of a customer record that has no corresponding loan records

(c) The deletion of a loan record with a corresponding customer record

(d) All of the above

2. Which of the following will cause a problem of referential integrity when there is a one-to-many relationship between customers and loans?
   (a) The addition of a new customer prior to entering loans for that customer
   (b) The addition of a new loan that references an invalid customer
   (c) Both (a) and (b)
   (d) Neither (a) nor (b)

3. Which of the following is true about a database that monitors players and the teams to which those players are assigned?
   (a) The PlayerID will be defined as a primary key within the Teams table
   (b) The TeamID will be defined as a primary key within the Players table
   (c) The PlayerID will appear as a foreign key within the Teams table
   (d) The TeamID will appear as a foreign key within the Players table

4. Which of the following best expresses the relationships within the expanded National Bank database as it appeared at the end of the chapter?
   (a) There is a one-to-many relationship between customers and loans
   (b) There is a one-to-many relationship between loans and payments
   (c) Both (a) and (b)
   (d) Neither (a) nor (b)

5. A database has a one-to-many relationship between branches and employees (one branch can have many employees). Which of the following is a true statement about that database?
   (a) The EmployeeID will be defined as a primary key within the Branches table
   (b) The BranchID will be defined as a primary key within the Employees table
   (c) The EmployeeID will appear as a foreign key within the Branches table
   (d) The BranchID will appear as a foreign key within the Employees table

6. Every table in an Access database:
   (a) Must be related to every other table
   (b) Must have one or more foreign keys
   (c) Both (a) and (b)
   (d) Neither (a) nor (b)

7. Which of the following is true of a main form and subform that are created in conjunction with the one-to-many relationship between customers and loans?
   (a) The main form should be based on the Customers table
   (b) The subform should be based on the Loans table
   (c) Both (a) and (b)
   (d) Neither (a) nor (b)

8. Which of the following is true regarding the navigation buttons for a main form and its associated subform?
   (a) The navigation buttons pertain to just the main form
   (b) The navigation buttons pertain to just the subform
   (c) There are separate navigation buttons for each form
   (d) There are no navigation buttons at all

9. How do you open a subform?
   (a) Go to the Design view of the associated main form, click anywhere in the main form to deselect the subform, then double click the subform
   (b) Go to the Database window, select the subform, then click the Open or Design buttons, depending on the desired view
   (c) Both (a) and (b)
   (d) Neither (a) nor (b)

10. Which of the following is true?
    (a) A main form may contain multiple subforms
    (b) A subform may contain another subform
    (c) Both (a) and (b)
    (d) Neither (a) nor (b)

11. Which command displays the open tables in an Access database in equal-sized windows one on top of another?
    (a) The Tile command in the Window menu
    (b) The Cascade command in the Window menu
    (c) The Tile command in the Relationships menu
    (d) The Cascade command in the Relationships menu

12. Which of the following describes how to move and size a field list within the Relationships window?
    (a) Click and drag the title bar to size the field list
    (b) Click and drag a border or corner to move the field list
    (c) Both (a) and (b)
    (d) Neither (a) nor (b)

13. Which of the following is true regarding entries in a Criteria row of a select query?
    (a) A text field may be entered with or without quotation marks
    (b) A date field may be entered with or without surrounding number (pound) signs
    (c) Both (a) and (b)
    (d) Neither (a) nor (b)

14. Which of the following is true about a select query?
    (a) It may reference fields in one or more tables
    (b) It may have one or more criteria rows
    (c) It may sort on one or more fields
    (d) All of the above

15. A report may be based on:
    (a) A table
    (b) A query
    (c) Both (a) and (b)
    (d) Neither (a) nor (b)

ANSWERS

1. a	6. d	11. b
2. b	7. c	12. d
3. d	8. c	13. c
4. c	9. c	14. d
5. d	10. c	15. c

1. **Adding Clip Art:** Figure 5.13 contains a modified version of the Customers form and its associated subforms. Complete the hands-on exercises in the chapter, then modify the completed Customers form so that it matches Figure 5.13. Follow the steps below to add the clip art image.

   a. Open the Loans subform in the Design view. Move the control for the Payments subform to the left to allow room for the OLE object.

   b. Click the Unbound Object Frame tool on the toolbox. (If you are unsure as to which tool to click, just point to the tool to display its name.)

   c. Click and drag in the Loans subform to size the frame, then release the mouse to display an Insert Object dialog box. Click the Create New Option button. Select the Microsoft Clip Gallery as the object type. Click OK.

   d. Click the Pictures tab. Choose the category and picture you want from within the Clip Gallery. Click the Insert Clip button to insert the picture into the Access form and simultaneously close the Clip Gallery dialog box.

   e. Right click the newly inserted object to display a shortcut menu, then click Properties to display the Properties dialog box. Click the Format tab, then select (click) the Size Mode property and select Stretch from the associated list. Change the Back Style property to Transparent, the Special Effect property to Flat, and the Border Style property to Transparent.

   f. You should see the entire clip art image, although it may be distorted. Click and drag the sizing handles on the frame to size the object so that its proportions are correct.

   g. Close the Loans subform, then open the Customer Form. Print the completed form with your customer information. Remember to click the selection area prior to printing. (You are still customer C11.)

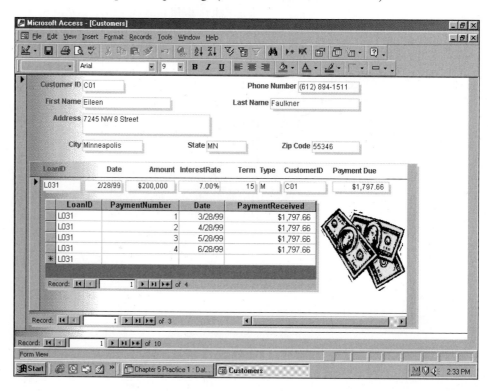

FIGURE 5.13   Adding Clip Art (Exercise 1)

2. The Report Wizard: Interest rates have come down and National Bank has decided to run a promotion on car loans. The loan officer would like to contact all existing customers with a car loan to inform them of their new rates. Create a report similar to the one in Figure 5.14 in response to the request from the loan officer.

The report should be based on a query that contains fields from both the Customers and the Loans tables. Note, too, the clip art image, which is required in the Report heading and which can be added using the techniques described in the previous problem. Be sure to add your name to the heading so that your instructor will know the report came from you.

Customers with Car Loans

Prepared by Brian Frew

Last Name	First Name	Address			Phone Number
Frew	Brian	1199 Dickinson Drive			(305) 284-5656
		Coral Gables	FL	33146	
Grauer	Benjamin	10000 Sample Road			(305) 444-5555
		Coral Springs	FL	33073	
Rey	Alex	3456 Main Highway			(303) 555-6666
		Denver	CO	80228	
Solomon	Wendy	7500 Reno Road			(713) 427-3104
		Houston	TX	77090	
Wit	Scott	5660 NW 175 Terrace			(410) 753-0345
		Baltimore	MD	21224	
Wit	Scott	5660 NW 175 Terrace			(410) 753-0345
		Baltimore	MD	21224	
Zacco	Michelle	488 Gold Street			(904) 374-5660
		Gainesville	FL	32601	

Sunday, February 21, 1999   **Page 1 of 1**

FIGURE 5.14   The Report Wizard (Exercise 2)

3. Employees by Location: Use the Look Ahead database in the Exploring Access folder to create the main and subform combination shown in Figure 5.15. There is a one-to-many relationship between locations and employees (one location contains many employees). You may have to create the relationships within the database, depending on whether or not you completed the assignments from earlier chapters, Note, too, that you need not follow the figure exactly, and are free to improve on the design in any way you deem appropriate.

Add your name as an Account Exec in Atlanta at a salary of $100,000 a year. Click the form selector bar to select the Atlanta location, then print this record for your instructor as proof you completed the exercise. Close the form, then open the Employees table to verify that your record has been added to the database.

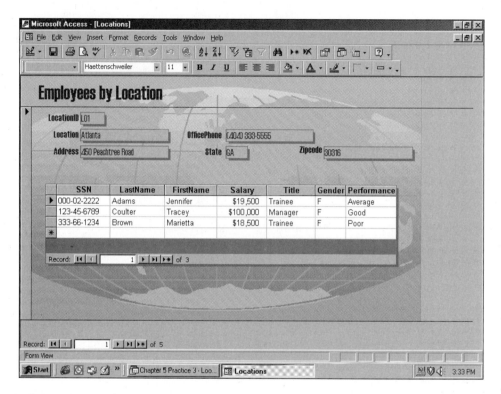

FIGURE 5.15 Employees by Location (Exercise 3)

4. Employees by Title: The form in Figure 5.16 is also based on the Look Ahead database that is referenced in the previous exercise. This time, however, the forms are based on the one-to-many relationship that exists between titles and employees (one title may pertain to many employees). You may have to create the relationships within the database, depending on whether or not you completed the assignments from earlier chapters. Once again, you need not follow the figure exactly, and are free to improve on the design in any way you deem appropriate.

Your name should appear automatically within the list of account executives (given that you added your name in the previous exercise). Click the form selector bar to select this form, then print the list of account executives for your instructor.

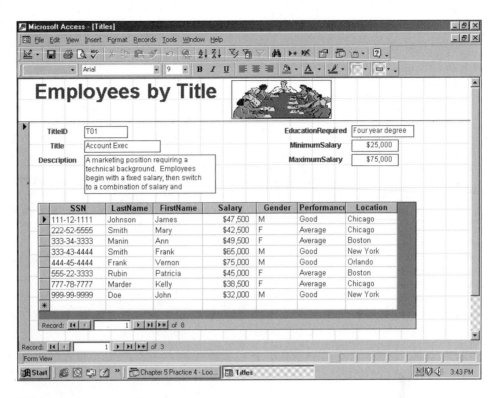

FIGURE 5.16   Employees by Title (Exercise 4)

5. The Switchboard: Complete the various hands-on exercises and end-of-chapter problems, then create a switchboard similar to Figure 5.17. You need not follow our design exactly, but you should include at least four menu options. Be sure to include a button to exit from the database.

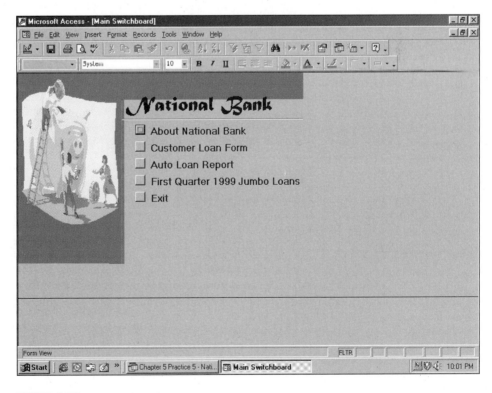

FIGURE 5.17   The Switchboard (Exercise 5)

6. **The Table Analyzer Wizard:** The Fly By Night Banking database is similar to the National Bank example we have used throughout the chapter, except that its design is flawed through duplicate data. The Table Analyzer Wizard will explain how redundant data wastes space and leads to errors, and then it will suggest ways in which to improve your design.

   a. Open the database, click the Tables button, and select the Loans table. Can you spot the flaw in the design that leads to redundant data?

   b. Pull down the Tools menu, click the Analyze command, then choose Tables to display the Table Analyzer Wizard in Figure 5.18. Let the Wizard examine the Loans table for you and suggest ways in which to split the data into two or more tables. How does the Wizard's design compare to the design of the National Bank database?

   c. Close The Fly By Night Banking database, then open the National Bank database you have used throughout the chapter. Start the Table Analyzer Wizard and let it analyze the Customers, Loans, and Payments tables. What suggestions does the Wizard have for changing these tables?

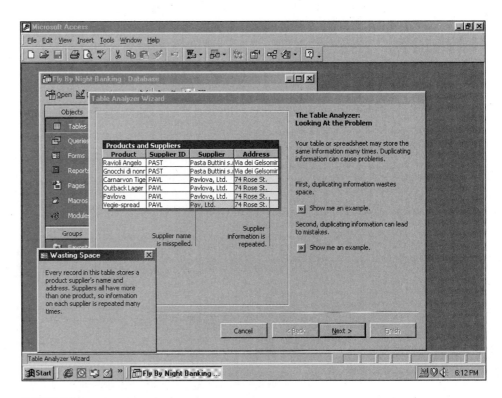

FIGURE 5.18   The Table Analyzer Wizard (Exercise 6)

7. **Synchronizing Reports:** The report in Figure 5.19 displays information about a specific customer, followed by information on all loans for that customer, followed by information about the next customer, his or her loans, and so on. It is similar in concept to the combination of a main form/subform that was created in the chapter. You can create the report in Figure 5.19 by selecting fields from both the Customers table and the Loans table, when you start the Report wizard.

   Alternatively, you can create the Customers report initially, change to the Design view, then click and drag the Subform/Subreport tool to start the Subreport Wizard to create the Loan report. This approach creates two separate reports that combine to produce the equivalent information in Figure 5.19. The reports are linked automatically through the CustomerID field that appears in both the Customers and the Loans tables. Which technique do you prefer?

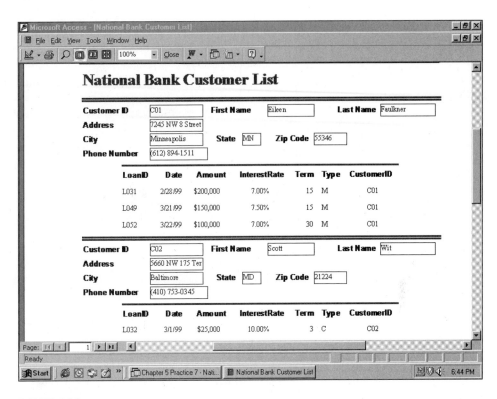

FIGURE 5.19   Synchronizing Reports (Exercise 7)

8. Data Access Pages: The report in Figure 5.20 displays information for customers and their loans. Look closely, however, and you will see that the report is an HTML document and that it is displayed in Internet Explorer rather than Microsoft Access. The report is known as a Data Access Page and it is created through the corresponding Wizard.

   a. Open the National Bank database. Click the Pages button from within the Database Window, then double click the option to create a data access page using the Wizard. Supply the information requested by the Wizard, but be sure to select all of the fields from both the Customers table and the Loans table.

   b. The Wizard will prompt you for additional information. Group the page by CustomerID. Sort the page by LoanID.

   c. The Wizard ends by letting you view the page or modify its design. Save the page as National Bank Customer List. As with any other Access object, you can go back and forth between the two views until you have the page the way you want it.

   d. You can view the page from within Access. You can also view it from within Internet Explorer, since a copy of the page is stored as a separate HTML document in the folder you specify when you save the page. Either way, click the plus sign to the left of CustomerID to see the loan information associated with that customer. Use the navigation bar at the bottom of the page to view the other loans for this customer and/or to view information on other customers.

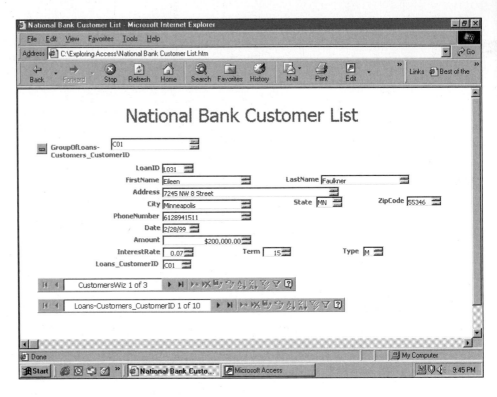

FIGURE 5.20   Data Access Pages (Exercise 8)

CASE STUDIES

Recreational Sports League

Design a database for a recreational sports league that will monitor players, coaches, and sponsors. There may be any number of teams in the league, with each team having any number of players. A player is associated with only one team.

Each team has at least one coach. The league also imposes the rule that a person may not coach more than one team. Each team has one sponsor, such as a local business. One sponsor can be associated with multiple teams.

Your solution should make the system as realistic as possible. The player table, for example, requires not only the identifying information for each player (name, address, phone, and so on) but additional fields such as birth date (to implement age limits on various teams), ability ratings, and so on. Your system should be capable of producing reports that will display all information about a specific team, such as its players, coach, and sponsor. The league administrators would also like master lists of all teams, players, coaches, and sponsors.

Show the required tables in the database, being sure to indicate the primary key and foreign keys in each table. Indicate one or two other fields in each table (you need not list them all).

The Personnel Director

You have been hired as a personnel director for a medium-sized company with offices in several cities. You require the usual personal data for each employee (birth date, hire date, home address, and so on). You also need to reach an employee at work, and must be able to retrieve the office address, office phone number, and office fax number for each employee. Each employee is assigned to only one branch office.

Your duties also include the administration of various health plans offered by the company. Each employee is given his or her choice of several health plans. Each plan has a monthly premium and deductible amount. Once the deductible is reached, each plan pays a designated percentage of all subsequent expenses.

Design a database that will include the necessary data to provide all of the information you need. Show the required tables in the database, being sure to indicate the primary key and foreign keys in each table. Indicate one or two other fields in each table (you need not list them all).

The Franchise

The management of a national restaurant chain is automating its procedure for monitoring its restaurants, restaurant owners (franchisees), and the contracts that govern the two. Each restaurant has one owner (franchisee). There is no limit on the number of restaurants an individual may own, and franchisees are encouraged to apply for multiple restaurants.

The payment from the franchisee to the company varies according to the contract in effect for the particular restaurant. The company offers a choice of contracts, which vary according to the length of the contract, the franchise fee, and the percentage of the restaurant's sales paid to the company for marketing and royalty fees. Each restaurant has one contract, but a given contract may pertain to many restaurants.

The company needs a database capable of retrieving all data for a given restaurant, such as its annual sales, location, phone number, owner, and type of contract in effect. It would also like to know all restaurants owned by one person as well as all restaurants governed by a specific contract type.

Widgets of America

Widgets of America gives its sales staff exclusive rights to specific customers. Each salesperson has many customers, but a specific customer always deals with the same sales representative. The company needs to know all of the orders placed by a specific customer as well as the total business generated by each sales representative. The data for each order includes the date the order was placed and the amount of the order. Design a database capable of producing the information required by the company.

Show the required tables in the database, being sure to indicate the primary key and foreign keys in each table. Indicate one or two other fields in each table (you need not list them all).

chapter 6

MANY-TO-MANY RELATIONSHIPS: A MORE COMPLEX SYSTEM

OBJECTIVES

After reading this chapter you will be able to:

1. Define a many-to-many relationship and explain how it is implemented in Access.
2. Use the Cascade Update and Cascade Delete options in the Relationships window to relax enforcement of referential integrity.
3. Explain how the AutoNumber field type simplifies the entry of a primary key for a new record.
4. Create a main and subform based on a query; discuss the advantage of using queries rather than tables as the basis for a form or report.
5. Create a parameter query; explain how a parameter query can be made to accept multiple parameters.
6. Use aggregate functions in a select query to perform calculations on groups of records.
7. Use the Get External Data command to add external tables to an existing database.

OVERVIEW

This chapter introduces a new case study to give you additional practice in database design. The system extends the concept of a relational database to include both a one-to-many and a many-to-many relationship. The case solution reviews earlier material on establishing relationships in Access and the importance of referential integrity. Another point of particular interest is the use of an AutoNumber field to facilitate the addition of new records.

The chapter extends what you already know about subforms and queries, and uses both to present information from related tables. The forms created in this chapter are based on multiple table queries rather than tables. The queries themselves are of a more advanced nature. We show you how to create a parameter query, where the user is prompted to enter the criteria when the query is run. We also review queries that use the aggregate functions built into Access to perform calculations on groups of records.

The chapter contains four hands-on exercises to implement the case study. We think you will be pleased with what you have accomplished by the end of the chapter, working with a sophisticated system that is typical of real-world applications.

CASE STUDY: THE COMPUTER SUPER STORE

The case study in this chapter is set within the context of a computer store that requires a database for its customers, products, and orders. The store maintains the usual customer data (name, address, phone, etc.). It also keeps data about the products it sells, storing for each product a product ID, description, quantity on hand, quantity on order, and unit price. And finally, the store has to track its orders. It needs to know the date an order was received, the customer who placed it, the products that were ordered, and the quantity of each product ordered.

Think, for a moment, about the tables that are necessary and the relationships between those tables, then compare your thoughts to our solution in Figure 6.1. You probably have no trouble recognizing the need for the Customers, Products, and Orders tables. Initially, you may be puzzled by the Order Details table, but you will soon appreciate why it is there and how powerful it is.

You can use the Customers, Products, and Orders tables individually to obtain information about a specific customer, product, or order, respectively. For example:

Query: What is Jeffrey Muddell's phone number?
Answer: Jeffrey Muddell's phone is (305) 253-3909.

Query: What is the price of a Pentium II laptop? How many are in stock?
Answer: A Pentium II laptop sells for $2,599. Fifteen systems are in stock.

Query: When was order O0003 placed?
Answer: Order O0003 was placed on April 18, 1999.

Other queries require you to relate the tables to one another. There is, for example, a *one-to-many relationship* between customers and orders. One customer can place many orders, but a specific order can be associated with only one customer. The tables are related through the CustomerID, which appears as the *primary key* in the Customers table and as a *foreign key* in the Orders table. Consider:

Query: What is the name of the customer who placed order number O0003?
Answer: Order O0003 was placed by Jeffrey Muddell.

Query: How many orders were placed by Jeffrey Muddell?
Answer: Jeffrey Muddell placed four orders: O0003, O0014, O0016, and O0024.

These queries require you to use two tables. To answer the first query, you would search the Orders table to find order O0003 and obtain the CustomerID (C0006 in this example). You would then search the Customers table for the customer with this CustomerID and retrieve the customer's name. To answer the

Customer ID	First Name	Last Name	Address	City	State	Zip Code	Phone Number
C0001	Benjamin	Lee	1000 Call Street	Tallahassee	FL	33340	(904) 327-4124
C0002	Eleanor	Milgrom	7245 NW 8 Street	Margate	FL	33065	(305) 974-1234
C0003	Neil	Goodman	4215 South 81 Street	Margate	FL	33065	(305) 444-5555
C0004	Nicholas	Colon	9020 N.W. 75 Street	Coral Springs	FL	33065	(305) 753-9887
C0005	Michael	Ware	276 Brickell Avenue	Miami	FL	33131	(305) 444-3980
C0006	Jeffrey	Muddell	9522 S.W. 142 Street	Miami	FL	33176	(305) 253-3909
C0007	Ashley	Geoghegan	7500 Center Lane	Coral Springs	FL	33070	(305) 753-7830
C0008	Serena	Sherard	5000 Jefferson Lane	Gainesville	FL	32601	(904) 375-6442
C0009	Luis	Couto	455 Bargello Avenue	Coral Gables	FL	33146	(305) 666-4801
C0010	Derek	Anderson	6000 Tigertail Avenue	Coconut Grove	FL	33120	(305) 446-8900
C0011	Lauren	Center	12380 S.W. 137 Avenue	Miami	FL	33186	(305) 385-4432
C0012	Robert	Slane	4508 N.W. 7 Street	Miami	FL	33131	(305) 635-3454

(a) Customers Table

Product ID	Product Name	Units In Stock	Units On Order	Unit Price
P0001	Pentium II/400 MHz	50	0	$1,899.00
P0002	Pentium II/450 MHz	25	5	$1,999.00
P0003	Pentium III/450 MHz	125	15	$2,099.00
P0004	Pentium III/500 MHz	25	50	$2,299.00
P0005	Pentium II laptop/300 MHz	15	25	$2,599.00
P0006	17" SVGA Monitor	50	0	$499.00
P0007	19" SVGA Monitor	25	10	$899.00
P0008	21" Multisync Monitor	50	20	$1,599.00
P0009	6.4 GB IDE Hard Drive	15	20	$399.00
P0010	10 GB Ultra ATA Hard Drive	25	15	$799.00
P0011	17 GB Ultra ATA Hard Drive	10	0	$1,245.00
P0012	CD-ROM: 32X	40	0	$249.00
P0013	DVD-ROM	50	15	$449.95
P0014	HD Floppy Disks	500	200	$9.99
P0015	Zip Cartridges	100	50	$14.79
P0016	Internal Zip Drive	15	3	$179.95
P0017	Serial Mouse	150	50	$69.95
P0018	Trackball	55	0	$59.95
P0019	Joystick	250	100	$39.95
P0020	Fax/Modem 56 Kbps	35	10	$189.95
P0021	Fax/Modem 33.6 Kbps	20	0	$65.95
P0022	Laser Printer (network)	100	15	$1,395.00
P0023	Ink Jet Printer	50	50	$249.95
P0024	Laser Printer (personal)	125	25	$569.95
P0025	Windows 95	400	200	$95.95
P0026	Windows 98	150	50	$75.95
P0027	Norton Anti-Virus	150	50	$115.95
P0028	Microsoft Scenes Screen Saver	75	25	$29.95
P0029	Microsoft Bookshelf	250	100	$129.95
P0030	Microsoft Cinemania	25	10	$59.95
P0031	Professional Photos on CD-ROM	15	0	$45.95

(b) Products Table

Order ID	Customer ID	Order Date
O0001	C0004	4/15/99
O0002	C0003	4/18/99
O0003	C0006	4/18/99
O0004	C0007	4/18/99
O0005	C0001	4/20/99
O0006	C0001	4/21/99
O0007	C0002	4/21/99
O0008	C0002	4/22/99
O0009	C0001	4/22/99
O0010	C0002	4/22/99
O0011	C0001	4/24/99
O0012	C0007	4/24/99
O0013	C0004	4/24/99
O0014	C0006	4/25/99
O0015	C0009	4/25/99
O0016	C0006	4/26/99
O0017	C0011	4/26/99
O0018	C0011	4/26/99
O0019	C0012	4/27/99
O0020	C0012	4/28/99
O0021	C0010	4/29/99
O0022	C0010	4/29/99
O0023	C0008	4/30/99
O0024	C0006	5/1/99

(c) Orders Table

Order ID	Product ID	Quantity
O0001	P0013	1
O0001	P0014	4
O0001	P0027	1
O0002	P0001	1
O0002	P0006	1
O0002	P0020	1
O0002	P0022	1
O0003	P0005	1
O0003	P0020	1
O0003	P0022	1
O0004	P0003	1
O0004	P0010	1
O0004	P0022	2
O0005	P0003	2
O0005	P0012	2
O0005	P0016	2
O0006	P0007	1
O0006	P0014	10
O0007	P0028	1
O0007	P0030	3
O0008	P0001	1
O0008	P0004	3
O0008	P0008	4
O0008	P0011	2
O0008	P0012	1
O0009	P0006	1
O0010	P0002	2
O0010	P0022	1
O0010	P0023	1
O0011	P0016	2
O0011	P0020	2
O0012	P0021	10
O0012	P0029	10
O0012	P0030	10
O0013	P0009	4
O0013	P0016	10
O0013	P0024	2
O0014	P0019	2
O0014	P0028	1
O0015	P0018	1
O0015	P0020	1
O0016	P0029	2
O0017	P0019	2
O0018	P0009	1
O0018	P0025	2
O0018	P0026	2
O0019	P0014	25
O0020	P0024	1
O0021	P0004	1
O0022	P0027	1
O0023	P0021	1
O0023	P0028	1
O0023	P0029	1
O0024	P0007	1
O0024	P0013	5
O0024	P0014	3
O0024	P0016	1

(d) Order Details Table

FIGURE 6.1   Super Store Database

second query, you would begin in the Customers table and search for Jeffrey Mud-dell to determine the CustomerID (C0006), then search the Orders table for all records with this CustomerID.

The system is more complicated than earlier examples in that there is a *many-to-many relationship* between orders and products. One order can include many products, and at the same time a specific product can appear in many orders. The implementation of a many-to-many relationship requires an additional table, the Order Details table, containing (at a minimum) the primary keys of the individual tables.

The Order Details table will contain many records with the same OrderID, because there is a separate record for each product in a given order. It will also contain many records with the same ProductID, because there is a separate record for every order containing that product. However, the *combination* of OrderID and ProductID is unique, and this **combined key** becomes the primary key in the Order Details table. The Order Details table also contains an additional field (Quantity) whose value depends on the primary key (the *combination* of OrderID and ProductID). Thus:

Query: How many units of product P0014 were included in order O0001?
Answer: Order O0001 included four units of product P0014. (The order also included one unit of Product P0013 and one unit of P0027.)

The Order Details table has four records with a ProductID of P0014. It also has three records with an OrderID of O0001. There is, however, only one record with a ProductID P0014 *and* an OrderID O0001, which is for four units.

The Order Details table makes it possible to determine all products in a given order or all orders for a given product. You can also use the Products table in conjunction with the Order Details table to determine the names of those products. Consider:

Query: Which orders include a Pentium II/400MHz computer?
Answer: A Pentium II/400MHz computer is found in orders O0002 and O0008.

Query: Which products were included in Order O0003?
Answer: Order O0003 consisted of products P0005 (a Pentium II laptop), P0020 (a 56Kbps fax/modem), and P0022 (a laser printer).

To answer the first query, you would begin in the Products table to find the ProductID for a Pentium II/400MHz (P0001). You would then search the Order Details table for records containing a ProductID of P0001, which in turn identifies orders O0002 and O0008. The second query is processed in similar fashion except that you would search the Order Details table for an OrderID of O0003. This time you would find three records with ProductIDs P0005, P0020, and P0022, respectively. You would then go to the Products table to look up the ProductIDs to return the name of each product.

We've emphasized that the power of a relational database comes from the inclusion of multiple tables and the relationships between those tables. As you already know, you can use data from several tables to compute the answer to more complex queries. For example:

Query: What is the total cost of order O0006? Which products are in the order and how many units of each product?
Answer: The total cost of order O0006 is $998.90. The order consists of one 19-inch monitor at $899 and ten boxes of HD floppy disks at $9.99 each.

To determine the cost of an order, you must first identify all of the products associated with that order, the quantity of each product, and the price of each product. The previous queries have shown how you would find the products in an order and the associated quantities. The price of a specific product is obtained from the Products table, which enables you to compute the invoice by multiplying the price of each product by the quantity. Thus, the total cost of order O0006 is $998.90. (One unit of P0007 at $899.00 and ten units of product P0014 at $9.99.)

The AutoNumber Field Type

Look carefully at the Customer, Order, and Product numbers in their respective tables and note that each set of numbers is consecutive. This is accomplished by specifying the *AutoNumber field* type for each of these fields in the design of the individual tables. The AutoNumber specification automatically assigns the next sequential number to the primary key of a new record. If, for example, you were to add a new customer to the existing Customers table, that customer would be assigned the number 13. In similar fashion, the next order will be order number 26, and the next product will be product number 32. (Deleting a record does not, however, renumber the remaining records in the table; that is, once a value is assigned to a primary key, the primary key will always retain that value.)

The C, O, and P that appear as the initial character of each field, as well as the high-order zeros, are *not* part of the fields themselves, but are displayed through the *Format property* associated with each field. Our Customers table, for example, uses the format \C0000, which displays a "C" in front of the field and pads it with high-order zeros. The Format property determines how a value is displayed, but does not affect how it is stored in the table. Thus, the CustomerID of the first customer is stored as the number 1, rather than C0001. The zeros provide a uniform appearance for that field throughout the table.

The Relationships Window

The Relationships window in Figure 6.2 shows the Computer Store database as it will be implemented in Access. The database contains the Customers, Orders, Products, and Order Details tables as per the previous discussion. The field lists display the fields within each table, with the primary key shown in bold. The OrderID and ProductID are both shown in bold in the Order Details table, to indicate that the primary key consists of the combination of these fields.

The many-to-many relationship between Orders and Products is implemented by a *pair* of one-to-many relationships. There is a one-to-many relationship between the Orders table and the Order Details table. There is a second one-to-many relationship between the Products table and the Order Details table. In other words, the Orders and Products tables are related to each other through the pair of one-to-many relationships with the Order Details table.

The *relationship lines* show the relationships between the tables. The number 1 appears next to the Products table on the relationship line connecting the Products table and the Order Details table. The infinity symbol appears at the end of the relationship line next to the Order Details table. The one-to-many relationship between these tables means that each record in the Products table can be associated with many records in the Order Details table. Each record in the Order Details table, however, is associated with only one record in the Products table.

In similar fashion, there is a second one-to-many relationship between the Orders table and the Order Details table. The number 1 appears on the relationship line next to the Orders table. The infinity symbol appears at the end of the line next to the Order Details table. Thus, each record in the Orders table can be associated with many records in the Order Details table, but each record in the Order Details table is associated with only one order.

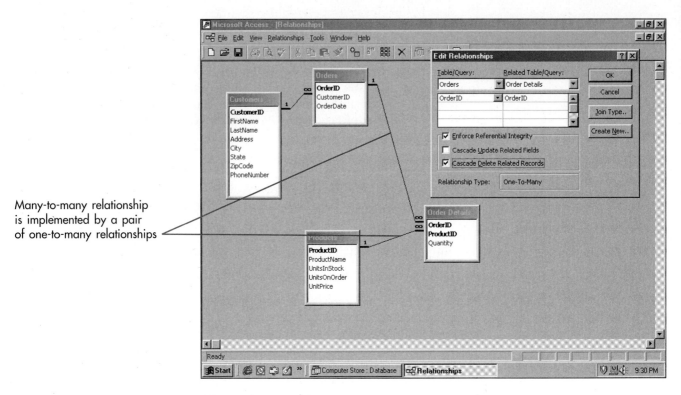

Many-to-many relationship is implemented by a pair of one-to-many relationships

FIGURE 6.2   The Relationships Window

Referential integrity ensures that the records in related tables are consistent with one another by preventing you from adding a record to a related table with an invalid foreign key. You could not, for example, add a record to the Order Details table that referenced a nonexistent order in the Orders table. The enforcement of referential integrity will also prevent you from deleting a record in the primary (Orders) table when there are corresponding records in the related (Order Details) table.

There may be times, however, when you want to delete an order and simultaneously delete the corresponding records in the Order Details table. This is accomplished by enabling the *cascaded deletion* of related records (as shown in Figure 6.2), so that when you delete a record in the Orders table, Access automatically deletes the associated records in the Order Details table. If, for example, you were to delete order number O0006 from the Orders table, any records with this OrderID in the Order Details table would be deleted automatically.

You might also want to enable the *cascaded updating* of related fields to correct the value of an OrderID. Enforcement of referential integrity would ordinarily prevent you from changing the value of the OrderID field in the Orders table when there are corresponding records in the Order Details table. You could, however, specify the cascaded updating of related fields so that if you were to change the OrderID in the Orders table, the corresponding fields in the Order Details table would also change.

PRACTICE WITH DATABASE DESIGN

An Access database contains multiple tables, each of which stores data about a specific entity. To use Access effectively, you must be able to relate the tables to one another, which in turn requires knowledge of database design. Appendix B provides additional examples that enable you to master the principles of a relational database.

Relationships and Referential Integrity

Objective: To create relationships between existing tables in order to demonstrate referential integrity; to edit an existing relationship to allow the cascaded deletion of related records. Use Figure 6.3 as a guide in the exercise.

STEP 1: Add a Customer Record (the AutoNumber field type)

➤ Start Access. Open the **Computer Store database** in the **Exploring Access folder**.

➤ The **Tables button** is already selected in the Database window. Open the **Customers table**, then click the **Maximize button** (if necessary) so that the table takes the entire screen as shown in Figure 6.3a.

➤ Click the **New Record button**, then click in the **First Name field**. Enter the first letter of your first name (e.g., "J" as shown in the figure):

- The record selector changes to a pencil to indicate that you are in the process of entering a record.

- The CustomerID is assigned automatically as soon as you begin to enter data. *Remember your customer number as you will use it throughout the chapter.* (Your CustomerID is 13, not C0013. The prefix and high-order zeros are displayed through the Format property. See boxed tip.)

➤ Complete your customer record, pressing the **Tab key** to move from one field to the next. Press **Tab** after you have entered the last field (phone number) to complete the record. Close the Customers table.

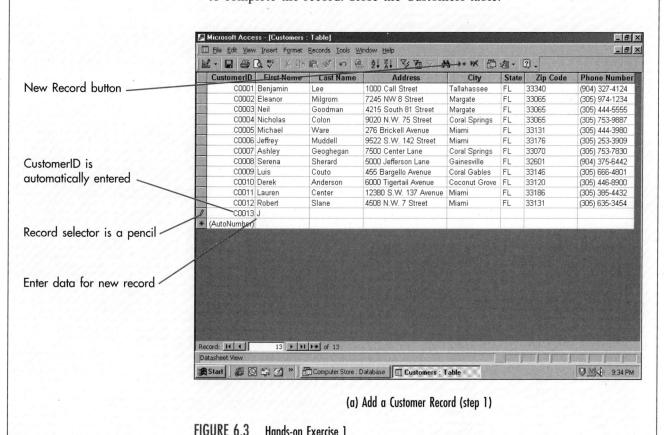

New Record button

CustomerID is automatically entered

Record selector is a pencil

Enter data for new record

CustomerID	First Name	Last Name	Address	City	State	Zip Code	Phone Number
C0001	Benjamin	Lee	1000 Call Street	Tallahassee	FL	33340	(904) 327-4124
C0002	Eleanor	Milgrom	7245 NW 8 Street	Margate	FL	33065	(305) 974-1234
C0003	Neil	Goodman	4215 South 81 Street	Margate	FL	33065	(305) 444-5555
C0004	Nicholas	Colon	9020 N.W. 75 Street	Coral Springs	FL	33065	(305) 753-9887
C0005	Michael	Ware	276 Brickell Avenue	Miami	FL	33131	(305) 444-3980
C0006	Jeffrey	Muddell	9522 S.W. 142 Street	Miami	FL	33176	(305) 253-3909
C0007	Ashley	Geoghegan	7500 Center Lane	Coral Springs	FL	33070	(305) 753-7830
C0008	Serena	Sherard	5000 Jefferson Lane	Gainesville	FL	32601	(904) 375-6442
C0009	Luis	Couto	455 Bargello Avenue	Coral Gables	FL	33146	(305) 666-4801
C0010	Derek	Anderson	6000 Tigertail Avenue	Coconut Grove	FL	33120	(305) 446-8900
C0011	Lauren	Center	12380 S.W. 137 Avenue	Miami	FL	33186	(305) 385-4432
C0012	Robert	Slane	4508 N.W. 7 Street	Miami	FL	33131	(305) 635-3454
C0013	J						
(AutoNumber)							

(a) Add a Customer Record (step 1)

FIGURE 6.3 Hands-on Exercise 1

STEP 2: Create the Relationships

➤ Pull down the **Tools menu** and click **Relationships** to open the Relationships window as shown in Figure 6.3b. Maximize the Relationships window.

➤ Pull down the **Relationships menu** and click **Show Table** (or click the **Show Table button**) to display the Show Table dialog box.

➤ The **Tables tab** is selected within the Show Table dialog box, and the **Customers table** is selected. Click the **Add Command button**.

➤ Add the **Order Details**, **Orders**, and **Products** tables in similar fashion. Close the Show Table dialog box.

➤ Point to the bottom border of the **Customers field list**, then click and drag the border until all of the fields are visible.

➤ If necessary, click and drag the bottom border of the other tables until all of their fields are visible. Click and drag the title bars to move the field lists.

➤ Click and drag the **CustomerID field** in the Customers field list to the **CustomerID field** in the Orders field list. You will see the Relationships dialog box in Figure 6.3b when you release the mouse.

➤ Click the **Enforce Referential Integrity** check box. Click the **Create Command button** to establish the relationship.

➤ Click and drag the **OrderID field** in the Orders field list to the **OrderID field** in the Order Details field list. Click the **Enforce Referential Integrity** check box, then click the **Create Command button**.

➤ Click and drag the **ProductID field** in the Products field list to the **ProductID field** in the Order Details field list. Click the **Enforce Referential Integrity** check box, then click the **Create Command button**.

➤ Click the **Save button**. Close the Relationships window.

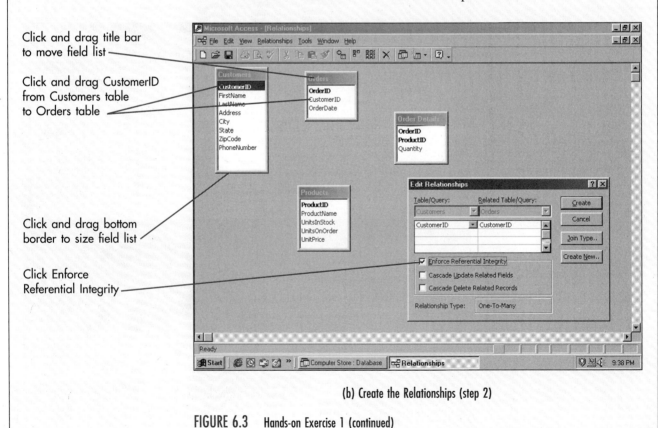

Click and drag title bar to move field list

Click and drag CustomerID from Customers table to Orders table

Click and drag bottom border to size field list

Click Enforce Referential Integrity

(b) Create the Relationships (step 2)

FIGURE 6.3   Hands-on Exercise 1 (continued)

STEP 3: Delete an Order Details Record

➤ You should be in the Database window. If necessary, click the **Tables button**, then open the **Orders table** as shown in Figure 6.3c.

➤ Click the **plus sign** next to order O0005. The plus sign changes to a minus sign and you see the order details for this record. Click the **row selector column** to select the Order Details record for product **P0016** in order **O0005**.

➤ Press the **Del key**. You will see a message indicating that you are about to delete one record. Click **Yes**. The Delete command works because you are deleting a "many record" in a one-to-many relationship.

➤ Click the **minus sign** next to **Order O0005**. The minus sign changes to a plus sign and you no longer see the order details. Click the **row selector column** to select the record, then press the **Del key** to (attempt to) delete the record.

➤ You will see a message indicating that you cannot delete the record. The Delete command does not work because you are attempting to delete the "one record" in a one-to-many relationship. Click **OK**.

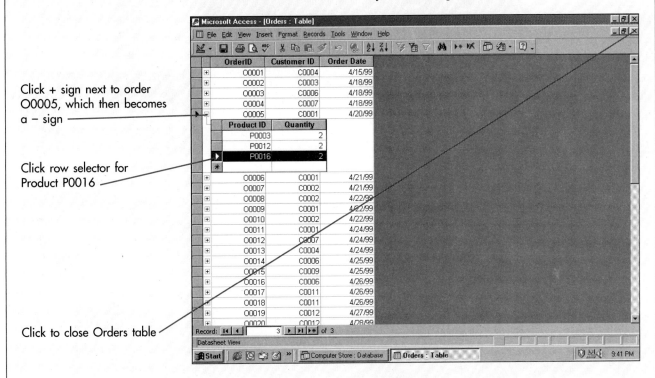

Click + sign next to order O0005, which then becomes a − sign

Click row selector for Product P0016

Click to close Orders table

(c) Delete an Order Details Record (step 3)

FIGURE 6.3   Hands-on Exercise 1 (continued)

WHAT YOU CAN AND CANNOT DELETE

You can always delete a record from the "many" table, such as the Order Details table in this example. The enforcement of referential integrity, however, will prevent you from deleting a record in the "one" table (i.e., the Orders table) when there are related records in the "many" table (i.e., the Order Details table). Thus you may want to modify the relationship to permit the cascaded deletion of related records, in which case deleting a record from the "one" table will automatically delete the related records.

STEP 4: Edit a Relationship

➤ Close the Orders table. (The tables in a relationship must be closed before the relationship can be edited.)

➤ Pull down the **Tools menu** and click **Relationships** to reopen the Relationships window (or click the **Relationships button** on the toolbar). Maximize the window.

➤ Point to the line connecting the Orders and Order Details tables, then click the **right mouse button** to display a shortcut menu. Click **Edit Relationship** to display the Relationships dialog box in Figure 6.3d.

➤ Check the box to **Cascade Delete Related Records**, then click **OK** to accept the change and close the dialog box. Click the **Save button** to save the edited relationship. Close the Relationships window.

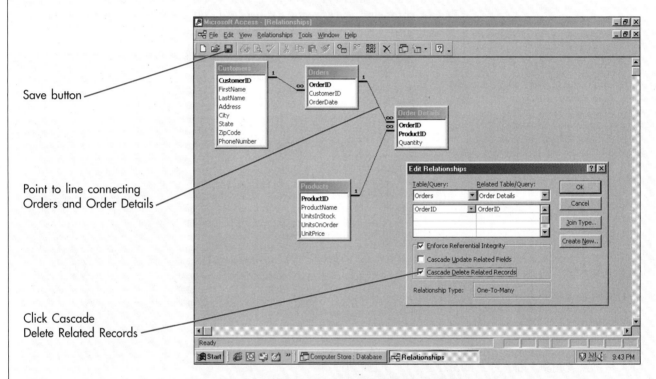

Save button

Point to line connecting
Orders and Order Details

Click Cascade
Delete Related Records

(d) Edit a Relationship (step 4)

FIGURE 6.3   Hands-on Exercise 1 (continued)

RELATED FIELDS AND DATA TYPE

The related fields on both sides of a relationship must be the same data type—for example, both number fields or both text fields. (Number fields must also have the same field size setting.) You cannot, however, specify an AutoNumber field on both sides of a relationship. Accordingly, if the related field in the primary table is an AutoNumber field, the related field in the related table must be specified as a number field, with the Field Size property set to Long Integer.

STEP 5: Delete a Record in the Orders Table

➤ You should be back in the Database window. Open the **Orders table**. Click the record selector column for **Order O0005**. Press the **Del key**.

➤ Record O0005 is deleted from the table (although you can cancel the deletion by clicking No in response to the message that is displayed on your screen). We want you to delete the record, however. Thus, click **Yes** in response to the message in Figure 6.3e.

➤ Order O0005 is permanently deleted from the Orders table as are the related records in the Order Details table. The Delete command works this time (unlike the previous attempt in step 4) because the relationship was changed to permit the deletion of related records.

➤ Close the Orders table. Close the database. Click **Yes** if prompted to save the tables or relationships.

➤ Exit Access if you do not want to continue with the next exercise at this time.

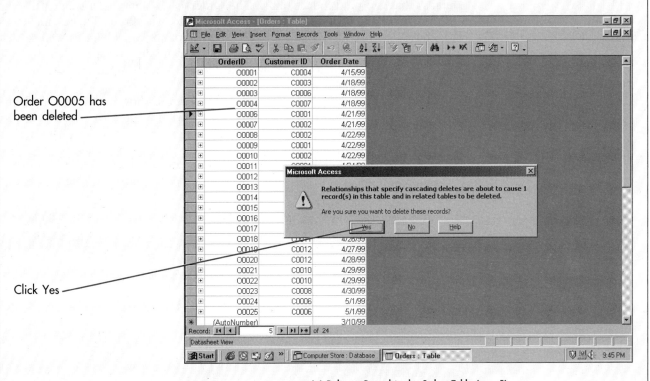

Order O0005 has been deleted

Click Yes

(e) Delete a Record in the Orders Table (step 5)

FIGURE 6.3   Hands-on Exercise 1 (continued)

USE WITH CAUTION

The cascaded deletion of related records relaxes referential integrity and eliminates errors that would otherwise occur during data entry. That does not mean, however, that the option should always be selected, and in fact, most of the time it is disabled. What would happen, for example, in an employee database with a one-to-many relationship between branch offices and employees, if cascade deleted records was in effect and a branch office was deleted?

The main and subform combination in Figure 6.4 is used by the store to enter a new order for an existing customer. The forms are based on queries (rather than tables) for several reasons. A query enables you to display data from multiple tables, to display a calculated field, and to take advantage of AutoLookup, a feature that is explained shortly. A query also lets you display records in a sequence other than by primary key.

The main form contains fields from both the Orders table and the Customers table. The OrderID, OrderDate, and CustomerID (the join field) are taken from the Orders table. The other fields are taken from the Customers table. The query is designed so that you do not have to enter any customer information other than the CustomerID; that is, you enter the CustomerID, and Access will automatically look up (*AutoLookup*) the corresponding customer data.

The subform is based on a second query containing fields from the Order Details table and the Products table. The OrderID, Quantity, and ProductID (the join field) are taken from the Order Details table. The ProductName and Unit-Price fields are from the Products table. AutoLookup works here as well so that when you enter the ProductID, Access automatically displays the Product Name and Unit Price. You then enter the quantity, and the amount (a calculated field) is determined automatically.

The queries for the main form and subform are shown in Figures 6.5a and 6.5b, respectively. The upper half of the Query window displays the field list for each table and the relationship between the tables. The lower half of the Query window contains the design grid.

The following exercise has you create the main and subform in Figure 6.4. We supply the query for the main form (Figure 6.5a), but we ask you to create the query for the subform (Figure 6.5b).

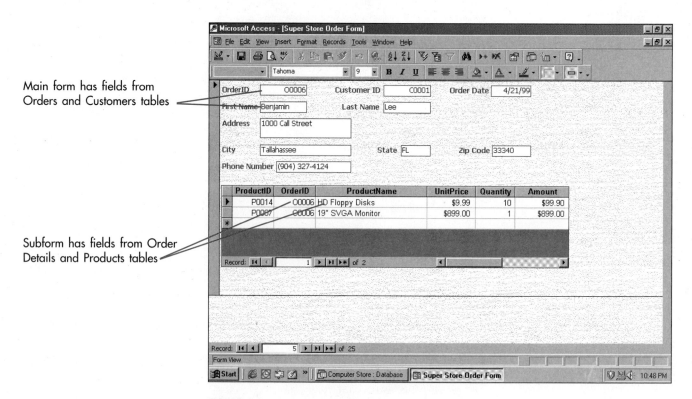

Main form has fields from Orders and Customers tables

Subform has fields from Order Details and Products tables

FIGURE 6.4   The Super Store Order Form

Join field from "one"
table is unique

Tables have a
one-to-many relationship

Join field used in query
is from "many" table

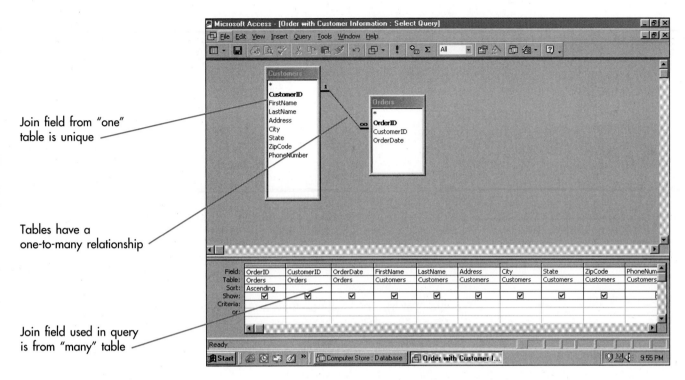

(a) Order with Customer Information Query (used for the main form)

Join field from "one"
table is unique

Tables have a
one-to-many relationship

Join field used in query
is from "many" table

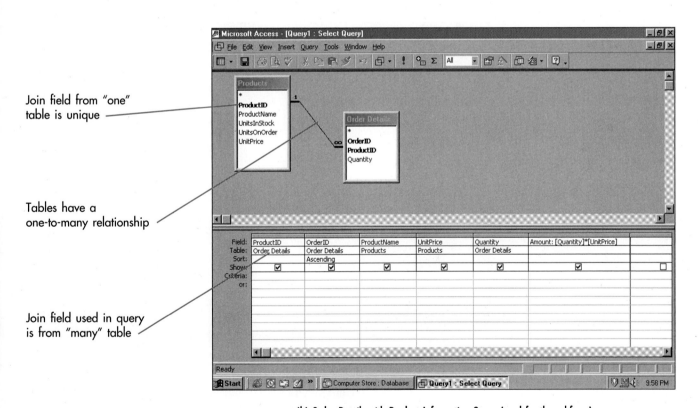

(b) Order Details with Product Information Query (used for the subform)

FIGURE 6.5   Multiple Table Queries

Subforms and Multiple Table Queries

Objective: To use multiple table queries as the basis for a main form and its associated subform; to create the link between a main form and subform manually. Use Figure 6.6 as a guide in the exercise.

STEP 1: Create the Subform Query

➤ Open the **Computer Store database** from the previous exercise. Click the **Queries button** in the Database window.

➤ Double click **Create query in Design view** to display the Query Design window in Figure 6.6c.

➤ The Show Table dialog box appears as shown in Figure 6.6a with the Tables tab already selected.

➤ Double click the **Products table** to add this table to the query. Double click the **Order Details table** to add this table to the query. A join line showing the one-to-many relationship between the Products and Order Details table appears automatically.

➤ Click **Close** to close the Show Table dialog box. If necessary, click the **Maximize button**. Resize the field lists as necessary.

Double click the Order Details table to add it to the query

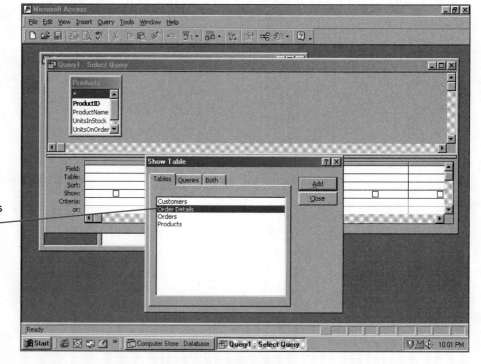

(a) Create the Subform Query (step 1)

FIGURE 6.6   Hands-on Exercise 2

STEP 2: Create the Subform Query (continued)

➤ Add the fields to the query as follows:
- Double click the **ProductID** and **OrderID fields** in that order from the Order Details table.
- Double click the **ProductName** and **UnitPrice fields** in that order from the Products table.
- Double click the **Quantity field** from the Order Details table.

➤ Click the **Sort row** under the **OrderID field**. Click the **drop-down arrow**, then specify an **ascending** sequence.

➤ Click the first available cell in the Field row. Type **=[Quantity]*[UnitPrice]**. Do not be concerned if you cannot see the entire expression.

➤ Press **enter**. Access has substituted Expr1: for the equal sign you typed. Drag the column boundary so that the entire expression is visible as in Figure 6.6b. (You may need to make the other columns narrower in order to see all of the fields in the design grid.)

➤ Click and drag to select **Expr1**. (Do not select the colon.) Type **Amount** to substitute a more meaningful field name.

➤ Point to the expression and click the **right mouse button** to display a short-cut menu. Click **Properties** to display the Field Properties dialog box in Figure 6.6b.

➤ Click the box for the **Format property**. Click the **drop-down arrow**, then scroll until you can click **Currency**. Close the Properties dialog box.

➤ Save the query as **Order Details with Product Information**. Click the **Run button** to test the query so that you know the query works prior to using it as the basis of a form.

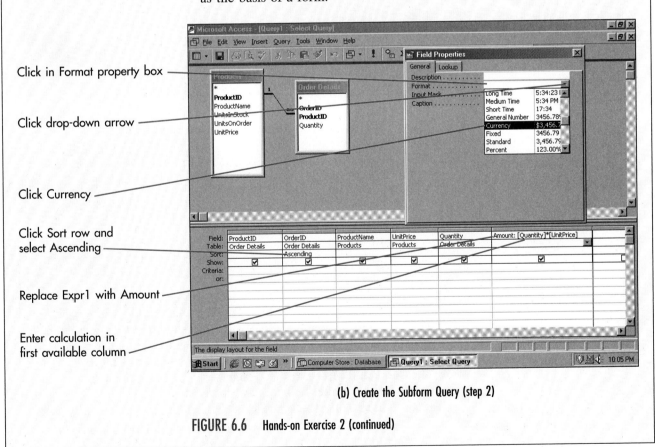

(b) Create the Subform Query (step 2)

FIGURE 6.6   Hands-on Exercise 2 (continued)

STEP 3: Test the Query

➤ You should see the dynaset shown in Figure 6.6c. (See the boxed tip if the dynaset does not appear.)

➤ Enter **1** (not P0001) to change the ProductID to 1 (from 14) in the very first record. (The Format property automatically displays the letter P and the high-order zeros.)

➤ Press **enter.** The Product Name changes to a Pentium II/400MHz system as you hit the enter key. The unit price also changes, as does the computed amount.

➤ Click the **Undo button** to cancel the change. The ProductID returns to P0014, and the Product Name changes back to HD Floppy Disks. The unit price also changes, as does the computed amount.

➤ Close the query. Save the changes to the query design if prompted to do so.

Undo button

Enter 1

Product data will change when you press enter key, as will calculated amount

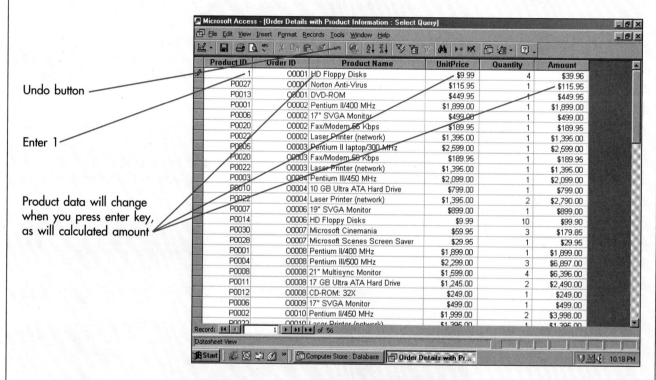

(c) Test the Query (step 3)

FIGURE 6.6 Hands-on Exercise 2 (continued)

A PUZZLING ERROR

If you are unable to run a query, it is most likely because you misspelled a field name in the design grid. Access interpets the misspelling as a parameter query (see page 280) and asks you to enter a parameter value (the erroneous field name is displayed in the dialog box). Press the Esc key to exit the query and return to the Design view. Click the field row for the problem field and make the necessary correction.

STEP 4: Create the Orders Form

➤ Click the **Forms button** in the Database window, then double click the **Create form by using Wizard icon** to start the Form Wizard. You should see the dialog box in Figure 6.6d except that no tables have been selected at this time.

➤ Click the **drop-down arrow** on the Tables/Queries list box to display the tables and queries in the database. Select **Order with Customer Information** (the query we provided), then click the **>> button** to enter all of the fields from the query onto the form.

➤ Click the **drop-down arrow** to redisplay the tables and queries in the database. Click **Order Details with Product Information** to select this query as shown in Figure 6.6d. Click the **>> button**.

➤ Be sure that the Selected Fields area contains the fields from both queries. Click **Next**. The Wizard will prompt you for the additional information it needs to create the form and its associated subform:

- The next screen suggests that you view the data by **Order with Customer Information** and that you create a form with subforms. Click **Next**.

- The **Datasheet option button** is selected as the default layout for the subform. Click **Next**.

- Click **Sumi Painting** as the style for your form. Click **Next**.

- Enter Super Store Order form as the title of the form, but accept the Wizard's suggestion for the name of the subform (**Order Details with Product Information subform**).

- Click the option button to **Modify the form's design**, then click the **Finish command button** to create the form and exit the Form Wizard.

➤ You should be in the Design view of the Super Store Order form you just created. Click the **Save button** to save the form and continue working.

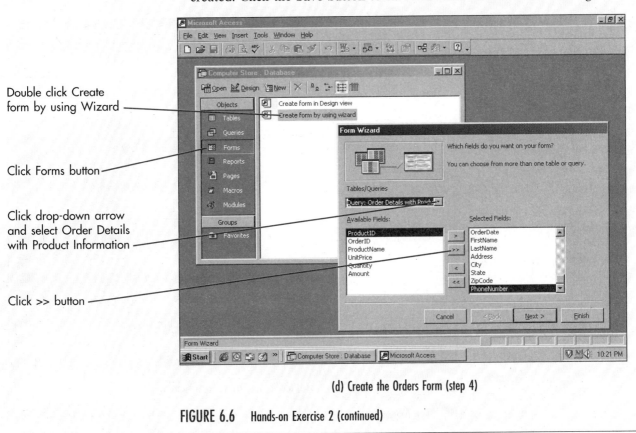

Double click Create form by using Wizard

Click Forms button

Click drop-down arrow and select Order Details with Product Information

Click >> button

(d) Create the Orders Form (step 4)

FIGURE 6.6   Hands-on Exercise 2 (continued)

STEP 5: Modify the Orders Form

➤ You are in the Design view. Maximize the window (if necessary), then **click and drag the bottom of the Details section** down to give yourself additional room in which to work.

➤ It takes time (and a little practice) to move and size the controls within a form. Try the indicated command, then click the **Undo button** if you are not satisfied with the result.

➤ Click and drag the control for the subform and its label toward the form footer. Select the label of the subform control, then press the **Del key** to delete the label as shown in Figure 6.6e. Click and drag the left border of the subform control toward the left to make the subform wider.

➤ Click the **PhoneNumber control** to select the control and display the sizing handles, then drag the control above the subform control.

➤ Click and drag the controls for **City**, **State**, and **ZipCode** (one at a time) on the line above the PhoneNumber control.

➤ Click and drag the **LastName control** so that it is next to the FirstName control. Click and drag the **Address control** under the control for FirstName.

➤ Move the **CustomerID** control to the right of the OrderID control. Click and drag the **OrderDate** control so that it is next to the CustomerID. The width of the form will change automatically if the form is not wide enough. You may, however, need to extend the width a little further when you release the mouse.

➤ Select the **Page Break** tool then click below the subform control to insert a page break on the form. The page break will print one order per page.

➤ Adjust the size, spacing, and alignment of the labels as necessary, switching back and forth between Form view and Design view. Save the form.

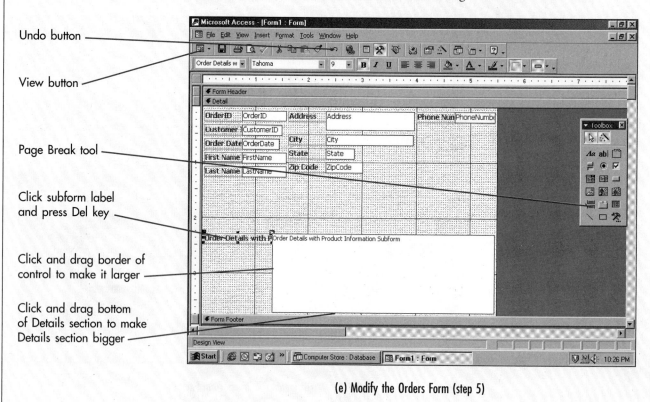

Undo button

View button

Page Break tool

Click subform label and press Del key

Click and drag border of control to make it larger

Click and drag bottom of Details section to make Details section bigger

(e) Modify the Orders Form (step 5)

FIGURE 6.6 Hands-on Exercise 2 (continued)

STEP 6: Change the Column Widths

➤ Click the **View button** to change to the Form view. You should see the first order in the database together with the associated product information. You may, however, have to adjust the width of the columns within the subform and/or change the size and position of the subform within the main form.

➤ To change the width of the columns within the subform:

• Click the **down arrow** on the **View button** and change to the **Datasheet view**. Click the **plus sign** next to the OrderID column for the first order to display the related records as shown in Figure 6.6f.

• Click and drag the various column headings until you can read all of the information. Click the **Save button** to save the new layout, then close the form. You must close the main form, then reopen the form in order for the changes in the subform to be visible.

• You should be back in the Database window. Double click the **Super Store Order form** to reopen the form and check the width of the columns in the subform. If necessary, click the **down arrow** on the **View button** to return to the Datasheet view to further adjust the columns.

➤ It may also be necessary to change the size or position of the subform within the main form. Click the **View button** and change to the **Design view**.

➤ Click and drag a sizing handle to change the size of the subform. Click and drag the subform control to change its position. If necessary, extend the width of the form.

➤ The process is one of trial and error, but it should take only a few minutes to size the subform properly. Save the completed form.

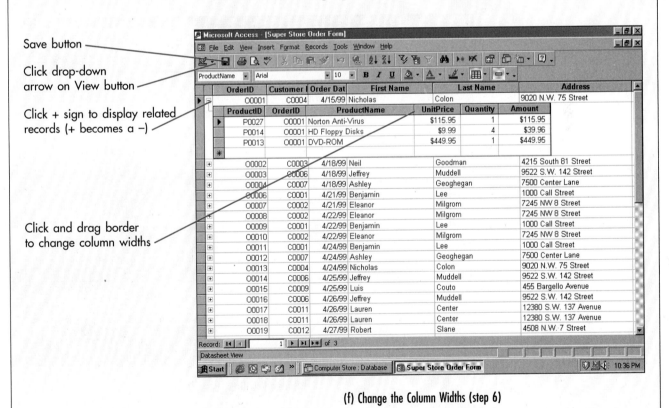

(f) Change the Column Widths (step 6)

FIGURE 6.6 Hands-on Exercise 2 (continued)

STEP 7: Enter a New Order

➤ Change to the **Form view** of the Orders form as shown in Figure 6.6g. The navigation buttons on the main form let you move from one order to the next. The navigation buttons on the subform move between products in an order.

➤ Click the **New Record button** on the main form to display a blank form so that you can place an order.

➤ Click in the **Customer ID text box**. Enter **13** (your customer number from exercise 1), then press the **Tab** or **enter key** to move to the next field.

• The OrderID is entered automatically as it is an AutoNumber field and assigned the next sequential number.

• All of your customer information (your name, address, and phone number) is entered automatically because of the AutoLookup feature that is built into the underlying query.

• Today's date is entered automatically because of the default value (=Date( ) that is built into the Orders table.

➤ Click the **ProductID text box** in the subform. Enter **1** (not P0001) and press the **enter key** to move to the next field. The OrderID (O0026) is entered automatically, as is the Product Name and Unit Price.

➤ Press the **Tab key** three times to move to the Quantity field, enter **1**, and press the **Tab key** twice more to move to the ProductID field for the next item. (The amount is calculated automatically.)

➤ Complete your order as shown in Figure 6.6g.

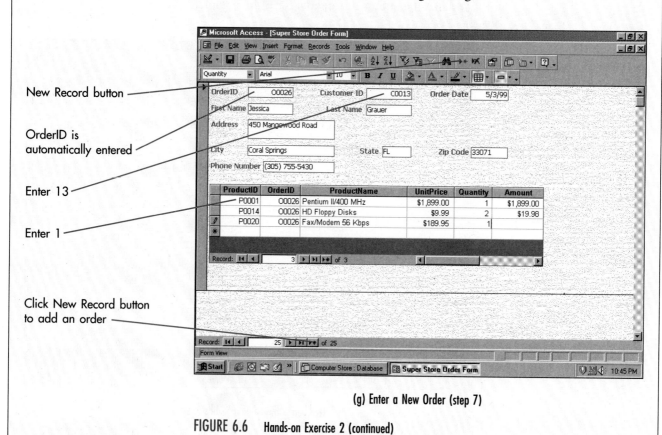

(g) Enter a New Order (step 7)

FIGURE 6.6   Hands-on Exercise 2 (continued)

STEP 8: Print the Completed Order

➤ Click the **Selection Area** to select the current record (the order you just completed).

➤ Pull down the **File menu**. Click **Page Setup** to display the Page Setup dialog box as shown in Figure 6.6h. Click the **Page tab**, then click the **Landscape option** button so that your form will fit on the page. (Alternatively, you could click the Margins tab and decrease the left and right margins.) Click **OK**.

➤ Pull down the **File menu**, click **Print** to display the Print dialog box, then click the option button to specify **Selected Record(s)** as the print range. (You cannot click the Print button on the toolbar, as that will print every record.)

➤ Click **OK** to print the form. Close the form, then close the database. Answer **Yes** if asked to save the changes.

➤ Exit Access if you do not want to continue with the next exercise at this time.

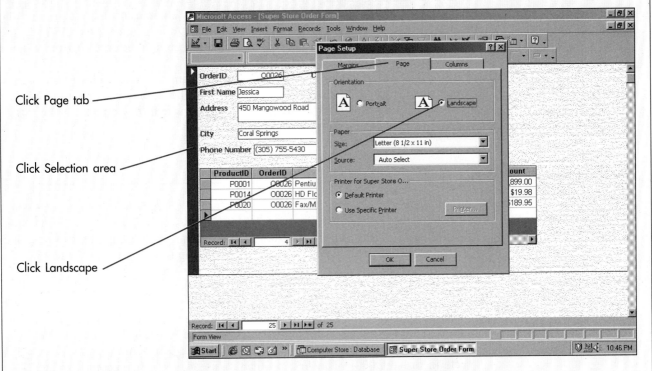

(h) Print the Completed Order (step 8)

FIGURE 6.6   Hands-on Exercise 2 (continued)

ADDING CUSTOMERS

The order form enables you to add an order for a new customer in the process of creating an order for that customer. Click the New Record button to add a new order, leave the Customer ID field blank, then complete the customer information (name, address, etc.) in the upper part of the form. (You need to enter at least one field after which the CustomerID will be created automatically since it was defined as an AutoNumber field.) Press the enter key after you have entered the last field (telephone number) of customer information.

PARAMETER QUERIES

A select query, powerful as it is, has its limitations. It requires you to enter the criteria directly in the query, which means you have to change the query every time you vary the criteria. What if you wanted to use a different set of criteria (e.g., a different customer's name) every time you ran the "same" query?

A *parameter query* prompts you for the criteria each time you execute the query. It is created in similar fashion to a select query and is illustrated in Figure 6.7. The difference between a parameter query and an ordinary select query is the way in which the criteria are specified. A select query contains the actual criteria. A parameter query, however, contains a *prompt* (message) that will request the criteria when the query is executed.

The design grid in Figure 6.7a creates a parameter query that will display the orders for a particular customer. The query does not contain the customer's name, but a prompt for that name. The prompt is enclosed in square brackets and is displayed in a dialog box in which the user enters the requested data when the query is executed. Thus, the user supplies the customer's name in Figure 6.7b, and the query displays the resulting dynaset in Figure 6.7c. This enables you to run the same query with different criteria; that is, you can enter a different customer name every time you execute the query.

A parameter query may prompt for any number of variables (parameters), which are entered in successive dialog boxes. The parameters are requested in order from left to right, according to the way in which they appear in the design grid.

TOTAL QUERIES

A *total query* performs calculations on a *group* of records using one of several summary (aggregate) functions available within Access. These include the Sum, Count, Avg, Max, and Min functions to determine the total, number of, average, maximum, and minimum values, respectively. Figure 6.8 illustrates the use of a total query to compute the total amount for each order.

Figure 6.8a displays the dynaset from a select query with fields from both the Products and Order Details tables. (The dynaset contains one record for each product in each order and enables us to verify the results of the total query in Figure 6.8c.) Each record in Figure 6.8a contains the price of the product, the quantity ordered, and the amount for that product. There are, for example, three products in order O0001. The first product costs $449.95, the second product costs $39.96 (four units at $9.99 each), and the third product costs $115.95). The total for the order comes to $605.86, which is obtained by (manually) adding the amount field in each of the records for this order.

Figure 6.8b shows the Design view of the total query to calculate the cost of each order. The query contains only two fields, OrderID and Amount. The QBE grid also displays a *Total row* in which each field in the query has either a Group By or aggregate entry. The *Group By* entry under OrderID indicates that the records in the dynaset are to be grouped (aggregated) according to the like values of OrderID; that is, there will be one record in the total query for each distinct value of OrderID. The *Sum function* specifies the arithmetic operation to be performed on that field for each group of records.

The dynaset in Figure 6.8c displays the result of the total query and contains *aggregate* records, as opposed to *individual* records. There are three records for order O0001 in Figure 6.8a, but only one record in Figure 6.8c. This is because each record in a total query contains a calculated result for a group of records.

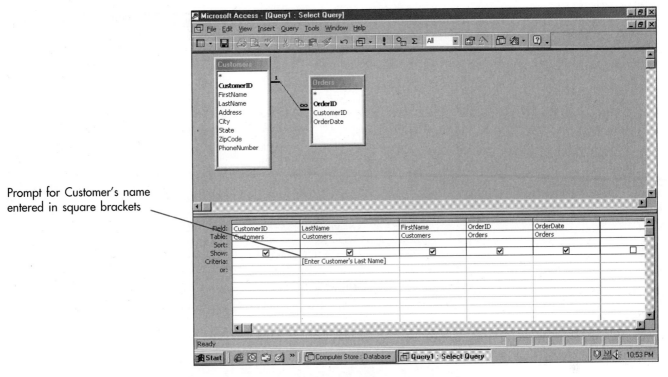

Prompt for Customer's name entered in square brackets

(a) Design Grid

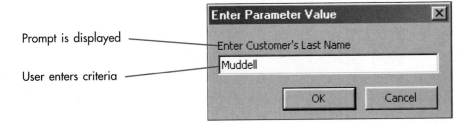

Prompt is displayed

User enters criteria

(b) Dialog Box

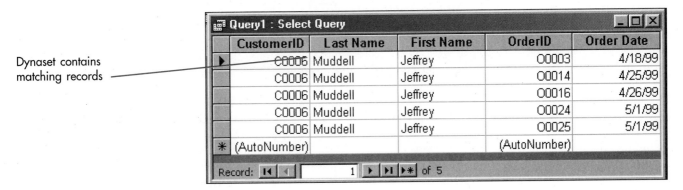

Dynaset contains matching records

(c) Dynaset

FIGURE 6.7   Parameter Query

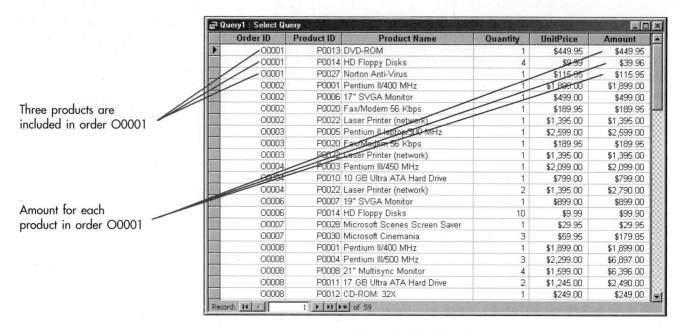

Three products are
included in order O0001

Amount for each
product in order O0001

(a) Order Details with Product Information Dynaset

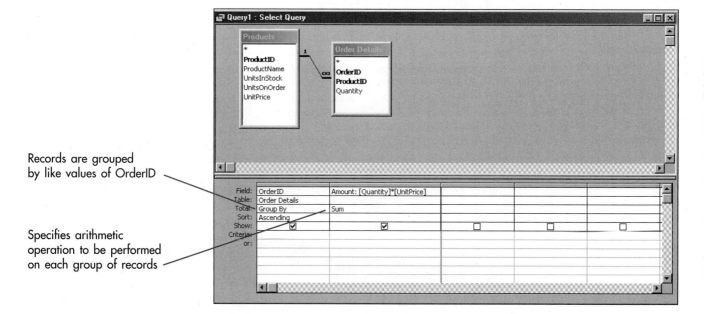

Records are grouped
by like values of OrderID

Specifies arithmetic
operation to be performed
on each group of records

(b) Design Grid

Order ID	Amount
O0001	$605.86
O0002	$3,982.95
O0003	$4,183.95
O0004	$5,688.00
O0006	$998.90
O0007	$209.80
O0008	$17,931.00

(c) Dynaset

FIGURE 6.8   Total Query

The exercise that follows begins by having you create the report in Figure 6.9. The report is a detailed analysis of all orders, listing every product in every order. The report is based on a query containing fields from the Orders, Customers, Products, and Order Details tables. The exercise also provides practice in creating parameter queries and total queries.

Sales Analysis by Order

Prepared by: Jessica Grauer

			Product Name	Quantity	UnitPrice	Amount
O0001	Colon	4/15/99				
			DVD-ROM	1	$449.95	$449.95
			HD Floppy Disks	4	$9.99	$39.96
			Norton Anti-Virus	1	$115.95	$115.95
					Sum	$605.86
O0002	Goodman	4/18/99				
			17" SVGA Monitor	1	$499.00	$499.00
			Fax/Modem 56 Kbps	1	$189.95	$189.95
			Laser Printer	1	$1,395.00	$1,395.00
			Pentium II/400 MHz	1	$1,899.00	$1,899.00
					Sum	$3,982.95
O0003	Muddell	4/18/99				
			Fax/Modem 56 Kbps	1	$189.95	$189.95
			Laser Printer	1	$1,395.00	$1,395.00
			Pentium II laptop/300 MHz	1	$2,599.00	$2,599.00
					Sum	$4,183.95
O0004	Geoghegan	4/18/99				
			10 GB Ultra ATA	1	$799.00	$799.00
			Laser Printer	2	$1,395.00	$2,790.00
			Pentium III/450 MHz	1	$2,099.00	$2,099.00
					Sum	$5,688.00
O0006	Lee	4/21/99				
			19" SVGA Monitor	1	$899.00	$899.00
			HD Floppy Disks	10	$9.99	$99.90
					Sum	$998.90
O0007	Milgrom	4/21/99				
			Microsoft Cinemania	3	$59.95	$179.85
			Microsoft Scenes Screen Saver	1	$29.95	$29.95

Thursday, April 22, 1999   **Page 1 of 4**

FIGURE 6.9   Sales Analysis by Order

Advanced Queries

Objective: To copy an existing query; to create a parameter query; to create a total query using the Aggregate Sum function. Use Figure 6.10 as a guide.

STEP 1: Create the Query

➤ Open the **Computer Store database** from the previous exercise. Click the **Queries button** in the Database window. Double click **Create query in Design view** to display the Query Design window.

➤ By now you have had sufficient practice creating a query, so we will just outline the steps:

- Add the **Customers**, **Orders**, **Products**, and **Order Details** tables. Move and size the field lists within the Query window to match Figure 6.10a. Maximize the window.

- Add the indicated fields to the design grid. Be sure to take each field from the appropriate table.

- Add the calculated field to compute the amount by multiplying the quantity by the unit price. Point to the expression, click the **right mouse button** to display a shortcut menu, then change the Format property to **Currency**.

- Check that your query matches Figure 6.10a. Save the query as **Sales Analysis by Order**.

➤ Click the **Run button** (the exclamation point) to run the query. The dynaset contains one record for every item in every order. Close the query.

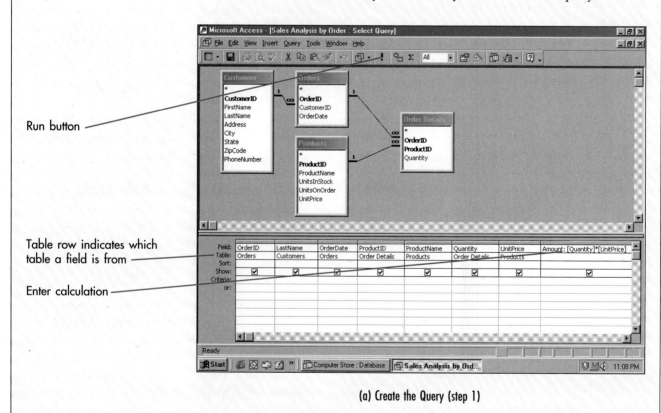

(a) Create the Query (step 1)

FIGURE 6.10   Hands-on Exercise 3

STEP 2: The Report Wizard

➤ Click the **Reports button** in the Database window. Double click the **Create report by using Wizard** icon to start the Report Wizard.

➤ Click the **drop-down arrow** to display the tables and queries in the database, then select **Sales Analysis by Order** (the query you just created). Click **OK**.

➤ By now you have had sufficient practice using the Report Wizard, so we will just outline the steps:

 • Select all of the fields in the query *except* the ProductID. Click the **>> button** to move every field in the Available Fields list box to the Selected Fields list, then select the **ProductID field** within the Selected Fields list and click the **< button** to remove this field. Click **Next**.

 • Group the report by **OrderID**. Click **Next**.

 • Sort the report by **ProductName**. Click the **Summary Options button** to display the Summary Options dialog box in Figure 6.10b. Check **Sum** under the Amount field. The option button to **Show Detail and Summary** is selected. Click **OK** to close the Summary Options dialog box. Click **Next**.

 • The **Stepped Layout** is selected, as is **Portrait orientation**. Be sure the box is checked to **Adjust field width so all fields fit on a page**. Click **Next**.

 • Choose **Bold** as the style. Click **Next**.

 • **Sales Analysis by Order** is entered as the title of the report. The option button to **Preview the Report** is selected. Click **Finish**.

➤ The report you see approximates the finished report, but requires several modifications to improve the formatting. The OrderDate and LastName, for example, are repeated for every product in an order, when they should appear only once in the group (OrderID) header.

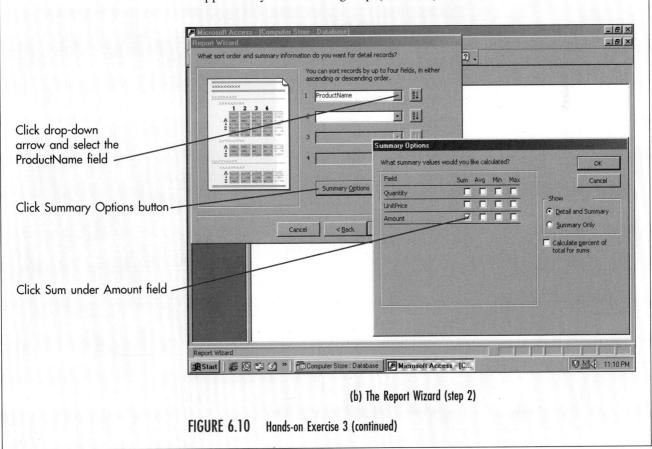

(b) The Report Wizard (step 2)

FIGURE 6.10   Hands-on Exercise 3 (continued)

STEP 3: Modify the Report Design

➤ Click the **Close button** to change to the Design view to modify the report as shown in Figure 6.10c.

➤ Press and hold the **Shift key** as you click the **OrderDate** and **LastName** controls to select both controls, then drag the controls to the group header next to the OrderID.

➤ Click anywhere in the report to deselect the controls after they have been moved. Press and hold the **Shift key** to select the **OrderID**, **OrderDate**, and **LastName** labels in the Page Header. Press the **Del key** to delete the labels.

➤ Size the **Quantity**, **UnitPrice**, and **Amount controls** (and their **labels**). Move the **ProductName control** and its **label** closer to the other controls.

➤ Click the **OrderID control** in the OrderID header. Click the **right mouse button**, click **Properties**, and change the Border Style to **Transparent**. Close the Properties dialog box.

➤ Click the **Label tool**, then click and drag in the report header to create an unbound control under the title of the report. Type **Prepared by:** followed by your name as shown in Figure 6.10c.

➤ Select (click) the first control in the OrderID footer (which begins with "Summary for"). Press the **Del key**. Click and drag the unbound control containing the word **Sum** to the right of the group footer so that the label is next to the computed total for each order. Do the same for the Grand Total label in the Report footer.

➤ Click the **Save button** to save the report, then click the **View button** to preview the report.

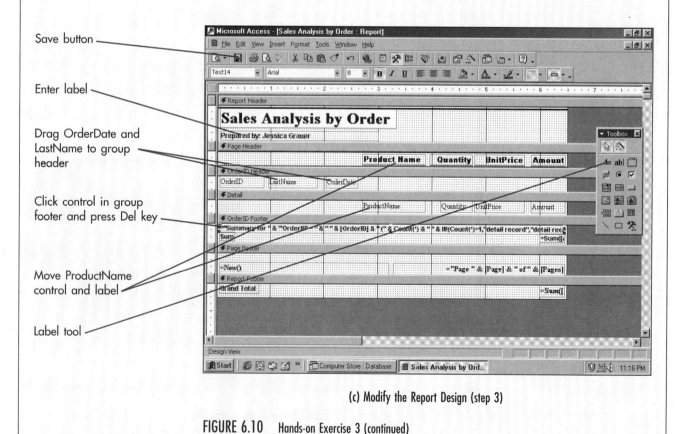

Save button

Enter label

Drag OrderDate and LastName to group header

Click control in group footer and press Del key

Move ProductName control and label

Label tool

(c) Modify the Report Design (step 3)

FIGURE 6.10   Hands-on Exercise 3 (continued)

SELECTING MULTIPLE CONTROLS

Select (click) a column heading in the page header, then press and hold the Shift key as you select the corresponding control in the Detail section. This selects both the column heading and the bound control and enables you to move and size the objects in conjunction with one another. Continue to work with both objects selected as you apply formatting through various buttons on the Formatting toolbar, or change properties through the property sheet. Click anywhere on the report to deselect the objects when you are finished.

STEP 4: Print the Report

➤ You should see the report in Figure 6.10d, which groups the reports by OrderID. The products are in alphabetical order within each order.

➤ Click the **Zoom button** to see the entire page. Click the **Zoom button** a second time to return to the higher magnification.

➤ Click the **Printer button** if you are satisfied with the appearance of the report, or return to the Design view to make any needed changes.

➤ Pull down the **File menu** and click **Close** to close the report. Click **Yes** if asked whether to save the changes.

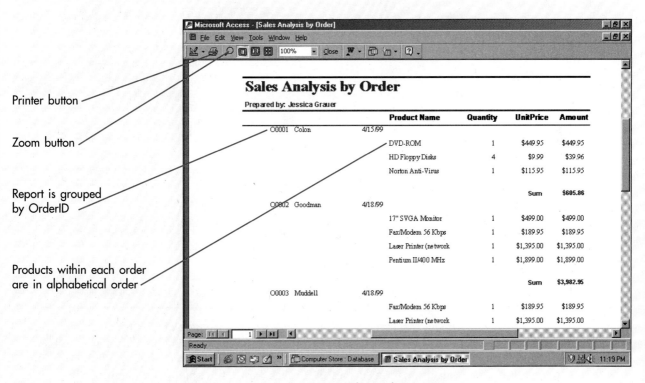

Printer button

Zoom button

Report is grouped by OrderID

Products within each order are in alphabetical order

(d) Print the Report (step 4)

FIGURE 6.10   Hands-on Exercise 3 (continued)

STEP 5: Copy an Existing Query

➤ If necessary, return to the Database window, then click the **Queries button** in the Database window.

➤ Click the **Sales Analysis by Order query** to select the query as shown in Figure 6.10e.

➤ Pull down the **Edit menu** and click **Copy** (or use the Ctrl+C shortcut) to copy the query to the clipboard.

➤ Pull down the **Edit menu** and click **Paste** (or use Ctrl+V shortcut) to produce the Paste As dialog box in Figure 6.10e. Type **Sales Totals**. Click **OK**.

➤ The Database window contains the original query (Sales Analysis by Order) as well as the copied version (Sales Totals) you just created.

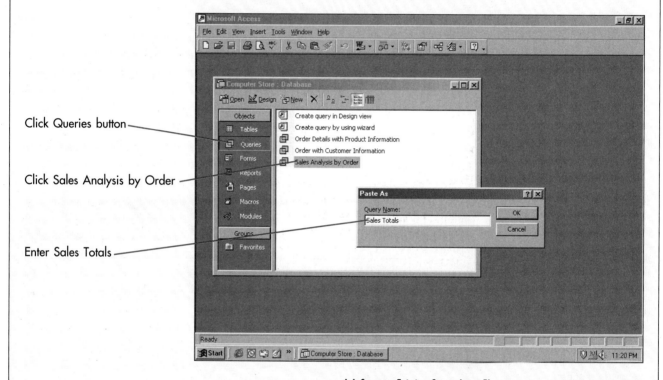

Click Queries button

Click Sales Analysis by Order

Enter Sales Totals

(e) Copy an Existing Query (step 5)

FIGURE 6.10   Hands-on Exercise 3 (continued)

COPY, DELETE, OR RENAME A REPORT

The Database window enables you to copy, delete, or rename any object (a table, form, query, or report) in an Access database. To copy an object, select the object, pull down the Edit menu, and click Copy. Pull down the Edit menu a second time, click Paste, then enter the name of the copied object. To delete or rename an object, point to the object, then click the right mouse button to display a shortcut menu, and select the desired operation.

STEP 6: Create a Total Query

➤ Select the newly created **Sales Totals query**. Click the **Design button** to open the Query Design window in Figure 6.10f.

➤ Click the **column selector** for the **OrderDate field** to select the column. Press the **Del key** to delete the field from the query. Delete the **ProductID, ProductName, Quantity**, and **UnitPrice fields** in similar fashion.

➤ Pull down the **View menu** and click **Totals** to display the Total row (or click the **Totals button** on the toolbar).

➤ Click the **Total row** under the Amount field, then click the **drop-down arrow** to display the summary functions. Click **Sum** as shown in the figure.

➤ Save the query.

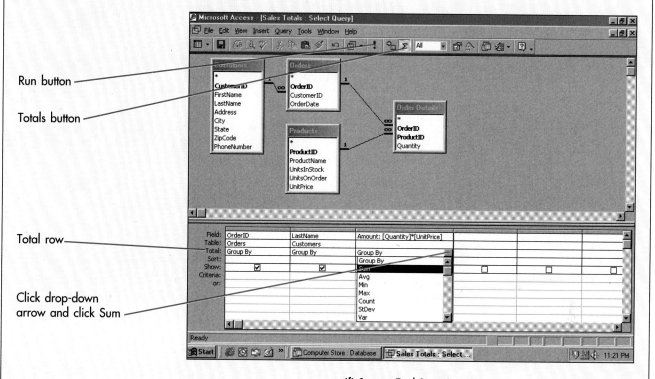

(f) Create a Total Query (step 6)

FIGURE 6.10   Hands-on Exercise 3 (continued)

THE DESCRIPTION PROPERTY

A working database will contain many different objects of the same type, making it all too easy to forget the purpose of the individual objects. The Description property helps you to remember. Point to any object within the Database window, click the right mouse button to display a shortcut menu, click Properties to display the Properties dialog box, enter an appropriate description, then click OK to close the Properties sheet. Once a description has been created, you can right click any object in the Database window, then click the Properties command from the shortcut menu to display the information.

STEP 7: Run the Query

➤ Pull down the **Query menu** and click **Run** (or click the **Run button**) to run the query. You should see the datasheet in Figure 6.10g, which contains one record for each order with the total amount of that order.

➤ Click any field and attempt to change its value. You will be unable to do so as indicated by the beep and the message in the status bar, indicating that the recordset is not updatable.

➤ Click the **Design View button** to return to the Query Design view.

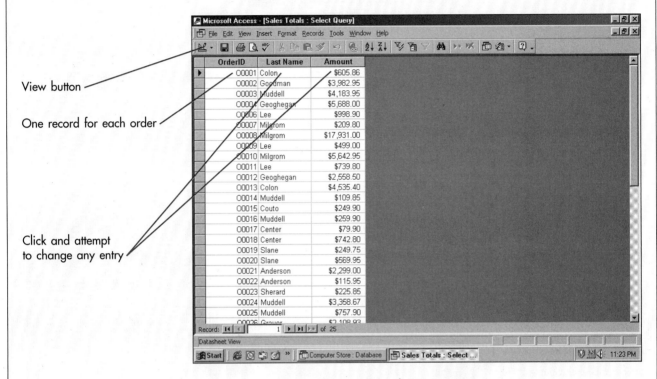

View button —

One record for each order —

Click and attempt to change any entry —

(g) Run the Query (step 7)

FIGURE 6.10 Hands-on Exercise 3 (continued)

UPDATING THE QUERY

The changes made to a query's dynaset are automatically made in the underlying table(s). Not every field in a query is updatable, however, and the easiest way to determine if you can change a value is to run the query, view the dynaset, and attempt to edit the field. Access will prevent you from updating a calculated field, a field based on an aggregate function (such as Sum or Count), or the join field on the "one side" of a one-to-many relationship. If you attempt to update a field you cannot change, the status bar will display a message indicating why the change is not allowed.

STEP 8: Create a Parameter Query

➤ Click the **Criteria row** under **LastName**. Type **[Enter Customer's Last Name]**. Be sure to enclose the entry in square brackets.

➤ Pull down the **File menu**. Click **Save As**. Enter **Customer Parameter Query** in the Save Query "Sales Total" To box. Click **OK**.

➤ Run the query. Access will display the dialog box in Figure 6.10h, asking for the Customer's last name. Type **your name** and press **enter**. Access displays the information for your order(s). Close the query.

Run button

Enter your name

Enter prompt in square brackets

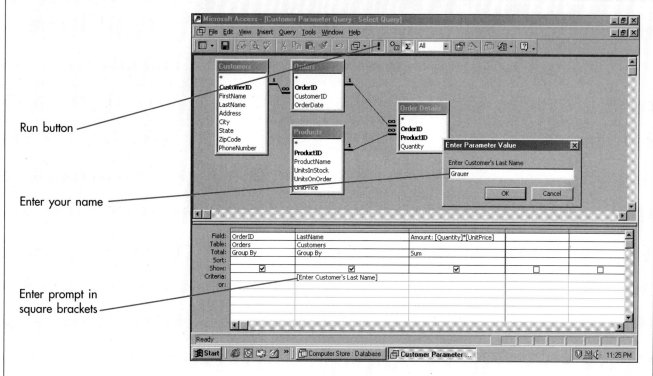

(h) Create a Parameter Query (step 8)

FIGURE 6.10   Hands-on Exercise 3 (continued)

THE TOPVALUES PROPERTY

The TopValues property returns a designated number of records rather than the entire dynaset. Open the query in Design view, then click the right mouse button *outside* the design grid to display a shortcut menu. Click Properties, click the box for TopValues, and enter the desired value as either a number or a percent; for example, 5 to list the top five records, or 5% to display the records that make up the top five percent. The dynaset must be in sequence according to the desired field in order for the TopValues property to work properly.

STEP 9: Exit Access

➤ Exit Access if you do not want to continue with the next exercise. (Do not be concerned if Access indicates it will empty the clipboard.)

One of the advantages of an Access database is that it can be easily expanded to include additional data without disturbing the existing tables. The database used throughout the chapter consisted of four tables: a Customers table, a Products table, an Orders table, and an Order Details table. Figure 6.11 extends the database to include a Sales Persons table with data about each member of the sales staff.

The salesperson helps the customer as he or she comes into the store, then receives a commission based on the order. There is a one-to-many relationship between the salesperson and orders. One salesperson can generate many orders, but an order can have only one salesperson. The Sales Persons and Orders tables are joined by the SalesPersonID field, which is common to both tables.

Figure 6.11 is similar to Figure 6.1 at the beginning of the chapter except that the Sales Persons table has been added and the Orders table has been expanded to include a SalesPersonID. This enables management to monitor the performance of the sales staff. Consider:

Query: How many orders has Cori Rice taken?
Answer: Cori has taken five orders.

The query is straightforward and easily answered. You would search the Sales Persons table for Cori Rice to determine her SalesPersonID (S03). You would then search the Orders table and count the records containing S03 in the SalesPersonID field.

The Sales Persons table is also used to generate a report listing the commissions due to each salesperson. The store pays a 5% commission on every sale. Consider:

Query: Which salesperson is associated with order O0003? When was this person hired?
Answer: Cori Rice is the salesperson for order O0003. Ms. Rice was hired on March 15, 1993.

The determination of the salesperson is straightforward, as all you have to do is search the Orders table to locate the order and obtain the SalesPersonID (S03). You then search the Sales Persons table for this value (S03) and find the corresponding name (Cori Rice) and hire date (3/15/93).

Query: What is the commission on order O0003?
Answer: The commission on order O0003 is $209.20.

The calculation of the commission requires a fair amount of arithmetic. First, you need to compute the total amount of the order. Thus, you would begin in the Order Details table, find each product in order O0003, and multiply the quantity of that product by its unit price. The total cost of order O0003 is $4,183.95, based on one unit of product P0005 at $2,599, one unit of product P0020 at $189.95, and one unit of product P0022 at $1,395. (You can also refer to the sales report in Figure 6.9 that was developed in the previous exercise to check these calculations.)

Now that you know the total cost of the order, you can compute the commission, which is 5% of the total order, or $209.20 (.05 × $4,183.95). The complete calculation is lengthy, but Access does it automatically, and therein lies the beauty of a relational database.

(a) Customers Table

Customer ID	First Name	Last Name	Address	City	State	Zip Code	Phone Number
C0001	Benjamin	Lee	1000 Call Street	Tallahassee	FL	33340	(904) 327-4124
C0002	Eleanor	Milgrom	7245 NW 8 Street	Margate	FL	33065	(305) 974-1234
C0003	Neil	Goodman	4215 South 81 Street	Margate	FL	33065	(305) 444-5555
C0004	Nicholas	Colon	9020 N.W. 75 Street	Coral Springs	FL	33065	(305) 753-9887
C0005	Michael	Ware	276 Brickell Avenue	Miami	FL	33131	(305) 444-3980
C0006	Jeffrey	Muddell	9522 S.W. 142 Street	Miami	FL	33176	(305) 253-3909
C0007	Ashley	Geoghegan	7500 Center Lane	Coral Springs	FL	33070	(305) 753-7830
C0008	Serena	Sherard	5000 Jefferson Lane	Gainesville	FL	32601	(904) 375-6442
C0009	Luis	Couto	455 Bargello Avenue	Coral Gables	FL	33146	(305) 666-4801
C0010	Derek	Anderson	6000 Tigertail Avenue	Coconut Grove	FL	33120	(305) 446-8900
C0011	Lauren	Center	12380 S.W. 137 Avenue	Miami	FL	33186	(305) 385-4432
C0012	Robert	Slane	4508 N.W. 7 Street	Miami	FL	33131	(305) 635-3454
C0013	Jessica	Grauer	758 Mangowood Road	Coral Springs	FL	33071	(305) 755-5430

(b) Products Table

Product ID	Product Name	Units In Stock	Units On Order	Unit Price
P0001	Pentium II/400 MHz	50	0	$1,899.00
P0002	Pentium II/450 MHz	25	5	$1,999.00
P0003	Pentium III/450 MHz	125	15	$2,099.00
P0004	Pentium III/500 MHz	25	50	$2,299.00
P0005	Pentium II laptop/300 MHz	15	25	$2,599.00
P0006	17" SVGA Monitor	50	0	$499.00
P0007	19" SVGA Monitor	25	10	$899.00
P0008	21" Multisync Monitor	50	20	$1,599.00
P0009	6.4 GB IDE Hard Drive	15	20	$399.00
P0010	10 GB Ultra ATA Hard Drive	25	15	$799.00
P0011	17 GB Ultra ATA Hard Drive	10	0	$1,245.00
P0012	CD-ROM: 32X	40	0	$249.00
P0013	DVD-ROM	50	15	$449.95
P0014	HD Floppy Disks	500	200	$9.99
P0015	Zip Cartridges	100	50	$14.79
P0016	Internal Zip Drive	15	3	$179.95
P0017	Serial Mouse	150	50	$69.95
P0018	Trackball	55	0	$59.95
P0019	Joystick	250	100	$39.95
P0020	Fax/Modem 56 Kbps	35	10	$189.95
P0021	Fax/Modem 33.6 Kbps	20	0	$65.95
P0022	Laser Printer (network)	100	15	$1,395.00
P0023	Ink Jet Printer	50	50	$249.95
P0024	Laser Printer (personal)	125	25	$569.95
P0025	Windows 95	400	200	$95.95
P0026	Windows 98	150	50	$75.95
P0027	Norton Anti-Virus	150	50	$115.95
P0028	Microsoft Scenes Screen Saver	75	25	$29.95
P0029	Microsoft Bookshelf	250	100	$129.95
P0030	Microsoft Cinemania	25	10	$59.95
P0031	Professional Photos on CD-ROM	15	0	$45.95

(c) Orders Table

Order ID	Customer ID	Order Date	SalesPersonID
O0001	C0004	4/15/99	S01
O0002	C0003	4/18/99	S02
O0003	C0006	4/18/99	S03
O0004	C0007	4/18/99	S04
O0006	C0001	4/21/99	S05
O0007	C0002	4/21/99	S01
O0008	C0002	4/22/99	S02
O0009	C0001	4/22/99	S03
O0010	C0002	4/22/99	S04
O0011	C0001	4/24/99	S05
O0012	C0007	4/24/99	S01
O0013	C0004	4/24/99	S02
O0014	C0006	4/25/99	S03
O0015	C0009	4/25/99	S04
O0016	C0006	4/26/99	S05
O0017	C0011	4/26/99	S01
O0018	C0011	4/26/99	S02
O0019	C0012	4/27/99	S03
O0020	C0012	4/28/99	S04
O0021	C0010	4/29/99	S05
O0022	C0010	4/29/99	S01
O0023	C0008	4/30/99	S02
O0024	C0006	5/1/99	S03
O0025	C0006	5/1/99	S04
O0026	C0013	5/3/99	S05

(d) Order Details Table

Order ID	Product ID	Quantity
O0001	P0013	1
O0001	P0014	4
O0001	P0027	1
O0002	P0001	1
O0002	P0006	1
O0002	P0020	1
O0002	P0022	1
O0003	P0005	1
O0003	P0020	1
O0003	P0022	1
O0004	P0003	1
O0004	P0010	1
O0004	P0022	2
O0006	P0007	1
O0006	P0014	10
O0007	P0028	1
O0007	P0030	3
O0008	P0001	1
O0008	P0004	3
O0008	P0008	4
O0008	P0011	2
O0008	P0012	1
O0009	P0006	1
O0010	P0002	2
O0010	P0022	1
O0010	P0023	1
O0011	P0016	2
O0011	P0020	2
O0012	P0021	10
O0012	P0029	10
O0012	P0030	10
O0013	P0009	4
O0013	P0016	10
O0013	P0024	2
O0014	P0019	2
O0014	P0028	1
O0015	P0018	1
O0015	P0020	1
O0016	P0029	2
O0017	P0019	2
O0018	P0009	1
O0018	P0025	2
O0018	P0026	2
O0019	P0014	25
O0020	P0024	1
O0021	P0004	1
O0022	P0027	1
O0023	P0021	1
O0023	P0028	1
O0023	P0029	1
O0024	P0007	1
O0024	P0013	5
O0024	P0014	3
O0024	P0016	1
O0025	P0012	2
O0025	P0029	2
O0026	P0001	1

(e) Sales Persons Table

SalesPersonID	First Name	Last Name	Work Phone	Hire Date
S01	Linda	Black	(305) 284-6105	2/3/93
S02	Michael	Vaughn	(305) 284-3993	2/10/93
S03	Cori	Rice	(305) 284-2557	3/15/93
S04	Karen	Ruenheck	(305) 284-4641	1/31/94
S05	Richard	Linger	(305) 284-4662	1/31/94

FIGURE 6.11   Super Store Database

The Sales Commission Query

Figure 6.12a displays the design view of a parameter query to calculate the commissions for a specific salesperson. (This query determines the commissions for Cori Rice, which you computed manually in the previous discussion.) Enter the last name of the sales associate, Rice, and the query returns the dynaset in Figure 6.12b, showing all of her commissions. Note, too, that the commission returned for order O0003 is $209.20, which corresponds to the amount we arrived at earlier.

The query in Figure 6.12a includes fields from all five tables in the database. The relationships are shown graphically in the top half of the query window and reflect the earlier discussion—for example, the one-to-many relationship between salespersons and orders. These tables are joined through the SalesPersonID field, which is the primary key in the Sales Persons table but a foreign key in the Orders table. (The Orders table has been modified to include this field.)

The following exercise has you import the Sales Persons table from another Access database. It then directs you to modify the existing Orders table to include a SalesPersonID, which references the records in the Sales Persons table, and to modify the Super Store Order Form to include the salesperson data.

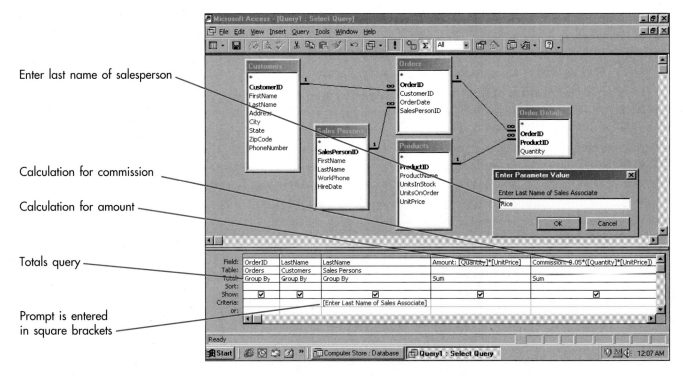

(a) Design View

(b) Dynaset

FIGURE 6.12   Sales Commission

Expanding the Database

Objective: To import a table from another database; to modify the design of an existing table. Use Figure 6.13 as a guide in the exercise.

STEP 1: Import the Sales Persons Table

➤ Open the **Computer Store database**. Click the **Tables button**. Pull down the **File menu**. Click **Get External Data**, then click the **Import** command.

➤ Click (select) the **Sales Persons database** from the **Exploring Access folder**, then click **Import** to display the Import Objects dialog box in Figure 6.13a.

➤ If necessary, click the **Tables button**, click **SalesPersons** (the only table in this database), then click **OK**. A dialog box will appear briefly on your screen as the Sales Persons table is imported into the Computer Store database.

Click Tables tab

Click SalesPersons

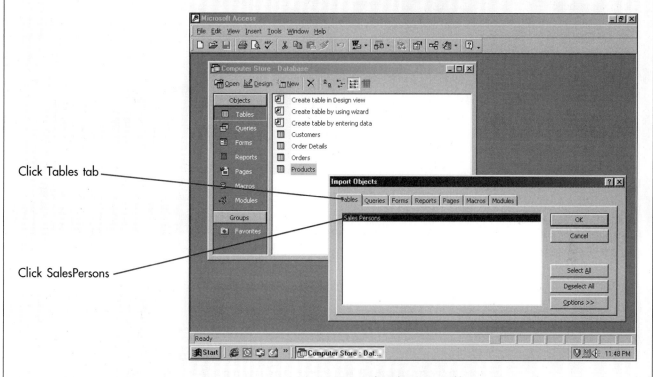

(a) Import the Sales Persons Table (step 1)

FIGURE 6.13   Hands-on Exercise 4

THE DOCUMENTS SUBMENU

The Documents menu contains shortcuts to the last 15 files that were opened. Click the Start button, click (or point to) the Documents menu, then click the document you wish to open (e.g., Computer Store), assuming that it appears on the menu. Windows will start the application, then open the indicated document.

STEP 2: Modify the Orders Table Design

➤ Select the **Orders table** from the Database window as shown in Figure 6.13b. Click the **Design button**.

➤ Click in the first available row in the **Field Name** column. Enter **SalesPersonID** as shown in Figure 6.13b. Choose **Number** as the data type. The Field Size property changes to Long Integer by default.

- Click the **Format** property. Enter **\S00**.
- Click the **Default Value** property and delete the **0**.

➤ Click the **Save button** to save the modified design of the Orders table.

View button

Save button

Click Design button

Click Orders table

Enter new field

Enter \S00

Delete 0

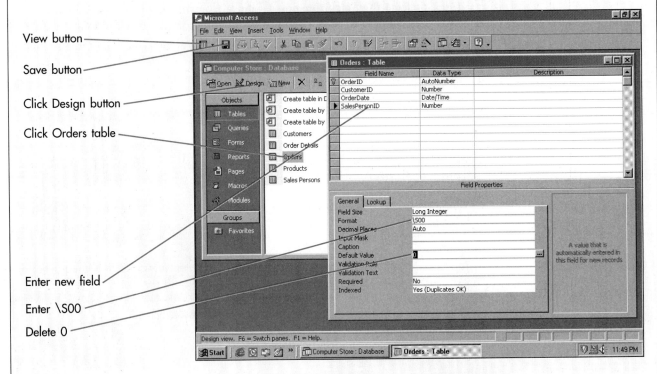

(b) Modify the Orders Table Design (step 2)

FIGURE 6.13   Hands-on Exercise 4 (continued)

RELATIONSHIPS AND THE AUTONUMBER FIELD TYPE

The join fields on both sides of a relationship must be the same data type—for example, both number fields or both text fields. The Auto-Number field type, however, cannot be specified on both sides of a relationship. Thus, if the join field (SalesPersonID) in the primary table (Sales Persons) is an AutoNumber field, the join field in the related table (Orders) must be specified as a Number field, with the Field Size property set to Long Integer.

STEP 3: Add the SalesPerson to Existing Orders

➤ Click the **Datasheet View button** to change to the Datasheet view as shown in Figure 6.13c. Maximize the window.

➤ Enter the **SalesPersonID** for each existing order as shown in Figure 6.13c.

➤ Enter only the number (e.g., 1, rather than S01) as the S and leading 0 are displayed automatically through the Format property. (Orders O0001 and O0002 are associated with salespersons 1 and 2 respectively, and are not visible in the figure.)

➤ Close the Orders table.

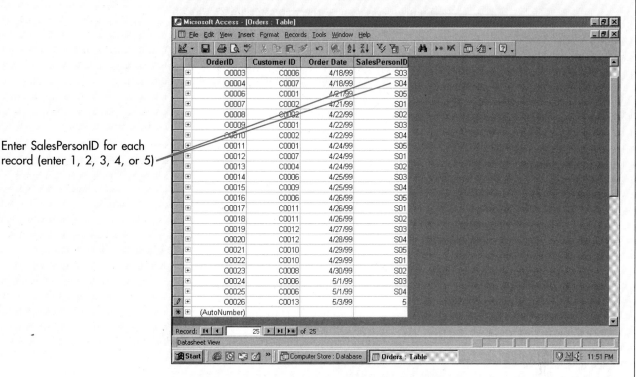

Enter SalesPersonID for each record (enter 1, 2, 3, 4, or 5)

(c) Add the SalesPerson (step 3)

FIGURE 6.13   Hands-on Exercise 4 (continued)

HIDE THE WINDOWS TASKBAR

The Windows taskbar is great for novices because it makes task switching as easy as changing channels on a TV. It also takes up valuable real estate on the desktop, and hence you may want to hide the taskbar when you don't need it. Point to an empty area on the taskbar, click the right mouse button to display a shortcut menu, and click Properties to display the Taskbar Properties dialog box. Click the Taskbar Options tab (if necessary), check the box to Auto hide the taskbar, and click OK. The taskbar should disappear. Now point to the bottom of the screen (or the edge where the taskbar was last displayed), and it will reappear.

STEP 4: Create the Relationship

➤ Pull down the **Tools menu**. Click **Relationships** to open the Relationships window as shown in Figure 6.13d. (The Sales Persons table is not yet visible.) Click the **Maximize button**.

➤ If necessary, drag the bottom border of the **Orders table** until you see the SalesPersonID (the field you added in step 2).

➤ Pull down the **Relationships menu**. Click **Show Table**. Click the **Tables button** if necessary, select the **Sales Persons table**, then click the **Add button**. Close the Show Table dialog box.

➤ Drag the title bar of the **SalesPersons table** to position the table as shown in Figure 6.13d. Drag the **SalesPersonID field** from the Sales Persons table to the SalesPersonID in the Orders table.

➤ Check the box to **Enforce Referential Integrity**. Click the **Create Command button** to create the relationship. Click the **Save button** to save the Relationships window. Close the Relationships window.

Click and drag SalesPersonID from SalesPersons table to Orders table

Click and drag to size Orders field list

Click Enforce Referential Integrity

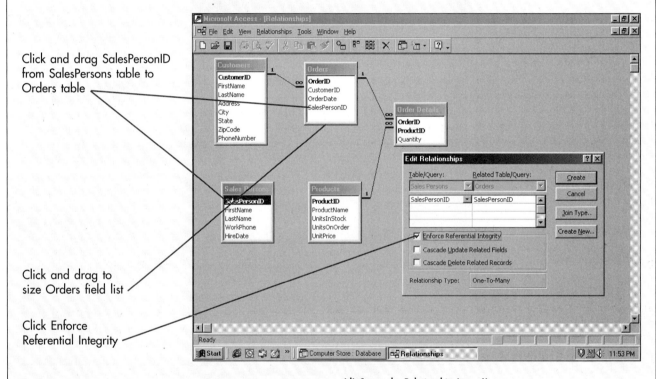

(d) Create the Relationship (step 4)

FIGURE 6.13 Hands-on Exercise 4 (continued)

PRINT THE RELATIONSHIPS

Pull down the Tools menu and click Relationships to open the Relationships window, then pull down the File menu and click the Print Relationships command. You will see the Print Preview screen of a report that displays the contents of the Relationships window. Click the Print button to print the report, or change to the Design view to modify the report, perhaps by adding your name. Save the report after printing so that it will be available at a later time.

STEP 5: Modify the Order with Customer Information Query

➤ You should be back in the Database window. Click the **Queries button**, select the **Order with Customer Information query**, then click the **Design button** to open the query in the Design view as shown in Figure 6.13e.

➤ If necessary, click and drag the border of the **Orders table** so that the newly added SalesPersonID field is displayed. Click the **horizontal scroll arrow** until a blank column in the design grid is visible.

➤ Click and drag the **SalesPersonID** from the Orders table to the first blank column in the design grid.

➤ Save the query. Close the query.

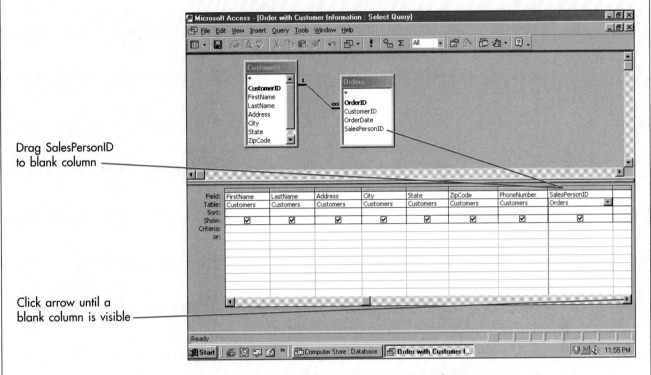

Drag SalesPersonID to blank column

Click arrow until a blank column is visible

(e) Modify the Order with Customer Information Query (step 5)

FIGURE 6.13 Hands-on Exercise 4 (continued)

OPTIMIZE QUERIES USING INDEXES

The performance of a database becomes important as you progress from a "student" database with a limited number of records to a real database with large tables. Thus it becomes advantageous to optimize the performance of individual queries by creating indexes in the underlying tables. Indexes should be specified for any criteria field in a query, as well as for any field that is used in a relationship to join two tables. To create an index, open the table in Design view and set the indexed property to Yes.

STEP 6: Modify the Order Form

➤ You should be back in the Database window. Click the **Forms button**, select the **Super Store Order Form**, then click the **Design** button.

➤ Right click the **form selector box**. Click **Properties** to display the Form Properties box. Click the **Data tab**, click the **Record Source property**, click the **drop-down arrow,** then select **Order with Customer Information**.

➤ Move and size the controls as shown in Figure 6.13f.

➤ Click the **Combo Box tool**, then click and drag in the form where you want the combo box to go. Release the mouse to start the Combo Box Wizard.

 • Check the option button that indicates you want the combo box to look up values in a table or query. Click **Next**.

 • Choose the **Sales Persons table** in the next screen. Click **Next**.

 • Select the **SalesPersonID** and **LastName**. Click **Next**.

 • Adjust the column width if necessary. Be sure the box to hide the key column is checked. Click **Next**.

 • Click the option button to store the value in the field. Click the **drop-down arrow** to display the fields and select the **SalesPersonID** field. Click **Next**.

 • Enter **Salesperson** as the label for the combo box. Click **Finish**.

➤ Move and/or size the combo box and its label so that it is spaced attractively on the form. Point to the combo box, click the **right mouse button** to display a shortcut menu, and click **Properties**. Click the **Other tab**.

➤ Change the name of the box to **Sales Person.** Close the dialog box.

➤ Pull down the **View menu** and click **Tab Order**. Click the **AutoOrder button**. Click **OK**. Save the form. Change to the Form view.

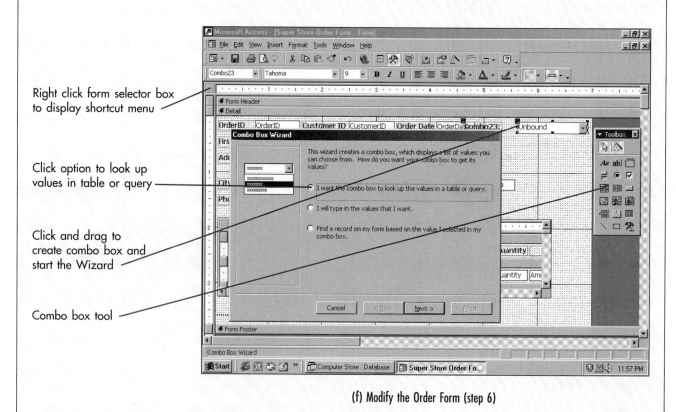

Right click form selector box to display shortcut menu

Click option to look up values in table or query

Click and drag to create combo box and start the Wizard

Combo box tool

(f) Modify the Order Form (step 6)

FIGURE 6.13   Hands-on Exercise 4 (continued)

STEP 7: The Completed Order Form

➤ You should see the completed form as shown in Figure 6.13g. Click the **New Record button** on the Form View toolbar to display a blank form so that you can place an order.

➤ Click in the **Customer ID text box**. Enter **13** (your customer number from the first exercise), then press the **Tab key** to move to the next field.
  - The OrderID is entered automatically as it is an AutoNumber field and assigned the next sequential number.
  - All of your customer information (your name, address, and phone number) is entered automatically because of the AutoLookup feature that is built into the underlying query.
  - Today's date is entered automatically because of the default value (=Date( )) that is built into the Orders table.

➤ Click the **drop-down arrow** on the Sales Person combo box. Select **Black** (or click in the box and type **B**), and the complete name is entered automatically.

➤ Click the **ProductID text box** in the subform. Enter **2** (not P0002) and press the **enter key** to move to the next field. The OrderID (O0027) is entered automatically, as is the Product Name and Unit Price.

➤ Press the **Tab key** three times to move to the Quantity field and enter **1**. The amount is computed automatically.

➤ Move to the ProductID field for the next item. Choose any item and enter a quantity.

➤ Close the Order form.

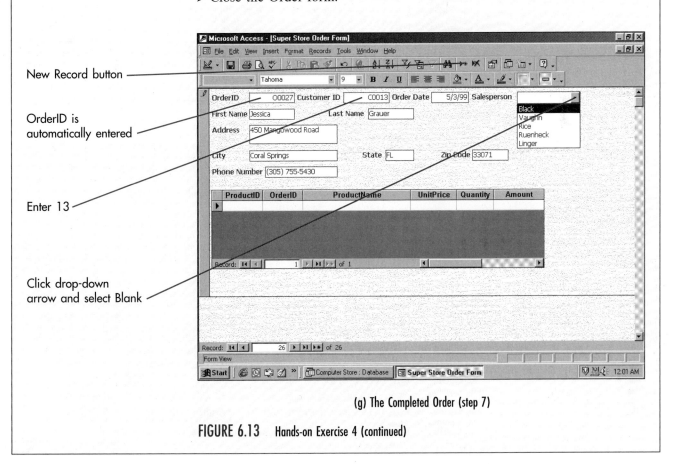

(g) The Completed Order (step 7)

FIGURE 6.13   Hands-on Exercise 4 (continued)

STEP 8: Database Properties

➤ You should be back in the Database window. Pull down the **File menu** and click **Database Properties** to display the dialog box in Figure 6.13h. Click the **Contents tab** to display the contents of the Computer Store database.

- There are five tables (Customers, Order Details, Orders, Products, and Sales Persons).
- There are five queries, which include the Total and Parameter queries you created in exercise 3.
- There are two forms—the main form, which you have completed in this exercise, and the associated subform.
- There is one report, the report you created in exercise 3.

➤ Click OK to close the dialog box. Close the Computer Store database. Exit Access.

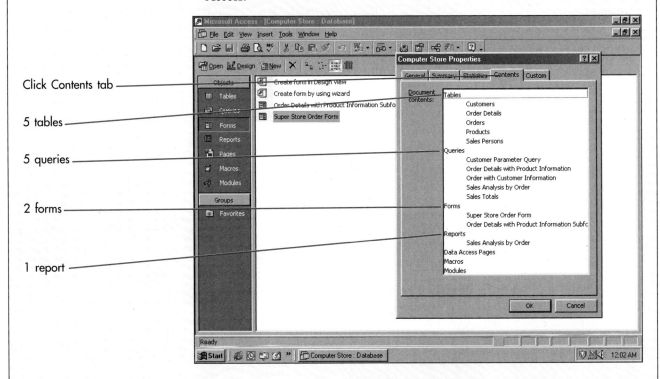

Click Contents tab

5 tables

5 queries

2 forms

1 report

(h) Database Properties (step 8)

FIGURE 6.13   Hands-on Exercise 4 (continued)

THE STARTUP PROPERTY

The Startup property determines how a database will appear when it is opened. One very common option is to open a form automatically so that the user is presented with the form without having to navigate through the Database window. Pull down the Tools menu, click Startup to display the Startup dialog box, then click the drop-down arrow in the Display Form list box. Select the desired form (e.g., the Super Store Order form developed in this exercise), then click OK. The next time you open the database the designated form will be opened automatically. See exercise 7 at the end of the chapter.

SUMMARY

The implementation of a many-to-many relationship requires an additional table whose primary key consists of (at least) the primary keys of the individual tables. The many-to-many table may also contain additional fields whose values are dependent on the combined key. All relationships are created in the Relationships window by dragging the join field from the primary table to the related table. A many-to-many relationship in the physical system is implemented by a pair of one-to-many relationships in an Access database.

Enforcement of referential integrity prevents you from adding a record to the related table if that record contains an invalid value of the foreign key. It also prevents the deletion and/or updating of records on the "one" side of a one-to-many relationship when there are matching records in the related table. The deletion (updating) can take place, however, if the relationship is modified to allow the cascaded deletion (updating) of related records (fields).

There are several reasons to base a form (or subform) on a query rather than a table. A query can contain a calculated field; a table cannot. A query can contain fields from more than one table and take advantage of AutoLookup. A query can also contain selected records from a table and/or display those records in a different sequence from that of the table on which it is based.

A parameter query prompts you for the criteria each time you execute the query. The prompt is enclosed in square brackets and is entered in the Criteria row within the Query Design view. Multiple parameters may be specified within the same query.

Aggregate functions (Avg, Min, Max, Sum, and Count) perform calculations on groups of records. Execution of the query displays an aggregate record for each group, and individual records do not appear. Updating of individual records is not possible in this type of query.

Tables may be added to an Access database without disturbing the data in existing tables. The Get External Data command enables you to import an object(s) from another database.

KEY WORDS AND CONCEPTS

AutoLookup
AutoNumber field
Cascaded deletion
Cascaded updating
Combined key
Description property
Foreign key
Format property
Get External Data
   command
Group By

Join field
Join line
Main form
Many-to-many
   relationship
One-to-many
   relationship
Parameter query
Primary key
Prompt
Referential integrity

Startup property
Sum function
Table row
TopValues property
Total query
Total row
Unmatched Query
   Wizard
Zoom box

1. Which tables are necessary to implement a many-to-many relationship between students and the courses they take?
   (a) A Students table
   (b) A Courses table
   (c) A Students-Courses table
   (d) All of the above

2. Which of the following would be suitable as the primary key in a Students-Courses table, where there is a many-to-many relationship between Students and Courses, and further, when a student is allowed to repeat a course?
   (a) The combination of StudentID and CourseID
   (b) The combination of StudentID, CourseID, and semester
   (c) The combination of StudentID, CourseID, semester, and grade
   (d) All of the above are equally appropriate

3. Which of the following is necessary to add a record to the "one" side in a one-to-many relationship in which referential integrity is enforced?
   (a) A unique primary key for the new record
   (b) One or more matching records in the many table
   (c) Both (a) and (b)
   (d) Neither (a) nor (b)

4. Which of the following is necessary to add a record to the "many" side in a one-to-many relationship in which referential integrity is enforced?
   (a) A unique primary key for the new record
   (b) A matching record in the primary table
   (c) Both (a) and (b)
   (d) Neither (a) nor (b)

5. Under which circumstances can you delete a "many" record in a one-to-many relationship?
   (a) Under all circumstances
   (b) Under no circumstances
   (c) By enforcing referential integrity
   (d) By enforcing referential integrity with the cascaded deletion of related records

6. Under which circumstances can you delete the "one" record in a one-to-many relationship?
   (a) Under all circumstances
   (b) Under no circumstances
   (c) By enforcing referential integrity
   (d) By enforcing referential integrity with the cascaded deletion of related records

7. Which of the following would be suitable as the primary key in a Patients-Doctors table, where there is a many-to-many relationship between patients and doctors, and where the same patient can see the same doctor on different visits?

(a) The combination of PatientID and DoctorID

(b) The combination of PatientID, DoctorID, and the date of the visit

(c) Either (a) or (b)

(d) Neither (a) nor (b)

8. How do you implement the many-to-many relationship between patients and doctors described in the previous question?

   (a) Through a one-to-many relationship between the Patients table and the Patients-Doctors table

   (b) Through a one-to-many relationship between the Doctors table and the Patients-Doctors table

   (c) Both (a) and (b)

   (d) Neither (a) nor (b)

9. A database has a one-to-many relationship between teams and players, which is implemented through a common TeamID field. Which data type and field size should be assigned to the TeamID field in the Players table, if TeamID is defined as an AutoNumber field in the Teams table?

   (a) AutoNumber and Long Integer

   (b) Number and Long Integer

   (c) Text and Long Integer

   (d) Lookup Wizard and Long Integer

10. Which of the following is true about a main form and an associated subform?

    (a) The main form can be based on a query

    (b) The subform can be based on a query

    (c) Both (a) and (b)

    (d) Neither (a) nor (b)

11. A parameter query:

    (a) Displays a prompt within brackets in the Criteria row of the query

    (b) Is limited to a single parameter

    (c) Both (a) and (b)

    (d) Neither (a) nor (b)

12. Which of the following is available as an aggregate function within a select query?

    (a) Sum and Avg

    (b) Min and Max

    (c) Both (a) and (b)

    (d) Neither (a) nor (b)

13. A query designed to take advantage of AutoLookup requires:

    (a) A unique value for the join field in the "one" side of a one-to-many relationship

    (b) The join field to be taken from the "many" side of a one-to-many relationship

    (c) Both (a) and (b)

    (d) Neither (a) nor (b)

14. Which of the following can be imported from another Access database?

    (a) Tables and forms

    (b) Queries and reports

    (c) Both (a) and (b)

    (d) Neither (a) nor (b)

15. Which of the following is true of the TopValues query property?
  (a) It can be used to display the top 10 records in a dynaset
  (b) It can be used to display the top 10 percent of the records in a dynaset
  (c) Both (a) and (b)
  (d) Neither (a) nor (b)

ANSWERS

1. d	**6.** d	**11.** a
2. b	**7.** b	**12.** c
3. a	**8.** c	**13.** c
4. a	**9.** b	**14.** c
5. a	**10.** c	**15.** c

PRACTICE WITH ACCESS 2000

1. The Sales Commission report in Figure 6.14 is based on a query similar to the parameter query used to determine the commissions for a particular salesperson. Create the necessary query, then use the Report Wizard to create the report in Figure 6.14.

You need not match our report exactly and are free to improve its design, perhaps by adding clip art to the report header. Print the completed report for your instructor. This exercise illustrates the power of Access as both the report and underlying query are based on five different tables.

2. The query in Figure 6.15 identifies products that have never been ordered. The query was created through the Find Unmatched Query Wizard according to the instructions below.

  a. Click the Queries button in the Database window. Click the New button, select the Find Unmatched Query Wizard, then click OK.

  b. Choose Products as the table whose records you want to see in the query results. Click Next.

  c. Choose Order Details as the table that contains the related records. Click Next.

  d. ProductID is automatically selected as the matching field. Click Next.

  e. Select every field from the Available Fields list. Click Next.

  f. Products without Matching Order Details is entered as the name of the query. Click the Finish Command button to exit the Wizard and see the results of the query.

  g. What advice will you give to management regarding unnecessary inventory?

  h. What advantage (if any) is there in using the Find Unmatched Query Wizard to create the query, as opposed to creating the query by entering the information directly in the Query Design view?

  i. Could you use the unmatched Query Wizard to determine which sales persons have not placed an order?

Sales Commission Report

	OrderID	Order Date	Last Name	Amount	Commission
Black					
	O0001	4/15/99	Colon	$605.86	$30.29
	O0007	4/21/99	Milgrom	$209.80	$10.49
	O0012	4/24/99	Geoghegan	$2,558.50	$127.93
	O0017	4/26/99	Center	$79.90	$4.00
	O0022	4/29/99	Anderson	$115.95	$5.80
	O0027	5/ 3/99	Grauer	$1,999.00	$99.95
			Sum:	$5,569.01	$278.45
Linger					
	O0006	4/21/99	Lee	$998.90	$49.95
	O0011	4/24/99	Lee	$739.80	$36.99
	O0016	4/26/99	Muddell	$259.90	$13.00
	O0021	4/29/99	Anderson	$2,299.00	$114.95
	O0026	5/ 3/99	Grauer	$2,108.93	$105.45
			Sum:	$6,406.53	$320.33
Rice					
	O0003	4/18/99	Muddell	$4,183.95	$209.20
	O0009	4/22/99	Lee	$499.00	$24.95
	O0014	4/25/99	Muddell	$109.85	$5.49
	O0019	4/27/99	Slane	$249.75	$12.49
	O0024	5/ 1/99	Muddell	$3,358.67	$167.93
			Sum:	$8,401.22	$420.06
Ruenheck					
	O0004	4/18/99	Geoghegan	$5,688.00	$284.40
	O0010	4/22/99	Milgrom	$5,642.95	$282.15
	O0015	4/25/99	Couto	$249.90	$12.50
	O0020	4/28/99	Slane	$569.95	$28.50
	O0025	5/ 1/99	Muddell	$757.90	$37.90
			Sum:	$12,908.70	$645.44
Vaughn					
	O0002	4/18/99	Goodman	$3,982.95	$199.15
	O0008	4/22/99	Milgrom	$17,931.0	$896.55
	O0013	4/24/99	Colon	$4,535.40	$226.77
	O0018	4/26/99	Center	$742.80	$37.14
	O0023	4/30/99	Sherard	$225.85	$11.29
			Sum:	$27,418.00	$1,370.90

Monday, May 31, 1999   **Page 1 of 1**

FIGURE 6.14   Sales Commission Report (Exercise 1)

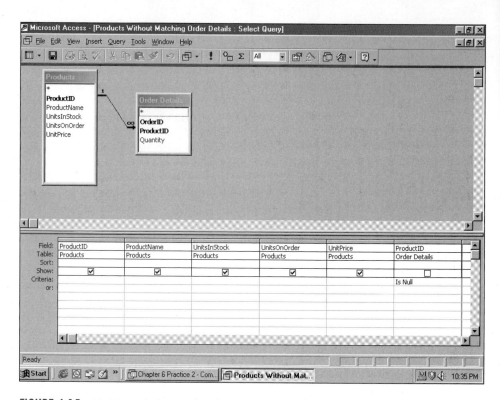

FIGURE 6.15   Find Unmatched Query Wizard (Exercise 2)

3. Create the form in Figure 6.16, which displays either the information for an existing customer or a blank form to add a new customer. This is accomplished by basing the form on a parameter query rather than the Customers table. Execution of the query displays a blank form when the customer's name is not in the database (as in Figure 6.16), or it will display a completed form when it finds the name. Create the necessary parameter query that requests the customer's last name followed by the customer's first name, then create the form based on the parameter query. You are free to improve upon our design.

4. The best way to open the Customer form that was created in the previous exercise is by adding a command button to the Super Store Order form as shown in Figure 6.17. The user would click the Find/Add Command button to display the Parameter Value dialog box, then he or she would enter the customer's last name as indicated. The system would return a completed Customer form for an existing customer (from which to obtain the CustomerID) or a blank form to add a new customer. Closing the customer form, in either case, would return you to the Order form where you can enter the CustomerID and the data for the new order.

   a. Open the Super Store Order form that was completed in Hands-on Exercise 4, then use the Command Button Wizard to add the buttons in Figure 6.17. The Find/Add a Customer button should open the form from the previous problem. The Add Order button should add a new order, and the Close Form button should close the Order form.

   b. Add the Form Header to improve the appearance of the form.

   c. Add a new order for yourself consisting of a Pentium 400, 17-inch monitor, laser printer, and 56k bps modem.

   d. Print this order (be sure to print only a single order) and submit it to your instructor.

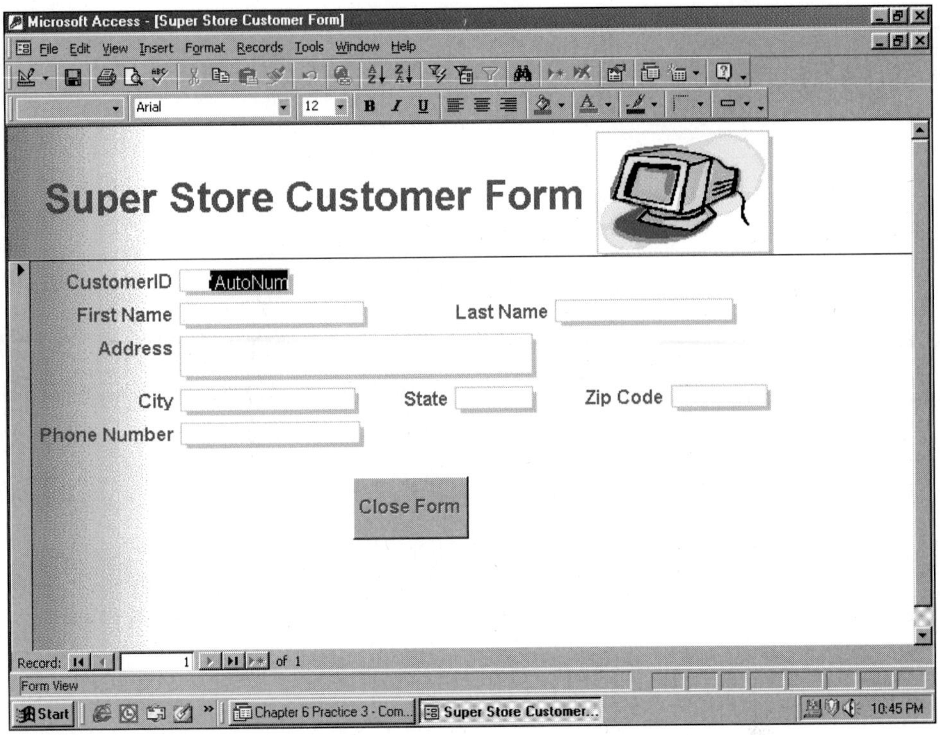

FIGURE 6.16   Super Store Customer Form (Exercise 3)

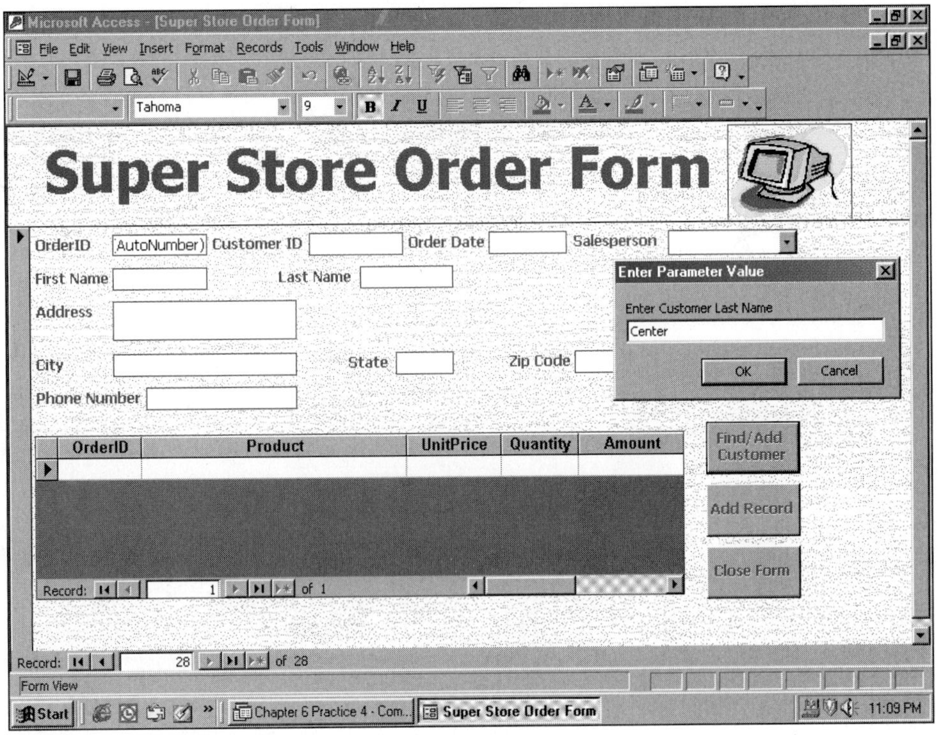

FIGURE 6.17   Improved Super Store Order Form (Exercise 4)

5. Figure 6.18 displays the final version of our Super Store Order form, which contains one additional element—the total amount for the displayed order. Proceed as follows:

a. Open the Super Store Order form in Design view. Click the Subform/Subreport Wizard tool, then click and drag on the design grid under the existing subform control to create a new subform to display the total amount of the order. The subform should be based on the Sales Total query that was created in the third hands-on exercise.

b. Add the OrderID and Amount fields to the new form. Select the option to Show Sales Totals for each record in the Order with Customer Information. Accept the suggested name for the subform.

c. You may need to temporarily make the subform control larger in order to see what you are doing. Delete the label on the subform header section and then click the Form header. Delete the OrderID control in the Detail section, size the Amount control, then size the subform control accordingly.

d. Right click the Form Selector box to display the Properties dialog box. Change the Default View property to Single Form and the Scroll Bars property to Neither. Suppress the record selectors and the navigation buttons. Save the form.

e. Size and move the Sales Total subform within the Order Form. Delete the current label and add a new label for the Order total. Save the form.

f. Change to the Form view, then use the Navigation buttons to move from one order to the next. Each time you view a new order, the total amount is visible at the bottom of the screen.

g. The completed form should match Figure 6.18. This is truly a useful form, and it contains all the information associated with one order.

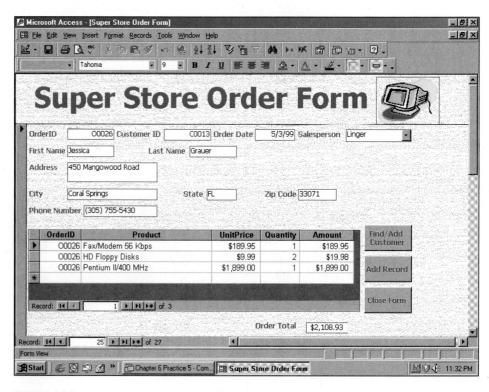

FIGURE 6.18   Final Super Store Order Form (Exercise 5)

6. The Switchboard: Complete the various hands-on exercises and end-of-chapter problems, then create a switchboard similar to Figure 6.19. You need not follow our design exactly, but you should include at least four menu options. Be sure to include a button to exit from the database. Do you see how a switchboard simplifies the selection of various Access objects?

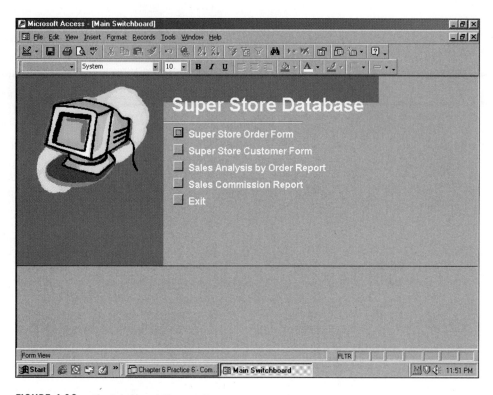

FIGURE 6.19 The Switchboard (Exercise 6)

7. The Startup Property: The Startup property can be used to display the switchboard automatically and/or to further customize the application when it is opened initially. Pull down the Tools menu, click Startup to display the Startup dialog box as shown in Figure 6.20, then experiment with the various options.

You can give the application a customized look by including a title that is displayed in the title bar for Microsoft Access. You can also hide the Database window from the nontechnical user, to prevent unintended changes to the database. Be sure, however, that if you choose to hide the Database window, you know how to display it later so that you will be able to access the objects in the database. (Pull down the Windows menu and click the Unhide command.)

You can also hide menus and/or toolbars from the user by clearing the respective check boxes. *A word of caution, however—once the menus are hidden it is difficult to get them back.* Start Access, pull down the File menu, and click Open to display the Open dialog box, select the database to open, then press and hold the Shift key when you click the Open button. (This is a powerful technique that is a treasured secret of Access developers.) Write a brief note to your instructor to summarize the options you have selected.

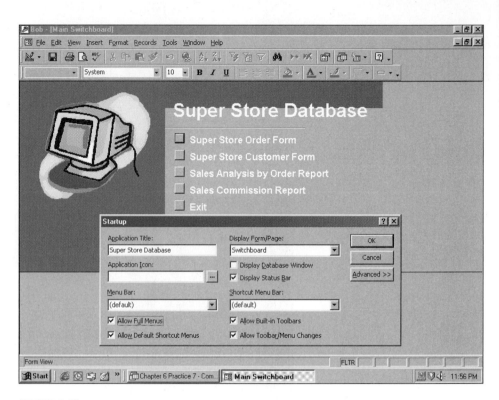

FIGURE 6.20 The Startup Property (Exercise 7)

CASE STUDIES

Medical Research

Design a database for a medical research project that will track specific volunteers and/or specific studies. A study will require several subjects, but a specific person may participate in only one study. The system should also be able to track physicians. Many physicians can work on the same study. A given physician may also work on multiple studies.

The system should be able to display all facts about a particular volunteer (subject) such as name, birth date, sex, height, weight, blood pressure, and cholesterol level. It should be able to display all characteristics associated with a particular study—for example, the title, beginning date, ending date, as well as the names of all physicians who work on that study. It should also show whether the physician is a primary or secondary investigator in each study.

Show the required tables in the database, being sure to indicate the primary key and foreign keys in each table. Indicate one or two other fields in each table as appropriate. (You need not list them all.)

The Stockbroker

You have been hired as a consultant to a securities firm that wants to track its clients and the stocks they own. The firm prides itself on its research and maintains a detailed file for the stocks it follows. Among the data for each stock are its symbol (ideal for the primary key), the industry it is in, its earnings, dividend, etc.

The firm requires the usual client data (name, address, phone number, social security number, etc.). One client can hold many different stocks, and the same stock can be held by different clients. The firm needs to know the date the client purchased the stock, the number of shares that were purchased, and the purchase price. Show the required tables in the database, being sure to indicate the primary key and foreign keys in each table.

The Video Store

You have been hired as a database consultant to the local video store, which rents and/or sells tapes to customers. The store maintains the usual information about every customer (name, address, phone number, and so on). It also has detailed information about every movie, such as its duration, rating, rental price, and purchase price. One customer can rent several tapes, and the same tape will (over time) be rented to many customers.

The owner of the store needs a detailed record of every rental that identifies the movie, the customer, the date the rental was made, and the number of days the customer may keep the movie without penalty.

Class Scheduling

Class scheduling entails the coordination of course offerings as published in a registration schedule together with faculty assignments. All courses have a formal title but are more commonly known by a six-position course-id. Microcomputer Applications, for example, is better known as CIS120. The first three characters in the course-id denote the department (e.g., CIS stands for Computer Information Systems). The last three indicate the particular course.

The university may offer multiple sections of any given course at different times. CIS120, for example, is offered at four different times: at 9:00, 10:00, 11:00, and 12:00, with all sections meeting three days a week (Mondays, Wednesdays, and Fridays). The information about when a class meets is summarized in the one-letter section designation; for example, section A meets from 9:00 to 9:50 on Mondays, Wednesdays, and Fridays.

The published schedule should list every section of every course together with the days, times, and room assignments. It should also display the complete course title, number of credits, and the name of the faculty member assigned to that section. Design a relational database to satisfy these requirements.

Career Planning and Placement

Design a database that will keep track of the interviews that are being conducted in the Center. Information is needed on which companies are conducting on-campus interviews at the Center, as well as which students are being interviewed, and by which company. A company can interview many students, and a student has the option of interviewing with as many companies as he/she wishes. In addition, note that each student is assigned to one of the Center's three counselors, and that counselor will work with that student until he/she graduates.

The system must be able to generate reports on the counselors (name, office, phone number, fax number), students (name, campus address, campus phone number, major, GPA, graduation date), and companies (name, interviewer, address, phone number, industry). It should also create reports that list the students interviewed by a given company, the companies that a given student has interviewed with, the position(s) that a student has applied for with a particular company, and the students assigned to a given counselor.

chapter 7

BUILDING APPLICATIONS: THE SWITCHBOARD, MACROS, AND PROTOTYPING

OBJECTIVES

After reading this chapter you will be able to:

1. Use the Switchboard Manager to create and/or modify a switchboard; explain why multiple switchboards may be required within one application.

2. Use the Link Tables command to associate tables in one database with objects in a different database.

3. Describe how macros are used to automate an application; explain the special role of the AutoExec macro.

4. Describe the components of the Macro window; distinguish between a macro action and an argument.

5. Explain how prototyping facilitates the development of an application; use the MsgBox action as the basis of a prototype macro.

6. Use the Unmatched Query Wizard to identify records in one table that do not have a corresponding record in another table.

7. Create a macro group; explain how macro groups simplify the organization of macros within a database.

OVERVIEW

This chapter revisits the concept of a user interface (or switchboard) that ties the objects in a database together, so that the database is easy to use. The switchboard displays a menu, often a series of menus, which enables a nontechnical person to move easily from one Access object to another. Any database containing a switchboard is known as an application and, unlike an ordinary Access database, it does not require knowledge of Microsoft Access on the part of the user.

The development of an application may also entail the splitting of a database into two files—one containing the tables and the other containing the remaining objects (the forms, reports, queries, and macros). The tables are then linked to the other objects through the Link Tables command. It sounds complicated but this approach has several advantages, as you will see.

The chapter also covers macros and prototyping, two techniques that are used by developers in creating applications. A macro automates common command sequences and further simplifies the system for the end user. Prototyping is used in conjunction with developing the various switchboards to demonstrate the "look and feel" of an application, even before the application is complete. Three hands-on exercises are included in the chapter to progressively build the application as you develop your skills in Access.

CASE STUDY: A RECREATIONAL SPORTS LEAGUE

You have probably played in a sports league at one time or another, whether in Little League as a child or in an intramural league at school or work. Whatever the league, it had teams, players, and coaches. The typical league registers the players and coaches individually then holds a draft among the coaches to divide the players into teams according to ability. The league may have been organized informally, with manual procedures for registering the participants and creating the teams. Now we automate the process.

Let's think for a moment about the tables and associated relationships that will be necessary to create the database. There are three tables, one each for players, coaches, and teams. There is a one-to-many relationship between teams and players (one team has many players, but a player is assigned to only one team). There is also a one-to-many relationship between teams and coaches (one team has many coaches, but a coach is assigned to only one team).

In addition to the tables, the database will contain multiple forms, queries, and reports based on these tables. A Players form is necessary in order to add a new player, or edit or delete the record of an existing player. A similar form should exist for Coaches. There might also be a sophisticated main and subform combination for the Teams table that displays the players and coaches on each team, and through which data for any table (Team, Player, or Coach) can be added, edited, or deleted. And, of course, there will be a variety of reports and queries.

Let's assume that this database has been created. It would not be difficult for a person knowledgeable in Access to open the database and select the various objects as the need arose. He or she would know how to display the Database window and how to select the various buttons in order to open the appropriate object. But what if the system is to be used by someone who does not know Access, which is typically the case? You can see that the user interface becomes the most important part of the system, at least from the viewpoint of the end user. An interface that is intuitive and easy to use will be successful. Conversely, a system that is difficult to use or visually unappealing is sure to fail.

Figure 7.1a displays the switchboard that will be created for this application. We have added a soccer ball as a logo, but the application applies to any type of recreational sports league. The interface is intuitive and easy to use. Click the About Sports button, the first button on our menu, and the system displays the informational screen we like to include in all of our applications. Click any other button, and you display the indicated form. Click the Teams button, for example, and you see the form in Figure 7.1b where you can add a new team, view, edit, or print the data for any existing team, then click the Close Form button to return to the main menu.

The switchboard in Figure 7.1a exists as a form within the database. Look closely, however, and you will see it is subtly different from the forms you have developed in previous chapters. The record selector and navigation buttons, for example, have been suppressed because they are not needed. In other words, this

Click About Sports button to
display informational message ⎯

Hyperlink ⎯

Click Teams button to
display Team form

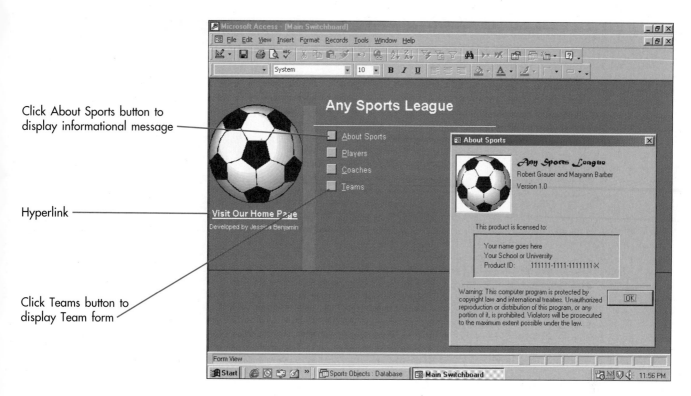

(a) The Main Menu

Add, edit, delete a team ⎯

Add, edit, delete a coach

Add, edit, delete a player

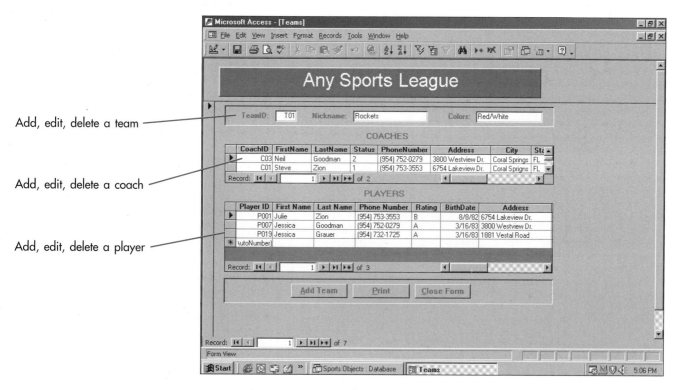

(b) The Teams Form

FIGURE 7.1   Building a User Interface

Record Source for switchboard is
Switchboard Items table

Switchboard can have
eight menu items

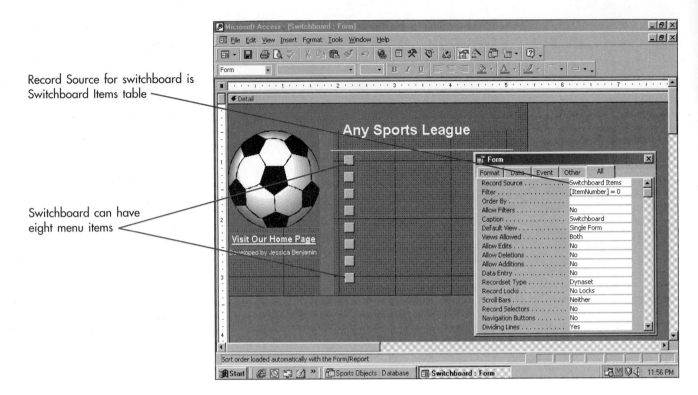

(c) Design View

SwitchboardID identifies which
switchboard item belongs to

ItemNumber identifies position
of item on switchboard

ItemText specifies text shown
on switchboard for that item

Command determines action
taken when that item is selected

Argument determines object to
be acted on (form to be opened)

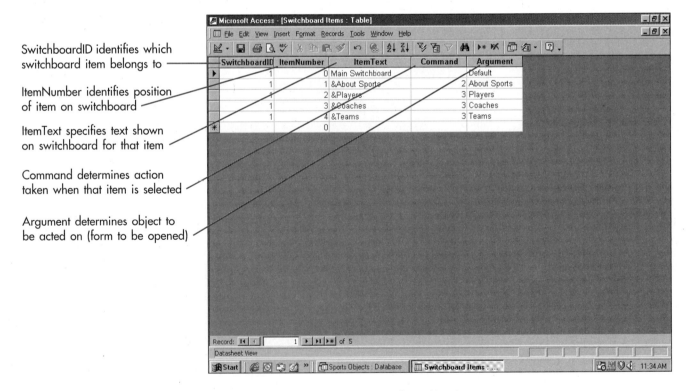

(d) Switchboard Items

FIGURE 7.1   Building a User Interface (continued)

form is not used for data entry, but as the basis of a menu for the user. You can even visit the league's Web site by clicking the indicated hyperlink.

The essence of the form, however, lies in the command buttons that enable the user to open the other objects in the database. Thus, when a user clicks a button, Access interprets that action as an event and responds with an action that has been assigned to that event. Clicking the Teams button, for example, causes Access to open the Teams form. Clicking the Players button is a different event, and causes Access to open the Players form.

The Switchboard Manager

The *Switchboard Manager* creates a switchboard automatically, by prompting you for information about each menu item. You supply the text of the item as it is to appear on the switchboard, together with the underlying command. Access does the rest. It creates a *switchboard form* that is displayed to the user and a *Switchboard Items table* that stores information about each command.

The switchboard form is shown in both the Form view and the Design view, in Figures 7.1a and 7.1c, respectively. At first, the views do not appear to correspond to one another, in that text appears next to each button in the Form view, but it is absent in the Design view. This, however, is the nature of a switchboard, because the text for each button is taken from the Switchboard Items table in Figure 7.1d, which is the record source for the form, as can be inferred from the Form property sheet. In other words, each record in the Switchboard Items table has a corresponding menu item in the switchboard form. Note, too, that you can modify the switchboard form after it has been created, perhaps by inserting a picture or a hyperlink as was done in Figure 7.1.

As indicated, the Switchboard Items table is created automatically and can be modified through the Switchboard Manager or by directly opening the table. It helps, therefore, to have an appreciation for each field in the table. The SwitchboardID field identifies the number of the switchboard, which becomes important in applications with more than one switchboard. Access limits each switchboard to eight items, but you can create as many switchboards as you like, each with a different value for the SwitchboardID. Every application has a main switchboard by default, which can in turn display other switchboards as necessary.

The ItemNumber and ItemText fields identify the position and text of the item, respectively, as it appears on the switchboard form. (The & that appears within the ItemText field will appear as an underlined letter on the switchboard to enable a keyboard shortcut; e.g., &Teams is displayed as Teams and recognizes the Alt+T keyboard shortcut in lieu of clicking the button.) The Command and Argument fields determine the action that will be taken when the corresponding button is clicked. Command number 3, for example, opens a form.

The Linked Tables Manager

Every application consists of tables *and* objects (forms, queries, reports, macros, and modules) based on those tables. The tables and objects may be stored in the same database (as has been done throughout the text) or they may be stored in separate databases, as will be done for the soccer application. Look closely at the Database window in Figure 7.2a. The title bar displays "Sports Objects" and indicates the name of the database that is currently open. Note, however, the arrows that appear next to the icons for the Players, Teams, and Coaches tables to indicate that the tables are stored in a different database. The name of the second database, "Sports Tables," is seen in the Linked Table Manager dialog box in Figure 7.2b.

The tables and objects are associated with one another through the **Link Tables command** and/or through the **Linked Table Manager**. Once the linking has been established, however, it is as though the Players, Coaches, and Teams tables were in the Sports Objects database with respect to maintaining the data. In other words, you can add, edit, and delete a record in any of the three tables as if the tables were physically in the Sports Objects database.

The advantage to storing the tables and objects in separate databases is that you can enhance an application by creating a new version of the Sports Objects database, without affecting the underlying tables. The new version has the improved features, such as a new form or report but attaches to the original data, and thus retains all of the transactions that have been processed.

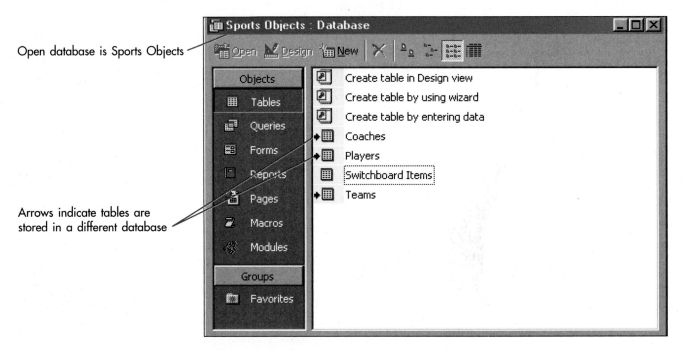

Open database is Sports Objects

Arrows indicate tables are stored in a different database

(a) The Database Window

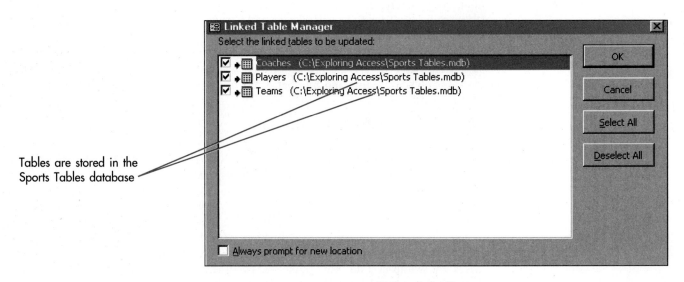

Tables are stored in the Sports Tables database

(b) The Linked Table Manager

FIGURE 7.2   Linking Tables

The Switchboard Manager

Objective: To create a switchboard; to use the Link Tables command to associate tables in one database with the objects in a different database. Use Figure 7.3 as a guide in the exercise.

STEP 1: The Sports Objects Database

➤ Start Access. Change to the **Exploring Access folder** as you have been doing through the text.

➤ Open the **Sports Objects database** as shown in Figure 7.3a, then click the various buttons in the Database window to view the contents of this database. This database contains the various objects (forms, queries, and reports) in the soccer application, but not the tables.

   • Click the **Tables button**. There are currently no tables in the database.
   • Click the **Queries button**. There is one query in the database.
   • Click the **Forms button**. There are six forms in the database.
   • Click the **Reports button**. There are currently no reports in the database.

➤ Pull down the **File menu**, click **Database Properties**, then click the **Contents tab** to see the contents of the database as shown in Figure 7.3a. The Database Properties command enables you to see all of the objects on one screen.

➤ Click **OK** to close the dialog box.

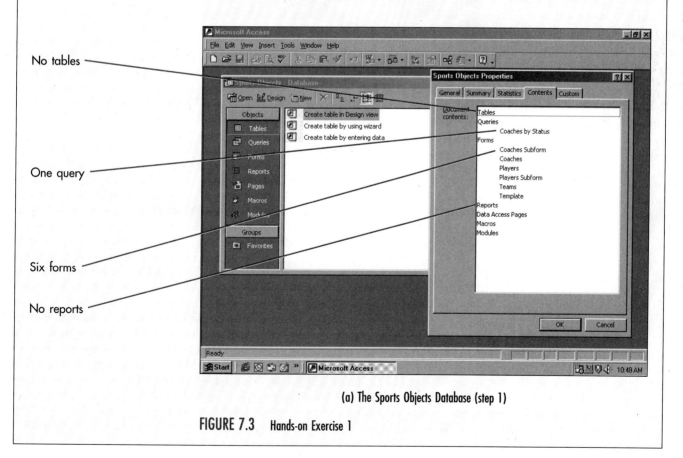

(a) The Sports Objects Database (step 1)

FIGURE 7.3   Hands-on Exercise 1

STEP 2: The Link Tables Command

➤ Pull down the **File menu**. Click **Get External Data**, then click **Link Tables** from the cascaded menu. You should see the **Link** dialog box (which is similar in appearance to the Open dialog box).

➤ Select the **Exploring Access folder**, the folder you have been using throughout the text. Scroll (if necessary) until you can select the **Sports Tables** database, then click the **Link command button**.

➤ You should see the Link Tables dialog box in Figure 7.3b. Click the **Select All command button** to select all three tables, then click **OK**.

➤ The systems (briefly) displays a message indicating that it is linking the tables, after which the tables should appear in the Database window. (If necessary, click the **Tables button** in the Database window.) The arrow next to each table indicates that the table physically resides in another database.

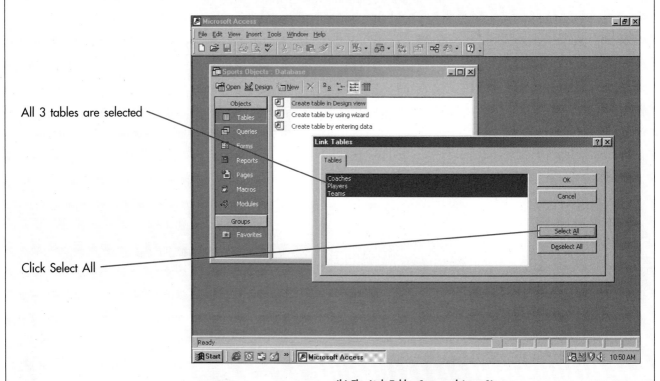

All 3 tables are selected

Click Select All

(b) The Link Tables Command (step 2)

FIGURE 7.3   Hands-on Exercise 1 (continued)

THE DATABASE SPLITTER

The tables and associated objects should always be stored in separate databases. But what if you created the application prior to learning about the ability to link tables and objects to one another? Open the existing database, pull down the Tools menu, click (or point to the Database Utilities), select the Database Splitter command, and follow the onscreen instructions. You will wind up with two separate databases, a back end that contains the tables, and a front end that contains the other objects. See exercise 3 at the end of the chapter.

STEP 3: Import the About Sports Form

➤ Pull down the **File menu**, click the **Get External Data** command, then click **Import** to display the Import dialog box. Select the **Exploring Access folder**, the folder you have been using throughout the text.

➤ Scroll (if necessary) until you can select the **About Sports database**, then click the **Import button** to display the Import Objects dialog box in Figure 7.3c. Click the **Forms button**, select the **About Sports** form, and click **OK**. The system pauses as the About Sports form is brought into this database.

➤ Once the importing is complete, the Database window changes to display the forms in this database, which now includes the About Sports form. Open the form in the Design view, then modify its contents to include your name and school. Save your changes, then close the form.

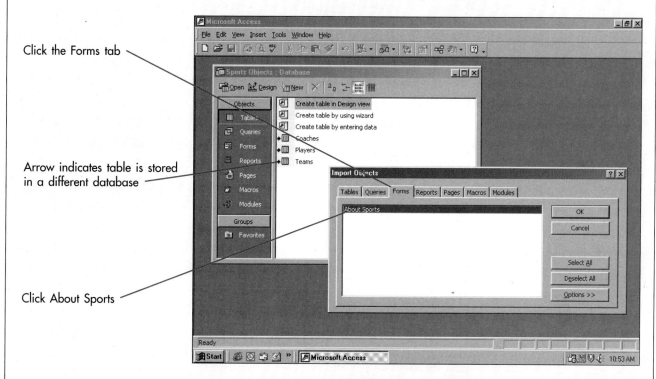

Click the Forms tab

Arrow indicates table is stored in a different database

Click About Sports

(c) Import the About Sports Form (step 3)

FIGURE 7.3   Hands-on Exercise 1 (continued)

IMPORTING VERSUS LINKING

The Get External Data command displays a cascaded menu to import or link an object from another database. Importing a table brings a copy of the table into the current database and does not maintain a tie to the original table. Linking, on the other hand, does not bring the table into the database but only a pointer to the table. All changes are stored in the original table and are reflected automatically in any database that is linked to the original table. Any type of object can be imported into a database. A table is the only type of object that can be linked.

STEP 4: Start the Switchboard Manager

➤ Minimize the Database window. Pull down the **Tools menu**, click the **Database Utilities command**, and choose **Switchboard Manager**.

➤ Click **Yes** if you see a message indicating that there is no valid switchboard. You should see the Switchboard Manager dialog box in Figure 7.3d.

➤ Click the **Edit command button** to display the Edit Switchboard Page dialog box. Click the **New command button** to add an item to this page, which in turn displays the Edit Switchboard item dialog box.

➤ Click in the Text list box and type **&About Sports**, which is the name of the command as it will appear in the switchboard.

➤ Click the **drop-down arrow** on the Command list box. Choose the command to open the form in either Add or Edit mode (it doesn't matter for this form).

➤ Click the **drop-down arrow** in the Form list box and choose **About Sports**.

➤ Click **OK** to create the switchboard item. The Edit Switchboard Item dialog box closes and the About Sports item appears in the Main Switchboard.

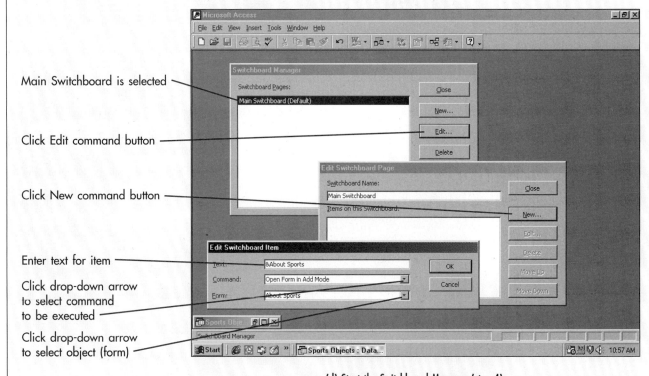

Main Switchboard is selected

Click Edit command button

Click New command button

Enter text for item

Click drop-down arrow
to select command
to be executed

Click drop-down arrow
to select object (form)

(d) Start the Switchboard Manager (step 4)

FIGURE 7.3   Hands-on Exercise 1 (continued)

CREATE A KEYBOARD SHORTCUT

The & has special significance when used within the name of an Access object because it creates a keyboard shortcut to that object. Enter "&About Sports", for example, and the letter A (the letter immediately after the ampersand) will be underlined and appear as "A̲bout Sports" on the switchboard. From there, you can execute the item by clicking its button, or you can use the Alt+A keyboard shortcut.

STEP 5: Complete the Switchboard

➤ Click the **New command button** in the Edit Switchboard Page dialog box to add a second item to the switchboard. Once again, you see the Edit Switchboard dialog box.

➤ Click in the Text list box and type **&Players**. Click the **drop-down arrow** on the Command list box and choose **Open Form in Edit Mode**. Click the **drop-down arrow** in the Form list box and choose **Players**.

➤ Click **OK** to close the Edit Switchboard item dialog box. The &Players command appears as an item on the switchboard.

➤ Create two additional switchboard items for **&Coaches** and **&Teams** in similar fashion. Your switchboard should contain four items as shown in Figure 7.3e. Click **Close** to close the Edit Switchboard Page dialog box. Click **Close** to close the Switchboard Manager dialog box.

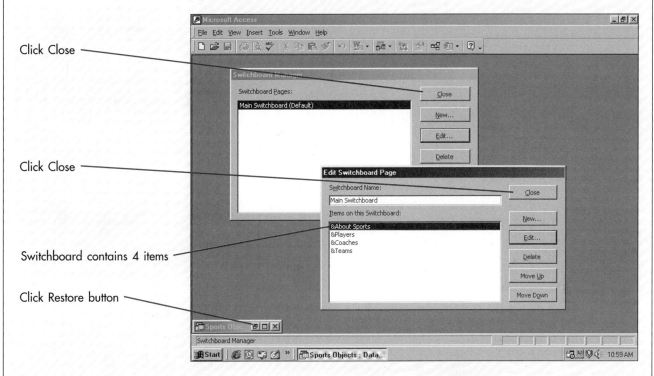

Click Close

Click Close

Switchboard contains 4 items

Click Restore button

(e) Complete the Switchboard (step 5)

FIGURE 7.3   Hands-on Exercise 1 (continued)

ADD MODE VERSUS EDIT MODE

It's easy to miss the difference between opening a form in the Add mode versus the Edit mode. The Add mode lets you add new records to a table, but it precludes you from viewing records that are already in the table. The Edit mode is more general and lets you add new records and/or edit existing records. Select the Add mode if you want to prevent a user from modifying existing data. Choose the Edit mode to give the user unrestricted access to the table.

STEP 6: Test the Switchboard

➤ Click the **Restore button** in the Database window to view the objects in the database, then click the **Forms tab**. The Switchboard form has been created automatically by the Switchboard Manager.

➤ Double click the **Switchboard form** to open the Main Switchboard. Do not be concerned about the design of the switchboard at this time, as your immediate objective is to make sure that the buttons work. (We modify the design of the switchboard later in the end of the exercise.) Maximize the window.

➤ Click the **About Sports button** (or use the **Alt+A** shortcut) to display the About Sports form as shown in Figure 7.3f. Click the **OK button** to close the form.

➤ Click the **Players button** (or use the **Alt+P** shortcut) to open the Players form. Click the **Maximize button** so that the Players form takes the entire window.

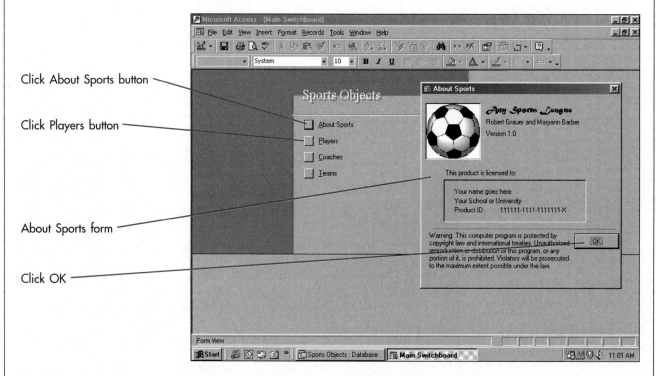

(f) Test the Switchboard (step 6)

FIGURE 7.3   Hands-on Exercise 1 (continued)

THE SWITCHBOARD ITEMS TABLE

You can modify an existing switchboard in one of two ways—by using the Switchboard Manager or by making changes directly in the underlying table of switchboard items. Press the F11 key to display the Database window, click the Tables button, then open the Switchboard Items table where you can make changes to the various entries on the switchboard. We encourage you to experiment, but start by changing one entry at a time. The ItemText field is a good place to begin.

STEP 7: Add Your Record

➤ Click the **Add Player button** on the bottom of the form (or use the **Alt+A** shortcut) to display a blank record where you will enter data for yourself as shown in Figure 7.3g.

➤ Click the **text box** to enter your first name. (The PlayerID is an AutoNumber field that is updated automatically.) Enter your name, then press the **Tab key** to move to the next field.

➤ Continue to enter the appropriate data for yourself, but please assign yourself to the **Comets team**. The team is entered via a drop-down list. Type **C** (the first letter in Comets) and Comets is entered automatically from the drop-down list for teams.

➤ The player rating is a required field (all players are evaluated for ability in order to balance the teams) and must be A, B, C, or D.

➤ Click the **Close Form button** to return to the switchboard.

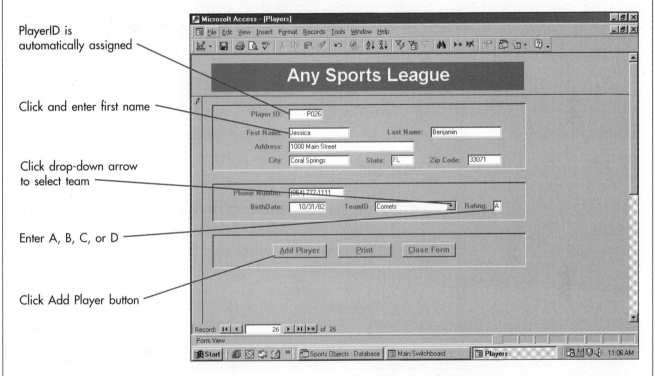

PlayerID is automatically assigned

Click and enter first name

Click drop-down arrow to select team

Enter A, B, C, or D

Click Add Player button

(g) Add Your Record (step 7)

FIGURE 7.3   Hands-on Exercise 1 (continued)

A LOOK AHEAD

The Add Record button in the Players form was created through the Command Button Wizard. The Wizard in turn creates an *event procedure* that creates a blank record at the end of the underlying table and enables you to add a new player. The procedure does not, however, position you at a specific control within the Players form; that is, you still have to click in the First Name text box to start entering the data. You can, however, create a macro that displays a blank record *and* automatically moves to the First Name control. See exercise 7 at the end of the chapter.

STEP 8: Complete the Data Entry

➤ You should once again see the switchboard. Click the **Coaches button** (or use the **Alt+C** shortcut) to open the Coaches form.

➤ Click the **Add Coach button** at the bottom of the form. Click the text box to enter the coach's first name. (The CoachID is entered automatically.)

➤ Enter data for your instructor as the coach. Click the appropriate **option button** to make your instructor a **Head Coach**. Assign your instructor to the Comets. Click the **Close Form button** to return to switchboard.

➤ Click the **Teams command button** on the switchboard to open the Teams form and move to Team T02 (the Comets). You should see your instructor as the head coach and yourself as a player as shown in Figure 7.3h.

➤ Pull down the **Edit menu** and click **Select Record** (or click the selection area), then click the **Print button** to print the roster for your team.

➤ Click the **Close Form button** to return to the switchboard.

Team T02 (Comets)

Instructor is head coach

Click in selection area

You are player on the team

Click to move to Comets record

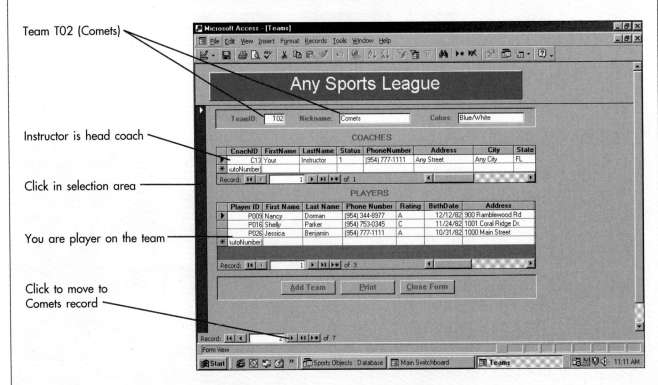

(h) Complete the Data Entry (step 8)

FIGURE 7.3 Hands-on Exercise 1 (continued)

THE DISPLAY WHEN PROPERTY

The Add, Print, and Close Form command buttons appear on the various forms (Team, Player, or Coach) when the forms are displayed on the screen, but not when the forms are printed. Open a form in Design view, point to an existing command button, then click the right mouse button to display a shortcut menu. Click the Properties command, click on the line for the Display When property and choose when you want the button to appear; i.e., when the form is displayed, printed, or both.

STEP 9: Insert the Clip Art

➤ Change to the Design View. **Right click** in the Picture area of the form to display a context-sensitive menu, then click the **Properties command** to display the Property sheet.

➤ The Picture property is currently set to "none" because the default switchboard does not contain a picture. Click in the Picture box, then click the **Build button** to display the Insert Picture dialog box.

➤ Click the **down arrow** in the Look In box to change to the **Exploring Access folder**, then select the **SoccerBall** as shown in Figure 7.3i. Click **OK**.

➤ Size the picture as appropriate. The dimensions of the soccer ball should be changed to a square, e.g., 1.7 inches × 1.7 inches. Close the property sheet.

➤ Right click below the picture in the Detail area of the form. Point to the **Fill/Back Color command** from the context-sensitive menu to display a color palette. Choose the same shade as appears on the rest of the form. (It is the fifth square from the left in the second row.)

➤ Click the **Undo button** if the color does not match. Save the form.

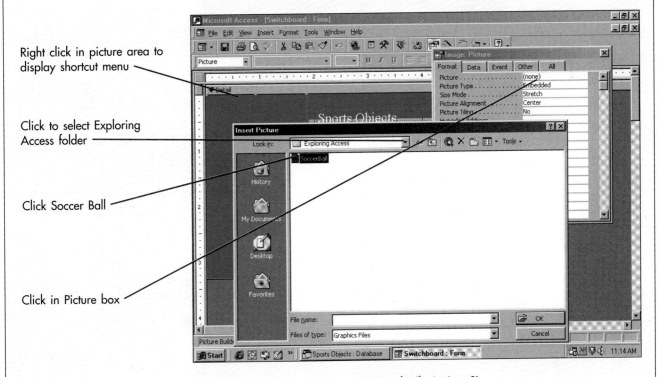

Right click in picture area to display shortcut menu

Click to select Exploring Access folder

Click Soccer Ball

Click in Picture box

(i) Insert the Clip Art (step 9)

FIGURE 7.3   Hands-on Exercise 1 (continued)

THE OBJECT BOX

The easiest way to familiarize yourself with the design of the switchboard is to click the down arrow on the object box on the Formatting toolbar, scrolling as necessary to see the various objects. Select (click) any object in the Object box and it is selected automatically in the form. Right click the selected object to display its property sheet.

STEP 10: Complete the Design

➤ Click the **Label tool**, then click and drag to create a text box under the picture. Enter your name in an appropriate font, point size, and color. Move and/or size the label containing your name as appropriate.

➤ Press and hold the **Shift key** as you click each text box in succession. The boxes appear to be empty, but the text will be drawn from the Switchboard items table.

➤ Be sure that you selected all text boxes. Click the **drop-down arrow** on the Font/Fore color button and change the font to white as shown in Figure 7.3j. Change the font and point size to **Arial** and **10pt**, respectively. Save the form.

➤ Change to the Form view to see the result of your changes. Exit Access if you do not want to continue with the next exercise at this time.

Undo button ——

Font/Fore Color tool ——

Size picture to 1.7" x 1.7" ——

Click and drag to create text box ——

Select all 8 menu item text boxes ——

Label tool ——

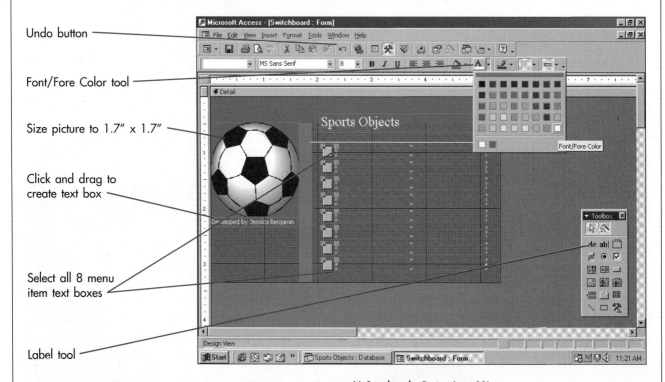

(j) Complete the Design (step 10)

FIGURE 7.3   Hands-on Exercise 1 (continued)

SET A TIME LIMIT

It's easy to spend an hour or more on the design of the switchboard, but that is counterproductive. The objective of this exercise was to develop a user interface that provides the "look and feel" of a system by selecting various menu options. That has been accomplished. Yes, it is important to fine-tune the interface, but within reason. Set a time limit for your design, then move on to the next exercise.

The exercise just completed created a switchboard that enabled a nontechnical user to access the various tables within the database. It did not, however, automate the application completely in that the user still has to open the form containing the switchboard to get started, and further may have to maximize the switchboard once it is open. You can make the application even easier to use by including macros that perform these tasks automatically.

A *macro* automates a command sequence. Thus, instead of using the mouse or keyboard to execute a series of commands, you store the commands (actions) in a macro and execute the macro. You can create a macro to open a table, query, form, or report. You can create a macro to display an informational message, then beep to call attention to that message. You can create a macro to move or size a window, or to minimize, maximize, or restore a window. In short, you can create a macro to execute any command (or combination of commands) in any Access menu and thus make an application easier to use.

The Macro Window

A macro is created in the *Macro window*, as shown in Figure 7.4. The Macro window is divided into two sections. The *actions* (commands) that comprise the macro are entered at the top. The *arguments*, or information for those actions, are entered in the lower section. Access macros are different from those in Word or Excel, in that Access lacks the macro recorder that is common to those applications. Hence, you have to enter the actions explicitly in the Macro window rather than have the recorder do it for you. In any event, macros are stored as separate objects in a database. The macro name can contain up to 64 characters (letters, numbers, and spaces) and it appears in the title bar of the Macro window (e.g., Back Up in Figure 7.4).

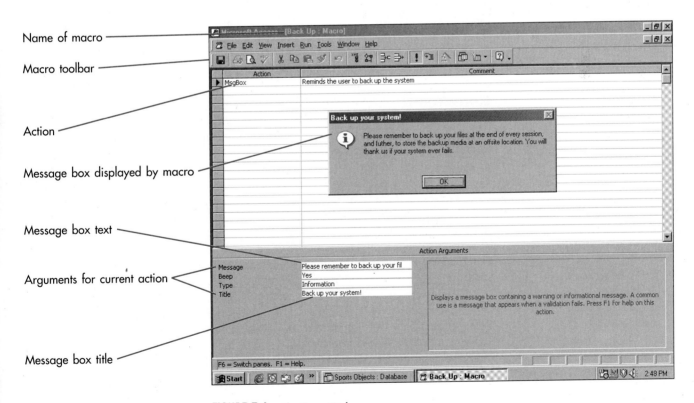

FIGURE 7.4   The Macro Window

To create a macro, select the Macros button in the Database window, then click the New button to display the Macro window. You add actions to a macro by clicking in Action area, then choosing the action from a drop-down list or by typing the name of the action. The arguments for an action are entered in similar fashion; that is, by choosing from a drop-down list (when available) or by typing the argument directly. The macro in Figure 7.4 consists of a single action with four arguments. As indicated, you specify the action, *MsgBox* in this example, in the top portion of the window, then you enter the values for the various arguments (Message, Beep, Type, and Title) in the bottom half of the window.

After the macro is created, you can execute it whenever the application is open. Execution of the macro in Figure 7.4, for example, will display the dialog box shown in the figure, to remind the user to back up his or her data. The contents of the dialog box are determined by the value of the arguments. The text of the dialog box is specified in the Message argument, only a portion of which is visible in the Macro window. The value of the Type argument determines the icon that is displayed within the dialog box (Information in this example). The Title argument contains the text that appears in the title bar of the dialog box.

The *macro toolbar* is displayed at the top of the Macro window and contains buttons that help create and test a macro. Many of the buttons (e.g., the Database window, Save, and Help buttons) are common to other toolbars you have used in conjunction with other objects. Other buttons are specific to the Macro window and are referenced in the Hands-on exercises. As with other toolbars, you can point to a button to display its ScreenTip and determine its purpose.

The AutoExec Macro

The *AutoExec macro* is unique in that it is executed automatically whenever the database in which it is stored is opened. The macro is used to automate a system for the end user. It typically contains an OpenForm action to open the form containing the main switchboard. It may also perform other housekeeping chores, such as maximizing the current window.

Every database can have its own AutoExec macro, but there is no requirement for the AutoExec macro to be present. We recommend, however, that you include an AutoExec macro in every application to help the user get started.

Debugging

Writing a macro is similar to writing a program, in that errors occur if the actions and/or the associated arguments are specified incorrectly. Should Access encounter an error during the execution of a macro, it displays as much information as it can to help you determine the reason for the error.

Figure 7.5 contains an erroneous version of the AutoExec macro that attempts to open the Switchboard form. The macro contains two actions, Maximize and OpenForm. The Maximize action maximizes the Database window and affects all subsequent screens that will be displayed in the application. The Open-Form macro is intended to open the switchboard from the previous exercise. The name of the form is deliberately misspelled.

When the AutoExec macro is executed, Access attempts to open a form called "Switchboards", but is unable to do so, and hence it displays the informational message in the figure. Click OK, and you are presented with another dialog box which attempts to step you through the macro and discover the cause of the error. As indicated, the error is due to the fact that the name of the form should have been "switchboard" rather than "switchboards". The errors will not always be this easy to find, and hopefully, you will not make any. Should a bug occur, however, you will know where to begin.

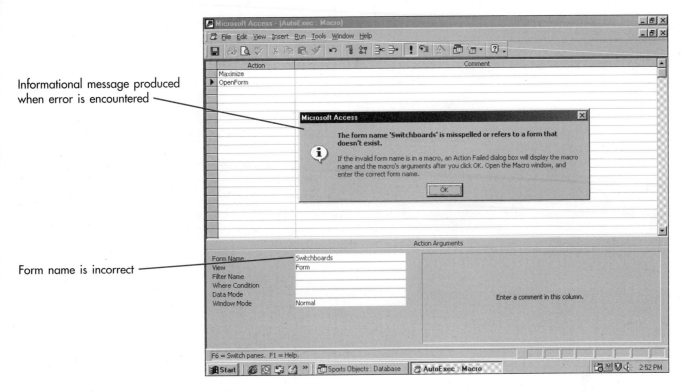

Informational message produced when error is encountered

Form name is incorrect

FIGURE 7.5 Debugging

THE FIRST BUG

A bug is a mistake in a computer program; hence debugging refers to the process of correcting program errors. According to legend, the first bug was an unlucky moth crushed to death on one of the relays of the electromechanical Mark II computer, bringing the machine's operation to a halt. The cause of the failure was discovered by Grace Hopper, who promptly taped the moth to her logbook, noting, *"First actual case of bug being found."*

APPLICATION DEVELOPMENT

The key to creating a successful application is to maintain a continual dialog between the end-user (client) and the developer. The developer creates an initial version of an application and presents it to the user for testing and feedback. The user experiments with the system and responds with various comments. The developer incorporates the suggestions and delivers a new version (release) of the application, whereupon the user does further testing, and so on.

This type of iterative development is known as **prototyping** and it continually presents the user with a "complete" system that captures the "look and feel" of the finished application. Consider, for example, Figure 7.6a that displays an updated version of the main switchboard that includes a report menu, which in turn displays the report switchboard in Figure 7.6b. The latter was created using the Switchboard Manager and it, in turn, expanded the Switchboard Items table as shown in Figure 7.6c. The SwitchboardID field assumes significance in this version of the application in that there are two different switchboards, the main switchboard and the report switchboard, with values of one and two, respectively.

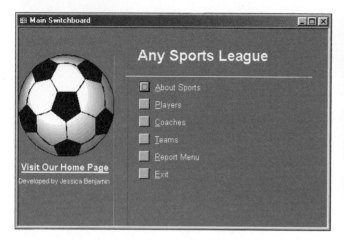

(a) Main Switchboard

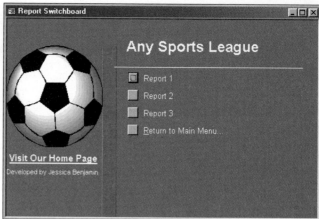

(b) Report Switchboard

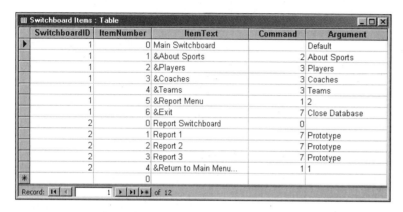

(c) Switchboard Items

Switchboard Items : Table				
SwitchboardID	ItemNumber	ItemText	Command	Argument
1	0	Main Switchboard		Default
1	1	&About Sports	2	About Sports
1	2	&Players	3	Players
1	3	&Coaches	3	Coaches
1	4	&Teams	3	Teams
1	5	&Report Menu	1	2
1	6	&Exit	7	Close Database
2	0	Report Switchboard	0	
2	1	Report 1	7	Prototype
2	2	Report 2	7	Prototype
2	3	Report 3	7	Prototype
2	4	&Return to Main Menu...	1	1
	0			

Record: 1 of 12

Under Development...

This object will be implemented in the next version. In the meantime, you can gain an appreciation for the "look and feel" of the system by stepping through the various commands on the switchboard.

OK

(d) Prototype Macro

FIGURE 7.6   Prototyping

The reports, however, have not yet been created, nor do they need to be. The user can still click any of the buttons on the Report Switchboard and see the message in Figure 7.6d that provides an appreciation for how the eventual system will work. The application is "complete" in the sense that every option works, but it is incomplete in that the reports have not been fully developed. Nevertheless, the prototype lets the user see a working system, and further, enables the user to provide immediate feedback to the developer. The sooner the user communicates the requested changes to the developer, the easier (and cheaper) it is for the developer to incorporate those changes. It's time now for our next hands-on exercise in which you develop the next release of the recreational sports league application.

AVOID CLUTTER—USE SUBSERVIENT MENUS

Don't clutter a switchboard by displaying too much information or too many command buttons. (Access limits the number of menu items to eight.) Develop subservient (lower-level) menus if you find yourself with too many buttons on one screen. Be sure to provide a consistent means of navigation to enable the user to move easily from one switchboard (menu) to the next.

Objective: To create an AutoExec and a Close Database macro; to create a subsidiary switchboard. Use Figure 7.7 as a guide in the exercise.

STEP 1: Create the AutoExec Macro

➤ Start Access. Open the **Sports Objects database** from the previous exercise. Click the **Macros button** in the Database window.

➤ Click the **New button** to create a new macro. If necessary, click the **maximize button** so that the Macro window takes the entire screen as in Figure 7.7a.

➤ Click the **drop-down arrow** to display the available macro actions. Scroll until you can select **Maximize**. (There are no arguments for this action.)

➤ Click the **Action box** on the second line, click the **drop-down arrow** to display the macro actions, then scroll until you can click the **OpenForm action**. Click the text box for the **Form Name** argument in the lower section of the Macro window.

➤ Click the **drop-down arrow** to display the list of existing forms and select **Switchboard** (the form you created in the previous exercise).

➤ Click the **Save button** to display the Save As dialog box in Figure 7.7a. Type **AutoExec** as the macro name and click **OK**. Click the **Run button** to run the macro and open the switchboard.

➤ Close the switchboard. Close the AutoExec macro.

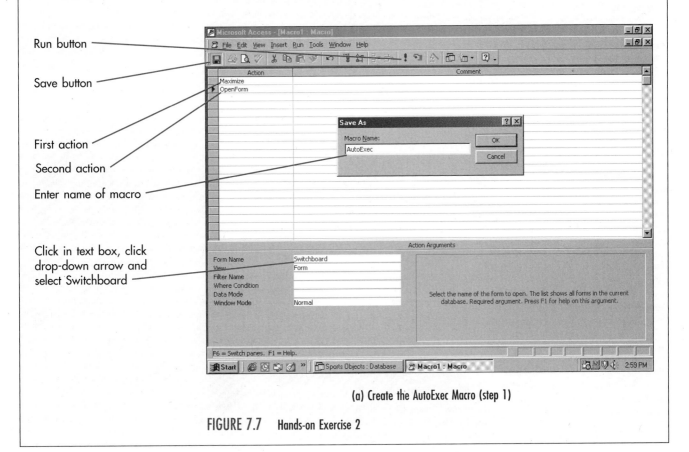

(a) Create the AutoExec Macro (step 1)

FIGURE 7.7 Hands-on Exercise 2

STEP 2: Create the Prototype Macro

➤ You should be back in the Database window, which should display the name of the AutoExec macro. Click the **New button** to create a second macro.

➤ Type **MS** (the first two letters in the MsgBox action) then press **enter** to accept this action. Enter the comment shown in Figure 7.7b.

➤ Click the text box for the **Message** argument, then press **Shift+F2** to display the zoom box so that you can see the contents of your entire message. Enter the message in Figure 7.7b. Click **OK**.

➤ Click the text box for the **Type argument**, click the **drop-down arrow** to display the list of message types, and select **Information**.

➤ Click in the text box for the **Title argument**, and enter "**Under Development**".

➤ Click the **Run button** to test the macro. You will see a message indicating that you have to save the macro. Click **Yes** to save the macro, type **Prototype** as the name of the macro, and click **OK**.

➤ You will see a dialog box containing the message you just created. Click **OK**. Close the macro.

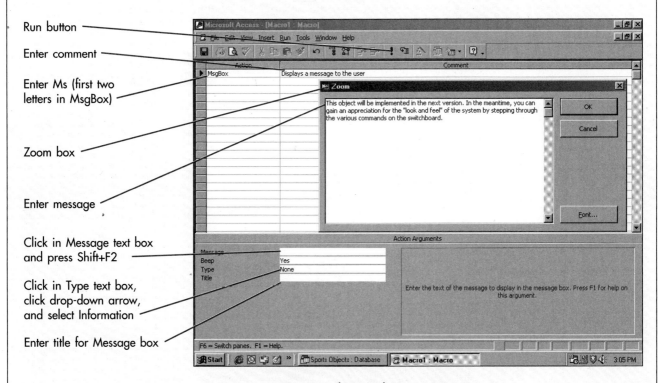

(b) Create the Prototype Macro (step 2)

FIGURE 7.7   Hands-on Exercise 2 (continued)

TYPE ONLY THE FIRST LETTER(S)

Click the Action box, then type the first letter of a macro action to move immediately to the first macro action beginning with that letter. Type an M, for example, and Access automatically enters the Maximize action. If necessary, type the second letter of the desired action; for example, type the letter I (after typing an M), and Access selects the Minimize action.

STEP 3: Create the Close Database Macro

➤ Click the **New button** once again to create the third (and last) macro for this exercise. Specify the **MsgBox** action as the first command in the macro. Enter the comment shown in Figure 7.7c.

➤ Enter an appropriate message that stresses the importance of backup. Select Warning as the message type. Enter an appropriate title for the message box.

➤ Click the **Action box** on the second line. Type **Cl** (the first two letters in Close) and press **enter**. Enter the indicated comment as shown in Figure 7.7c.

➤ Click the text box for the **Object Type** argument. Click the **drop-down arrow** and choose **Form** as the Object type. Click the **Object Name** argument, click the **drop-down arrow**, and choose **Switchboard** as the Object (form) name.

➤ Click the Action box on the third line. Type **Cl** (the first two letters in Close) and press **enter**. Click the comments line for this macro action and enter the comment shown in the figure. No arguments are necessary.

➤ Save the macro as **Close Database**, then close the macro. If necessary, press the **F11 key** to return to the Database window where you should see three macros: AutoExec, Close Database, and Prototype.

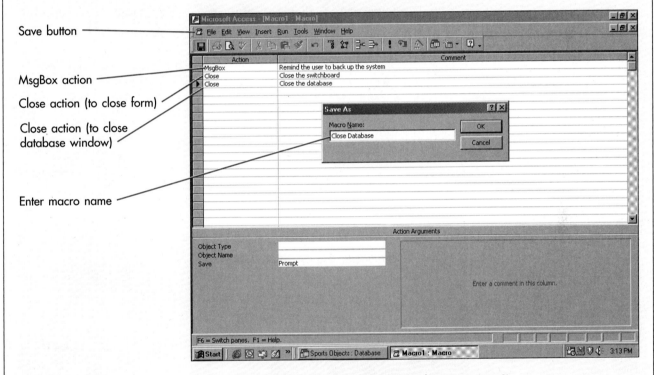

(c) Create the Close Databases Macro (step 3)

FIGURE 7.7   Hands-on Exercise 2 (continued)

USE KEYBOARD SHORTCUTS—F6, F11, AND SHIFT+F2

Use the F6 key to move back and forth between the top and bottom halves of the Macro window. Press Shift+F2 to display a zoom box that enables you to view long arguments in their entirety. Use the F11 key at any time to display the Database window.

STEP 4: Create the Report Switchboard

➤ Minimize the Database window to give yourself more room in which to work. Pull down the **Tools menu**, click the **Database Utilities command**, and choose **Switchboard Manager** to display the Switchboard Manager dialog box.

➤ Click **New**. Enter **Report Switchboard** as the name of the switchboard page. Click **OK**. The Create New dialog box closes and the Report Switchboard Page appears in the Switchboard Manager dialog box.

➤ Select the **Report Switchboard**, click the **Edit button** to open the Edit Switchboard Page dialog box, then click **New** to open the Edit Switchboard Item dialog box as shown in Figure 7.7d.

➤ Add the first switchboard item. Click in the Text list box and type **Report 1**, the name of the command, as it will appear in the switchboard. Press the **Tab key** to move to the Command list box and type **R** (the first letter in Run macro). Press the **Tab key** to move to the Macro list box, and type **P** (the first letter in the Prototype macro).

➤ Click **OK** to create the switchboard item. The Edit Switchboard Item dialog box closes and Report 1 appears on the Report Switchboard Page. Repeat this process to create two additional items, Report 2 and Report 3.

➤ Add an additional item that will return the user to the main switchboard. Click **New** to open the Edit Switchboard Item dialog box. Click in the Text list box and type "**&Return to Main Menu . . .**"

➤ Press the **Tab key** to move to the Command list box where the Go to Switchboard command is entered by default. Press the **Tab key** to move to the Switchboard list box, and type **M** (the first letter in the "Main Switchboard"). Click **OK** to create the switchboard item.

➤ Close the Edit Switchboard Page.

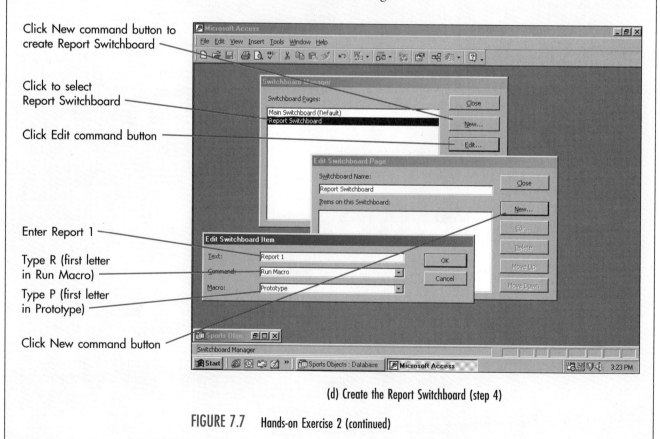

Click New command button to create Report Switchboard

Click to select Report Switchboard

Click Edit command button

Enter Report 1

Type R (first letter in Run Macro)

Type P (first letter in Prototype)

Click New command button

(d) Create the Report Switchboard (step 4)

FIGURE 7.7   Hands-on Exercise 2 (continued)

STEP 5: Modify the Main Switchboard

➤ Select the **Main Switchboard** in the Switchboard Manager dialog box, click the **Edit button** to open the Edit Switchboard Page dialog box, then click **New** to open the Edit Switchboard Item dialog box as shown in Figure 7.7d.

➤ Add a new switchboard item to open the Report Switchboard. Click in the Text list box and type "**&Report Menu . . .**", the name of the command as it will appear in the switchboard.

➤ Press the **Tab key** to move to the Command list box where "Go to Switchboard" is already entered, then press the **Tab key** a second time to move to the Switchboard list box. Type **R** (the first letter in the "Report Switchboard"). Click **OK** to create the switchboard item.

➤ The Edit Switchboard Item dialog box closes and "&Report Menu" appears on the main switchboard.

➤ The main switchboard needs one last command to close the database. Thus, click **New** to open the Edit Switchboard Item dialog box. Type **&Exit** as the name of the command.

➤ Press the **Tab key** to move to the Command list box and type **R** (the first letter in "Run Macro"). Press the **Tab key** a second time to move to the Macro list box, and type **C** (the first letter in the "Close Database" macro). Click **OK** to create the switchboard item.

➤ The main switchboard should contain six items—&About Sports, &Players, &Coaches, and &Teams, from the first exercise, and &Report Menu and &Exit from this exercise.

➤ Close the Edit Switchboard Page dialog box. Close the Switchboard Manager.

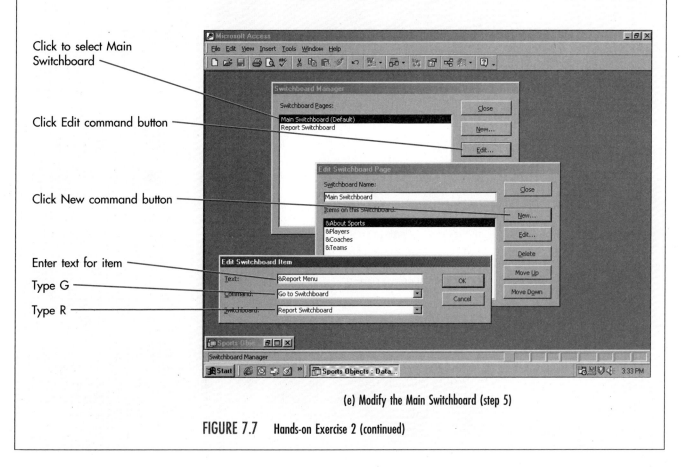

Click to select Main Switchboard

Click Edit command button

Click New command button

Enter text for item

Type G

Type R

(e) Modify the Main Switchboard (step 5)

FIGURE 7.7   Hands-on Exercise 2 (continued)

STEP 6: Test the Main Switchboard

➤ Click the **Restore button** in the Database window to view the objects in the database, click the **Forms button**, then double click the **Switchboard form** to open the main switchboard.

➤ Click the **Exit button** (or use the **Alt+E** shortcut):

- You should see an informational message similar to the one shown in the figure. (The message is displayed by the MsgBox action in the Close Database macro.)

- Click **OK** to accept the message. The Close Database macro then closes the database.

➤ Pull down the **File menu** then click **Sports Objects** from the list of recently opened databases. The AutoExec macro executes automatically, maximizes the current window, and displays the main switchboard.

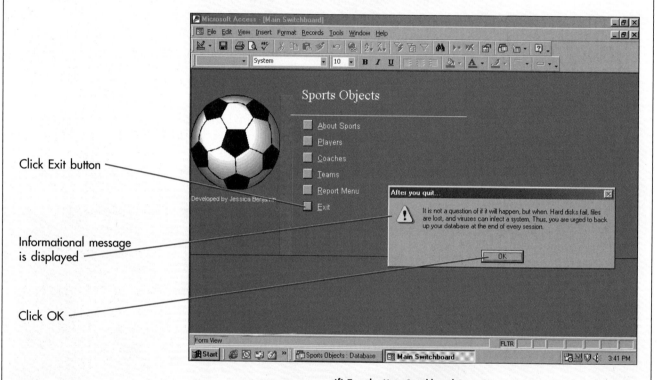

Click Exit button

Informational message is displayed

Click OK

(f) Test the Main Switchboard (step 6)

FIGURE 7.7   Hands-on Exercise 2 (continued)

ADD A HYPERLINK

You can enhance the appeal of your switchboard through inclusion of a hyperlink. Open the switchboard form in Design view, then click the Insert Hyperlink button to display the Insert Hyperlink dialog box. Enter the text to be displayed and the Web address, then click OK to close the dialog box and return to the Design view. Right click the hyperlink to display a shortcut menu, click the Properties command to display the Properties dialog box, then change the caption, font, and/or point size as appropriate. See exercise 8 at the end of the chapter.

STEP 7: Test the Report Switchboard

➤ Click the **Report Menu button** (or use the **Alt+R** keyboard shortcut) on the main switchboard to display the Report switchboard in Figure 7.7g. Click the command buttons for any of the reports, then click **OK** in response to the informational message.

➤ Click the **Return to Main Menu button** to exit the Report Menu and return to the main switchboard.

• To continue working, click the **Close button** on the title bar (or pull down the **File menu** and click the **Close command**) to close the form and continue working on this database. (You cannot click the Exit command button as that would close the database.) You should be back in the Database window where you can continue with the next hands-on exercise.

• To close the database, click the **Exit button** (or use the **Alt+E** shortcut).

➤ Either way, you have demonstrated the "look and feel" of the system to the extent that you can step through the various menus. Good work.

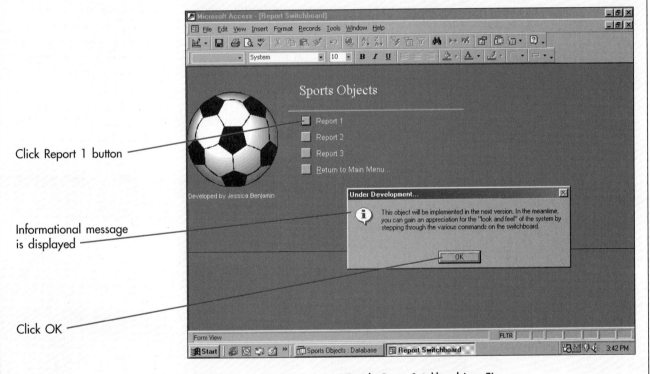

Click Report 1 button

Informational message is displayed

Click OK

(g) Test the Report Switchboard (step 7)

FIGURE 7.7 Hands-on Exercise 2 (continued)

BE CONSISTENT

Consistency within an application is essential to its success. Similar functions should be done in similar ways to facilitate learning and build confidence in the application. The sports application, for example, has similar screens for the Players, Coaches, and Teams forms, each of which contains the identical command buttons to add or print a record and close the form.

The development of the application is progressing nicely, but there is an additional function that must be included, namely the implementation of a player draft. Players sign up for the coming season at registration, after which the coaches meet to select players for their teams. All players are rated as to ability, and the league strives to maintain a competitive balance between teams. This is accomplished through a draft in which the coaches take turns selecting players from the pool of unassigned players.

The draft is implemented through the form in Figure 7.8. The form is based on a query, which identifies the players who have not yet been assigned to a team. To aid in the selection process, the unassigned players are listed by ability and alphabetically within ability. Note, too, the use of a combo box to simplify data entry in conjunction with the team assignment. The user is able to click the drop-down arrow to display a list of team nicknames (or enter the nickname directly) rather than having to remember the associated team number. The combo box facilitates data entry and helps to ensure its accuracy.

In addition to displaying the list of unassigned players, the form in Figure 7.8 also contains three command buttons that are used during the player draft. The Find Player button moves directly to a specific player, and enables a coach to see whether a specific player has been assigned to a team, and if so, to which team. The Update List button refreshes the underlying query on which the list of unassigned players is based. It is used periodically during the draft as players are assigned to teams, to remove those players from the list of unassigned players. The End Draft button closes the form and returns to the Switchboard. Note, too, that the appearance of the form matches the other forms in the application. This type of consistency is important to give your application a professional look.

Players are listed by ability and alphabetically within ability

Click drop-down arrow and select team name

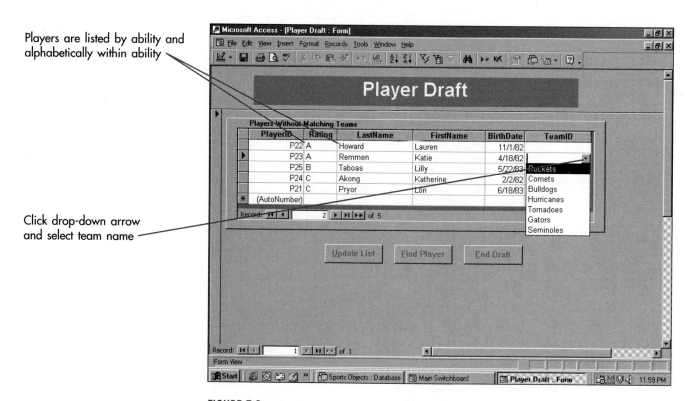

FIGURE 7.8   The Player Draft

LIST BOXES VERSUS COMBO BOXES

The choice between a list box and a combo box depends on how you want the control to appear in the form. The advantage of a list box is that multiple options are visible, and further, that the user is restricted to entering a value from the list. A combo box, however, takes less space because only the selected option is shown, and the other options are not displayed until you open it. A combo box also enables you to control whether the user can enter just the values in the list or whether additional values are permitted. (The Limit to List property is set to Yes and No, respectively.) A combo box also lets you enter the first few characters in a value to move directly to that value. A list box, however, accepts only the first letter.

The Unmatched Query Wizard

Let's think, for a moment, about how Access is able to display the list of unassigned players. Recall that there is a one-to-many relationship between teams and players (one team has many players, but a player has only one team) and that this relationship is implemented through the common TeamID field that appears in both tables. The TeamID is the primary key in the Teams table and it is a foreign key in the Players table. A player is assigned to a team by entering the team number into the TeamID field in the Players table. Conversely, any player without a value in his or her TeamID field is an unassigned player.

To display a list of unassigned players, you need to create a query based on the Players table, which selects records without an entry in the TeamID field. This can be done by creating the query explicitly (and specifying the Is Null criterion for TeamID) or more easily through the Unmatched Query Wizard which creates the query for you. The Wizard asks you a series of questions, as shown in Figure 7.9, then generates the query for you.

The *Unmatched Query Wizard* identifies the records in one table (e.g., the Players table) that do not have matching records in another table (e.g., the Teams table). The Wizard begins by asking for the table that contains the unmatched records (Figure 7.9a) and for the related table (Figure 7.9b). It identifies the join field (TeamID in Figure 7.9c), then gives you the opportunity to select the fields you want to see in the query results (Figure 7.9d). The Wizard even suggests a name for the query (Players Without Matching Teams in Figure 7.9e), then displays the dynaset in Figure 7.9f.

The Unmatched Query Wizard has multiple applications within the Sports league database. It can identify players without teams (as in Figure 7.9), or conversely, teams without players. It can also identify coaches who have not been assigned to a team, and, conversely, teams without coaches.

Macro Groups

Implementation of the player draft requires three macros, one for each command button. Although you could create a separate macro for each button, it is convenient to create a macro group that contains the individual macros. The macro group has a name, as does each macro in the group. Only the name of the macro group appears in the Database window.

Figure 7.10 displays a Player Draft macro group containing three individual macros (Update List, Find Player, and End Draft) which run independently of one

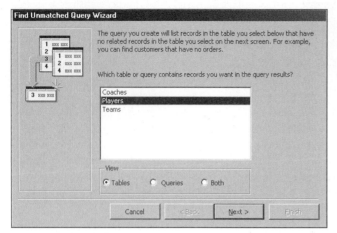

(a) Table Containing the Unmatched Records

(b) The Related Table

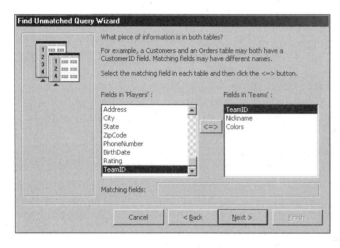

(c) Join Field

(d) Fields for Dynaset

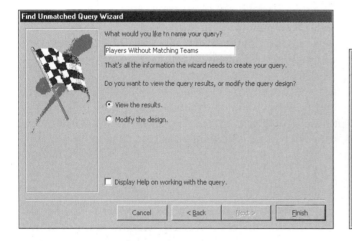

(e) Suggested Name

(f) Dynaset

FIGURE 7.9 The Find Unmatched Query Wizard

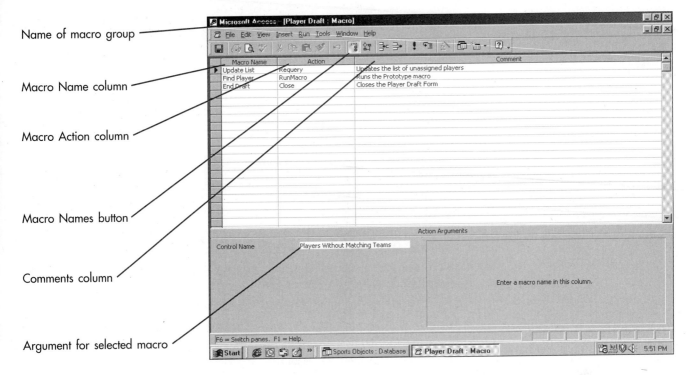

Name of macro group

Macro Name column

Macro Action column

Macro Names button

Comments column

Argument for selected macro

FIGURE 7.10   Macro Group

another. The name of each macro appears in the Macro Name column (which is displayed by clicking the Macro Names button on the Macro toolbar). The actions and comments for each macro are shown in the corresponding columns to the right of the macro name.

The advantage of storing related macros in a macro group, as opposed to storing them individually, is purely organizational. Large systems often contain many macros, which can overwhelm the developer as he or she tries to locate a specific macro. Storing related macros in macro groups limits the entries in the Database window, since only the (name of the) macro group is displayed. Thus, the Database window would contain a single entry (Player Draft, which is the name of the macro group), as opposed to three individual entries (Update List, Find Player, and End Draft, which correspond to the macros in the group).

Access must still be able to identify the individual macros so that each macro can be executed at the appropriate time. If, for example, a macro is to be executed when the user clicks a command button, the On Click property of that command button must specify both the individual macro and the macro group. The two names are separated by a period; for example, Player Draft.Update List to indicate the Update List macro in the Player Draft macro group.

As indicated, each macro in Figure 7.10 corresponds to a command button in the Player Draft form of Figure 7.8. The macros are created in the following hands-on exercise that implements the player draft.

USE THE MACRO BUILDER

Use the Macro Builder to create a macro and assign it to an event in a single operation. Right click an existing command button to display its property sheet, click the Event tab, select the event, then click the build button (the three dots at the right of the text box). Select the Macro Builder to open the macro window where you create the macro.

Objective: Create a macro group containing three macros to implement a player draft. Use Figure 7.11 as a guide in the exercise.

STEP 1: The Unmatched Query Wizard

➤ Start Access and open the **Sports Objects database**. Pull down the **File menu** and click **Close** (or click the **Close button**) to close the Main Menu form but leave the database open.

➤ Click the **Queries button** in the Database window. Click **New**, select the **Find Unmatched Query Wizard**, then click **OK** to start the Wizard:

• Select **Players** as the table whose records you want to see in the query results. Click **Next**.

• Select **Teams** as the table that contains the related records. Click **Next**.

• **TeamID** is automatically selected as the matching field. Click **Next**.

• Select the following fields from the Available Fields list: **PlayerID**, **Rating**, **LastName**, **FirstName**, **BirthDate**, and **TeamID**. Click **Next**.

• **Players Without Matching Teams** is entered as the name of the query. Check that the option button to **View the results** is selected, then click **Finish** to exit the Wizard and see the results of the query.

➤ You should see a dynaset containing five players (Pryor, Howard, Remmen, Akong, and Taboas) as shown in Figure 7.11a. The TeamID field for each of these players is blank, indicating that these players have not yet been assigned.

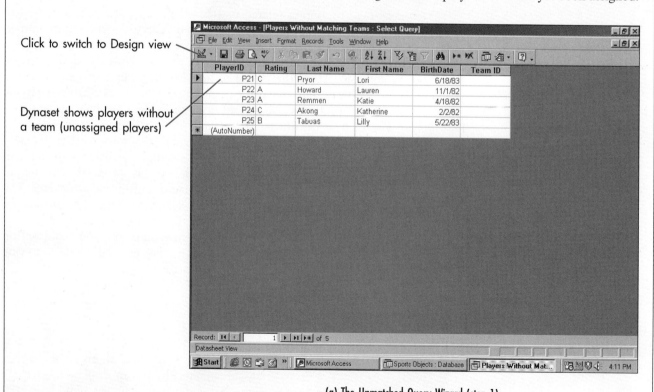

Click to switch to Design view

Dynaset shows players without a team (unassigned players)

(a) The Unmatched Query Wizard (step 1)

FIGURE 7.11   Hands-on Exercise 3

STEP 2: Modify the Query

➤ Change to Design view to see the underlying query as displayed in Figure 7.11b.

➤ Click and drag the line separating the upper and lower portions of the window. If necessary, click and drag the field lists to match the figure.

➤ Click in the **Sort row** for **Rating**, then click **Ascending** from the drop-down list. Click in the **Sort row** for **LastName**, then click **Ascending** from the drop-down list.

➤ Click the **Run button** to view the revised query which lists players according to their player rating and alphabetically within rating.

➤ Close the query. Click **Yes** if asked whether to save the changes to the Players Without Matching Teams query.

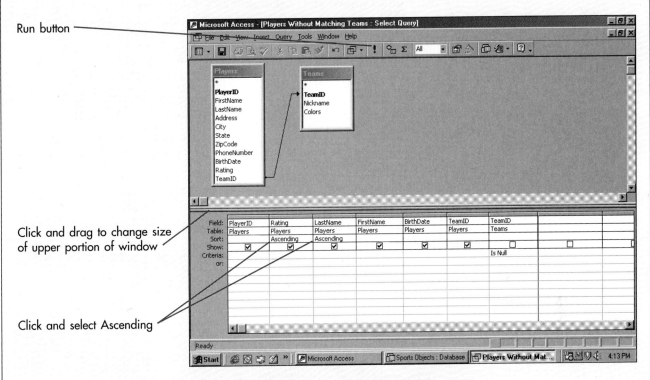

Run button

Click and drag to change size of upper portion of window

Click and select Ascending

(b) Modify the Query (step 2)

FIGURE 7.11   Hands-on Exercise 3 (continued)

THE IS NULL CRITERION

The Is Null criterion selects those records which do not have a value in the designated field. It is the essence of the Unmatched Query Wizard which uses the criterion to identify the records in one table that do not have a matching record in another table. The NOT operator can be combined with the Is Null criterion to produce the opposite effect; that is, the criterion Is Not Null will select records with any type of entry (including spaces) in the specified field.

STEP 3: Create the Unmatched Players Form

➤ Click the **Forms button** in the Database window, click **New** to display the New Form dialog box and select **AutoForm:Datasheet**.

➤ Click the **drop-down arrow** to choose a table or query. Select the **Players Without Matching Teams** (the query created in step 2). Click **OK**.

➤ Maximize the window if necessary, then change to the Design view. Select the **TeamID control** in the Detail section, then press the **Del key**.

➤ Click the **Combo Box tool**. Click and drag in the Detail section, then release the mouse to start the Combo Box Wizard:

- Check the option button that indicates you want the combo box to **look up values in a table or query**. Click **Next**.
- Choose the **Teams** table in the next screen. Click **Next**.
- Select the **TeamID** and **Nickname** fields. Click **Next**.
- Adjust the column width if necessary. Be sure the box to **Hide the key column** is checked. Click **Next**.
- Click the option button to store the value in the field. Click the **drop-down arrow** to display the fields and select the **TeamID** field. Click **Next**.
- Enter **TeamID** as the label for the combo box. Click **Finish**.

➤ Click (select) the label next to the control you just created. Press the **Del key**.

➤ Point to the combo box, click the **right mouse button** to display a shortcut menu, and click **Properties**. Change the name of the control to **TeamID**. Close the Properties box.

➤ Click the **Save button** to display the Save As dialog box in Figure 7.11c. (Players Without Matching Teams is already entered as the default name.)

➤ Click **OK** to save the form, then close the form.

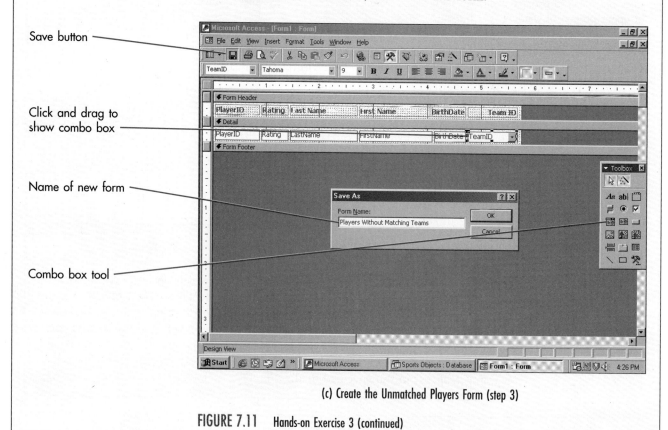

Save button

Click and drag to show combo box

Name of new form

Combo box tool

(c) Create the Unmatched Players Form (step 3)

FIGURE 7.11   Hands-on Exercise 3 (continued)

STEP 4: Create the Player Draft Macro Group

➤ Click the **Macros button** in the Database window. Click **New** to create a new macro. Click the **maximize button** to maximize the Macro window.

➤ If you do not see the Macro Names column, pull down the **View menu** and click **Macro Names** to display the column.

➤ Enter the macro names, comments, and actions, as shown in Figure 7.11d.

- The Requery action (in the Update List macro) has a single argument in which you specify the control name (the name of the query). Type **Players Without Matching Teams**, which is the query you created in step one.

- The Find Player macro will be implemented as an assignment (see practice exercise 6), but in the interim, it will access the Prototype macro developed earlier. Choose **RunMacro** as the action and specify **Prototype**.

- The arguments for the End Draft macro are visible in Figure 7.11d. The **Player Draft form** will be created in the next step. (You must enter the name manually since the form has not yet been created.)

➤ Save the Macro group as **Player Draft**. Close the Macro window.

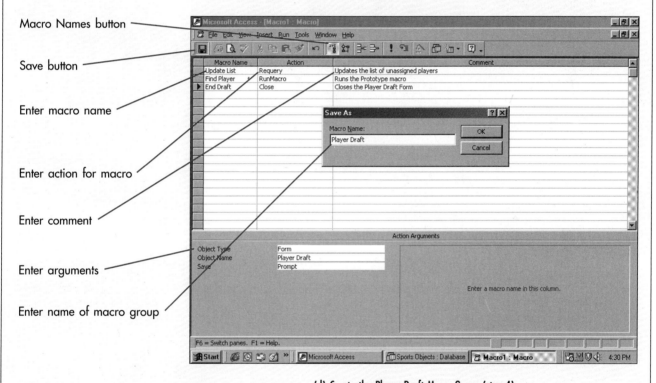

(d) Create the Player Draft Macro Group (step 4)

FIGURE 7.11   Hands-on Exercise 3 (continued)

REQUERY COMMAND NOT AVAILABLE

The macros in the Player Draft group are designed to run only when the Player Draft form is open. Do not be concerned, therefore, if you attempt to test the macros at this time and the Action Failed dialog box appears. The macros will work correctly at the end of the exercise, when the entire player draft is in place.

STEP 5: Create the Player Draft Form

➤ Click the **Forms button** in the Database window. Select the **Template form**, click the **Copy button** to copy the form to the clipboard, then click the **Paste button** to complete the copy operation. Type **Player Draft** as the name of the copied form. Click **OK**.

➤ Open the Player Draft form in **Design view**. Pull down the **Window menu** and click **Tile Horizontally** to arrange the windows as shown in Figure 7.11e. (If necessary, close any open windows besides the two in our figure, then retile the windows.)

➤ Click in the **Database window**. Click and drag the **Players Without Matching Teams form** into the Detail section of the Player Draft form as shown in Figure 7.11e. Maximize the Player Draft window.

Click and drag Players Without Matching Teams form to Detail Section of Player Draft form

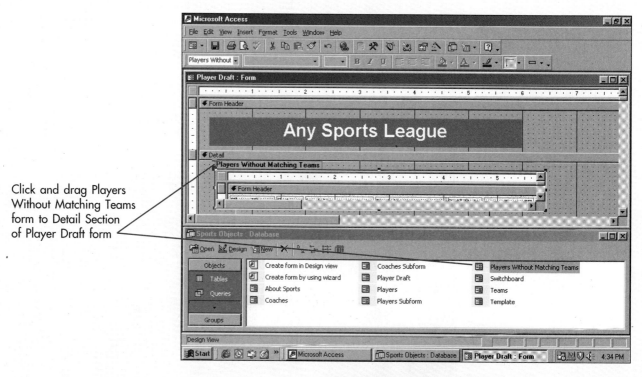

(e) Create the Player Draft Form (step 5)

FIGURE 7.11   Hands-on Exercise 3 (continued)

USE A TEMPLATE

Avoid the routine and repetitive work of creating a new form by basing all forms for a given application on the same template. A template is a partially completed form that contains graphic elements and other formatting specifications. A template does not, however, have an underlying table or query. We suggest that you create a template for your application and store it within the database, then use that template whenever you need to create a new form. It saves you time and trouble. It also promotes a consistent look that is critical to the application's overall success.

STEP 6: Modify the Player Draft Form

➤ Click and drag the decorative box so that it is larger than the Players Without Matching Forms control. Move the control within the decorative box.

➤ Select the control for the form, then click and drag the **sizing handles** in the Players Without Matching Team form so that its size approximates the form in Figure 7.11f.

➤ Select (click) the label, **Players Without Matching Teams** as shown in Figure 7.11f, then press the **Del key** to remove the label.

➤ Change to the **Form view**. You should see the Form view of the subform, which displays the players who have not yet been assigned to a team. Change the column widths if necessary.

➤ Return to the Form Design view to change the width of the subform. Continue to switch back and forth between the Form view and the Design view until you are satisfied. Save the form.

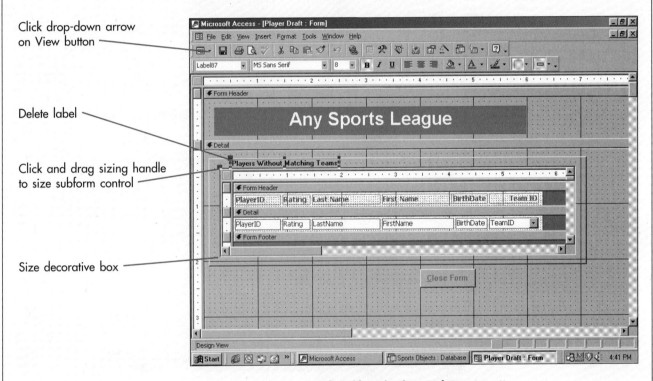

(f) Modifying the Player Draft Form (step 6)

FIGURE 7.11   Hands-on Exercise 3 (continued)

SUPPRESS THE RECORD SELECTOR AND NAVIGATION BUTTONS

You can suppress the Record Selector and Navigation buttons on the Player Draft form, which have no active function and only confuse the user. Change to the Design view, right click the Form selector box to the left of the ruler, then click the Properties command to display the Properties dialog box. Click the Record Selectors text box and click No to disable it. Click the Navigation Buttons text box and click No to disable it. Close the Properties dialog box, then return to the Form view to see the effect of these changes, which are subtle but worthwhile.

STEP 7: Add the Command Buttons

➤ Click and drag the **Command Button tool** to create a command button, as shown in Figure 7.11g. Click **Miscellaneous** in the Categories list box. Select **Run Macro** from the list of actions. Click **Next**.

➤ Select **Player Draft.Update List** from the list of existing macros. Click **Next**.

➤ Click the **Text option button**. Click and drag to select the default text (Run Macro), then type **&Update List** as the text to display. Click **Next**.

➤ Enter **Update List** (in place of the button number). Click **Finish**.

➤ Create a second command button to find a player. The caption of the button should be **&Find Player** and it should run the Find Player macro.

➤ Change the caption property of the existing button on the template that closes the form to **&End Draft**.

➤ Size, align, space, and color the command buttons. Save the form.

➤ Change to the Form view. Click the **End Draft button** to close the form.

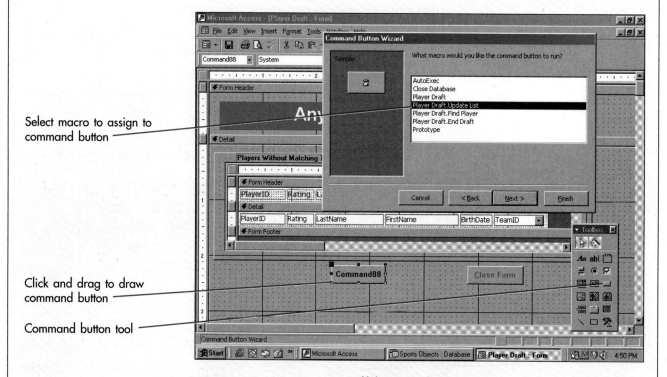

Select macro to assign to command button

Click and drag to draw command button

Command button tool

(g) Add the Command Buttons (step 7)

FIGURE 7.11   Hands-on Exercise 3 (continued)

ASSIGN MACROS TO CONTROLS AND COMMAND BUTTONS

Right click any command button or control to display a context-sensitive menu in which you click the Properties command, then click the Event tab in the resulting property sheet. Click in the text box of the desired event, then click the down arrow to assign an existing macro to the control or command button. Note, too, that you can click the Build button, instead of the down arrow, to select the Macro Builder and create a macro if it does not yet exist.

STEP 8: Modify the Main Switchboard

➤ Pull down the **Tools menu**, click the **Database Utilities command**, and choose **Switchboard Manager**. Select the **Main Switchboard** in the Switchboard Manager dialog box, then click the **Edit button**.

➤ Click **New** to open the Edit Switchboard Item dialog box. Click in the Text list box and type **Player &Draft**. (The ampersand in front of the letter "D" establishes Alt+D as a shortcut for this button.)

➤ Press the **Tab key** to move to the Command list box. Select the command to open the form in the Edit mode. Press the **Tab key** to move to the Form list box and select the Player Draft form as shown in Figure 7.11h.

➤ Click **OK** to create the switchboard item. The Edit Switchboard Item dialog box closes and Player &Draft appears on the Main Switchboard. Select the Player &Draft entry, then click the **Move Up button** to move this command above the &Exit command.

➤ Close the Edit Switchboard page, then close the Switchboard Manager.

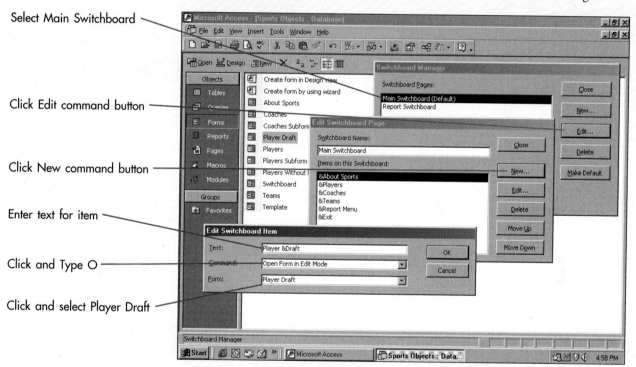

(h) Modify the Main Switchboard (step 8)

FIGURE 7.11   Hands-on Exercise 3 (continued)

REPLICATE THE DATABASE

You can create a copy of a database, known as a replica, then take the replica with you on a laptop computer. This lets you work with the database even if you are not connected to the network, but you will eventually have to synchronize your replica with the network version. Start Windows Explorer, click and drag the Access database to the My Briefcase icon on the desktop, then follow the onscreen instructions. Use the Access Help facility for additional information.

STEP 9: Test the Completed System

➤ Click the **Macros button** in the Database window. Double click the **AutoExec macro** to execute this macro, as though you just opened the database.

➤ Click the **Player Draft** button on the Main Switchboard to display the form you just created, as shown in Figure 7.11i.

➤ Click the **TeamID field** for Katie Remmen. Type **R** (the first letter in Rockets) and Katie is assigned automatically to this team. Click the **Update List command button**. Katie disappears from the list of unassigned players.

➤ Click the **Find Player button**. Click **OK** when you see the message indicating this function has not been implemented. Click the **End Draft button**.

➤ Click the **Teams command button** to view the team rosters. Team T01 (Rockets) is the first team you see, and Katie Remmen is on the roster. Click the **Close Form** button to return to the switchboard.

➤ Click the **Exit button**. Click **OK** in response to the message for backup.

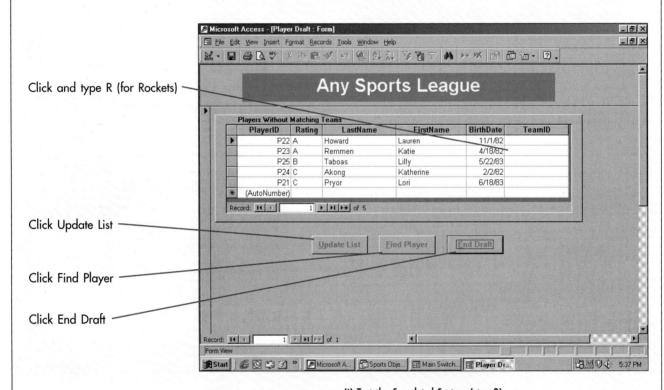

Click and type R (for Rockets)

Click Update List

Click Find Player

Click End Draft

(i) Test the Completed System (step 9)

FIGURE 7.11   Hands-on Exercise 3 (continued)

PASSWORD PROTECT A DATABASE

Protect your database from unauthorized access through imposition of a password. It's a two-step process. First, close the database, then pull down the File menu, click the Open command to display the Open dialog box, select the database, then click the drop-down Open button and choose Open Exclusive. Next, pull down the Tools menu, click Security, click Set Database password, and follow the onscreen prompts. Be careful, however, because you cannot open the database if you forget the password.

An Access application is different from an ordinary database in that it contains an intuitive user interface known as a switchboard. The switchboard can be created automatically using the Switchboard Manager, a tool that prompts you for each item you want to include. You supply the text of the menu item, as it is to appear on the switchboard, together with the underlying command. Access does the rest and creates the switchboard form and associated table of switchboard items.

The tables in a database can be separated from the other objects to enable the distribution of updated versions of the application without disturbing the data. The tables are stored in one database and the objects in another. The Link Tables command associates the tables with the objects.

A macro automates a command sequence and consists of one or more actions. The Macro window has two sections. The upper section contains the name (if any) of the macro and the actions (commands) that make up the macro. The lower section specifies the arguments for the various actions. A macro group consists of multiple macros and is used for organizational purposes.

The AutoExec macro is executed automatically whenever the database in which it is stored is opened. Each database can have its own AutoExec macro, but there is no requirement for an AutoExec macro to be present.

The Unmatched Query Wizard identifies the records in one table (e.g., the Players table) that do not have matching records in another table (e.g., the Teams table).

A prototype is a model (mockup) of a completed application that demonstrates the "look and feel" of the application. Prototypes can be developed quickly and easily through the use of simple macros containing the MsgBox action. Continual testing through prototyping is essential to the success of a system.

A database can be protected from unauthorized use through imposition of a password.

Action
Application
Argument
AutoExec macro
Combo box
Command button
Database properties
Database splitter
Debugging
Display When property
Event
Event procedure
Get External Data command

Import command
Is Null criterion
Linked Table Manager
Link Tables command
List box
Macro
Macro group
Macro toolbar
Macro window
MsgBox Action
On Click property
Prototyping
Requery command

Splitting a database
Switchboard
Switchboard Items table
Switchboard Manager
Template
Top-down implementation
Unmatched Query Wizard
User interface
Zoom box

1. Which of the following is created automatically by the Switchboard Manager?
   (a) A form to hold the switchboard
   (b) A table containing the commands associated with the switchboard
   (c) Both (a) and (b)
   (d) Neither (a) nor (b)

2. Which of the following describes the storage of the tables and objects for the application developed in the chapter?
   (a) Each table is stored in its own database
   (b) Each object is stored in its own database
   (c) The tables are stored in one database and the objects in a different database
   (d) The tables and objects are stored in the same database

3. Which of the following is true regarding the Link Tables command as it was used in the chapter?
   (a) It was executed from the Sports Objects database
   (b) It was executed from the Sports Tables database
   (c) Both (a) and (b)
   (d) Neither (a) nor (b)

4. What happens when an Access database is opened initially?
   (a) Access executes the AutoExec macro if the macro exists
   (b) Access opens the AutoExec form if the form exists
   (c) Both (a) and (b)
   (d) Neither (a) nor (b)

5. Which statement is true regarding the AutoExec macro?
   (a) Every database must have an AutoExec macro
   (b) A database may have more than one AutoExec macro
   (c) Both (a) and (b)
   (d) Neither (a) nor (b)

6. Which of the following are examples of arguments?
   (a) MsgBox and OpenForm
   (b) Message type (e.g., critical) and Form name
   (c) Both (a) and (b)
   (d) Neither (a) nor (b)

7. Which of the following can be imported from another Access database?
   (a) Tables and forms
   (b) Queries and reports
   (c) Both (a) and (b)
   (d Neither (a) nor (b)

8. How do you change the properties of a command button on an existing form?
   (a) Open the form in Form view, then click the left mouse button to display a shortcut menu
   (b) Open the form in Form view, then click the right mouse button to display a shortcut menu
   (c) Open the form in Form Design view, then click the left mouse button to display a shortcut menu
   (d) Open the form in Form Design view, then click the right mouse button to display a shortcut menu

9. Which of the following is true regarding the Unmatched Query Wizard with respect to the Sports league database?
   (a) It can be used to identify teams without players
   (b) It can be used to identify players without teams
   (c) Both (a) and (b)
   (d) Neither (a) nor (b)

10. Which of the following can be associated with the On Click property of a command button?
    (a) An event procedure created by the Command Button Wizard
    (b) A macro created by the user
    (c) Either (a) or (b)
    (d) Neither (a) nor (b)

11. Which of the following was suggested as essential to a backup strategy?
    (a) Backing up files at the end of every session
    (b) Storing the backup file(s) at another location
    (c) Both (a) and (b)
    (d) Neither (a) nor (b)

12. Which of the following is true if the On Click property of a command button contains the entry, *Player Draft.Update List*?
    (a) Update List is an event procedure
    (b) Player Draft is an event procedure
    (c) Player Draft is a macro in the Update List macro group
    (d) Update List is a macro in the Player Draft macro group

13. Which of the following is true?
    (a) An existing database may be split into two separate databases, one containing the tables, and one containing the other objects
    (b) Once the objects in a database have been linked to the tables in another database, the name and/or location of the latter database can never be changed
    (c) Both (a) and (b)
    (d) Neither (a) nor (b)

14. The F6 and F11 function keys were introduced as shortcuts. Which of the following is true about these keys?
    (a) The F6 key switches between the top and bottom sections of the Macro window
    (b) The F11 key makes the Database window the active window
    (c) Both (a) and (b)
    (d) Neither (a) nor (b)

15. Which of the following was suggested as a way to organize macros and thus limit the number of macros that are displayed in the Database window?
    (a) Avoid macro actions that have only a single argument
    (b) Avoid macros that contain only a single action
    (c) Create a macro group
    (d) All of the above

ANSWERS

1. c	**6.** b	**11.** c
2. c	**7.** c	**12.** d
3. a	**8.** d	**13.** a
4. a	**9.** c	**14.** c
5. d	**10.** c	**15.** c

PRACTICE WITH ACCESS 2000

1. Do the three hands-on exercises in the chapter, then complete the application by creating the reports that are referenced on the Report switchboard. The requirements for each report are described below:

   a. Report 1 is a master list of all players in alphabetical order. Include the player's first and last name, date of birth, rating, phone, and address, in that order. Create the report in landscape rather than portrait orientation.

   b. Report 2 is a master list of all coaches in alphabetical order. Include the coach's first and last name, phone, and address, in that order. Create the report in landscape rather than portrait orientation.

   c. Report 3 is to print the team rosters in sequence by TeamID. Each roster is to begin on a new page. The header line should contain the TeamID, nickname, and team colors as well as the name and phone number of the head coach. A detail line, containing the player's first and last name, telephone number, and date of birth is to appear for each player. Players are to be listed alphabetically.

   d. Modify the Report Switchboard to include the report names, and further, modify the action associated with each button to open the indicated report.

   e. Submit each of the reports to your instructor as proof that you did this exercise.

2. The Linked Table Manager: Look carefully at the screen in Figure 7.12 and notice that the Coaches table is linked to a different database than the Players or Teams tables. Open the Sports Objects database, pull down the Tools menu, click (or point to) the Database Utilities command, then select the Linked Table Manager. Click the box next to the Coaches table, then check the box to Always prompt for new location. Click OK to update the link. Choose the New Coaches table in the Exploring Access folder and the Linked Table Manager will update the link to reflect the New Coaches database. Print the updated coaches' roster using report number 2 from the previous exercise.

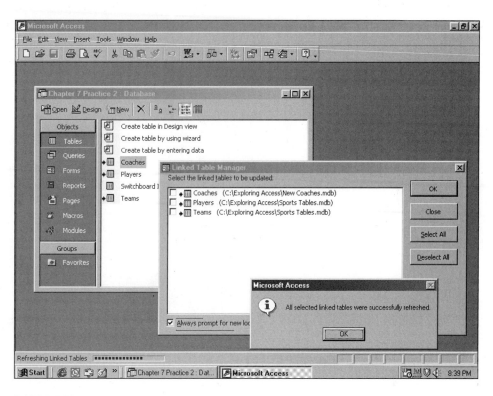

FIGURE 7.12 The Linked Table Manager (Exercise 2)

3. **Splitting a Database:** Open the Computer Store database from Chapter 6 and use the Compact and Repair command to compact the database. Pull down the Tools menu, click (or point to) the Database Utilities command, then select the Database Splitter to display a screen similar to Figure 7.13. Click the button to Split the Database, then follow the onscreen instructions.

   a. What is the size of the Computer Store database after it has been compacted?

   b. How many databases do you have after the split is complete?

   c. What are the contents of each database after the split?

   d. What is the size of each database after the split?

   e. What is the advantage to splitting the database if the size increases?

4. **The Tech Support Macro:** Modify the About Sports form to include a Tech Support button as shown in Figure 7.14. The On Click property of the new button is to be associated with a Technical Support macro (that you are to create) which displays your e-mail address. Submit a disk with the Sports league database to your instructor.

5. **Establishing Conditions:** Figure 7.15 on page 361 illustrates the use of the Condition column in the Macro window. The intent of the macro in Figure 7.15 is to display a message to "A"-rated players inviting them to try out for an All-City competitive team that plays against teams from other cities.

   a. Create the macro shown in Figure 7.15. (Click the Conditions button on the Macro toolbar to display the Conditions column in the Macro window.)

   b. Open the Players form in Design view. Right click the Rating control to display its Property sheet, then assign the macro you just created to the On Exit property.

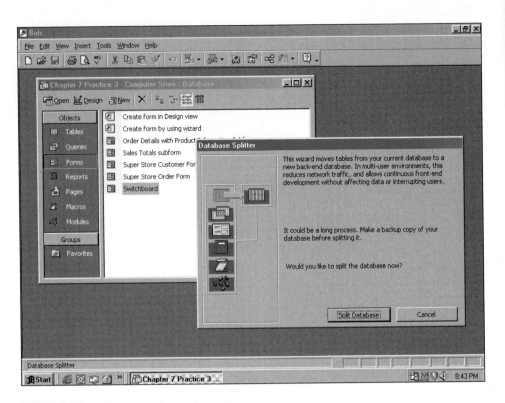

FIGURE 7.13   Splitting a Database (Exercise 3)

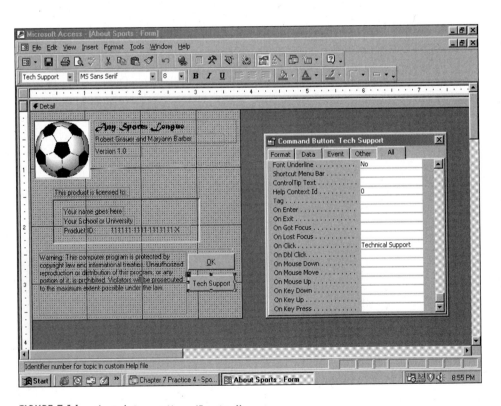

FIGURE 7.14   The Tech Support Macro (Exercise 4)

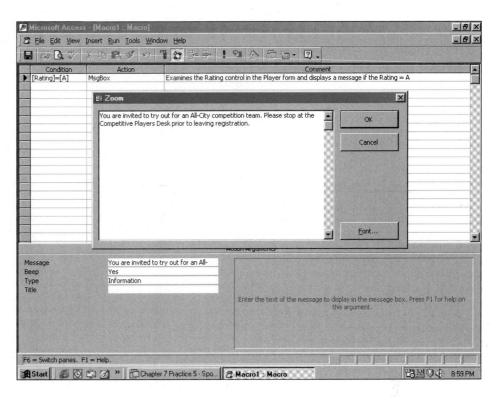

FIGURE 7.15   Establishing Conditions (Exercise 5)

c. Change to Form view, then move to the record containing the information you entered for yourself in step 3 of the first hands-on exercise. Click the text box containing the player rating, enter "A", then press the Tab key to move to the next control. Change your rating to a "B" and press the Tab key a second time. Reenter an "A" as your player rating.

d. Submit a disk with the Sports league database to your instructor.

6. Completing the Find Player Function: The player draft was only partially completed in the third hands-on exercise and still requires the completion of the Find Player function. After this has been accomplished, you will be able to click the Find Player button in Figure 7.16 to display the Find Parameter Value dialog box to enter a player name, and then view the information for that player. Accordingly:

a. Create a parameter query that requests the last name of a player, then returns *all* fields for that player.

b. Copy the existing Players Form to a new form called Find Player. Change the Record Source property of the Find Player form to the parameter query you created in part (a).

c. Change the Find Player macro in the Player Draft group so that it opens the Find Player form you just created.

d. Test the Find Player button.

e. Submit the completed disk to your instructor.

7. The Add Player Macro: Open the Players form, click the button to add a player, then note that in order to add a player you must first click the First Name text box. You can, however, automate the process by creating a macro to move automatically to the First Name text box, then associating that macro with the On Click property of the Add Player button. Close the form, then follow the instructions on the next page.

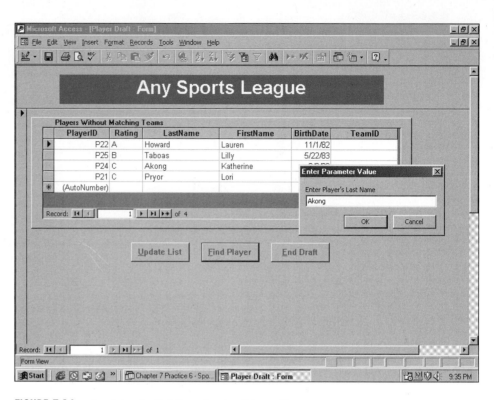

FIGURE 7.16   Completing the Find Player Function (Exercise 6)

a. Create the Add Player macro, which consists of two actions, RunCommand, and GoToControl. The first action, RunCommand, has a single argument, Command. Click in the text box for the Command argument. Click the drop-down arrow and select RecordsGoToNew.

b. The second action, GoToControl, has a single argument (FirstName) that specifies the name of the control on the Players form. Save the macro as Add Player. Do not attempt to run the macro at this time.

c. Open the Players form in Design view as shown in Figure 7.17. Point to the Add Player command button, then click the right mouse button to display a shortcut menu. Click Properties to display the Properties dialog box. Click the down arrow on the vertical scroll bar until you can see the On Click property, which is currently set to [Event Procedure]. Click the On Click property box, then click the drop-down arrow to display the existing macros. Click Add Player (the macro you just created). Close the Properties dialog box.

d. Click the Form View button to switch to Form view and test the Add Player macro. Click the Add Player command button. You are automatically positioned in the First Name box (because of the Add Player macro) and can start typing immediately.

e. Click the Close Form command button when you have completed the record. Click Yes if prompted to save the changes to the Players form.

f. This may seem like a lot of trouble, but the end-user appreciates this type of convenience. You can modify the Coaches form in similar fashion.

g. Submit the completed disk to your instructor as proof you completed the exercise.

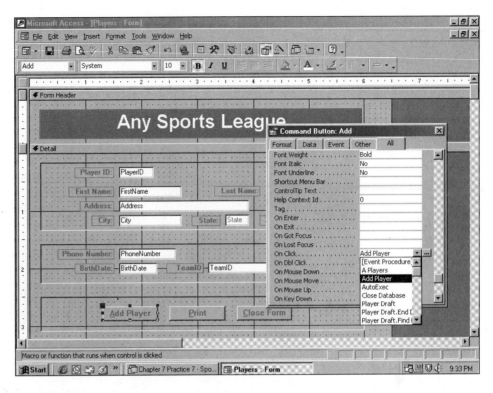

FIGURE 7.17   The Add Player Macro (Exercise 7)

8. Inserting a Hyperlink: Complete the Switchboard as described in the chapter, then open the completed switchboard in Design view as shown in Figure 7.18. Click the Insert Hyperlink button to display the Insert Hyperlink dialog box, then indicate the text to display and the associated Web

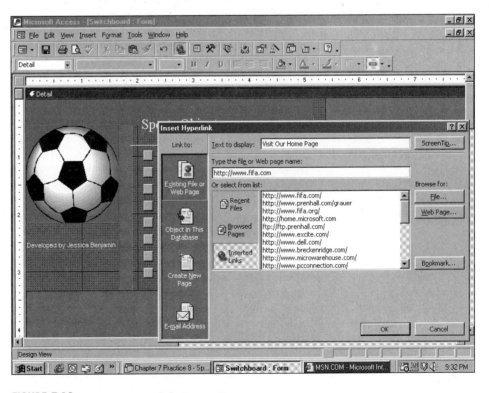

FIGURE 7.18   Inserting a Hyperlink (Exercise 8)

site. Try the Fifa Web site www.fifa.com if you do not have an alternative Web site. Right click the hyperlink after it has been created to display a shortcut menu, click the Properties command to display the Properties dialog box, then change the caption, font, and/or point size as appropriate.

9. Password Protection: Close the Soccer database. Pull down the File menu, click the Open command to display the Open dialog box, then click the drop-down Open button and choose Open Exclusive. You must open the database in this way or else you will not be able to set a password. Next pull down the Tools menu, click Security, click Set Database password, and follow the onscreen prompts. Be careful, however, because once you save a database with a password, you cannot open it if you forget the password.

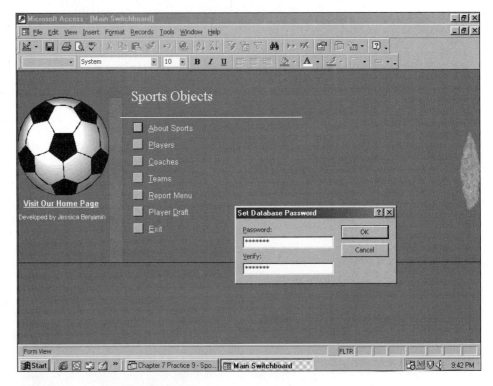

FIGURE 7.19   Password Protection (Exercise 9)

CASE STUDIES

Client/Server Applications

The application for the Coral Springs Soccer Association was developed to run on a single PC; in practice, however, it would most likely be implemented on a network. Investigate the additional steps needed to load the Sports Tables database on a server and enable multiple users (clients) to access the database simultaneously. How does Access prevent two users from modifying the same record simultaneously? What security features are available? How would backup be implemented? Where would the Sports Objects database be stored?

Security Options

Setting a password is the first step in protecting a database. You can also set different levels of password protection, by giving different permissions to different users. Pull down the Tools menu, click Security, then click User and Group Permissions to display the associated dialog box. Use Help to explore the options within this dialog box. You can also encrypt a database through a different command within the Security menu. Explore the various security options, then summarize your findings in a short note to your instructor.

A Project for the Semester

Choose any of the eight cases at the end of Chapter 5 or 6 (with the exception of the Recreational Sports League in Chapter 5) and develop a complete system. Design the tables and relationships and provide a representative series of forms to enter and edit the data. Create a representative set of queries and reports. And finally, tie the system together via a system of menus similar to those that were developed in the chapter.

The Database Wizard

The Database Wizard provides an easy way to create a database as it creates the database for you. The advantage of the Wizard is that it creates the tables, forms, and reports, together with a Main Menu (called a switchboard) in one operation. The disadvantage is that the Wizard is inflexible compared to creating the database yourself. Use the online Help facility to learn about the Database Wizard, then use the Wizard to create a simple database for your Music Collection. Is the Wizard a useful shortcut or is it easier to create the database yourself?

Compacting versus Compressing

The importance of adequate backup has been stressed throughout the text. As a student, however, your backup may be limited to what you can fit on a single floppy disk, which in turn creates a problem if the size of your database grows beyond 1.4Mb. Two potential solutions involve compacting and/or compressing the database. Compacting is done from within Access whereas compressing requires additional software. Investigate both of these techniques with respect to the Sports league database created in the chapter. Be sure to indicate to your instructor the reduction in file size that you were able to achieve.

The AutoKeys Macro

Use the Access Help command to discover the AutoKeys macro, a little-known feature that truly customizes an application. Extend the Sports League database in this chapter to include an AutoKeys macro that recognizes the F2 key; i.e., pressing this key from any screen in the application should display a dialog box with your name, class, semester, and e-mail address. Submit the completed disk to your instructor as proof you completed this exercise.

chapter 8

CREATING MORE POWERFUL APPLICATIONS: INTRODUCTION TO VBA

OBJECTIVES

After reading this chapter you will be able to:

1. Describe the relationship of VBA to Microsoft Office 2000; list several reasons to use VBA in creating an Access application.
2. Describe the components of the Module window; differentiate between the Procedure view and the Full Module view.
3. Describe two different ways to create an event procedure; explain how to navigate between existing procedures.
4. Explain how the Quick Info and Complete Word features facilitate the entry of VBA statements.
5. Create a combo box to locate a record on a form; explain why an event procedure is required for the combo box to function properly.
6. Describe the arguments of the MsgBox function; explain how the use of a VBA constant displays a uniform message in the title bar of every message box.
7. Create an event procedure to facilitate data entry through keyboard shortcuts.
8. Create an event procedure that substitutes application-specific messages for the standard Access error messages.
9. Describe several types of data validation; create an event procedure that warns the user a field has been omitted, giving the user the option to save the record without entering the data.

OVERVIEW

You can accomplish a great deal in Access without using Visual Basic. You can create an Access database consisting of tables, forms, queries, and reports, by executing commands from pull-down menus. You can use macros to create menus that tie those objects together so that the database is easier to use. Nevertheless, there comes a point where you need the power of a programming language in order to develop a truly useful application. Hence, this introduction to *Visual Basic for Applications* (or *VBA*), a subset of Visual Basic that is accessible from every application in Microsoft Office 2000.

VBA is different from traditional programming languages in that it is event-driven. An *event* is any action that is recognized by Access. Opening or closing a form is an event. So is clicking a button in a form or entering data in a text box or other control on the form. The essence of VBA is the creation of *procedures* (or sets of VBA statements) that respond to specific events. Hence, the term *event procedure* will be used throughout the chapter.

To enhance an application through VBA, you decide which events are significant and what is to happen when those events occur. Then you develop the appropriate event procedures. You can, for example, create an event procedure that displays a splash (introductory) screen for the application every time a user opens the database. You can write an event procedure that creates a keyboard shortcut for data entry that executes when the user presses a particular keystroke combination. You can create an event procedure to display a specific message in place of the standard error message supplied by Access. In all instances, the execution of your procedures depends entirely on the user, because he or she triggers the underlying events through an appropriate action.

You can also use VBA to modify the event procedures that Access has created for you. If, for example, you used the Command Button Wizard to create a button to close a form, Access created the event procedure for you. The user clicks the button and the event procedure closes the form. You can, however, use VBA to improve the procedure created by Access by adding a statement that reminds the user to back up the database after closing the form.

This chapter provides a general introduction to VBA through four hands-on exercises that enhance an application in different ways. Our approach is very different from that of other texts that run several hundred pages and cover the subject in extended detail. Our objective is to provide you with an appreciation for what can be accomplished, rather than to cover VBA in detail. We will show you how to create and modify simple procedures. We will also provide you with the conceptual framework to explore the subject in greater detail on your own.

One last point before we begin is that VBA is common to every application in Microsoft Office, and thus anything that you learn about VBA from within Access is applicable to the other applications as well. If, for example, you create a macro in Word or Excel, the macro recorder captures the keystrokes and then generates a VBA procedure that is accessible through the Word document or Excel workbook, respectively. You can modify the procedure by changing existing statements and/or by adding additional statements using the techniques in this chapter.

EVENT-DRIVEN VERSUS TRADITIONAL PROGRAMMING

A traditional program is executed sequentially, beginning with the first line of code and continuing in order through the remainder of the program. It is the program, not the user, that determines the order in which the statements are executed. VBA, on the other hand, is event driven, meaning that the order in which the procedures are executed depends on the events that occur. It is the user, rather than the program, that determines which events occur, and consequently which procedures are executed.

The form in Figure 8.1 will be used throughout the chapter as the basis of our VBA examples. The form itself is unremarkable and parallels many of the forms that were developed throughout the text. It was created initially through the Form Wizard, then modified by moving and sizing controls as appropriate. What then is so special about the form, and how does it utilize VBA?

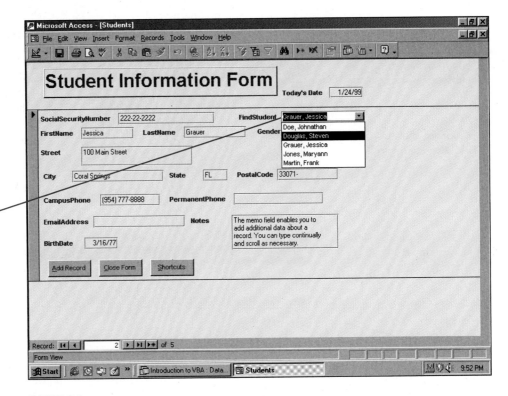

Find Student Combo box

FIGURE 8.1   User Form

The answer lies beneath the surface and is best explained in conjunction with the dialog boxes in Figure 8.2. At first glance, the dialog boxes look like typical messages displayed by Microsoft Access. Look closely at the title bar of any message, however, and note that it has been changed to reflect the authors' introduction to Visual Basic. This is a subtle change that is easily implemented through VBA, and it gives your application a personal touch. Note, too, the different icons that are displayed in the various messages. This, too, is a subtle touch that further customizes the application and its messages.

Look closely at the content of each dialog box to learn more about the underlying VBA capability. The message in Figure 8.2a indicates that the user has omitted the e-mail address, then asks if the record should be saved anyway. This is an improvement over the built-in routines for data validation, which use the Required property to reject any record that omits the e-mail address. Should this occur, the user is notified that the field is required, but he or she cannot save the record unless a value is specified. Through VBA, however, the user has a choice and can opt to save the record even when there is no e-mail address.

The dialog box in Figure 8.2b is displayed as a result of clicking the Shortcuts command button on the form. The message implies that the user can use keyboard shortcuts to enter the city, state, and zip code for Miami or Coral Springs. True, the user could enter the data manually, but think how much time can be saved when there is extensive data entry.

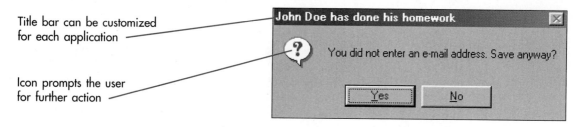

Title bar can be customized for each application

Icon prompts the user for further action

(a) Data Validation

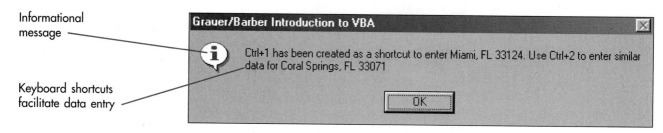

Informational message

Keyboard shortcuts facilitate data entry

(b) Facilitating Data Entry

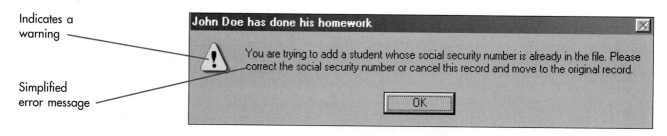

Indicates a warning

Simplified error message

(c) Error Trapping

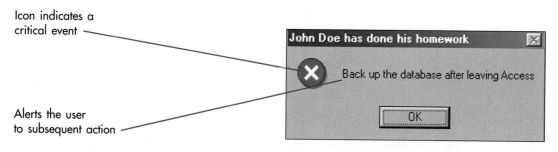

Icon indicates a critical event

Alerts the user to subsequent action

(d) Enhanced Communication with User

FIGURE 8.2   Dialog Boxes

Figure 8.2c displays a message indicating that one is attempting to add a student whose social security number is already in the file. The text is very straightforward and that is exactly the point. The default Access error message would not be as clear, and would have indicated that changes to the table were not successful because they would have created a duplicate value of the primary key. In other words, we used VBA to first detect the error, and then substituted a more explicit message. Finally, the message in Figure 8.2d simply reminds the user to back up the database upon exiting Access.

Modules and Procedures

There are, in essence, two different ways to learn VBA. The first is to immerse yourself in the theory and syntax before you attempt to develop any applications on your own. The second, and the one we follow, is to start with an overall appreciation of what it can do, then plunge right in. You need some basic vocabulary, but after that you can model your procedures on ours and create some very powerful applications in the process.

Visual Basic code is developed in units called procedures. There are two types of procedures, general procedures and event procedures. ***Event procedures*** are the essence of an Access application and run automatically in response to an event such as clicking a button or opening a form. ***General procedures*** do not run automatically, but are called explicitly from within another procedure. We focus exclusively on event procedures.

All (general and event) procedures are stored in modules; that is, one module contains one or more procedures. Every form in an Access database has its own module (known as a ***class module***) which contains the procedures for that form. A procedure is either public or private. A ***private procedure*** is accessible only from within the module in which it is contained. A ***public procedure*** is accessible from anywhere.

The procedures in a module are displayed and edited through the ***Module window***. Figure 8.3, for example, displays the Module window for the student form shown earlier in Figure 8.1. Four different procedures are visible, each of which is associated with a different event. Each procedure begins with a procedure header that names the procedure. This is followed by the executable statements within the procedure, followed by the End Sub statement to mark the end of the procedure. Do not be concerned if you do not understand the precise syntax of every statement. Try, instead, to gain an overall appreciation for what the procedures do.

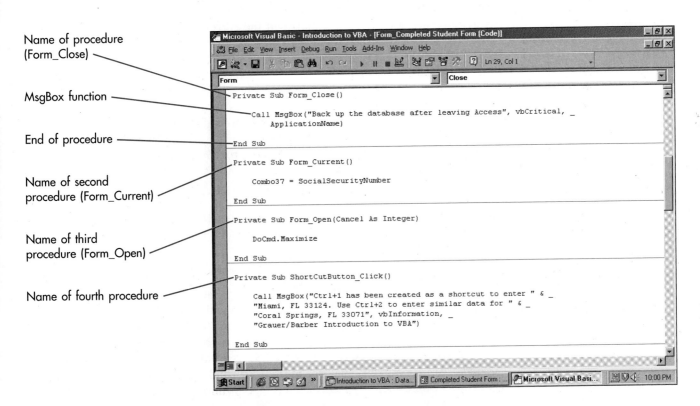

FIGURE 8.3 The Module Window

The first event procedure is for the **Close Form event**. The procedure header contains the key word Sub, followed by the procedure name (Form_Close). The **MsgBox function** within the procedure displays the message box (shown earlier in Figure 8.2d) when the event occurs. Thus whenever the user closes the form, either by clicking the Close button on the form or by clicking the Close button in the document window, the event procedure is triggered and one is reminded to back up the database. (See boxed tip.)

The syntax of the MsgBox function is typical of many VBA statements and is best understood if you view the statement as it might appear in a help screen *MsgBox (prompt, buttons, title)*. The entries in parentheses are known as **arguments** (or **parameters**) and determine the contents of the message box. The first argument is contained in quotation marks and it specifies the prompt (or message text) that appears within the message box. The second argument indicates the type of command buttons (if any) and the associated icon that appear within the dialog box. This argument is specified as an **intrinsic** (or previously defined) **constant** (vbCritical in this example) and it determines the icon that is to appear in the message box. The third argument contains the text that appears in the title bar of the message box. It, too, appears in quotation marks.

The second event procedure is associated with the **Current event** of the form and is the focus of our first hands-on exercise. The nature of this procedure is much less intuitive than the previous example, yet this event procedure is critical to the success of the form. Return to the Student Form shown earlier in Figure 8.1 and note the presence of a combo box to find a specific student. The user clicks the drop-down arrow on the combo box and selects a student from the displayed list, after which the data for that student is displayed in the form.

The combo box was created through the Combo Box Wizard, and it works well, but it does have one limitation. If the user elects to move from one record to the next by clicking a navigation button at the bottom of the form, the combo box is out of sync in that it does not reflect the name of the new student. Hence the need to write a VBA procedure for the Current event to change the value in the combo box to match the current record. In other words, the VBA procedure will move the SocialSecurityNumber of the current record to the combo box control whenever the record changes.

The third event procedure is associated with the Open Form event, and it needs almost no explanation. The single executable statement will maximize the form when it is opened. Again, do not be concerned if you do not understand the precise syntax of every statement in our initial examples as we add further explanation in the chapter. The fourth and final procedure is associated with the Click event of the ShortCut command button and it contains another example of the MsgBox function. Note, too, that for this procedure to make sense, other event procedures have to be created to implement the shortcuts as described.

We would be misleading you if we said that VBA is easy. It's not, but neither is it as complicated as you might think. And more importantly, VBA is extremely powerful. We think you will be pleased with what you can accomplish by the end of this chapter. Once again, it is time for a hands-on exercise.

A SIMPLE STRATEGY FOR BACKUP

We cannot overemphasize the importance of adequate backup. Backup procedures are personal and vary from individual to individual as well as from installation to installation. Our suggested strategy is very simple, namely that you back up whatever you cannot afford to lose and that you do so at the end of every session. Be sure to store the backup at a different location from the original file.

Create a Combo Box and Associated VBA Procedure

Objective: To create a combo box to locate a record; to create a VBA procedure to synchronize the combo box with the current record. Use Figure 8.4.

STEP 1: Open the Introduction to VBA Database

➤ Start Access. Open the **Introduction to VBA database** in the **Exploring Access folder** as shown in Figure 8.4a.

➤ If necessary, click the **Forms button**. Select (click) the **Original Student Form**. Pull down the **Edit menu** and click the **Copy command** (or click the **Copy button** on the Database toolbar). The form is copied to the clipboard.

➤ Pull down the **Edit menu** a second time and click the **Paste command** (or click the **Paste button** on the Database toolbar) to display the Paste As dialog box. Type **Completed Student Form** and press **enter**.

Copy button

Paste button

Forms button

Enter name of new form

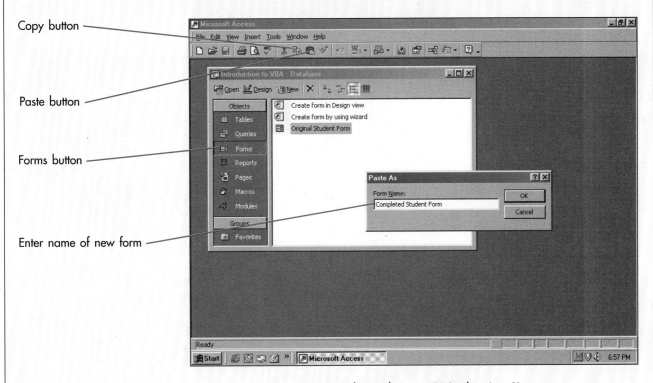

(a) Open the Introduction to VBA Database (step 1)

FIGURE 8.4   Hands-on Exercise 1

KEYBOARD SHORTCUTS—CUT, COPY, AND PASTE

Ctrl+X, Ctrl+C, and Ctrl+V are shortcuts to cut, copy, and paste, respectively, and apply to Windows applications in general. The shortcuts are easier to remember when you realize that the operative letters X, C, and V are next to each other at the bottom left side of the keyboard.

STEP 2: The Combo Box Wizard

➤ Open the newly created **Completed Student Form** in Design view. Maximize the window.

➤ Click the **Combo Box tool** on the Toolbox toolbar, then click and drag on the form next to the SSN control to create a combo box and start the Wizard.

➤ Select the option button to **Find a record on my form based on the value I selected in my combo box** as shown in Figure 8.4b. Click **Next**.

➤ Double click the **SocialSecurityNumber field** to move it from the list box of available fields (on the left of the Combo Box Wizard) to the list of selected fields. Double click the **LastName field** to move this field as well. Click **Next**.

➤ You should see the columns in the combo box as they will appear in the form. Be sure the Check box to Hide key column is checked. Click **Next**.

➤ Change the label of the combo box to **FindStudent** (do not use a space in the label). Click **Finish** to exit the Combo Box Wizard.

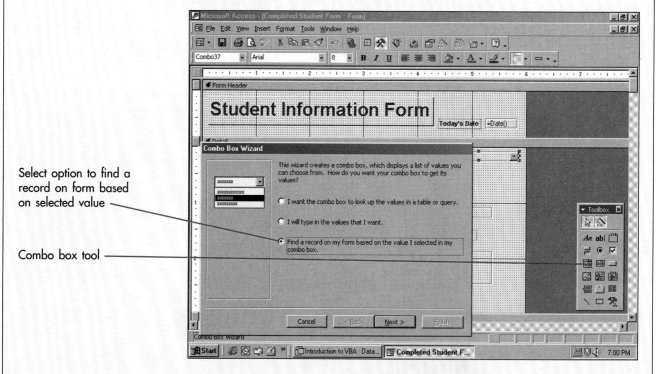

Select option to find a record on form based on selected value

Combo box tool

(b) The Combo Box Wizard (step 2)

FIGURE 8.4   Hands-on Exercise 1 (continued)

SIZING AND MOVING A COMBO BOX AND ITS LABEL

A combo box is always created with an attached label. Select (click) the combo box, and it will have sizing handles and a move handle, but the label has only a move handle. Select the label (instead of the combo box) and the opposite occurs. To move a combo box and its label, click and drag the border of either object. To move either the combo box or its label, click and drag the move handle (a tiny square in the upper left corner) of the appropriate object.

STEP 3: Move and Size the Combo Box

➤ Move and size the newly created combo box to match the layout in Figure 8.4c. The Properties sheet is not yet visible. You will most likely have to decrease the size of the combo box and/or increase the size of the label.

➤ To align the combo box and/or its label with the other controls on the same row of the form, press and hold the **Shift key** to select the controls you want to align. Pull down the **Format menu**, click **Align**, then click **Top** to align the top of all selected elements.

➤ Point to the combo box, click the **right mouse button** to display a shortcut menu, then click **Properties** to display the Properties dialog box in Figure 8.4c. If necessary, click the **All tab**.

➤ Write down the name of the combo box (Combo37 in our figure) as you will need it in step 7. The name of your control may be different from ours.

➤ Click the **Row Source property** to select it, then click the **Build button** (the button with three dots) that appears when the row is selected.

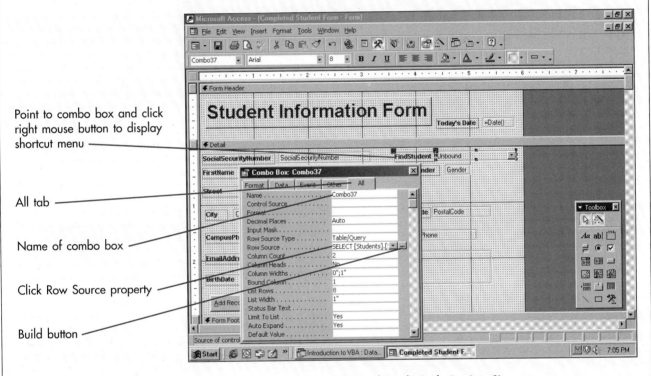

Point to combo box and click right mouse button to display shortcut menu

All tab

Name of combo box

Click Row Source property

Build button

(c) Move and Size the Combo Box (step 3)

FIGURE 8.4   Hands-on Exercise 1 (continued)

THE PROPERTY DIALOG BOX

You can change the appearance or behavior of a control in two ways—by changing the actual control on the form itself or by changing the underlying properties. Anything you do to the control automatically changes the associated property, and conversely, any change to the property sheet is reflected in the appearance or behavior of the control. We find ourselves continually switching back and forth between the two techniques.

STEP 4: Update the Row Source

➤ You should see the query in Figure 8.4d, except that your query has not yet been completed. Click in the second column of the Field row, immediately after the LastName control.

➤ Press the **space bar** then type **& ", " & FirstName**. Leave a space after the comma within the quotation marks. Press **enter**.

➤ Double click the border between this cell and the next to increase the column width so that you can see the entire expression. Note that Expr1: has been entered automatically in front of the expression.

➤ Click in the **Sort row** of the same column, click the **down arrow** if necessary, then click **Ascending** to display the records in alphabetical order by last name.

➤ Close the query. Click **Yes** when asked whether to save the changes that were made to the SQL statement. Close the Properties sheet.

➤ Click the **View button** to return to Form view.

Close button ——

Add & "," & [FirstName] ——

Double click border to increase column width

Click in Sort row and select Ascending

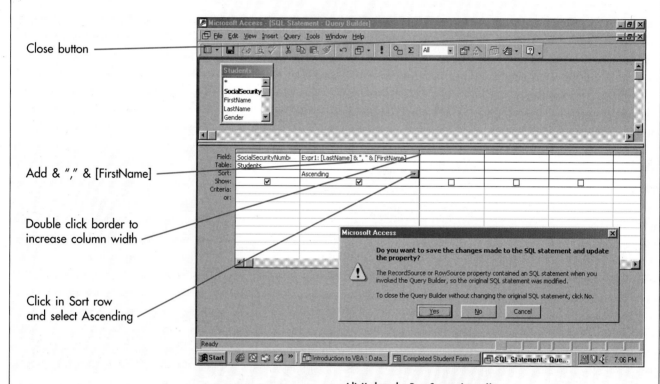

(d) Update the Row Source (step 4)

FIGURE 8.4   Hands-on Exercise 1 (continued)

CONCATENATING A STRING

The ampersand (&), or concatenation operator, indicates that the elements on either side of an expression are to appear adjacent to one another when the expression is displayed. You can also concatenate a literal and a fieldname such as "The employee's last name is" & LastName to display "The employee's last name is Smith," assuming that Smith is the current value in the LastName field.

STEP 5: Test the Find Student Combo Box

➤ If necessary, click the **Navigation button** above the status bar to return to the first record in the table, Maryann Jones, as shown in Figure 8.4e.

➤ Click the **drop-down arrow** on the combo box you just created to display a list of students in alphabetical order. (If you do not see the list of students, press **Esc** to cancel whatever operation is in effect, then return to Design view to repeat the instructions in the previous steps.)

➤ Select (click) **Grauer, Jessica** from the list of names in the combo box. The form is updated to display the information for this student. Click the **drop-down arrow** a second time and select **Douglas, Steven** from the combo box. Again the form is updated.

➤ Click the **navigation button** to return to the first student. The form displays the record for Maryann Jones, but the combo box is *not* updated; i.e., it still displays Douglas, Steven.

➤ Click the **View button** to return to Design view.

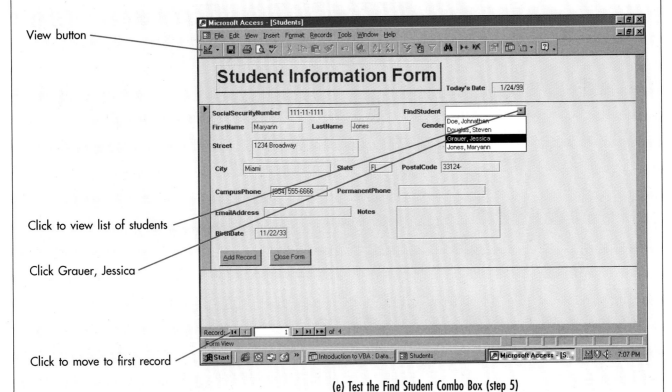

(e) Test the Find Student Combo Box (step 5)

FIGURE 8.4   Hands-on Exercise 1 (continued)

WHY USE VBA?

The combo box enables you to select a name from an alphabetical list, then updates the form to display the data for the corresponding record. All of this has been accomplished without the use of VBA. The problem is that the combo box is not updated automatically when records are selected via the navigation buttons. The only way to correct this problem is by writing a VBA procedure.

STEP 6: Create an Event Procedure

➤ Point to the **form selector box** (the tiny square at the upper left of the form), click the **right mouse button** to display a shortcut menu, then click **Properties** to display the Form property sheet.

➤ Click the **Event tab**. Click the **On Current** event, then click the **Build button** to display the Choose Builder dialog box as shown in Figure 8.4f.

➤ Click (select) **Code Builder**, then click **OK**. A VBA window will open containing the module for the Completed Student Form.

➤ If necessary, maximize the VBA window and/or click the **Procedure View button** above the status bar. The insertion point is positioned automatically within a newly created event procedure.

➤ You should see a statement beginning Private Sub Form_Current( ) corresponding to the On Current event. You should also see the line ending End Sub, but no code appears between the Sub and End Sub statements.

Point to form selector box and click right mouse button to display shortcut menu

Event tab

Click On Current

Click Code Builder

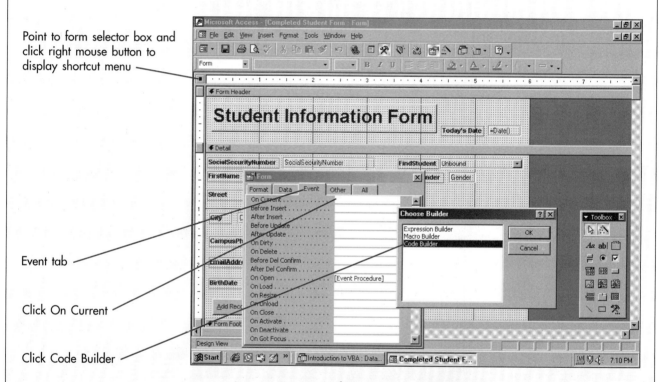

(f) Create an Event Procedure (step 6)

FIGURE 8.4 Hands-on Exercise 1 (continued)

CREATING AN EVENT PROCEDURE

There are two basic ways to create an event procedure. It can be done from the Form design view, as is done in this exercise, by right clicking the form selector box to display the form properties, clicking the Event tab to select the desired event, then clicking the Build button and selecting the Code Builder. You can also create an event procedure directly in the Module window. Either way, the procedure header and end statements are created automatically for you.

STEP 7: Complete the On Current Event Procedure

➤ The insertion point should be on a blank line, between the Sub and End Sub statements. If not, click on the blank line. Press the **Tab key** to indent. Indentation makes your code easier to read, but is not a syntactical requirement.

➤ Type **Combo37** (use the number of your combo box as determined in step 5). If you do not remember the name of the combo box, click the button on the taskbar to return to the Form window, click in the combo box and click the **All tab**. Look at the entry in the **Name property**.

➤ Press the **space bar** after you have entered the name of your combo box, type an **equal sign**, and press the **space bar** a second time. Type **Social** (the first several letters in the name of the SocialSecurityNumber control).

➤ Pull down the **Edit menu** and click **Complete Word** (or press **Ctrl+Space**) to display all of the objects, properties, and methods that start with these letters.

➤ SocialSecurityNumber is already selected as shown in Figure 8.4g. Press the **space bar** to copy the selected item and complete the statement.

➤ Click the **Save button** on the Visual Basic toolbar. Close the VBA window.

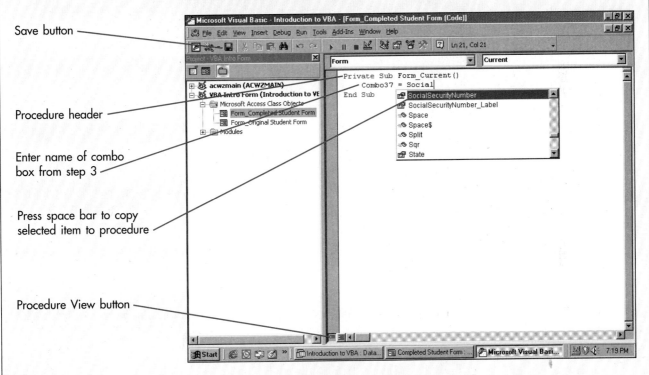

Save button

Procedure header

Enter name of combo box from step 3

Press space bar to copy selected item to procedure

Procedure View button

(g) Complete the On Current Event Procedure (step 7)

FIGURE 8.4   Hands-on Exercise 1 (continued)

USE THE RIGHT MOUSE BUTTON

The Quick Info and AutoList features are activated automatically as you create a VBA statement. The features can also be activated at any time by pulling down the Edit menu and selecting the Quick Info or List Properties/Methods commands, respectively. You can also point to any portion of a VBA statement and click the right mouse button to display a shortcut menu with options to display this information.

STEP 8: Add Your Record

➤ If necessary, click the button for the Access form on the task bar. Close the properties sheet. Click the **View button** to return to Form view.

➤ You should see the Student Information form. Click the **navigation button** to move to the next record. The data in the form are updated.

➤ Click the **navigation button** to return to the first record. Once again the data in the form are updated, as is the name in the combo box.

➤ Click the form's **Add Record command button**. You should see a blank form as shown in Figure 8.4h.

➤ Click in the SocialSecurityNumber text box and enter your social security number. Continue to enter your personal data.

➤ Close the form when you have finished entering data. Exit Access if you do not want to continue with the next exercise at this time.

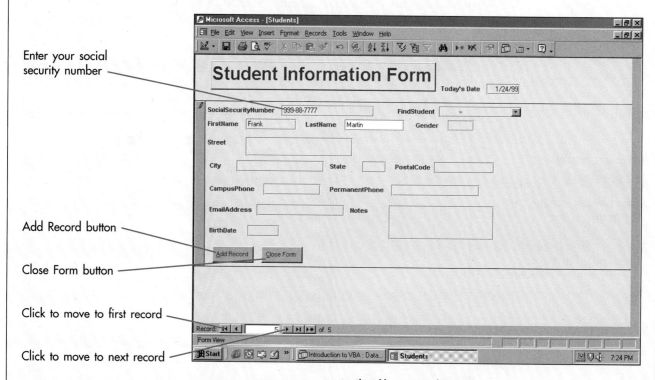

Enter your social security number

Add Record button

Close Form button

Click to move to first record

Click to move to next record

(h) Add Your Record (step 8)

FIGURE 8.4   Hands-on Exercise 1 (continued)

THE SET FOCUS METHOD

Ideally, clicking the Add Record button should position you in the SocialSecurityNumber field, without you having to click in the field to begin entering data. Open the Student form in Design view, right click the Add Record button and display the Properties dialog box. Click the Event tab, click the On Click property, then click the Build button. Insert the statement SocialSecurityNumber.SetFocus immediately after the DoCmd statement. Go to Form view, then click the Add button. You should be positioned in the SocialSecurityNumber field.

FACILITATING DATA ENTRY

One of the most useful things you can accomplish through VBA is to provide the user with shortcuts for data entry. Many forms, for example, require the user to enter the city, state, and zip code for incoming records. In certain systems, such as a local store or company, this information is likely to be repeated from one record to the next. One common approach is to use the ***Default property*** in the table definition to specify default values for these fields, so that the values are automatically entered into a record.

What if, however, there are several sets of common values? Our local store, for example, may draw customers from two or three different cities, and we need to constantly switch between the different cities. The Default property is no longer effective because it is restricted to a single value. A better solution is to use VBA to provide a set of keyboard shortcuts such as Ctrl+1 for the first city, state, and zip code, Ctrl+2 for the next set of values, and so on. The user selects the appropriate shortcut and the city, state, and zip code are entered automatically. The VBA code is shown in Figure 8.5.

Figure 8.5a displays the ***KeyDown event procedure*** to implement two shortcuts, Ctrl+1 and Ctrl+2, corresponding to Miami and Coral Springs respectively. Figure 8.5b displays the ***Click event procedure*** for the shortcut button on the data entry form (which was shown earlier in Figure 8.1). The user clicks the button and a message is displayed that describes the shortcuts. The latter is very important because the system must communicate the availability of the shortcuts to the user, else how is he or she to know that they exist?

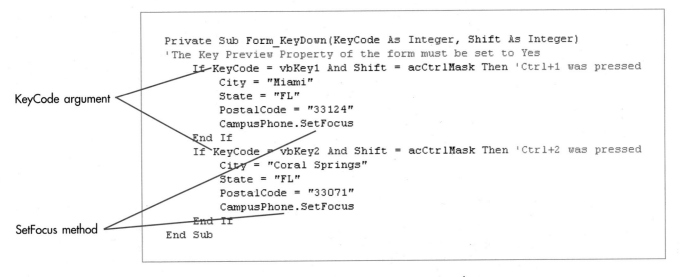

KeyCode argument

```
Private Sub Form_KeyDown(KeyCode As Integer, Shift As Integer)
'The Key Preview Property of the form must be set to Yes
    If KeyCode = vbKey1 And Shift = acCtrlMask Then 'Ctrl+1 was pressed
        City = "Miami"
        State = "FL"
        PostalCode = "33124"
        CampusPhone.SetFocus
    End If
    If KeyCode = vbKey2 And Shift = acCtrlMask Then 'Ctrl+2 was pressed
        City = "Coral Springs"
        State = "FL"
        PostalCode = "33071"
        CampusPhone.SetFocus
    End If
End Sub
```

SetFocus method

(a) Form KeyDown Event Procedure

MsgBox function

```
Private Sub ShortCutButton_Click()
    Call MsgBox("Ctrl+1 has been created as a shortcut to enter " & _
        "Miami, FL 33124. Use Ctrl+2 to enter similar data for " & _
        "Coral Springs, FL 33071", vbInformation, _
        "Grauer/Barber Introduction to VBA")
End Sub
```

(b) ShortCutButton Click Event Procedure

FIGURE 8.5   Procedure for Exercise 2

Consider now the event procedure in Figure 8.5a and think about what it takes to implement a keyboard shortcut. In essence, the procedure must determine whether the user has used any of the existing shortcuts, and if so, enter the appropriate values in the form. There are different ways to accomplish this, the easiest being through a series of If statements, each of which checks for a specific shortcut. In other words, check to see if the user pressed Ctrl+1, and if so, enter the appropriate data. Then check to see if the user pressed Ctrl+2, etc. (If you have a previous background in programming, you may recognize alternate ways to implement this logic, either through the Else clause in the If statement, or through a Case statement. We explore these alternate structures later in the chapter, but for the time being, we want to keep our statements as simple as possible.)

Once again, we ask that you try to gain an overall appreciation for the procedure as opposed to concerning yourself with every detail in every statement. You should recognize, for example, that the KeyDown event procedure requires two arguments, KeyCode and Shift, as can be seen from the parenthetical information in the procedure header. (The procedure header is created automatically as you shall see in the following hands-on exercise.)

The **KeyCode argument** tests for a specific number or letter; for example, KeyCode = vbKey1 determines whether the number 1 has been pressed by the user. (VBA defines several intrinsic constants such as vbKey1 or vbKeyA corresponding to the number 1 and letter A, respectively.) In similar fashion, the Shift argument tests for the Ctrl, Shift, or Alt key by checking for the intrinsic constants acCtrlMask, acShiftMask, and acAltMask, respectively. The And operator ensures that both keys (Ctrl and the number 1) have been pressed simultaneously.

Once a determination has been made as to whether a shortcut has been used, the corresponding values are moved to the indicated controls (City, State, and PostalCode) on the form. The **SetFocus method** then moves the insertion point to the CampusPhone control where the user can continue to enter data in the form.

The Click event procedure in Figure 8.5b contains a single VBA statement to call the MsgBox function, which displays information about the shortcuts to the user when he or she clicks the Shortcuts button. The MsgBox function has three arguments—a literal that is continued over two lines containing the text of the message, an intrinsic constant (vbInformation) indicating the icon that is to be displayed with the message, and a second literal indicating the text that is to appear in the title bar of the message dialog box.

The statement is straightforward, but it does illustrate the rules for continuing a VBA statement from one line to the next. To continue a statement, leave a space at the end of the line to be continued, type the underscore character, then continue the statement on the next line. You may not, however, break a line in the middle of a character string. Thus you need to complete the character string with a closing quotation mark, add an ampersand (as the concatenation operator to display this string with the character string on the next line), then leave a space followed by the underscore to indicate continuation.

BUILD CODE BY OBSERVATION AND INFERENCE

VBA is a powerful language with a subtle syntax and an almost endless variety of intrinsic constants. The expertise required to build the procedures for the keyboard shortcuts is beyond the novice, but once you are given the basic code, it is relatively easy to extend or modify the code to accommodate a specific application. Look at the code in Figure 8.5, for example, and decide how you would change the existing Ctrl+1 keyboard shortcut to reflect a different city. Can you add a third If statement to create a Ctrl+3 shortcut for a new city?

Facilitating Data Entry

Objective: Create keyboard shortcuts to facilitate data entry. Use Figure 8.6 as a guide in the exercise.

STEP 1: Create the KeyDown Event Procedure

➤ Open the **Introduction to VBA database** from the previous exercise. Click the **Forms button** then open the **Completed Student Form** in Design view.

➤ Pull down the **View menu** and click **Code** (or click the **Code button**) on the Database toolbar. If you are in Full Module view, click within any procedure, then click the **Procedure view button** above the status bar.

➤ Click the **down arrow** in the Event list box and select **Form**.

➤ Click the **down arrow** in the Procedure list box to display the list of events for the form. Click **KeyDown** to create a procedure for this event.

Click drop-down arrow in Event list box

Click drop-down arrow in Procedure list box

Click KeyDown

Procedure View button

Full Module View button

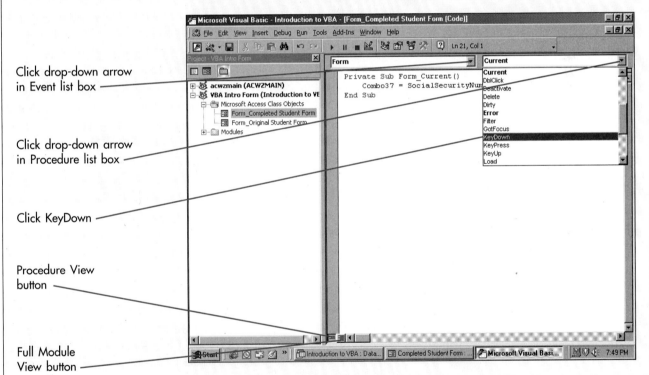

(a) Create the KeyDown Event Procedure (step 1)

FIGURE 8.6 Hands-on Exercise 2

PROCEDURE VIEW VERSUS FULL MODULE VIEW

Procedures can be displayed individually, or multiple procedures can be viewed simultaneously. Click the Procedure View button to display one procedure or click the Full Module View button to show multiple procedures. Either way, you can press Ctrl+PgDn and Ctrl+PgUp to move between procedures in the Module window.

STEP 2: Correct the Compile Error

➤ The Procedure header and End Sub statements for the KeyDown event procedure are created automatically as shown in Figure 8.6b. The insertion point is positioned on the blank line between these two statements.

➤ Type an **apostrophe** (to indicate a comment), then enter the text of the comment as shown in the figure. Press **enter** when you have completed the comment. The line turns green to indicate it is a comment.

➤ Press the **Tab key** to indent the first line of code, then enter the statement exactly as it appears in the figure. Press **enter**. You should see the error message because we made a (deliberate) error in the If statement to illustrate what happens when you make an error.

➤ Click **OK** if you know the reason for the error, or click **Help** to display a screen describing the error, then close the Help window.

➤ Now return to the VBA statement, type a space at the end of the line, and add the key word **Then** to correct the error. Press **enter** to complete the statement. The error message should not appear.

Click to close
Project Explorer window

Enter comment

Enter first line of code

A compilation error
has occurred

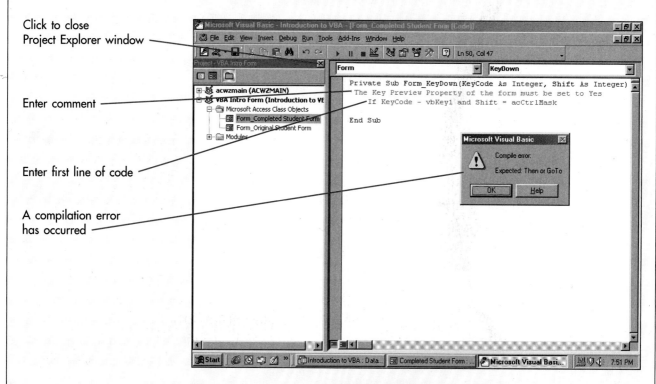

(b) Correct the Compile Error (step 2)

FIGURE 8.6 Hands-on Exercise 2 (continued)

RED, GREEN, AND BLUE

Visual Basic for Applications uses different colors for different types of statements (or a portion of those statements). Any statement containing a syntax error appears in red. Comments appear in green. Key words, such as Sub and End Sub, appear in blue.

STEP 3: Complete the KeyDown Event Procedure

➤ Close the Project Explorer window and complete the KeyDown procedure as shown in Figure 8.6c. Use what you know about the Cut, Copy, and Paste commands to facilitate entering the code.

➤ You could, for example, copy the first If statement, then modify the code as appropriate, rather then typing it from scratch. Select the statements to cut or copy to the clipboard, then paste them elsewhere in the module.

➤ If the results are different from what you expected or intended, click the Undo command immediately to reverse the effects of the previous command.

➤ Be sure that your code matches the code in Figure 8.6c. The indentation is not a syntactical requirement of VBA, but is used to make the statements easier to read. Click the **Save button** to save the module.

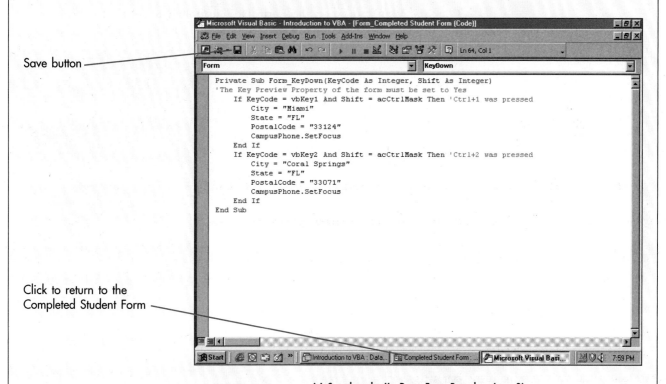

(c) Complete the KeyDown Event Procedure (step 3)

FIGURE 8.6   Hands-on Exercise 2 (continued)

THE COMPLETE WORD TOOL

You know that your form contains a control to reference the postal code, but you are not quite sure of the spelling. The Complete Word tool can help. Enter the first several characters, then press Ctrl+Space (or pull down the Edit menu and click Complete Word). VBA will complete the term for you if you have entered a sufficient number of letters, or it will display all of the objects, properties, and methods that begin with the letters you have entered. Use the down arrow to scroll through the list until you find the item, then press the space bar to complete the entry.

STEP 4: Set the Key Preview Property

➤ The Key Preview property of the form must be set to Yes in order to complete the keyboard shortcut. Click the taskbar button to return to the **Completed Student Form**.

➤ Point to the **form selector box** (the tiny square at the upper left of the form). Click the **right mouse button** to display a context-sensitive menu with commands for the entire form.

➤ Click **Properties** to display the Form Properties dialog box. Click the **Event tab** and scroll until you can click the **Key Preview property**. Change the property to **Yes** as shown in Figure 8.6d.

➤ Close the Form Property dialog box. Save the form which now contains the new procedure for the keyboard shortcut. The procedure should be tested as soon as it completed.

➤ Click the **View button** on the Form Design toolbar to return to Form view.

View button

Point to the form selector box and click the right mouse button

Event tab

Click Key Preview property

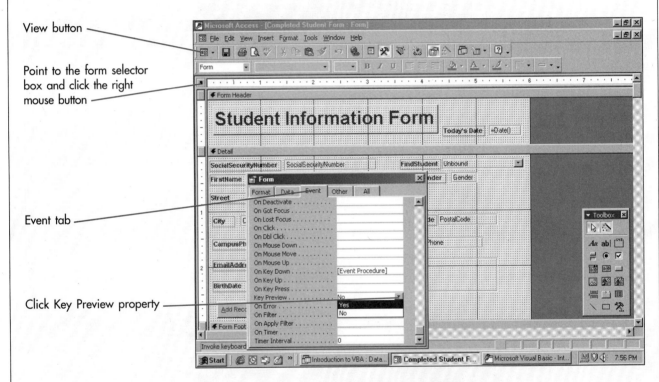

(d) Set the Key Preview Property (step 4)

FIGURE 8.6   Hands-on Exercise 2 (continued)

USE THE PROPERTY SHEET

Every object on a form has its own property sheet. This enables you to change the appearance or behavior of a control in two ways—by changing the control through application of a menu command or toolbar button, or by changing the underlying property sheet. Anything you do to the control changes the associated property, and conversely, any change to the property sheet is reflected in the appearance or behavior of the control.

STEP 5: Test the Procedure

➤ Click the **navigation button** to move to the first record in the table as shown in Figure 8.6e. Press **Ctrl+1** to change the City, State, and Postal Code to reflect Miami, as per the shortcut you just created.

➤ The data change automatically and you are automatically positioned on the Campus Phone field. The record selector changes to a pencil to indicate that the data has been edited, but not yet saved.

➤ If the shortcut does not work, return to step 4 and check that the Key Preview property has been set to Yes. If the shortcut still does not work, return to the module for the form and check the VBA statements.

➤ Press **Ctrl+2** to change the city to Coral Springs. The data should change automatically, after which you are positioned in the Campus Phone field.

➤ Click the **View button** to return to the Design view of the form.

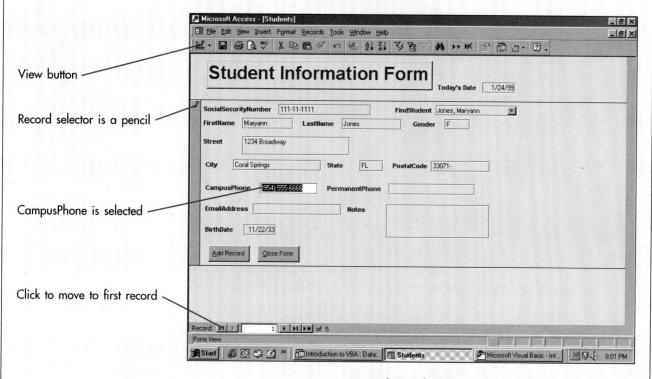

(e) Test the Procedure (step 5)

FIGURE 8.6 Hands-on Exercise 2 (continued)

CHANGE THE TAB ORDER

The Tab key provides a shortcut in the finished form to move from one field to the next; that is, you press Tab to move forward to the next field and Shift+Tab to return to the previous field. The order in which fields are selected corresponds to the sequence in which the controls were entered onto the form, and need not correspond to the physical appearance of the actual form. To restore a left-to-right, top-to-bottom sequence, pull down the View menu, click Tab Order, then select AutoOrder.

STEP 6: Create the ShortCut Command Button

➤ Click and drag the **Command Button tool** on the Toolbox toolbar to create a new command button as shown in Figure 8.6f.

➤ The Command Button Wizard starts automatically. This time, however, you want to create the Click event procedure for this button yourself.

➤ Click the **Cancel button** as soon as you see the Wizard. Right click the newly created command button and display its property sheet. Click the **All tab**.

➤ Change the Name property to **ShortCutButton**. Change the Caption property to **&ShortCuts**.

➤ Click the **Event tab**. Click the **On Click property**, click the **Build button**, click **Code Builder**, then click **OK** to display the Module window.

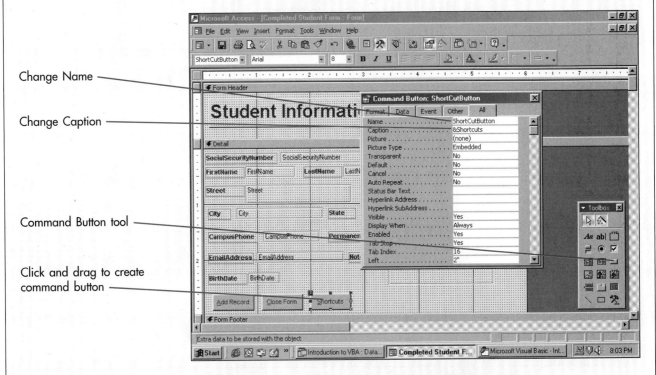

Change Name

Change Caption

Command Button tool

Click and drag to create
command button

(f) Create the ShortCut Command Button (step 6)

FIGURE 8.6 Hands-on Exercise 2 (continued)

ACCELERATOR KEYS AND THE CAPTION PROPERTY

The Caption property enables you to create a keyboard shortcut for a command button. Right click the button in the Form Design view to display the Properties dialog box for the command button. Click the All tab, then modify the Caption property to include an ampersand immediately in front of the letter that will be used in the shortcut (e.g., &Help if you have a Help button). Close the dialog box then go to Form view. The command button will contain an underlined letter (e.g., Help) that can be activated in conjunction with the Alt key (e.g. Alt+H) as a shortcut or accelerator key.

STEP 7: Create the OnClick Procedure

➤ You should be positioned on the blank line in the ShortCutButton_Click procedure, as shown in Figure 8.6g. Press the **Tab key** to indent, then enter the VBA statement exactly as it is shown in the figure. Note the following:

- A tip (known as "Quick Info") appears as soon as you type the left parenthesis after the MsgBox function. The tip displays the syntax of the function and lists its arguments.

- Indentation is not a requirement of VBA per se, but is done to make the VBA code easier to read. Continuation is also optional and is done to make the code easier to read.

➤ Complete the statement exactly as shown in the figure, except substitute your name for Grauer/Barber. Click the **Save button**. Close the Module window.

➤ Size and align the new button. Save the form. Click the **View button**.

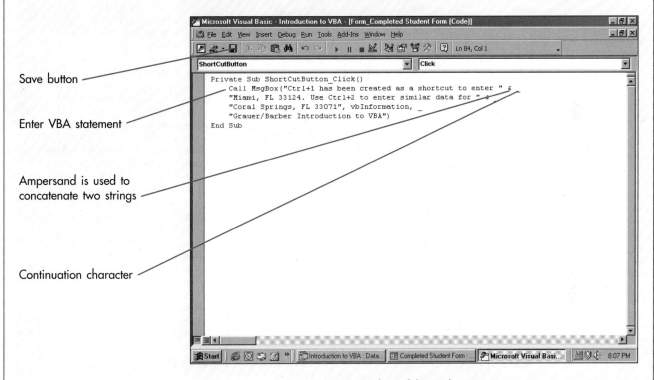

(g) Create the OnClick Procedure (step 7)

FIGURE 8.6   Hands-on Exercise 2 (continued)

THE MSGBOX FUNCTION

The MsgBox function has three arguments—the text of the message to be displayed, the number of buttons and type of message, and the text that appears on the title bar. The message itself is divided into multiple character strings, which continue from one line to the next. The ampersand concatenates the two character strings to display a single message. The underscore character indicates that the statement is continued to the next line.

STEP 8: Test the ShortCuts Button

➤ Click the **ShortCuts button**. You can also use the keyboard shortcut, Alt+S, as indicated by the underlined letter on the button name that was established through the Caption property for the button.

➤ You should see the message box that is displayed in Figure 8.6h. Your name should appear in the title bar of the dialog box rather than ours. Click **OK** to close the dialog box.

➤ Try the other shortcuts that have been built into the form. Press **Ctrl+1** and **Ctrl+2** to switch back and forth between Miami and Coral Springs, respectively. Press **Alt+C** to close the form. Not everyone prefers the keyboard to the mouse, but you have nonetheless created a powerful set of shortcuts.

➤ Exit Access if you do not want to continue with the next exercise at this time.

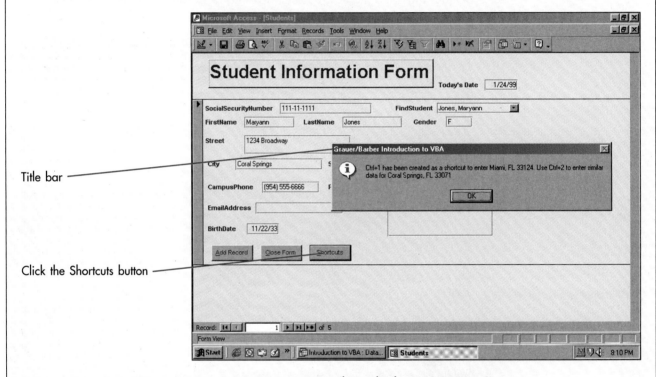

Title bar

Click the Shortcuts button

(h) Test the ShortCuts Button (step 8)

FIGURE 8.6   Hands-on Exercise 2 (continued)

CREATE UNIFORM COMMAND BUTTONS

A form is made more appealing if all of its command buttons have similar properties. Change to Design view, then press and hold the Shift key as you select each of the command buttons. Pull down the Format menu, click Size, then choose the desired parameters for all of the buttons such as widest and tallest. (You have to execute the command once for each parameter.) Leave the buttons selected, pull down the Format menu, select the Align command, then choose the desired alignment. Pull down the Format menu a final time, select the Horizontal Spacing command, then implement the desired (e.g., uniform) spacing for the buttons.

It is not a question of whether errors in data entry will occur, but rather how quickly a user will understand the nature of those errors in order to take the appropriate corrective action. If, for example, a user attempts to add a duplicate record for an existing customer, Access will display an error message of the form, "changes to the table were not successful because they would create duplicate values of the primary key." The issue is whether this message is clear to the nontechnical individual who is doing the data entry.

An experienced Access programmer will realize immediately that Access is preventing the addition of the duplicate record because another record with the same primary key (e.g., a social security or account number) is already in the file. A nontechnical user, however, may not understand the message because he or she does not know the meaning of "primary key." Wouldn't it be easier if the system displayed a message indicating that a customer with that social security or account number is already in the file? In other words, errors invariably occur, but it is important that the message the user sees clearly indicates the problem.

Figure 8.7 displays the event procedure that is developed in the next hands-on exercise to display application-specific error messages in place of the standard messages provided by Access. The procedure is triggered any time there is an error in data entry. Realize, however, that there are literally hundreds of errors and it is necessary to test for each error for which we want a substitute message. Each error has a unique error number, and thus the first task is to determine the number associated for the error you want to detect. This is accomplished by forcing the error to occur, then printing the error number in the *Immediate window* (a special window within the VBA editor that enables you to display results of a procedure as it is executing). It's easier than it sounds, as you will see in the hands-on exercise.

Once you know the error numbers, you can complete the procedure by checking for the errors that you wish to trap, then displaying the appropriate error messages. One way to implement this logic is through a series of individual If statements, with one If statement for each error. It is more efficient, however, to use a Case statement as shown in Figure 8.7.

The *Case statement* tests the value of an incoming variable (DataErr in our example, which contains the error number), then goes to the appropriate set of statements depending on the value of that variable. Our procedure tests for two errors, but it could be easily expanded to check for additional errors. Error 2237 occurs if the user attempts to find a record that is not in the table. Error 3022 results when the user attempts to add a duplicate record. Once an error is detected, the Call MsgBox function is used to display the error message we create, after which Access will continue processing without displaying the default error message.

Note, too, the last case (Else) which is executed when Access detects an error other than 2237 or 3022. This time we do not display our own message because we do not know the nature of the error. Instead we set the Response variable to the intrinsic constant acDataErrContinue, which causes Access to display the default error message for the error that occurred.

Figure 8.7b displays the *General Declarations section,* which contains statements that apply to every procedure in the form. The section defines the constant ApplicationName as a string and sets it to the literal value "John Doe did his homework." Note, too, how the two MsgBox statements in Figure 8.7a reference this constant as the third argument and recall that this argument contains the text that is displayed on the title bar of the message box. In other words we can change the value of the ApplicationName constant in one place, and have that change reflected automatically in every MsgBox function.

```
Private Sub Form_Error(DataErr As Integer, Response As Integer)
' You need to determine the specific error number in order to trap the error. Thus:
'    1. Create the error in Access to determine the error number
'    2. Use the Print method of the Debug object to display the error
'    3. Press Ctrl+G to open the Immediate window where the error will be displayed

    Debug.Print "Error Number = ", DataErr

    Select Case DataErr
        Case 2237
            Call MsgBox("The student is not in our file. Please " & _
                "check the spelling and reenter correctly, or click the " & _
                "Add button to enter a new record.", vbExclamation, _
                ApplicationName)
            Response = acDataErrContinue
        Case 3022
            Call MsgBox("You are trying to add a student whose " & _
                "social security number is already in the file. Please " & _
                "correct the social security number or cancel this " & _
                "record and move to the original record.", vbExclamation, _
                ApplicationName)
            Response = acDataErrContinue

        Case Else
            Response = acDataErrDisplay
    End Select
End Sub
```

Error numbers

Call MsgBox displays
error message

(a) Form Error Event Procedure

ApplicationName
constant

```
Option Compare Database
Option Explicit

Const ApplicationName As String = "John Doe has done his homework"
```

(b) General Declarations Section

FIGURE 8.7   Procedures for Exercise 3

THE CASE STATEMENT

The Case statement tests the value of a variable, then branches to one of several sets of statements depending on the value of that variable. You may not be able to write a Case statement intially, but once you see the statement you can extend the code to accommodate any application. Look at the code in Figure 8.7, for example, and decide the required modifications to reflect employees rather than students. How would you extend the existing Case statement to include an additional error message?

Error Trapping

Objective: To create an event procedure that substitutes application-specific messages for the standard Access error messages. Use Figure 8.8 as a guide.

STEP 1: Force the Error Message

➤ Open the **Introduction to VBA database**. If necessary, click the **Forms button**, then open the **Completed Student Form** in Form view.

➤ Click and drag to select the name in the Find Student combo box. Type **XXXX** (an obviously invalid name). Press **enter**. You should see the error message in Figure 8.8a, which may be confusing to a nontechnical user.

➤ Click **OK** to close the message box. Press the **Esc key** to erase the XXXX, since we are not interested in finding this student. Change to Design view.

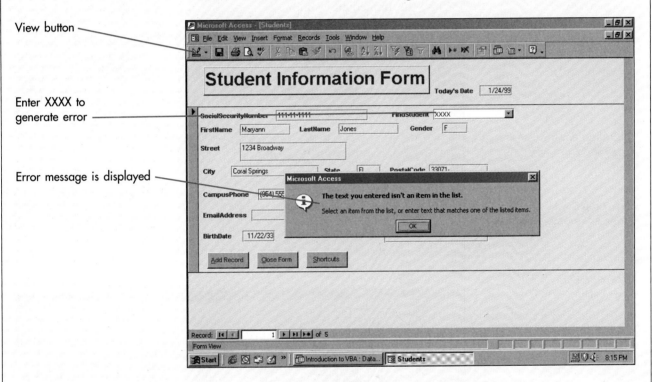

View button

Enter XXXX to generate error

Error message is displayed

(a) Force the Error Message (step 1)

FIGURE 8.8 Hands-on Exercise 3

THE MOST RECENTLY OPENED FILE LIST

The easiest way to open a recently used database is to select it from the Microsoft Access dialog box that appears when Access is started initially. Check to see if your database appears on the list of the four most recently opened databases, and if so, simply double click the database to open it. The list of the most recently opened databases can also be found at the bottom of the File menu.

STEP 2: Determine the Error Number

➤ Pull down the **View menu** and click **Code** (or click the **Code button** on the Form Design toolbar) to display the Module window. If necessary, click the **down arrow** for the Object box and select the **Form object**.

➤ Click the **down arrow** in the Procedure box and click **Error** to display the event procedure that will execute when an error occurs in the form. Click the **Procedure View button** as shown in Figure 8.8b.

➤ We created this procedure for you. It consists of a single executable statement, to print a literal, followed by the number of the error. The comments explain how to use the procedure.

➤ Pull down the **View menu** and click **Immediate window** (or press **Ctrl+G**) to open the Immediate window. You should see number 2237.

➤ This is the error number reserved by Access to indicate that the value that was entered in the text portion of a combo box does not match any of the entries in the associated list.

➤ Close the Immediate window.

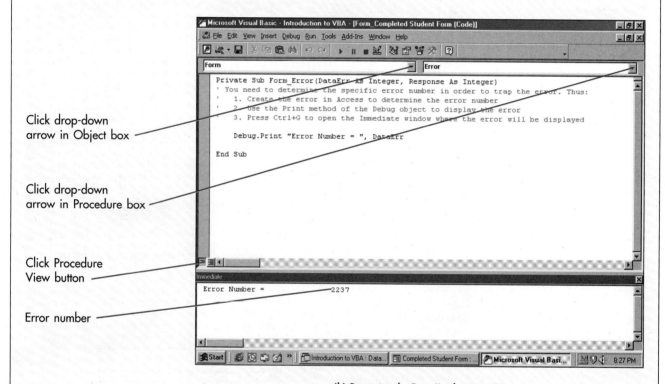

Click drop-down arrow in Object box

Click drop-down arrow in Procedure box

Click Procedure View button

Error number

(b) Determine the Error Number (step 2)

FIGURE 8.8   Hands-on Exercise 3 (continued)

INSTANT CALCULATOR

Use the Print method (action) in the Immediate window to use VBA as a calculator. Press Ctrl+G at any time to display the Immediate window. Type the statement Debug.Print, followed by your calculation, for example, Debug.Print 2+2, then press enter. The answer is displayed on the next line in the Immediate window.

STEP 3: Trap the First Error

➤ Click in the event procedure at the end of the Debug statement, press the **enter key** twice, then enter the code in Figure 8.8c. Note the following:

- Comments appear at the beginning of the procedure.

- The Case statement tests the value of an incoming variable (DataErr), then goes to the appropriate set of statements depending on the value of that variable. The procedure currently tests for only one error, but it will be expanded later in the exercise to check for additional errors.

- The indentation and blank lines within the procedure are not requirements of VBA per se, but are used to make the code easier to read.

- A "Quick Info" tip appears as soon as you type the left parenthesis after the MsgBox function. The tip displays the syntax of the function.

➤ Complete the statement exactly as shown in Figure 8.8c. Save the procedure.

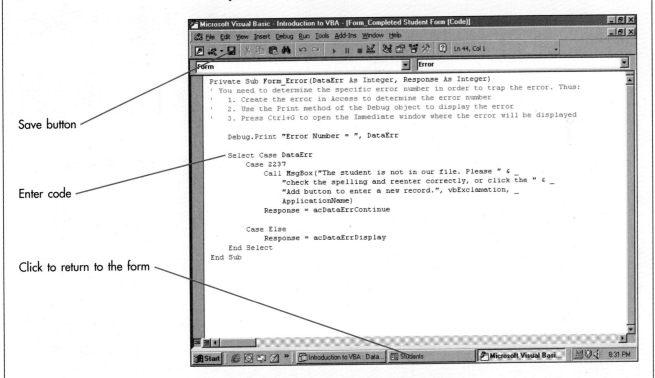

(c) Trap the First Error (step 3)

FIGURE 8.8   Hands-on Exercise 3 (continued)

CONTINUING A VBA STATEMENT—THE & AND THE UNDERSCORE

A VBA statement can be continued from one line to the next by leaving a space at the end of the line to be continued, typing the underscore character, then continuing on the next line. You may not, however, break a line in the middle of a literal (character string). Thus you need to complete the character string with a closing quotation mark, add an ampersand (as the concatenation operator to display this string with the character string on the next line), then leave a space followed by the underscore to indicate continuation.

STEP 4: Test the Error Event Procedure

➤ Click the taskbar button to return to the **Completed Student Form**. Change to the Form view. Click and drag to select the name in the Find Student combo box. Type **XXXX** (an obviously invalid name). Press **enter**.

➤ This time you should see the error message in Figure 8.8d corresponding to the text you entered in the previous step. (Note the title bar on the dialog box indicating that your name goes here. We tell you how to modify the title bar later in the exercise.)

➤ Click **OK** to close the message box. Press the **Esc key** to erase the XXXX. Return to Design view.

➤ Pull down the **View menu** and click **Code** (or click the **Code button** on the Form Design toolbar) to display the Module window.

Enter XXXX to create the error

The modified error message is displayed

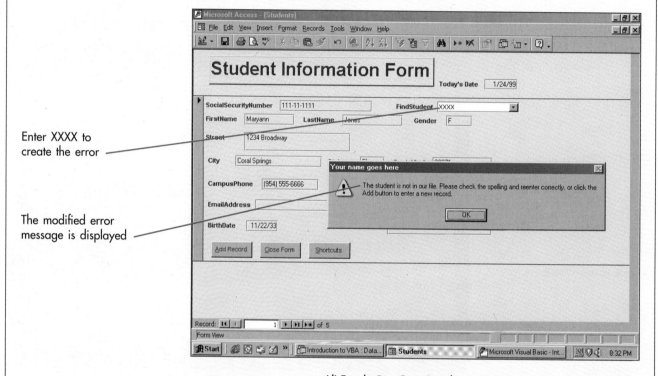

(d) Test the Error Event Procedure (step 4)

FIGURE 8.8   Hands-on Exercise 3 (continued)

THE FIRST BUG

A bug is a mistake in a computer program; hence debugging refers to the process of correcting program errors. According to legend, the first bug was an unlucky moth crushed to death on one of the relays of the electro-mechanical Mark II computer, bringing the machine's operation to a halt. The cause of the failure was discovered by Grace Hopper, who promptly taped the moth to her logbook, noting, "First actual case of bug being found."

STEP 5: Change the Application Name

➤ Click the **down arrow** for the Object box and select **(General)** at the beginning of the list of objects.

➤ We have defined the Visual Basic constant **ApplicationName**, and initialized it to "Your name goes here." This was the text that appeared in the title bar of the dialog box in the previous step.

➤ Click and drag to select **Your name goes here**. Enter **John Doe has done his homework**, substituting your name for John Doe.

➤ Pull down the **Edit menu**, click the **Find command** to display the Find dialog box. Enter ApplicationName in the Find What text box. Specify the option to search the **Current module** and specify **All** as the direction.

➤ Click the **Find Next command button** to locate all occurrences of the ApplicationName constant. Can you appreciate the significance of this technique to customize your application? Save the procedure.

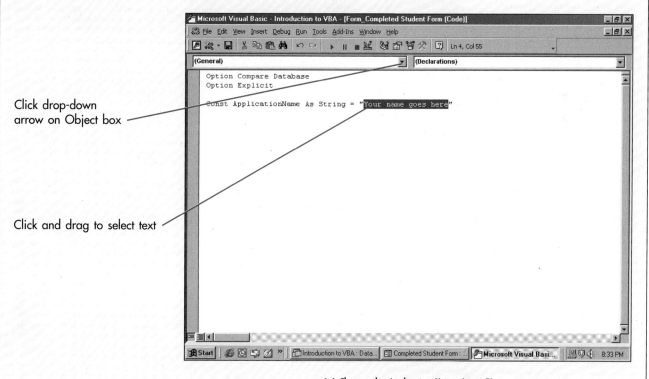

Click drop-down arrow on Object box

Click and drag to select text

(e) Change the Application Name (step 5)

FIGURE 8.8   Hands-on Exercise 3 (continued)

THE MSGBOX FUNCTION—CONSTANTS VERSUS LITERALS

The third argument of the MsgBox function can be entered as a literal such as "John Doe's Application." It's preferable, however, to specify the argument as a constant such as ApplicationName, then define that constant in the Declarations section. That way, you can change the name of the application in one place, and have the change automatically reflected in every MsgBox statement that references the constant.

STEP 6: Complete the Error Event Procedure

➤ Click the **down arrow** for the Object box and select the **Form object**. Click the **down arrow** for the Procedure box and click the **Error procedure**.

➤ Click immediately before the Case Else statement, then enter the additional code shown in Figure 8.8f. Use the Copy and Paste commands to enter the second Case statement. Thus:

- Click and drag to select the first Case statement, click the Copy button, click above the Case Else statement, and click the Paste button.

- Modify the copied statements as necessary, rather than typing the statements from scratch. Use the Ins key to toggle between insertion and replacement. Be sure that your code matches ours.

➤ Click the **Save button** to save the procedure. Click the taskbar button to return to the **Completed Student Form**.

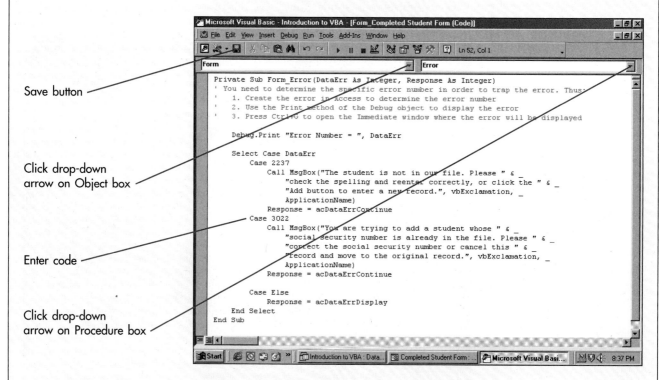

(f) Complete the Error Event Procedure (step 6)

FIGURE 8.8 Hands-on Exercise 3 (continued)

THE OBJECT AND PROCEDURE BOXES

The Object box at the top left of the Module window displays the current object, such as a form or a control on the form. The Procedure box displays the name of the current procedure for the selected object. To create or navigate between events for a form, click the down arrow on the Object box to select the Form object, then click the down arrow on the Procedure box to display the list of events. Events that already have procedures appear in bold. Clicking an event that is not bold creates the procedure header and End Sub statements for that event.

STEP 7: Complete the Testing

➤ You should be back in Design view of the Completed Student Form. Pull down the **View menu** and change to the **Datasheet view** as shown in Figure 8.8g. (You can also click the **down arrow** next to the View button on the Form Design view and select Datasheet view.)

➤ Enter **222-22-2222** as a duplicate social security number for the first record. Press the **down arrow** (or click the appropriate navigation button) to attempt to move to the next record.

➤ You should see the error message in Figure 8.8g. The title bar displays the value of the application name entered earlier in the exercise.

➤ Click **OK** (or press **Esc**) to close the dialog box. Press **Esc** (a second time) to restore the original value of the social security number. Close the window.

➤ Exit Access if you do not want to continue with the next exercise at this time.

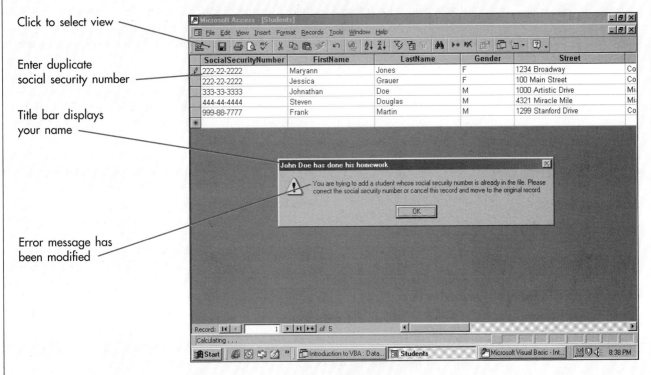

Click to select view

Enter duplicate social security number

Title bar displays your name

Error message has been modified

(g) Complete the Testing (step 7)

FIGURE 8.8 Hands-on Exercise 3 (continued)

LISTEN TO YOUR USER

One source of continual frustration to the end user are error messages steeped in technical jargon. What's obvious to you as a developer or student is often beyond the unsophisticated end user. Thus, anything that you can do to simplify a system will increase its chances for success. Listen to your users. Find out where they are having trouble and what they don't understand, then act accordingly.

DATA VALIDATION

Data validation is a crucial component of any system. The most basic type of validation is implemented automatically, without any additional effort on the part of the developer. A user cannot, for example, enter data that does not conform to the designated field type. The user cannot enter text into a numeric field, nor can one enter an invalid date such as February 30 into a date field. Access also prevents you from entering a duplicate record (i.e., a record with the same primary key as another record).

Other validation checks are implemented by the developer, at either the field or record level. The former performs the validation as soon as you move from one field to the next within a table or form. The latter waits until all of the fields have been completed, then checks the entire record prior to updating the record. Both types of validation are essential to prevent invalid data from corrupting the system.

The developer can also use VBA to extend the data validation capabilities within Access. You can, for example, write an event procedure to remind the user that a field is empty and ask whether the record should be saved anyway. The field is not required and hence the Required property is not appropriate. However, you do not want to ignore the omitted field completely, and thus you need to create a VBA procedure.

The VBA code in Figure 8.9 implements this type of check through a ***nested If*** statement in which one If statement is contained inside of another. The second (inner) If statement is executed only if the first statement is true. Thus, we first check to see whether the e-mail address has been omitted, and if it has, we ask the user whether he or she wants to save the record anyway.

The outer If statement in Figure 8.9, *If IsNull (EmailAddress),* checks to see if the e-mail address is blank, and if it is, it executes the second If statement that contains a MsgBox function. Recall that the MsgBox function has three arguments—the text of the message, the Visual Basic intrinsic constant that specifies the command buttons and/or the type of icon that appear within the message box, and the text that is to appear on the title bar of the message.

Look carefully at the second argument, *vbYesNo + vbQuestion* within Figure 8.9. The intrinsic constant vbYesNo displays two command buttons (Yes and No) within the message box. The If in front of the message box function enables VBA to test the user's response and branch accordingly. Thus, if the user clicks the No button, the save operation is cancelled and the focus moves to the EmailAddress control in the form where the user enters the address. If, however, the user clicks the Yes button, the If statement is false and the record is saved without the e-mail address.

If statement —

Nested If statement —

```
Private Sub Form_BeforeUpdate(Cancel As Integer)
    If IsNull(EmailAddress) Then
        If MsgBox("You did not enter an e-mail address. Save anyway?", _
            vbYesNo + vbQuestion, ApplicationName) = vbNo Then
            Cancel = True
            EmailAddress.SetFocus
        End If
    End If
End Sub
```

FIGURE 8.9   Procedure for Exercise 4

Data Validation

Objective: To use Field and Table properties to implement different types of data validation. Use Figure 8.10 as a guide in the exercise.

STEP 1: Set the Field Properties

➤ Open the **Introduction to VBA database**. Click the **Tables button**, then open the **Students table** in Design view as shown in Figure 8.10a.

➤ Click the field selector column for the **Gender**. Click the **Validation Rule** box. Type **="M" or "F"** to accept only these values on data entry.

➤ Click the **Validation Text** box. Type **Please enter either M or F as the gender**.

➤ Click the **Required property** and change its value to **Yes**.

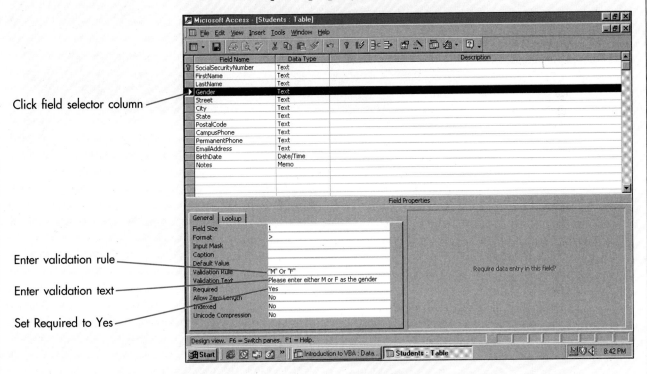

(a) Set the Field Properties (step 1)

FIGURE 8.10 Hands-on Exercise 4

OPTIMIZE DATA TYPES AND FIELD SIZES

The data type property determines the data that can be accepted into a field and the operations that can be performed on that data. Any field that is intended for use in a calculation should be given the numeric data type. You can, however, increase the efficiency of an Access database by specifying the appropriate value for the Field Size property of a numeric field. The Byte, Integer, and Long Integer field sizes hold values up to 256, 32,767, and 2,147,483,648, respectively.

STEP 2: Set the Table Properties

➤ Point to the **selector box** in the upper left corner, then click the **right mouse button** and display the Table Properties dialog box as shown in Figure 8.10b.

➤ Click in the **Validation Rule box** and enter **[CampusPhone] Is Not Null Or [PermanentPhone] Is Not Null** to ensure that the user enters one phone number or the other. (The field names should not contain any spaces and are enclosed in square brackets.)

➤ Press **enter**, then type, **You must enter either a campus or permanent phone number** (which is the validation text that will be displayed in the event of an error).

➤ Click the **Save button** to save the table. Click **No** when you see the message asking whether existing data should be tested against the new rules.

➤ Close the Table Properties dialog box. Close the Students table.

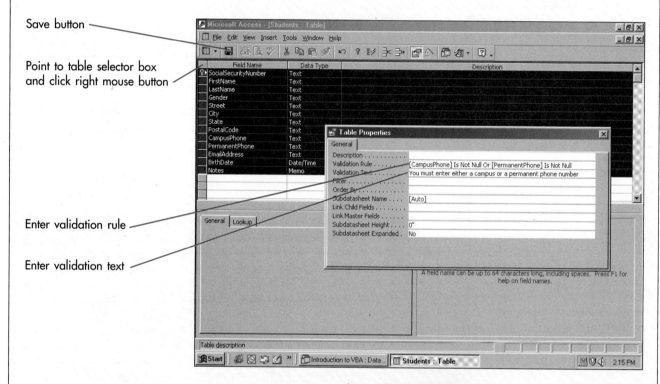

Save button

Point to table selector box and click right mouse button

Enter validation rule

Enter validation text

(b) Set the Table Properties (step 2)

FIGURE 8.10   Hands-on Exercise 4 (continued)

DAY PHONE OR PERMANENT PHONE

You can set the required property of a field to force the user to enter data for that field. But what if you wanted the user to enter one of two fields and were indifferent to which field was chosen? Setting the Required property of either or both fields would not accomplish your goal. Thus, you need to implement this type of validation at the record (rather than the field) level by setting the properties of the table as a whole, rather than the properties of the individual fields.

STEP 3: Test the Validation Rules

➤ Open the Completed Student Form in Form view. If necessary, move to Maryann Jones, the first record in the table.

➤ Click and drag to select the gender field, then type **X** to replace the gender. Press **enter**. You will see an error message pertaining to the gender field.

➤ Press **Esc** (or click **OK**) to close the dialog box. Press **Esc** a second time to restore the original value.

➤ Click and drag to select the existing Campus Phone number, then press the **Del key** to erase the phone number. Press the **Tab key** to move to the Permanent Phone field. Both phone numbers should be blank.

➤ Click the ➤ **button** to move to the next record. You should see the error message in Figure 8.10c pertaining to the table properties.

➤ Press **Esc** (or click **OK**) to close the dialog box. Press **Esc** a second time to restore the original value.

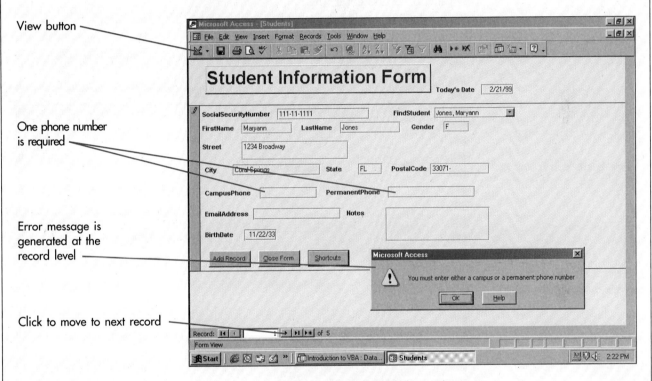

(c) Test the Validation Rules (step 3)

FIGURE 8.10   Hands-on Exercise 4 (continued)

VALIDATING AT THE FIELD VERSUS THE RECORD LEVEL

Data validation is performed at the field or record level. If it is done at the field level (e.g., by specifying the Required and Validation Rule properties for a specific field), Access checks the entry immediately as soon as you exit the field. If it is done at the record level, however (e.g., by checking that one of two fields has been entered), Access has to wait until it has processed every field in the record. Thus, it is only on attempting to move to the next record that Access informs you of the error.

STEP 4: Create the BeforeUpdate Event Procedure

➤ Change to the Form Design view. Pull down the **View menu** and click **Code** (or click the **Code button**) on the Form Design toolbar. If necessary, click the **Procedure view button** to view one procedure at a time.

➤ Click the **down arrow** on the Objects list box and click **Form**. Click the **down arrow** on the Procedure list box to display the list of events for the form. Click **BeforeUpdate** to create a procedure for this event.

➤ Press the **Tab key** to indent, then enter the statements exactly as shown in Figure 8.10d. Note that as soon as you enter "EmailAddress," Access displays the methods and properties for the EmailAddress control.

➤ Type **set** (the first three letters in the SetFocus method), watching the screen as you enter each letter. Access moves through the displayed list automatically, until it arrives at the **SetFocus method**. Press **enter**.

➤ Add an **End If** statement to complete the If statement testing the MsgBox function. Press **enter**, then enter a second **End If** statement to complete the If statement testing the IsNull condition. Save the procedure.

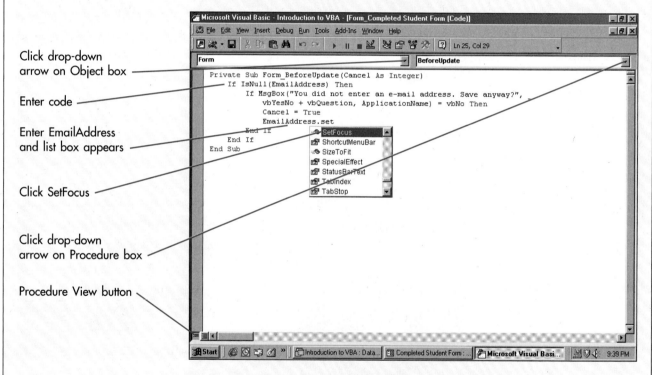

Click drop-down arrow on Object box

Enter code

Enter EmailAddress and list box appears

Click SetFocus

Click drop-down arrow on Procedure box

Procedure View button

(d) Create the BeforeUpdate Event Procedure (step 4)

FIGURE 8.10 Hands-on Exercise 4 (continued)

AUTOLIST MEMBERS—HELP IN WRITING CODE

Access displays the methods and properties for a control as soon as you enter the period after the control name. Type the first several letters to select the method or property. Press the space bar to accept the selected item and remain on the same line or press the enter key to accept the item and begin a new line.

STEP 5: Test the BeforeUpdate Event Procedure

➤ Click the taskbar button for the Access form. Change to the Form view. Click in the **memo field** and enter the text shown in Figure 8.10e.

➤ Check the remaining fields, but be sure to leave the e-mail address blank. Click the navigation button to (attempt to) move to the next record.

➤ You should see the error message in Figure 8.10e. Note the entry in the title bar that corresponds to the value of the ApplicationName constant you entered earlier.

➤ Click **No** to cancel the operation, close the dialog box, and automatically position the insertion point within the text box for the e-mail address.

➤ Enter an e-mail address such as **mjones@anyschool.edu**, then move to the next record. This time Access does not display the error message and saves the record.

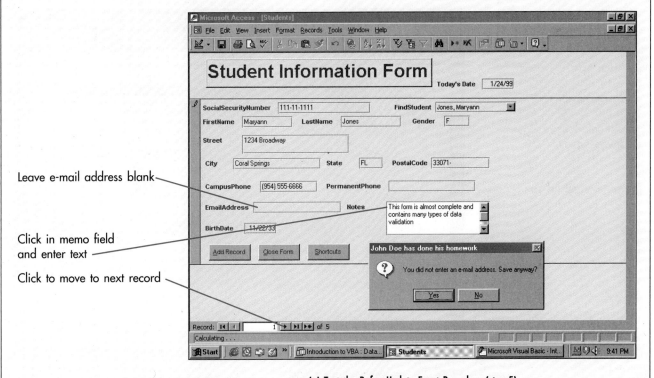

Leave e-mail address blank

Click in memo field and enter text

Click to move to next record

(e) Test the BeforeUpdate Event Procedure (step 5)

FIGURE 8.10   Hands-on Exercise 4 (continued)

MEMO FIELDS VERSUS TEXT FIELDS

A text field can store up to 255 characters. A memo field, however, can store up to 64,000 characters and is used to hold descriptive data that runs for several sentences, paragraphs, or even pages. A vertical scroll bar appears in the Form view when the memo field contains more data than is visible at one time. Note, too, that both text and memo fields store only the characters that have been entered; i.e., there is no wasted space if the data does not extend to the maximum field size.

STEP 6: Create the CloseForm Event Procedure

➤ Change to the **Form Design view**, then click the **Code button** on the Form Design toolbar to display the Module window. If necessary, click the **Object box** to select Form, then click the **Procedure box** to select the **Close event**.

➤ You should see the partially completed event procedure in Figure 8.10f. Press **Tab** to indent the statement, then enter **Call MsgBox** followed by a **left parenthesis**. The Quick Info feature displays the syntax of this function.

➤ Complete the message, ending with the closing quotation mark and comma. The AutoList feature displays the list of appropriate arguments. Type **vbc**, at which point you can select the **vbCritical** parameter by typing a **comma**.

➤ Type a **space** followed by an **underscore** to continue the statement to the next line. Enter **ApplicationName** as the last parameter by a closing **right parenthesis**. Save the module.

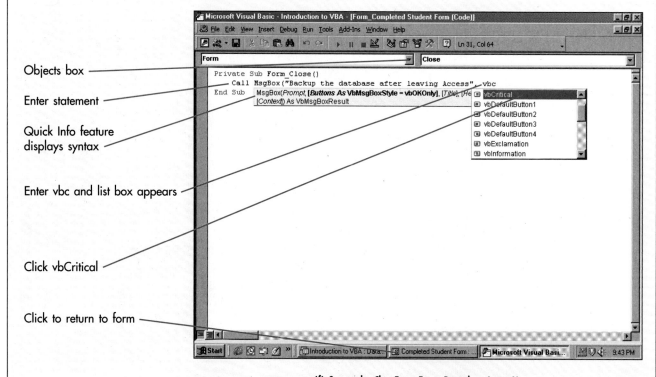

Objects box

Enter statement

Quick Info feature displays syntax

Enter vbc and list box appears

Click vbCritical

Click to return to form

(f) Create the CloseForm Event Procedure (step 6)

FIGURE 8.10   Hands-on Exercise 4 (continued)

CHOOSE THE RIGHT EVENT

We associated the message prompting the user to back up the database with the Close event for the form. Would it work equally well if the message were associated with the Click event of the Close Form command button? The answer is no, because the user could bypass the command button and close the form by pulling down the File menu and choosing the Close command, and thus never see the message. Choosing the right object and associated event is one of the subtleties in VBA.

STEP 7: Close the Form

➤ Click the Access form button on the taskbar. Return to Form view. The form looks very similar to the form with which we began, but it has been enhanced in subtle ways:

- The drop-down list box has been added to locate a specific student.
- Accelerator keys have been created for the command buttons (e.g., Alt+A to add a record).
- The SetFocus property was used to position the insertion point directly in the Social Security text box to add a new record.
- The Ctrl+1 and Ctrl+2 keyboard shortcuts have been created.
- The data validation has been enhanced through custom error messages.
- The application has been customized through the entry on the title bar.

➤ Click the **Close Form button** to display the dialog box in Figure 8.10g. Click **OK** to close the dialog box, which in turn closes the form.

➤ Close the database. Exit Access. Congratulations on a job well done.

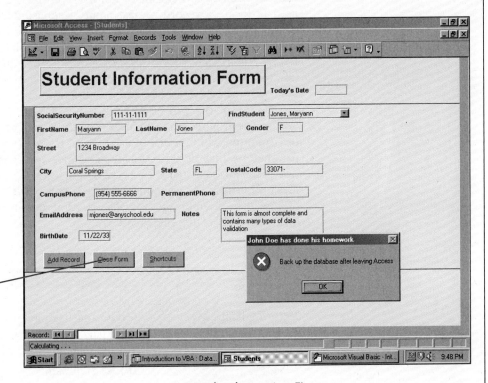

Click Close Form button

(g) Close the Form (step 7)

FIGURE 8.10   Hands-on Exercise 4 (continued)

BACK UP IMPORTANT FILES

It's not a question of if it will happen, but when—hard disks die, files are lost, or viruses may infect a system. It has happened to us and it will happen to you, but you can prepare for the inevitable by creating adequate backup before the problem occurs. Decide which files to back up, how often to do the backup, and where to keep the backup. Do it!

Visual Basic for Applications (VBA) is a subset of Visual Basic that is accessible from every application in Microsoft Office 2000. VBA is different from traditional programming languages in that it is event driven. An event is any action that is recognized by Access. Visual Basic code is developed in units called event procedures that run automatically, in response to an event such as clicking a button or opening a form.

All VBA procedures are stored in modules. Every form in an Access database has its own module that contains the event procedures for that form. All procedures are either public or private. A private procedure is accessible only from within the module in which it is contained. A public procedure is accessible from anywhere. All procedures are displayed and edited in the Module window within Access. Additional procedures can be developed by expanding the existing code through inference and observation.

Several event procedures were created in this chapter to illustrate how VBA can be used to enhance an Access application. Hands-on exercise 1 focused on the Current event to synchronize the displayed record in a form with a combo box used to locate a record by last name. Exercise 2 developed a Key Down event procedure to facilitate data entry. Exercise 3 used the Error event to substitute application-specific error messages for the default messages provided by Access. Exercise 4 created a Before Update event procedure to enhance the data validation for the form. Additional procedures can be developed by expanding the existing code through inference and observation.

Many of the procedures used the MsgBox function to display a message and/or accept input from the user (i.e., to determine whether the user clicks a Yes or No button within a dialog box). The MsgBox function has three arguments (or parameters) that describe the type of message. The first argument contains the text of the message and is enclosed in quotation marks. The second argument specifies an intrinsic (or previously defined) constant that determines the icon that is to appear in the message box. The third argument contains the text that appears in the title bar of the message box.

KEY WORDS AND CONCEPTS

Before Update event	GIGO (garbage in, garbage out)	On Open event
Case statement	If statement	Parameter
Class module	If/Else statement	Private procedure
Click event	Immediate window	Procedure box
Comment	Intrinsic constant	Procedure header
Complete Word feature	Key Down event	Procedure view
Complete Word tool	Key Preview property	Public procedure
Current event	KeyCode argument	Quick Info feature
Data validation	Module view	Quick Info tool
Default property	Module window	SetFocus method
Error trapping	MsgBox function	Shift argument
Event	Object box	VBA
Event procedure	On Current event	Visual Basic for Applications
Full Module view	On Error event	
General procedure		

1. Which of the following applications in Microsoft Office 2000 can be enhanced through VBA?
   (a) Word and Excel
   (b) Access and PowerPoint
   (c) Outlook
   (d) All of the above

2. Which of the following enhancements to an application are accomplished by using VBA event procedures?
   (a) Improved data validation
   (b) Creation of keyboard shortcuts for data entry
   (c) Substitution of customized error messages for the standard messages provided by Access
   (d) All of the above

3. Which of the following is necessary in order to establish a keyboard short-cut to facilitate data entry on a form?
   (a) Create a procedure for the Key Up event of the form and set the Key Preview property to No
   (b) Create a procedure for the Key Up event of the form and set the Key Preview property to Yes
   (c) Create a procedure for the Key Down event of the form and set the Key Preview property to No
   (d) Create a procedure for the Key Down event of the form and set the Key Preview property to Yes

4. Which of the following characters is used to continue a VBA statement from one line to the next?
   (a) A hyphen
   (b) An underscore
   (c) A hyphen and an ampersand
   (d) An underscore and an ampersand

5. Which of the following types of data validation requires that an event procedure be developed in VBA?
   (a) Checking that a required field has been entered
   (b) Checking that one of two fields has been entered
   (c) Prompting the user with a message indicating that an optional field has been omitted, and asking for further instruction
   (d) All of the above

6. Which of the following is *not* used to implement a validation check that requires the user to enter a value of Atlanta or Boston for the City field?
   (a) Set the Required property for the City field to Yes
   (b) Set the Validation Rule property for the City field to either "Atlanta" or "Boston"
   (c) Set the Default property for the City field to either "Atlanta" or "Boston"
   (d) Set the Validation Text property for the City field to display an appropriate error message if the user does not enter either Atlanta or Boston

7. Which of the following techniques would you use to require the user to enter either a home phone or a business phone?
   (a) Set the Required property of each field to Yes
   (b) Set the Validation Rule property for each field to true
   (c) Set the Validation Rule for the table to [HomePhone] or [Business-Phone]
   (d) All of the above are equally acceptable

8. Which of the following is true about the Procedure box in the Module window?
   (a) Events that have procedures appear in bold
   (b) Clicking an event that appears in boldface displays the event procedure
   (c) Clicking an event that is not in bold creates a procedure for that event
   (d) All of the above

9. Which event procedure was created in conjunction with the combo box to locate a record on the form?
   (a) An On Current event procedure for the combo box control
   (b) An On Current event procedure for the form
   (c) A Key Down event procedure for the combo box control
   (d) A Key Down event procedure for the form

10. Which event procedure was created to warn the user that the e-mail address was omitted and asking whether the record is to be saved anyway?
    (a) An On Error event procedure for the combo box control
    (b) An On Error event procedure for the form
    (c) A Before Update event procedure for the e-mail control
    (d) A Before Update event procedure for the form

11. Which of the following does *not* create an event procedure for a form?
    (a) Display the Properties box for the form in Design View, click the Event tab, select the event, then click the Build button
    (b) Select the form in the Object box of the Module window, then click the event (displayed in regular as opposed to boldface) in the Procedure box
    (c) Pull down the View menu in the Database window and click the code command or click the Code button on the Database toolbar
    (d) All of the above create an event procedure

12. You want to display a message in conjunction with closing a form. Which of the following is the best way to accomplish this?
    (a) Write a VBA procedure for the Close Form event
    (b) Create a Close command button for the form, then write a VBA procedure for the On Click event of the command button to display the message
    (c) Either (a) or (b)
    (d) Neither (a) nor (b)

13. Which of the following is not an Access-intrinsic constant?
    (a) ApplicationName
    (b) vbCritical
    (c) acCtrlMask
    (d) vbKey1

14. What advantage, if any, is gained by using VBA to create a keyboard short-cut to enter the city, state, and zip code in an incoming record as opposed to using the Default Value property in the table definition?
    (a) It's much easier to use VBA than it is to specify the Default Value property
    (b) The Default Value property cannot be applied to multiple fields for the same record, and thus VBA is the only way to accomplish this task
    (c) VBA can be used to create different shortcuts for different sets of values, whereas the Default Value property is restricted to a single value
    (d) All of the above

15. Which of the following statements was used to display the Error Number associated with an error in data entry?
    (a) Debug.Print "Error Number = "
    (b) Debug.Print "Error Number = ", DataErr
    (c) Print "Error Number = "
    (d) Print "Error Number = ", DataErr

ANSWERS

1. d	**6.** c	**11.** c
2. d	**7.** c	**12.** a
3. d	**8.** d	**13.** a
4. b	**9.** b	**14.** c
5. c	**10.** d	**15.** b

PRACTICE WITH ACCESS 2000 AND VBA

1. Do the four hands-on exercises in the chapter, then modify the completed form at the end of the fourth hands-on exercise to:
   a. Prompt the user if birth date is omitted, indicating that the birth date has not been entered and asking whether the record should be saved anyway.
   b. Create a keyboard shortcut, Ctrl13, that will enter data for New York, NY, 10010 in the city, state, and zip code, respectively.
   c. Supply a descriptive error message if the user attempts to add a record without the social security number.
   d. Change the color of the combo box and associated label that were created in the first hands-on exercise so that these elements stand out on the form.
   e. Submit a disk containing the completed form to your instructor.

2. Open the *Chapter 8 Practice 2* database in the Exploring Access folder, then modify the customer form in Figure 8.11 to accommodate all of the following:
   a. Create a command button to add a new customer. The button should be created in such a way so that clicking the button takes the user directly to the FirstName field. (The CustomerID is created automatically and thus there is no need to position the user here.)

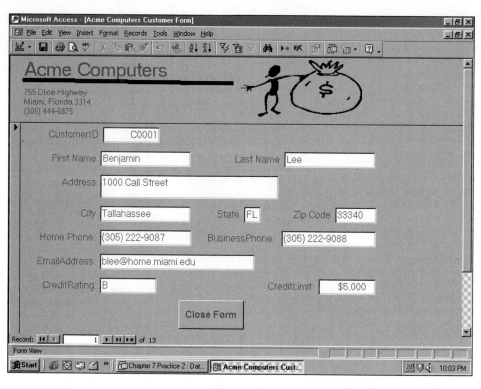

FIGURE 8.11 Acme Computers Customer Form (Exercise 2)

   b. Supply a descriptive error message (in place of the standard error message) if the user attempts to add a record without customer's first name.

   c. Change the table properties so that the user is required to enter either the home phone or e-mail address.

   d. Create a BeforeUpdate event procedure for the form that asks if the record should be saved in the event that the zip code is not entered.

   e. Add a combo box to find a customer record and format it to match the other controls. Be sure to change the On Current event so that the value shown in the Find Customer control matches the customer information currently displayed on the form.

   f. Create a KeyDown procedure so that Ctrl+1 enters a credit rating of A and a credit limit of $10,000, Ctrl+2 enters a credit rating of B and a credit limit of $5,000, and Ctrl+3 enters a credit rating of C and a credit limit of $1,000. Don't forget to set the KeyPreview property for the form to Yes.

   g. Create a command button that allows the user to view the shortcuts.

   h. Change the application name that appears in the title bar of various message boxes to "Acme Computers".

   i. Create a Close event procedure for the form that displays a message to back up the data that is displayed when the form is closed.

3. Help for VBA: Review the hands-on exercises in the chapter to recall the various ways that you can obtain help in VBA. In addition, you can click on any Visual Basic key word, then press the F1 key to display a context-sensitive help screen as shown in Figure 8.12. Summarize this information in a short note to your instructor. It will be an invaluable reference as you continue to explore VBA in Access as well as other applications in Office 2000.

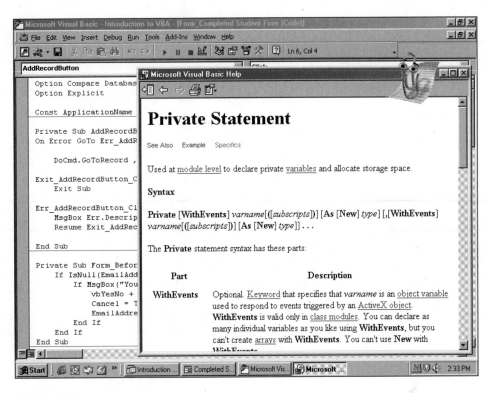

FIGURE 8.12   Help for VBA (Exercise 3)

 4. The Developer's Forum: Go to the Access Developer's page at the Microsoft site as shown in Figure 8.13. Scan through one or more articles, then summarize your findings in a short note to your instructor. Explore the site further to determine what other pages may be of interest to the developer.

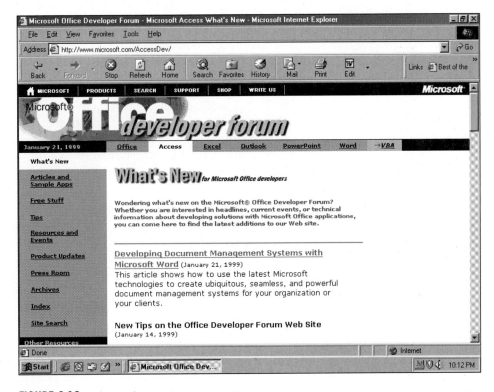

FIGURE 8.13   The Developer's Forum (Exercise 4)

The Importance of Backup

Go to a real installation such as a doctor or an attorney's office, the company where you work, or the computer lab at school. Determine the backup procedures that are in effect then write a one-page report indicating whether the policy is adequate and, if necessary, offering suggestions for improvement. Your report should be addressed to the individual in charge of the business and it should cover all aspects of the backup strategy. Be sure to indicate which files are backed up, the individual responsible, how often the files are backed up, and where the backup copies are stored.

Return to Soccer

Open the Soccer database that you created in the previous chapter, choose one or more of the forms in that database, and add macros as appropriate. Does the addition of the macros enhance the appeal of the database to the end user? Do the macros help to ensure the validity of the underlying data? Summarize your findings in a brief note to your instructor.

The Database Wizard

The Database Wizard is intended to help you create an entire database from your answers to a few simple questions. Pull down the File menu, click the New command, click the Databases tab, then explore the various databases that are available. At first glance, the Database Wizard seems wonderful. After additional study, however, you may realize that it is fairly limited and has virtually no flexibility. What is your opinion of this tool? Summarize your thoughts in a brief note to your instructor.

Debugging

The Debug toolbar contains several tools to help you debug a procedure if it does not work as intended. The Step Into command is especially useful as it executes the procedure one statement at a time. Choose any of the procedures you created in this chapter, then investigate the procedure in detail using the Debug toolbar. Summarize your results in a short note to your instructor.

appendix a

TOOLBARS

Microsoft Access has 24 predefined toolbars that provide access to commonly used commands. The toolbars are displayed in Figure A.1 and are listed here for convenience: Alignment and Sizing, Database, Filter/Sort, Form Design, Form View, Formatting (Datasheet), Formatting (Form/Report), Formatting (Page), Macro Design, Page Design, Page View, Print Preview, Query Datasheet, Query Design, Relationship, Report Design, Shortcut Menus, Source Code Control, Table Datasheet, Table Design, Toolbox, Utility 1, Utility 2, and Web.

The buttons on the toolbars are intended to indicate their functions. Clicking the Printer button (the fourth button from the left on the Database toolbar), for example, executes the Print command. If you are unsure of the purpose of any toolbar button, point to it, and a ScreenTip will appear that displays its name.

You can display multiple toolbars at one time, move them to new locations on the screen, customize their appearance, or suppress their display.

➤ To display or hide a toolbar, pull down the View menu and click the Toolbars command. Select (deselect) the toolbar(s) that you want to display (hide). The selected toolbar(s) will be displayed in the same position as when last displayed. You may also point to any toolbar and click with the right mouse button to bring up a shortcut menu, after which you can select the toolbar to be displayed (hidden).

➤ To change the size of the buttons, suppress the display of the Screen-Tips, pull down the View menu, click Toolbars, and click Customize to display the Customize dialog box. If necessary, click the Options tab, then select (deselect) the appropriate check box. Alternatively, you can right click on any toolbar, click the Customize command from the context-sensitive menu, then select (deselect) the appropriate check box from within the Options tab in the Customize dialog box.

➤ Toolbars are either docked (along the edge of the window) or floating (in their own window). A toolbar moved to the edge of the window will dock along that edge. A toolbar moved anywhere else in the window will float in its own window. Docked toolbars are one tool wide (high).

Floating toolbars can be resized by clicking and dragging a border or corner as you would with any window.

- To move a docked toolbar, click anywhere in the gray background area and drag the toolbar to its new location. You can also click and drag the move handle (the vertical line) at the left of the toolbar.
- To move a floating toolbar, drag its title bar to its new location.

➤ To customize a toolbar, display the toolbar on the screen, pull down the View menu, click Toolbars, and click Customize to display the Customize dialog box. Alternatively, you can click on any toolbar with the right mouse button and select Customize from the shortcut menu.

- To move a button, drag the button to its new location on that toolbar or any other displayed toolbar.
- To copy a button, press the Ctrl key as you drag the button to its new location on that toolbar or any other displayed toolbar.
- To delete a button, drag the button off the toolbar and release the mouse button.
- To add a button, click the Commands tab in the Customize dialog box, select the category from the Categories list box which contains the button you want to add, then drag the button to the desired location on the toolbar. (To see a description of a tool's function prior to adding it to a toolbar, select the tool, then click the Description command button.)
- To restore a predefined toolbar to its default appearance, click the Toolbars tab, select (highlight) the desired toolbar, and click the Reset command button.

➤ Buttons can also be moved, copied, or deleted without displaying the Customize dialog box.

- To move a button, press the Alt key as you drag the button to the new location.
- To copy a button, press the Alt and Ctrl keys as you drag the button to the new location.
- To delete a button, press the Alt key as you drag the button off the toolbar.

➤ To create your own toolbar, pull down the View menu, click Toolbars, click Customize, click the Toolbars tab, then click the New command button. Alternatively, you can click on any toolbar with the right mouse button, select Customize from the shortcut menu, click the Toolbars tab, and then click the New command button.

- Enter a name for the toolbar in the dialog box that follows. The name can be any length and can contain spaces. Click OK.
- The new toolbar will appear on the screen. Initially it will be big enough to hold only one button. Add, move, and delete buttons following the same procedures as outlined above. The toolbar will automatically size itself as new buttons are added and deleted.
- To delete a custom toolbar, pull down the View menu, click Toolbars, click Customize, and click the Toolbars tab. *Verify that the custom toolbar to be deleted is the only one selected (highlighted).* Click the Delete command button. Click OK to confirm the deletion. (Note that a predefined toolbar cannot be deleted.)

Alignment and Sizing Toolbar

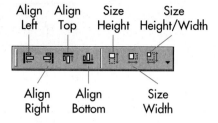

Align Left · Align Top · Size Height · Size Height/Width · Align Right · Align Bottom · Size Width

Database Toolbar

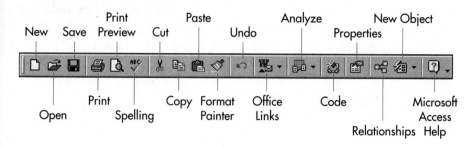

New · Save · Print Preview · Cut · Paste · Undo · Analyze · Properties · New Object · Open · Print · Spelling · Copy · Format Painter · Office Links · Code · Relationships · Microsoft Access Help

Filter/Sort

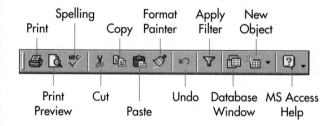

Print · Spelling · Copy · Format Painter · Apply Filter · New Object · Print Preview · Cut · Paste · Undo · Database Window · MS Access Help

Form Design

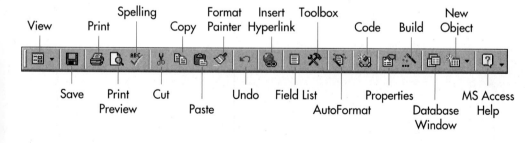

View · Print · Spelling · Copy · Format Painter · Insert Hyperlink · Toolbox · Code · Build · New Object · Save · Print Preview · Cut · Paste · Undo · Field List · AutoFormat · Properties · Database Window · MS Access Help

Form View

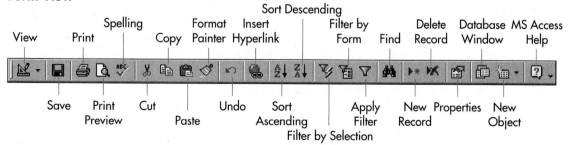

View · Print · Spelling · Copy · Format Painter · Insert Hyperlink · Sort Descending · Filter by Form · Find · Delete Record · Database Window · MS Access Help · Save · Print Preview · Cut · Paste · Undo · Sort Ascending · Filter by Selection · Apply Filter · New Record · Properties · New Object

FIGURE A.1   Access Toolbars

Formatting (Datasheet)

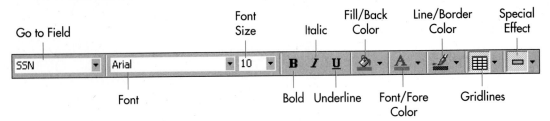

Formatting (Form/Report)

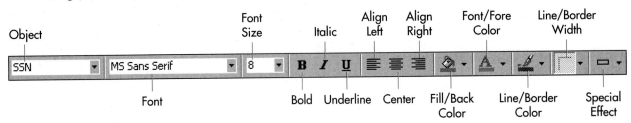

Formatting (Page)

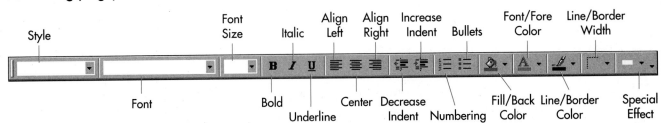

Macro Design

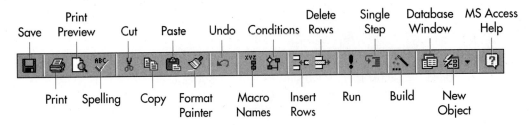

Page Design

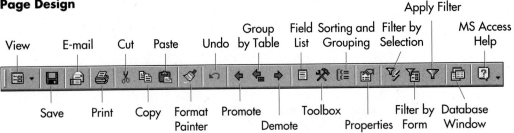

FIGURE A.1   Access Toolbars (continued)

Page View

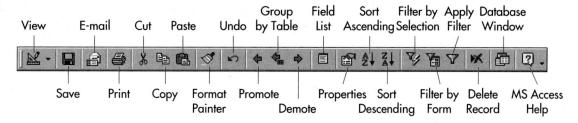

Print Preview

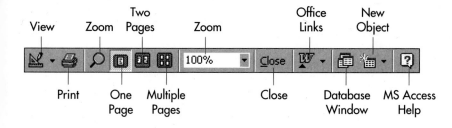

Query Datasheet

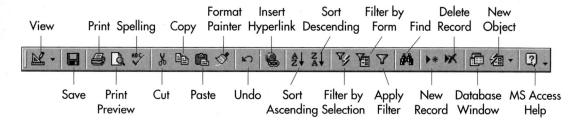

Query Design

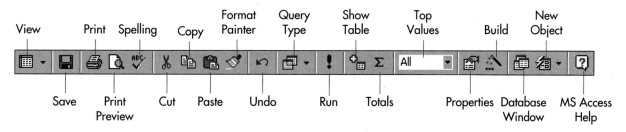

Relationship

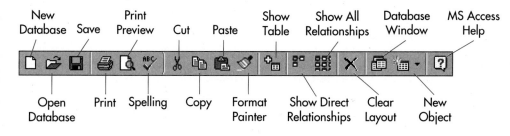

FIGURE A.1   Access Toolbars (continued)

Report Design

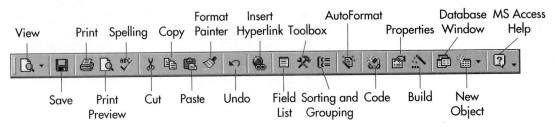

Shortcut Menus

Source Code Control

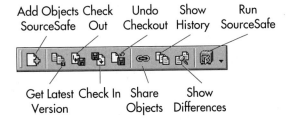

Table Datasheet

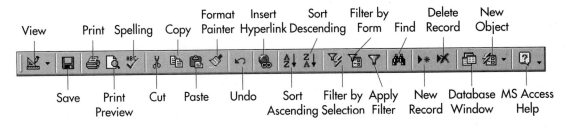

Table Design

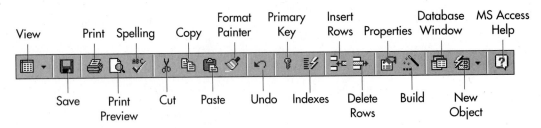

FIGURE A.1 Access Toolbars (continued)

Toolbox

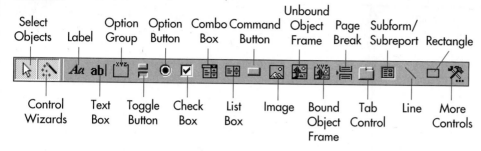

Select
Objects   Label   Option
Group   Option
Button   Combo
Box   Command
Button   Unbound
Object
Frame   Page
Break   Subform/
Subreport   Rectangle

Control
Wizards   Text
Box   Toggle
Button   Check
Box   List
Box   Image   Bound
Object
Frame   Tab
Control   Line   More
Controls

Utility 1

Utility 2

Add or Remove
Buttons   Add or Remove
Buttons

Web

Back   Stop Current
Jump   Start
Page   Favorites
Menu   Show Only
Web Toolbar

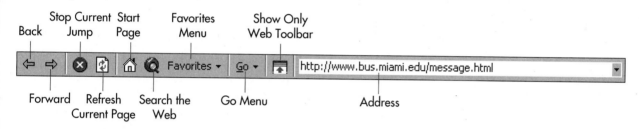

Forward   Refresh
Current Page   Search the
Web   Go Menu   Address

FIGURE A.1   Access Toolbars (continued)

appendix b

DESIGNING A RELATIONAL DATABASE

OVERVIEW

An Access database consists of multiple tables, each of which stores data about a specific subject. To use Access effectively, you must relate the tables to one another. This in turn requires a knowledge of database design and an understanding of the principles of a relational database under which Access operates.

Our approach to teaching database design is to present two case studies, each of which covers a common application. The first case centers on franchises for fast food restaurants and incorporates the concept of a one-to-many relationship. One person can own many restaurants, but a given restaurant is owned by only one person. The second case is based on a system for student transcripts and incorporates a many-to-many relationship. One student takes many courses, and one course is taken by many students. The intent in both cases is to design a database capable of producing the desired information.

CASE STUDY: FAST FOOD FRANCHISES

The case you are about to read is set within the context of a national corporation offering franchises for fast food restaurants. The concept of a franchise operation is a familiar one and exists within many industries. The parent organization develops a model operation, then franchises that concept to qualified individuals (franchisees) seeking to operate their own businesses. The national company teaches the franchisee to run the business, aids the person in site selection and staffing, coordinates national advertising, and so on. The franchisee pays an initial fee to open the business followed by subsequent royalties and marketing fees to the parent corporation.

The essence of the case is how to relate the data for the various entities (the restaurants, franchisees, and contracts) to one another. One approach is to develop a single restaurant table, with each restaurant record containing data about the owner and contract arrangement. As we shall see, that design leads to problems of redundancy whenever the same person owns more than one restaurant or when several restaurants are governed by the same contract type. A better approach is to develop separate tables, one for each of the objects (restaurants, franchisees, and contracts).

The entities in the case have a definite relationship to one another, which must be reflected in the database design. The corporation encourages individuals to own multiple restaurants, creating a *one-to-many relationship* between franchisees and restaurants. One person can own many restaurants, but a given restaurant is owned by only one person. There is also a one-to-many relationship between contracts and restaurants because the corporation offers a choice of contracts to each restaurant.

The company wants a database that can retrieve all data for a given restaurant, such as the annual sales, type of contract in effect (contract types are described below), and/or detailed information about the restaurant owner. The company also needs reports that reflect the location of each restaurant, all restaurants in a given state, and all restaurants managed by a particular contract type. The various contract arrangements are described below:

Contract 1: 99-year term, requiring a one-time fee of $250,000 payable at the time the franchise is awarded. In addition, the franchisee must pay a royalty of 2 percent of the restaurant's gross sales to the parent corporation, and contribute an additional 2 percent of sales to the parent corporation for advertising.

Contract 2: 5-year term (renewable at franchisee's option), requiring an initial payment of $50,000. In addition, the franchisee must pay a royalty of 4 percent of the restaurant's gross sales to the parent corporation, and contribute an additional 3 percent of sales to the parent corporation for advertising.

Contract 3: 10-year term (renewable at franchisee's option), requiring an initial payment of $75,000. In addition, the franchisee must pay a royalty of 3 percent of the restaurant's gross sales to the parent corporation, and contribute an additional 3 percent of sales to the parent corporation for advertising.

Other contract types may be offered in the future. The company currently has 500 restaurants, of which 200 are company owned. Expansion plans call for opening an additional 200 restaurants each year for the next three years, all of which are to be franchised. There is no limit on the number of restaurants an individual may own, and franchisees are encouraged to apply for multiple restaurants.

Single Table Solution

The initial concern in this, or any other, system is how best to structure the data so that the solution satisfies the information requirements of the client. We present two solutions. The first is based on a single restaurant table and will be shown to have several limitations. The second introduces the concept of a relational database and consists of three tables (for the restaurants, franchisee, and contracts).

The single table solution is shown in Figure B.1a. Each record within the table contains data about a particular restaurant, its franchisees (owner), and contract type. There are five restaurants in our example, each with a *unique* restaurant number. At first glance, Figure B.1a appears satisfactory; yet there are three specific types of problems associated with this solution. These are:

1. Difficulties in the modification of data for an existing franchisee or contract type, in that the same change may be made in multiple places.
2. Difficulties in the addition of a new franchisee or contract type, in that these entities must first be associated with a particular restaurant.

Restaurant Number	Restaurant Data (Address, annual sales . . .)	Franchisee Data (Name, telephone, address . . .)	Contract Data (Type, term, initial fee . . .)
R1	Restaurant data for Miami . . .	Franchisee data (Grauer . . .)	Contract data (Type 1 . . .)
R2	Restaurant data for Coral Gables . . .	Franchisee data (Moldof . . .)	Contract data (Type 1 . . .)
R3	Restaurant data for Fort Lauderdale. . .	Franchisee data (Grauer . . .)	Contract data (Type 2 . . .)
R4	Restaurant data for New York . . .	Franchisee data (Glassman . . .)	Contract data (Type 1 . . .)
R5	Restaurant data for Coral Springs . . .	Franchisee data (Coulter . . .)	Contract data (Type 3 . . .)

(a) Single Table Solution

Restaurant Number	Restaurant Data	Franchisee Number	Contract Type
R1	Restaurant data for Miami . . .	F1	C1
R2	Restaurant data for Coral Gables . . .	F2	C1
R3	Restaurant data for Fort Lauderdale. . .	F1	C2
R4	Restaurant data for New York . . .	F3	C1
R5	Restaurant data for Coral Springs . . .	F4	C3

Contract Type	Contract Data
C1	Contract data. . .
C2	Contract data. . .
C3	Contract data. . .

Franchisee Number	Franchisee Data (Name, telephone, address, . . .)
F1	Grauer. . .
F2	Moldof. . .
F3	Glassman. . .
F4	Coulter. . .

(b) Multiple Table Solution

FIGURE B.1   Single versus Multiple Table Solution

3. Difficulties in the deletion of a restaurant, in that data for a particular franchisee or contract type may be deleted as well.

The first problem, modification of data about an existing franchisee or contract type, stems from redundancy, which in turn requires that any change to duplicated data be made in several places. In other words, any modification to a duplicated entry, such as a change in data for a franchisee with multiple restaurants (e.g., Grauer, who owns restaurants in Miami and Fort Lauderdale), requires a search through the entire table to find all instances of that data so that the identical modification can be made to each of the records. A similar procedure would have to be followed should data change about a duplicated contract (e.g., a change in the royalty percentage for contract Type 1, which applies to restaurants R1, R2, and R4). This is, to say the least, a time-consuming and error-prone procedure.

The addition of a new franchisee or contract type poses a different type of problem. It is quite logical, for example, that potential franchisees must apply to the corporation and qualify for ownership before having a restaurant assigned to them. It is also likely that the corporation would develop a new contract type prior to offering that contract to an existing restaurant. Neither of these events is easily accommodated in the table structure of Figure B.1a, which would require the creation of a dummy restaurant record to accommodate the new franchisee or contract type.

The deletion of a restaurant creates yet another type of difficulty. What happens, for example, if the company decides to close restaurant R5 because of insufficient sales? The record for this restaurant would disappear as expected, but so too would the data for the franchisee (Coulter) and the contract type (C3), which is not intended. The corporation might want to award Coulter another restaurant in the future and/or offer this contract type to other restaurants. Neither situation would be possible as the relevant data has been lost with the deletion of the restaurant record.

Multiple Table Solution

A much better solution appears in Figure B.1b, which uses a different table for each of the entities (restaurants, franchisees, and contracts) that exist in the system. Every record in the restaurant table is assigned a unique restaurant number (e.g., R1 or R2), just as every record in the franchisee table is given a unique franchisee number (e.g., F1 or F2), and every contract record a unique contract number (e.g., C1 or C2).

The tables are linked to one another through the franchisee and/or contract numbers, which also appear in the restaurant table. Every record in the restaurant table is associated with its appropriate record in the franchisee table through the franchisee number common to both tables. In similar fashion, every restaurant is tied to its appropriate contract through the contract number, which appears in the restaurant record. This solution may seem complicated, but it is really quite simple and elegant.

Assume, for example, that we want the name of the franchisee for restaurant R5, and further, that we need the details of the contract type for this restaurant. We retrieve the appropriate restaurant record, which contains franchisee and contract numbers of F4 and C3, respectively. We then search through the franchisee table for franchisee F4 (obtaining all necessary information about Coulter) and search again through the contract table for contract C3 (obtaining the data for this contract type). The process is depicted graphically in Figure B.1b.

The multiple table solution may require slightly more effort to retrieve information, but this is more than offset by the advantages of table maintenance. Consider, for example, a change in data for contract C1, which currently governs restaurants R1, R2, and R4. All that is necessary is to go into the contract table, find record C1, and make the changes. The records in the restaurant table are *not* affected because the restaurant records do not contain contract data per se, only the number of the corresponding contract record. In other words, the change in data for contract C1 is made in one place (the contract table), yet that change would be reflected for all affected restaurants. This is in contrast to the single table solution of Figure B.1a, which would require the identical modification in three places.

The addition of new records for franchisees or contracts is done immediately in the appropriate tables of Figure B.1b. The corporation simply adds a franchisee or contract record as these events occur, without the necessity of a corresponding restaurant record. This is much easier than the approach of Figure B.1a, which required an existing restaurant in order to add one of the other entities.

The deletion of a restaurant is also easier than with the single table organization. You could, for example, delete restaurant R5 without losing the associated franchisee and contract data as these records exist in different tables.

Queries to the Database

By now you should be convinced of the need for multiple tables within a database and that this type of design facilitates all types of table maintenance. However, the ultimate objective of any system is to produce information, and it is in this area that the design excels. Consider now Figure B.2, which expands upon the multiple table solution to include additional data for the respective tables.

To be absolutely sure you understand the multiple table solution of Figure B.2, use it to answer the questions at the top of the next page. Check your answers with those provided.

Restaurant Number	Street Address	City	State	Zip Code	Annual Sales	Franchisee Number	Contract Type
R1	1001 Ponce de Leon Blvd	Miami	FL	33361	$600,000	F1	C1
R2	31 West Rivo Alto Road	Coral Gables	FL	33139	$450,000	F2	C1
R3	333 Las Olas Blvd	Fort Lauderdale	FL	33033	$250,000	F1	C2
R4	1700 Broadway	New York	NY	10293	$1,750,000	F3	C1
R5	1300 Sample Road	Coral Springs	FL	33071	$50,000	F4	C3

(a) Restaurant Table

Franchisee Number	Franchisee Name	Telephone	Street Address	City	State	Zip Code
F1	Grauer	(305) 755-1000	2133 NW 102 Terrace	Coral Springs	FL	33071
F2	Moldof	(305) 753-4614	1400 Lejeune Blvd	Miami	FL	33365
F3	Glassman	(212) 458-5054	555 Fifth Avenue	New York	NY	10024
F4	Coulter	(305) 755-0910	1000 Federal Highway	Fort Lauderdale	FL	33033

(b) Franchisee Table

Contract Type	Term (years)	Initial Fee	Royalty Pct	Advertising Pct
C1	99	$250,000	2%	2%
C2	5	$50,000	4%	3%
C3	10	$75,000	3%	3%

(c) Contract Table

FIGURE B.2   Fast Food Franchises

Questions

1. Who owns restaurant R2? What contract type is in effect for this restaurant?
2. What is the address of restaurant R4?
3. Which restaurant(s) are owned by Mr. Grauer?
4. List all restaurants with a contract type of C1.
5. Which restaurants in Florida have gross sales over $300,000?
6. List all contract types.
7. Which contract type has the lowest initial fee? How much is the initial fee? Which restaurant(s) are governed by this contract?
8. How many franchisees are there? What are their names?
9. What are the royalty and advertising percentages for restaurant R3?

Answers

1. Restaurant R2 is owned by Moldof and governed by contract C1.
2. Restaurant R4 is located at 1700 Broadway, New York, NY 10293.
3. Mr. Grauer owns restaurants R1 and R3.
4. R1, R2, and R4 are governed by contract C1.
5. The restaurants in Florida with gross sales over $300,000 are R1 ($600,000) and R2 ($450,000).
6. The existing contract types are C1, C2, and C3.
7. Contract C2 has the lowest initial fee ($50,000); restaurant R3 is governed by this contract type.
8. There are four franchisees: Grauer, Moldof, Glassman, and Coulter.
9. Restaurant R3 is governed by contract C2 with royalty and advertising percentages of four and three percent, respectively.

THE RELATIONAL MODEL

The restaurant case study illustrates a ***relational database,*** which requires a separate table for every entity in the physical system (restaurants, franchisees, and contracts). Each occurrence of an entity (a specific restaurant, franchisee, or contract type) appears as a row within a table. The properties of an entity (a restaurant's address, owner, or sales) appear as columns within a table.

Every row in every table of a relational database must be distinct. This is accomplished by including a column (or combination of columns) to uniquely identify the row. The unique identifier is known as the ***primary key.*** The restaurant number, for example, is different for every restaurant in the restaurant table. The franchisee number is unique in the franchisee table. The contract type is unique in the contract table.

The same column can, however, appear in multiple tables. The franchisee number, for example, appears in both the franchisee table, where its values are unique, and in the restaurant table, where they are not. The franchisee number is the primary key in the franchisee table, but it is a ***foreign key*** in the restaurant table. (A foreign key is simply the primary key of a related table.)

The inclusion of a foreign key in the restaurant table enables us to implement the one-to-many relationship between franchisees and restaurants. We enter the franchisee number (the primary key in the franchisee table) as a column in the restaurant table, where it (the franchisee number) is a foreign key. In similar fashion, contract type (the primary key in the contract table) appears as a foreign key in the restaurant table to implement the one-to-many relationship between contracts and restaurants.

It is helpful perhaps to restate these observations about a relational database in general terms:

1. Every entity in a physical system requires its own table in a database.
2. Each row in a table is different from every other row because of a unique column (or combination of columns) known as a primary key.
3. The primary key of one table can appear as a foreign key in another table.
4. The order of rows in a table is immaterial.
5. The order of columns in a table is immaterial, although the primary key is generally listed first.
6. The number of columns is the same in every row of the table.

THE KEY, THE WHOLE KEY, AND NOTHING BUT THE KEY

The theory of a relational database was developed by Dr. Edgar Codd, giving rise to the phrase, *"The key, the whole key, and nothing but the key . . . so help me Codd."* The sentence effectively summarizes the concepts behind a relational database and helps to ensure the validity of a design. Simply stated, the value of every column other than the primary key depends on the key in that row, on the entire key, and on nothing but that key.

Referential Integrity

The concept of **referential integrity** requires that the tables in a database be consistent with one another. Consider once again the first row in the restaurant table of Figure B.2a, which indicates that the restaurant is owned by franchisee F1 and governed by contract Type C1. Recall also how these values are used to obtain additional information about the franchisee or contract type from the appropriate tables in Figures B.2b and B.2c, respectively.

What if, however, the restaurant table referred to franchisee number F1000 or contract C9, neither of which exists in the database of Figure B.2? There would be a problem because the tables would be inconsistent with one another; that is, the restaurant table would refer to rows in the franchisee and contract tables that do not exist. It is important, therefore, that referential integrity be strictly enforced and that such inconsistencies be prevented from occurring. Suffice it to say that data validation is critical when establishing or maintaining a database, and that no system, relational or otherwise, can compensate for inaccurate or incomplete data.

CASE STUDY: STUDENT TRANSCRIPTS

Our second case is set within the context of student transcripts and expands the concept of a relational database to implement a *many-to-many relationship.* The system is intended to track students and the courses they take. The many-to-many relationship occurs because one student takes many courses, while at the same time, one course is taken by many students. The objective of this case is to relate the student and course tables to one another to produce the desired information.

The system should be able to display information about a particular student as well as information about a particular course. It should also display information about a student-course combination, such as when a student took the course and the grade he or she received.

Solution

The (intuitive and incorrect) solution of Figure B.3 consists of two tables, one for courses and one for students, corresponding to the two entities in the physical system. The student table contains the student's name, address, major, date of entry into the school, cumulative credits, and cumulative quality points. The course table contains the unique six-character course identifier, the course title, and the number of credits.

There are no problems of redundancy. The data for a particular course (its description and number of credits) appears only once in the course table, just as the data for a particular student appears only once in the student table. New courses will be added directly to the course table, just as new students will be added to the student table.

The design of the student table makes it easy to list all courses for one student. It is more difficult, however, to list all students in one course. Even if this were not the case, the solution is complicated by the irregular shape of the student table. The rows in the table are of variable length, according to the number of courses taken by each student. Not only is this design awkward, but how do we know in advance how much space to allocate for each student?

Course Number	Course Description	Credits
ACC101	Introduction to Accounting	3
CHM100	Survey of Chemistry	3
CHM101	Chemistry Lab	1
CIS120	Microcomputer Applications	3
ENG100	Freshman English	3
MTH100	Calculus with Analytic Geometry	4
MUS110	Music Appreciation	2
SPN100	Spanish I	3

(a) Course Table

Student Number	Student Data	Courses Taken with Grade and Semester											
S1	Student data (Adams...)	ACC101	SP99	A	CIS120	FA98	A	MU100	SP98	B			
S2	Student data (Fox...)	ENG100	SP99	B	MTH100	SP99	B	SPN100	SP99	B	CIS120	FA98	A
S3	Student data (Baker...)	ACC101	SP99	C	ENG100	SP99	B	MTH100	FA98	C	CIS120	FA98	B
S4	Student data (Jones...)	ENG100	SP99	A	MTH100	SP99	A						
S5	Student data (Smith...)	CIS120	SP99	C	ENG100	SP99	B	CIS120	FA98	F			

(b) Student Table

FIGURE B.3   Student Transcripts (repeating groups)

The problems inherent in Figure B.3 stem from the many-to-many relationship that exists between students and courses. The solution is to eliminate the **repeating groups** (course number, semester, and grade), which occur in each row of the student table in Figure B.3, in favor of the additional table shown in Figure B.4. Each row in the new table is unique because the *combination* of student number, course number, and semester is unique. Semester must be included since students are allowed to repeat a course. Smith (student number S5), for example, took CIS120 a second time after failing it initially.

The implementation of a many-to-many relationship requires an additional table, with a **combined key** consisting of (at least) the keys of the individual entities. The many-to-many table may also contain additional columns, which exist as a result of the combination (intersection) of the individual keys. The combination of student S5, course CIS120, and semester SP99 is unique and results in a grade of C.

Note, too, how the design in Figure B.4 facilitates table maintenance as discussed in the previous case. A change in student data is made in only one place (the student table) regardless of how many courses the student has taken. A new student may be added to the student table prior to taking any courses. In similar fashion, a new course can be added to the course table before any students have taken the course.

Review once more the properties of a relational database, then verify that the solution in Figure B.4 adheres to these requirements. To be absolutely sure

Course Number	Course Description	Credits
ACC101	Introduction to Accounting	3
CHM100	Survey of Chemistry	3
CHM101	Chemistry Lab	1
CIS120	Microcomputer Applications	3
ENG100	Freshman English	3
MTH100	Calculus with Analytic Geometry	4
MUS110	Music Appreciation	2
SPN100	Spanish I	3

(a) Course Table

Student Number	Student Data
S1	Student data (Adams. . .)
S2	Student data (Fox. . .)
S3	Student data (Baker. . .)
S4	Student data (Jones. . .)
S5	Student data (Smith. . .)

(b) Student Table

Student Number	Course Number	Semester	Grade
S1	ACC101	SP99	A
S1	CIS120	FA98	A
S1	MU100	SP98	B
S2	ENG100	SP99	B
S2	MTH100	SP99	B
S2	SPN100	SP99	B
S2	CIS120	FA98	A
S3	ACC101	SP99	C
S3	ENG100	SP99	B
S3	MTH100	FA98	C
S3	CIS120	FA98	B
S4	ENG100	SP99	A
S4	MTH100	SP99	A
S5	CIS120	SP99	C
S5	ENG100	SP99	B
S5	CIS120	FA98	F

(c) Student-Course Table

FIGURE B.4   Student Transcripts (improved design)

that you understand the solution, and to illustrate once again the power of the relational model, use Figure B.4 to answer the following questions about the student database.

Questions

1. How many courses are currently offered?
2. List all three-credit courses.
3. Which courses has Smith taken during his stay at the university?
4. Which students have taken MTH100?
5. Which courses did Adams take during the Fall 1998 semester?
6. Which students took Microcomputer Applications in the Fall 1998 semester?
7. Which students received an A in Freshman English during the Spring 1999 semester?

Answers

1. Eight courses are offered.
2. The three-credit courses are ACC101, CHM100, CIS120, ENG100, and SPN100.
3. Smith has taken CIS120 (twice) and ENG100.
4. Fox, Baker, and Jones have taken MTH100.
5. Adams took CIS120 during the Fall 1998 semester.
6. Adams, Fox, Baker, and Smith took Microcomputer Applications in the Fall 1998 semester.
7. Jones was the only student to receive an A in Freshman English during the Spring 1999 semester.

SUMMARY

A relational database consists of multiple two-dimensional tables. Each entity in a physical system requires its own table in the database. Every row in a table is unique due to the existence of a primary key. The order of the rows and columns in a table is immaterial. Every row in a table contains the same columns in the same order as every other row.

A one-to-many relationship is implemented by including the primary key of one table as a foreign key in the other table. Implementation of a many-to-many relationship requires an additional table whose primary key combines (at a minimum) the primary keys of the individual tables. Referential integrity ensures that the information in a database is internally consistent.

KEY WORDS AND CONCEPTS

Column
Combined key
Entity
Foreign key
Many-to-many
 relationship

One-to-many
 relationship
Primary key
Query
Redundancy
Referential integrity

Relational database
Repeating group
Row
Table

appendix c

COMBINING AN ACCESS DATABASE WITH A WORD FORM LETTER

OVERVIEW

One of the greatest benefits of using the Microsoft Office suite is the ability to combine data from one application with another. An excellent example is a *mail merge*, in which data from an Access table or query are input into a Word document to produce a set of individualized form letters. You create the *form letter* using Microsoft Word, then you merge the letter with the *records* in the Access table or query. The merge process creates the individual letters, changing the name, address, and other information as appropriate from letter to letter. The concept is illustrated in Figure C.1, in which John Smith uses a mail merge to seek a job upon graduation. John writes the letter describing his qualifications, then merges that letter with a set of names and addresses to produce the individual letters.

The mail merge process uses two input files (a main document and a data source) and produces a third file as output (the set of form letters). The *main document* (e.g., the cover letter in Figure C.1a) contains standardized text together with one or more *merge fields* that indicate where the variable information is to be inserted in the individual letters. The *data source* (the set of names and addresses in Figure C.1b) contains the data that varies from letter to letter and is a table (or query) within an Access database. (The data source may also be taken from an Excel list, or alternatively it can be created as a table in Microsoft Word.)

The main document and the data source work in conjunction with one another, with the merge fields in the main document referencing the corresponding fields in the data source. The first line in the address of Figure C.1a, for example, contains three merge fields, each of which is enclosed in angle brackets, *<<Title>> <<FirstName>> <<LastName>>*. (These entries are not typed explicitly but are entered through special commands as described in the hands-on exercise that follows shortly.) The merge process examines each record in the data source and substitutes the appropriate field values for the corresponding merge fields as it creates

John H. Smith

426 Jenny Lake Drive • Coral Gables, FL 33146 • (305) 666-4801

April 13, 1999

<<Title>> <<FirstName>> <<LastName>>
<<JobTitle>>
<<Company>>
<<Address1>>
<<City>>, <<State>> <<PostalCode>>

Dear <<Title>> <<LastName>>:

I am writing to inquire about a position with <<Company>> as an entry-level computer programmer. I have just graduated from the University of Miami with a bachelor's degree in Computer Information Systems (May 1999), and I am very interested in working for you. I have a background in both microcomputer applications (Windows 95, Word, Excel, PowerPoint, and Access) as well as extensive experience with programming languages (Visual Basic, C++, and COBOL). I feel that I am well qualified to join your staff as over the past two years I have had a great deal of experience designing and implementing computer programs, both as a part of my educational program and during my internship with Personalized Computer Designs, Inc.

I am eager to put my skills to work and would like to talk with you at your earliest convenience. I have enclosed a copy of my résumé and will be happy to furnish the names and addresses of my references, if you so desire. You may reach me at the above address and phone number. I look forward to hearing from you.

Sincerely,

John H. Smith

(a) The Form Letter (a Word document)

FIGURE C.1   The Mail Merge

the individual form letters. For example, the first three fields in the first record will produce *Mr. Jason Frasher;* the same fields in the second record will produce, *Ms. Lauren Howard,* and so on.

In similar fashion, the second line in the address contains the *<<JobTitle>>* field. The third line contains the *<<Company>>* field. The fourth line references the *<<Address1>>* field, and the last line contains the *<<City>>, <<State>,* and *<<PostalCode>>* fields. The salutation repeats the *<<Title>>* and *<<LastName>>* fields. The first sentence in the letter uses the *<<Company>>* field a second time. The mail merge prepares the letters one at a time, with one letter created for every record in the data source until the file of names and addresses is exhausted. The individual form letters are shown in Figure C.1c. Each letter begins automatically on a new page.

	Title	First Name	Last Name	JobTitle	Company	Address1	City	State	Postal Code
▶	Mr	Jason	Frasher	President	Frasher Systems	100 S. Miami Avenue	Miami	FL	33103-
	Ms.	Lauren	Howard	Director of Human Resources	Unique Systems	475 LeJeune Road	Coral Gables	FL	33146-
	Ms.	Elizabeth	Scherry	Director of Personnel	Custom Computing	8180 Kendall Drive	Miami	FL	33156-
*									

Record: 14 4 | 1 | ▶ ▶I ▶* of 3

(b) The Data Source (an Access Table or Query)

John H. Smith

426 Jenny Lake Drive • Coral Gables, FL 33146 • (305) 666-4801

April 13, 1999

Ms. Elizabeth Scherry
Director of Personnel
Custom Computing
8180 Kendall Drive
Miami, FL 33156

Dear Ms. Scherry:

I am writing to inquire about a position with Custom Computing as an entry-level computer
programmer. I have just graduated from the U...
Computer Information Systems (May 1999), a...
background in both microcomputer applicatio...
Access) as well as extensive experience with ...
COBOL). I feel that I am well qualified to jo...
great deal of experience designing and impler...
educational program and during my internshi...

I am eager to put my skills to work and woul...
have enclosed a copy of my résumé and will ...
references, if you so desire. You may reach m...
forward to hearing from you.

Sincerely,

John H. Smith

John H. Smith

426 Jenny Lake Drive • Coral Gables, FL 33146 • (305) 666-4801

April 13, 1999

Ms. Lauren Howard
Director of Human Resources
Unique Systems
475 LeJeune Road
Coral Gables, FL 33146

Dear Ms. Howard:

I am writing to inquire about a position with Unique Systems as an entry-level computer
programmer. I have just graduated from th...
Computer Information Systems (May 1999...
background in both microcomputer applica...
Access) as well as extensive experience wi...
COBOL). I feel that I am well qualified to ...
great deal of experience designing and imp...
educational program and during my intern...

I am eager to put my skills to work and w...
have enclosed a copy of my résumé and w...
references, if you so desire. You may reac...
forward to hearing from you.

Sincerely,

John H Smith

John H. Smith

426 Jenny Lake Drive • Coral Gables, FL 33146 • (305) 666-4801

April 13, 1999

Mr. Jason Frasher
President
Frasher Systems
100 S. Miami Avenue
Miami, FL 33103

Dear Mr. Frasher:

I am writing to inquire about a position with Frasher Systems as an entry-level computer
programmer. I have just graduated from the University of Miami with a bachelor's degree in
Computer Information Systems (May 1999), and I am very interested in working for you. I have a
background in both microcomputer applications (Windows 95, Word, Excel, PowerPoint, and
Access) as well as extensive experience with programming languages (Visual Basic, C++, and
COBOL). I feel that I am well qualified to join your staff as over the past two years I have had a
great deal of experience designing and implementing computer programs, both as a part of my
educational program and during my internship with Personalized Computer Designs, Inc.

I am eager to put my skills to work and would like to talk with you at your earliest convenience. I
have enclosed a copy of my résumé and will be happy to furnish the names and addresses of my
references, if you so desire. You may reach me at the above address and phone number. I look
forward to hearing from you.

Sincerely,

John H. Smith

(c) The Printed Letters

FIGURE C.1   The Mail Merge (continued)

APPENDIX C: COMBINING ACCESS AND WORD

Mail Merge Helper

A mail merge can be started from either **_Microsoft Word_** or **_Microsoft Access_**. Either way two input files are required—the form letter (main document) and the data source. The order in which these files are created depends on how the merge is initiated. When starting in Microsoft Word, you begin with the form letter, then create the data source. The process is reversed in Access—you start with a table or query, then exit to Word to create the form letter. The merge itself, however, is always performed from within Microsoft Word through the **_Mail Merge Helper_** as indicated in the next hands-on exercise.

The Mail Merge Helper guides you through the process. It enables you to create (or edit) the main document, to create or edit the data source, and finally, it enables you to merge the two.

PAPER MAKES A DIFFERENCE

Most of us take paper for granted, but the right paper can make a significant difference in the effectiveness of the document. Reports and formal correspondence are usually printed on white paper, but you would be surprised how many different shades of white there are. Other types of documents lend themselves to colored paper for additional impact. In short, the paper you use is far from an automatic decision. Our favorite source for paper is a company called Paper Direct (1-800-APAPERS). Ask for a catalog, then consider the use of a specialty paper the next time you have an important project, such as the cover letter for your résumé.

HANDS-ON EXERCISE 1

Mail Merge

Objective: To combine an Access table and a Word form letter to implement a mail merge and produce a set of form letters. Use Figure C.2 as a guide in the exercise.

STEP 1: Open the Names and Addresses Database

➤ Start Access. Open the **Names and Addresses** database in the **Exploring Access folder**. The **Tables button** is selected. The **Contacts table** is the only table within the database.

➤ Pull down the **Tools menu**, click **Office Links** to display a cascaded menu in Figure C.2a, then click **Merge It with MS Word** to begin the mail merge.

➤ The dialog box for the Microsoft Word Mail Merge Wizard appears after a few seconds.

➤ The option button to link your data to an existing Microsoft Word document is already selected. (We have created the form letter for you on the data disk.) Click **OK**.

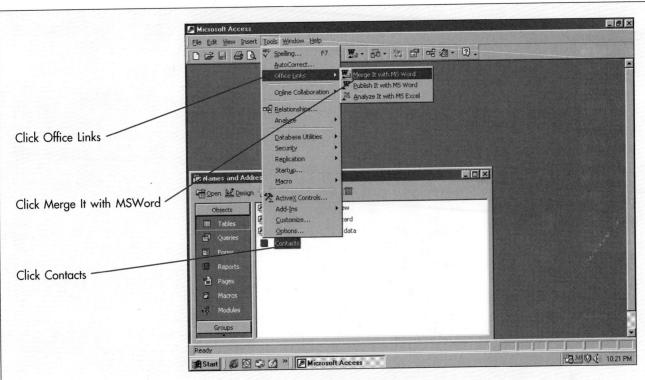

Click Office Links

Click Merge It with MSWord

Click Contacts

(a) Open the Names and Addresses Database (step 1)

FIGURE C.2   Hands-on Exercise 1 (continued)

STEP 2: Open the Form Letter

➤ You should see the dialog box to select the form letter as shown in Figure C.2b. If necessary, change to the **Exploring Access folder**, then select the **Form Letter document**. Click **Open**.

➤ Click the **Microsoft Word button** on the taskbar, then maximize the window containing the Word document (Form Letter).

➤ Pull down the **File menu**, click the **Save As** command to display the Save As dialog box, enter **Finished Form Letter** as the name of the document, then click the **Save command button**.

➤ There are now two identical copies of the file on disk: "Form Letter," which we supplied, and "Finished Form Letter," which you just created. The title bar references the latter, which is the document in memory. (You can always return to the original document if you modify this one beyond repair.)

THE MAIL MERGE TOOLBAR

The Microsoft Word Mail Merge toolbar is displayed automatically as soon as a merge is initiated. The toolbar contains various buttons that are used in conjunction with a mail merge and is referenced explicitly in step 5 of this exercise. Remember, too, that you can right click any toolbar in any Office application to display a shortcut menu, which enables you to explicitly display or hide the toolbars in that application.

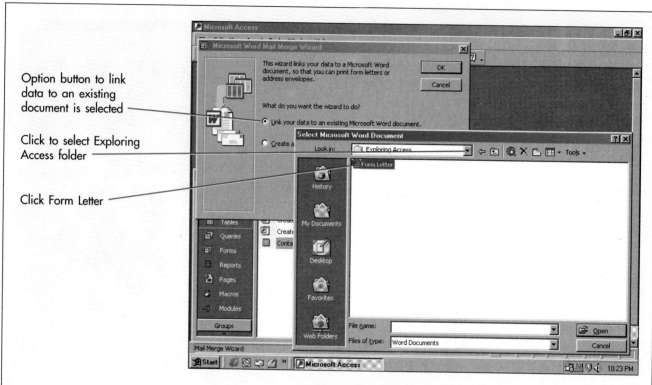

Option button to link
data to an existing
document is selected

Click to select Exploring
Access folder

Click Form Letter

(b) Open the Form Letter (step 2)

FIGURE C.2   Hands-on Exercise 1 (continued)

STEP 3: Insert Today's Date

➤ The form letter should be visible on your monitor as shown in Figure C.2c.
  • If necessary, pull down the **View menu** and click **Print Layout** (or click the Print Layout button above the status bar).
  • If necessary, click the **Zoom control arrow** on the Standard toolbar to change to **Page Width**.

➤ Click to the left of the "D" in Dear Sir, then press **enter** twice to insert two blank lines. Press the **up arrow** two times to return to the first line you inserted.

➤ Pull down the **Insert menu** and click the **Date and Time** command to display the dialog box in Figure C.2c.

➤ Select (click) the date format you prefer and, if necessary, check the box to update automatically. Click **OK** to close the dialog box.

FIELD CODES VERSUS FIELD RESULTS

All fields in Microsoft Word are displayed in a document in one of two formats, as a *field code* or as a *field result*. A field code appears in braces and indicates instructions to insert variable data when the document is printed; a field result displays the information as it will appear in the printed document. You can toggle the display between the field code and field result by selecting the field and pressing Shift+F9 during editing.

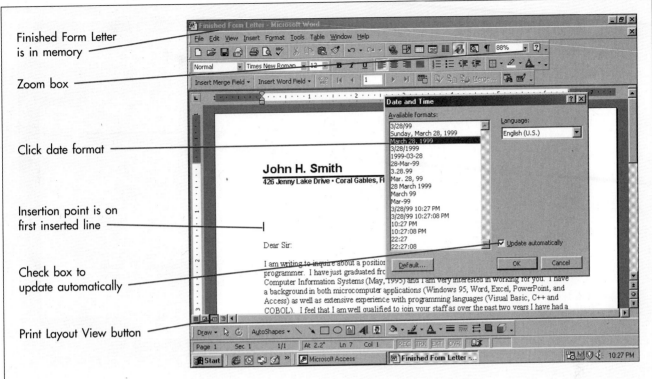

Finished Form Letter is in memory

Zoom box

Click date format

Insertion point is on first inserted line

Check box to update automatically

Print Layout View button

(c) Insert Today's Date (step 3)

FIGURE C.2 Hands-on Exercise 1 (continued)

STEP 4: Insert the Merge Fields

➤ Click in the document immediately below the date. Press **enter** to insert a blank line between the date and the first line of the address.

➤ Click the **Insert Merge Field** button on the Mail Merge toolbar to display the fields within the data source, then select (click) **Title** from the list of fields. The title field is inserted into the main document and enclosed in angle brackets as shown in Figure C.2d.

➤ Press the **space bar** to add a space between the words. Click the **Insert Merge Field** button a second time. Click **FirstName**. Press the **space bar**.

➤ Click the **Insert Merge Field** button again. Click **LastName**.

➤ Press **enter** to move to the next line. Enter the remaining fields in the address as shown in Figure C.2d. Be sure to add a comma as well as a space after the **City field**.

➤ Delete the word "Sir" in the salutation and replace it with the **Title** and **Last Name fields** separated by spaces. Delete the words "your company" in the first sentence and replace them with the **Company field**.

➤ Save the document.

STEP 5: The Mail Merge Toolbar

➤ The Mail Merge toolbar enables you to preview the form letters before they are created. Click the **<<abc>> button** on the Mail Merge toolbar to display field values rather than field codes.

➤ You will see, for example, Mr. Jason Frasher (instead of <<Title>> <<First-Name>> <<LastName>>) as shown in Figure C.2e.

Insert Merge Field button

Click to insert merge field
at insertion point

Merge Field codes

Insertion point

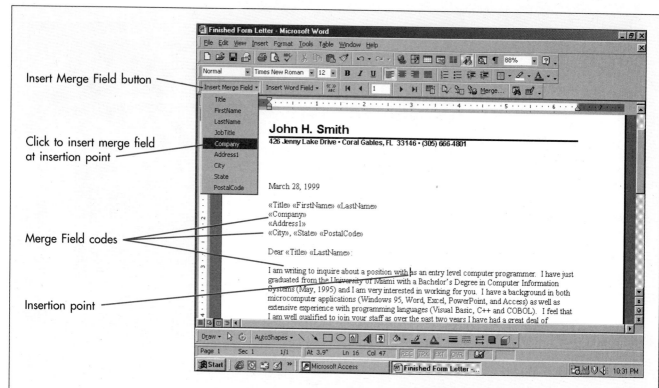

(d) Insert the Merge Fields (step 4)

<<abc>> button

Go to first record

Go to previous record

Go to next record

Go to last record
Mail Merge Helper button

Field values are displayed

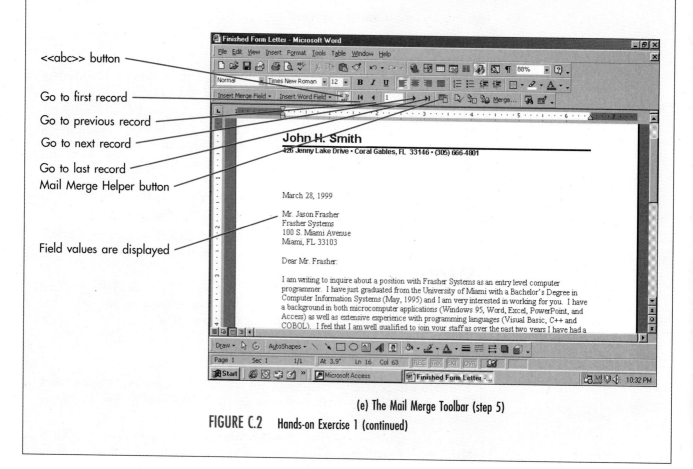

(e) The Mail Merge Toolbar (step 5)

FIGURE C.2   Hands-on Exercise 1 (continued)

➤ The **<<abc>> button** functions as a toggle switch. Click it once and you switch from field codes to field values; click it a second time and you go from field values back to field codes. End with the field values displayed.

➤ Look at the text box on the Mail Merge toolbar, which displays the number 1 to indicate that the first record is displayed. Click the ▶ **button** to display the form letter for the next record (Ms. Lauren Howard, in our example).

➤ Click the ▶ **button** again to display the form letter for the next record (Ms. Elizabeth Scherry). The toolbar indicates you are on the third record. Click the ◀ **button** to return to the previous (second) record.

➤ Click the |◀ **button** to move directly to the first record (Jason Frasher). Click the ▶| **button** to display the form letter for the last record (Elizabeth Scherry).

➤ Toggle the **<<abc>> button** to display the field codes.

STEP 6: The Mail Merge Helper

➤ Click the **Mail Merge Helper button** on the Merge toolbar to display the dialog box in Figure C.2f.

➤ The Mail Merge Helper shows your progress thus far:

- The main document has been created and saved as Finished Form Letter on drive C.

- The data source is the Contacts table within the Names and Addresses database.

➤ Click the **Merge command button** to display the Merge dialog box in Figure C.2f. The selected options should already be set, but if necessary, change your options to match those in the figure.

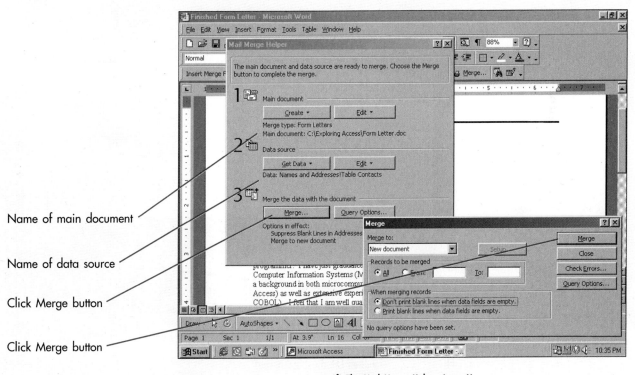

Name of main document

Name of data source

Click Merge button

Click Merge button

(f) The Mail Merge Helper (step 6)

FIGURE C.2   Hands-on Exercise 1 (continued)

➤ Click the **Merge command button**. Word pauses momentarily, then generates the three form letters in a new document, which becomes the active document and is displayed on the monitor. The title bar of the active window changes to Form Letters1.

STEP 7: The Form Letters

➤ Scroll through the individual letters in the FormLetters1 document to review the letters one at a time.

➤ Pull down the **View menu**. Click **Zoom**. Click **Many Pages**. Click the **monitor icon**, then click and drag the icon within the resulting dialog box to display three pages side by side. Click **OK**. You should see the three form letters as shown in Figure C.2g.

➤ Print the letters to prove to your instructor that you did this exercise.

➤ Pull down the **File menu** and click **Exit** to exit Word. Pay close attention to the informational messages that ask whether to save the modified file(s):

• There is no need to save the merged document (Form Letters1) because you can always re-create the merged letters, provided you have saved the main document and data source.

• Save the Finished Form Letter if you are asked to do so.

➤ Exit Access. Congratulations on a job well done. We wish you good luck in your job hunting!

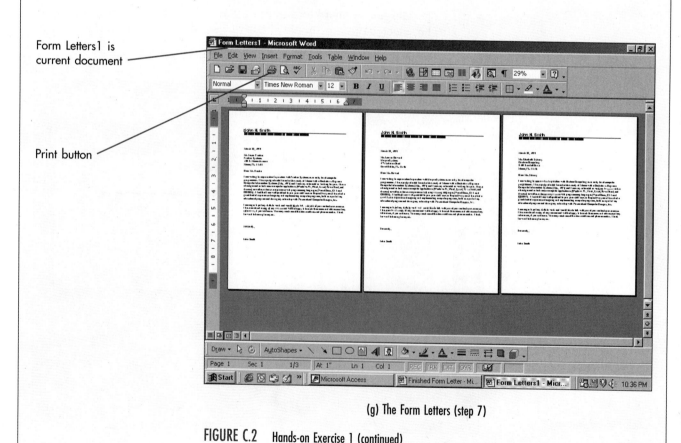

Form Letters1 is current document

Print button

(g) The Form Letters (step 7)

FIGURE C.2   Hands-on Exercise 1 (continued)

appendix d

A PROJECT
FOR THE SEMESTER

OVERVIEW

This appendix describes the student project we require in our course in Microsoft Access at the University of Miami. It is intended for both student and instructor, as it describes the various milestones in the administration of a class project. Our experience has been uniformly positive. Students work hard, but they are proud of the end result and we are continually impressed at the diversity and quality of student projects. The project is what students remember most about our course and it truly enhances the learning experience.

We begin our course with an overview of Access as it is presented in Chapter 1. We focus on the Bookstore and Employee databases, each of which contains a single table. We also touch on the concept of a relational database through the "Look Ahead" database at the end of the chapter. The initial emphasis in the course, however, is on databases with a single table, since students must develop proficiency with basic skills. This is accomplished through detailed coverage of Chapters 2 and 3, where students learn how to create tables, forms, queries, and reports.

We then move into a discussion of relational databases and database design. Students want to be proficient in Access, but it is equally important that they are comfortable with database design. Thus we present several different examples, starting in Chapter 4, followed by Appendix A, then reinforced through the opening sections in Chapters 5 and 6, and the associated case studies at the end of these chapters. It is at this point that we introduce the class project, which becomes the focal point of our course for the rest of the semester.

The Groups

The class is divided into groups of three or four students each, and students work together to submit a collective project. It is critical that the groups are balanced with respect to student abilities, and hence our groups are always formed after the first exam when we have additional information with which to create the groups. We distribute a questionnaire in which we ask students whom they want to work with (and conversely, if there is anyone they would be uncomfortable working with). We try to honor the former requests, but will always honor the latter, so that the groups work as smoothly as possible.

Once the groups have been formed, we establish a series of milestones that are described in the remainder of the appendix. There is absolutely no requirement for you or your class to follow our milestones exactly. We have found, however, that providing detailed feedback through a series of continual assignments is the most effective way to move each group toward its final goal.

One other suggestion is to have the groups engage in a continuing presentation to the class as a whole. We allocate the beginning of each class period to group presentations of 10 to 15 minutes each on the current class assignment. The group presentations accomplish two goals—they enable students to learn from each other, and they provide valuable practice in presenting one's work to an audience.

Phase I—Preliminary Design

Describe, in a one- or two-page narrative, the relational database that your group will design and implement. You can select any of the case studies at the end of the chapters on one-to-many or many-to-many relationships, or alternatively you can choose an entirely different system. Regardless of which system you choose, the preliminary design is one of the most important aspects of the entire project since it is the foundation for the project. A good design will enable you to implement the project successfully, and hence you should give considerable thought to the document you prepare. Your project need not be unduly complex, but it must include at least three tables. The relationships between the tables can be one-to-many or many-to-many. The information can be contained in a written document to your instructor and/or a PowerPoint presentation for the class. Either way, it must do all of the following:

1. Describe the physical system for which you will create the database.
2. Develop a "wish list" describing in general terms the information the system is to produce.
3. Design a database capable of producing the required information. List the tables in the database, the fields in each table, and the relationships between the tables.
4. Describe in general terms how the database will be able to produce at least three of the reports on the wish list by describing the underlying queries, each of which references fields from multiple tables in the database.

Phase II—Detailed Design

Implement the refinements (if any) to the preliminary design from phase I, then expand that design to include all of the necessary fields in each table. You are also asked to develop the properties for each field at this time. Be sure to include adequate data validation and to use input masks as appropriate. One additional requirement is that the primary key of at least one table is an AutoNumber field.

After you have completed the design, create an Access database containing the necessary tables, with the All fields in each table, but no other objects. You do not have to enter any data at this time, but you are required to document your work. Use the Print Relationships command in the File menu to create a one-page document that gives you a visual overview of your database. Submit this document to your instructor.

You are also asked to provide detailed documentation for each table. Pull down the Tools menu, click Analyze, click Documentor. Select Tables in the Object Type drop-down list box, then select all of the tables. Click the Options button, then include for each table the Properties and Relationships but not the Permissions by User and Group. Include for each field Names, Data types, Sizes, and Properties. Do not include any information on indexes. Print the information for each table in the database and submit it to your instructor for review.

Phase III—The User Interface

Phase III focuses on the switchboard and associated template that will be replicated throughout the system. The switchboard, or user interface, is critical to the success of any system as a user spends his or her day in front of the screen. It should be functional and visually compelling. We have found that the best way for the group to arrive at a switchboard is for each member to submit a design independently, after which the group can select the best design.

The main switchboard should contain a logo for the project and establish a color scheme. The initial version need contain only two buttons—one to display the "Help About" form that is illustrated throughout the text and one button to exit from the application. Use clip art as appropriate, but clip art for the sake of clip art is often juvenile. You may want to use different fonts and/or simple graphics (e.g., horizontal or vertical lines are often quite effective). A simple design is generally the best design.

After the switchboards and help forms have been created, they are to be merged into a database that will consist solely of the switchboards and associated help forms (you will have to rename the switchboards). Use the Get External Data command in the File menu to import the objects from the other databases. Bring this database to class and be prepared to show off the competing designs for your project. Choose the winning switchboard for your system, then use that switchboard to design a template that will be the basis for the forms and other objects.

Phase IV—Create the Forms and Enter Test Data

Phase IV has you create the forms in which to enter test data, based on the template of Phase III. You need a form (or subform) for every table that will enable you to add, edit, and delete records in that table. You are also required to have at least one subform, and you must structure your forms to facilitate data entry in a logical way. All forms should have a consistent look (via a common template).

The forms should be user-friendly and display command buttons so that there is no requirement on the part of the end user to know Access. Each form is to include buttons to add, delete, find and print a record, and to close the form. A Help button is a nice touch. Include drop-down list boxes to facilitate data entry in at least two places. The forms should be designed so that they fit on one screen and do not require the user to scroll to access all of the fields and/or the command buttons. Decide on a common resolution, either 640 × 480 or 800 × 600, and follow that throughout.

Use the forms after they have been created to enter test data for each table. (Each table should contain 10 to 15 records.) Be sure that the data will adequately test all of the queries and reports that will be in your final system. Submit a print-out of the data in each table to your instructor. (You can print the Datasheet view of each table.) In addition, submit a printed copy of each form to your instructor.

Phase V—Prototyping

Phase V has you develop a "complete" system using a switchboard and prototyping as described in Chapter 7. The main menu should be displayed automatically (via an AutoExec macro) when the database is opened and the user should be able to step through the entire system. The final reports and queries need not be implemented at this time (a "not yet implemented" message is fine at this stage). The user should, however, be able to go from one form to the next without leaving Access or encountering an error message.

Phase VI—The Finishing Touches

The system should be "up and running" as you continue to build the various objects during the testing phase. It is at this point that you can add the finishing touches through VBA as described in Chapter 8, if in fact you are able to cover that material during the semester. Another finishing touch to consider is the creation of a Web page for the group. The page can be simple and contain descriptive information about the project and the members in the group. Load the page onto your school server, then include a hyperlink on the main switchboard to display the page.

Phase VII—The Completed System

Submit the completed Access database that should contain all of the reports and/or queries needed to satisfy the initial wish list. To obtain a grade of A, you will need to satisfy the following requirements (many of which have been completed) in the earlier phases:

1. An approved design of sufficient complexity similar to the completed soccer database in Chapter 7.
2. Separation of the objects and tables into separate databases that are subsequently linked to one another.
3. Use of the Data Validation and Input Mask properties to validate and facilitate data entry. In addition, at least one table is to contain an AutoNumber field as its primary key.
4. Existing data in all tables with 10 to 15 records in each table.
5. An AutoExec macro to load the main menu and maximize the document window.
6. A help button on one or more screens that displays the name of the group and an appropriate help message (e.g., a phone number). An "About" button on the opening switchboard that opens a form with introductory information about the project.
7. A working form (or subform) for each table in the database so that you can maintain each table. You must have at least one subform in your system. The forms should have a consistent look (via a common template). The system and especially the forms are to make sense; i.e., just because you have all of the forms does not mean you satisfy the requirements of the project. Your forms should be designed to facilitate data entry in a logical way.

8. The forms should be user-friendly and display command buttons so that there is no requirement on the part of the end user to know Access. Each form is to include buttons to add, delete, find and print a record, and to close the form. Include drop-down list boxes to facilitate data entry in at least two places.

9. All forms should be designed for a common resolution, either 640 × 480 or 800 × 600. The screens should be sufficiently compact so that no scrolling is required.

10. Three working reports, at least one of which is a group/total report.

11. Inclusion of a parameter query to drive a form or report.

12. At least one unmatched query. A top-value query is a nice touch, but depends on the system.

13. Two optional components are the "finishing touches" that are described in Phase VI. Your instructor may require you to include VBA modules and/or a group Web page.

14. The completed system should be as visually compelling as possible. Clip art for the sake of clip art tends to be juvenile without effect. In general, a consistent logo (one image) is much better from slide to slide than multiple images. No clip art is better than poor clip art or too much clip art.

15. You will be judged on whether your system actually works; i.e., the instructor will enter and/or modify data at random. The effects of the new data should be manifest in the various reports and queries. In addition, the system cannot break; i.e., the user must be able to go from one menu (form) to the next without difficulty.

The Written Document

In addition to demonstrating a working system, you are to submit a written document as described below. The submission of the written project will be an impressive (lengthy) document but easily generated, as much of the material is created directly from Access. The objective is for you to have a project of which you will be proud and something that you can demonstrate in the future. Include the following:

1. Title page plus table (list) of the contents; pages need not be numbered, but please include "loose-leaf" dividers for each section.

2. A one- or two-page description of the system taken from the earlier presentation to the class.

3. Technical documentation that includes the relationships diagram and table properties, as prepared in the detailed design phase.

4. Hard copy of each form (one per page).

5. Hard copy of each report (one per page).

6. A working disk.

Peer Evaluations

Sealed peer evaluations are to be submitted with each phase. Each member in the group is to evaluate every other member in the group including themselves by awarding a total of 19 points; (e.g., 5, 5, 5, and 4 in a group with four people). The rationale for requesting evaluations at every milestone is to prevent problems before they occur. In assigning a final grade, I am not looking for small differences, but rather instances where one member is simply not doing his or her share. Should this occur, the instructor will meet privately with the group to correct the problem.

A Final Word

Throughout the project, you will be working with different versions of your database on different machines. You will also need to share your work with other members of your group. And, of course, you need to back up your work. The floppy disk is the medium of choice, but its capacity is only 1.4MB and an Access database can quickly exceed that. It becomes critical, therefore, that you understand the various ways of reducing the storage requirements.

In particular, you should learn how to *compact* an Access database, after which you can take advantage of a *file compression program* to reduce the size even further. You might also explore the use of *FTP* as an alternate means of transferring a file. You should also learn how to separate the data from the other objects in a database to further reduce storage requirements. And finally, you should realize that clip art and other bit map images are one of the primary reasons for a large database. Ask yourself whether you really need it.

prerequisites

ESSENTIALS OF WINDOWS 95/98: DISK AND FILE MANAGEMENT

OBJECTIVES

After reading this supplement you will be able to:

1. Describe the objects on the Windows desktop; distinguish between the Classic style and the Web style.
2. Explain the significance of the common user interface; identify several elements that are present in every window.
3. Use the Help command to learn about Windows 98.
4. Format a floppy disk.
5. Define a file; differentiate between a program file and a data file; describe the rules for naming a file.
6. Explain how folders are used to organize the files on a disk; explain how to compress and expand a folder or drive within Windows Explorer.
7. Distinguish between My Computer and Windows Explorer with respect to viewing files and folders; explain the advantages of the hierarchical view available within Windows Explorer.
8. Use Internet Explorer to access the Internet and download the practice files for the Exploring Windows series.
9. Copy and/or move a file from one folder to another; delete a file, then recover the deleted file from the Recycle Bin.
10. Describe how to view a Web page from within Windows Explorer.

OVERVIEW

Windows 98 is a computer program (actually many programs) that controls the operation of a computer and its peripherals. Windows 98 is the third major release of the Windows operating system and it improves upon its immediate predecessor, Windows 95, in two important ways. First, there are many enhancements "under the surface" that make the PC run more efficiently. Second, Windows 98 brings the Internet to the desktop. Unlike Windows 95, however, Windows 98 has two distinct interfaces, a "Classic Style" and a "Web Style." The Classic style works identically to Windows 95, and thus we have titled this section, "Essentials of Windows 95/98" in that the Classic Style applies to both operating systems.

We begin with a discussion of the Windows desktop and describe the common user interface and consistent command structure that is present in every Windows application. We identify the basic components of a window and discuss how to execute commands and supply information through different elements in a dialog box. We introduce you to My Computer, an icon on the Windows desktop, and show you how to use My Computer to access the various components of your system. We also describe how to access the Help command.

The supplement focuses, however, on disk and file management. We present the basic definitions of a file and a folder, then describe how to use My Computer to look for a specific file or folder. We introduce Windows Explorer, which provides a more efficient way of finding data on your system, then show you how to move or copy a file from one folder to another. We discuss other basic operations such as renaming and deleting a file. We also describe how to recover a deleted file (if necessary) from the Recycle Bin.

There are also four hands-on exercises that enable you to apply the conceptual discussion in the text at the computer. The exercises refer to a set of practice files (known as a data disk) that we have created for you. You can obtain the practice files from our Web site (www.prenhall.com/grauer) or from a local area network if your professor has downloaded the files for you.

WINDOWS NT VERSUS WINDOWS 98

The computer you purchase for home use will have Windows 98. The computer you use at school or the office, however, will most likely have *Windows NT*, a more secure version of Windows that is intended for networked environments. This is significant to system personnel, but transparent to the user because Windows NT 5.0 (which will be called *Windows 2000*) has the same user interface as Windows 98. There are subtle differences, but for the most part, the screens are identical, and thus you will be able to use this text with either operating system.

THE DESKTOP

All versions of Windows create a working environment for your computer that parallels the working environment at home or in an office. You work at a desk. Windows operations take place on the *desktop.* There are physical objects on a desk such as folders, a dictionary, a calculator, or a phone. The computer equivalents of those objects appear as *icons* (pictorial symbols) on the desktop. Each object on a real desk has attributes (properties) such as size, weight, and color. In similar fashion, Windows assigns properties to every object on its desktop. And just as you can move the objects on a real desk, you can rearrange the objects on the Windows desktop.

Figure 1 displays three different versions of the *Windows 98* desktop. Figures 1a and 1b illustrate the desktop when Windows 98 is first installed on a new computer. These desktops have only a few objects and are similar to the desk in a new office, just after you move in. Figure 1a is displayed in the *Classic style,* which for all practical purposes is identical to the *Windows 95* desktop. Figure 1b

Click icon to select it;
double click icon to open it —

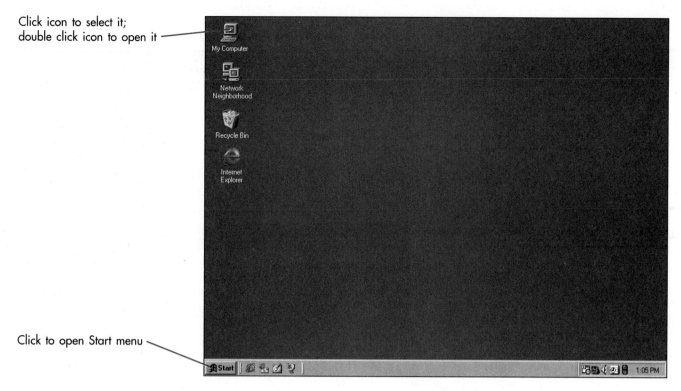

(a) Classic Style

Click to open Start menu —

Point to icon to select it;
click icon to open it —

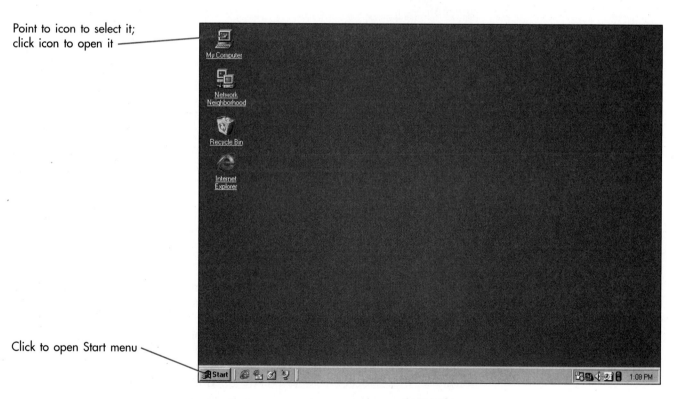

(b) Web Style

Click to open Start menu —

FIGURE 1   The Different Faces of Windows 98

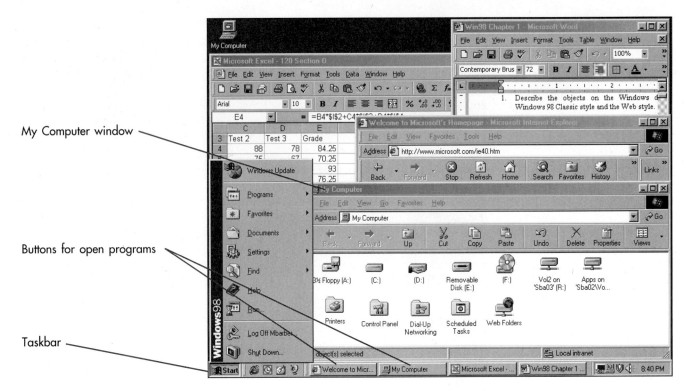

My Computer window

Buttons for open programs

Taskbar

(c) A Working Desktop

FIGURE 1   The Different Faces of Windows 98 (continued)

is displayed in the **Web style,** which is new to Windows 98. The icons on a Web style desktop are underlined and function identically to the hyperlinks within a browser such as Internet Explorer or Netscape Communicator.

The styles differ in visual appearance and in the way the icons work. In the Classic style, you click an icon to select it (mouse operations are described on page 10), and you double click the icon to open it. In the Web style, however, you point to an icon to select it, and you click the icon to open it. These operations mimic those of a Web browser—hence the term, "Web style." (It is a misnomer of sorts, in that the Web style has nothing to do with the Web per se, as you are not necessarily connected to the Internet nor are you viewing any Web pages.) You can display your desktop in either style by setting the appropriate option through the View menu in My Computer, as will be described later in a hands-on exercise. The choice depends entirely on personal preference.

Do not be concerned if your desktop is different from ours. Your real desk is arranged differently from those of your friends, and so your Windows desktop will also be different. What is important is that you recognize the capabilities inherent in Windows 98, as illustrated in Figure 1. Thus, it is the simplicity of the desktops in Figures 1a and 1b that helps you to focus on what is important. The **Start button,** as its name suggests, is where you begin. Click the Start button and you see a menu that lets you start any program installed on your computer. Starting a program opens a window on the desktop and from there you go to work.

Look now at Figure 1c, which displays an entirely different desktop, one with four open windows, that is similar to a desk in the middle of a working day. Each window in Figure 1c displays a program that is currently in use. The ability to run several programs at the same time is known as **multitasking,** and it is a major benefit of the Windows environment. Multitasking enables you to run a word processor in one window, create a spreadsheet in a second window, surf the Internet in a third window, play a game in a fourth window, and so on. You can work in a program as long as you want, then change to a different program by clicking its program.

You can also change from one program to another by using the taskbar at the bottom of the desktop. The *taskbar* contains a button for each open program, and it enables you to switch back and forth between those programs by clicking the appropriate button. The taskbars in Figures 1a and 1b do not contain any buttons (other than the Start button) since there are no open applications. The taskbar in Figure 1c, however, contains four additional buttons, one for each open program.

The icons on the desktop in Figures 1a and 1b are used to access programs or other functions in Windows 98. The *My Computer* icon is the most basic, and it enables you to view the devices on your system. Open My Computer in either Figure 1a or 1b, for example, and you see the objects in the My Computer window of Figure 1c. The contents of the My Computer window depend on the hardware of the specific computer system. Our system, for example, has one floppy drive, two hard (fixed) disks, a removable disk (an Iomega Zip drive), a CD-ROM, and access to two network drives. The My Computer window also contains the Control Panel, Printers, Dial-Up Networking, Web Folders, and Scheduled Tasks folders, which allow access to functions that control other elements in the environment on your computer. (These capabilities are not used by beginners and are generally "off limits" in a lab environment, and thus are not discussed further.)

The other icons on the desktop in Figures 1a and 1b are also noteworthy. *Network Neighborhood* extends your view of the computer to include the accessible drives on the network to which your machine is attached, if indeed it is part of a network. (You will not see this icon if you are not connected to a network.) The *Recycle Bin* allows you to restore a file that was previously deleted. The Internet Explorer icon starts *Internet Explorer,* the Web browser that is built into Windows 98. Indeed, the single biggest difference between Windows 98 and its predecessor, Windows 95, is the tight integration with the Internet and the World Wide Web.

THE COMMON USER INTERFACE

All Windows applications share a *common user interface* and possess a consistent command structure. This is a critically important concept and one of the most significant benefits of the Windows environment, as it provides a sense of familiarity from one application to the next. In essence, every Windows application follows the same conventions and works essentially the same way. Thus, once you learn the basic concepts and techniques in one application, you can apply that knowledge to every other application. The next several pages present this material, after which you will have an opportunity to practice in a hands-on exercise.

Anatomy of a Window

Figure 2 displays a typical window and labels its essential elements. Figure 2a displays the window in the Classic style. Figure 2b shows the identical window using the Web style. Regardless of the style, each window has a title bar, a minimize button, a maximize or restore button, and a close button. Other elements, which may or may not be visible, include a horizontal and/or vertical scroll bar, a menu bar, a status bar, and one or more toolbars. A window may also contain additional objects (icons) that pertain specifically to the programs or data associated with that window.

Title bar

Menu bar

Toolbars

Minimize button

Maximize button

Close button

Status bar

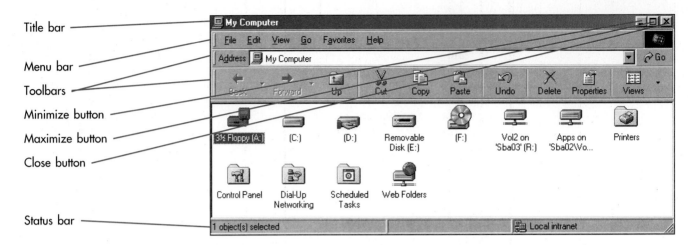

(a) Classic Style

Title bar

Menu bar

Toolbars

Minimize button

Maximize button

Close button

Status bar

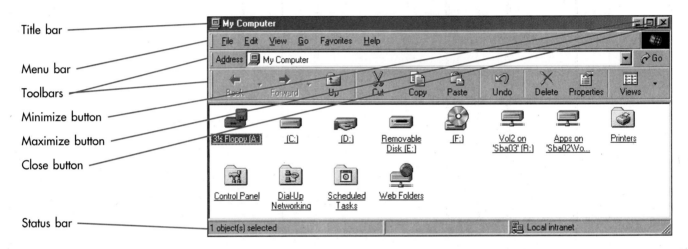

(b) Web Style

FIGURE 2   Anatomy of a Window

The *title bar* appears at the top of the window and displays the name of the window; for example, My Computer in both Figures 2a and 2b. The icon at the extreme left of the title bar provides access to a control menu that lets you select operations relevant to the window such as moving it or sizing it. The *minimize button* shrinks the window to a button on the taskbar, but leaves the application in memory. The *maximize button* enlarges the window so that it takes up the entire desktop. The *restore button* (not shown in Figure 2) appears instead of the maximize button after a window has been maximized, and restores the window to its previous size. The *close button* closes the window and removes it from memory and the desktop.

The *menu bar* appears immediately below the title bar and provides access to pull-down menus (as discussed later). Two toolbars, the *Address bar* and *Standard Buttons bar,* appear below the menu bar. The *status bar* at the bottom of the window displays information about the window as a whole or about a selected object within a window.

A *vertical* (or *horizontal*) *scroll bar* appears at the right (or bottom) border of a window when its contents are not completely visible and provides access to the unseen areas. Scroll bars do not appear in Figure 2 since all of the objects in the window are visible at the same time.

Moving and Sizing a Window

A window can be sized or moved on the desktop through appropriate actions with the mouse. To *size a window,* point to any border (the mouse pointer changes to a double arrow), then drag the border in the direction you want to go—inward to shrink the window or outward to enlarge it. You can also drag a corner (instead of a border) to change both dimensions at the same time. To *move a window* while retaining its current size, click and drag the title bar to a new position on the desktop.

Pull-down Menus

The menu bar provides access to *pull-down menus* that enable you to execute commands within an application (program). A pull-down menu is accessed by clicking the menu name or by pressing the Alt key plus the underlined letter in the menu name; for example, press Alt+V to pull down the View menu. Three pull-down menus associated with My Computer are shown in Figure 3.

Commands within a menu are executed by clicking the command or by typing the underlined letter (for example, C to execute the Close command in the File menu) once the menu has been pulled down. Alternatively, you can bypass the menu entirely if you know the equivalent keystrokes shown to the right of the command in the menu (e.g., Ctrl+X, Ctrl+C, or Ctrl+V to cut, copy, or paste as shown within the Edit menu). A *dimmed command* (e.g., the Paste command in the Edit menu) means the command is not currently executable, and that some additional action has to be taken for the command to become available.

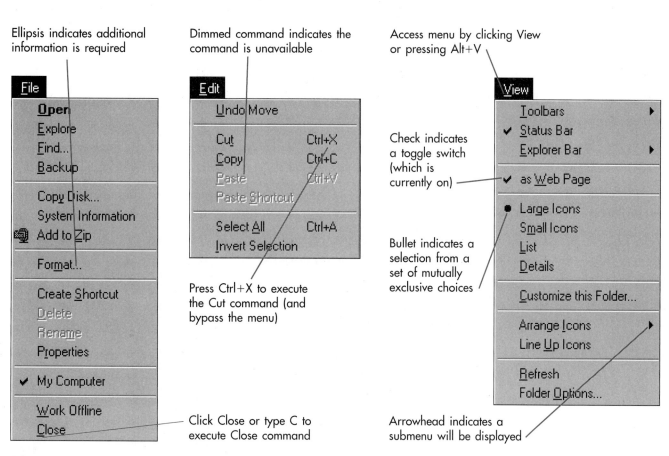

FIGURE 3   Pull-down Menus

An *ellipsis* (...) following a command indicates that additional information is required to execute the command; for example, selection of the Format command in the File menu requires the user to specify additional information about the formatting process. This information is entered into a dialog box (discussed in the next section) which appears immediately after the command has been selected.

A *check* next to a command indicates a toggle switch, whereby the command is either on or off. There is a check next to the Status Bar command in the View menu of Figure 3, which means the command is in effect (and thus the status bar will be displayed). Click the Status Bar command, and the check disappears, which suppresses the display of the status bar. Click the command a second time, and the check reappears, as does the status bar in the associated window.

A *bullet* next to an item (e.g., Large Icons in Figure 3c) indicates a selection from a set of mutually exclusive choices. Click another option within the group (e.g., Small Icons), and the bullet will disappear from the previous selection (Large Icons) and appear next to the new selection (Small Icons).

An *arrowhead* after a command (e.g., the Arrange Icons command in the View menu) indicates that a *submenu* (also known as a cascaded menu) will be displayed with additional menu options.

Dialog Boxes

A *dialog box* appears when additional information is needed to execute a command. The Format command, for example, requires information about which drive to format and the type of formatting desired.

Option (radio) buttons indicate mutually exclusive choices, one of which must be chosen; for example, one of three Format Type options in Figure 4a. Click a button to select an option, which automatically deselects the previously selected option.

Check boxes are used instead of option buttons if the choices are not mutually exclusive or if an option is not required. Multiple boxes can be checked as in Figure 4a, or no boxes may be checked as in Figure 4b. Individual options are selected and cleared by clicking the appropriate check box.

A *text box* is used to enter descriptive information—for example, Bob's Disk in Figure 4a. A flashing vertical bar (an I-beam) appears within the text box when the text box is active, to mark the insertion point for the text you will enter.

A *list box* displays some or all of the available choices, any one of which is selected by clicking the desired item. A *drop-down list box,* such as the Capacity list box in Figure 4a, conserves space by showing only the current selection. Click the arrow of a drop-down list box to display the list of available options. An *open list box,* such as those in Figure 4b, displays multiple choices at one time. (A scroll bar appears within an open list box if all of the choices are not visible and provides access to the hidden choices.)

A *tabbed dialog box* provides multiple sets of options. The dialog box in Figure 4c, for example, has six tabs, each with its own set of options. Click a tab (the Web tab is currently selected) to display the associated options.

The *Help button* (a question mark at the right end of the title bar) provides help for any item in the dialog box. Click the button, then click the item in the dialog box for which you want additional information. The close button (the X at the extreme right of the title bar) closes the dialog box.

All dialog boxes also contain one or more *command buttons,* the function of which is generally apparent from the button's name. The Start button, in Figure 4a, for example, initiates the formatting process. The OK command button in Figure 4b accepts the settings and closes the dialog box. The Cancel button does just the opposite, and ignores (cancels) any changes made to the settings, then closes the dialog box without further action.

Drop-down list box shows current selection (click arrow to see list of available options)

Start button begins formatting (executes command)

Option buttons indicate mutually exclusive choices

Text box is used to enter descriptive information

Check boxes indicate choices that are not mutually exclusive

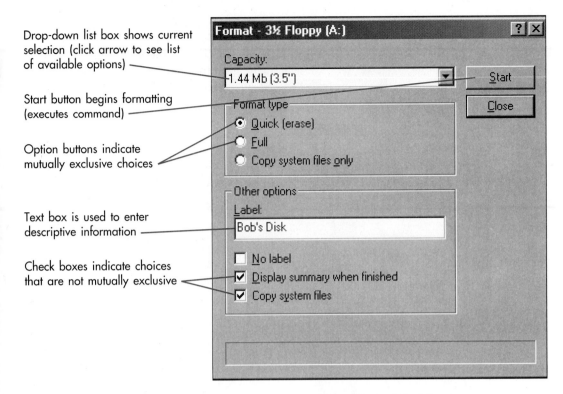

(a) Option Boxes and Check Boxes

Open list box displays multiple options

Scroll bar indicates that not all choices are visible

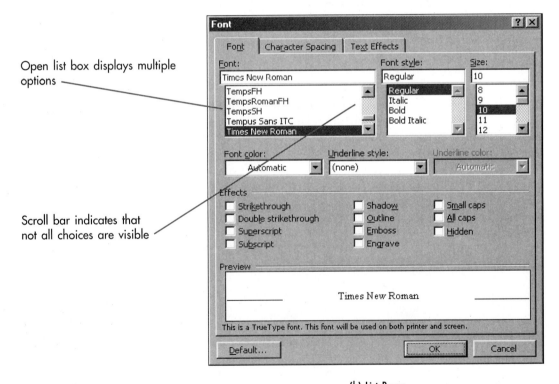

(b) List Boxes

FIGURE 4   Dialog Boxes

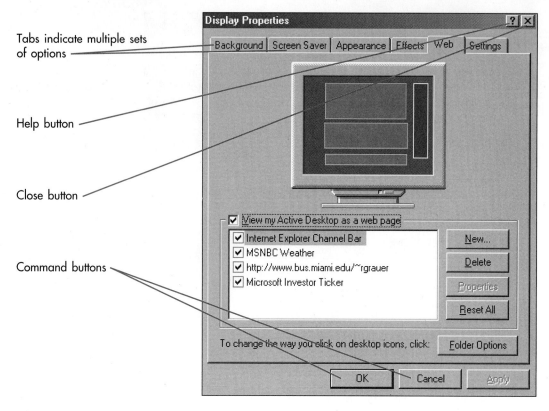

Tabs indicate multiple sets of options

Help button

Close button

Command buttons

(c) Tabbed Dialog Box

FIGURE 4   Dialog Boxes (continued)

THE MOUSE

The mouse is indispensable to Windows and is referenced continually in the hands-on exercises throughout the text. There are five basic operations with which you must become familiar:

- To *point* to an object, move the mouse pointer onto the object.
- To *click* an object, point to it, then press and release the left mouse button.
- To *right click* an object, point to the object, then press and release the right mouse button.
- To *double click* an object, point to it, then quickly click the left button twice in succession.
- To *drag* an object, move the pointer to the object, then press and hold the left button while you move the mouse to a new position.

The mouse is a pointing device—move the mouse on your desk and the *mouse pointer,* typically a small arrowhead, moves on the monitor. The mouse pointer assumes different shapes according to the location of the pointer or the nature of the current action. You will see a double arrow when you change the size of a window, an I-beam as you insert text, a hand to jump from one help topic to the next, or a circle with a line through it to indicate that an attempted action is invalid.

The mouse pointer will also change to an hourglass to indicate Windows is processing your command, and that no further commands may be issued until the action is completed. The more powerful your computer, the less frequently the hourglass will appear.

The Mouse versus the Keyboard

Almost every command in Windows can be executed in different ways, using either the mouse or the keyboard. Most people start with the mouse and add keyboard shortcuts as they become more proficient. There is no right or wrong technique, just different techniques, and the one you choose depends entirely on personal preference in a specific situation. If, for example, your hands are already on the keyboard, it is faster to use the keyboard equivalent. Other times, your hand will be on the mouse and that will be the fastest way. Toolbars provide still other ways to execute common commands.

In the beginning, you may wonder why there are so many different ways to do the same thing, but you will eventually recognize the many options as part of Windows' charm. It is not necessary to memorize anything, nor should you even try; just be flexible and willing to experiment. The more you practice, the faster all of this will become second nature to you.

THE HELP COMMAND

Windows 98 includes extensive documentation with detailed information about virtually every area in Windows. It is accessed through the *Help command* on the Start menu, which provides three different ways to search for information.

The *Contents tab* in Figure 5a is analogous to the table of contents in an ordinary book. The topics are listed in the left pane, and the information for the selected topic is displayed in the right pane. The list of topics can be displayed in varying amounts of detail, by opening and closing the various book icons that appear.

A closed book (e.g., Troubleshooting) indicates that there are subtopics that can be seen by opening (clicking) the book. An open book (e.g., How the Screen Looks) indicates that all of the subtopics are visible. (You can click an open book to close it and gain additional space in the left pane.) A question mark (e.g., Set up a screen saver) indicates the actual topic, the contents of which are displayed in the right side of the screen. An underlined entry (e.g., Related Topics) indicates a hyperlink, which you can click to display additional information. You can also print the information in the right pane by pulling down the Options menu and selecting the Print command.

The *Index tab* in Figure 5b is analogous to the index of an ordinary book. You enter the first several letters of the topic to look up (e.g., Internet), choose a topic from the resulting list, and then click the Display button to view the information in the right pane. The underlined entries represent hyperlinks, which you can click to display additional topics. And, as in the Contents window, you can print the information in the right pane by pulling down the Options menu and selecting the Print command.

The *Search tab* (not shown in Figure 5) contains a more extensive listing of entries than does the Index tab. It lets you enter a specific word or phrase, then it returns every topic containing that word or phrase.

GET HELP ONLINE
The Windows 98 Help file is a powerful tool, but it may not have the answer to every question. Click the Start button, click Help to display the Windows Help dialog box, then click the Web Help button on the toolbar. Click the link to Support online and you will be connected to the Microsoft technical support site, where you can search the Microsoft Knowledge base.

Index tab

Search tab

Open book indicates that
subtopics are listed; click to
close book and hide subtopics

Selected topic; contents
displayed in right pane

Hyperlink; click to display
additional information

Click to open book and
see list of subtopics

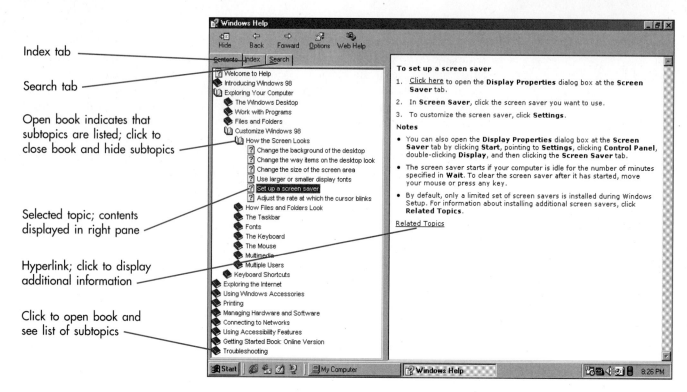

(a) Contents Tab

Enter topic

Click specific topic

Click specific topic

Click display

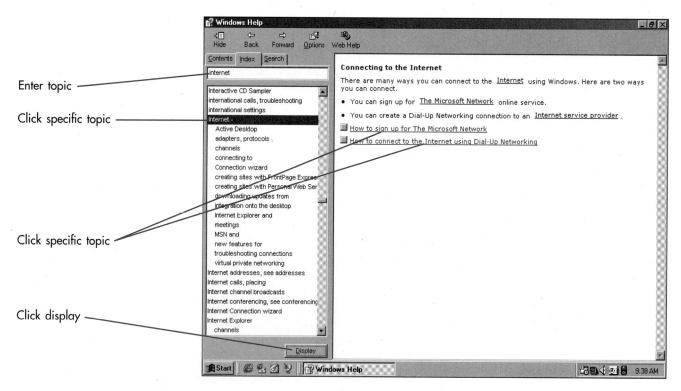

(b) Index Tab

FIGURE 5   The Help Command

FORMATTING A FLOPPY DISK

You will soon begin to work on the computer, which means that you will be using various applications to create different types of documents. Each document is saved in its own file and stored on disk, either on a hard disk (e.g., drive C) if you have your own computer, or on a floppy disk (drive A) if you are working in a computer lab at school.

All disks have to be formatted before they can hold data. The formatting process divides a disk into concentric circles called tracks, then further divides each track into sectors. You don't have to worry about formatting a hard disk, as that is done at the factory prior to the machine being sold. You do, however, have to format a floppy disk in order to write to that disk. Realize, too, that you will need to use one or more floppy disks even if you have your own computer in order to copy important files (such as your term paper) from your hard drive to the floppy disks. The latter will serve as backup should anything happen to the file on the hard disk.

In any event, you need to purchase floppy disks, and format them so that they will be able to store the files you create. (You can purchase preformatted floppy disks, but it is very easy to format your own, and we provide instructions in the hands-on exercise that follows.) Be aware, however, that formatting erases any data that was previously on a disk, so be careful not to format a disk with important data (e.g., one containing today's homework assignment).

Formatting is accomplished through the *Format command*. The process is straightforward and has you enter all of the necessary information into a dialog box. One of the box's options is to copy system files onto the disk while formatting it. These files are necessary to start (boot) your computer, and if your hard disk were to fail, you would need a floppy disk with the system (and other) files in order to start the machine. (See Help for information on creating a *boot disk* containing the system files.) For ordinary purposes, however, you do not put the system files on a floppy disk because they take up space you could use to store data.

FORMAT AT THE PROPER CAPACITY

A floppy disk should be formatted at its rated capacity, or else you may be unable to read the disk. There are two types of 3½-inch floppy disks, double-density (720KB and obsolete) and high-density (1.44MB). The easiest way to determine the type of disk you have is to look at the disk itself for the label DD or HD, for double- and high-density, respectively. You can also check the number of square holes in the disk; a double-density disk has one, whereas a high-density disk has two.

LEARNING BY DOING

Learning is best accomplished by doing, and so we come to the first of two hands-on exercises in this chapter. The exercises enable you to apply the concepts you have learned, then extend those concepts to further exploration on your own. Our opening exercise welcomes you to the Windows desktop, directs you to open My Computer, then has you move and size a window. It describes how to format a floppy disk and how to use the Help command. The exercise provides instructions for both the Classic style and Web style and illustrates how to switch between the two.

Welcome to Windows 98

Objective: To turn on the computer, start Windows, and open My Computer; to move and size a window; to format a floppy disk and use the Help command. Use Figure 6 as a guide in the exercise.

STEP 1: Open My Computer

➤ Start the computer by turning on the various switches appropriate to your system. Your system will take a minute or so to boot up, after which you should see the desktop in Figure 6a. (The My Computer window is not yet open.) Close the Welcome to Windows 98 window if it appears.

➤ Do not be concerned if your desktop differs from ours. The way in which you open My Computer depends on the style in effect on your desktop. Thus:

- In the Classic style, double click the **My Computer icon** (shown in Figure 6a).

- In the Web style, click the **My Computer icon** (not shown in Figure 6a).

- In either style, right click the **My Computer icon** to display a context-sensitive menu, then click the **Open command.**

➤ The My Computer window will open as shown in Figure 6a. The contents of your window and/or its size and position on the desktop will be different from ours.

Click My Computer icon (Classic style)

Click View menu

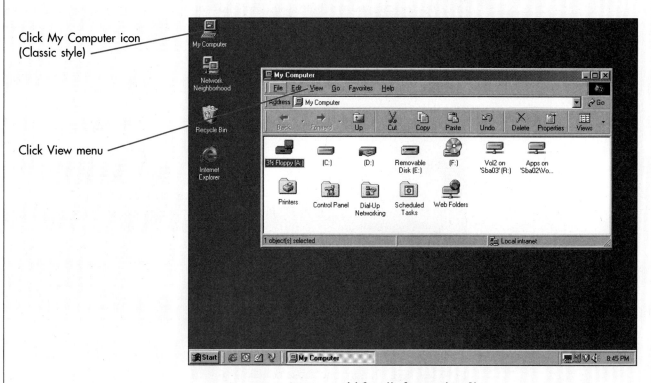

(a) Open My Computer (step 1)

FIGURE 6   Hands-on Exercise 1

STARTING YOUR COMPUTER

The number and location of the on/off switches depend on the nature and manufacturer of the devices connected to the computer. The easiest possible setup is when all components of the system are plugged into a surge protector, in which case only a single switch has to be turned on. In any event, turn on the monitor, printer, and system unit. Note, too, that new-comers to computing often forget that the floppy drive should be empty prior to starting a computer. This ensures that the system starts by reading files from the hard disk (which contains the Windows files) as opposed to a floppy disk (which does not).

STEP 2: Customize My Computer

➤ Pull down the **View menu,** then click (or point to) the **Toolbars command** to display a cascaded menu as shown in Figure 6b. If necessary, check the commands for the **Standard Buttons** and **Address Bar,** and clear the commands for Links and Text Labels.

➤ If necessary, pull down the **View menu** a second time to make or verify the selections in Figure 6b. (You have to pull down the menu each time you choose a different command.)

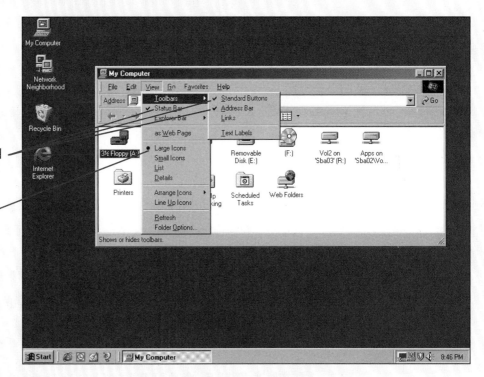

Status Bar, Standard Buttons, and Address Bar are checked

Large Icons is selected

(b) Customize My Computer (step 2)

FIGURE 6   Hands-on Exercise 1 (continued)

- The **Status Bar command** should be checked. The Status Bar command functions as a toggle switch. Click the command, and the status bar is displayed; click the command a second time, and the status bar disappears.
- **Large Icons** should be selected as the current view. (The Large Icons view is one of four mutually exclusive views in My Computer.)

➤ Pull down the **View menu** once again, click (or point to) the **Explorer Bar command** and verify that none of the options are checked. Each option functions as a toggle switch; i.e., click an option to check it, and click it a second time to remove the check.

➤ Pull down the **View menu** a final time. Click (or point to) the **Arrange Icons command** and (if necessary) click the **AutoArrange command** so that a check appears. Click outside the menu (or press the **Esc key**) if the command is already checked.

DESIGNATING THE DEVICES ON A SYSTEM

The first (usually only) floppy drive is always designated as drive A. (A second floppy drive, if it were present, would be drive B.) The first (often only) hard disk on a system is always drive C, whether or not there are one or two floppy drives. A system with one floppy drive and one hard disk (today's most common configuration) will contain icons for drive A and drive C. Additional hard drives (if any) and/or the CD-ROM are labeled from D on.

STEP 3: Move and Size a Window

➤ Click the **maximize button** so that the My Computer window expands to fill the entire screen. Click the **restore button** (which replaces the maximize button and is not shown in Figure 6c) to return the window to its previous size.

➤ Pull down the **View menu** and click **Details**. (Alternatively, you can click the **Down Arrow** for the **Views button** on the toolbar and select **Details** from the resulting menu.)

➤ Move and size the My Computer window on your desktop to match the display in Figure 6c.
- To change the width or height of the window, click and drag a border (the mouse pointer changes to a double arrow) in the direction you want to go. Thus you drag the border inward to shrink the window or drag it outward to enlarge it.
- To change the width and height at the same time, click and drag a corner rather than a border.
- To change the position of the window, click and drag the title bar.

➤ Click the **minimize button** to shrink the My Computer window to a button on the taskbar. My Computer is still active in memory although its window is no longer visible.

➤ Click the **My Computer button** on the taskbar to reopen the window.

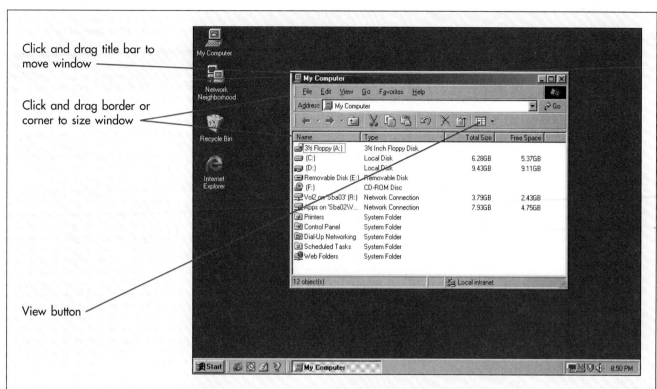

Click and drag title bar to
move window

Click and drag border or
corner to size window

View button

(c) Move and Size a Window (step 3)

FIGURE 6   Hands-on Exercise 1 (continued)

MINIMIZING VERSUS CLOSING AN APPLICATION

Minimizing an application leaves the application open in memory and available at the click of the taskbar button. Closing it, however, removes the application from memory, which also causes it to disappear from the taskbar. The advantage of minimizing an application is that you can return to the application immediately. The disadvantage is that leaving too many applications open will degrade the performance of your system.

STEP 4: Format a Floppy Disk

➤ Place a floppy disk in drive A. The formatting process erases anything that is on the disk, so be sure that you do not need anything on the disk.

➤ The way you select drive A and display the Format dialog box depends on the style in effect. Thus:

- In the Classic style, click (do not double click) the icon for **drive A,** then pull down the **File menu** and click the **Format command.**

- In the Web style, point to (do not click) the icon for **drive A,** then pull down the **File menu** and click the **Format command.**

- In either style, right click the icon for **drive A** to select it and display a context-sensitive menu, then click the **Format command.**

➤ Move the Format dialog box by clicking and dragging its **title bar** so that the display on your desktop matches ours. Set the formatting parameters as shown in Figure 6d:

- Set the **Capacity** to match the floppy disk you purchased (1.44MB for a high-density disk and 720KB for a double-density disk).

- Click the **Full option button** to choose a full format, which checks a disk for errors as it is formatted. This option is worth the extra time as compared to a quick format; the latter erases the files on a previously formatted disk but does not check for errors.

- Click the **Label text box** if it's empty or click and drag over the existing label if there is an entry. Enter a new label (containing up to 11 characters) such as **Bob's Disk.**

- Click the **Start command button** to begin the formatting operation. This will take a minute or two. You can see the progress of the formatting process at the bottom of the dialog box.

➤ After the formatting process is complete, you will see the Format Results message box. Read the information, then click the **Close command button** to close the informational dialog box.

➤ Click the **close button** to close the Format dialog box. Save the formatted disk for use with various exercises later in the text.

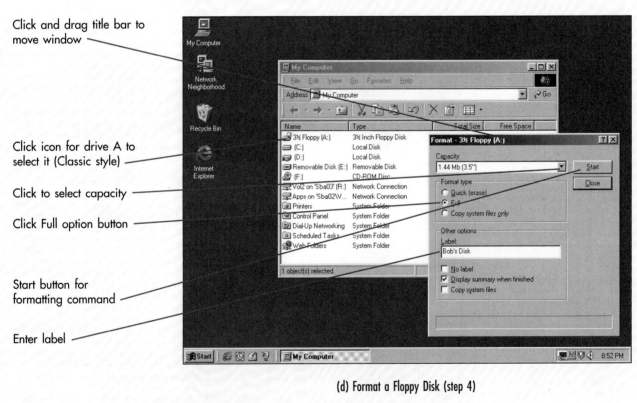

Click and drag title bar to move window

Click icon for drive A to select it (Classic style)

Click to select capacity

Click Full option button

Start button for formatting command

Enter label

(d) Format a Floppy Disk (step 4)

FIGURE 6   Hands-on Exercise 1 (continued)

THE HELP BUTTON

The Help button (a question mark) appears in the title bar of almost every dialog box. Click the question mark, then click the item you want information about (which then appears in a pop-up window). To print the contents of the pop-up window, click the right mouse button inside the window, and click Print Topic. Click outside the pop-up window to close the window and continue working.

STEP 5: Change the Style

➤ Pull down the **View menu** and click the **Folder Options command** to display the Folder Options dialog box in Figure 6e. Click the **General tab,** click the option button for **Web style,** then click **OK** to accept the settings and close the Folder Options dialog box.

➤ The icons in the My Computer window should be underlined because you have changed to the Web style. Click the icon for **drive A** to view the contents of the floppy disk. The contents of the Address bar change to reflect drive A. The disk is empty, so you do not see any files.

➤ Close the My Computer window. Click the (underlined) **My Computer icon** on the desktop to open My Computer. You click (rather than double click) the icon to open it because you are in the Web style.

➤ Close My Computer.

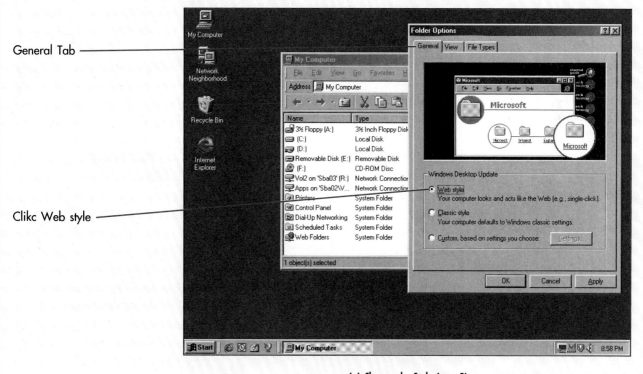

General Tab

Clikc Web style

(e) Change the Style (step 5)

FIGURE 6   Hands-on Exercise 1 (continued)

STEP 6: The Help Command

➤ Click the **Start button** on the taskbar, then click the **Help command** to display the Help window in Figure 6f. Do not be concerned if the size or position of your window is different from ours.

➤ Click the **Index tab,** then click in the text box to enter the desired topic. Type **Web st** (the first letters in "Web style," the topic you are searching for). Note that when you enter the last letter, the Help window displays "Web style folders" in the list of topics.

➤ Click (select) **Web style mouse selection,** then click the **Display button** to view the information in Figure 6f. Read the instructions carefully.

➤ Pull down the **Options menu** and click the **Print command** to display the Print dialog box. Click **OK** to print the selected page.

➤ Click the **close button** to close the Help window.

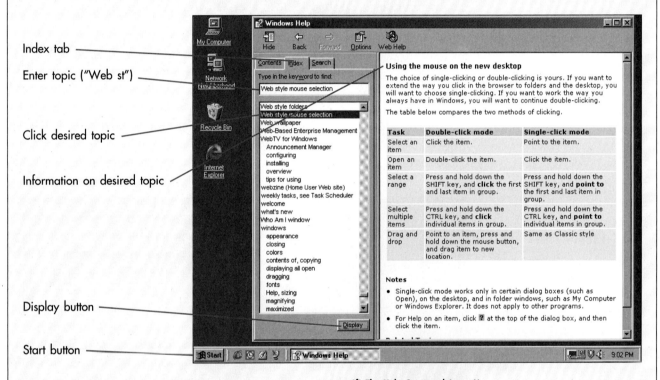

(f) The Help Command (step 6)

FIGURE 6 Hands-on Exercise 1 (continued)

STEP 7: Shut Down the Computer

➤ Click the **Start button,** click the **Shut Down command** to display the Shut Down Windows dialog box, and if necessary, click the option button to shut down the computer.

➤ Click the **Yes command button,** then wait as Windows gets ready to shut down your system. Wait until you see another screen indicating that it is OK to turn off the computer.

FILES AND FOLDERS

A *file* is a set of instructions or data that has been given a name and stored on disk. There are two basic types of files, program files and data files. Microsoft Word and Microsoft Excel are examples of program files. The documents and workbooks created by these programs are examples of data files.

A *program file* is an executable file because it contains instructions that tell the computer what to do. A *data file* is not executable and can be used only in conjunction with a specific program. As a student, you execute (run) program files, then you use those programs to create and/or modify the associated data files.

Every file must have a *file name* so that it can be identified. The file name may contain up to 255 characters and may include spaces and other punctuation. (This is very different from the rules that existed under MS-DOS, which limited file names to eight characters followed by an optional three-character extension.) Long file names permit descriptive entries such as *Term Paper for Western Civilization* (as opposed to *TPWCIV* that would be required under MS-DOS).

Files are stored in *folders* to better organize the hundreds (often thousands) of files on a hard disk. A Windows folder is similar in concept to a manila folder in a filing cabinet into which you put one or more documents (files) that are somehow related to each other. An office worker stores his or her documents in manila folders. In Windows, you store your files (documents) in electronic folders on disk.

Folders are the keys to the Windows storage system. Some folders are created automatically; for example, the installation of a program such as Microsoft Office automatically creates one or more folders to hold the various program files. Other folders are created by the user to hold the documents he or she creates. You could, for example, create one folder for your word processing documents and a second folder for your spreadsheets. Alternatively, you can create a folder to hold all of your work for a specific class, which may contain a combination of word processing documents and spreadsheets. Anything at all can go into a folder—program files, data files, even other folders.

Figure 7 displays a My Computer window for a folder containing six documents. Figure 7a shows the folder in the Classic style whereas Figure 7b shows it in the Web style. The choice between the two is one of personal preference and has to do with the action of the mouse. In the Classic style, you click an icon to select it, and you double click the icon to open it. In the Web style, you point to an icon to select it, and you click the icon to open it. (These operations mimic those of a Web browser.)

Regardless of the style in effect, the name of the folder (Homework) appears in the title bar next to the icon of an open folder. The minimize, maximize, and close buttons appear at the right of the title bar. A menu bar with six pull-down menus appears below the title bar. The Address bar appears below the menu bar and the toolbar appears below that. As with any toolbar, you can point to any button to display a ScreenTip that is indicative of the button's function. A status bar appears at the bottom of both windows, indicating that the Homework folder contains six objects (documents) and that the total file size is 333KB.

The Homework folder in both Figures 7a and 7b is displayed in *Details view,* one of four views available in My Computer. (The other views are Large Icons, Small Icons, and List view. The choice of view depends on your personal preference.) The Details view contains the maximum amount of information for each file and is used more frequently than the other views. It shows the file size, the type of file, and the date and time the file was last modified. The Details view also displays a small icon to the left of each file name that represents the application that is associated with the file. The Views button is the easiest way to switch from one view to another.

Name of folder

Menu bar

Address bar

Tool bar

Views button

Icon indicates associated application

Status bar

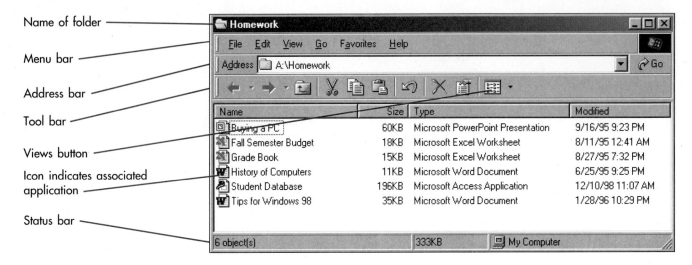

(a) Classic Style

Type column

Web Style has underlined icons

Icon indicates a Word document

Number of objects in window

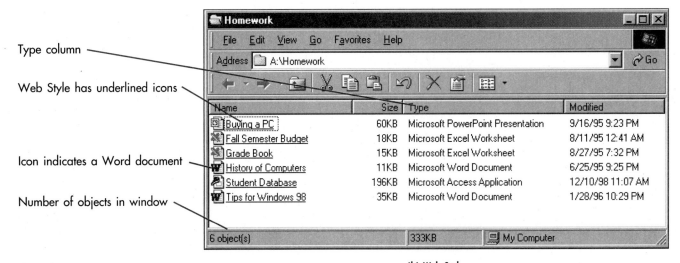

(b) Web Style

FIGURE 7   The Homework Folder

CLASSIC STYLE OR WEB STYLE

The Classic style and Web style are very different from one another, but neither style is a "better" style. The choice is one of personal preference, and depends on how you want to view the desktop and how you want to open its objects, by double clicking or clicking, respectively. We encourage you to experiment with both styles, and indeed, we find ourselves switching back and forth between the two. Use the Folder Options command in the View menu to change the style.

File Type

Every data file has a specific *file type* that is determined by the application used to create the file. One way to recognize the file type is to examine the Type column in the Details view as shown in Figure 7a. The History of Computers file, for example, is a Microsoft Word document. The Grade Book is a Microsoft Excel worksheet.

You can also determine the file type (or associated application) in any view by examining the application icon displayed next to the file name. Look carefully at the icon next to the History of Computers document in Figure 7a or 7b, for example, and you will recognize the icon for Microsoft Word. The application icon is recognized more easily in Large Icons view, as shown in Figure 8. Each application in Microsoft Office has a distinct icon.

Still another way to determine the file type is through a three-character *extension*, which is appended to the file name, but which is not shown in Figure 7. (A period separates the file name from the extension.) Each application has a unique extension that is automatically assigned to the file name when the file is created. DOC and XLS, for example, are the extensions for Microsoft Word and Excel, respectively. The extension may be suppressed or displayed according to an option in the View menu, but is better left suppressed.

My Computer

My Computer enables you to browse through the various folders on your system so that you can locate a document and go to work. Let's assume that you're looking for your term paper on the History of Computers, which you began yesterday, and which you saved in a folder called Homework.

My Computer can be used to locate the Homework file, and as indicated earlier, you can use either the Classic style in Figure 8a or the Web style in Figure 8b. The concepts are identical, but there are differences in the appearance of the icons (they are underlined in the Web style) and in the way the commands are executed. One other difference is that the Classic style opens a new window for each open folder, whereas the Web style uses a single window throughout the process.

In the Classic style in Figure 8a, you begin by double clicking the My Computer icon on the desktop to open the My Computer window, which in turn displays the devices on your system. Next, you double click the icon for drive C to open a second window that displays the folders on drive C. From there, you double click the icon for the Homework folder to open a third window containing the documents in the Homework folder. Once in the Homework folder, you can double click the icon of an existing document, which starts the associated application and opens the document, enabling you to begin work.

The Web style in Figure 8b follows the same sequence, but has you click rather than double click. Equally important, it uses a single window throughout the process as opposed to the multiple windows in the Classic style. You begin by clicking the My Computer icon on the desktop to display the contents of My Computer, which includes an icon for drive C. Then you click the icon for drive C, which in turn lets you click the Homework folder, from which you can click the icon for the data file to start the associated application and open the document. Note, too, the back arrow on the toolbar in Figure 8b, which is active throughout the Web style. You can click the back arrow to return to the previous folder (drive C in this example), just as you can click the back arrow on a Web browser to return to the previous Web page.

Double click My Computer icon —

Double click icon for Drive C —

Double click icon for
Homework folder —

Double click to start Excel and
open Grade Book file —

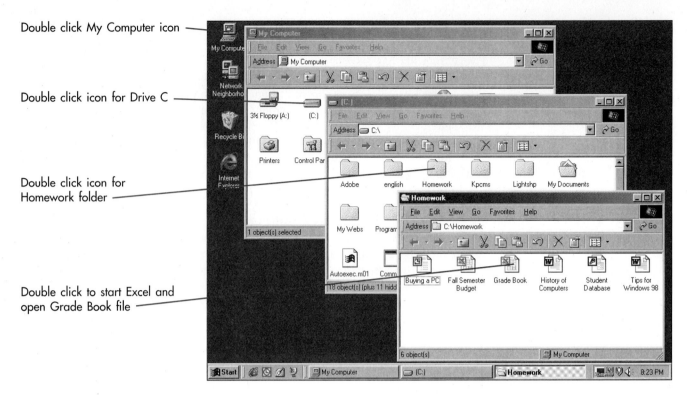

(a) Classic Style

Click to open My computer —

Click Back arrow to
return to previous folder —

Click to start Excel and
open Grade Book file —

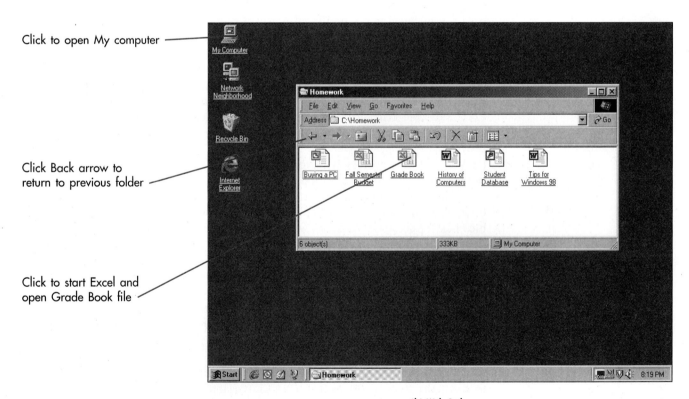

(b) Web Style

FIGURE 8   Browsing My Computer

The Exploring Windows Home Page

Objective: To download a file from the Web to a PC using the Classic and/or Web style. The exercise requires a formatted floppy disk and access to the Internet. Use Figure 9 as a guide in the exercise.

STEP 1: Start Internet Explorer

➤ Start Internet Explorer by clicking its icon on the desktop. If necessary, click the **maximize button** so that Internet Explorer takes the entire desktop.

➤ Enter the address of the site you want to visit:

- Pull down the **File menu,** click the **Open command** to display the Open dialog box, and enter **www.prenhall.com/grauer** (the http:// is assumed). Click **OK.**

- *Or,* click in the **Address bar** below the toolbar, which automatically selects the current address (so that whatever you type replaces the current address). Enter the address of the site, **www.prenhall.com/grauer** (the http:// is assumed). Press **Enter.**

➤ You should see the Exploring Windows series home page as shown in Figure 9a. Click the book for **Office 2000,** which takes you to the Office 2000 home page. Click the **Student Resources link** (at the top of the window) to go to the Student Resources page.

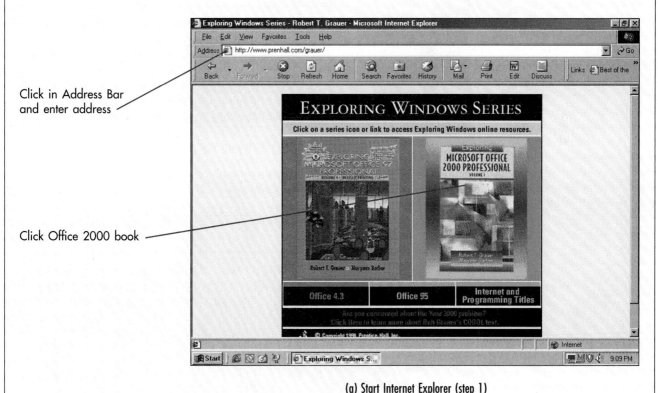

Click in Address Bar and enter address

Click Office 2000 book

(a) Start Internet Explorer (step 1)

FIGURE 9   Hands-on Exercise 2

STEP 2: Download the Practice Files

➤ Click the link to **Student Data Disk** (in the left frame), then scroll down the page until you see Windows 98 Prerequisites. Click the indicated link to download the student data disk as shown in Figure 9b.

➤ You will see the File Download dialog box asking what you want to do. The option button to save this program to disk is selected. Click **OK.** The Save As dialog box appears.

➤ Place a formatted floppy disk in drive A, click the **drop-down arrow** on the Save in list box, and select (click) **drive A.** Click **Save** to begin downloading the file.

Click Student Resources link

Click link to Student Data Disk

Click Save

Click link to download Windows 98 Prerequisites Data Disk

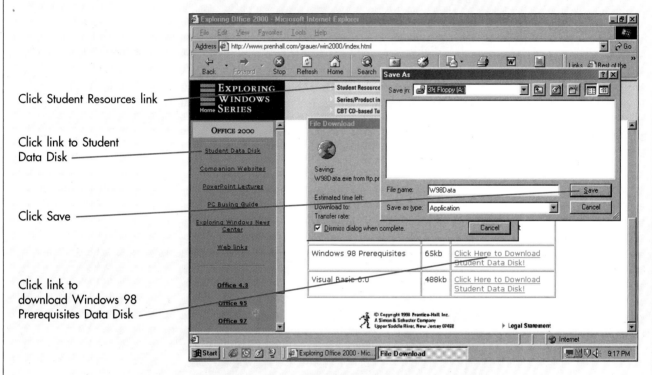

(b) Download the Practice Files (step 2)

FIGURE 9   Hands-on Exercise 2 (continued)

REMEMBER THE LOCATION

It's easy to download a file from the Web. The only tricky part, if any, is remembering where you have saved the file. This exercise is written for a laboratory setting, and thus we specified drive A as the destination, so that you will have the file on a floppy disk at the end of the exercise. If you have your own computer, however, it's faster to save the file to the desktop or in a temporary folder on drive C. Just remember where you save the file so that you can access it after it has been downloaded. And, if you really lose a file, click the Start button, then click the Find command. Use Help to learn more about searching for files on your PC.

- The File Download window will reappear on your screen and show you the status of the downloading operation. Be patient as this may take a few minutes.

- The File Download window will close automatically when the downloading is complete. If necessary, click **Close** when you see the dialog box indicating that the download is complete. Close Internet Explorer.

STEP 3: Classic Style or Web Style

- The instructions for opening My Computer and installing the practice files vary slightly, depending on which style is in effect on your desktop.
  - In the Classic style you click an icon to select it, and you double click the icon to open it.
  - In the Web style you point to an icon to select it, and you click the icon to open it. These operations mimic those of a Web browser—hence the term "Web style."

- You can switch from one style to the other using **My Computer.** Pull down the **View menu,** click the **Folder Options command,** then click the **General tab.** Select the option button for **Web style** or **Classic style** as desired, then click **OK** to accept the settings and close the Folder Options dialog box.

- Go to **step 4** or **step 6,** depending on which style is in effect on your desktop. You might even want to do the exercise both ways, in order to determine which style you prefer.

TO CLICK OR DOUBLE CLICK

The choice between Web style and Classic style is personal and depends on how you want to open a document, by clicking or double clicking, respectively. One way to change from one style to the other is to point to the desktop, click the right mouse button to display a context-sensitive menu, then click the Properties command to open the Display Properties dialog box. Click the Web tab, click the Folder Options command button, click Yes when prompted whether to view the folder options, then choose the style you want.

STEP 4: Install the Practice Files in Classic Style

- Double click the **My Computer icon** on the desktop to open the My Computer window. Double click the icon for **drive A** to open a second window as shown in Figure 9c. The size and/or position of these windows on your desktop may differ from ours; the second window, for example, may appear directly on top of the existing window.

- Double click the **W98Data icon** to install the data disk. You will see a dialog box thanking you for selecting the Exploring Windows series. Click **OK** when you have finished reading the dialog box to continue the installation and display the WinZip Self-Extractor dialog box in Figure 9c.

- Check that the Unzip To Folder text box specifies **A:**, which will extract the files to the floppy disk. (You can enter a different drive and/or folder if you prefer.)

- Click the **Unzip button** to extract (uncompress) the practice files and copy them onto the designated drive. Click **OK** after you see the message indicating that the files have been unzipped successfully. Close the WinZip dialog box.

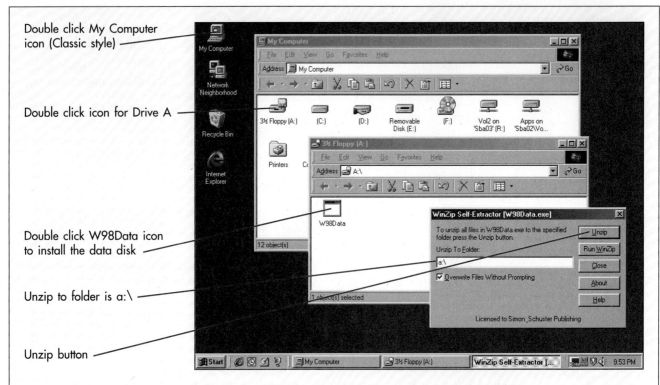

Double click My Computer icon (Classic style)

Double click icon for Drive A

Double click W98Data icon to install the data disk

Unzip to folder is a:\

Unzip button

(c) Install the Practice Files in Classic Style (step 4)

FIGURE 9 Hands-on Exercise 2 (continued)

CUSTOMIZE MY COMPUTER

You can customize the My Computer window regardless of whether you choose the Classic style or Web style. Pull down the View menu, click the Toolbars command to display a cascaded menu, then check the commands for the Standard Buttons and Address Bar, and clear the commands for Links and Text Labels. Pull down the View menu a second time and select (click) the desired view. Pull down the View menu a final time, click the Arrange Icons command, and (if necessary) click the AutoArrange command so that a check appears. Click outside the menu (or press the Esc key) if the command is already checked.

STEP 5: Delete the Compressed File in Classic Style

➤ The practice files have been extracted to drive A and should appear in the drive A window. If you do not see the files, pull down the **View menu** and click the **Refresh command.**

➤ You should see a total of six files in the drive A window. Five of these are the practice files on the data disk; the sixth is the original file that you downloaded earlier.

➤ If necessary, pull down the **View menu** and click **Details** (or click the **Views button** repeatedly) to change to the Details view. Your display should match Figure 9d.

➤ Select (click) the **W98Data icon.** Pull down the **File menu** and click the **Delete command** or click the **Delete button** on the toolbar. Click **Yes** when asked to confirm the deletion. The ie4datadisk file disappears from the drive A window.

➤ Go to **step 8** to complete this exercise; that is, you can skip steps 6 and 7, which illustrate the Web style.

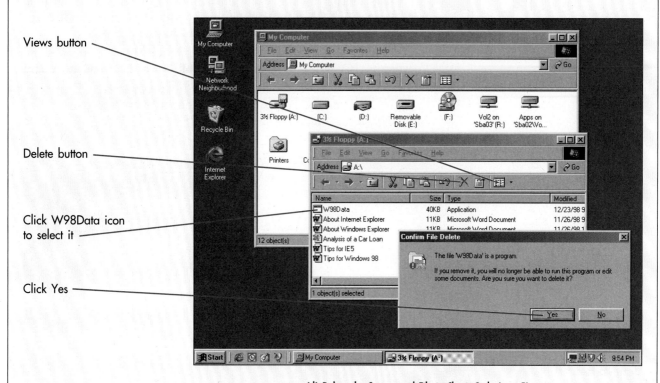

Views button

Delete button

Click W98Data icon
to select it

Click Yes

(d) Delete the Compressed File in Classic Style (step 5)

FIGURE 9   Hands-on Exercise 2 (continued)

ONE WINDOW OR MANY

The Classic style opens a new window every time you open a new drive or folder using My Computer, which can quickly lead to a cluttered desktop. You can, however, customize the Classic style to display the objects in a single window. Pull down the View menu, click the Folder Options command, click the option button for Custom based on the settings you choose, then click the Settings command button to display the Custom Settings dialog box. Click the option button in the Browse folders area to open each folder in the same window, click OK to close the Custom Settings dialog box, then click OK to close the Folder Options dialog box.

STEP 6: Install the Practice Files in Web Style

➤ Click the **My Computer icon** on the desktop to open the My Computer window, then click the icon for **drive A** within My Computer. Click the **W98Data icon** to install the data disk.

➤ You will see a dialog box thanking you for selecting the Exploring Windows series. Click **OK** when you have finished reading the dialog box to continue the installation and display the WinZip Self-Extractor dialog box in Figure 9e.

➤ Check that the Unzip To Folder text box specifies **A:**, which will extract the files to the floppy disk. (You can enter a different drive and/or folder if you prefer.)

➤ Click the **Unzip button** to extract the practice files and copy them onto the designated drive. Click **OK** after you see the message indicating that the files have been unzipped successfully. Close the WinZip dialog box.

➤ The practice files have been extracted to drive A and should appear in the drive A window. If you do not see the files, pull down the **View menu** and click the **Refresh command.**

➤ Pull down the **View menu.** Toggle the command **as Web Page** on or off as you prefer. The command is off in Figure 9e.

Click My Computer icon (Web style)

Click W98Data icon to install the data disk

Unzip to folder is a:\

Click OK

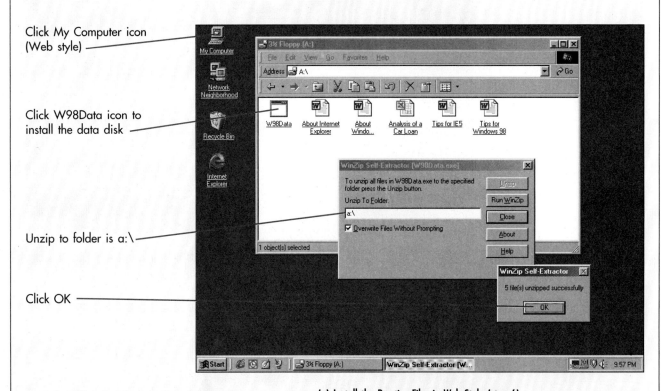

(e) Install the Practice Files in Web Style (step 6)

FIGURE 9   Hands-on Exercise 2 (continued)

THE BACK AND FORWARD BUTTONS IN MY COMPUTER

The Web style is so named because it follows the conventions of a Web browser. Unlike the Classic style, which displays a separate window for each drive or folder, the Web style uses a single window throughout. Thus, you can click the Back button on the My Computer toolbar to return to a previous folder. In similar fashion you can click the Forward button from a previously viewed folder to go to the next folder.

STEP 7: Delete the Compressed File in Web Style

➤ You should see a total of six files in the drive A window. Five of these are the practice files on the data disk; the sixth is the original file that you downloaded earlier.

➤ If necessary, pull down the **View menu** and click **Details** to change to the Details view in Figure 9f so that your display matches ours.

➤ Point to the **W98Data icon,** which in turn selects the file. Pull down the **File menu** and click the **Delete command** or click the **Delete button** on the toolbar. Click **Yes** when asked to confirm the deletion. The W98Data file disappears from the drive A window.

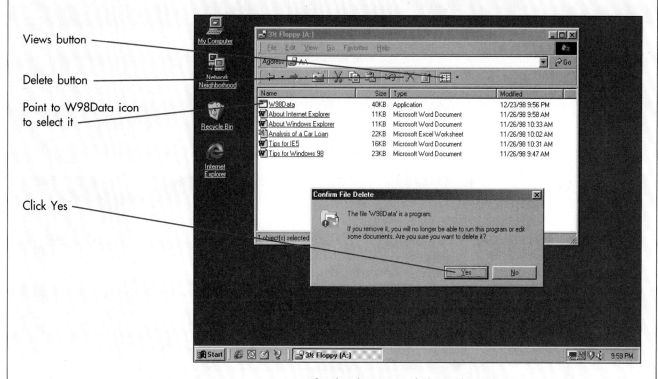

Views button ——

Delete button ——

Point to W98Data icon to select it ——

Click Yes ——

(f) Delete the Compressed File in Web Style (step 7)

FIGURE 9   Hands-on Exercise 2 (continued)

CHANGE THE VIEW

The contents of drive A are displayed in the Details view, one of four views available in My Computer. Details view displays the maximum amount of information for each file and is our general preference. You can, however, click the Views button on the My Computer toolbar to cycle through the other views (Large Icons, Small Icons, and List). You can also pull down the View menu and toggle the As Web Page command on, which will display additional information in the My Computer window.

STEP 8: Modify a File

➤ It doesn't matter whether you are in the Web style or the Classic style. (Our figure displays the Web style.) What is important, however, is that you have successfully downloaded the practice files.

➤ Open the **About Internet Explorer** document:

  • Click the icon in Web style.

  • Double click the document icon in Classic style.

➤ If necessary, maximize the window for Microsoft Word. (The document will open in the WordPad accessory if Microsoft Word is not installed on your machine.)

➤ Read the document, then click inside the document window and press **Ctrl+End** to move to the end of the document. Add the sentence shown in Figure 9g followed by your name.

➤ Pull down the **File menu,** click **Print,** then click **OK** to print the document and prove to your instructor that you did the exercise. Pull down the **File menu** and click **Exit** to close the application. Click **Yes** if prompted whether to save the file.

➤ Exit Windows if you do not want to continue with the next exercise at this time.

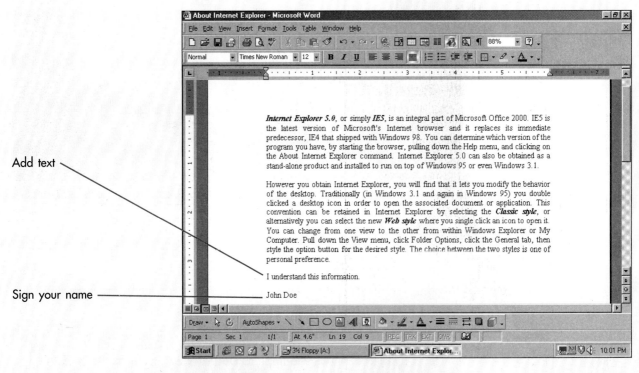

(g) Modify a File (step 8)

FIGURE 9   Hands-on Exercise 2 (continued)

There are two programs that manage the files and folders on your system, My Computer and Windows Explorer. My Computer is intuitive, but less efficient, as you have to open each folder in succession. Windows Explorer is more sophisticated, as it provides a hierarchical view of the entire system in a single window. A beginner might prefer My Computer whereas a more experienced user will most likely opt for Windows Explorer.

Assume, for example, that you are taking four classes this semester, and that you are using the computer in each course. You've created a separate folder to hold the work for each class and have stored the contents of all four folders on a single floppy disk. Assume further that you need to retrieve your third English assignment so that you can modify the assignment, then submit the revised version to your instructor.

Figure 10 illustrates how *Windows Explorer* could be used to locate your assignment. As with My Computer, you can display Windows Explorer in either the Classic style or the Web style. The concepts are identical, but there are differences in the appearance of the icons (they are underlined in the Web style) and in the way the commands are executed. The choice is one of personal preference and you can switch back and forth between the two. (Pull down the View menu and click the Folder Options command to change from one style to the other.)

The Explorer window in both Figure 10a and Figure 10b is divided into two panes. The left pane contains a tree diagram (or hierarchical view) of the entire system showing all drives and, optionally, the folders in each drive. The right pane shows the contents of the active (open) drive or folder. Only one object (a drive or folder) can be active in the left pane, and its contents are displayed automatically in the right pane.

Look carefully at the icon for the English folder in the left pane of either figure. The folder is open, whereas the icon for every other folder is closed. The open folder indicates that the English folder is the active folder. (The name of the active folder also appears in the title bar of Windows Explorer and in the address bar on the toolbar.) The contents of the active folder (three Word documents in this example) are displayed in the right pane. The right pane is displayed in Details view, but could just as easily have been displayed in another view (e.g., Large or Small Icons).

As indicated, only one folder can be open (active) at a time in the left pane. Thus, to see the contents of a different folder such as Accounting, you would open (click on) the Accounting folder, which automatically closes the English folder. The contents of the Accounting folder would then appear in the right pane.

Look carefully at the tree structure in either Figure 10a or Figure 10b and note that it contains an icon for Internet Explorer, which when selected, starts Internet Explorer and displays a Web page in the contents pane of Windows Explorer. Thus you can use Windows Explorer to view Web pages, and conversely, you can use Internet Explorer to view documents and/or folders that are stored locally.

ORGANIZE YOUR WORK

Organize your folder in ways that make sense to you, such as a separate folder for every class you are taking. You can also create folders within folders; for example, a correspondence folder may contain two folders of its own, one for business correspondence and one for personal letters.

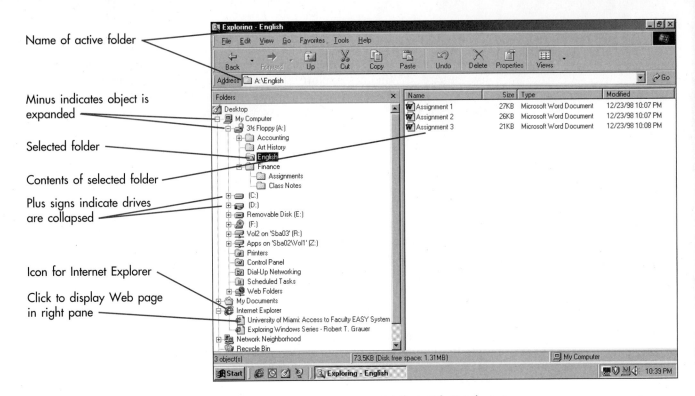

Name of active folder

Minus indicates object is expanded

Selected folder

Contents of selected folder

Plus signs indicate drives are collapsed

Icon for Internet Explorer

Click to display Web page in right pane

(a) Classic Style (Details view)

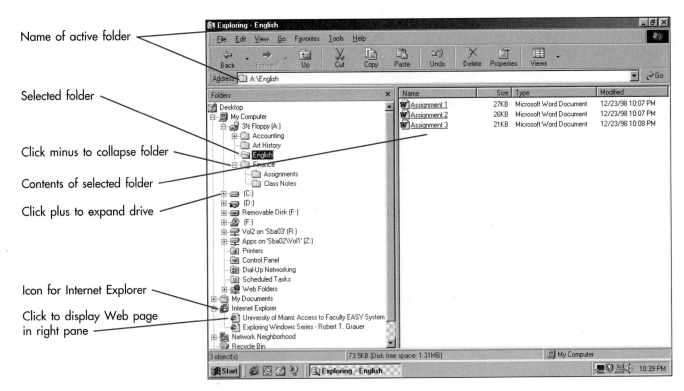

Name of active folder

Selected folder

Click minus to collapse folder

Contents of selected folder

Click plus to expand drive

Icon for Internet Explorer

Click to display Web page in right pane

(b) Web Style (Details view)

FIGURE 10   Windows Explorer

Expanding and Collapsing a Drive

The tree diagram in Windows Explorer displays the devices on your system in hierarchical fashion. The desktop is always at the top of the hierarchy, and it contains various icons such as My Computer, the Recycle Bin, Internet Explorer, and Network Neighborhood. My Computer in turn contains the various drives that are accessible from your system, each of which contains folders, which in turn contain documents and/or additional folders. Each *icon* may be *expanded* or *collapsed* by clicking the plus or minus sign, respectively. Click either sign to toggle to the other. Clicking a plus sign, for example, expands the drive, then displays a minus sign next to the drive to indicate that its subordinates are visible.

Return to either Figure 10a or 10b and look at the icon next to My Computer. It is a minus sign (as opposed to a plus sign), and it indicates that My Computer has been expanded to show the devices on the system. There is also a minus sign next to the icon for drive A to indicate that it too has been expanded to show the folders on the disk. There is also a minus sign next to the Internet Explorer icon, which displays the Web sites that were visited in this session. Note, however, the plus sign next to drives C and D, indicating that these parts of the tree are currently collapsed and thus their subordinates (in this case, folders) are not visible.

A folder may contain additional folders, and thus individual folders may also be expanded or collapsed. The minus sign next to the Finance folder, for example, indicates that the folder has been expanded and contains two additional folders, for Assignments and Class Notes, respectively. The plus sign next to the Accounting folder, however, indicates the opposite; that is, the folder is collapsed and its subordinate folders are not currently visible. A folder with neither a plus or minus sign, such as Art History, does not contain additional folders and cannot be expanded or collapsed.

The hierarchical view within Windows Explorer, and the ability to expand and collapse the various folders on a system, enables the user to quickly locate a specific file or folder. If, for example, you wanted to see the contents of the Art History folder, all you would do is click its icon in the left pane, which automatically changes the display in the right pane to show the documents in that folder.

Windows Explorer is ideal for moving or copying files from one folder or drive to another. You simply select (open) the folder that contains the files, use the scroll bar in the left pane (if necessary) so that the destination folder is visible, then click and drag the files from the right pane to the destination folder. Windows Explorer is a powerful tool, but it takes practice to master. It's time for another hands-on exercise in which we use Windows Explorer to copy the practice files from a network drive to a floppy disk. (The exercise assumes that your instructor has placed our files on your local area network.)

THE DOCUMENT, NOT THE APPLICATION

Windows 98 is document oriented, meaning that you are able to think in terms of the document rather than the application that created it. You can still open a document in traditional fashion, by starting the application that created the document, then using the File Open command in that program to retrieve the document. It's often easier, however, to open the document from within My Computer (or Windows Explorer) by clicking its icon in Web view, or double clicking the icon in Classic view. Windows then starts the application and opens the data file. In other words, you can open a document without explicitly starting the application.

The Practice Files (via a local area network)

Objective: To use Windows Explorer to copy the practice files from a network drive to a floppy disk. The exercise requires a formatted floppy disk and access to a local area network. Use Figure 11 as a guide in the exercise.

CONVERGENCE OF THE EXPLORERS

Windows Explorer and Internet Explorer are separate programs, but each includes some functionality of the other. You can use Windows Explorer to display a Web page by clicking the Internet Explorer icon within the tree structure in the left pane. Conversely, you can use Internet Explorer to display a local drive, document, or folder. Start Internet Explorer in the usual fashion, click in the Address bar, then enter the appropriate address such as C: to display the contents of drive C.

STEP 1: Start Windows Explorer

➤ Click the **Start button,** click (or point to) the **Programs command,** then click **Windows Explorer** to start this program. Click the **maximize button.**

➤ Make or verify the following selections using the **View menu** as shown in Figure 11a. You have to pull down the **View menu** each time you choose a different command.

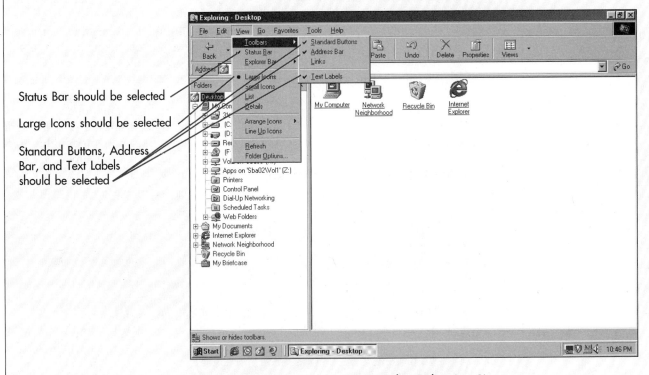

Status Bar should be selected

Large Icons should be selected

Standard Buttons, Address Bar, and Text Labels should be selected

(a) Start Windows Explorer (step 1)

FIGURE 11   Hands-on Exercise 3

- The **Standard Buttons, Address Bar,** and **Text Labels** should be checked.
- The **Status Bar command** should be checked.
- The **Large Icons view** should be selected.

➤ Click (select) the **Desktop icon** in the left pane to display the contents of the desktop in the right pane. Our desktop contains icons for My Computer, Network Neighborhood, the Recycle Bin, and Internet Explorer.

➤ Your desktop may have different icons from ours, but your screen should otherwise match the one in Figure 11a, given that you are in Web style.

CLASSIC STYLE OR WEB STYLE

Which do you prefer, Coke or Pepsi? They are both good, and the choice is one of personal preference. So it is with Classic style and Web style. They are different, but neither is clearly better than the other, and indeed we find ourselves switching between the two. This exercise is written for the Classic style.

STEP 2: Change to Classic Style (if necessary)

➤ You can skip this step if your desktop is already in Classic style. Pull down the **View menu,** click the **Folder Options command** to display the Folder Options dialog box, then click the **General tab** as shown in Figure 11b.

➤ Click the **Classic style option button,** then click **OK** to accept this setting and close the Folder Options dialog box. The icons within Windows Explorer should be displayed in Classic style.

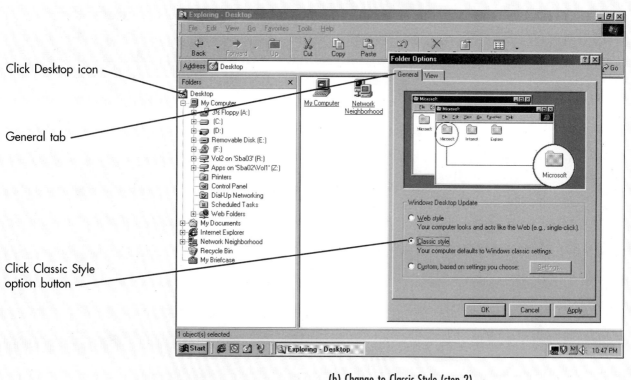

(b) Change to Classic Style (step 2)

FIGURE 11   Hands-on Exercise 3 (continued)

FILE EXTENSIONS

Long-time DOS users remember a three-character extension at the end of a file name to indicate the file type; for example, DOC or XLS to indicate a Word document or Excel workbook, respectively. The extensions are displayed or hidden according to the option you choose through the View menu of Windows Explorer. Pull down the View menu, click the Folder Options command to display the Folder Options dialog box, click the View tab, then check (or clear) the box to hide (or show) file extensions for known file types. Click OK to accept the setting and exit the dialog box.

STEP 3: Collapse the Individual Drives

➤ Click the **minus** (or the **plus**) **sign** next to My Computer to collapse (or expand) My Computer. Toggle the signs back and forth a few times for practice. End with a minus sign next to My Computer.

➤ Place a formatted floppy disk in drive A. Click the drive icon next to **drive A** to select the drive and display its contents in the right pane as shown in Figure 11c. The disk does not contain any files, and hence the right pane is empty.

➤ Click the **plus sign** next to drive A. The plus sign disappears, as drive A does not have any folders.

➤ Click the **sign** next to the other drives to toggle back and forth between expanding and collapsing the individual drives on your system. End this step with every drive collapsed; that is, there should be a **plus sign** next to every drive except drive A, as shown in Figure 11c.

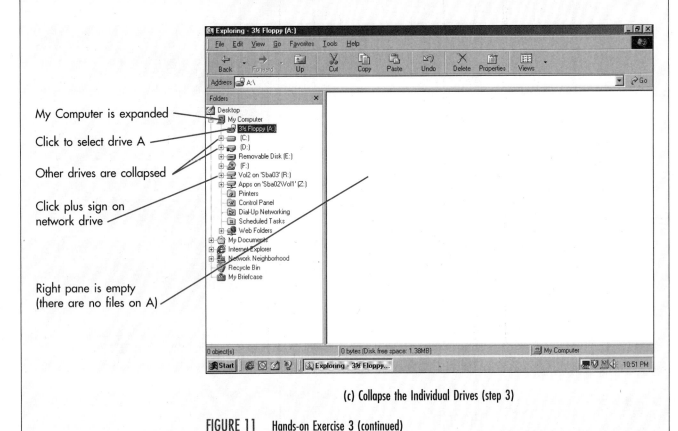

(c) Collapse the Individual Drives (step 3)

FIGURE 11   Hands-on Exercise 3 (continued)

THE PLUS AND MINUS SIGNS

Any drive, be it local or on the network, may be expanded or collapsed to display or hide its folders. A minus sign indicates that the drive has been expanded and that its folders are visible. A plus sign indicates the reverse; that is, the device is collapsed and its folders are not visible. Click either sign to toggle to the other. Clicking a plus sign, for example, expands the drive, then displays a minus sign next to the drive to indicate that the folders are visible. Clicking a minus sign has the reverse effect; that is, it collapses the drive, hiding its folders.

STEP 4: Select the Network Drive

➤ Click the **plus sign** for the network drive that contains the files you are to copy (e.g., **drive R** in Figure 11d). Select (click) the **Exploring Windows 98 folder** to open this folder.

➤ You may need to expand other folders on the network drive (such as the Datadisk folder on our network) as per instructions from your professor. Note the following:

- The Exploring Windows 98 folder is highlighted in the left pane, its icon has changed to an open folder, and its contents are displayed in the right pane.

- The status bar indicates that the folder contains five objects and the total file size is 82.5KB.

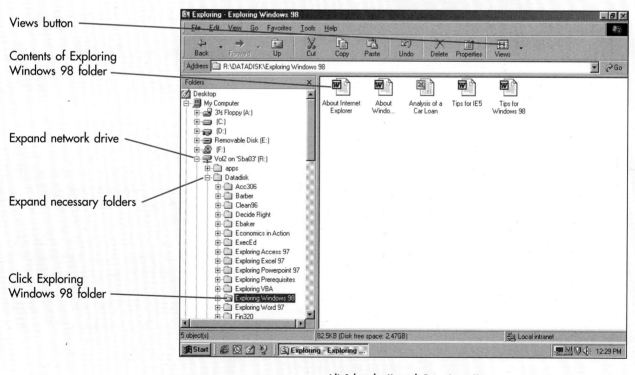

Views button

Contents of Exploring Windows 98 folder

Expand network drive

Expand necessary folders

Click Exploring Windows 98 folder

(d) Select the Network Drive (step 4)

FIGURE 11   Hands-on Exercise 3 (continued)

➤ Click the icon next to any other folder to select the folder, which in turn deselects the Exploring Windows 98 folder. (Only one folder in the left pane can be active at a time.)

➤ Reselect (click) the **Exploring Windows 98 folder,** and its contents are again visible in the right pane.

➤ Pull down the **View menu** and select **Details** (or click the arrow on the **Views button** on the toolbar to display the different views, then **Details**). This enables you to see the file sizes of the individual files.

SORT BY NAME, DATE, FILE TYPE, OR SIZE

The files within a folder can be displayed in ascending or descending sequence by name, date modified, file type, or size. Change to the Details view. Select the desired folder in the left pane, then click the desired column heading in the right pane; click size, for example, to display the contents of the selected folder according to the size of the individual files. Click the column heading a second time to reverse the sequence—that is, to switch from ascending to descending, and vice versa.

STEP 5: Copy the Individual Files

➤ Select (click) the file called **About Windows Explorer,** which highlights the file as shown in Figure 11e. The Exploring Windows 98 folder is no longer highlighted because a different object has been selected. The folder is still open, however, and its contents are displayed in the right pane.

➤ Click and drag the selected file in the right pane to the **drive A icon** in the left pane:

  • You will see the ⊘ symbol as you drag the file until you reach a suitable destination (e.g., until you point to the icon for drive A). The ⊘ symbol will change to a plus sign when the icon for drive A is highlighted, indicating that the file can be copied successfully.

  • Release the mouse to complete the copy operation. You will see a pop-up window, which indicates the status of the copy operation. This may take several seconds depending on the size of the file.

➤ Select (click) the file **Tips for Windows 98,** which automatically deselects the previously selected file (About Windows Explorer). Copy the selected file to drive A by dragging its icon from the right pane to the drive A icon in the left pane.

➤ Copy the three remaining files to drive A as well. (You can select multiple files at the same time by pressing and holding the **Ctrl key** as you click each file in turn. Point to any of the selected files, then click and drag the files as a group.)

➤ Select (click) **drive A** in the left pane, which in turn displays the contents of the floppy disk in the right pane. You should see the five files you have copied to drive A.

Click About Windows
Explorer to select it

Drag file to icon for drive A

Click minus to
collapse network drive

+ indicates file is
being copied

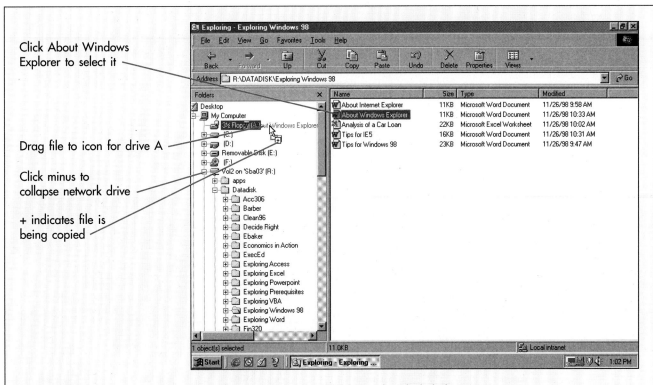

(e) Copy the Individual Files (step 5)

FIGURE 11   Hands-on Exercise 3 (continued)

SELECT MULTIPLE FILES

Selecting (clicking) one file automatically deselects the previously selected file. You can, however, select multiple files by pressing and holding the Ctrl key as you click each file in succession. You can also select multiple files that are adjacent to one another by using the Shift key; that is, click the icon of the first file, then press and hold the Shift key as you click the icon of the last file. You can also select every file in a folder through the Select All command in the Edit menu (or by clicking in the right pane and pressing Ctrl+A). The same commands work in the Web style, except that you hover over an icon (point to it and pause) rather than click it; for example, point to the first file, then press the Ctrl key as you hover over each subsequent file that you want to select.

STEP 6: Display a Web Page

➤ This step requires an Internet connection. Click the **minus sign** next to the network drive to collapse that drive. Click the **minus sign** next to any other expanded drive so that the left pane in Windows Explorer is similar to Figure 11f.

➤ Click the **Internet Explorer icon** to start Internet Explorer and display the starting page for your configuration. Click in the Address bar near the top of the window. Type **www.prenhall.com/grauer** to go to the *Exploring Windows* home page.

➤ Look closely at the icons on the toolbar, which have changed to reflect the tools associated with viewing a Web page.

➤ Click the **Back button** to return to drive A, which was the previously displayed item in Windows Explorer. The icons on the toolbar return to those associated with a folder.

➤ Click the **Forward button** to return to the Web page. The icons on the toolbar change back to those associated with the Internet.

➤ Close Windows Explorer. Shut down the computer if you do not want to continue with the next exercise at this time.

Icons on toolbar reflect those associated with a Web page

Back button

Forward button

Click Internet Explorer icon to display your start page

Click a site to display Web page in right pane

Web page is displayed

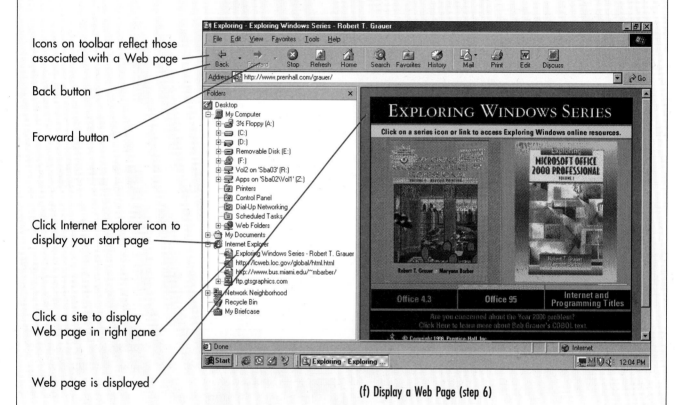

(f) Display a Web Page (step 6)

FIGURE 11 Hands-on Exercise 3 (continued)

THE SMART TOOLBAR

The toolbar in Windows Explorer recognizes whether you are viewing a Web page or a set of files and folders, and changes accordingly. The icons that are displayed when viewing a Web page are identical to those in Internet Explorer and include the Search, History, Favorites, and buttons that show various sets of Internet links. The buttons that are displayed when viewing a file or folder include the Undo, Delete, and Views buttons that are used in file management. Both sets of icons include the Back button to return to the previous object.

THE BASICS OF FILE MANAGEMENT

As you grow to depend on the computer, you will create a variety of files in applications such as Microsoft Word or Excel. Learning how to manage those files is one of the most important skills you can acquire. The purpose of Hands-on Exercises 2 and 3 was to give you a set of files with which to practice. That way, when you have your own files, you will be comfortable executing the various file management commands you will need on a daily basis. Accordingly, we discuss the basic commands you will use, then present another hands-on exercise in which you apply those commands.

Moving and Copying a File

Moving and copying a file from one location to another is the essence of file management. It is accomplished most easily by clicking and dragging the file icon from the source drive or folder to the destination drive or folder, within Windows Explorer. There is a subtlety, however, in that the result of dragging a file (i.e., whether the file is moved or copied) depends on whether the source and destination are on the same or different drives. Dragging a file from one folder to another folder on the same drive moves the file. Dragging a file to a folder on a different drive copies the file. The same rules apply to dragging a folder, where the folder and every file in it are moved or copied as per the rules for an individual file.

This process is not as arbitrary as it may seem. Windows assumes that if you drag an object (a file or folder) to a different drive (e.g., from drive C to drive A), you want the object to appear in both places. Hence, the default action when you click and drag an object to a different drive is to copy the object. You can, however, override the default and move the object by pressing and holding the Shift key as you drag.

Windows also assumes that you do not want two copies of an object on the same drive, as that would result in wasted disk space. Thus, the default action when you click and drag an object to a different folder on the same drive is to move the object. You can override the default and copy the object by pressing and holding the Ctrl key as you drag.

You don't have to remember these conventions, however. Just click and drag with the right mouse button and you will be presented with a context-sensitive menu asking whether to move or copy the files. It's not as complicated as it sounds, and you get a chance to practice in the hands-on exercise, which follows shortly.

Deleting a File

The **Delete command** deletes (removes) a file from a disk. The command can be executed in different ways, most easily by selecting a file, then pressing the Del key. Even after a file is deleted, however, you can usually get it back because it is not physically deleted from the hard disk, but moved instead to the Recycle Bin from where it can be recovered.

The **Recycle Bin** is a special folder that contains all files that were previously deleted from any hard disk on your system. Think of the Recycle Bin as similar to the wastebasket in your room. You throw out (delete) a report by tossing it into a wastebasket. The report is gone (deleted) from your desk, but you can still get it back by taking it out of the wastebasket as long as the basket wasn't emptied. The Recycle Bin works the same way. Files are not deleted from the hard disk per se, but moved instead to the Recycle Bin from where they can be restored to their original location.

The Recycle Bin will eventually run out of space, in which case the files that have been in the Recycle Bin the longest are deleted to make room for additional files. Accordingly, once a file is removed from the Recycle Bin, it can no longer be restored, as it has been physically deleted from the hard disk. Note, too, that the protection afforded by the Recycle Bin does not extend to files deleted from a floppy disk. Such files can be recovered, but only through utility programs outside of Windows 98.

Backup

It's not a question of *if* it will happen, but *when*—hard disks die, files are lost, or viruses may infect a system. It has happened to us and it will happen to you, but you can prepare for the inevitable by creating adequate backup *before* the problem occurs. The essence of a **backup strategy** is to decide which files to back up, how often to do the backup, and where to keep the backup. Once you decide on a strategy, follow it, and follow it faithfully!

Our strategy is very simple—back up what you can't afford to lose, do so on a daily basis, and store the backup away from your computer. You need not copy every file, every day. Instead, copy just the files that changed during the current session. Realize, too, that it is much more important to back up your data files than your program files. You can always reinstall the application from the original disks or CD, or if necessary, go to the vendor for another copy of an application. You, however, are the only one who has a copy of the term paper that is due tomorrow.

We cannot overemphasize the importance of adequate backup and urge you to copy your data files to floppy disks and store those disks away from your computer. You might also want to write-protect your backup disks so that you cannot accidentally erase a file. It takes only a few minutes, but you will thank us, when (not if) you lose an important file and wish you had another copy.

Write-protection

A floppy disk is normally **write-enabled** (the square hole is covered with the movable tab) so that you can change the contents of the disk. Thus, you can create (save) new files to a write-enabled disk and/or edit or delete existing files. Occasionally, however, you may want to **write-protect** a floppy disk (by sliding the tab to expose the square hole) so that its contents cannot be modified. This is typically done with a backup disk where you want to prevent the accidental deletion of a file and/or the threat of virus infection.

Our Next Exercise

As we have indicated throughout this supplement, the ability to move and copy files is of paramount importance. The only way to master these skills is through practice, and so we offer our next exercise in which you execute various commands for file management.

The exercise begins with the floppy disk containing the five practice files in drive A. We ask you to create two folders on drive A (step 1) and to move the various files into these folders (step 2). Next, you copy a folder from drive A to drive C (step 3), modify one of the files in the folder on drive C (step 4), then copy the modified file back to drive A (step 5). We ask you to delete a file in step 6, then recover it from the Recycle Bin in step 7. We also show you how to write-protect a floppy disk in step 8. Disk and file management is a critical skill, and you will want to master the exercise in its entirety. There is a lot to do, so let's get started.

HANDS-ON EXERCISE 4

Windows Explorer

Objective: Use Windows Explorer to move, copy, and delete a file. Use Figure 12, which was done using the Classic style, as a guide.

STEP 1: Create a New Folder

➤ Start Windows Explorer. Place the floppy disk from Hands-on Exercise 2 or 3 in drive A. Select (click) the icon for **drive A** in the left pane of the Explorer window. Drive A should contain the files shown in Figure 12a.

➤ You will create two folders on drive A, using two different techniques:

- Point to a blank area anywhere in the **right pane,** click the **right mouse button** to display a context-sensitive menu, click (or point to) the **New command,** then click **Folder** as the type of object to create. The icon for a new folder will appear with the name of the folder (New Folder) highlighted. Type **Computing 101** to change the name of the folder. Press **Enter.**

- Click the icon for **drive A** once again. Pull down the **File menu,** click (or point to) the **New command,** and click **Folder** as the type of object to create. Type **IE Documents** to change the name of the folder. Press **Enter.** The right pane should now contain five documents and two folders.

➤ Pull down the **View menu.** Click (or point to) the **Arrange Icons command** to display a submenu, then click the **By Name command.**

Click Folder

Click icon for drive A

Point to a blank area in right pane and click right mouse button to display shortcut menu

Click new

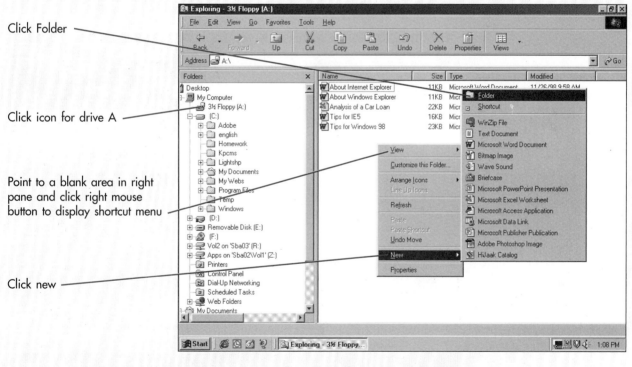

(a) Create a New Folder (step 1)

FIGURE 12 Hands-on Exercise 4

RENAME COMMAND

Every file or folder is assigned a name at the time it is created, but you may want to change that name at some point in the future. Point to a file or a folder, then click the right mouse button to display a menu with commands pertaining to the object. Click the Rename command. The name of the file or folder will be highlighted with the insertion point (a flashing vertical line) positioned at the end of the name. Enter a new name to replace the selected name, or click anywhere within the name to change the insertion point and edit the name.

STEP 2: Move a File

➤ Pull down the **View** menu and click **Refresh.** Click the **plus sign** next to drive A to expand the drive as shown in Figure 12b. Note the following:

- The left pane shows that drive A is selected. The right pane displays the contents of drive A (the selected object in the left pane). The folders are shown first and appear in alphabetical order. The file names are displayed after the folders and are also in alphabetical order.

- There is a minus sign next to the icon for drive A in the left pane, indicating that it has been expanded and that its folders are visible. Thus, the folder names also appear under drive A in the left pane.

➤ Click and drag the icon for **About Windows Explorer** from the right pane to the **Computing 101 folder** in the left pane to move the file into that folder.

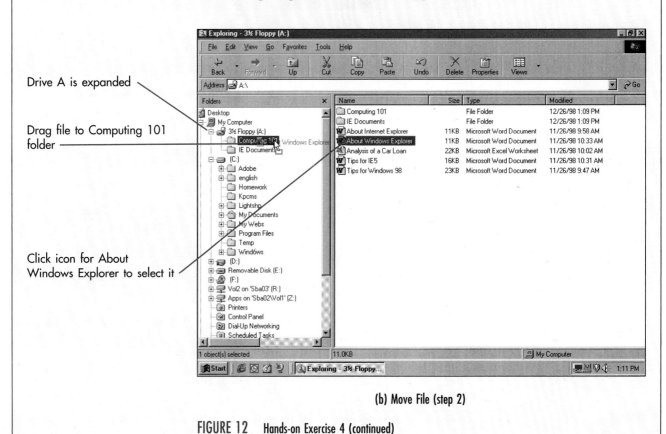

Drive A is expanded

Drag file to Computing 101 folder

Click icon for About Windows Explorer to select it

(b) Move File (step 2)

FIGURE 12   Hands-on Exercise 4 (continued)

➤ Click and drag the **Tips for Windows 98 icon** and the **Analysis of a Car Loan icon** to the **Computing 101 folder** in similar fashion.

➤ Click the **Computing 101 icon** in the left pane to select the folder and display its contents in the right pane. You should see the three files.

➤ Click the icon for **drive A** in the left pane, then click and drag the remaining files, **About Internet Explorer** and **Tips for IE5,** to the **IE Documents folder.**

RIGHT CLICK AND DRAG

The result of dragging a file with the left mouse button depends on whether the source and destination folders are on the same or different drives. Dragging a file to a folder on a different drive copies the file. Dragging the file to a folder on the same drive moves the file. If you find this hard to remember, click and drag with the right mouse button to display a shortcut menu asking whether you want to copy or move the file. This simple tip can save you from making a careless (and potentially serious) error.

STEP 3: Copy a Folder

➤ If necessary, click the **plus sign** next to the icon for drive C to expand the drive and display its folders as shown in Figure 12c.

➤ Do *not* click the icon for drive C, as drive A is to remain selected. (You can expand or collapse an object without selecting it.)

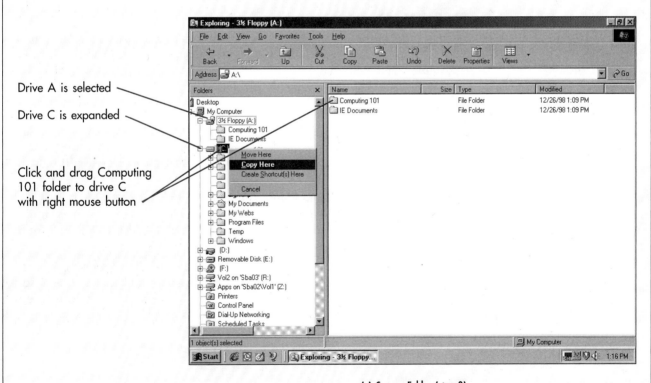

Drive A is selected

Drive C is expanded

Click and drag Computing 101 folder to drive C with right mouse button

(c) Copy a Folder (step 3)

FIGURE 12   Hands-on Exercise 4 (continued)

➤ Point to the **Computing 101 folder** in either pane, click the **right mouse button,** and drag the folder to the icon for **drive C** in the left pane, then release the mouse to display a shortcut menu. Click the **Copy Here command.**

- You may see a Copy files dialog box as the individual files within the folder are copied from drive A to drive C.

- If you see the Confirm Folder Replace dialog box, it means that the previous student forgot to delete the Computing 101 folder when he or she did this exercise. Click the **Yes to All button** so that the files on your floppy disk will replace the previous versions on drive C.

➤ Please remember to **delete** the Computing 101 folder on drive C, when you get to step 9 at the end of the exercise.

CUSTOMIZE WINDOWS EXPLORER

Increase or decrease the size of the left pane within Windows Explorer by dragging the vertical line separating the left and right panes in the appropriate direction. You can also drag the right border of the various column headings (Name, Size, Type, and Modified) in the right pane to increase or decrease the width of the column and see more or less information in that column. And best of all, you can click any column heading to display the contents of the selected folder in sequence by that column. Click the heading a second time, and the sequence changes from ascending to descending and vice versa.

STEP 4: Modify a Document

➤ Click the **Computing 101 folder** on drive C to make this folder the active folder and display its contents in the right pane. Open the **About Windows Explorer** document:

- Double click the document icon in Classic style.

- Click the icon in Web style.

➤ Do not be concerned if the size and/or position of the Microsoft Word window is different from ours. All that matters is that you see the document. If necessary, click inside the document window, then press **Ctrl+End** to move to the end of the document.

➤ Add the sentence shown in Figure 12d followed by your name. Pull down the **File menu** and click **Save** to save the modified file (or click the **Save button** on the Standard toolbar). Pull down the **File menu** and click **Exit** to exit from Microsoft Word.

➤ Pull down the **View menu** in Windows Explorer and click **Refresh** (or press the **F5 key**) to update the contents of the right pane. The date and time associated with the About Windows Explorer file has been changed to indicate that the file has just been modified.

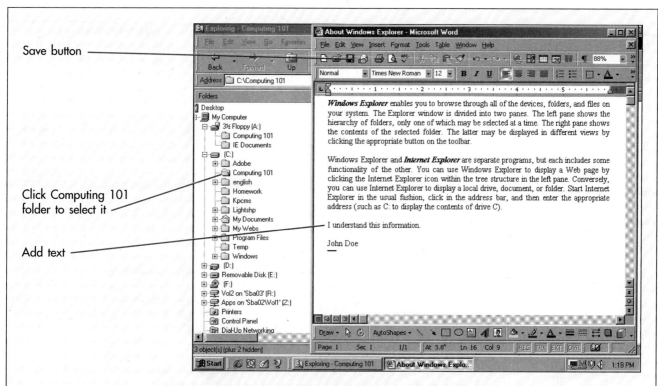

Save button

Click Computing 101
folder to select it

Add text

(d) Modify a Document (step 4)

FIGURE 12   Hands-on Exercise 4 (continued)

KEYBOARD SHORTCUTS

Most people begin with the mouse, but add keyboard shortcuts as they become more proficient. Ctrl+B, Ctrl+I, and Ctrl+U are shortcuts to boldface, italicize, and underline, respectively. Ctrl+X (the X is supposed to remind you of a pair of scissors), Ctrl+C, and Ctrl+V correspond to Cut, Copy, and Paste, respectively. Ctrl+Home and Ctrl+End move to the beginning or end of a document. These shortcuts are not unique to Microsoft Word, but are recognized in virtually every Windows application.

STEP 5: Copy (Back Up) a File

➤ Verify that the **Computing 101 folder** on drive C is the active folder as denoted by the open folder icon. Click and drag the icon for the **About Windows Explorer** file from the right pane to the **Computing 101 folder** on **drive A** in the left pane.

➤ You will see the message in Figure 12e, indicating that the folder (drive A) already contains a file called About Windows Explorer and asking whether you want to replace the existing file. Click **Yes** because you want to replace the previous version of the file on drive A with the updated version from drive C.

➤ You have just backed up the file; in other words, you have created a copy of the file on drive C on the disk in drive A. Thus, you can use the floppy disk to restore the file on drive C should anything happen to it. We cannot overemphasize the importance of adequate backup!

Click and drag About Windows Explorer file to Computing 101 folder on drive A

Computing 101 folder on drive C is selected

Click Yes

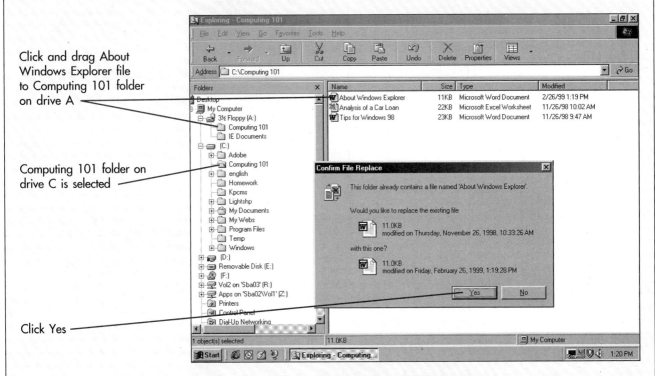

(e) Copy (Back Up) a File (step 5)

FIGURE 12   Hands-on Exercise 4 (continued)

COPYING FROM ONE FLOPPY DISK TO ANOTHER

You've learned how to copy a file from drive C to drive A, or from drive A to drive C, but how do you copy a file from one floppy disk to another? It's easy when you know how. Place the first floppy disk in drive A, select drive A in the left pane of the Explorer window, then copy the file from the right pane to a temporary folder on drive C in the left pane. Remove the first floppy disk, and replace it with the second. Select the temporary folder on drive C in the left pane, then click and drag the file from the right pane to the floppy disk in the left pane.

STEP 6: Delete a Folder

➤ Select (click) the **Computing 101 folder** on drive C in the left pane. Pull down the **File menu** and click **Delete** (or press the **Del key**).

➤ You will see the dialog box in Figure 12f asking whether you are sure you want to delete the folder (i.e., send the folder and its contents to the Recycle Bin). Note the green recycle logo within the box, which implies that you will be able to restore the file.

➤ Click **Yes** to delete the folder. The folder disappears from drive C. Pull down the **Edit menu.** Click **Undo Delete.**

➤ The deletion is cancelled and the folder reappears in the left pane. If you don't see the folder, pull down the **View menu** and click the **Refresh command.**

Click Computing 101
folder on drive C

Recycle logo

Click Yes

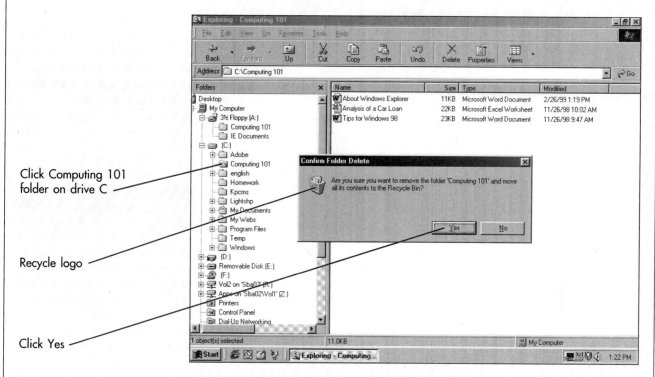

(f) Delete a Folder (step 6)

FIGURE 12   Hands-on Exercise 4 (continued)

THE UNDO COMMAND

The Undo command is present not only in application programs such as Word or Excel, but in Windows Explorer as well. You can use the command to undelete a file if it is executed immediately (within a few commands) after the Delete command. To execute the Undo command, right click anywhere in the right pane to display a shortcut menu, then select the Undo action. You can also pull down the Edit menu and click Undo to reverse (undo) the last command. Some operations cannot be undone (in which case the command will be dimmed), but Undo is always worth a try.

STEP 7: The Recycle Bin

➤ The Recycle Bin can also be used to recover a deleted file provided that the network administrator has not disabled this function.

➤ If necessary, select the **Computing 101 folder** on drive C in the left pane. Select (click) the **About Windows Explorer** file in the right pane. Press the **Del key,** then click **Yes** when asked whether to send the file to the Recycle Bin.

➤ Click the **down arrow** in the vertical scroll bar in the left pane until you see the icon for the **Recycle Bin.** (You can also open the Recycle Bin from the desktop.) Click the icon to make the Recycle Bin the active folder and display its contents in the right pane.

➤ The Recycle Bin contains all files that have been previously deleted from drive C, and hence you will see a different set of files than those displayed in Figure 12g. Pull down the **View menu,** click (or point to) **Arrange Icons,** then click **By Delete Date** to display the files in this sequence.

➤ Click in the **right pane.** Press **Ctrl+End** or scroll to the bottom of the window. Point to the **About Windows Explorer** file, click the **right mouse button** to display the shortcut menu in Figure 12g, then click **Restore.**

➤ The file disappears from the Recycle Bin because it has been returned to the Computing 101 folder. You can open the Computing 101 folder on drive C to confirm that the file has been restored.

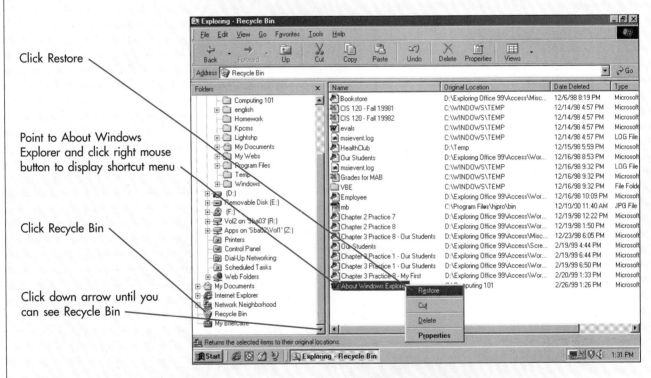

Click Restore

Point to About Windows Explorer and click right mouse button to display shortcut menu

Click Recycle Bin

Click down arrow until you can see Recycle Bin

(g) The Recycle Bin (step 7)

FIGURE 12   Hands-on Exercise 4 (continued)

THE SHOW DESKTOP BUTTON

The Show Desktop button on the taskbar enables you to minimize all open windows with a single click. The button functions as a toggle switch. Click it once and all windows are minimized. Click it a second time and the open windows are restored to their position on the desktop. If you do not see the Show Desktop button, right click a blank area of the taskbar to display a context-sensitive menu, click Toolbars, then check the Quick Launch toolbar, which contains the Show Desktop button.

STEP 8: Write-protect a Floppy Disk

➤ You can write-protect a floppy disk so that its contents cannot be modified. Remove the floppy disk from drive A, then move the built-in tab on the disk so that the square hole on the disk is open. The disk is now write-protected.

➤ If necessary, expand drive A in the left pane, select the **Computing 101 folder,** select the **Analysis of a Car Loan document** in the right pane, then press the **Del key.** Click **Yes** when asked whether to delete the file.

➤ You will see the message in Figure 12h indicating that the file cannot be deleted because the disk is write-protected. Click **OK.** Remove the write-protection by moving the built-in tab to cover the square hole.

➤ Repeat the procedure to delete the **Analysis of a Car Loan document.** Click **Yes** in response to the confirmation message asking whether you want to delete the file. Note, however, the icon that appears in this dialog box is a red exclamation point, rather than a recycle emblem, indicating you cannot (easily) recover a deleted file from a floppy disk.

➤ The file disappears from the right pane indicating it has been deleted. The Computing 101 folder on drive A should contain only two files.

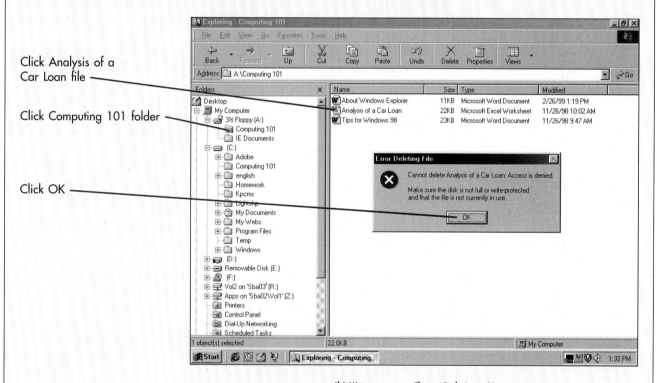

(h) Write-protect a Floppy Disk (step 8)

FIGURE 12   Hands-on Exercise 4 (continued)

STEP 9: Complete the Exercise

➤ Delete the **Computing 101 folder** on drive C as a courtesy to the next student in the Computer Lab.

➤ Exit Windows Explorer. Welcome to Windows 98!

Windows 98 is a computer program (actually many programs) that controls the operation of your computer and its peripherals. It is the third major release of the Windows operating system, following Windows 3.1 and Windows 95.

All Windows operations take place on the desktop, which is displayed in either the Classic style or the Web style. The choice between the two is one of personal preference. The Classic style is virtually identical to the Windows 95 desktop and requires you to click an icon to select it, and double click the icon to open it. The Web style uses underlined icons that function identically to the hyperlinks in a browser; thus you point to an icon to select it, and click the icon to open it.

All Windows applications share a common user interface and possess a consistent command structure. Every window on the desktop contains the same basic elements, which include a title bar, a minimize button, a maximize or restore button, and a close button. Other elements that may be present include a menu bar, vertical and/or horizontal scroll bars, a status bar, and a toolbar. All windows may be moved and sized.

Multitasking is a major benefit of the Windows environment as it enables you to run several programs at the same time. The taskbar contains a button for each open program and enables you to switch back and forth between those programs by clicking the appropriate button.

The mouse is essential to Windows and has five basic actions: pointing, clicking, right clicking, double clicking, and dragging. The mouse pointer assumes different shapes according to the nature of the current action.

A dialog box supplies information needed to execute a command. Option buttons indicate mutually exclusive choices, one of which must be chosen. Check boxes are used if the choices are not mutually exclusive or if an option is not required. A text box supplies descriptive information. A (drop-down or open) list box displays multiple choices, any of which may be selected. A tabbed dialog box provides access to multiple sets of options.

The Help command on the Start menu provides access to detailed information about Windows 98. You can search for information three ways—through the Contents, Index, and Find tabs. You can also go to the Microsoft Web site, where you have access to the Windows Knowledge Base of current information.

A floppy disk must be formatted before it can store data. Formatting is accomplished through the Format command within the My Computer window. My Computer enables you to browse the disk drives and other devices attached to your system. My Computer is present on every desktop, but its contents depend on your specific configuration.

A file is a set of data or set of instructions that has been given a name and stored on disk. There are two basic types of files—program files and data files. A program file is an executable file, whereas a data file can be used only in conjunction with a specific program. Every file has a file name and a file type. The file name can be up to 255 characters in length and may include spaces.

Files are stored in folders to better organize the hundreds (or thousands) of files on a disk. A folder may contain program files, data files, and/or other folders. There are two basic ways to search through the folders on your system—My Computer and Windows Explorer. My Computer is intuitive but less efficient than Windows Explorer, as you have to open each folder in succession. Windows Explorer is more sophisticated as it provides a hierarchical view of the entire system.

Windows Explorer is divided into two panes. The left pane displays all of the devices and, optionally, the folders on each device. The right pane shows the contents of the active (open) drive or folder. Only one drive or folder can be active in the left pane. Any device, be it local or on the network, may be expanded or collapsed to display or hide its folders. A minus sign indicates that the drive has been expanded and that its folders are visible. A plus sign indicates the reverse; that is, the device is collapsed and its folders are not visible.

The result of dragging a file (or folder) from one location to another depends on whether the source and destination folders are on the same or different drives. Dragging the file to a folder on the same drive moves the file. Dragging the file to a folder on a different drive copies the file. It's easier, therefore, to click and drag with the right mouse button to display a menu from which you can select the desired operation.

The Delete command deletes (removes) a file from a disk. A file deleted from a hard disk can be restored from the Recycle Bin. This is not true, however, for files that are deleted from a floppy disk.

The choice between Web style and Classic style is strictly one of personal preference and depends on how you want to open a document, by clicking or double clicking, respectively. The Folder Options command in the View menu of My Computer or Windows Explorer enables you to switch from one style to the other.

KEY WORDS AND CONCEPTS

Backup strategy	Folder	Rename a file
Check box	Format command	Restore a file
Classic style	Help command	Restore button
Close button	Horizontal scroll bar	Search tab
Collapsed icon	Index tab	Smart toolbar
Command button	Internet Explorer	Start button
Common user interface	List box	Status bar
Contents tab	Maximize button	Tabbed dialog box
Copy a file	Menu bar	Taskbar
Data file	Minimize button	Text box
Delete a file	Mouse operations	Title bar
Desktop	Move a file	Vertical scroll bar
Dialog box	Multitasking	Web style
Dimmed command	My Computer	Windows 2000
Drop-down list box	Network Neighborhood	Windows 95
Expanded icon	Option button	Windows 98
Extension	Program file	Windows NT
File	Pull-down menu	Windows Explorer
File name	Radio button	Write-enabled
File type	Recycle Bin	Write-protected

1. What is the significance of a faded (dimmed) command in a pull-down menu?
   (a) The command is not currently accessible
   (b) A dialog box will appear if the command is selected
   (c) A Help window will appear if the command is selected
   (d) There are no equivalent keystrokes for the particular command

2. Which of the following is true regarding a dialog box?
   (a) Option buttons indicate mutually exclusive choices
   (b) Check boxes imply that multiple options may be selected
   (c) Both (a) and (b)
   (d) Neither (a) nor (b)

3. Which of the following is the first step in sizing a window?
   (a) Point to the title bar
   (b) Pull down the View menu to display the toolbar
   (c) Point to any corner or border
   (d) Pull down the View menu and change to large icons

4. Which of the following is the first step in moving a window?
   (a) Point to the title bar
   (b) Pull down the View menu to display the toolbar
   (c) Point to any corner or border
   (d) Pull down the View menu and change to large icons

5. How do you exit Windows?
   (a) Click the Start button, then click the Shut Down command
   (b) Right click the Start button, then click the Shut Down command
   (c) Click the End button, then click the Shut Down command
   (d) Right click the End button, then click the Shut Down command

6. How do you open My Computer?
   (a) Double click the My Computer icon in the Windows 98 Classic style
   (b) Click the My Computer icon in the Windows 98 Web style
   (c) Both (a) and (b)
   (d) Neither (a) nor (b)

7. Which button appears immediately after a window has been maximized?
   (a) The close button
   (b) The restore button
   (c) The maximize button
   (d) All of the above

8. What happens to a window that has been minimized?
   (a) The window is still visible but it no longer has a minimize button
   (b) The window shrinks to a button on the taskbar
   (c) The window is closed and the application is removed from memory
   (d) The window is still open but the application has been removed from memory

9. What is the significance of three dots next to a command in a pull-down menu?
   (a) The command is not currently accessible
   (b) A dialog box will appear if the command is selected
   (c) A Help window will appear if the command is selected
   (d) There are no equivalent keystrokes for the particular command

10. The Recycle Bin enables you to restore a file that was deleted from:
    (a) Drive A
    (b) Drive C
    (c) Both (a) and (b)
    (d) Neither (a) nor (b)

11. The left pane of Windows Explorer may contain:
    (a) One or more folders with a plus sign
    (b) One or more folders with a minus sign
    (c) Both (a) and (b)
    (d) Neither (a) nor (b)

12. Which of the following was suggested as essential to a backup strategy?
    (a) Back up all program files at the end of every session
    (b) Store backup files at another location
    (c) Both (a) and (b)
    (d) Neither (a) nor (b)

13. Which of the following is true regarding a disk that has been write protected?
    (a) Existing files cannot be modified or erased
    (b) A new file cannot be added to the disk
    (c) Both (a) and (b)
    (d) Neither (a) nor (b)

14. How do you open a file from within My Computer or Windows Explorer?
    (a) Click the file icon if you are in the Classic style
    (b) Double click the file icon if you are in the Web style
    (c) Both (a) and (b)
    (d) Neither (a) nor (b)

15. How do you change from the Web style to the Classic style?
    (a) Open My Computer, pull down the View menu, click Options, click the General tab, and specify Classic style
    (b) Open Windows Explorer, pull down the View menu, click Folder Options, click the General tab, and specify Classic style
    (c) Both (a) and (b)
    (d) Neither (a) nor (b)

Answers

1. a	**6.** c	**11.** c
2. c	**7.** b	**12.** b
3. c	**8.** b	**13.** c
4. a	**9.** b	**14.** d
5. a	**10.** b	**15.** c

1. **My Computer:** Figure 13 displays a document that was created using the WordPad program, a simple word processor that is included in Windows 98. You can do the exercise using WordPad, or alternatively you can use Microsoft Word. Our directions are for WordPad:

   a. Open My Computer. Pull down the View menu and switch to the Details view. Size the window as necessary.

   b. Press Alt+Print Screen to copy the My Computer window to the clipboard.

   c. Click the Start menu, click Programs, click Accessories, then click WordPad to open the word processor. Maximize the window.

   d. Pull down the Edit menu. Click the Paste command to copy the contents of the clipboard to the document you are about to create. The My Computer window should be pasted into your document.

   e. Click below the graphic, press Ctrl+End to move to the end of your document. Press the enter key three times (to leave three blank lines).

   f. Type a modified form of the memo in Figure 13 so that it conforms to your configuration. Type just as you would on a regular typewriter except do not press the enter key at the end of a line as the program will automatically wrap from one line to the next. If you make a mistake, just press the backspace key to erase the last character, and continue typing.

   g. Finish the memo and sign your name. Pull down the File menu, click the Print command, then click OK in the dialog box to print the document.

2. **Windows Explorer:** Prove to your instructor that you have completed the four hands-on exercises by capturing a screen similar to Figure 14 that displays the contents of the floppy disk at the end of the exercise. Follow these instructions to create the document in Figure 14 on page 60:

   a. Do the hands-on exercises as described in the text. Place the floppy disk used in the exercise in drive A, and select the Computing 101 folder to display its contents in the right pane of Windows Explorer. If necessary, change to Details view.

   b. Press the Print Screen key to copy the screen to the clipboard (an area of memory that is available to every Windows application).

   c. Click the Start button, click Programs, click Accessories, then click Paint to open the Paint accessory. If necessary, click the maximize button so that the Paint window takes the entire desktop.

   d. Pull down the Edit menu. Click Paste to copy the screen from the clipboard to the drawing. Click Yes if you are asked to enlarge the bitmap.

   e. Click the text tool (the capital A), then click and drag in the drawing area to create a dotted rectangle that will contain the message to your instructor. Type the text indicating that you did your homework. (If necessary, pull down the View menu and check the command for the Text toolbar. This enables you to change the font and/or point size). Click outside the text to deselect it.

   f. Pull down the File menu and click the Page Setup command to display the Page Setup dialog box. Click the Landscape option button. Change the margins to one inch all around. Click OK.

   g. Pull down the File menu a second time. Click Print. Click OK.

   h. Exit Paint. You do not have to save the file. Submit the document to your instructor.

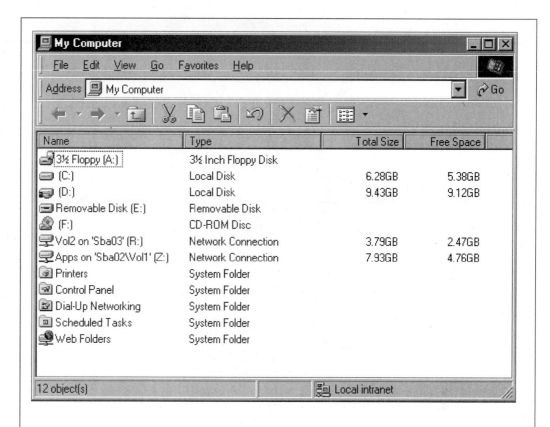

Dear Professor,

Please find above the contents of My Computer (displayed in the Classic style) as it exists on my computer system. As you can see, I have one floppy drive, labeled drive A, and two hard drives, labeled C and D. There are 5.38Gb free on drive C and 9.12Gb free on drive D. I still have a lot of free space left. I have a high-capacity removable disk drive (drive E) and a CD-ROM drive (drive F). In addition to my local drives, I have access to two network drives, drives R and Z.

I enjoyed reading the chapter and I look forward to learning more about the Active Desktop and Internet Explorer.

Sincerely,

Eric Simon

FIGURE 13   My Computer (Exercise 1)

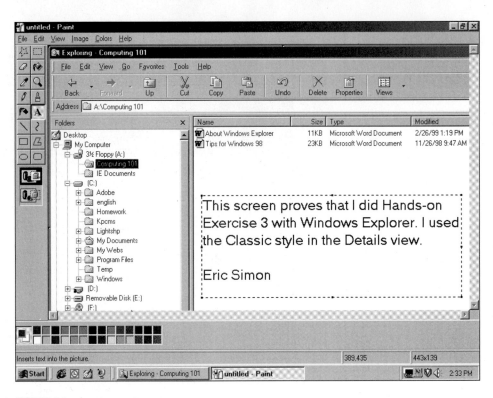

FIGURE 14   Windows Explorer (Exercise 2)

3. Companion Web Sites: Each book in the *Exploring Microsoft® Office 2000* series is accompanied by an online study guide or Companion Web site as shown in Figure 15. Start Internet Explorer and go to the Exploring Windows home page at www.prenhall.com/graucr. Click the book to Office 2000, click the Companion Web site link at the top of the screen, then choose the appropriate text (e.g., *Exploring Microsoft Office Professional Volume I*) and chapter within the text (e.g., *Essentials of Windows 95/98*).

   Each study guide contains a series of short-answer exercises (multiple-choice, true/false, and matching) to review the material in the chapter. You can take practice quizzes by yourself and/or e-mail the results to your instructor. You can try the essay questions for additional practice and engage in online chat sessions. We hope you will find the online guide to be a valuable resource.

4. Organize Your Work: A folder may contain documents, programs, or other folders. The My Classes folder in Figure 16, for example, contains five folders, one folder for each class you are taking this semester, and in similar fashion, the Correspondence folder contains two additional folders according to the type of correspondence. We use folders in this fashion to organize our work, and we suggest you do likewise. The best way to practice with folders is on a floppy disk, as was done in Figure 16. Accordingly:

   a. Format a floppy disk or alternatively, use the floppy disk you have been using throughout the chapter.

   b. Create a Correspondence folder. Create a Business and Personal folder within the Correspondence folder as shown in Figure 16.

   c. Create a My Courses folder. Create a separate folder for each course you are taking within the My Courses folder as shown in Figure 16.

   d. Use the technique described in problem 2 to capture the screen shown in Figure 16. Add your name to the captured screen, and then submit it to your instructor as proof that you have done the exercise.

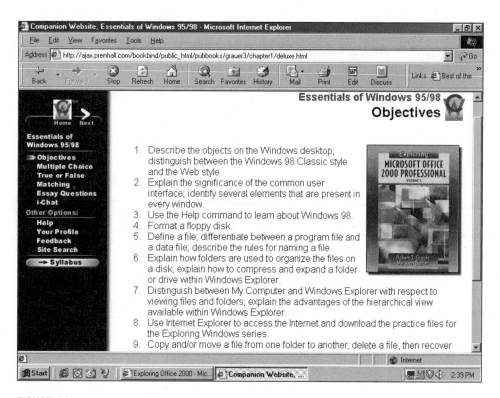

FIGURE 15   Companion Web Sites (Exercise 3)

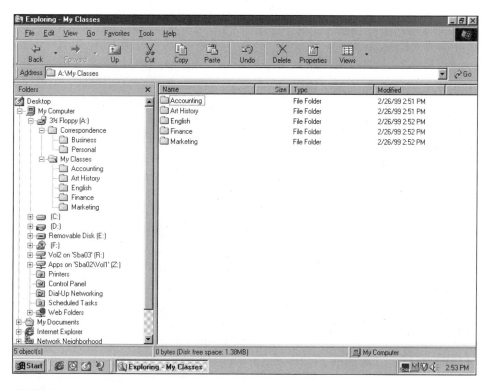

FIGURE 16   Organize Your Work (Exercise 4)

5. View Folders as a Web Page: Windows 98 enables you to view a folder as a Web page, as shown in Figure 17. Start Windows Explorer, collapse all of the drives on your system, select the My Computer icon, then pull down the View menu and click the As Web Page command. Click the Views button to cycle through the different views until your screen matches ours. Use the Folder Options command in the Views menu to experiment with additional ways to view the folders on your system. Summarize your option of this feature in a brief note to your instructor.

FIGURE 17 View Folders as a Web Page (Exercise 5)

6. Discover Windows 98: This exercise requires the Windows 98 CD. The opening screen in Windows 98 displays a Welcome window that invites you to take a discovery tour of Windows 98. (If you do not see the Welcome window, click the Start button, click Run, enter C:\windows\welcome in the Open text box, and press enter.) Click the option to discover Windows 98, which in turn displays the screen in Figure 18. Take a tour of Windows 98, then summarize the highlights in a short note to your instructor.

7. Implement a Screen Saver: A screen saver is a program that protects your monitor by producing a constantly changing pattern after a designated period of inactivity. This is not something you can do in a laboratory setting, but it is well worth doing on your own machine.

Point to a blank area of the desktop, click the right mouse button to display a context-sensitive menu, then click the Properties command to open the Display Properties dialog box in Figure 19. Click the Screen Saver tab, click the down arrow in the Screen Saver list box and select Scrolling Marquee. Click the Settings command button, enter the text and other options for your message, then click OK to close the Options dialog box. Click OK a second time to close the Display Properties dialog box.

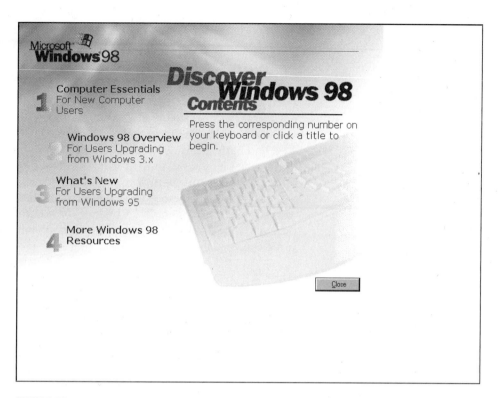

FIGURE 18   Discover Windows 98 (Exercise 6)

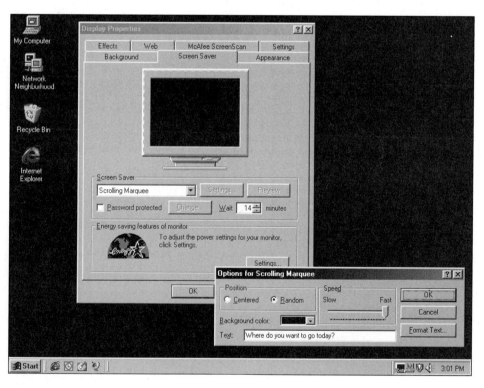

FIGURE 19   Implement a Screen Saver (Exercise 7)

Planning for Disaster

Do you have a backup strategy? Do you even know what a backup strategy is? You had better learn, because sooner or later you will wish you had one. You will erase a file, be unable to read from a floppy disk, or worse yet suffer a hardware failure in which you are unable to access the hard drive. The problem always seems to occur the night before an assignment is due. The ultimate disaster is the disappearance of your computer, by theft or natural disaster. Describe, in 250 words or less, the backup strategy you plan to implement in conjunction with your work in this class.

The Boot Disk

We don't want to give you undue cause for concern, but there is a real possibility that the hard drive on your machine will fail some time in the future and hence you will be unable to start your system. Should that occur, you will want to have a boot (startup) disk at your disposal to start the system from the floppy drive in order to access your hard drive. Use the Help command to learn how to create a startup disk, then follow the instructions if you haven't yet created one. Put the disk in a safe place. We hope you never have to use it, but you should be prepared.

File Compression

You've learned your lesson and have come to appreciate the importance of backing up all of your data files. The problem is that you work with large documents that exceed the 1.44MB capacity of a floppy disk. Accordingly, you might want to consider the acquisition of a file compression program to facilitate copying large documents to a floppy disk in order to transport your documents to and from school, home, or work. You can download an evaluation copy of the popular WinZip program at www.winzip.com. Investigate the subject of file compression, then submit a summary of your findings to your instructor.

The Threat of Virus Infection

A computer virus is an actively infectious program that attaches itself to other programs and alters the way a computer works. Some viruses do nothing more than display an annoying message at an inopportune time. Most, however, are more harmful, and in the worst case, erase all files on the disk. When is a computer subject to infection by a virus? What precautions does your school or university take against the threat of virus infection in its computer lab? What precautions, if any, do you take at home? What is the difference between the scan function in an antivirus program versus leaving the antivirus program active in memory? Can you feel confident that your machine will not be infected if you faithfully use a state-of-the-art antivirus program that was purchased in January 1997?

INDEX

J

Join line, 171
Join properties, 228–229

K

Key Down event, 381, 383, 385
Key Preview property, 386
Keyboard shortcut (creation of), 324
KeyCode argument, 382

L

Link Tables command, 320, 322
Linked data, 174, 200
Linked subforms, 239–246
Linked Table Manager, 319–320, 358–359
List box (versus combo box), 333
Lookup Wizard, 80–81

M

Macro, 4, 331–333
Macro group, 343, 345
Macro toolbar, 331
Macro window, 331
Mail merge, 433–442
Mail Merge Helper, 436
Mail Merge toolbar, 437
Main document, 433–434
Main form, 217
Make-table query, 140–142
Many-to-many relationship, 260–263,
    429–431
Max function, 129
Memo field, 53, 405
Menus (changing of), 22
Merge field, 433
Microsoft Access
    introduction to, 3–4
    starting of, 7
    version of, 11
Microsoft Excel
    exporting data to, 173–174
    importing data from, 165, 167
    pivot tables and charts, 202
Microsoft Graph, 175, 177
Microsoft Word (with mail merge), 436
Min function, 129
Module, 4
Module window, 371

MsgBox
    macro action, 331–332
    VBA function, 372, 397
Multiple-table queries, 163–164, 171–172

N

Navigation buttons
    suppression of, 351
    with subforms, 217–218, 239, 246
Nested If statement, 400
Not function, 119–120
Now function, 111, 169
Null criterion, 347
Number field, 53

O

Object box, 329, 398
Office Assistant, 17, 24, 38
Office Clipboard, 204
OLE field, 53
One-to-many relationship, 33, 163, 207,
    424–427
Open command, 7
Option group, 82–83
OR condition, 118–119

P

Page, 4
Page footer, 104–105, 129
Page header, 104–105, 127–128
Page Setup command, 65, 87
Parameter query, 280–281, 291
Password protection, 354, 364
Pencil (as record selector symbol), 5, 10
Pivot chart, 202
Pivot table, 202
PMT function, 217, 218, 225
Practice files (downloading of), 7
Primary key, 5, 53–54, 209, 428
    changing of, 60
    concatenated, 237
Print preview, 110
Private procedure, 371
Procedure box, 398
Procedure view, 383
Prompt (*see* Parameter query)
Property (definition of), 55
Property sheet, 55, 67–68, 74–75
Prototyping, 333–334, 336
Public procedure, 371

Q

Query, 14–15, 115–148
 copying of, 178, 288
 multiple tables in, 228–229, 230–232
 optimizing of, 299
 updating of, 290
Query window, 116–117, 179
 customization of, 121
Quick Info tool, 379

R

Record, 2
 adding of, 10
Record selector, 4–5, 19
 suppression of, 351
Referential integrity, 36, 164, 168, 209, 216, 264, 266, 429
Related records (deletion of), 267
Relational database, 32–40, 428
Relational operators, 119
Relationship
 creation of, 211–212, 240, 263, 266, 298
 data types in , 213
 deletion of, 213
 editing of, 268
 printing of, 298
Relationship line, 209, 263
Relationships window, 34–35, 168, 209–210, 211–212, 263
 printing of, 169
Remove Filter button, 25
Rename (Access object), 143, 288
Repeating group, 431
Replace command, 13–14, 22
Replica, 353
Report, 4, 16, 23, 102–114
 copying or renaming, 288
 properties of, 114
 synchronization of, 235
Report footer, 104–105, 129, 138
Report header, 104–105, 127–128
Report Wizard, 104, 106, 108–109, 135, 234, 285
Requery command, 349
Required property, 55
Row source, 376

S

ScreenTip (with keyboard shortcut), 61
Select query, 115–116, 120–127
 multiple tables in, 228–229, 230–232

Selection area (in a form), 88
SetFocus method, 380, 382
Show row, 115–116
Simple query Wizard, 120
Sort, 25, 30
 on multiple fields, 31
Sort ascending button, 25, 30
Sort descending button, 25, 30
Sort row, 115–116
 with multiple fields, 130, 172
Sorting and Grouping command, 112
Splitting a database, 322, 359–360
SQL, 228–229
SQL view, 116
Startup property, 192, 244, 302, 311
String (concatenation of), 376
Structured Query Language (*see* SQL)
Subdatasheet, 170, 209, 210, 215, 223
Subform, 217–227, 239, 240–246, 270, 272–279
Sum function, 129, 280
Summary functions, 175
Switchboard, 185–187, 316–319, 333–334
Switchboard Items table, 187, 319, 326
Switchboard Manager, 187, 188–190, 319, 324–325, 338–339

T

Tab order, 86, 387
Table, 2, 4–5
 creation of, 57–65
 design of, 50–55
 modification of, 80
 moving in, 8–9
 opening of, 8
Table Analyzer Wizard, 212, 254
Table properties (for data validation), 402
Table row, 228–229
Table Wizard, 53, 57–59
Tabular report, 102–103
Taskbar (hiding of), 297
Template, 350
Text field, 53
Tip of the day, 23
Toolbars, 415–421
Top Values property, 133, 291
Total query, 175–176, 179, 280, 282, 289
Total row, 175, 179, 280, 282, 289
Triangle (as record selector symbol), 5

U

Unbound control, 65, 106
 adding to a report, 112